DIAMONDS

ISBN: 2-84576-032-9

Copyright deposit: October 2001

Printed in Italy

DIAMONDS

In the heart of the Earth, in the heart of Stars, at the heart of Power

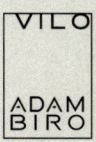

under the direction
of **Hubert Bari**
and **Violaine Sautter**

original translation by Michael Hing

Museum National d'Histoire Naturelle
Mouawad since 1890
VILO ADAM BIRO

ACKNOWLEDGEMENTS

This publication is the catalogue of the Diamonds exhibition, which was originally created by the French Muséum national d'histoire naturelle in Paris, under the administration of Jean-Claude Moreno.

The exhibition would not have been possible without the financial support of the Mouawad Group, subsidies from the French Education and Culture Ministries, and contributions from Brink's, American Airlines, Fichet-Bauche and the DTC.

EXHIBITION

Exhibition Commissaires:
Hubert Bari and Violaine Sautter,
Muséum national d'histoire naturelle, Paris

Production assistance:
Administration: Sonia Wille
Architecture: Jean Lossel
Administrator of Works: Michael Hing

General administration:
Mineralogy Laboratory
Directed by Professor Michel Guiraud
Assisted by Benjamin Rondeau and Gian Carlo Parodi

Administration of the Central Services of the Muséum national d'histoire naturelle:
Surveillance: Régis Cardoville
Security: Michel Garmier
Communications: Agnès Dejean de la Bâtie
Legal services: Philippe Falgayrette
Heritage and Works services: Jean-François Bénet

The scientific committee comprised the authors of this book. The committee would like to acknowledge the contribution made by special adviser Pierre Lemoine, honorary inspector-general of the Museums of France.

Production:
Art Concept, Strasbourg
Lighting:
SACER, Strasbourg
Graphic design:
2exVia, Strasbourg

Secure transportation of the jewels:
Brink's
Air freight and transport:
American Airlines
Physical security for the exhibits:
Fichet-Bauche

CATALOGUE

Editorial team:
Publishers: Éditions Adam Biro (Marlyne Kherlakian, editor;
Mara Mariano, publishing management;
Bulnes & Robaglia, assisted by Nathalie Bigard, graphics;
Yaëlle Biro, editorial administration)

Mouawad Group

Muséum national d'histoire naturelle
(Hubert Bari and Violaine Sautter, project directors)

The organisers would like to extend their grateful thanks to the institutions, colleagues and private collectors who helped gather an extraordinary collection of treasures, of both art and natural history:

Madame the Countess of Paris
HSH Prince Georg Friedrich of Prussia
HE Sheikh Saud Mohamed Ali Abdullah Al-Thani, Doha, Qatar
National Palace of Ajuda, Lisbon (Isabel Silveira Godinho, Teresa Maranhas)
Ultramarino Historical Archive, Lisbon (Maria Luisa Abrantes)
Silver Museum, Florence (Marilena Mosco)
National Ancient Art Museum, Lisbon (Leonor D'Orey)
Historical Museum, Basel (Marie-Claire Berkemeier-Favre)
Fine Arts Museum, Bordeaux (Dominique Cante)
Inter-University Medical Library, Paris (Guy Cobolet)
French National Library, Paris (Rare and Precious Book Reserve, Antoine Coron, Magali Vène; Map Department, Catherine Hoffman; Print And Drawing Department, Laure Beaumont-Maillet; Western and Eastern Manuscript Department, Monique Cohen)
St. Geneviève Library, Paris (Simone Breton)
Cartier International (Renée Frank)
Cartier Art Collection, Geneva (Eric Nussbaum and Anne-Christine Charbonnaz) and other team members from Cartier
De Beers Group, London (Lesley Coldham)
De Beers Archives, Kimberley, South Africa (Brenda Feder)
Diamond Museum, Diamantina, Brazil (Till Pestana)
Ralph Esmerian Collection, New York (Penny Proddow, Marion Fasel)
Thomas Faerber, Geneva
Ricardo Do Espirito Santo Silva Foundation, Lisbon (Maria Joao Espirito Santo Bustorff Silva)
Gem Tech Lab, Geneva (Franck Notari, Pierre-Yves Boillat)
Guyanor (Carlos Bertoni)
De Grisogono, Geneva
Guimet National Asiatic Art Museum, Paris (Francis Macouin)
Grünes Gewölbe, Staatliche Kunstsammlungen, Dresden (Dr. Dirk Syndram, Dr. Sybile Erbert-Schifferer)
Olivier Guichet and Kiet Tran Van Mang Collection, Chiang Mai, Thailand
Robert Haag Collection, Tucson, Arizona
INPI, Paris (Serge Chambaud)
National Museum, Jakarta (Dr. Endang, Dr. Ernawati, Dr. Suhardini)
Louvre Museum, Paris (Objets d'Art Department, Daniel Alcouffe, Gérard Mabille; Department of Oriental Antiquities, Islamic Section, Marthe Bernus-Taylor)
Metropolitan Opera Guild, New York (Susan Braddock, Robert Tuggle)
Robert Mouawad Collection, Geneva
Perfect Stone Investments Ltd., Guernsey
Pitti Palace, Florence (Serena Padovani, Marco Chiarini)
Rainbow Gems International, Antwerp (Eddy Elzas)
National Renaissance Museum, Écouen (Alain Erlande-Brandebourg, Pierre Ennès)
Rijksmuseum, Amsterdam (Dr. J. P. Filedt Kok, Dr. Gertie van Berge)
Rosenborg Castle, Copenhagen (Niels Knud-Liebgott)
Smithsonian Institution, Mineralogy Department, Washington DC (Jeffrey Post)
D. K. Surana Inc. Collection, New York
Tiffany, New York (Annamarie Sandecki, Fernanda Kellogg)
Uffizi Gallery, Florence (Caterina Caneva)
Cape Town University (Prof. John Gurney)
National Museum of Versailles and the Trianons, Versailles (Pierre Arizzoli-Clementel)
Hélène Vetsch Collection
Wejer-de-Groodt and Kunz-de-Groodt collection
With special thanks to Katharina and Thomas Faerber, for their advice and their photographic work.

Many individuals and institutions have contributed to this exhibition or to this publication. We would like to extend our warmest thanks to all of them:

The people of the Mineralogy Laboratory of the Muséum national d'histoire naturelle in Paris and Chantal Adler, Jean-François Ahon, Yves-Marie Allain, Claude-Jean Allègre, Bernard Bodo, David Caméo, Ramon Capdevilla, Pierre Cartigny, Pierre-Jacques Chiappero, Jean-Pierre Chalain, Christie's (François Curiel, Jean-Marc Lunnel, Jean-René Saillard), Shadia Clot, Eole Colin, Jean Dejax, Patrick De Wever, Norbert Engel, Patricia Galliou, Heja Garcia-Guillerminet, Gemological Institute of America, Alix Gicquel, Philippe Gillet, Geneviève Giraud-Boulinier, Eric Gonthier, Michel Grégoire, John N. Hatleberg, Herbert Horowitz, Serge Kirszbaum Conseil (Serge Kirszbaum and Jérôme Loeb), Véronique Jeanneau, John Koivula, French laboratory of gemmology, David Lam (OPA), Shane F. McClure, Pr Adolphe Nicolas, Laetitia Paquerot, Catherine Perrier, Camille Pisani, Hugo Plumel, Stephen Richardson, Christian Sautter, Dr James E. Shigley, SSEF, Pr I. Sunagawa, Philippe Taquet, Dominique Tissot, Catherine Trautmann, Jean-Dominique Wahiche.

Finally, we would not have been able to set up this exhibition as quickly as we did without the assistance of Dr. George E. Harlow, Curator of the Earth Sciences Department of the American Museum of Natural History, New York.

PARTNERS

This project could never have taken place without help from our partners, for which the Museum extends its most grateful thanks.

The project took place thanks to financial support from the Mouawad group, which underwrote the exhibition's finances and provided invaluable support. We would particularly like to extend our personal thanks to the group's president, Robert Mouawad. His commitment to the project has confirmed his firm's reputation as a patron of the arts, with a commitment to supporting exceptional artistic and cultural events. We would also like to thank Lina El Bawab for her skilled and comprehensive project management, and Antoine Khairallah and Georges Coutya for their invaluable advice.

Mouawad
since 1890

The safe international transport of the diamonds was skilfully managed by Brink's, in accordance with their unrivalled reputation. Once in place, the diamonds also benefited from constant surveillance and protection by Brink's security guards. We would like to thank Jean-Michel Houry and his team.

BRINK'S

Thanks to its worldwide network of flights, American Airlines was able to undertake the aerial transportation of the most important works, along with their accompanying personnel. We are deeply grateful to the staff of American Airlines worldwide for their assistance.

AA
AmericanAirlines®

Ensuring the physical security of the diamonds in the exhibition was an enormous challenge. This challenge was undertaken by the Fichet-Bauche company, a subsidiary of the Gunnebo group, the worldwide leader in security installations. We are deeply grateful to Fichet-Bauche for its assistance in finding solutions to our security requirements, for the protection of exhibits and personnel alike. We would particularly like to thank Christian Selosse, President, and Olivier Bianchi, Group Communications Director, along with their team.

Fichet-Bauche
for a s@fer world

We would also like to thank the DTC, Diamond Trading Company, part of the De Beers group. It enabled us to gather an extraordinary collection of rough diamonds. Thanks to our unlimited access to the group's archives, the organisers have been able to exhibit valuable documents that shed light on a little-understood era of human history. Finally, the DTC provided an unforgettably splendid atmosphere for the inauguration events, and helped to publicise the exhibition thanks to its peerless public relations department. We would like to personally thank Anthony Oppenheimer, Hazel Kay, Lesley Coldham and Brenda Feder.

DTC
A DIAMOND IS FOREVER

THE AUTHORS

Patrick Absalon
Art historian, Lecturer at Marc-Bloch University, Strasbourg.

Hubert Bari
Specialist museum exhibition organiser, based at the Muséum national d'histoire naturelle in Paris. He also has long experience in the diamond field, in his capacity as an amateur mineralogist.

Michèle Bimbenet-Privat
Head Curator of the French National Archives. Specialist in Parisian jewellery and goldwork from the 16th and 17th centuries.

Robyn Fréchet
Art historian, specialising in the study of medieval manuscripts.

Emmanuel Fritsch
Physics Professor at Nantes University, specialising in the study of gem materials. He is also Vice-President of the French Gemmology Association and of the Jean-Pierre-Chenet gemmology research centre.

Michel Guiraud
Professor at the Muséum national d'histoire naturelle, Paris, Director of the Mineralogy Laboratory. He specialises in minerals in metamorphic rocks, and studies the conditions behind their formation.

Hugh Hill
Astrophysics Researcher, currently based at NASA.

Alfred A. Levinson
Professor in the Department of Geology and Geophysics, Calgary University, Canada.

Jean-Pierre Lorand
CNRS Research Director. He is based at the Mineralogy Laboratory of the Muséum national d'histoire naturelle in Paris, and works on rocks from the Earth's mantle.

Alan R. Miciak
Teaches marketing at the University of Management, Canada.

Bernard Morel
Precious stone historian, honorary member of the Association Française de Gemmologie.

Amina Okada
Curator at the Musée national des arts asiatiques - Guimet (Musée Guimet), Paris, in charge of the Indian Art collections. She has organised numerous art exhibitions, particularly on painting and Mughal miniatures.

Violaine Sautter
CNRS Research Director. She works at the Mineralogy Laboratory in the Muséum national d'histoire naturelle, Paris, working on samples of rock from the ultra-deep terrestrial mantle.

Michael Seal
A specialist in the study of diamond's properties, with particular regard to its industrial applications. Former President of the European Federation of Abrasive Product Manufacturers, Paris.

Menahem Sevdermish
Founder and President of the European Gemmological Center and College, Ramat Gan, Israel.

CONTENTS

Jean-Claude Moreno
Provisional Administrator of the Muséum national d'histoire naturelle, Paris

Superficially, museums seem complacent, fixed in the past. This is, however, a false impression. Museums are complex, dynamic places. They are the domains of men and women who dedicate their lives to research in the myriad fields of the natural and human sciences. In fact, some fields are a hybrid between art and science.

The truth is that museums have a bountiful inventory of precious manuscripts, extinct creatures, mineral samples, gems, sculptures, paintings and rare plants. This is particularly true of the French Natural History Museum in Paris (the Muséum national d'histoire naturelle). In addition to this treasury, museum staff have the expertise to enable us to make sense of it all, thanks to researchers and teaching staff who study, technicians who protect and the exhibition organisers who create the magnificent displays. These interlocking, interdisciplinary skills are the bedrock of any museum. All that is needed is to find a suitable topic, and to allow the museum to bring it vividly to life, as if painting a picture using carefully-selected colours from a vast, all-encompassing palette.

Diamonds are an ideal subject for such a task. They are quintessential treasures of nature, yet they defied comprehension by early mineralogists. Once their secrets were uncovered, they allowed geologists to understand the inner workings of the deepest reaches of planet Earth. Over two millennia, a vast body of symbolism has built up around this exceptional stone, in Indian, Arabic and European literature. This symbolism cannot be put into context without an understanding of the gem's physical properties. Finally, the allure of a diamond is based upon the stone's optical properties. A knowledge of physics and optics is needed on the part of the gem-cutter before a diamond's true beauty can be revealed. Finally, as if to add to the mystique, astrophysicists have discovered diamonds within stars, and this discovery has had a profound impact upon the electronics industry. This wondrous depth of interest is why the Muséum national d'histoire naturelle set up a diamond exhibition in Paris, which ultimately went on tour throughout the world. When examined in such a light, the stone doesn't simply display a sparkling play of colour: it gives us insight into a whole range of different fields. It is the perfect subject for an interdisciplinary exhibition, allowing us to appreciate the most beautiful aspect of science itself: the quest to understand a great mystery.

Appropriately enough, the Museum was formerly the King's Botanical Garden. It has been intimately associated with power ever since its foundation in the 17th century and, of course, diamond is the ultimate symbol of power.

The Museum's history starts with the Revolution and the assignation of Royal gemstones to our collection. Later, in 1887, the lovely Marie-Louise Portrait Diamond was added to the Museum's collection by the Law of Alienation of the Crown Jewels, whilst the Louvre received the famous *Regent* diamond. The Muséum national d'histoire naturelle is a temple to nature, and the Louvre is a temple to the arts. However, this is a simplistic distinction: the natural sciences cannot be separated from the arts, and diamonds are particularly suited to emphasise this point. The Diamonds exhibition is vivid proof of that, and this book is a beautiful souvenir: scholars from a multitude of different fields have come together to tell this gemstone's extraordinary story, and every page is a surprise.

A very rare surviving example of the series of flower jewels made by Frédéric Boucheron around 1890. It is a masterwork of the jeweller's art, as can be seen in the setting of the diamonds, particularly those in the delicate flower stamens. The stem is also daring: it is made from a steel wire sheathed in silver. Its suppleness allows the necklace to flex gently during wear, bringing the whole jewel to life. Private collection, Geneva.

"Spider" brooch by Tiffany, around 1875. New York, from the collection of Tiffany & Co.

Before he became independent and made his own name as a designer, René Lalique worked for major jewellery houses like Cartier, Spaulding or Tiffany. He designed this ruby and diamond "Singing Bird" brooch for the house of Vever, in 1889. Private collection, New York.

PREFACE

Robert Mouawad

President of the Mouawad Group

Sometimes it's amusing to hear the way that people describe me. In fact, sometimes I'm a little worried that a kind of legend is being built up around me. It's really not appropriate. I seem to be known as "the crazy diamond man" or even just simply as "the collector", with so much emphasis it might just as well be written with a capital C. People look out for me at the leading diamond auctions in Geneva, London or New York. If I appear, apparently a whisper starts going through the crowd: it's going to be a good auction. People selling superb diamonds begin to smile, but prospective buyers don't, because it's assumed in advance that I will win the auction. In fact, this is all an exaggeration, that conceals the underlying truth. Quite simply, I have a passion for diamonds, the way some other people have a passion for Poussin paintings, or for Khmer art. To tell the truth, I am not a diamond collector myself. The collection that people believe I own - the most fabulous one in existence - doesn't really exist. My purchases are destined for the top-quality jewels made by the group that I run. The Mouawad group's reputation is based upon our ability to offer jewels containing famous diamonds to our prestigious clients.

It's enough for me to own an exceptional diamond, albeit temporarily. I gain immense pleasure from turning it in my hands, while I take the time - sometimes several years - to design a beautiful setting for it, and to find the person who will be right for it. It's during this period that I really get to know the stone. This heavenly gem accumulates history as much as it scatters light. Often, I get lost in a stone. One moment, there are some gems laid out on a table, and the next, they've carried me away into their world: a world of ancient European palaces or exotic ancient Mughal kingdoms. Sometimes, a single diamond's long history enables me to piece together a string of life stories: lives that made European or Oriental history. These are the moments that I have savoured, when I came to own the *Jubilee* or the *Taylor-Burton*, the Indore Pears or the *Ahmedabad*. I remember losing myself in the marvellously deep blue of the *Tereschenko*, and I write these lines with the unfathomable *Idol's Eye* lying by the side of the page.

It's true that few people ever get to experience such moments. It is impossible for the majority of people ever to have access to the world's greatest or most beautiful diamonds. The true beauty of this gem, which is most evident in large sizes, is a pleasure that is restricted to the immensely wealthy. When the exhibition proposal from the Muséum national d'histoire naturelle reached me, first of all I joked: who could have dared to make such a suggestion? It's the greatest collection of famous gems and fabulous jewels ever attempted. In fact, this daring came from an institution that is richly qualified to attempt the feat. It was founded by the Kings of France, formerly as the Botanical Garden, and later as a national museum. It has had diamonds in its blood, ever since its foundation. No other royal court sparkled as brightly as that of France, and the royal houses of Europe were dazzled by the glimmer of the *Sancy*, the *Bazu*, the *Blue Diamond of the French Crown*, the Regent and thousands of others.

I could not resist the offer to participate in such a project, and permit such an audacious event to proceed. I could see that this idea, to assemble dozens of famous gems in one place, was an insane dream about to become reality. Above all, I could see that it was an opportunity to open up the treasuries of the world: a world that is closed to most people, who are usually denied such pleasures. To take part in this exhibition became a personal crusade for me, and also a means of displaying the commitment of the group that I preside over. The Mouawad group originated from a small jewellery firm founded in 1890 by my grandfather, David Mouawad. Exhibitions are temporary and ephemeral. It is my hope that this book will serve as a permanent reminder of this great opportunity to contemplate the most beautiful material in nature. Not only to understand its natural history and to see masterpieces of the jeweller's art, but also to understand the cultural significance of a gem that is a religious talisman, an instrument of power, a source of literary inspiration and, ultimately, the stuff of legend.

A stunning diamond cascade: a Mouawad necklace with brilliant-cuts, emerald-cuts and triangles weighing 464 carats in total.

The glorious *Mouawad Magic*, an extraordinary 108.81-carat emerald-cut.

Michel Guiraud
Professor, Muséum national d'histoire naturelle

In search of *adamas*

We are most accustomed to seeing diamonds in the pages of magazines or jewellers' windows, rather than in technical papers or academic lectures attempting to unravel its secrets. In fact, it has an almost magical status as the stone of kings. However, this does not prevent it from being the subject of scientific research like any other topic. Even from this prosaic point of view, the stone shows us that there is nothing ordinary about it, and that it richly deserves its status as a very special gem.

Over the centuries since its discovery, diamond has had an important role to play in the history of science, as well as in human history. Pliny the Elder is reputed to have been the first Westerner to have classified the stone, and to have given it the name of *adamas*, from the Greek word meaning 'indomitable', with reference to its most formidable property, hardness. In fact, Pliny used the word both for diamond and for hard metals. Its hardness having been noted, no other great discoveries would be made about diamond throughout the Middle Ages: nothing was added to the sum of human knowledge apart from a succession of legends.

It has to be said that, for hundreds of years, very few Western scholars actually had the opportunity to examine a diamond directly. Moreover, the intellectual climate of the times did not encourage scientific experiments. It was not until the Renaissance, at the beginning of the 16th century, that the natural history of diamond began. Garcia da Orta (d. 1568), a Portuguese expelled from Europe by the Inquisition, found refuge in Goa, India, where he encountered the precious stone and its mines first-hand. His *Herbal ist Treatise* was the first text to demolish the ancient legends, and to describe the reality of diamond, stripped of its supernatural aspects.

However, it was not until the 18th century that diamond, the quintessential symbol of power, truly began to attract the scholars' attention. In the 18th century, France and indeed all of Europe effectively entered into the age of knowledge. This was the century when inquisitive knowledge-seekers such as Georges Louis de Buffon, Antoine Laurent de Jussieu, Carolus Linnaeus and others discovered the order of nature, and strove to understand its meaning. The Botanical Garden in Paris became the Muséum national d'histoire naturelle in 1793: it followed this line of study, and would carry this scientific approach to its greatest heights. Naturalists undertook great voyages to the ends of the Earth, in conjunction with the more sedentary labours of classification and nomenclature of the three kingdoms: animal, vegetable and mineral. This was the era of the Encyclopaedia: ancient alchemical beliefs disappeared, to be replaced by the rigour of mathematical logic, and the precision of chemical formulae and physical equations. In this era of nascent sciences, it was still possible for a single theme to affect all fields of knowledge. Encyclopaedic trends affected mineralogy, and had a parallel impact upon chemistry and physics. The study of diamonds shows to what extent the sciences nurtured each other, up until the beginning of the 19th century. The names Antoine Laurent de Lavoisier, Jöns Jacob Berzelius, René Just Haüy and even Isaac Newton can be found on treatises devoted to the gem. Today, this interdisciplinary cross-fertilisation seems a world away: now, specialists from neighbouring disciplines sometimes even have difficulty finding a common language.

Diamond science started at the end of the 17th century. The big news in the scientific world at the time was a discovery by the English chemist Robert Boyle (1627-1691): he found that diamond disappears without trace when subjected to very high temperatures in a furnace. This is because diamond is composed of pure carbon: at high temperatures, it combines with oxygen from the atmosphere to yield invisible carbon dioxide, without leaving any physical residue. But Boyle could not understand this, since his comprehension was constrained by the prevailing theory that all matter was composed of only four elements: earth, air fire and water. It took decades of trial and error to solve the mystery. This is why Boyle's discovery was greeted with such incredulity, since diamond's evanescence flew in the face of its well-known properties: hardness and inalterability. How could this invincible stone be so easily conquered by fire? A solution had to be found, and some diamonds had to be destroyed by wealthy aristocrats - the raw material was costly, after all - in order to repeat Boyle's experiment.

Therefore, Jean Gaston de Medici, last of the Tuscan Grand Dukes, ordered the combustion of some diamonds in 1694. The experiment was undertaken with a very large magnifying glass, by two Italian scholars: Giuseppe Averani and Cipriano Targioni-Tozzetti. Later, around 1760, François 1st of Habsburg-Lorraine, Emperor of Germany, donated a fortune in diamonds and rubies in order for them to be heated in furnaces. The result was that the rubies were unscathed, whereas the diamonds disappeared. Jean Darcet, Hilaire Marin Rouelle, Pierre-Joseph Macquer and Antoine Laurent de Lavoisier undertook a series of similar experiments, notably in the Botanical

From rough mineral to dazzling splendour, after cutting. At left, a mould of the original rough diamond crystal. The heavily etched surface was the result of dissolution forces. It was found around 1980 in ex-Zaire, currently the Democratic Republic of Congo. This 890-carat rough yielded the Incomparable (407.48 carats), a magnificent gem that is currently the third-largest cut diamond in existence. It is owned by Premier Gem Corp., New York, Marvin Samuels.

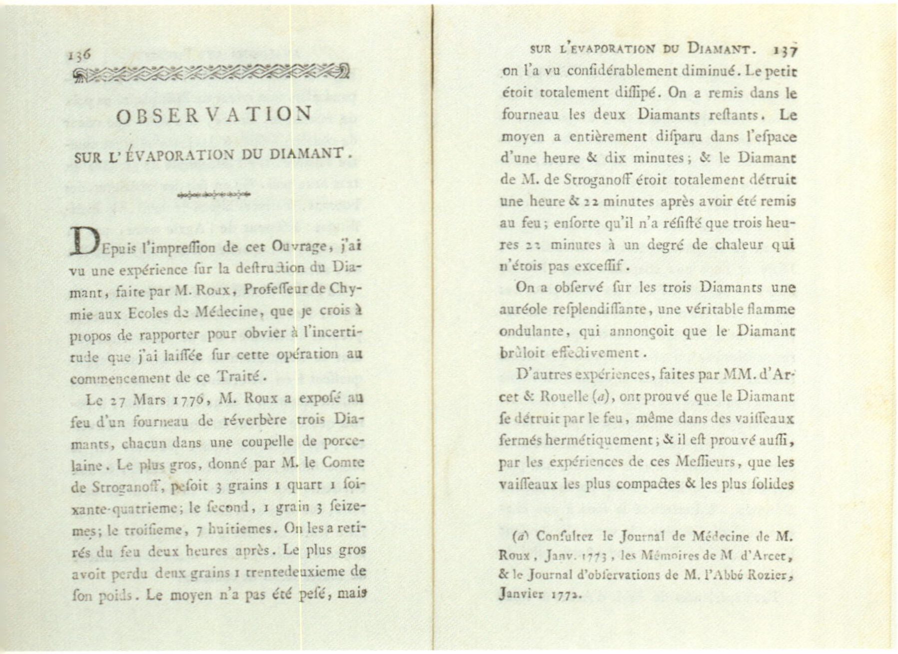

136

OBSERVATION

SUR L'ÉVAPORATION DU DIAMANT.

DEpuis l'impreſſion de cet Ouvrage, j'ai vu une expérience ſur la deſtruction du Diamant, faite par M. Roux, Profeſſeur de Chymie aux Ecoles de Médecine, que je crois à propos de rapporter pour obvier à l'incertitude que j'ai laiſſée ſur cette opération au commencement de ce Traité.

Le 27 Mars 1776, M. Roux a expoſé au feu d'un fourneau de réverbère trois Diamants, chacun dans une coupelle de porcelaine. Le plus gros, donné par M. le Comte de Stroganoff, peſoit 3 grains 1 quart 1 ſoixante-quatrieme; le ſecond, 1 grain 3 ſeizemes; le troiſieme, 7 huitiemes. On les a retirés du feu deux heures après. Le plus gros avoit perdu deux grains 1 trentedeuxieme de ſon poids. Le moyen n'a pas été peſé, mais

SUR L'EVAPORATION DU DIAMANT. 137

on l'a vu conſidérablement diminué. Le petit étoit totalement diſſipé. On a remis dans le fourneau les deux Diamants reſtants. Le moyen a entièrement diſparu dans l'eſpace d'une heure & dix minutes; & le Diamant de M. de Stroganoff étoit totalement détruit une heure & 22 minutes après avoir été remis au feu; enſorte qu'il n'a réſiſté que trois heures 22 minutes à un degré de chaleur qui n'étois pas exceſſif.

On a obſervé ſur les trois Diamants une auréole reſplendiſſante, une véritable flamme ondulante, qui annonçoit que le Diamant brûloit effectivement.

D'autres expériences, faites par MM. d'Arcet & Rouelle (a), ont prouvé que le Diamant ſe détruit par le feu, même dans des vaiſſeaux fermés hermétiquement; & il eſt prouvé auſſi, par les expériences de ces Meſſieurs, que les vaiſſeaux les plus compactes & les plus ſolides

(a) Conſultez le Journal de Médecine de M. Roux, Janv. 1773, les Mémoires de M. d'Arcet, & le Journal d'obſervations de M. l'Abbé Rozier, Janvier 1772.

Dutens, a chemist, analysed and summarised diamond combustion experiments at the end of the 18th century. Contemporaries were tantalisingly close to solving its mysterious composition: pure carbon. Paris, *Muséum national d'histoire naturelle*, central library

Garden in Paris, which would advance the understanding of diamond's properties. During one of these experiments, when Macquer took a stone out of the furnace, observers actually saw the diamond burning. Lavoisier came tantalisingly close to the answer in 1772. He put one diamond in each of three sealed crucibles. Before being sealed, the first crucible was topped up with graphite powder, the second with powdered chalk, and the third was left empty. When the three crucibles were heated, the diamond surrounded by graphite powder remained intact. The gem that was surrounded by chalk was altered. However, the third, which had been heated in the 'empty' crucible (it was, in fact, filled with air), had disappeared completely. This was because the graphite powder in the first crucible had protected the diamond: the small amount of oxygen in the crucible combined with the graphite to yield carbon dioxide. It was not until 1797 that the English chemist Smithson Tennant came up with the solution. He demonstrated that the combustion of a given quantity of diamonds would produce as much carbon dioxide as the combustion of the same mass of coal. In fact, it was realised that diamond consumed more oxygen because it was richer in carbon than coal, which has many impurities. Similar analytical difficulties would have to be overcome before the exact nature of graphite was discovered.

Nevertheless, by the dawn of the 19th century, it was known that diamond and graphite were both made from pure carbon. It was up to mineralogists to explain the enormous visual and physical differences between these two pure chemicals. They managed to demonstrate that, although diamond and graphite both have the same composition, their crystal structures are profoundly different. This is due to the arrangement of the carbon atoms in the two substances. Crystalline structure is defined by the distances between a carbon atom and each of its nearest neighbours. This definition implies that there is a single basic arrangement of a minimum number of atoms which, when repeated many times in three dimensions, will produce the overall crystal. This basic arrangement of atoms, the 'unit cell' is like a building block. It is not possible to go below the minimum number of atoms in the unit cell, without losing the repetitive nature of the atomic structure of the crystal. Therefore, the crystal can be considered to be a regular arrangement of these identical building blocks. This concept of crystallinity was demonstrated through the technique of X-ray diffraction, refined by English Nobel prize-winner, William Bragg, at the end of the 19th century. Basically, X-rays have a wavelength of approximately one Angstrom (one ten-billionth of a metre), similar to the distances between atoms. They can therefore penetrate matter, hence their well-known applications in medical diagnosis. When they penetrate a crystal, X-rays demonstrate another property: since the unit cell is repeated many times in three dimensions, the crystal's atoms are arranged in parallel planes that vary in density depending upon the way one looks at them. These parallel planes reflect X-rays according to the laws of optics, just as a mirror reflects visible light. X-rays have 'peaks' and 'troughs' in their wavelengths, just like visible light. From certain angles, the reflections are such that the distance between two atomic planes is exactly the same as an X-ray wavelength. Therefore, in this direction, the wavelengths will vibrate in phase. This effect is strong enough to be able to be detected, forming a characteristic 'stripe', indicating the alignment of a set of parallel planes. The greater the density of the atoms, the clearer the stripe. One can therefore determine the principal planes of the atoms in the crystal, and the distances between them. However, at the beginning of the 19th century, X-rays were unknown. It was thanks to René Just Haüy's genius, and his naturalist observations, that the nature of crystalline structures was discovered. Haüy's name is closely linked to the Muséum national d'histoire naturelle's history. He was preceded by Jean-Baptiste Romé de l'Isle, who measured and classified minerals. It was Romé de l'Isle who discovered that dihedral angles (the angles between crystal faces, measured perpendicularly from the ridge between them) are constant, across different samples of a given mineral. Basically, all the crystals of a single mineral are based on repetitive arrays of an identical arrangement of atoms: they therefore have identical geometrical parameters. Haüy followed on from this work, and discovered the principle of the 'unit cell', as described above. The story goes that Haüy dropped a large block of calcite, that shattered into fragments when it hit the ground. He realised that all the fragments had the same shape as the original large crystal. He conceived the theory that, if one could continue to break the pieces into smaller and smaller fragments, one would eventually reach a volume that would have all the properties of the original mineral, but which could not be fragmented further without destroying its integrity. The unit cell idea was born. He would refine the concept later on with the notion of the 'integral molecule': the unit cell is composed of chemical elements, present in whole-numbered proportions. This is the definition of a mineral, which is based on the superposition of an atomic structure upon a chemical composition.

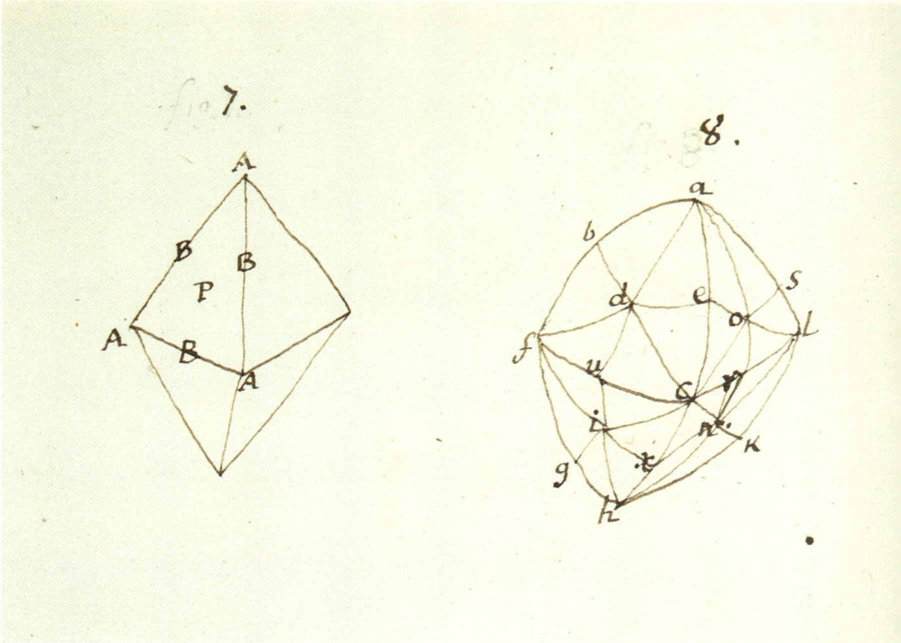

Two pages from manuscript number 1,399, written by René Just Haüy, the founding father of crystallography. A description of diamond is embellished with his observations of two crystals' shapes. Around 1800. Paris, *Muséum national d'histoire naturelle*, central library.

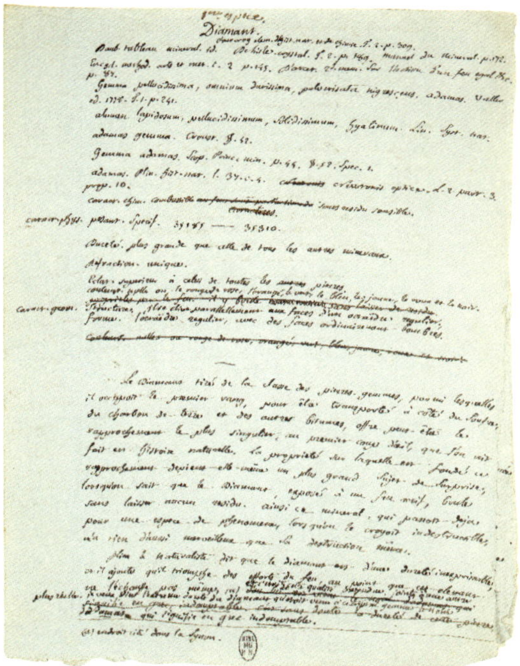

Therefore, Haüy could legitimately be considered as the founder of modern mineralogy. He would later show that all the crystalline shapes in nature stemmed from seven basic shapes: the seven crystal systems. He was, of course, interested in diamond. It is said that he was the one who demonstrated that its crystal forms and shapes were a result of its membership of the cubic crystal system. This was confirmed by the father-and-son team of the Braggs themselves, who achieved an X-ray diffraction pattern for diamond in 1913 and determined its structure. Every carbon atom is linked to four neighbours, each the same distance away, in the shape of a tetrahedron. By stacking tetrahedrons together, we arrive at the most compact and solid structure known. Graphite, on the other hand, has a different structure. It is composed of carbon atoms linked together in hexagonal shapes, forming layers. The distances between these layers is more than double the distance between the carbon atoms in a diamond molecule. As a result, the space between the layers is a weak spot in graphite's structure. This structural difference gives rise to the two minerals' contrasting physical properties. Diamond's compact, three-dimensional crystal structure makes it the hardest known material in existence, whereas the weakly layered structure of graphite makes it so soft that it can be used as an industrial lubricant. It is slippery because the hexagonal layers are weakly linked: they slide over each other. The comparatively large distance between the layers explains why there are fewer atoms of carbon in a given volume of graphite than for a comparable volume of diamond. As a result, the latter is 50% denser. Finally, light passes through a diamond very slowly because the atoms are arranged so compactly: this is why diamond refracts light so well.

Graphite and diamond are known as 'polymorphic minerals'. This is becau-

Crystalline structures of diamond (top) and graphite (bottom). Diamond displays a pyramidal structure of stacked tetrahedra, ensuring the overall structure's solidity. Graphite's structure has solidly linked hexagonal layers of carbon atoms that are, in turn, linked to each other. The links between the layers are, however, relatively weak. This makes the structure much less rigid: the layers can easily slide over each other. After Robert M. Hazen, *The Diamond Makers*, Cambridge University Press, 1999

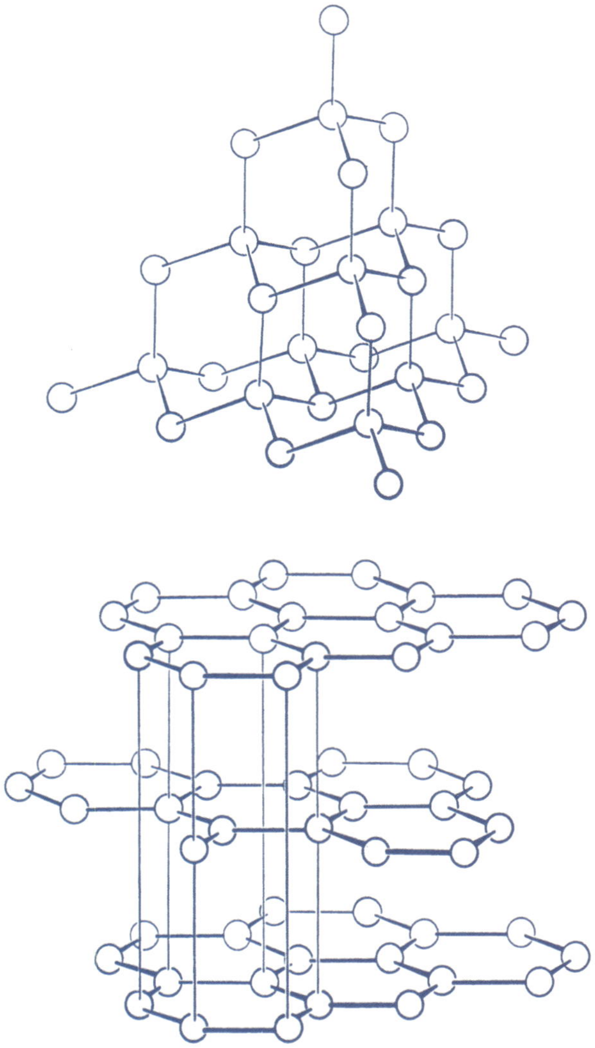

se they have the same chemical composition, but different crystal structures. This begs the question of how the two can coexist. To answer this question, we require thermodynamics, a science that originated in the 19th century. Thermodynamics effectively shows us that there is only one stable form for a given set of physical conditions. A 'phase diagram' is simply a graphical display that shows these stability conditions. We can use water to demonstrate this notion: at atmospheric pressure, water boils at 100°C. While it is boiling, it is present in two phases: liquid water and gaseous steam. Even if the temperature rises, the water/steam system will remain at 100°C until all the water has turned to steam: one cannot heat liquid water above 100°C at atmospheric pressure without it changing into a gas. This is thermodynamic equilibrium. However, if the pressure changes, the boiling point varies. Any mountain-climber who has ever had difficulty making a hot cup of tea at altitude will know this! Conversely, in a pressure cooker, high pressure raises the boiling point, hence resulting in a faster cooking time. A phase diagram shows a pressure/temperature line, marking the boundary to the conditions at which water will change from liquid to gas. Likewise, there is a phase diagram that marks out the boundaries of stability for graphite and diamond. Work began on this diagram in 1938, and its details would not be known exactly until 1955. This relatively recent date shows why synthesising diamond in the laboratory has been a long and difficult process. Basically, before 1938, nobody realised that it was necessary to reach pressures of at least 15,000 atmospheres at 500°C for diamond to be stable. Once this was understood, it took time to construct equipment that could reach these pressures. Defining the phase diagram has also been extremely useful for geologists. It proves that diamond could only have come from deep down inside planet Earth, where the extreme pressure needed to ensure its stability is found. The only thing that remained was to solve two mysteries: how it formed, and how it managed to reach the surface without changing into graphite. These were the topics of scientific research in the late 20th century: they are still not completely answered today in the early 21st.

Therefore, to understand diamond's formation is to understand the structure and the history of the Earth, and its functional dynamics. Although modern analytical techniques and the paradigm of plate tectonics have enabled us to see more clearly, we still have a long way to go before we can shed light on the complete story of this mineral's origins. And the story does not stop there! These small lumps of regularly stacked carbon atoms have many more surprises in store: they have not finished teaching us about our planet's history, or even taking us beyond that into interstellar space. The discovery that diamonds can tell us about the mysterious life and death of stars has aroused immense scientific interest. What other mineral could tell us so much?

The domains of existence of the various forms of carbon, such as diamond and graphite, were unknown for a long time. This lasted until the determination of carbon's phase diagram. This contemporary jewel by German designer Cornelia Rating summarises the dichotomy better than any lecture: the coexistence between a black, soft material and a colourless mineral that is harder than any other. This necklace is made out of pieces of coal, wrapped in diamond and platinum ribbons. De Beers Diamonds International Awards, 2000.

1 Diamonds: in the heart of the Earth, in the hearts of stars

Hubert Bari & Emmanuel Fritsch

CHAPTER I

The natural history of diamonds

Once a diamond is discovered, it has a very short life expectancy. Because of the enormous value involved, it is rapidly cleaved, sawn, cut and polished. It is, in a way, denatured. This is regrettable as far as mineralogists are concerned, because diamonds leave the natural history sphere when they are cut. It is an impossible dream for most people to view diamonds close to their source. That source is the head office of the DTC. DTC stands for Diamond Trading Company: it has recently been re-named, and used to be the CSO, or Central Selling Organisation. It is part of the all-powerful De Beers group, and the place to which almost all the mines in the world deliver their gems. However, for this book's authors, the dream came true. The DTC is headquartered in London, near the site of an ancient Carthusian monastery. It is not easy to get inside: passwords must be given, and numerous steel doors need to be opened. After a final security check, we enter a room with a long picture window, illuminated by north-facing daylight. There is a table about twenty metres long inside the room. In preparation for our visit, De Beers employees have set up several piles of diamonds on the table: each pile is worth $500,000. The piles vary in size: the more impure and tinted the diamonds are, the larger the piles get. Instinctively, we pass over the largest heaps and head for the smallest pile, containing a handful of the largest, purest diamonds. These marvels of natural history are staggering in their beauty, with beautiful crystal shapes and exquisite colours. For a mineralogist, the display is awe-inspiring. Diamond is such a simple mineral - pure carbon - yet it has such variety in terms of its crystal shapes and geometric forms, such as octahedra or cubes. Further along, there is a priceless collection of crystals that are not for sale: the famous 'De Beers Special Collection', assembled over many decades. When we wonder at the collection, we pay tribute to Rogan McLean, a retired CSO Director, preserved this collection of natural curiosities that would otherwise have been cut and destroyed.

The marvellous De Beers sorting table.
Each batch of diamonds is worth half a million dollars. The heap at the front is the smallest but, of course, the most interesting.

A diamond crystal mounted on a wooden base, from the collection of Abbot Haüy, the famous mineralogist from *the Muséum national d'histoire naturelle* in Paris. It is one of the representative mineral samples that were used to define diamond's crystallographic nature. Haüy's treatise on crystallography is in the background.

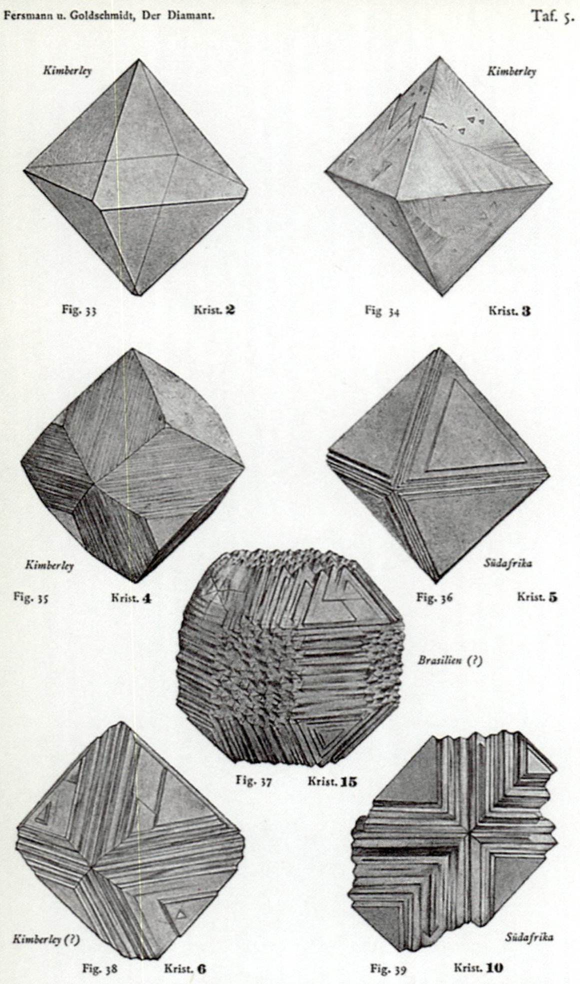

Illustration showing some of the basic diamond shapes, such as the octahedron and the dodecahedron. It was taken from Viktor Goldschmidt and Alexander von Fersmann's 1911 crystallography album. *Muséum national d'histoire naturelle*, Paris.

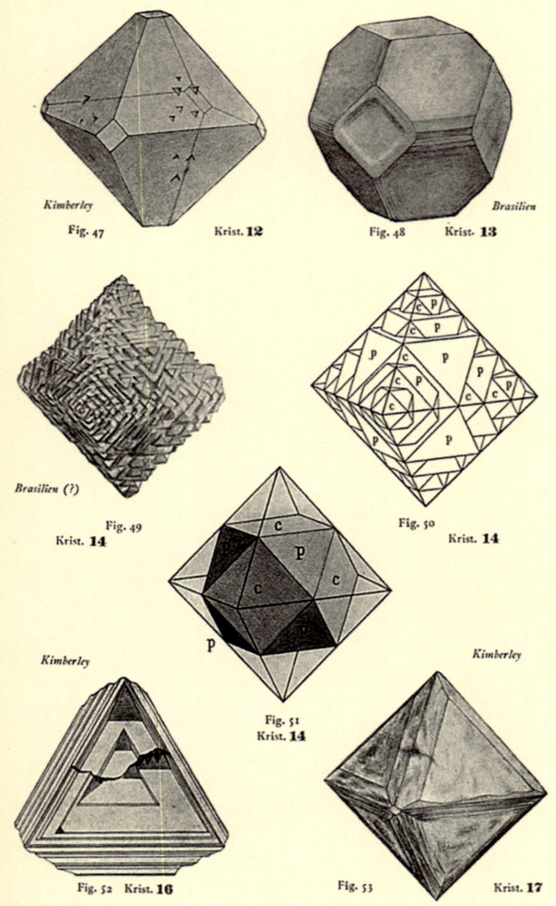

Face to face with diamonds

The table bears shapes that bring the origins of crystallography to mind. Before X-ray diffraction crystallography was introduced, the only way of deducing the regular internal atomic structure of crystalline materials was to observe their exterior crystal shapes and faces. This was the basis of crystallography. It was performed using goniometers, devices like adjustable protractors. When placed against two faces of a crystal, they give a measurement of the dihedral angle perpendicular to those faces. This was the time of the contact goniometer. Soon afterwards, the optical goniometer was invented - although this, too, is hardly used nowadays. It allows angles between crystal faces to be measured with great accuracy, by turning them along a crystallographic axis in front of a light source. One of the crystal faces acts like a mirror, and the crystallographer measures the position of its reflection on a graduated plate. The crystal is then turned, to acquire a reflection from another face. The difference between these two readings gives the dihedral angle between the two crystal faces. Diamonds were the subject of intensive optical goniometer research. This is hardly surprising: they are usually found in small crystals, which often have reflective faces because they are extremely hard. The French excelled in the goniometry technique, particularly Jean-Baptiste Romé de l'Isle (1736-1790) and René Just Haüy (1743-1822), who were trailblazers in the field. A famous early-20th-century mineralogist from Heidelberg University, Prof. Viktor Goldschmidt, compiled the work of hundreds of crystallographers in his *Atlas der Kristallformen.* It's one of the most beautiful mineralogy books in existence, in nine enormous volumes, and covers crystallographic research from the whole of the 19th century. In 1911, he published another book, with his Russian collaborator Alexander von Fersmann. It is in two small volumes, soberly entitled *Diamond: a Study.* These are two volumes of pure crystallography. The second volume is devoted entirely to plates of illustrations. It is a marvellous work of art, based upon hundreds of goniometer measurements undertaken by these two scholars. It is still one of the most beautiful graphical works ever devoted to diamonds. Goldschmidt and von Fersmann never had the opportunity to be dazzled by the treasures of the De Beers collection. If they could have seen these samples, they would have rediscovered, on the centimetre scale, some of the things that they could barely see at millimetre level. Their beautiful enlarged drawings give a glimpse into the subject's complexity.

The octahedron: perfection has eight sides and six points

There is one dominant diamond shape in this array of forms: the octahedron, a type of double-pyramid with a square cross-section. It used to be called the 'simple point' shape, because of its pointed corners. Two octahedra in the De Beers selection stand out. One is two centimetres across and is as clear as *glass* (in fact, such crystals are known as *glassies* in the trade). It is superb, with an almost magical, balanced double-pyramid shape and near-perfect crystal points, top and bottom. Looking at it, one can see why ancient alchemists, science-fiction writers and 'new-age' hippies attribute such shapes with supernatural energy powers. It is indisputably beautiful and impressive. Very few people ever have the privilege of handling such a gem. The second octahedron is yellow; its faces are slightly frosted and more irregular. It has many small, skin-deep indentations with triangular outlines. These are known in the trade as 'trigons'. However, although its surface is peppered with little geometrical markings, the inside is of gem quality, just like the first stone. Gem-cutters know that it is not possible to judge a diamond's clarity simply by looking at its surface. They perform a procedure known as 'windowing': polishing a smooth facet on the surface, in order to be able to see deep into the gem's interior.

The octahedron is by far the most common basic shape for rough diamond crystals. De Beers' magical table bears thousands of them, from diamond mines the world over. Centuries ago, Indian diamond-cutters had already noticed this. They believed that there was a kind of organic relationship between the stones. The large octahedra were the parents, and the smaller gems were their 'babies'. This belief in the sexuality and childbirth of diamonds seems quaint, even bizarre to our eyes. However, the table bears a strange gem that provides a simple explanation for the superstition: one of the octahedra, a centimetre across, has another, smaller, octahedral crystal trapped inside it. Such freaks of nature must surely have been seen two thousand years ago, well before the laws of crystallography and crystal growth were understood. They would have given rise to the belief that the outer diamonds were 'pregnant' with baby crystals. The next stage in gestation is also illustrated on the table: there is a magnificent octahedral crystal in the pile, attached to an agglomeration of smaller crystals. The ancient gem-cutters may have thought that such a gem resembled an Indian monkey, carrying her babies clutched to her body. Presumably, they would have assumed that the crystal had given birth to its babies, who would eventually grow on to adulthood. Hindu scholars believed that such gems grew in size as they got older, eventually reaching hundreds of carats should they survive to their dotage.

Although the ancient Indian idea of diamonds undergoing childbirth was mistaken, the part about diamonds eventually growing to great size was, in fact, closer to the mark. As we shall see, this is indeed what happens in the heart of the Earth's mantle, more than 120 kilometres deep. This is the place where diamond crystals form. Small crystals grow from 'seeds' for as long as they continue to be supplied with pure carbon to nourish their development - assuming, of course, that the physical and chemical conditions remain favourable for growth. This is how small octahedra turn into large crystals. Their growth patterns can be seen in rough diamond samples. It is possible to look inside the stones using a polarising microscope. The frosted surfaces begin to resemble skies full of triangular spaceships, hovering over strange landscapes furrowed with parallel grooves. These parallel lines are growth patterns: they show that the octahedron grew progressively, in the same way as tree rings show evidence of plant growth over the years. One of the De Beers crystals is broken in two, revealing its striations, which look like the growth marks of a tiny, angular tree. But nobody knows how long the stones took to grow: each line might have taken days, years or millennia to form.

Indian gem-cutters prized the octahedron above all other shapes, and they wrote highly detailed texts on the subject. Louis Finot was an eminent French specialist in ancient Sanskrit documents. He assembled a number of ancient Indian documents on the subject of gemstones, from the archives of many different libraries. He published his translations in an École des Hautes Études journal, in 1896. The results were extremely enlightening, with information on gem descriptions, their physical properties, how to evaluate their worth, gem-mining, how to identify imitations and, finally, their supernatural power for good or evil. This body of literature goes under the generic name of *Ratnapariksha* ("the art of gem appreciation"). All the texts start with the most precious gem of all: diamond. Here are some extracts, dating back at least as far as the 6th century AD: "the natural characteristics of diamond are points, facets and edges, numbering 6, 8, 12: fine, equal and sharp. A six-pointed diamond, pure and unmarked, with pronounced and sharp edges, a fine colour, light, with well-formed facets, flawless, illuminating the space around it with rainbow fires: such a diamond is not easy to find on this Earth". Followed by: "Diamond's five qualities consist of six-pointedness, with eight equal faces, sharp points, light and flawless[...] No good will come of a diamond that has truncated corners or edges, with imperfect facets, of rounded shape and without brilliance."

The ancients were fascinated by the octahedron, and associated it with perfection. This idea was, in fact, not far from the truth. The laws of crystalline growth have since taught us that, for diamond, a perfect octahedral shape results from slow growth, compared to the other growth forms (discussed below). Under these conditions, which are ideal for making a beautiful crystal, there are neither too many nor too few atoms bonding to the crystal surface as it grows. The atoms arrange themselves in a regular way, giving rise to smooth, flat faces, bordered by sharp edges. In diamonds, no other gem-quality crystallographic shape ever possesses such flat faces and sharp edges.

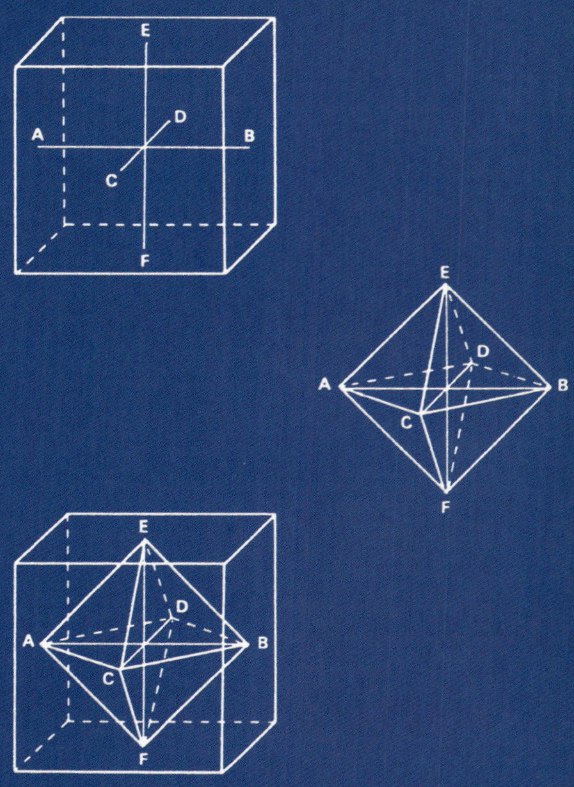

Drawing of a cube and an octahedron, showing how the octahedron fits within a cube. The symmetry axes are also shown.

The superb rough *Oppenheimer* diamond, 253.7 carats, found in the Dutoitspan mine, Kimberley. It is one of the most beautiful uncut diamond crystals in the world. Smithsonian Institution, Washington.

The *Cullinan*: a superb, but shapeless diamond! The rough stone weighed 3,106 carats. It is shown here being held by the director of the Premier mine, William McHardy, on the day of its discovery. On his left is Thomas Cullinan, president of the mine company. De Beers Archives, Kimberley.

Sharp-eyed Indian gem-cutters had observed that diamonds come in a variety of crystal forms, and they were already aware of the commonest: the 6-pointed octahedron, the 8-pointed cube and the 12-pointed dodecahedron. They were also aware that the crystals' faces were often irregularly developed. In fact, if a diamond crystal grows inside an irregularly shaped confined space, one face may grow more quickly than the others. This face will be smaller than the others, because it will gradually get narrower. Therefore, the De Beers rough diamond piles contain some surprises for the careful observer. One crystal is strangely lengthened, despite the fact that diamond crystallises in the cubic system and, theoretically, its crystals should fit neatly inside a sphere. The cubic crystal system is described as being 'isotropic': this means that its properties are the same in all directions, radiating from its centre. And yet, the De Beers crystal could easily be confused with baryte, a barium sulphate which is formed in many metallic seams in mines. It is, in fact, an octahedron. One growth direction was presented with more favourable growth conditions than the others, and the crystal lengthened in that direction. Such crystals are basically accidents of growth.

Great, shapeless monsters

Slow and regular growth can give rise to these marvellous octahedral diamonds, but it can also generate astonishing monsters: enormous stones of indeterminate shape. Most of the biggest diamonds in the world took this form: the *Cullinan*, the *Centenary* and, more recently, the *De Beers Millennium Star*. In fact, almost all large diamonds over 300 carats are of irregular form. There is only one notable exception: the famous *SixOneSix Diamond*, a rough octahedron of just under 616 carats, found in the Dutoitspan mine, Kimberley, on April 17, 1974. Master diamond-cutters have the heavy responsibility of proposing a cut for such large, apparently shapeless crystals. It can take months to locate the gem's crystallographic orientation. Why is it that these legendary rough crystals do not have smooth faces and clean edges? Paradoxically, it is because the perfect octahedral shape arises from a defect. When that defect is not present, the shape cannot be perfect any more.

How can this be? The explanation is as follows. In order to form a smooth, flat crystal face, crystal growth needs to take shape around a specific crystal defect. This defect is known as a spiral dislocation, and the ordered atomic structure grows around it. A spiral dislocation is a shift in the position of certain atoms in an atomic layer, relative to the rest of the crystal. This is not specific to diamond: the same thing happens in crystals of sugar or ordinary kitchen salt. This defect occurs in abundance in almost all diamonds, except for certain rare stones, which are chemically very pure. If the stone is absolutely pure, the spiral dislocation does not occur and a clean crystal face cannot develop around the defect. As a result, the crystal does not develop flat faces.

A tangled knot of diamond

We have discussed large, famous diamonds. But what of lower-quality diamonds, destined for industrial use? In this case, instead of having slow growth, which helps create perfection, we have fast, chaotic growth instead. If there is a lot of carbon in the growth medium, or if the temperature or pressure drops quickly, then diamond will tend to grow quickly. This kind of rapid crystal growth happens in everyday life: the spreading of hoar-frost crystals on window-panes, for example. Under fast growth conditions, diamond forms exactly the same kind of fibrous crystal structure, in a wide variety of shapes. The result can be disconcerting: sometimes it forms spheres made out of fibrous radiating diamond filaments, resembling a hedgehog or tangle of hair. This type of diamond growth is known as *ballas*. Curiously enough, industrial diamonds can also form rather beautiful crystal shapes with recognisable forms, although they are opaque and the crystal faces are roughened. These forms include cubes, octahedron/cube combinations, and some rarer shapes, such as the dodecahedron, for example. But how can fibrous clumps form into shapes with flat faces, such as cubes? The answer lies in a poorly understood process known as *fibre branching*. By some miracle of nature, diamond retains the 'memory' of its original small central seed. The fibres grow in rapid spurts from this perfectly formed seed, and the tips grow according to the resulting surfaces, whether they be cubic, octahedral, or dodecahedral faces. This remarkable property is unknown in other minerals, and its secret mechanism has yet to be deciphered.

Sometimes, gem-quality crystals are covered in layers of fibrous diamond. This results in a commodity best suited to risk-taking thrill-seekers: speculative rough, or *coated diamonds*. Certain diamond deposits produce stones that conceal beautiful, gem-quality crystals under an opaque, dirt-coloured skin. The only way of discovering whether there is a beautiful gem under the surface is by using the polishing wheel to grind a 'window' in the stone. There is a catch, however: the cutter has to decide to buy the stone first! It is possible to lose a lot of money on this addictive game. This category of diamonds is found in several diamond-bearing deposits: Brazil, Congo and British Guyana, for example. The skin follows the shape of the underlying crystal, and is of constant thickness all over. It is made of diamond fibres, which developed perpendicular to the flat, smooth crystalline faces of the diamond underneath. This strange juxtaposition is caused by an abrupt change in growth conditions: slow growth initially gives rise to a beautiful gem, followed by a period of very fast growth, when the crystal's growth becomes fibrous.

The two largest diamonds cut from the gigantic *Cullinan* stone, shown life-size: the *Great Star of Africa* (or *Cullinan I*: 530.20 carats) and the *Cullinan II* (317.40 carats). Jewel House, Tower of London.

A gem-quality diamond cuboid of exceptional size (2 cm). The crystal faces are not flat, and neither are the edges. For these reasons, it is not a true cube.
The term "cuboid" was therefore introduced, to describe such spectacular diamond crystals. In addition, the growth markings are not parallel to the edges: they are aligned with the diagonal directions of each square face. Michael J. Scott collection.

Almost a cube: the cuboid, or false cube

Under certain conditions, which are not yet fully understood, crystal cube edges seem to develop more quickly than the centres of the faces, which are therefore indented. These conditions give rise to objects that resemble cubes, but which are not true cubes. Their surfaces are rough, irregular, and only approximately aligned with cube faces. British researchers suggested the name "cuboid" in the 1970s, to avoid any confusion with true cube growth faces, which are flat and smooth. Some really resemble cubes. Others only have a cubic skeleton: they have a cube's edges, although they are not straight any more. They also have indentations, in the shape of inverted pyramids, on the sides. In even more extreme cases, some rare specimens are in the shape of a central ball covered with edges. These resemble old terrestrial globes, with curved ridges representing the equator and lines of longitude. At first glance, these perplexing stones seem not to resemble cubes at all. Indeed, one might believe that they were crystals that had been almost completely dissolved. However, they display crystal growth marks on their surfaces, and these growth marks have hardly faded. Some of them yield a three-pointed star, when cleaved along an octahedral face. Coincidentally, one famous car manufacturer has a three-pointed star as its motif, so these diamonds are sometimes used to make expensive key-rings!

Cuboid crystals can therefore develop into some extreme forms. Surprisingly, this rare morphology is often associated with an unusual chemical composition. They have abnormally high hydrogen levels, some degree of yellow fluorescence, specific types of micro-inclusions and, very rarely, they can possess

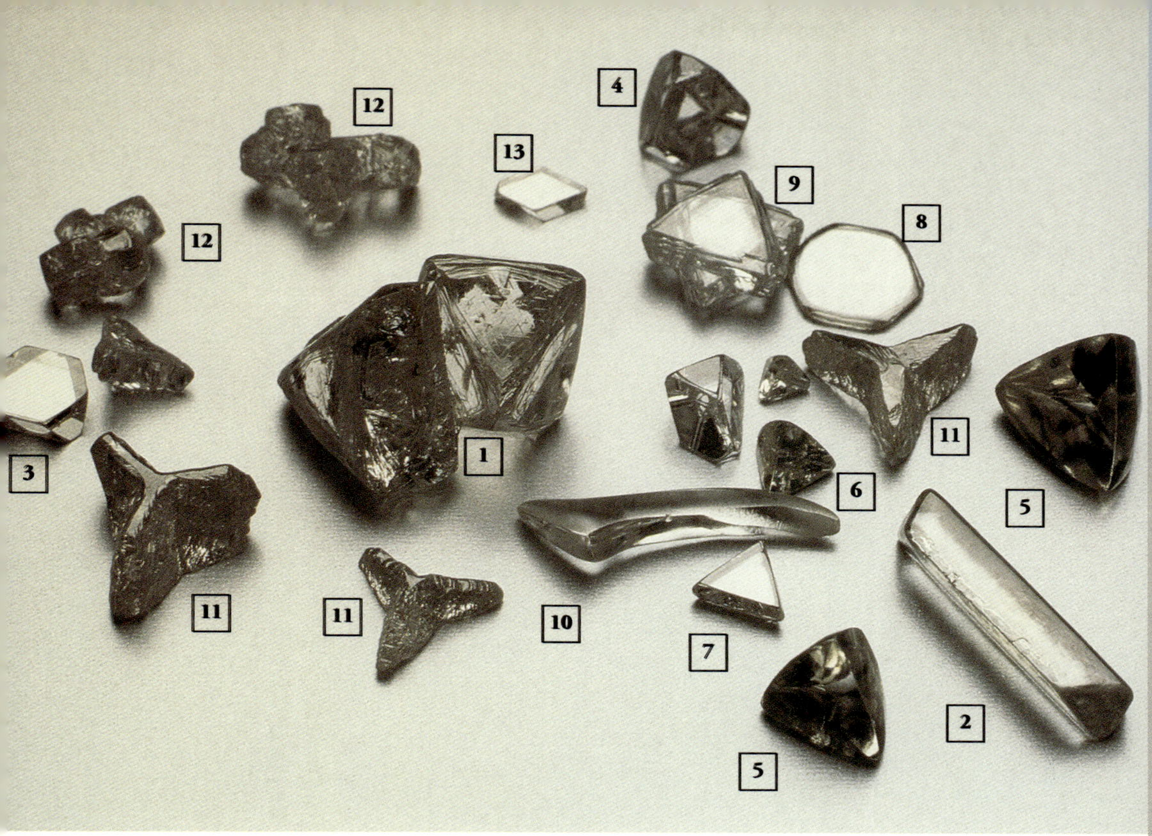

A group of rough diamonds of remarkable or unusual shapes. In the centre, there is an octahedron (1) twinned with a macle. The octahedral form can be modified in various ways. Preferential growth in one direction (or cleavage) could be the cause of the lengthened (2) or flattened crystals (3). Preferential growth of some faces or cleavages can give rise to a form close to a three-sided pyramid, the tetrahedron (forms 4 and 5). More rarely, this form can be due to the asymmetrical development of a twin (6). Macles commonly have a triangular shape (1, 7). A flattened hexagon shape is possible, but very rare (8). In Yakutia, they sometimes find twins of macles. These form two opposed triangles, in a Star-of-David shape (9). In very rare cases, if an octahedron is broken, cleaved and very dissolved, it can develop into a "hound's-tooth" (10). The Jwaneng mine occasionally produces "skeletonised", partly dissolved cubes. If the corners of the cube cleave off, this produces a three-pointed star (11). Of course, crystals of various forms can join together to produce strange or evocative shapes (12). The cause of number 13's lozenge shape is unknown, but it could possibly be the result of a cleavage. Special Collection, De Beers London.

a violet colour that is not found in any other diamond shape. Cuboid crystals are not only an unusual shape, they are a whole diamond category.

Octahedra, fibres and cuboids are the elementary diamond growth shapes. Nevertheless, these shapes can be modified by many other factors. While they are growing, crystals can join together to form twins. They will stay within the Earth for a long time: three billion years, in some cases. Many events and modifications can occur over such a long period. As we will see, diamonds are often dissolved, deformed, broken or cleaved. This can give rise to radically unusual shapes, thereby multiplying the number of forms found in natural diamonds.

Gemini crystals

Crystals have a peculiar habit: they sometimes grow into each other. Abbot Haüy was the founder of crystallography. He felt that the word 'coupled' was too risqué, so specialists use the word 'twin' or the slightly more obscure term 'macle'. Twins are a fascinating part of crystallography, just as they are fascinating to geneticists. They can be considered as 'Siamese crystals'. Twins are associations of two or more crystals from the same mineral species. The crystals do not link up in a random way: they follow very precise crystallographic rules (twinning laws), although there is only one twin law in diamonds. The crystals grow jointly, and share an element of symmetry. The boundary between the crystals can be an interpenetration, or a join. Generally, twins are detected by observing re-entrant angles between the crystal faces. By definition, such re-entrant angles are not normally present in a single crystal. Twins are, however, often very difficult to identify with the naked eye. Sometimes, the only indication is a break in the crystal's growth lines, with a 'fold' where the grooves on the crystal face change direction. Various crystal forms are possible when the different crystal shapes are combined with contact or interpenetrant twin crystals. Some of these are rarer than others. Naturally, twins pose problems for the diamond-cutter. The cutter has to contend with first one crystal, then the other within the same stone. When the crystallographic alignments change direction, so do the cleavages and hardness properties, which are not the same in all directions within the same stone.

Twin of two diamond cubes, known as a 'fluorite' twin. Private Collection.

Twins are usually flat, triangular crystals. They are also known as 'macles'. They are much in demand for specific uses. Ultra-sharp diamond blades can be cut from them, and so can 'glasses', or 'portrait diamonds', that can be used to cover a miniature or the face of a watch. Diamond

Mohs-Rose 'twin'. This splendid 4.98-carat crystal has a complex shape. It was thought to be two diamond tetrahedra twinned together. However, recent studies proved that it is not a twin, but a complex shape produced by the dissolution of a single octahedron. Michael J. Scott collection.

Three octahedra: the first is perfect, the other two are flattened. The fourth stone is a triangular macle. Private collection.

A rare example of a diamond on matrix (2 cm). It has a basically octahedral shape, and displays many parallel growth zones. This generates multiple small, reflective faces. Houston Natural History Museum.

This 1.5cm Russian diamond is an almost perfect octahedron, like the majority of diamonds from Yakutia. Slight surface dissolution has exposed successive growth layers on each triangular face. Private collection.

From perfection to dissolution:
a series of four slightly yellowish diamonds.
Three are octahedral, one is rounded.
The rounded diamond is the end result of the dissolution of an octahedral crystal, as can be seen by the rounded faces and curved edges.
It has a roughly dodecahedral shape, with curved, lozenge-shaped faces. This rounded shape is common in diamond deposits. Private collection.

watch-glasses are, of course, guaranteed to be unscratchable! Such crystals are known as rotated macles. They are formed from two half-octahedrons that are rotated and joined along an octahedral plane. The result is a triangle, with small re-entrant angles at the three corners. Two triangular macles can in turn rotate and join together, and this grouping of four diamonds provides the extraordinary and extremely rare 'Star of David' form. The diamond business has been dominated by Jewish merchants and cutters for many years, so one can easily imagine the kind of impact that this discovery must have had.

Goldschmidt and von Fersmann catalogued other diamond twins. Most of them would only be spotted by a trained crystallographer, except for one very beautiful variety, resulting from the interpenetration of two cubes. Mineralogists call it a 'fluorite' twin, because it is commonly found in the mineral fluorite. This twin also has a kind of star-shape, somewhat reminiscent of an aniseed flower. The Houston Natural History Museum has one in its collection: the two interpenetrating cubes are each 2cm wide!

Goldschmidt and von Fersmann believed that they had identified other twins. However, with the assistance of modern crystallographic methods based on X-rays, some of these findings have been disproved. Their Mohs-Rose twin, for example, superficially appears to be a rare tetrahedral twin. However, this curious crystal has rough crystal faces, which were discovered to be dissolution surfaces. It is a freak of nature, which appears to be unique to diamonds. It is so unexpected, one can easily understand why the two pioneers were mistaken.

A dissolute existence

After its initial growth period, which is of unknown duration, diamond resides at great depths for extremely long periods of time: up to three billion years. It would be extraordinary if diamonds were to remain unmodified during such a long period. It is thought that the crystals are subjected to convection currents that cause them to travel to the heart of the Earth before being ejected. Many diamonds have evidently been partly dissolved, and they can begin to resemble small, half-melted ice-cubes as a result. However, many such diamonds are discovered in solid rock, and have clearly not been subjected to any erosion at the surface. The dissolution events therefore occur deep within the Earth, but it is not known precisely where. They may occur in the mantle or, later, in the volcanic pipes that bring the crystals up to the surface, mixed with corrosive fluids.

Dissolution has a major impact on the shapes of diamonds before they reach the Earth's surface. The majority of crystals dissolve, starting at specific zones of weakness, such as the points and the edges, which become rounded. This gives rise to curved dissolution forms that look very different to growth features, which have flat faces and edges. The first stage of this metamorphosis is an octahedron with curved, three- or six-sided pyramidal faces. Crystallographically, these are known as trisoctahedra and hexoctahedra. The edges get so rounded that they become lozenge-shaped faces. The resulting form is a rhomboidal dodecahedron with curved faces, known as a rhombododecahedron. This complex, twelve-sided shape is common in garnets.

All the possible growth forms, including twins, can be subjected to dissolution in the same way as octahedra. Any fractures or growth defects are weak points; they are engulfed by the corrosive solutions. For example, if a triangular macle has a fracture along one of its sides, it may become a heart-shape, as the fracture opens up and the outline becomes rounded. In extreme and rare cases, holes can be dissolved in the diamond. Beyond this, of course, is complete dissolution. One might speculate about the number of magnificent diamonds that disappeared before ever arriving at the Earth's surface. These dissolution attacks leave traces that follow crystallographic rules. For example, shallow triangular indentations are often found on the surfaces of octahedral crystals. These are known as trigons. On pseudo-cubic faces, square indentations may be seen, with edges that are parallel to the octahedral crystal planes: although growth may have followed the cubic shape, dissolution follows the octahedral shape.

Hound's-teeth and other exotic shapes

When several events occur together to change a diamond's shape, the final result can be so far from the initial octahedral form that the species is almost unrecognisable. This is the case with certain stones from the Helam mine in Namibia. They have rounded, grooved shapes, sometimes decorated with little horns. Some of the vaguely prismatic crystals, with one rounded and one pointed end, are known as *hound's-tooth* crystals by diamond cutters. These probably result from fractures or cleavages, followed by dissolution. It seems that some diamonds are so abused deep within the Earth, they really lead a dog's life!

The tetrahedron: cleavage or twin

The tetrahedron, or three-sided pyramid, is a rare diamond shape. It has prompted much argument. Not long ago, De Beers launched a press release when it found one of them. This is because, if diamond does indeed grow in a tetrahedral form, it flies in the face of diamond's crystal symmetry. This is because the tetrahedron has less symmetry than the octahedron. Such a crystal would be highly interesting to researchers! In fact, recent studies proved that such tetrahedra generally result from the cleavage of octahedral stones. In rare cases, they can be the result of a twin that developed atypically. All is well, therefore: diamond's structure has high-order octahedral symmetry, and apparent cases of lower-order symmetry are merely accidents of growth or subsequent breakages, mimicking different forms.

Diamond has many characteristic forms, therefore: some are ordinary, and others extraordinary. Of all these forms, the octahedron is the only one that commonly displays smooth, flat faces, the result of slow and regular growth. The cube always has rough surfaces (except in synthetic diamonds, but that's another story). The rhombododecahedron always has curved, often striated faces, the result of the dissolution of a diamond that was originally octahedral. It is best to forget the idealised crystals that are often displayed in books. These are only a pale shadow of the truth. A diamond's shape is a record of its birth and its life history. Crystallographers are fortunate enough to be able to read it.

Batch of yellow and brown diamonds.
Almost all of them are dissolution shapes.
De Beers Collection.

Batch of diamonds, displaying an extraordinary variety of shapes, colours and sizes. De Beers collection.

Bastard diamonds

By reading this title, one might think that diamonds cross-breed with other minerals. This is not the case! The word *'bastard'* became corrupted in English to the word *boart*, generally denoting diamonds that are destined for industrial use. They are unsuitable crystals for jewellery. They may be eliminated because of their poor colour (dirty yellow, brown, etc.), their unusable shape (fractures, polycrystalline growths), or quite simply their opacity. Some crystals are suffused with black graphite inclusions. They are black, and are also destined for industrial use. De Beers has an impressive mass of *boart* in its collection. It weighs more than 200 grams.

But there are other types of non-gem-quality diamond. Carbonado is a term that indicates an aggregate of diamond and graphite (the high- and low-pressure forms of carbon, respectively). Carbonado was initially found in Brazil, hence the Portuguese-sounding name. This material has a slightly lower density than pure diamond: about 3.2 to 3.4, compared to 3.51. When crushed, car-

bonado yields grinding powder. When examined under the microscope, it reveals myriad, slightly flattened diamond crystals, stuck together with black carbon, primarily in the form of graphite. The exact formation conditions that give rise to these aggregates remain unknown.

As we have seen, diamond's shapes are far more varied than one might think. However, untrained observers generally look at these splendid, transparent shapes and assume that they are man-made. Nothing could be further from the truth. These shapes are the result of crystal growth processes, blasted to the surface by volcanic eruptions in a completely random manner, to be unearthed by adventurers or persistent geologists. The proof of this naturalness lies in rock samples that still have diamonds trapped inside them. As we will see, kimberlite is the rock that carries diamonds to the surface of the Earth. De Beers has a remarkable series of crystals that are still trapped in their rock matrix. They are the summit of diamond mineralogy: collectors' items that only the most privileged museums possess. They are also symbolic of diamond's qualities: transparency emerging from opacity, and sparkling light, trapped inside dull rock.

De Beers' exceptional rough diamond collection is not the only one, however. There is another, preserved in the Kremlin in Moscow. It is the Russian Diamond Fund, the official collection of the Russian Federation. This vault displays the Tsars' jewels, as well as an impressive series of rough diamonds. They were saved from cutting in order to display the exceptional beauty of Siberian diamonds. The collection has some stones that reach several hundred carats, each in its beautiful natural form. In accordance with tradition, these diamonds were given names. The majority of them were found in the Soviet era, so their names were often evocative, such as the *XXIVth Congress of the Soviet Union Communist Party* (324.50 carats), the *Soviet Constitution* (119.65 carats) or the *Fifty Years of Aeroflot* (65.63 carats).

The first over-100-carat diamond preserved by the USSR in a natural state is the *Maria* (105.98 carats). It was named in honour of Maria Markovna Konenkina, one of the first mine-workers in the Mir ("Peace") diamond mine in Yakutia. The *Maria* is the Communist counterpart to the 260-carat *Oppenheimer* crystal. The Oppenheimer was named in honour of Sir Ernest Oppenheimer, the De Beers chairman. It is a marvellous yellow octahedron, in the collection of the Smithsonian Institution, Washington. These names are reminders of the political chasm between the two great global ideologies of the time: depending on where the diamonds were found, they were named after either the worker or the manager.

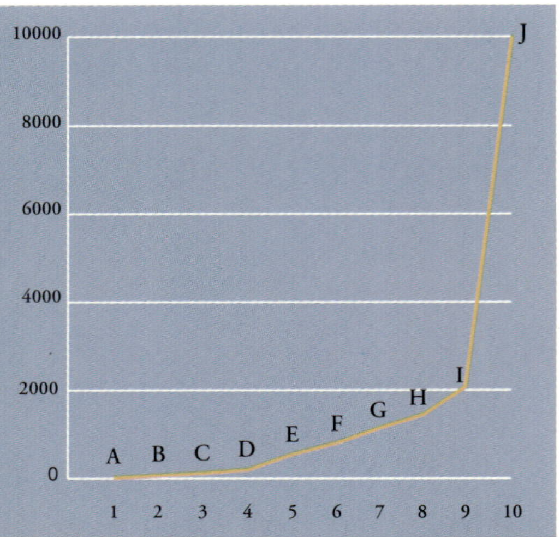

The hardness scale. The Mohs scale (from 1 to 10) is shown on the horizontal axis and the Knoop scale (from 1 to 10,000) on the Y-axis.
A. Talc (2.4)
B. Gypsum (35)
C. Calcite (109)
D. Fluorite (189)
E. Apatite (536)
F. Orthoclase (795)
G. Quartz (1,120)
H. Topaz (1,427)
I. Corundum (2,060)
J. Diamond (10,000)

So hard and yet so fragile

"Often woman changeth, a fool is he who trusteth": King François I engraved this sentence on a windowpane in Chambord castle. He certainly realised how useful diamond's hardness could be. In these ancient times, diamonds were cut in pointed shapes, following the original octahedral crystal form as far as possible. The King used his ring stone to scratch this very personal reflection on the glass, believing that he would thereby preserve it for eternity. He was wrong: Louis XIV had the window destroyed when he visited Chambord with his mistress, Madame de la Vallière, because the words were an insult to his partner. Courtiers imitated François I in Versailles, and the windows of the castle still bear famous signatures, engraved using the diamonds in their rings. Evidently, people have always been aware of diamond's hardness. Its name derives from the Greek word *adamas*, meaning invincible. In fact, diamond is still (at the time of writing) the hardest-known substance, although some artificial compounds appear to be catching up with it.

Diamond's hardness is best expressed in figures. Just as there is the Richter scale for earthquakes, there is hardness scale for minerals, and diamond is right at the top of this scale. The scale bears the name of an Austrian mineralogist, Dr. Mohs. He worked it out using direct, practical observation, which was the main technique available to him at the time (1826). He compared minerals to each other, and defined a scale with ten increments. Each position on the scale was occupied by a common mineral, enabling easy comparisons to be made. Any mineral on the scale will be able to scratch all of the minerals below it, and it will in turn be scratched by the ones above. The softest mineral on the scale is talc, and the second-softest is gypsum. Graphite is chemically equivalent to diamond, yet it ranks just above talc and below gypsum on the scale. Glass ranks between fifth and sixth, below quartz, a very common mineral that is in seventh place on the scale. The minerals begin to get very hard above seven on the scale. Topaz is the eighth-ranked mineral, corundum (sapphire and ruby) is ninth, and finally, diamond is enthroned at the top at number ten.

This scale has the advantage of being practical, but its artificial linearity does not give a true picture of the hardness phenomenon. For these purposes, there is a better method, using the Knoop scale. In order to measure hardness using this scale, a diamond point is set up under a microscope. The point is used to make an impression in the surface of the material being measured. The result is a pyramid-shaped indentation in the material, the depth and size of which are related to its hardness. The softer the mineral, the bigger the imprint. When the size of these indentations is expressed in terms of a scale, the picture is very different! By doing this, we find that the Mohs scale is not truly linear. Diamond, for example, is considerably harder than corundum, whereas the variations in hardness between the minerals at the bottom of the scale are much smaller. It also becomes evident that diamond's hardness varies according to the crystal's alignment: octahedral crystal faces are harder than cube faces!

Why is diamond the hardest known natural substance, and so considerably harder than the matter which precedes it? Clearly, its structure is responsible. This is also the key difference between diamond and graphite (one of the softest minerals), even though both of them are made up solely of carbon atoms. It is important to emphasise that diamond was formed under conditions of enormous pressure. This is the cause of its unusual structure and properties. Under this almost unimaginable pressure, the carbon atoms are forced much closer together than in graphite. Therefore, the atomic bonds, which are very short and very strong, are responsible for diamond's enormous hardness compared to graphite. The hardness is greatest on the octahedral crystal faces, which correspond to directions where the density of atoms is highest. This can be seen on a molecular model of diamond. Diamond-cutters noticed this characteristic centuries ago, and the octahedral faces gained the reputation of being uncuttable. In order to polish these faces, diamond-cutters had to 'force' the octahedral angles. Simply changing the polishing angle by 1° is enough to make the pyramidal crystal faces cuttable. For this reason, old point-cut diamonds do not have natural crystal angles: the pyramid is either flatter or more pointed, depending on the cutter's decision. In other words, diamonds have a 'grain', just like wood. In order to obtain a good polish on the diamond, the cutter must follow that grain. In other words, the cutter should not go against the layered atomic structure, but polish along these layers. These characteristics mean that cutters need years of experience before they can optimise their diamond-cutting skills to take account of the stone's hardness.

February 1908: Joseph Asscher, about to make history by cleaving the enormous *Cullinan* diamond.

Hardness does not necessarily mean toughness, however. Jade, for example, is much softer than diamond, but it is extremely difficult to break. Its toughness comes from the fibrous nature of its constituent minerals. These fibres are interlinked in all directions. On the other hand, diamond is the hardest mineral, but it is relatively fragile. There is a cleavage direction running parallel to the octahedral crystal faces. This means that a diamond crystal can be split apart along this direction, leaving a perfectly clean break with a mirror-smooth surface. Skilled cutters can even produce ultra-sharp diamond blades by splitting the gems in this way. This cleavage plane exists because of the relative weakness of the bonds between atomic layers parallel to the octahedral crystal face. There are many bonds parallel to the plane, but fewer perpendicular to the plane. Diamonds are brought to the surface with great violence during kimberlite eruptions, and this can be enough to cleave the crystals naturally. The most famous example is the enormous *Cullinan* diamond, which had a cleavage face on one side. The other piece has never been found. Judging by the size of this cleavage face, one can speculate on the probable weight of the complete stone: it is likely that the *Cullinan* originally weighed over a kilo in total!

These qualities of hardness and brittleness found their way into historical texts and diamond mythology. Hardness became the symbol of a whole series of associated qualities: inalterability, eternity (because of its permanent resistance to wear), power (due to its ability to pierce through anything) and invincibility. The texts also display knowledge of diamond's brittleness, although it was misinterpreted. Pliny was the first to mention a peculiar 'diamond test'. In common with many ancient authors, he believed that a diamond could be identified by placing it on an anvil and hitting it with a hammer. According to these texts, if the hammer broke (or, indeed, the anvil), the diamond was real! If the stone broke, then it must not have been a diamond to begin with. This mistaken belief would last up until the Renaissance, and one can only speculate on the number of stones that must have been broken and cleaved through the application of this useless 'test'. There was once a version of the *Physiologus*, a famous natural history book from the end of the Roman Empire, in the Turkish library of Smyrna. It was later destroyed, but it was copied and illustrated in Ethiopia in the 8th-9th centuries. An illumination showed a tester identifying a diamond. He raises a large, long-handled hammer and prepares to smash it down on the anvil, where an innocent diamond awaits its doom.

This octahedron has sharp edges and perfectly flat faces. It is a rare example of a crystal that has not been modified by dissolution, which alters the majority of natural diamonds. Under appropriate lighting conditions, the same diamond acts as a prism to disperse light into the colours of the rainbow (below). This is what causes diamond's multi-coloured 'fire'. Michael J. Scott collection.

This regrettable test has a modern-day equivalent. In diamond mines, it is necessary to crush the kimberlite rock to extract the diamonds. The crushing operations are done using mills that are calibrated to take account of the average size of the stones that are found in each mine. But, all too often, very large diamonds have been rescued in the nick of time, just before reaching the crushing mills' jaws. In the mines that are most likely to unearth large stones, a trained supervisor continuously monitors the conveyor belt delivering chunks of kimberlite to the crusher, in order to rescue any *Cullinans.* This supervisor is the only way of avoiding the modern anvil equivalent, which would shatter diamond even though it is the hardest natural substance. The Centenary diamond was saved in this manner. The *Centenary* is one of the most beautiful diamonds in existence: it was rescued from the Premier mine's conveyor belt in South Africa, in 1988.

Light atoms, heavy stone

Every mineralogy textbook mentions that diamond is dense. Its stated density is 3.51. In other words, a litre-sized container brim-full of diamonds would weigh just over three and half kilos (one litre of common granite would barely weigh 2.7 kilos). It is astonishing that a substance made solely of carbon atoms should achieve such a high density. Carbon is one of the 92 known natural elements, and is very light. It is in sixth place on the Periodic Table. Hydrogen is the lightest element, and uranium is the heaviest. This paradox is further illustrated by graphite: it is also composed of pure carbon, but only has a density of 2.2. What is the cause of this? Once again, it is the result of the enormous pressure exerted upon diamonds as they form. The atoms are compacted together by the pressure, so much so that they are much more numerous in a given volume of diamond than is the case in a comparable volume of graphite. This high density can be easily detected, by holding a diamond of 20 carats or above: it appears unusually heavy in the hand (although, admittedly, not everyone gets to perform this test!). This density is in fact a very useful quality: in sedimentary deposits, diamonds naturally concentrate in layers, because the flow of water cannot carry them easily. This observation brought about a 'diamond rush' in Brazil around 1730. Prospectors sought hollows in riverbeds, or preferably "potholes", caused by naturally occurring swirling whirlpools of water. Diamonds get trapped there because of their density, and some lucky prospectors discovered several hundred carats of diamonds in these natural deposits! For the same reason, diamond is often found in alluvial layers in association with gold nuggets.

Strangely enough, in ancient Hindu gem texts, it is mentioned that the purest diamonds are light - so light, in fact, that they are said to be able to float on water. Naturally, this runs counter to common sense. And yet... one particular geologist, a world-renowned diamond specialist who was, moreover, completely sober, once saw diamonds floating on water in a kimberlite-washing factory. All that was needed was to fish them out with a scoop, as if they were shrimp! There is an explanation for this strange phenomenon. Diamond is dense, but it detests water. Its surface does not get wet, and water flows off diamond like droplets touching an electric hotplate: the drops roll away, like water off a duck's back! This curious water-repelling phenomenon is one of diamond's strange surface properties (scientists describe it as a surface tension effect). Consider a very flat diamond, such as a macle or cleavage, for example: the surface tension of the diamond pushes the water away, and this can be sufficient to counterbalance the effect of its mass, which would normally make it break the surface of the water and sink. On the other hand, octahedral crystals will sink like... well, stones!

Fat-lover

Although diamonds hate water, they adore grease. The carbon atoms on the crystal surface are not surrounded by other carbon atoms, unlike the ones in the interior. They therefore seek to form bonds with whatever compatible substance first comes their way. As grease is a compatible compound, diamond tries to bond to it. This peculiar property is exploited by miners in South Africa, who developed a system to separate diamonds from ore in their washing plants, by covering their washing tables and conveyor belts with grease. The diamonds stick to the grease, whereas the ore fragments are washed away. A blade scrapes the table or conveyor belt at the end, thereby recovering diamonds. There are many small, independent South African companies washing diamond-bearing gravels on the banks of the Vaal river, and they still use this method. This property also explains why diamonds become dull when they have been worn for too long without being washed. They quickly become coated with a film of grease that they pick up from contact with the skin. Diamonds should be de-greased regularly with detergent, like crockery!

Grease tables are used to extract diamonds from alluvial deposits along the Vaal river, close to Kimberley. The other stones are washed away by the flow of water.

Darkness, light and the rainbow

Should mineralogists wander out of their natural history museums into fine-art museums, they might make an interesting observation: in portraits from the late Gothic period to the Renaissance, diamonds were painted in black! It was not some kind of artistic convention, since this manner of presenting diamonds was common to all schools of painting. This is an interesting paradox. Paintings from the Northern European School (Quentin Metsys, Pourbus, Rubens...), the German school (Dürer, Cranach the Elder...), and portraits of diamond-covered French, Italian or Spanish nobility (Fouquet, Cornelius of Lyon, Bellini, Pantoja de la Cruz...) all portray the same oddity. Diamonds do not sparkle. They are uniformly black and, for this reason, they are set in dull jewels that appear to lack colour and allure. However, beautiful jewellery was being manufactured at the time. This can be seen in numerous Flemish and Italian masterpieces, showing the Virgin Mary wearing sumptuous ruby- or sapphire-set clasps upon her mantle. Why did the nobility and the merchant bourgeoisie wear diamond jewels, when coloured gemstones had dominated Middle Ages jewellery? This choice was dictated by the two key facts discussed above: diamond's rarity made it possible to display financial power, and its hardness made it a symbol of eternity and invincibility. Its beauty, such as we know it today, was completely unknown at the time. Its sparkle was muted, and its 'fire' (the ability to disperse white light into the colours of the rainbow), would not be understood and maximised until much later.

Diamond's fire: it splits white light up into the colours of the rainbow, resulting in multi-coloured reflections.

Ancient texts hardly mention diamond's brilliance: it was a neglected property that was revealed only sporadically, on the rare occasions that ambient light hit the stone in the right way. Gem-cutters wrote about its greasy lustre. This is hardly a flattering description, but it is a property that some diamonds naturally display on their crystal faces. The stone's potential brilliance would only be realised once European gem-cutters refined their techniques. Diamond-cutting only reached this level in the 17th century. This was the era of Cardinal Mazarin, a famous diamond collector. From that point on, diamond's brilliance would be recognised as a significant part of its appeal, and gems would henceforth be cut accordingly. It was only then that diamond's ornamental value overtook its symbolic value: prior to that, diamond had been valued for symbolic reasons associated with its hardness.
Although early gem-cutting had finally enabled the stone's brilliance to be developed, it would nevertheless take a long time before diamond's formidable dispersion was properly exploited. Dispersion is the splitting of a ray of white light into the colours of the rainbow. The same effect is often seen in prisms. Certain special cuts are required in order to enable this play of light. The brilliant-cut is one of the most successful. Therefore, diamonds only became mesmerising, glittering symbols of beauty relatively recently, having previously been valued as symbols of eternity and inalterability.

Some understanding of diamond's optical properties is necessary. Brilliance is related to the reflection of light inside the stone. The speed of light in a vacuum is around 300,000 km per second. When a ray of light enters a diamond, it is slowed down and travels at a speed of only 124,000 km per second. This spectacular deceleration is caused by the molecular structure's density and the cohesion of the carbon atoms. This, in turn, causes the light ray to bend, which is known as refraction. The relationship between the speed of light in a vacuum and its speed in a given material is called the refractive index. Diamond's refractive index is very high: 300,000 divided by 124,000 gives 2.41, compared to 1.33 for water, for example. The higher the refractive index, the more light will be reflected by the stone. A ray of light that hits a diamond perpendicularly will be 17% reflected, compared to only 4% for ordinary window glass. The more the ray is tilted, the more light will be reflected: there is a 'critical angle' between the direction of the light ray and the facet surface which causes total reflection. Below this angle, the light ray will not pass through the stone, but will be reflected back. At a 30° angle of incidence, a third of the light will be reflected. These figures show that gemcutting and careful facet positioning are necessary in order to achieve maximum sparkle

Conductivity: contrasting extremes

Carbon atom electrons behave in very different ways in diamond and graphite. This results in visual differences (one is transparent, the other is opaque), and also other, more subtle differences. Diamond, for example, is a superb conductor of heat, unlike graphite. Diamond is a remarkably effective electrical insulator, whereas graphite conducts electricity. Diamond's heat conductivity is probably one of its most unusual properties. It exceeds that of any other known substance. Because of the very rigid crystal lattice, heat is quickly transmitted from one atom to another, like a kind of shockwave, until it leaves the stone. When a diamond is held in the hand, it feels cold due to the near-instantaneous transmission of heat away from the fingers. Diamond-cutters are familiar with this phenomenon, and put diamonds to their lips to check thermal conductivity. The lips have many nerve endings and are thus very sensitive. This quick test can be used, amongst others, to help check a stone's authenticity. Diamond hardly expands when heated: a red-hot diamond (at 800°C) can be plunged into liquid nitrogen (-195°C) without any ill effects! Any other non-metallic substance would shatter when subjected to such enormous thermal shock.

Brooch, from the island of Lombok, Indonesia. The polished faces show surface reflections that display diamond's brilliant lustre. However, the stone is of ancient, 17th-century cut, so the interior of the stone appears dark. National Museum, Jakarta.

A strongly coloured mineral

Diamond has the reputation of being the quintessential colourless stone. Generally, it is more highly prized the "whiter" (i.e. the more colourless) it is. However, this is not the whole story. Strangely, the majority of jewellery window-shoppers are unaware that diamonds come in all the colours of the rainbow. There are reds, greens, yellows, browns, blacks, oranges, pinks... Hollywood producers, at least, have discovered this fact. Apart from being an international blockbuster, the film *Titanic* performed a valuable role in educating the public about the existence of blue diamonds. In 1987, an event completely changed professionals' attitudes to coloured diamonds, although it has to be said that Leonardo di Caprio's on-screen capers proved more exciting to the general public. Christie's New York put a red diamond of 0.95 carat up for auction, causing much excitement. The market was already in a state of white-hot anticipation, thanks to a preceding series of incredible auctions. In a few minutes, bids soared. The stone, which was found in Brazil, was sold to an intermediary acting on behalf of the Sultan of Brunei for $879,700: the equivalent of $4,630 billion per kilo, in other words. It is possibly the most expensive substance in existence, except perhaps for some pharmaceutical proteins that have been crystallised in zero-gravity conditions aboard the space shuttle. The Sultan of Brunei is a passionate collector of coloured diamonds. He possesses the world's most beautiful known collection

Exceptional coloured diamond collection.
Michael J. Scott collection.

(although this does not prevent him from also having a magnificent collection of colourless diamonds). This is understandable, because coloured diamonds are so fascinating. The physical phenomena causing the colours are enthralling in themselves, and the gems are amongst the rarest and most beautiful natural wonders. Haüy called them the orchids of the mineral kingdom, and in his time orchids were extremely rare! Some people would have gone - and, indeed, would still go - to any lengths to possess the *Blue Diamond* of the French Crown, the *Dresden Green*, the Brazilian Red, the *Mouawad Pink*, or the Black Orlov. People who have caught the coloured diamond bug have seen their obsession richly rewarded. Coloured diamonds have become a highly specialised niche, alongside the colourless diamond market. There are several famous coloured diamond collections, such as the De Beers collection of over 200 stones, and Eddy Elzas' Rainbow Collection. Mr. Elzas runs a company in Antwerp called, appropriately enough, "Rainbow Gems". The collection has over 300 cut stones, displaying a dazzling panorama of all colours and shades. These are known as *fancy* colours. Formerly considered as mere collectors' curiosities, they have since had their revenge in spectacular fashion. The *Cullinan I* in the Tower of London's Royal Sceptre, has been overtaken by a golden-yellow diamond, the *Golden Jubilee*, which has been the largest cut diamond in the world since 1995.

The *Golden Jubilee*, the largest-known cut diamond in the world to date. It was found in the Premier mine, South Africa. It is of yellowish-gold colour and weighs 545.65 carats. It is now set in the King of Thailand's sceptre.

The Heart of Eternity, a fabulous blue heart-shaped diamond of 27.64 carats.It came from the Premier mine in South Africa and was unveiled by De Beers as part of the millennium celebrations

What happens inside a fancy coloured diamond? The light that enters it is obviously transformed, as it passes through the carbon crystal. White light is, as everybody knows, made up of a mixture of all the different colours of the rainbow. Inside the stone, an optical phenomenon absorbs one or more of these colours, and the light does not appear white any more. It lacks something in its mixture, and the diamond thus appears coloured. But how does this absorption occur? The answer lies in defects inside the stone. These defects allow the light to interact with diamond's electrons. The electrons absorb just enough light to create a beautiful colour. There are two main types of defect: impurities (particularly nitrogen), and flaws in the diamond crystal's molecular structure. For example, some diamonds contain nitrogen atoms dispersed throughout their crystal structure. Their electrons are excited into a kind of sub-atomic dance, by absorbing light energy that corresponds to the colours blue and purple. These two colours disappear from the light spectrum, which then appears to be an intense yellow (the famous "canary" yellow). If a diamond contains boron atoms, they drain the red and infra-red colours from incident light. Deprived of these colours, the transmitted light becomes blue before it reaches our eyes.

On an atomic scale, diamond crystals are not perfect. Their atomic arrangement is sometimes slightly askew: a missing atom here, a few disordered atoms there. These structural imperfections are known as colour centres. They are often caused by impurities. When they are sufficiently numerous, they cause certain light wavelengths to be absorbed, giving the diamond a distinct colour. Clearly, the cause of diamond's colours is not a simple topic. In order to understand the problem, an in-depth knowledge of optics and solid-state physics is required. However, this research has proved to be invaluable: it has enabled the detection of the artificial methods used by fraudsters to improve or alter a diamond's natural colour. Scientists can induce the appearance of these colour centres. For example, a dirty-brown diamond can be given a beautiful green colour by nuclear irradiation. This process was first performed experimentally at the beginning of the 20th century, by the physicist Henri Becquerel. He worked at the Muséum national d'histoire naturelle in Paris and, of course, he did not intend to make money from it. He was simply trying to test certain theories related to his discovery of natural radioactivity. The green diamonds he produced are still preserved in museum collections to this day. Nowadays, some diamonds have their colours artificially "enhanced". This can be a legitimate industry practice, although in a small number of cases it is done with the intention to deceive. Some artificial treatments (such as electron-beam, neutron or gamma irradiation) merely reproduce natural phenomena in a very short space of time. Therefore, it can be very difficult to detect diamonds that were coloured using these treatments. On the other hand, the *Blue Diamond of the French Crown* and the *Dresden Green* are known to be completely natural, since their colour was documented well before these techniques were developed! A stone's history, its provenance, and the detailed study of its absorption spectra may help distinguish it from artificially coloured stones. However, only specialists in very well-equipped laboratories can tell for sure. These expensive studies are therefore only performed on very valuable stones.

Brown is the commonest diamond colour, especially since the discovery of the Argyle mine in Australia, which produces such stones in great quantities. The mining company developed a promotional campaign to popularise the colour. Since "brown" was not a particularly catchy description, the diamonds were described as being of "cognac" colour, or "champagne" for the paler ones. The brown colour is caused by extremely thin coloured layers inside the stones; each layer is around a hundredth of a millimetre thick. These are believed to be structural defects. It is thought that they were caused by the crystals' deformation deep inside the Earth, before their volcanic ascent. There is another type of colour centre, associated with the presence of nitrogen atoms inside the crystal. This generally gives a yellow colour. Yellow is the second-commonest colour in diamonds, after brown. This yellow colour is almost absent in stones from the ancient Indian diamond mines, and only became commonplace when African deposits were discovered. The commonest yellow colour has a spectral absorption pattern that looks a little like a supermarket bar code. Specialists refer to these bars as the "Cape" lines, because they are very common in diamonds from the Cape of Good Hope, in South Africa. In the Dutoitspan mine, all large stones over 100 carats are yellow! The colour varies from straw yellow to golden yellow. The finest yellow stones are described as being "fancy intense" or "fancy vivid" yellow. This is more commonly referred to as "canary" yellow. The sumptuous *Tiffany* diamond is an extraordinary, fine yellow colour, like transparent gold. It was found in a French concession of the Kimberley mine. Irradiation and heating are sometimes used to intensify a diamond's yellow colour, or even turn it orange.

Pink is the most fascinating colour in diamonds. In rare cases, the colour can verge on purple, or even red. Pink diamonds are almost priceless, and their possession has always been a privilege restricted to the powerful. Some pink gems are of near-mythical importance, such as Queen Elizabeth II's *Williamson* Pink, the French Crown Jewels' *Hortensia* and *Grand Condé*, or the Iranian Crown Jewels' gigantic *Darya-I-Nur*. Originally, diamonds only came in a delicate pink colour. However, this subtlety was later disrupted, first by Brazil and then, once more, by Argyle. These deposits rapidly became famous for producing stones of a strong pink, almost purple colour. This intense colour is distributed in layers inside the stone. As with brown diamonds, the coloured layers are thought to be due to deformations.Really intense blue diamonds are exceptionally rare: large stones of this colour can be counted on the fingers of both hands. The most famous are: the *Blue Diamond* of the French Crown (today known as the *Hope*), the *Wittelsbach Blue* from the Bavarian Crown Jewels, the *Unzue* Heart (formerly wrongly known as the Eugénie), and the splendid *Tereschenko*. An additional series of blue diamonds has appeared recently such as the *Mouawad Blue* and various

Rough diamonds in a range of blue and pink colours.
De Beers collection.

A strange chameleon diamond. When it is first taken from its dark bank vault, it is of bright yellow colour. After being exposed to the light for one minute, it reverts to its stable but less attractive grey-green colour.

The second-largest-known black diamond in the world, displayed life-size. It weighs 300 carats. De Grisogono Collection.

blue diamonds from the Premier Mine cut by De Beers to celebrate the Millennium. Their blue colour is caused by the presence of a small number of boron atoms in the crystal, which substitute for carbon atoms. Unusually, and unlike any other type of diamond, these stones conduct electricity. Irradiation can cause an aquamarine-blue shade in some stones, but this is a long way away from the classic blue diamond colour, which is so deep it resembles sapphire. Irradiated blue diamonds do not acquire the ability to conduct electricity.
Green is one of the rarest diamond colours. In fact, there is only one large, historic green stone: the famous *Dresden Green*, preserved today in the Grünes Gewölbe Museum in Dresden. This splendid 41-carat pear is green throughout, in contrast to many diamonds that appear green in the rough but which subsequently lose their colour when cut. This is because the colour is often only skin-deep. The cause of the colour is complex but it is usually due to irradiation. These diamonds were exposed to natural radioactivity, in sands and gravels that were rich in radioactive minerals. This irradiation lasted for hundreds of thousands of years. It is possible to produce green diamonds artificially, using nuclear irradiation in a laboratory, and it is currently very difficult to distinguish the treated stones from the natural ones.

Another 'colour' is in fashion at the moment: black. Not so long ago, black diamonds were rejected as gemstones, and crushed for abrasives. Black diamonds get their colour from microscopic graphite inclusions. Sometimes, these inclusions are so regularly and densely distributed that the diamond can conduct electricity. There are two large, historic, black stones: the 67.50-carat *Black Orlov*, and the *Amsterdam Black*, a splendid stone that was cut during the 700th anniversary of the Dutch capital. It was cut from a rough stone weighing 55.85 carats, and the result was a 33.74 carats pear-shape with a remarkably deep black colour. There is a jeweller today who specialises in making pieces that play black and colourless diamonds against each other. Once again, intelligent marketing created demand where there was none, in order to maximise profits from a new market.

The colours described above are seen under natural light. However, they are only a small part of the rainbow of diamond shades. Other colours and colour effects appear under different circumstances. For example, diamonds are often luminescent. In other words, they often emit coloured light when exposed to light of particular wavelengths. Under ultraviolet radiation, approximately a third of diamonds fluoresce a blue or purplish colour, whilst others fluoresce yellow or green. Other colours are much rarer. One famous diamond owned by Pedro II, Emperor of Brazil, is yellow-brown in incandescent light (lightbulbs) and intense green in sunlight, because of the green luminescence caused by daylight. The famous blue *Hope* diamond glows orange-red under ultraviolet. Diamonds can also be phosphorescent: they can continue to emit light even after the light source that caused the original emission has been switched off. Ancient Indian gem-cutters believed that diamond possessed the ability to glow in the dark. However, it seems that the evasive phosphorescence effect cannot be triggered easily, for example by shining a torch on the stone during the night. Finally, there are chameleon diamonds. Like the eponymous lizard, they change colour depending on the circumstances. One specimen of this very special kind of diamond, in a New York collection, is grey-green in ordinary light, but turns vivid yellow when heated in a candle flame. Appropriately enough, according to zoology books, chameleon lizards turn yellow when they are in heat! If the diamond is moved away from the flame, it quickly reverts to its grey-green colour. However, if it is put into a dark vault, after a while it will emerge... yellow! Once it is exposed to light, its stable, dull colour returns in less than a minute. Under ultraviolet light, it displays an intense yellow colour, and after only one minute of exposure, it develops an intense phosphorescence that can last more than fifteen minutes! This is one of the rare gem-quality diamonds that should not really be set in jewellery, as it would be impossible to play with it in this way!

Octahedra or cuboids, canaries or chameleons, conductors or insulators: now, who could still say that diamond is only a simple arrangement of neatly stacked carbon atoms? This substance is still the subject of a great deal of research, and it has many potentially useful applications in industry, especially in high technology. As a result, many science laboratories are devoted to studying it. The stone is unusual as a result of its growth conditions, and exceptional in its properties. It is a challenge to our ability to understand the natural sciences and solid-state physics. How many people are aware of this, as they window-shop in front of jewellery stores?

The *Guinea Star*: a stunning 89.01-carat diamond, cut by the Goldberg company in New York. It was cut from a 255.1-carat rough stone that was the largest diamond ever found in Guinea (in 1988 or 1989). Some rough diamond crystals are displayed in the foreground, including several remarkable pink diamonds.

Dante's *Hell*, illustrated by Botticelli. In Dante's eyes, Hell was the 'frozen' centre of the Earth. The road to Hell passes through a succession of concentric circles. Lucifer reigns at the centre of the planet. Circa 1480.

CHAPTER II

Violaine Sautter
& Jean Pierre Lorand

Under the volcano:

discovering the invisible

Anyone who wishes to write about diamond needs to use superlatives: it is the most beautiful, hardest, most brilliant mineral. But its price is also due to its great scarcity. Is it rare for chemical or structural reasons? As we have seen, diamond's composition is simple: pure carbon. As for its crystal form, it comprises carbon atoms, packed together in a particularly compact cubic structure.

Therefore, its chemical complexity (or lack thereof) is unlikely to be the answer. In fact, carbon is abundant on the Earth's surface. It is found everywhere, as part of the basic chemical structure of living creatures: coral reefs, coal, oil, etc. Naturally, this carbon is not pure, as diamonds are, but clearly it is incorrect to say that carbon is rare. So, if the secret of diamonds' peculiar character has nothing to do with its chemical composition, then we need to look at how it formed, and how it attained that unusually compact crystal structure. Evidently (Chapter 1), in order to get from the crystalline structure of graphite to that of diamond, the carbon atoms need to be brought closer to each other. One way of achieving this is to put graphite under pressure. However, this is not enough: if the atoms are cold, they are unwilling to diffuse. They must also be heated, in order for them to move closer to each other and form atomic bonds. These particular formation conditions are only found in one place: in the depths of the Earth, well below the surface.

But if diamonds can only form and develop at great depths, why are they found on the Earth's surface? This is where the time factor comes into play. But, on this particular occasion, we are not talking about geological timescales, which are so long that it is difficult to imagine them. In fact, we are talking about minutes! Diamonds rise up to the surface incredibly quickly: so quickly, that they keep their compact crystal structure. They don't have time to change into their low-pressure alter ego, graphite.

In order to understand diamond's formation and its scarcity on the surface, we need to look at the structure of the Earth's deep interior, and its internal dynamics. We must penetrate this invisible, dark and secret world, and travel beneath the volcano. Only by doing so can we answer these key questions: what kind of environment does diamond form in? How does it grow? Is there the same amount of carbon deep inside the Earth as there is at the surface? When was diamond formed, and how does it relate to the long history of our planet? And finally, how does it get up to the surface?

Diamond's domain of existence, as a function of temperature and pressure

Right-hand drawing: phase diagram, showing the *theoretical* temperature and pressure conditions under which diamond will crystallise instead of graphite. The vertical pressure scale can be regarded as a depth scale. The red curve shows the boundary between the domains of existence of graphite and diamond. Deep inside the Earth, the domain of existence of diamonds proves to be restricted. Basically, temperature increases with depth, along with pressure. This law results in the green curve, known as a geotherm, which displays the conditions below the continents. The intersection between the red and green curves shows the temperature and pressure at which diamond begins to appear on Earth: 45,000 atmospheres, about 150 km deep, at a temperature of 1,200°C. Left-hand drawing: cross-section of the Earth, showing the actual domain of existence of graphite and diamond. The vertical axis shows the depth. Temperature and pressure increase simultaneously. The surface of the Earth is at a pressure of 1 atmosphere, and a temperature of 25°C on average. This corresponds to point 1 on the diagram on the right. The layer at which diamonds start crystallising, 150 km deep below the ancient continents, at a temperature of 1,200°C, corresponds to point 2.

Carbon in the pressure-cooker

Early experiments on the industrial synthesis of diamonds gave an idea of the possible formation conditions for natural diamonds. By playing with pressure and temperature, physicians managed to establish what is known as the 'phase diagram' for carbon (page 46). This outlines the domains of existence for graphite and diamond. By looking at this diagram, it is possible to see what pressure is needed in order to make diamond, for a given temperature. For example, at room temperature (25°C) and atmospheric pressure at ground level, graphite is the stable form of carbon, rather than diamond. The more the temperature increases, the more pressure is needed to make carbon crystallise into diamond instead of graphite. But this theoretical diagram does not enable us to determine at what depth inside the Earth diamonds actually form. For this, we need some vital additional information: what are the temperature and pressure conditions inside our planet, from the surface to the core?

The relationship between pressure and depth is easy to imagine by way of a simple analogy. Consider a scuba-diver: as the diver sinks deeper down into the water, the hydrostatic pressure increases. By hydrostatic pressure, we mean the pressure that is exerted by the water column above the diver: the further down one goes, the greater the pressure. Now imagine that the water has been replaced by rocks that are three times denser: the terrestrial mantle. The lithostatic pressure is simply the pressure exerted by the rock: the deeper below the surface, the higher the pressure. The same is true of temperature: it increases with depth, as one goes down inside the Earth. At the bottom of the world's deepest gold mines, 3 km deep below the surface in South Africa, the rocks are at a temperature of 60°C. Temperature and pressure thus simultaneously increase as one descends inside the Earth. Geologists refer to this variation in temperature with depth as the geothermal gradient. Broadly speaking, as one descends into the planet, the temperature increases 10°C with every additional kilometre below the continent. Therefore, the temperature is 600°C at a depth of 60 km. Physicists have managed to produce diamonds in the laboratory at this temperature, by increasing the pressure to 30,000 times atmospheric pressure (30 kilobars). However, at a depth of 60 km inside the Earth, where the temperature is 600°C, the lithostatic pressure is only 17 kilobars. Therefore, diamonds cannot exist there!

In order to find out at what depth diamonds naturally crystallise, we simply have to look at the phase diagram and find the point at which the geothermal gradient crosses the boundary line between graphite and diamond. The two lines intersect at around 120-150 km deep, that is, at a pressure of more than 50,000 times atmospheric pressure, and a temperature of more than 1,000°C. This is the minimum depth at which natural diamonds can begin to exist. According to the diagram, they could not exist any deeper than 1,000 km either: beyond that point, carbon turns into a liquid! If we are to understand the extraordinary natural conditions under which this beautiful gem is formed, we need to explore the zone of the Earth's interior between 120 and 1,000 km deep.

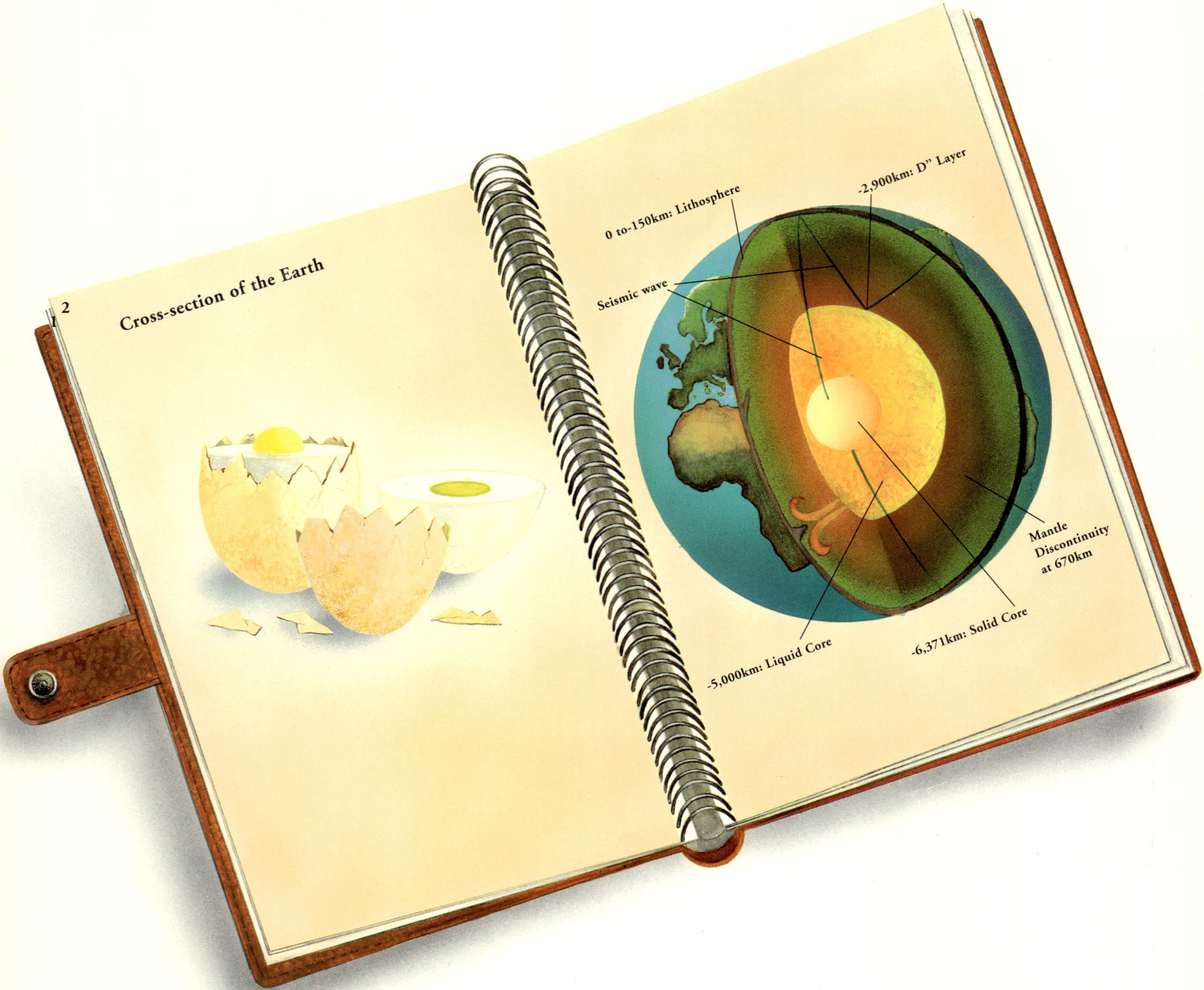

Anatomy of the Planet

Right-hand drawing:
Earthquakes emit seismic waves, which spread throughout the planet's interior. By studying them, we see how the Earth is divided up into different layers. The seismic waves are either transmitted through the layers, or bounce off the boundaries between them. The speed at which they travel is a function of the nature (i.e. solid or liquid) of the medium through which they are passing, and of its density. A sudden change in speed is an indication that the wave has passed from one medium to another. There are major discontinuities at 100, 670, 2,900 and 5,000 km, dividing the planet into five layers:
a) From 0 to 100 km: the rigid lithosphere, divided into plates. The Earth's crust is at the top.
b) From 100 to 670 km: the upper mantle. It is solid but plastic. At the 670 km transition, the temperature is around 2,000°C and the pressure is 240 kilobars.
c) From 670 to 2,900 km: the lower mantle. It is solid but plastic. The mantle-core transition area, known as zone D", contains a mixture of metals and silicates, at a temperature of 3,000°C and a pressure of 1,360 kilobars.
d) From 2,900 to 5,100 km: the external liquid mantle. At 5,000 km, the temperature is 5,000°C and the pressure is 3,300 kilobars.
e) from 5,100 to 6,371 km: the centre of the Earth. It is a solid metal core. The temperature is in excess of 6,000°C, and the pressure is 3,640 kilobars.

Left-hand drawing: the Earth, viewed as an egg. The thin external shell represents the crust, only a few dozen kilometres thick. The white is the mantle, more or less solid and 2,900 km thick. The yolk is the core, 3,500 km across.

The depths of the Earth: anatomy of our planet

Using a range of indirect techniques (such as seismology and gravimetry), we are now able to perform a kind of ultrasound scan of the Earth, in order to reveal its hidden anatomy (page 48). The Earth's crust, on the surface, is very thin. Immediately below it there lies the terrestrial mantle, the cradle of diamonds. It is completely solid, and divided into two parts: the upper and lower mantle. Finally, there is the metallic core, which is liquid towards the outside but solid in the centre. By scanning the Earth in this way, we discover something remarkable: our planet is primarily a crystalline solid, up to 2,900 km deep!

The crust is like a thin 'skin', covering the Earth's mineral 'flesh'. Its thickness and composition vary, depending on whether one is at the ocean floor or on a continent. The continents are granitic, and 30 to 40 km thick. They are rich in silica (the same substance as beach sand), and in other light elements like aluminium. These are less dense, so to some extent they lie on the surface, on top of the mantle. The basaltic oceanic crust, the water-covered blue part of our planet, accounts for 73% of the Earth's surface. It is thinner (7 to 12 km) but denser, because it is richer in heavy elements like iron and calcium. It can therefore sink into the mantle.

The mantle, located between the crust and the core, reaches to a depth of 2,900 km. Alone, it accounts for 83% of the Earth's volume. Its exact nature is more difficult to determine than that of the crust, since it is difficult to take direct samples from a depth greater than 10 km. In fact, the deepest drill-holes on the Earth's surface are a maximum of about 14 km deep. Although such deep operations are impressive feats of technology, they merely scratch the surface of our planet. However, earthquakes emit seismic waves. By studying their propagation velocity (the speed at which they spread through the planet), we can deduce some information. This research indicates that mantle rocks have a density that ranges between 3.2 and 4.5 g/cm^3. In addition, we know that when these rocks melted, they poured out millions of cubic kilometres of basalt over the Earth's surface. Only two types of rock satisfy these conditions: peridotite and eclogite. Peridotite (page 50) is a beautiful rock made up of olivine. As the name suggests, olivine is olive green (olivine, or peridot, is a magnesium-iron silicate). It also contains bronze-coloured pyroxenes (iron and magnesium silicate), dark green pyroxenes (calcium and magnesium silicate), and, finally, red garnets (magnesium-rich aluminium silicates). Eclogite (page 50) is a green and red rock, primarily composed of green pyroxene, and garnets that are richer in iron and calcium than the ones in the peridotites. These two rocks are also found in lava: as the lava rose up to the surface, it flowed past solid mantle rocks. As it flowed past the rocks, it sheared parts of them away, and brought them up to the surface. Peridotite is much more abundant than eclogite in these fragments. The samples brought to the surface by volcanoes therefore provide proof that the Earth's mantle is made of peridotites, at least up to 200 km deep. Let us take a more detailed look at this green rock: although it is not very well known to the public, it is the most abundant material on the planet. Its mineralogical composition means that the mantle has a simple basic chemical composition, that is fundamentally based on six essential elements. In decreasing order of importance, these are: oxygen, silicon, magnesium, iron, aluminium and calcium.

Peridotite: the 'mineral fabric' of the upper mantle (accounting for 95% of the rocks). The body of the rock is pale green olivine. It is also known as peridot, hence the name. It is studded with violet-red garnet and grass-green pyroxene. They are much less abundant. Muséum national d'histoire naturelle, Paris.

A block of eclogite: green pyroxene and red garnet are the two constituent minerals. Eclogite is the second most important rock in the mantle, although it only accounts for around 5%. Cape Town University.

It appears that the mantle's composition does not vary until 400 km deep. Between here and 670 km deep (the boundary between the upper and lower mantle), the propagation velocity of seismic waves dramatically increases. The mineralogical composition of the mantle therefore varies. Since no rock from these great depths has ever reached the surface, scientists have tried to discover the composition of this part of the mantle. They have reproduced these extreme conditions in the laboratory, using a type of apparatus that has revolutionised deep-Earth science: the diamond-anvil high pressure cell (page 51). By performing experiments with this equipment, scientists have discovered that olivine's crystal structure changes and becomes denser between 400 and 670 km deep. In addition, calcium-rich pyroxenes dissolve into the garnet. The deeper one goes below the surface, the simpler the mantle's mineralogy becomes: the amount of garnet increases, and the green mantle rocks turn pinkish and then red, until they eventually become garnetites (rocks with a composition that is more than 80% garnet). At a depth of 670 km, the temperature reaches 2,000°C. The mineral landscape then changes radically. At the lower mantle boundary, garnet and dense olivine are suddenly replaced by even denser magnesium or calcium silicates with a more compact structure (perovskite), and by a new magnesium and iron oxide, magnesio-wustite.

This brief lesson in terrestrial anatomy should not be considered as an unchangeable description of our planet. The Earth, unlike the Moon or Mercury, is a living planet, as can be seen in its intense volcanic activity. Now that we have outlined the static parts, we now have to discuss the planet's dynamics.

The diamond-anvil pressure cell.
This tool appeared in the early 1960s. It can reproduce the temperature and pressure conditions in any part of the Earth's mantle. Powdered rock is placed in the centre, a tenth of a millimetre across. It is placed between two 'jaws', each tipped with a one-carat diamond. The two mini-anvils are brought together with a simple hand-operated clamp. The sample can be exposed to exceptionally high pressure (equivalent to several million atmospheres), because the force is applied over a tiny surface area. The sample is then heated with an infra-red laser (which passes straight through the diamond), in order to recreate the temperature conditions in the heart of the Earth.
ENS, Lyon.

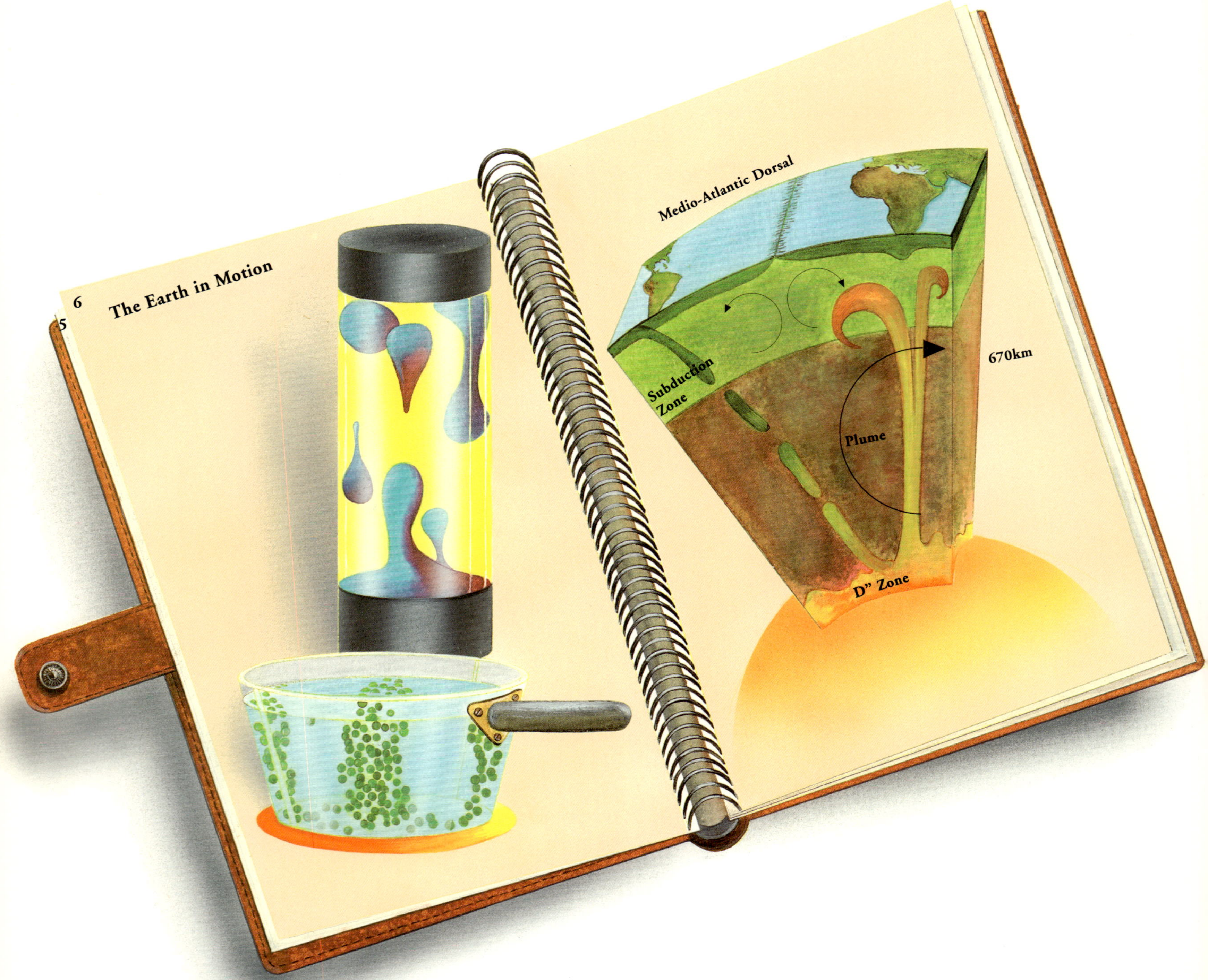

The movements that occur in the heart of the Earth

Right-hand drawing: cross-section of the Earth, through the Tropic of Capricorn, from the Andes to South Africa. *Convection* currents in the mantle are represented by circular arrows. Deep inside the Earth, the solid mantle is heated by the molten core below it. The rocks become less dense because of the heat, and they rise at a speed of a few centimetres per year. The basaltic ocean beds, which are cooled in contact with seawater, sink into the mantle through the *subduction zones*: these are the coldest rocks, so they are also the densest. Chunks of these cold plates sink down to the lower mantle after penetrating the 670 km boundary. Plumes start at zone D", at the interface between the mantle and the core, as a result of thermal and chemical instability. This causes material to rise. It is solid, but hotter than the convective mantle rock around it. It rises in thin channels, faster than the convection currents, cutting through the whole mantle without being deviated. Convection effects happen all over the planet and cause significant volcanism at the edges of the plates. The plumes, however, are very localised, and give rise to more random volcanism in the centres of the plates. When this happens in the centre of an ancient continent, kimberlites are the result.

Left-hand drawing: convection currents and plumes. Convection is illustrated by peas in a saucepan of simmering water. The plumes are equivalent to the movement inside the lamp, which contains two immiscible liquids of different viscosities.

Moving, yet standing still

The Earth's solid skin is known as the lithosphere (derived from the Greek: "stone sphere"). It is divided into movable plates. Some of them are referred to as continents: they drift endlessly across the surface of the planet. In contrast, the ocean floor plates have a distinct lifespan: they are formed and re-formed. When we look more closely, we can see that the lithosphere is made up of the crust, attached to part of the external layer of the upper mantle (the equivalent of a 'dermis', to the crustal 'epidermis'). Deeper down, there is a layer between the mantle, which is primarily made up of silicates, and the metal core. This layer is called the D" layer by geophysicists, and it is 200 km thick. It is a highly stressed zone, where the solid mantle silicates mix with the liquid iron of the outer core. The lower mantle is located between these two layers. It is known as the asthenosphere (derived from the Greek "sphere without resistance"). It is solid but, like putty, it can 'flow' on a geological timescale. In fact, it is much more malleable than the lithosphere above it. This plasticity is due to the heat, which makes the mantle rocks ductile, like red-hot metal. This viscous asthenosphere is the scene of much of the planet's internal activity. It experiences gigantic, very slow, mixing movements. They move at a speed of only a few centimetres per year, transporting minerals from the hot regions at the Earth's core to the much colder surface and vice-versa. They are, in effect, enormous convection currents (page 52). The rising part of the current brings hot matter up under the oceanic plates, producing basalts and pushing the adjacent plates aside.

The basalts of the ocean floor are then cooled by sea-water, and they return to where they came from, i.e. the mantle. This is known as subduction. During its return voyage, the basaltic floor recrystallises to form pyroxenes and garnets: these are eclogite minerals (page 50). This explains why there are far fewer eclogites than peridotites in the rocks that have been brought up to the surface: subduction is a phenomenon that is limited to the edges of the plates. Therefore, eclogitic rocks can only be local heterogeneities in a mantle that is dominated by peridotite. When the oceanic plate descends back down into the depths of the mantle, it forms the downwards part of the convection current. The layers dive under the continents (which are lighter), and descend along long slopes known as subduction planes, as far as 670 km deep. Some of them go down even deeper, to the D" zone, which is like a cemetery for these plates. As the cold rocks penetrate into the core-mantle boundary, they cause gigantic plumes of hotter, denser matter to rise up through the mantle. These plumes rise up at speeds of more than one metre per year, and they cut through the slower convection cells (moving at a speed of centimetres per year).

Diamond-bearing lithospheric roots under the ancient continents (cratons)

Right-hand drawing: seismic waves slow down when they reach a depth of 200 km beneath diamond-bearing regions. This is proof that there is a deep rock layer that is less dense than the asthenospheric mantle into which it penetrates. These diamond-bearing regions have deep roots, like molars. The roots are composed of lithospheric mantle, and they are over 150 km thick - in contrast to their upper surface, which has been flattened over time.

The base of the roots, beyond 150 km deep, literally dips into the area where graphite crystallises into diamond. On either side (at the same depth and pressure), the asthenospheric mantle is hotter. Graphite is therefore found here, rather than diamond, as indicated earlier in the phase diagram.
Left-hand drawing: crustal 'molar' and its lithospheric roots, buried deep into the diamond zone.

Like blowtorches, they bore through the thin oceanic plates, creating rows of volcanic islands like those of Hawaii. Under the very old continents, those dating back to the Archaean age (> 2,500 million years), it is much more difficult to create an opening. In fact, geophysicists have discovered that the roots of the lithospheric mantle reach down to more than 200 km deep (page 54). These roots are less dense, colder and much more rigid than the asthenosphere that surrounds them. As a result, the plumes produce a type of extremely rare and particularly explosive volcanism - in stark contrast to the comparatively gentle volcanoes on paradise islands. This very special volcanic activity is known as "kimberlitic volcanism", and it is the mechanism that brought up the majority of the Earth's diamonds to the surface. Diamonds are never found in oceanic basalts.

The *Ludwig II of Bavaria* diamond. This magnificent 1cm-wide, gem-quality octahedral diamond crystal was the first crystal to arrive in Europe with its kimberlite matrix still intact, in the 1870s. Reich der Kristalle Museum, Munich.

A piece of massive kimberlite: the lava is black. It is studded with olivine, red garnets, mica and small carbonate vesicles. Muséum national d'histoire naturelle, Paris.

Centimetre-sized megacrystals, brought up by kimberlitic magma. The glasses contain green pyroxene, red garnet and black ilmenite. The kimberlite sample displays a superb mica crystal. Natural History Museum, Cape Town, and Cape Town University.

Diamond's travelling companions

As we saw earlier, diamonds start to crystallise at below about 150 km deep, in the mantle (page 48). But in which rocks are they born? Are diamonds crystallised exclusively in the lithosphere, or are they also found in the convective asthenosphere? Are there diamonds deep in the heart of the Earth, at the mantle/core boundary?

To answer these questions, we must return to the surface, to take a closer look at the diamond deposits themselves. The kimberlite eruptions pierce through the world's oldest continents to reach the surface. The lava is often definitely younger than the over-2500-million-year-old ground that it has broken through (most South African kimberlites are less than 100 million years old). Like all volcanic rocks, it formed from a paste. In this case, the paste is anthracite-grey to bluish-black (page 56): various minerals were suspended in this paste as it solidified. There are large, round, green olivine crystals, red garnets, and often even flecks of brown mica. This group of minerals give kimberlite a unique chemical composition, which does not resemble any other lava: it is rich in magnesium and potassium. The lava also contains all kinds of rock and mineral debris. In fact, when they are brought up from the depths, diamonds never travel alone. They are accompanied by travelling companions: rounded inclusions (page 57) of garnet peridotite, eclogite, and large isolated crystals called megacrystals (page 56). How did they get there? The magma tore them away from the walls of rock that it passed when it rose. The inclusions are also called xenoliths, because these solid mantle rocks are obviously not related to the lava that transported them. Since the 1970s, scientists have managed to determine what pressure and temperature conditions the inclusions had been exposed to, shortly before the kimberlite magma snatched them away and bore them to the surface. The results varied between 30,000 and 80,000 atmospheres: equivalent to between 100 and 250 km deep. Most of these xenoliths had therefore been torn away from the cold lithospheric roots below the ancient continents. The kimberlitic volcanic activity therefore started at a much greater depth than the majority of lava eruptions. In fact, this is twice as deep as the basaltic lavas that are currently seen in volcanic eruptions on the Earth's surface. It probably starts at the lithosphere-asthenosphere boundary, under the old continents.

Professor Erlank, a geochemist, displays a pile of greenish nodules, brought up by kimberlitic magma. The xenoliths are in the shape of balls or flat wafers of varying sizes. The rounder they are, the deeper they originated, since they were corroded by the lava as it brought them to the surface.

A fragment of kimberlite, containing a xenolith. Cape Town University.

Inclusions inside diamonds.
Violet garnet inclusion from the Finsch mine (0.25 mm)
Colourless olivine inclusion (0.6 mm)
Chrome-rich, green diopside inclusion (0.3 mm)

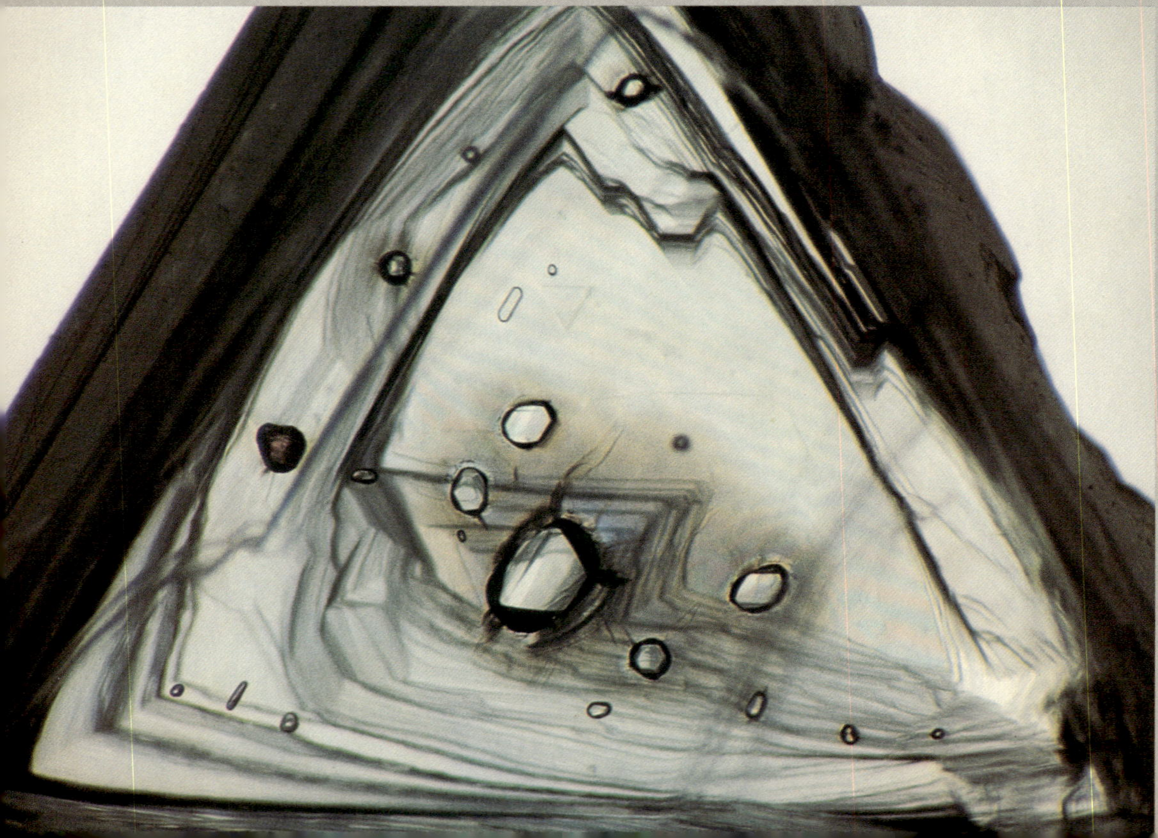

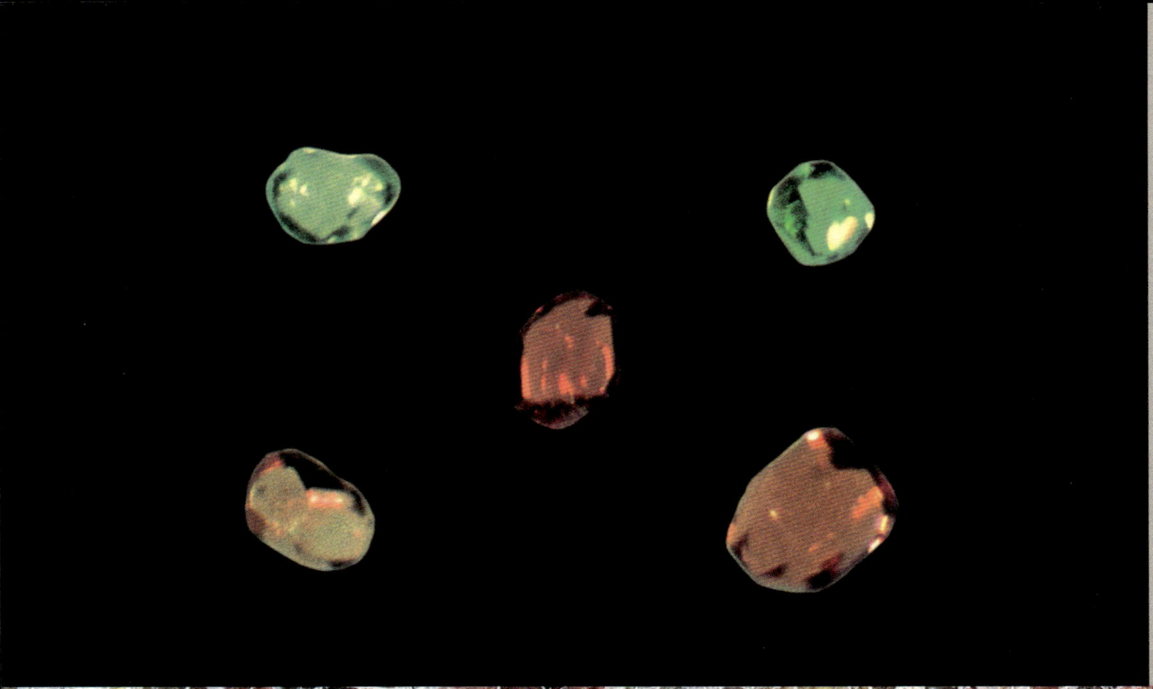

Peridotitic green pyroxene and garnet crystals, extracted from their diamond capsules.

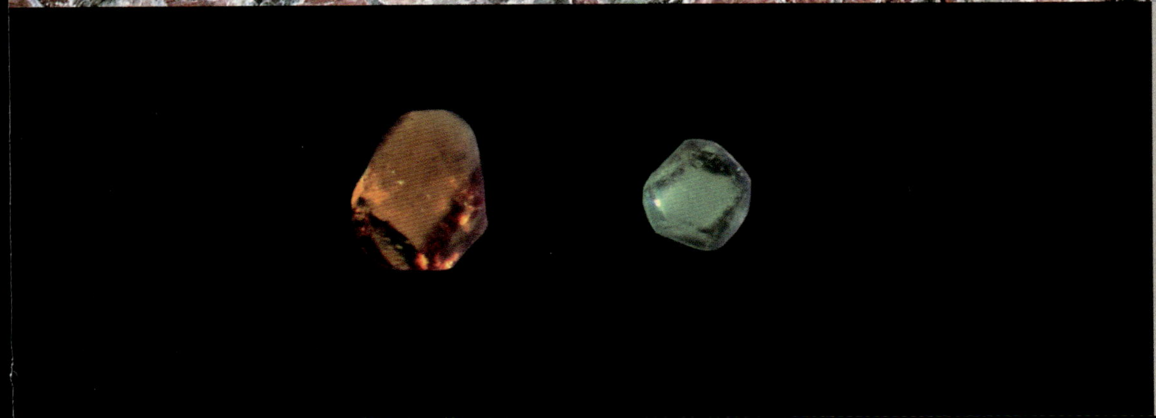

Red and green eclogite 'stained-glass window'. Diamonds sometimes form inside this rock.

Eclogitic orange garnet and bluish pyroxene crystals.

Inclusions in diamonds

Peridotitic	Eclogitic
Olivine	
Violet garnet	Orange garnet
Grass-green clinopyroxene	Bluish clinopyroxene
Orthopyroxene	Quartz
	Disthene
	Quartz-Coesite
	Sanidine
Spinel	Chromite
Ilmenite	
Sulphides	Sulphides
	Corundum
	Rutile
Diamond	Diamond

Unclassifiable:

Metallic iron, zircon and moissanite

As for diamonds, they are either found 'suspended' in the volcanic rock or, alternatively, inside the xenoliths, alongside the olivine, pyroxenes and garnet. Since they are therefore integral to the xenoliths' mineralogical composition, diamonds therefore also grew inside the deep roots of the ancient continents. This can be confirmed by looking inside the gems themselves. When they formed, they sometimes imprisoned tiny fragments of the minerals that surrounded them as they grew. Diamonds are effectively chemically inert carbon capsules that isolate the inclusions and protect them from any external forces. Because of these, the inclusions are priceless pieces of evidence because they have reached us, intact and untouched, from deep inside the Earth. More than twenty different minerals have been identified (page 60). The majority of diamonds studied to date contain minerals that are similar to those in the upper mantle peridotite nodules: olivine, pyroxenes, purplish garnets rich in magnesium, and chromium and iron oxides (page 58). These are indisputable signs that the diamonds formed in the upper mantle. However, there is an additional, less common type of diamond. These contain orangy garnets that are rich in calcium, and bluish pyroxenes that are rich in sodium (page 59). These diamonds appear to have formed in eclogite, rather than peridotite. Furthermore, the relative proportions of the two types of rock are adhered to, since for every three diamonds containing peridotitic inclusions, only one will contain eclogitic inclusions. Therefore, by studying diamonds' mineral impurities, we come to the same conclusions that we reached when we studied the xenoliths that accompany the diamonds. This is incontrovertible evidence that diamonds occur in mantle peridotites and eclogites. It suggests that most of the diamonds crystallise between 900 and 1,300°C, at pressures of 45,000 to 60,000 atmospheres (i.e. at depths of 150 to 200 km). Diamonds therefore crystallise at the bottom of the lithospheric roots.

However, diamonds and their kimberlitic travelling companions have some additional tales to tell! Garnetite xenoliths have also been discovered (page 61). These rocks, known as majorites, are made up of garnet, and come from depths of more than 350 km. This complicates matters. Moreover, certain extremely rare diamonds, which can be counted on the fingers of one hand, contain some very special inclusions: majorite garnet, perovskite-structured silicates and magnesio-wustite, minerals that make up the mantle at depths greater than 400 km. These observations confirm that diamond can also crystallise in the lower mantle. In this 'voyage to the centre of the Earth', some scientists have even claimed that some diamonds (ones containing metallic iron and silicon carbide inclusions) must have grown in the terrestrial core. However, at this point we have reached the limits of scientific knowledge, and we enter into the realm of speculation. It seems that carbon ought to liquefy under the colossal pressures that exist below 1,000 km deep, at the base of the mantle and in the external core. If true, this would make diamond formation impossible.

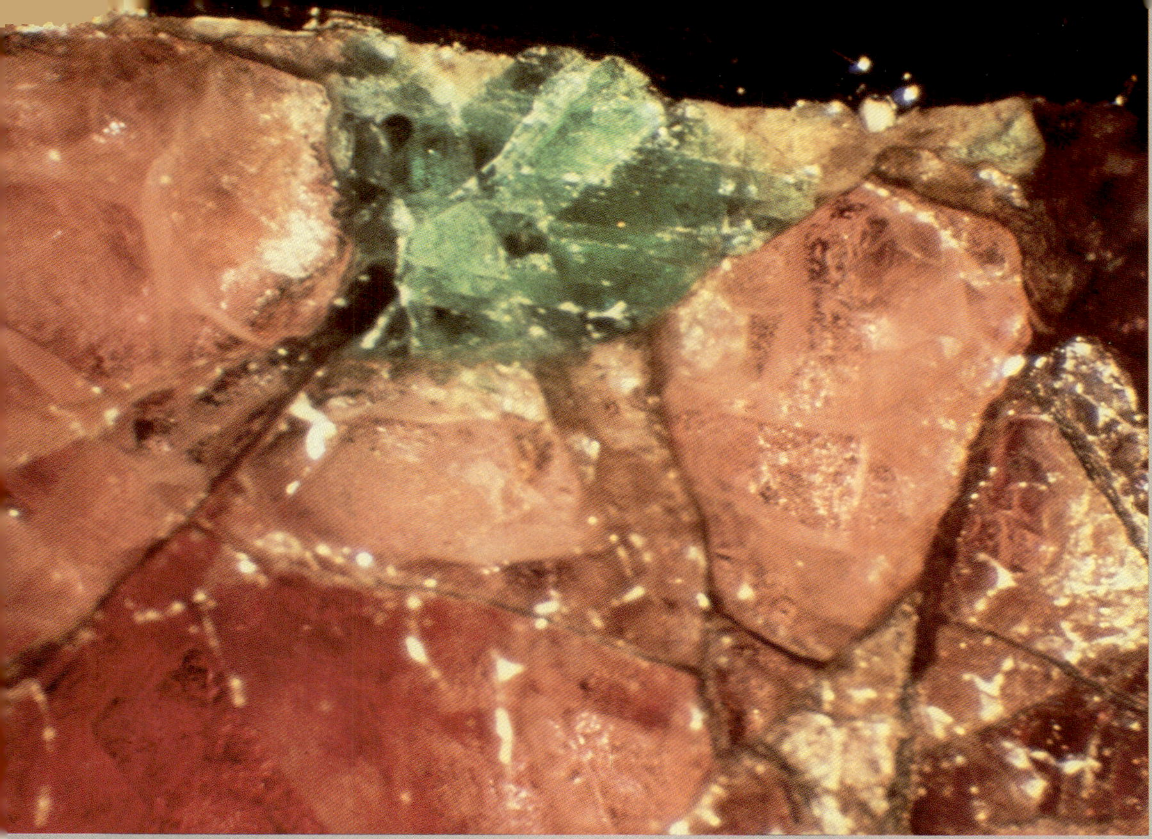

Garnetite xenolith, from Jagersfontein.
It is made out of pink garnet, associated with a small green pyroxene crystal. It contains little rods of colourless pyroxene, which can be seen under a binocular microscpe.

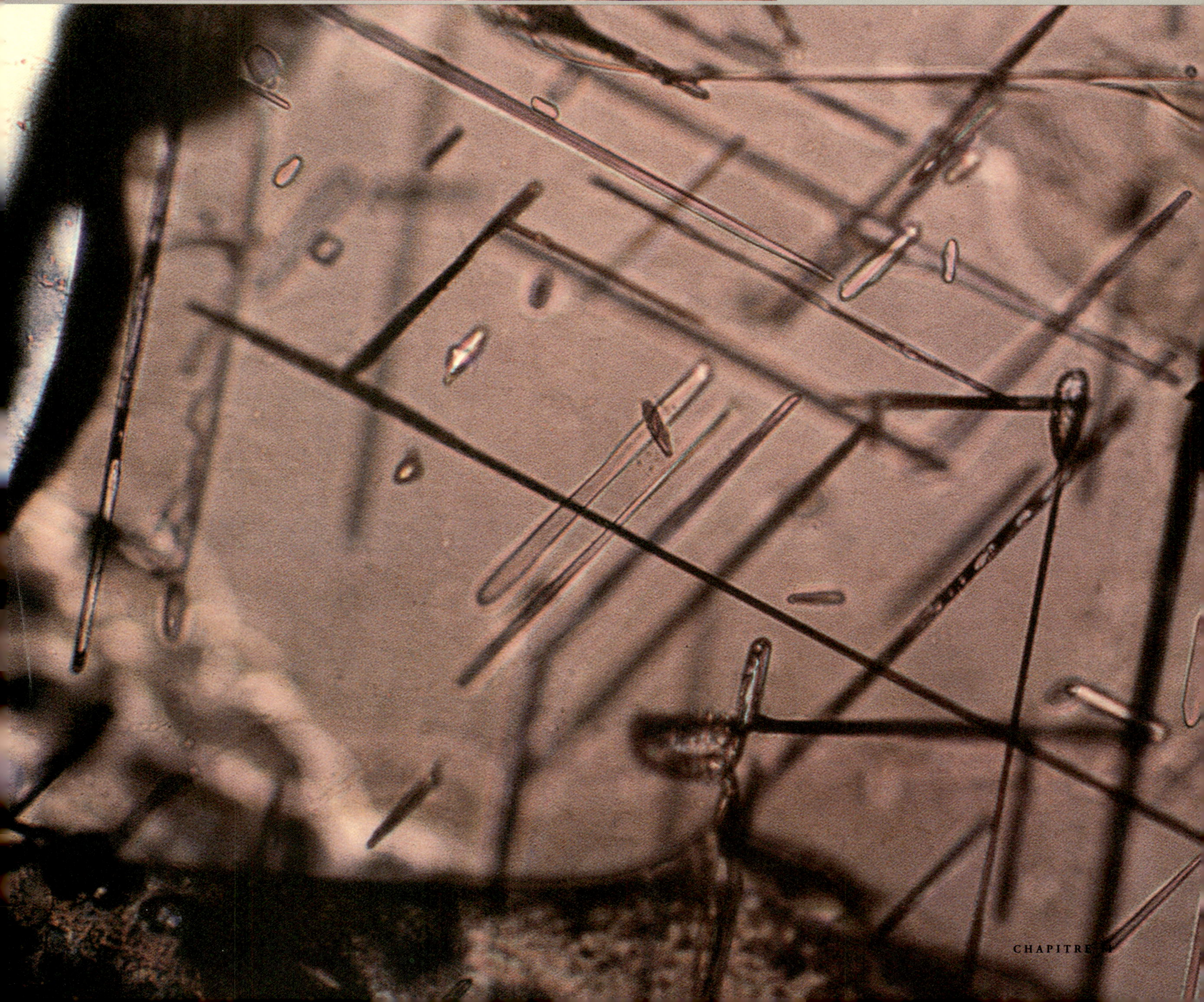

Diamond-making machines

We have seen how and where pressure and temperature conditions combine to cause diamonds to crystallise. However, in order for this to happen, the basic raw material needs to be available: elemental carbon. Carbon is not rare on our planet's surface, where it easily forms bonds with other light elements, such as oxygen, hydrogen or even nitrogen. The ocean contains 4×10^{13} (4 followed by thirteen zeroes!) tons of oxidised carbon, in the form of carbonates. The terrestrial biosphere contains an additional 2×10^{12} tons, in the form of organic carbon combined with hydrogen (in the form of oil or coal, for example). Finally, the biochemistry of living creatures is based on carbon, combined with hydrogen and oxygen.

In contrast, 99% of the volume of the terrestrial mantle is accounted for by six elements (O, Si, Al, Ca, Fe and Mg). Carbon is not on that list. According to analyses of volcanic gases, there may only be 300 grams of carbon per ton in the higher mantle, and possibly 3,000 in the lower mantle. Levels of carbon inside the planet are therefore 10 to 100 times lower than in the solar system as a whole, where carbon is amongst the four most abundant elements. What happened to the carbon when the Earth formed? At the present time, there are two hypotheses, and the truth is probably some where between the two. Some scientists have theorised that some of the carbon may be hiding in the centre of the Earth, in the metal core. Indeed, carbon has a strong chemical affinity with iron. Ancient metallurgists found this out the hard way, by forging iron tools that shattered if they contained too much carbon. The metal core could contain up to 1% carbon. However, there is another theory, which suggests that the primitive Earth's atmosphere may have been enriched with a massive injection of carbon dioxide gas. We should note that, during its earliest years, some 4,550 million years ago, the Earth did not have an atmosphere. This was because its gravity was too weak to attract the lightest gases, like hydrogen and helium. These were swept away by the powerful solar winds that swept the solar system at the time. Our planet's initial atmosphere would therefore have been composed of gases that had escaped from the mantle. Back then, when the metallic core was forming, the terrestrial mantle was much hotter than it is today. It was wracked with violent convection movements, that facilitated the massive release of imprisoned gases. Studies appear to suggest that there was very little oxygen in the primitive atmosphere, whereas carbon dioxide appears to have been very abundant (approximately 30% by mass, compared to 0.03% in the atmosphere today).

As a result of these ancient events, carbon would therefore not be very abundant in the mantle. However, this is not the only potential source of carbon for diamond formation. Part of the carbon present in the mantle also comes from the ocean floor, thanks to the subduction zones, which are like recycling factories for terrestrial waste. The sinking plates bring sedimentary rocks down with them as they sink into the mantle. These rocks may contain the sunken remains of calcareous-shelled sea creatures, and calcium-carbonate-rich sedimentary deposits. These contain carbon, which might be extracted by various possible chemical reactions, with the possibility that it could ultimately crystallise into diamond. One day, many millions of years hence, that might prove to be quite a reincarnation for these worthless seashells! There are therefore two categories of diamond. One category formed from carbon that came from the original 'stock' retained in the mantle. The other category probably crystallised from carbon that originally came from the ocean floor, and which was recycled in the mantle as a result of subduction. The diamonds that contain eclogitic mineral inclusions would therefore belong to this second category.

To reiterate, there is very little carbon deep within the Earth, in the places where the temperature and pressure conditions are right for diamond crystallisation. This is one of the reasons why diamond is such a rare mineral. We still do not know how long diamonds take to grow in the mantle. Clearly, the growth of crystalline mineral solids is very different from the growth of living creatures. In the animal and plant kingdoms, organisms grow as a result of cellular division, which takes place inside the body. This is the reverse of mineral growth processes. Mineral crystals grow on the outside, by adding successive layers of atoms to their surfaces, starting from a microscopic central crystal nucleus. When these atomic layers are added to the surface in three dimensions, following well-defined laws, this produces the flat, reflective faces characteristic of mineral crystals. Therefore, in order for diamonds to develop, the crystal nuclei need to be nourished from the outside, with carbon atoms that come from the growth medium (the mantle). But do the carbon atoms come from solids (such as compressed graphite under high pressure), from liquids (such as lava, containing dissolved carbon), or from a gas? This is still an open question, and scientists are still hypothesising over it. Because the mantle is under very high pressure, it obviously lacks cavities where crystals could form and freely express their crystalline faces. If diamonds grew from solid carbon in a solid medium (the mantle), they probably would not be able to develop the splendid octahedral crystals for which they are famous. Moreover, atoms move very slowly in solids, because they are trapped in a dense medium and tangled up in atomic bonds. If diamonds grew slowly from solid carbon, they would probably not entrap nearby minerals. However, as we saw earlier in this chapter, diamonds are often studded with mantle mineral inclusions and, conversely, it is very rare to find diamond imprisoned in these same minerals.

This paradox can only be explained by rapid growth, and only carbon-rich lava or very-high-pressure gases (in a state of fluid supercriticality) would be capable of supplying the necessary carbon atoms quickly enough. Therefore, not only are diamonds rare, they are also not distributed in a homogeneous way throughout the mantle. They are probably concentrated in channels, because fluids and lava tend to form well-defined paths as they travel through a solid. One can imagine a channel snaking through the heart of our planet, studded with a constellation of glittering crystals. If diamonds are distributed inside the mantle in this way, it must mean that they have very little chance of coming across a lava flow that would be capable of bringing them to the surface.

Billion-year-old diamonds

Diamonds are therefore formed at a great depth, between 150 and 670 km deep, in mantle peridotites and eclogites. There are lithospheric diamonds that develop in a relatively calm medium, and asthenospheric diamonds that crystallise in a moving environment. But are they all the same age? This question remained unanswered until relatively recently. However, in order to understand the mysterious origin of diamonds, and understand their history in the mantle, it is essential to know their age. There is a name for the geological science that determines the age of minerals and rocks: it is called geochronology. It exploits the fact that naturally radioactive elements like uranium disintegrate over time. Natural radioactive elements are found in minerals in infinitesimal quantities. The unstable atomic nuclei transform into specific successor nuclei over time. However, there are various radioactive elements, and they do not all disintegrate at the same speed. Some disintegrate over periods of several million (or even billion) years, like uranium. They can therefore be used to date ancient geological events. At the other end of the scale, carbon-14 disintegrates in a few thousand years. It is therefore only useful for relatively recent events, like those of human history.

But how can this tool be used to determine the age of diamonds? After all, diamonds are primarily composed of pure carbon, and they do not contain any radioactive elements with long lifespans. Fortunately, although diamonds themselves cannot be dated, their mineral inclusions can. Minerals like pyroxenes and garnets contain radioactive elements with long lifespans, such as samarium and neodymium. However, in order to be certain that the calculated age of the inclusion is also the age of the accompanying diamond, it is necessary to find inclusions that crystallised at the same time, and in the same place as their host. Fortunately, it is known that if an included mineral matches the shape of its diamond host (an octahedron or cuboctahedron, for example), instead of developing its own form (rhombohedron, etc.), then this essential condition has been met.

Twelve diamonds from the Premier mine. They were dated thanks to their inclusions. They weigh around 0.05 carat and are about 1,150 million years old. Cape Town University.

The ages of the Earth

Right-hand drawing: spiral timescale, showing the relative duration of the major periods in our planet's history. The Big Bang is the starting point: our universe was created 15 billion years ago.

Left-hand drawing:
Calendar, showing the condensed history of our planet. The start of the year coincides with the birth of our planet (4.5 billion years ago); the 31st of December marks the evolution of humans. Important points in the history of diamonds are interspersed throughout the year, compared to events in the history of the Earth.

In 1984, some garnet inclusions were dated for the first time. The garnets had been imprisoned in diamonds from the Finsch and Kimberley mines in South Africa. They were dated using neodymium-samarium and rubidium-strontium isotope techniques. All the diamonds had peridotitic inclusions, and had crystallised in the deep lithospheric roots (150-200 km), under Southern Africa. The results, shown in the adjoining table, are extraordinarily surprising. Most of the diamonds were indeed extremely old. For the most part, they had formed two or even three billion years ago. These diamonds came from great depths, but they were the same age as the ancient rocks of the surface crust. In Kimberley, 3.2-billion-year-old diamonds had been brought up to the surface by kimberlitic lava that was only 100 million years old (page 66). This was proof positive that kimberlite was not the 'host rock' for diamond formation, but merely the 'elevator' that had brought the gems and their travelling companions to the surface. Since that time, there have been further age measurements, using other techniques. These have been performed both on inclusions that were found trapped inside diamonds, and on minerals in the nodules and megacrystals that travelled up in the kimberlite, alongside the gems. All these findings reinforce the original basic conclusion: the lithospheric roots of the ancient continents were formed more than 3 billion years ago, and resisted the multiple geological upheavals that have shaken our planet over that period. This is a real record for longevity! For all this time, the roots sheltered the diamonds, until one day when a kimberlitic eruption came along and punched a hole through this diamond storage 'warehouse'. If we take these findings, and combine them with temperature and pressure data (obtained as before: 1200°C, pressure equivalent to a depth of 150 to 200 km), we come to the conclusion that the geothermal situation under the ancient continents was identical to the situation at the present time. Conditions favourable to diamond crystallisation thus already existed in Archaean times, at the base of the lithospheric roots (page 54).

On the other hand, diamonds encapsulating eclogitic inclusions are of more variable ages. On the whole, they are also more recent. This is easily explained, since eclogite, the host-rock for these diamonds, was formed by oceanic basalt subduction, a process that has only been active since the end of the Archaean period. Finally, there are also some very "young" diamonds, i.e. diamonds that are contemporary with the kimberlitic eruption. These can be identified thanks to their cubic form and their fibrous appearance (cf. Chapter 1).

What about deep mantle diamonds? They have been moved around by convection, and are undoubtedly not as old as the diamonds trapped at the base of the Archaean lithosphere. These diamonds could, in fact, have been formed throughout the Earth's history, perhaps sporadically. However, scientists are still faced with large gaps in the data, simply because this category of diamonds is extremely rare.

The ages of diamonds from different mines, in millions of years*

Peridotitic	**Eclogitic**
Kimberley 3,300	
Finsch 3,300	
	Finsch 1,580
	Premier 1,150
	Argyle 1,580
	Orapa 990

*After Richardson et al., 1984, 1986, 1990.

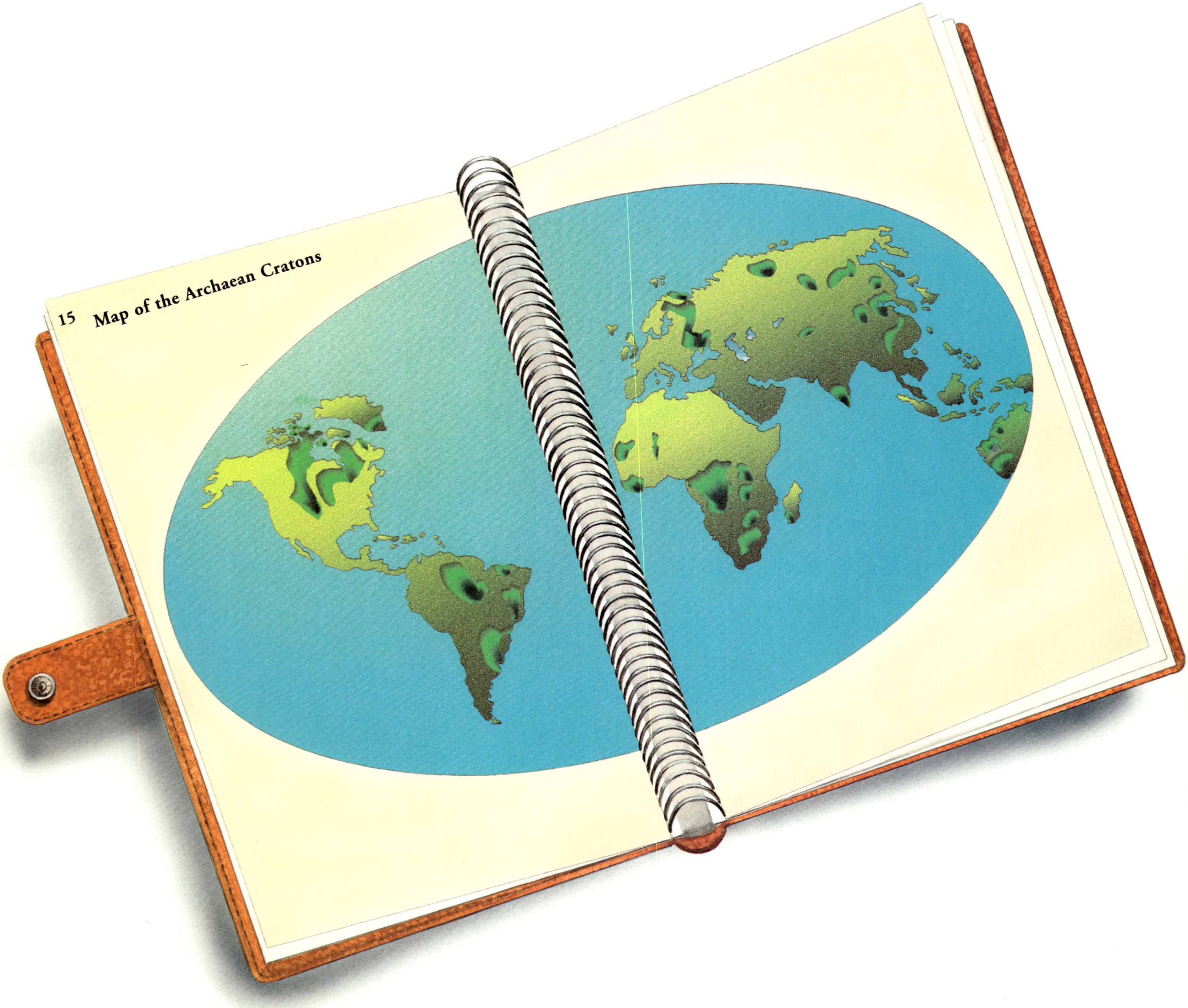

Map of the ancient cratons

World map showing the archaean nuclei, known as cratons. Their deep roots are diamond-bearing.

The ultrasonic elevator

As we have seen, diamonds come from the terrestrial mantle, more than 150 km deep. Diamonds are rare, because there is little carbon in the place where they form. Now, we need to understand how diamonds are brought up from such great depths. This mineral's zone of stability is very deep. Volcanoes that stem from such deep sources are exceptionally rare. Most basaltic volcanoes start from 100 km below the surface at best. We also know that diamonds should not exist on the Earth's surface (page 46). In order to prevent them from being transformed into graphite (the low-pressure form of carbon), the crystals must have been lifted up extremely quickly. Kimberlitic volcanism meets all these criteria. As we saw earlier, we can find out how deep its origins were by studying the state of crystallisation of the xenoliths, or by analysing the silicate inclusions inside diamonds. But how and why does volcanism form in the solid mantle at such great depths? What propels the kimberlitic magma towards the surface, at speeds that no other lava on Earth can match? These questions can be answered by studying two things: the way the kimberlite has formed deposits on the surface, and the structure of the lava itself.

From a geologist's point of view, the striking thing about diamonds is not so much that they are scarce, but that the diamond deposits are so strangely distributed. Diamond-bearing kimberlites are not randomly distributed at all. For example, no EU member state has a diamond deposit, except for Finland. Diamonds are found in a handful of locations around the world: India, Brazil, West and South Africa, Australia, Siberia, China and Canada. These areas have something in common: their age. They are extremely old: more than 3 billion years. They are remnants of the oldest continents that exist on the surface of our planet. Although there is only a limited number of these relics (page 68), they are, however, absolutely vast. They are known as cratons, from the Greek *kratos*, meaning 'empire'. Although these ancient cratons may seem as flat as pancakes on the surface, they have extremely deep roots, as we have seen. The lithospheric roots reach down more than 200 km deep. The kimberlitic chimneys that have blasted through the Earth's crust are clustered together in the centre of these cratons. These very narrow chimneys - barely more than a few hundred metres in diameter - are known as *pipes* (page 70). Kimberlites can also fill fissures, which are referred to as 'dykes' in geological terminology. There is therefore a cause-and-effect relationship between the magma's kimberlitic birth and the existence of deep roots under the ancient continents. We need to understand this relationship. For lava to form, it has to melt at a great depth, since the terrestrial mantle is solid. Basalts are widely distributed around the Earth's surface. Basically, they are formed at the edges of the lithospheric plates, when the asthenospheric mantle melts by decompression as it rises to the top on convection currents.

Geological cross-section through a kimberlite pipe

Right-hand drawing: 3 km-deep cross-section. In the Karroo desert, South Africa, the kimberlite *pipes* are vertical. They penetrate through the horizontal geological layers. The Kimberley mine reached a depth of 1,300m.

Left-hand drawing: a *pipe* is analogous to a champagne glass.

For kimberlite, the situation is very different - both at depth and on the surface. We know from the xenoliths that the melting depth is around 200 km, at the base of the lithospheric roots. Kimberlite appears either as breccia or in massive form on the surface. The breccia is widespread in the *pipes*, and has a chaotic appearance. It owes its name to the multiple, angular, variably-sized, foreign fragments of country rock that it contains. The lava acts like cement, holding these foreign blocks together. It is often soft and hardly recognizable. The Kimberley mines in South Africa were first studied by geologists from 1870 to 1900. The early geologists were misled by the presence of foreign rock fragments, and sometimes even tree trunks. They could not see that it was a volcanic phenomenon. This curious texture is actually a result of the eruption's cataclysmic nature: surface rocks were blasted into pieces by the eruption, and fell back down into the chimney before being 'cemented' together by the lava. Massive kimberlite can be distinguished from other lavas by the abundance of small white vesicles that they contain. These little vesicles are full of calcite and calcium carbonate. Originally, the vesicles were carbon dioxide bubbles.

Gases like water vapour and carbon dioxide are capable of lowering the solid mantle's melting point, in the same way as salt reduces the melting point of water (which is why salt is spread on the roads in wintertime, to get rid of ice). The explosive character of the volcanic eruptions leads us to surmise that enormous quantities of gas were initially stored where the magma was formed, at 200 km below the surface. But where did all this gas come from? It was not initially stored in gaseous form, but in the form of magnesium carbonates. In fact, carbonates withstand pressure very well, but not strong heat. This is why the are found in the mantle under the ancient continents, which is where they find the appropriate "mild" conditions. But if they are heated a little too much, they decompose and release carbon dioxide.

Like an uncorked champagne bottle, the lava contained carbon dioxide. Initially, at very great depths, it was gradually released in the form of millions of microscopic bubbles. Once released, its volume increased very rapidly as the magma rose. As a result, the pressure kept growing, thereby increasing the magma's rate of ascent until it carried everything around it in its wake. In fact, the kimberlites were capable of bringing up very many nodules, including some quite heavy ones, over a distance of more than 200 km. This would have required a considerable vertical stress and a very fast rate of ascent, in order to overcome the effects of gravity. This is when our 'elevator' analogy begins to look somewhat inadequate. Calculations indicate that, although the initial rate of ascent was fairly slow (10 to 30 km per hour - at that speed, the magma would have taken 4 to 5 hours to rise 110 km), it accelerated by several hundred kilometres per hour, until it reached the speed of sound over the last three kilometres of the journey. This is what caused the gigantic explosion that allowed the kimberlite to erupt to the surface. If the kimberlite rose a little too slowly, the 'elevator' would get stuck between the diamond and graphite zones, and the diamond would transform into graphite. Alternatively, if the lava had an excessive appetite for carbon, the diamonds would dissolve completely. Clearly, diamonds have to survive many extreme events before they reach the surface. Many diamonds still bear the scars of these events, in the shape of blunted corners and corroded crystal faces (cf. Chapter 1).

The Kimberley *pipe*. It is no longer being mined. The upper rock is comprised of yellow, oxidised kimberlite: *yellow ground*. The lower rock is fresh, darker rock: *blue ground*. Cape Town University.

The double-elevator hypothesis

Right-hand drawing: a plume brings up diamonds from the lower mantle. They contain inclusions of magnesio-wustite (Mw) and perovskites. Diamonds from the transition zone (between 670 and 400 km deep) contain inclusions of majorite (Mj). Diamonds also come from the lithospheric roots. They can be peridotitic (P) or eclogitic (E).

Left-hand drawing:
Diamonds initially rise up very slowly aboard plumes. Then, they rise up faster and faster in kimberlite, as they go up through the lithosphere.

If kimberlite forms at around 200 km deep, then there is a problem: as we have seen, some rare diamonds come from much greater depths. We need to infer the existence of two separate, successive elevators: the first would bring asthenospheric diamonds up to the base of the lithosphere, before they were grabbed by the kimberlite elevator, for their final rise through the lithosphere. There are plumes of hot material that rise up from the centre of the Earth, and these probably act as the first elevator. They could take deep asthenospheric mantle diamonds and transport them upwards, over a few million years, to the lithospheric roots (page 72). The lithospheric roots would act as a kind of storage space, where the diamonds would wait in the hope of finding a suitable kimberlite to take them to the surface. The tip of the rising plume would be deviated laterally when it came into contact with the hard lithospheric roots. Like a gigantic gas burner, it would also produces the heat required to warm the carbonates, thereby producing carbon dioxide and helping to make kimberlite. The kimberlitic elevator finally takes all its passengers to the surface: both the asthenospheric diamonds (initially brought up by the plumes) and the lithospheric diamonds (stored in the 'warehouse' for a billion years). However, given that the Earth only has a limited number of ancient continents, this process requires a random encounter between plume and root. Statistically, the plumes have a much better chance of rising up under young continents, and an even better chance of rising up under an ocean floor. They would then produce accumulations of basalt instead. This type of volcanism does not have kimberlite's energy, and it rises sufficiently slowly for all the diamonds to be irretrievably dissolved. In other words, diamonds don't get a 'window of opportunity' to escape from the mantle. They get a tiny crack in the wall.

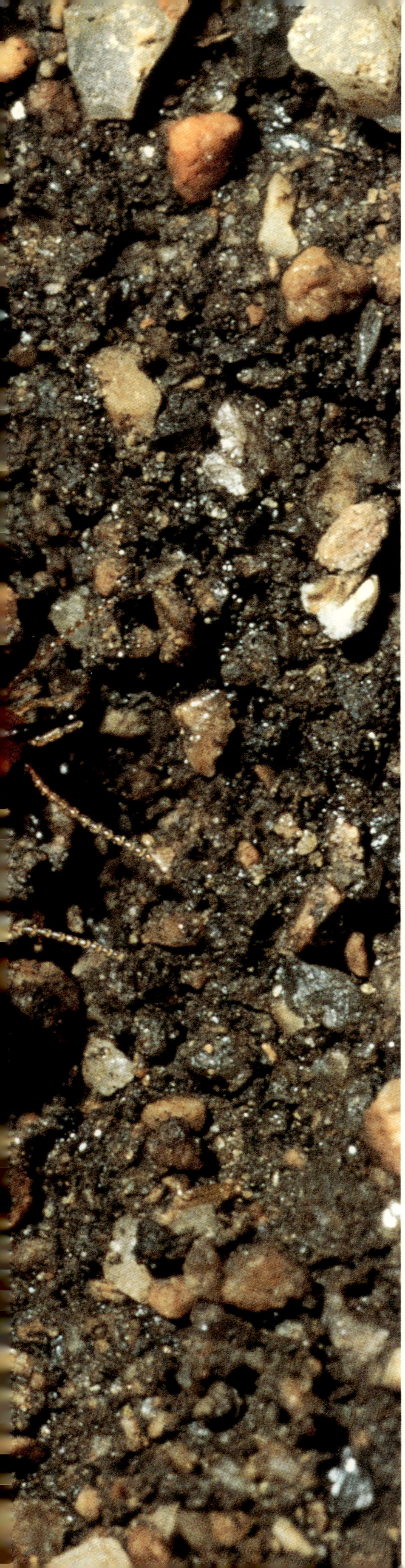

Diamonds on the surface: freaks of nature

When diamonds finally embark upon their final voyage towards surface in the kimberlite, they are in a minority, accompanied by many other mantle minerals. They are only saved from certain death by the fact that the voyage through the lithosphere is over after a very short period of time. Kimberlites brought them to the surface between 100 million and 1 billion years ago (depending on the deposit in question). There is only one simple reason why diamonds do not change back into graphite over a billion years on the surface: it is too cold. Crystalline structure changes can take place very slowly, over billion-year timescales, and their speed is dependant upon temperature. Heat facilitates crystalline transformations, because it agitates the atoms. They are therefore more likely to shift their original positions, break their chemical bonds with adjacent atoms, and build new bonds that are more suited to the ambient conditions. However, the temperature on the Earth's surface (and, indeed, in the first few kilometres of crust) is relatively low: around 25°C. In comparison, diamonds crystallise in a place where the temperature is an order of magnitude greater: 1200°C. As a result, it takes tens of billions of years for diamonds to turn into graphite when they are at the surface. People who own diamonds can rest assured that their sparkling jewels will not be turning into common pencil-lead any time soon!

Diamond's scarcity has an impact upon its price. A mine must crush more than 100 tons of kimberlite in order to extract a few carats (that is to say, a couple of grams) of this precious mineral. The reason for this scarcity is nothing to do with the difficulties of mining diamonds. It is because of the Earth itself. Basically, diamonds are rare because they only grow in the mantle, yet this is a place where the requisite raw material, carbon, is rare. Convection helps to compensate for this scarcity, by bringing some carbon to the diamond-formation zone: the carbon comes from the carbonates deposited on ocean floors. Then, in order for diamonds to rise up to the surface unharmed, they need to be stored at the base of the lithospheric roots underneath the oldest continents. They must then wait for their 'elevator' to arrive - an elevator that will travel fast enough for them to keep their crystalline structure. The kimberlite elevator itself is the result of a chance meeting between a hot matter plume, saturated with gas from the mantle's abyssal zone, and the cold, rigid roots at the base of the oldest continents. In addition, the elevator is likely to miss its invaluable cargo: many kimberlites failed to intercept the 'seams' of diamonds, and travelled up to the surface empty. Diamonds on the Earth's surface are therefore freaks of nature. A sequence of rare events had to occur in conjunction, in order for this exceptional mineral to be brought up from the darkness, and fuel our greed with its scintillating brilliance

An unusual type of sampling operation, performed by termites. One of them, near the bottom of the photo, is carrying a yellow diamond crystal. This might be a useful clue for diamond prospectors.

How do you hunt diamonds?

Over the past thirty years, scientific research on diamonds has not only enabled us to take fantastic imaginary voyages into the heart of our planet and back into the dawn of time. It has also advanced prospection methods considerably, helping to discover new diamond mines for the 21st century. Prospecting for diamonds is no easy task. For example, in South Africa there are 3,000 kimberlite pipes listed on geological survey maps. Barely 10% of them have been or will be mined. In fact, the majority are "sterile" (i.e. they do not contain enough diamonds to be profitable).

Until the 1950s, finding a diamond deposit was primarily a matter of luck (cf. Chapter 4). Since then, prospecting has became increasingly methodical, and it is now a high-tech operation (using sophisticated geophysics techniques and supercomputer digital simulations). However, the primary criterion is still geological: the identification of cratons, rock formations over 2.5 billion years old that form the oldest continents. In 1966, an English geologist by the name of Clifford formulated the following rule for diamond prospectors: the richest diamond kimberlites will be located in these cratons. Over the years, geological science became more sophisticated, and techniques to find the ages of rocks were refined. As a result, these cratons could be more accurately delineated geographically (page 68). Once this had been done, the kimberlites could be prospected more actively. Since 1973, economically viable kimberlites (0.5 to 1 carat per tonne) have been discovered in Western Russia (Arkanghelsk), Finland (Baltic craton), Venezuela (Guyanese craton), Australia (Ylgarn craton) and in the far north of Canada (Slave craton). This is in addition to the discovery of new pipes in traditionally productive areas, like Southern Africa, Siberia, Brazil or China. None of these discoveries contradicted Clifford's law. Its validity was underlined in 1991, when the fabulous Canadian deposits were identified. The Ekati mine (in Diavik district, North-Western Territory) kimberlites cut through the centre of the Slave craton. This craton contains the oldest rocks ever found on the surface of the Earth, with ages in excess of 4 billion years. The following

A heavy-mineral concentrate, such as one might find in a diamond-prospector's pan: olivine, garnet, pyroxene and ilmenite.

figures illustrate the discovery's importance: more than 200 kimberlite pipes were located, over a 10,000 km^2 area, more than two-thirds of these contain microdiamonds (< 0.5 mm in diameter), twelve are being mined (3,500,000 carats per year in the Panda mine) or will shortly be mined in the early 21st century. It has been announced that the Diavik mine contains reserves of almost 40 million tons, containing up to 3.3 carats of diamond per ton, often of gem quality. These deposits should propel Canada into the top league of diamond-producing countries, with output of more than 10 million carats per annum.

How can kimberlites be located, and how is their potential productivity measured? Kimberlites can be found by following the trail of its travelling companions, such as chromium garnet (uvarovite), magnesium- and chromium-rich ilmenite, chromite and green pyroxene. These minerals survived kimberlite's decomposition on the surface, and they are carried away by rivers. The rivers eroded the pipes over a geological timescale. These heavy minerals accumulate in alluvial 'placer' deposits. They are carefully washed and sorted during the final analysis process. Sometimes, some diamonds are also found. It is not easy to find the kimberlite pipe. Prospectors need to take samples at regular intervals, following a pre-determined grid pattern, that usually spreads in concentric circles around the area of dispersion. Prospectors try to approach the source methodically, like hunters converging on prey. However, the process is not always successful. This is because kimberlites are discrete rocks, whose outcrops seldom exceed a few hundred square metres in size. In addition, the pipes' surfaces are usually so oxidised, it is difficult to distinguish kimberlite from clay. This earthy looking kimberlite is known as yellow ground to diamond prospectors. Below this there is the blue ground, which is better-preserved. There is an additional complication: the kimberlite can be covered with a layer of more recent deposits. Finally, the kimberlite pipe can escape the prospectors' notice if the sampling grid pattern is too broadly spaced. Aerial methods of prospecting are becoming increasingly popular, because they are often more cost-effective and efficient. These methods can range from simply inspecting aerial site photographs, to taking satellite images of the infra-red radiation emitted by blue ground clays. This can sometimes permit pipes to be discovered even in tropical areas, where the ground has been altered considerably. However, helicopter-based magnetic and electric prospecting methods are the most sophisticated methods used to detect kimberlites. These measure electrical conductivity and magnetic field strength. Kimberlites are rich in iron-containing minerals, so they create disturbances in these readings. When the information from these anomalies is processed, it can be used to draw three-dimensional computer renderings of the pipe. The pipe can be inspected on screen, to give an idea of its size and shape. This information is essential, because it helps determine the tonnage of ore in the mine. Samples can then be taken on the ground, in order to refine the digital simulation. As an example, many core-shaped drill samples were taken when the Diavik mine in Canada was being mapped. Placed end to end, these cores would have been over 20 km long. The next stage was to statistically calculate the quantity of diamond that the kimberlite would produce. They took samples of kimberlites, ranging from 100 to 10,000 tons, and calculated the likely figures for the deposit as a whole. These procedures take time. They are highly dependent upon the economic outlook, and sometimes they have to be performed in remote areas where conditions are difficult. The whole process, from discovery to commercialisation, can take ten years.

There is an exception to every rule, no matter how rigid it may be. The huge Argyle mine is the exception to Clifford's law. It was discovered in 1979, in the north-western Australian desert. Surprisingly, the ground is proterozoic: much younger than the cratons, which are over 2.5 billion years old (page 68). It forms a belt around the Kimberley craton, in western Australia. However, the Argyle mines were not transported by kimberlite, but by a different volcanic rock: lamproite. On the surface, these rocks look like tabular bodies rather than pipes. They have a rather dark appearance, and could easily be overlooked. Since then, about thirty lamproite deposits have been mapped around the world, but only a few are diamond-bearing (Province of Guihzou, Yangtze, China; Ellendale-Argyle, Australia; Meadow Creek-Twin Knobs, Arkansas; Jack, British Columbia), and only Argyle proved to be world-class. A second exception to Clifford's law was discovered in 1999, in French Guyana. The diamonds were found in a third type of rock. The outcrops are located in the heart of the tropical Amazonian rainforest, in proterozoic-era rocks with no cratonic connections. It took a long time to identify the host rock, because there is a thick layer of laterite over the entire area. Surprisingly, it proved to be a komatiite. Unlike kimberlites, lamproites are very old. Their production virtually ceased 2 billion years ago. However, they are found in areas that are younger than the cratons. The rock itself differs from kimberlite and lamproite. It does not contain the small mica spangles that are typical of ultrapotassic diamond-bearing lava. On the other hand, it is extremely rich in magnesium. This new type of rock does not appear to be economically viable thus far (the diamonds usually weigh less than one carat), but it is nevertheless exceptional: it has higher concentrations of diamond than any other rock on the planet. In fact, it often contains up to 77 diamonds per kilogram, compared to kimberlites, which only produce a few carats per hundred tons. Could this type of rock simply turn out to be a dead end, sidetracking prospectors from their central objective, or is it a revolutionary discovery that will open new opportunities for the industry? It is still too early to tell. All we can do is make careful note of the fact that, more than 2,000 years after diamonds were discovered in India, diamond geology continues to surprise us.

Lamproite from Argyle, Australia.
Muséum national d'histoire naturelle, Paris.

Komatiite from the Dachine deposit in Guyana.
A 500-gram lump of rock yields about 50 diamonds. They are, unfortunately, of mediocre quality, but the yield is in stark contrast to that of kimberlite, which produces one carat of cut, gem-quality diamond for every hundred tons of ore. Rennes University.

CHAPTER III

Diamond Stardust

Hugh Hill
and Violaine Sautter

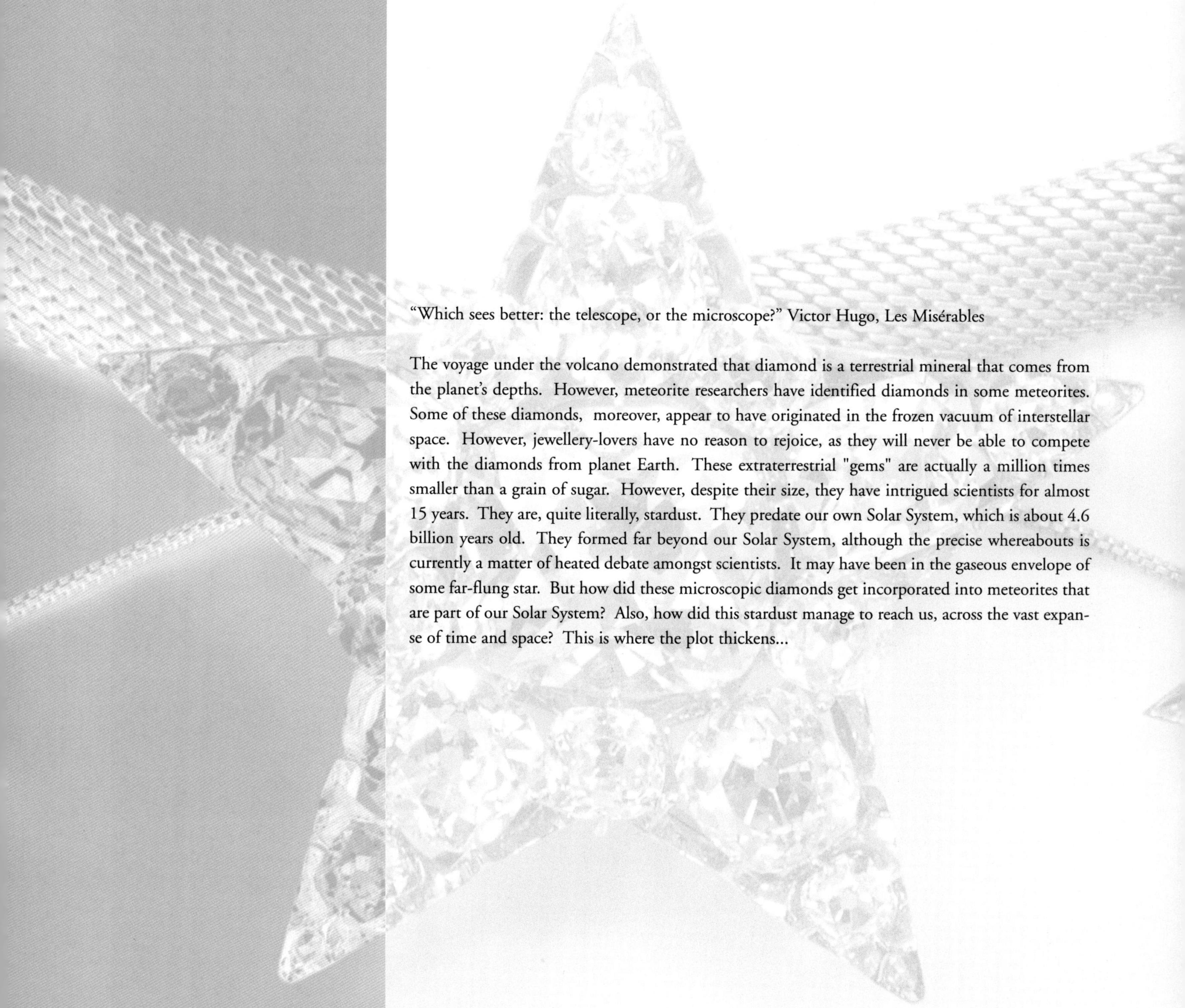

"Which sees better: the telescope, or the microscope?" Victor Hugo, Les Misérables

The voyage under the volcano demonstrated that diamond is a terrestrial mineral that comes from the planet's depths. However, meteorite researchers have identified diamonds in some meteorites. Some of these diamonds, moreover, appear to have originated in the frozen vacuum of interstellar space. However, jewellery-lovers have no reason to rejoice, as they will never be able to compete with the diamonds from planet Earth. These extraterrestrial "gems" are actually a million times smaller than a grain of sugar. However, despite their size, they have intrigued scientists for almost 15 years. They are, quite literally, stardust. They predate our own Solar System, which is about 4.6 billion years old. They formed far beyond our Solar System, although the precise whereabouts is currently a matter of heated debate amongst scientists. It may have been in the gaseous envelope of some far-flung star. But how did these microscopic diamonds get incorporated into meteorites that are part of our Solar System? Also, how did this stardust manage to reach us, across the vast expanse of time and space? This is where the plot thickens...

Star necklace, made in 1865 by Estavao de Sousa, a Portuguese jeweller, for Queen María Pia of Portugal. There are 198 diamonds in the stars, which are attached to a flexible gold collar. Lisbon, Ajuda Palace National Museum.

Mysterious "fingerprints" from dying stars

When we look at the heavens through a small telescope, on a clear, moonless night, interstellar space appears to be a cold, dark void. However, in the past 30 years, modern astronomical techniques have demonstrated that the truth is quite the opposite and deep space is not completely empty. Rather, it is strewn with innumerable chemical species, and dust grains of many types. We can detect these remote entities thanks to the way they absorb and emit radiation. Interstellar dust grains and chemical species have characteristic spectral features ("fingerprints") in various parts of the electromagnetic spectrum that permit astronomers to detect them from the Earth. More recently, a new generation of space-based telescopes, such as the Hubble Space Telescope, has also allowed detection, with incredible clarity, from beyond the Earth's unhelpfully absorbing atmosphere. In order to obtain the spectral fingerprints of the interstellar species, large telescopes analyse the radiation emitted or absorbed by them, and decipher the signals using various filters. Using modern detectors, it is possible to record the spectra of simple atoms, complex molecules and even minerals. Infrared telescopes have yielded the most spectacular results: they have, for example, been used to detect the spectra of more than two hundred carbon-based compounds, including many compounds that are familiar to organic chemists on Earth. These range from simple elemental carbon to fullerene (C_{60}), a complex molecule shaped like a soccer ball, that contains 60 carbon atoms arranged geometrically in a sphere. Many of these chemicals can be identified quite easily: scientists simply take the unknown astronomical spectra, and compare them to spectra that have been recorded in the laboratory, from known materials. Although most spectra can be readily identified, some are painfully difficult to interpret. For example, in 1984, astronomers from Calgary University in Canada observed a peculiar type of carbon-rich star. Specifically, this star had an unidentified spectral feature in the infrared part of the spectrum with a wavelength of 21 micrometers (Figure 1). What chemical species or mineral could have caused this mysterious feature?

Pre-solar "fossils" in primitive meteorites

Our story begins on the 14th of ay, 1864, when a meteorite fell on Orgueil, a small French village in the Tarn-et-Garonne region, 80 km from Toulouse. It was a rare type of carbon-rich meteorite and, hence, known as a carbonaceous chondrite (Figure 2). Meteorites are tiny fragments of minor planets that formed at the same time as the Earth. They come from the asteroid belt, which consists of small planets (up to approximately 1000 km across) orbiting between Mars and Jupiter. For researchers, they are literally gifts from heaven. This is because they contain important geological and chemical evidence that helps them understand the origin and early history of our Solar System. Meteorites are the oldest dated rocks known to science, and are considerably older than the oldest terrestrial rocks. They were formed at the same time as the Earth, some 4.6 billion years ago. Over 80% of them are referred to as chondrites. These come from planets which were so small that their composition remained similar to the material from which the Solar System was formed. Larger planets (such as Venus, the Earth, and Mars) partially melted when they were formed, due to the interior heating, and underwent a process of redistribution of matter into distinct layers. The denser, metallic materials migrated towards the centre to form the core, whereas the silicates were concentrated closer to the surface to form the mantle and the crust. This process is known as planetary fractionation or differentiation. However, most of the minor planets (asteroids) were too small to generate the requisite heat needed for this differentiation, and remained essentially similar (in terms of their mineralogy and chemical composition) to the primordial material that accreted to form the sun. The minor planets that did end up in the asteroid belt (within the orbits of Jupiter and Mars) violently collided with each other, generating countless billions of rocky fragments. When these fragments collide with the Earth and land on its surface, they are known as meteorites. As already mentioned, the most numerous and interesting meteorites are known as chondrites. They are espe-

The Orgueil meteorite, which fell on the eponymous village, 80 km north of Toulouse, in 1864. It is a chondrite: a type of primitive meteorite that is rich in small spherules. The dark colour is caused by its rich carbon content. The grey interior is covered by a black fusion crust. The Allende and Murchison meteorites also contain nanodiamonds, but the Orgueil meteorite has the highest levels of them. Paris, Muséum national d'histoire naturelle.

cially interesting to many types of scientists, as they have changed so little in 4.6 billion years. In fact, chondrites are actually defined as those meteorites that have almost the same elemental composition as the Sun's visible surface (known as the photosphere) with the exception of the volatile gases.

The Orgueil meteorite, however, was particularly unheated (primitive) within its parent asteroid and, therefore, preserved virtually all of its original minerals and chemical components. In the 1960s, it was even discovered that it contained several exotic isotopes from very far away, from a part of the galaxy far beyond our Solar System. A word about isotopes...

Atoms are made up of a nucleus with orbiting electrons. Most of the mass is concentrated in the nucleus. An atom is smaller than an angström unit (one angström = 10^{-10} metres). The nucleus is made up of two different types of particle: protons and neutrons. Different atoms of the same chemical element may have slightly different masses. This is because they can have different numbers of neutrons. For example, hydrogen is the simplest and most abundant element in the universe. The majority of hydrogen atoms have a mass of 1, because they have one proton and no neutrons. However, a very small proportion of hydrogen atoms in the universe are slightly heavier, with a mass of 2 or 3, because their nuclei contain a proton and one or two neutrons. Collectively, these variants are known as isotopes: atoms of the same element, but with different masses. Carbon has three isotopes. There are carbon atoms with a mass of 12, which are the most abundant, some of mass 13, and those of mass 14, which are the rarest. Different isotopes of the same element have the same number of protons and electrons. The electrons permit chemical reactions to take place, by forming

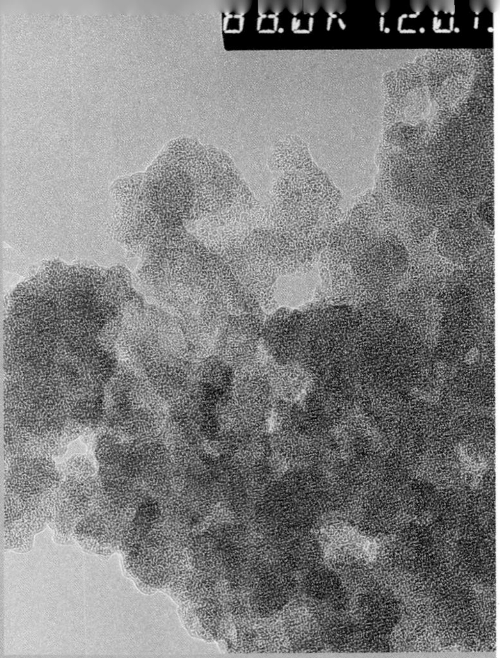

Electron microscope images of the Orgeuil meteorite's nanodiamonds, taken at different levels of magnification. The image with the pale background was taken at 88,000x magnification, and shows nanodiamond aggregates, on a scale of 1.5 cm representing 100 nanometres.

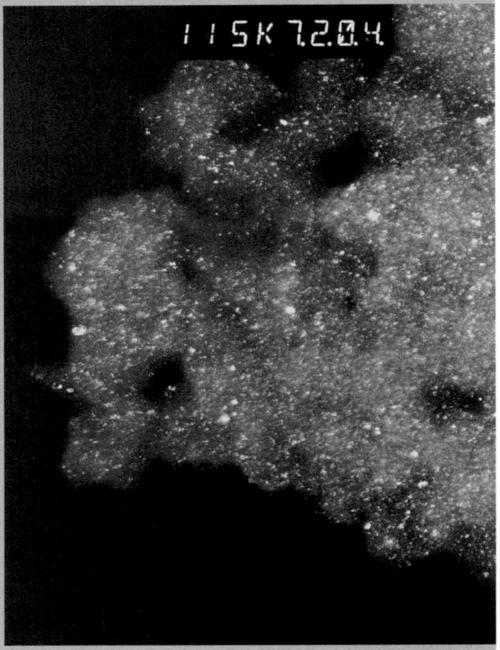

This picture, with a dark background, was taken at 115,000x magnification. It shows individual brilliant nanodiamond grains, on a scale of 2 cm, representing 100 nanometres.

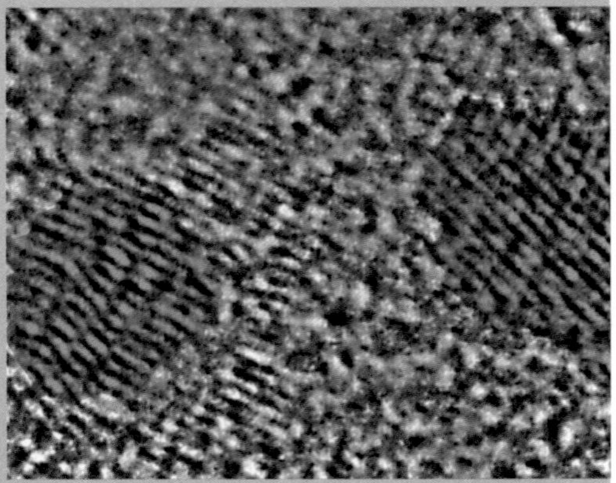

This ultra-high-resolution image was taken at 500,000x magnification. Two individual nanodiamond granules have been highlighted in blue: one can just begin to see the parallel layers of atoms.

or breaking bonds with other atoms. Assuming that a given element neither undergoes radioactive decay, nor is consumed as a result of other processes that preferentially enrich or reduce one isotope rather than another, the isotopic ratio of an element remains constant for a given element over billions of years. However, scientists sometimes detect isotopic anomalies: samples with isotopic ratios that initially don't appear to make sense.

The isotopic anomalies found in the Orgueil meteorite were determined by comparing them to materials from the Solar System, whose isotopic signatures were used as a frame of reference. Analysis showed that the Orgueil meteorite had a 'dual' isotopic signature: one normal, and the other abnormal. This means that it consisted of a mixture of two types of material. One type originated in the solar nebula that gave rise to the Sun, and the other type predated our Solar System. The most intriguing anomalies were the high levels (compared to our Solar System) of the light and heavy isotopes of the rare gas xenon. Scientists have known since 1975 that this isotopic anomaly indicates that the material came from a remote star, outside our Solar System. To be precise, this strange Xe-HL ("Xenon-Heavy, Light") mixture was caused by a process known as explosive nucleosynthesis, in supernovae. A supernova is a massive star that explodes violently at the end of its life (Figure 3). The anomalous xenon component in the Orgueil meteorite came from such an event, and is therefore older than the Solar System. To find out more, and discover which material carried this anomaly in the primitive meteorite, Chicago University researchers decided to carefully dissolve it, using strong acids. One of the scientists involved, Edward Anders, summarised the destructive recipe as follows: "It's like searching for a needle in a haystack. All that you have to do is burn the haystack, and then recover the needle from the ashes". To their great surprise, the mineral carrying the Xe-HL anomaly resisted the most aggressive chemical recipes that they could muster. However, they eventually separated a powdery, white residue from the meteorite, whose composition was exclusively carbon. They assumed that the carbon grains were amorphous (not crystals), but X-ray analysis revealed that they were, in fact, tiny diamond crystals. The diamonds were so small that they were only visible with the aid of an electron microscope (figure 4). Such grains are called nanodiamonds (a nanometre is one millionth of a metre). By way of comparison, one nanodiamond consists of a several hundred to a few thousand carbon atoms, whereas a normal diamond weighing a few carats contains several billion atoms. Hence the mystery: why was the meteorite studded with tiny diamonds from a far-off star?

It is important to note that the presence of diamonds in meteorites is not exceptional in itself. Well before the discovery of these pre-solar nanodiamonds, much larger diamonds had been discovered in less primitive, differentiated meteorites. However, these diamonds crystallised as a result of high pressure and temperature. These conditions were caused by impacts: either from the meteorite impacting carbonaceous rocks when it fell to Earth, or as the result of two rocky bodies striking each other in space. Terrestrial diamonds also crystallise under high pressure and temperature conditions, in the hot rocks of the Earth's mantle. Such diamonds are the result of processes inside our Solar System. They have little in common with presolar nanodiamonds in meteorites. Nanodiamonds are 'fossil' remnants of ancient stars, and they have a very different origin and history. In order to understand the link between diamonds and stars, we need to go back in time to the primordial Big Bang, the likely beginning of the Universe some 12-15 billion years ago...

A spectacular image of the Crab nebula, taken by the Palomar telescope in the 1960s. The Crab nebula is a gas envelope that was produced by a stellar explosion known as a supernova. In the centre, there is a pulsar, the collapsed core of the exploded star. This incredible explosion has observed by Chinese astronomers in the year 1054. The 'new star' (ten times the mass of the Sun) was so brilliant, it was visible in broad daylight for several weeks. The nebula is 7,000 light-years away from us, in the Taurus constellation. The green, yellow and red filaments around the edge are the remnants of the star, ejected into space by the explosion. The different colours correspond to different chemical elements present in the expanding gas. As the filaments progressively dissolve into the interstellar void, they will seed it with heavy elements that had been formed in the supernova. This is exactly the kind of star that would expel carbon, in the form of nanodiamonds, in its death throes.

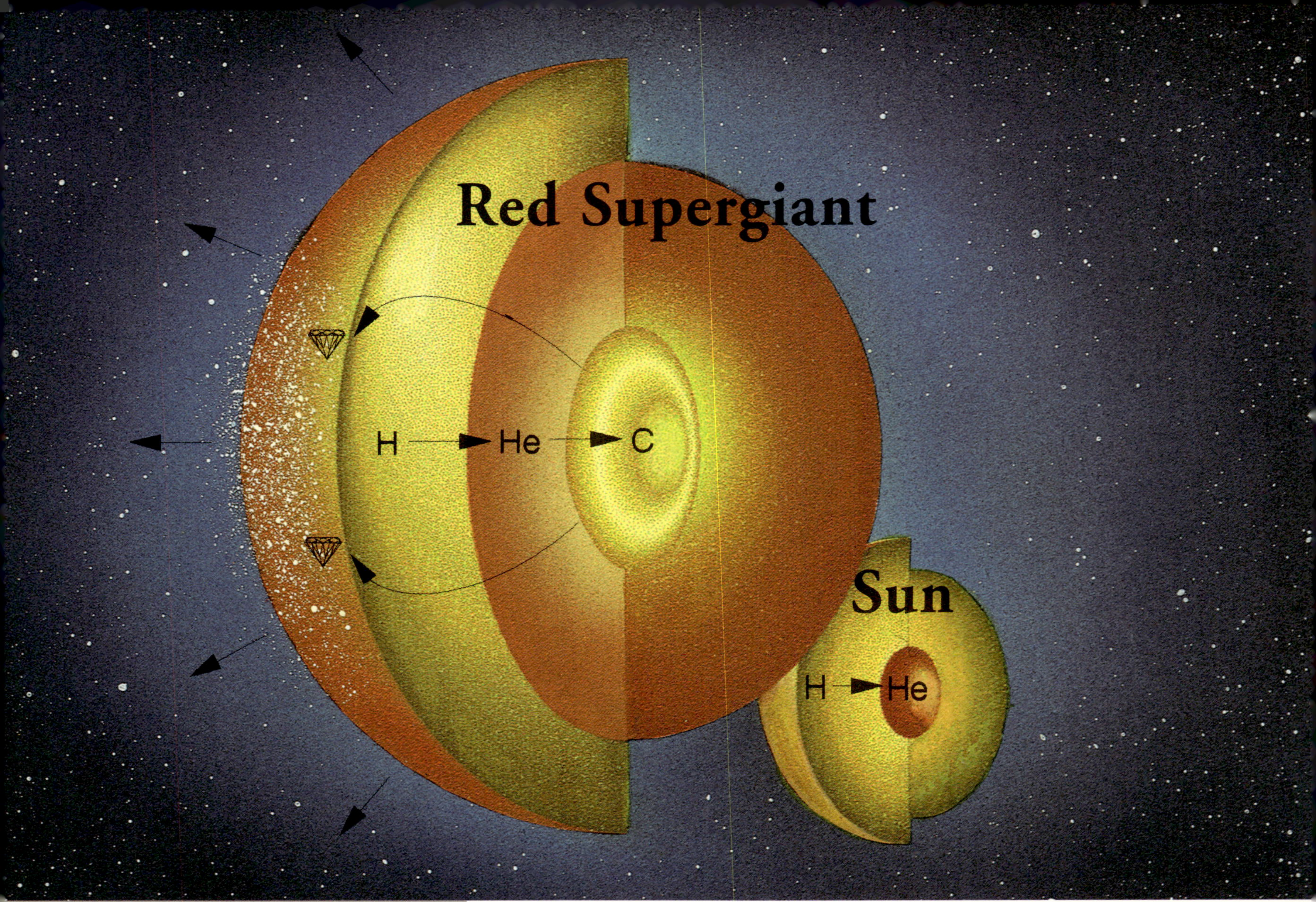

A carbon factory: the red giant. Inside stars, most elements are made from hydrogen, by nuclear reactions. The first reactions result in the fusion of hydrogen to form helium, and then helium into carbon. In more massive stars (more than ten solar masses), nuclear synthesis produces elements up to iron. these stars end up resembling an onion, with the end products forming into layers, with the heaviest in the core. In a red giant of between 4 and 8 solar masses, the helium envelope surrounds a thermically unstable carbon core, and the star shines brightly, producing flashes. This liberates energy that creates a convection zone, which brings the carbon up from the depths of the star towards the surface. Between pulses, the star's external convective envelope mixes hydrogen, helium and a little carbon, putting these elements into the star's atmosphere. These elements were created from nucleosynthesis in the heart of the star, and they are then disseminated throughout the cosmos by strong stellar winds. According to one theory, this expelled carbon condenses into nanodiamonds, in the gaseous plasma of the stellar corona.

Stars: nuclear power stations of the cosmos

In order to understand how interstellar nanodiamonds formed, we need to know how carbon came into being in the universe. Although it is the fourth most abundant element in our galaxy today, it was not generated in the Big Bang. This gigantic explosion created only two elements: hydrogen (in great abundance), and a little helium. These are the two lightest elements. They have the atomic numbers 1 and 2 respectively. Other, heavier elements in the Periodic Table were formed later on, by nucleosynthesis (i.e. the synthesis of atomic nuclei in the core of stars). In order to form new, heavier atoms, you need to start with lighter elements, and make their atomic nuclei fuse together. For example, six helium nuclei make one carbon nucleus. In order to achieve these nuclear fusions, gigantic pressures and temperatures are needed. These conditions are far in excess of those in the Earth's core. They are found in the hearts of stars (Figure 5). Nuclear fusion reactions are quite distinct from chemical reactions: chemistry combines different atoms merely by bonding the electrons that orbit around their nuclei. For example, when iron reacts chemically with oxygen to make rust, the atomic nuclei are preserved separately within the resulting iron oxide molecule.

Nucleosynthesis makes it possible for small atomic nuclei to be transformed into increasingly large ones in the hearts of stars. It commences when the temperature and pressure exceed a certain threshold value. In fact, several million degrees are necessary before the collisions between adjacent particles become so violent that the initial nuclear fusion reactions occur. However, shortly afterwards, a chain reaction starts, causing hydrogen nuclei to combine, releasing blasts of energy. This released energy is what makes a star "shine". The larger the star, the more nuclear fusion chain reactions occur. Familiar natural elements (such as carbon, silicon, calcium, magnesium and iron, as well as gases such as oxygen, nitrogen) were manufactured by nucleosynthesis reactions in various types of star. Stars are analogous to nuclear power stations, in space. All things on our planet, including human beings, the ocean, rocks and trees, are children of the cosmos. They are made from atoms that were initially synthesised in the hearts of stars or as result of supernova explosions, well before the our own sun existed. Stars are born and die, a little like living creatures. Since the Big Bang, generations of stars have come and gone. The matter (gas and dust) ejected upon the death of a star is then re-used to form new ones. Generations of stars came and went in our galaxy before the Sun's formation, 4.6 billion years ago. Consider a star like the Sun: its core facilitates hydrogen fusion reactions for about 10 billion years. These reactions produce helium, which is stored deep inside the star whilst the sun radiates its energy at various wavelengths. This is known as the main sequence, and is the longest part of the star's lifespan. Then the ageing process abruptly starts, and will last for a further, final, one billion years. The sun will expand, dilating so much so that it will engulf Mars. It will produce more and more energy, and will become a Red Giant: between ten and a thousand times bigger (by volume) than the Sun, shining a thousand times brighter. Once it has burnt all its fuel, it will shrink into a small, White Dwarf star, 1,000 to 10,000 times smaller in size than the Sun. However, not all stars evolve into White Dwarfs. In fact, after the Red Giant stage, some stars explode and release an vast amount of energy in a few seconds: these are known as supernovae. For the first few seconds, the star shines as much as a whole galaxy (cf. Figure 3).

But where does carbon fit in to this process ? In which type of star does it form? Red Giant and related stars are the most productive carbon factories. These have grown to approximately 1,000 times larger than their initial size, and their core temperature has risen to 100 million degrees. Inside the core, helium nuclei fuse to form carbon-12, as well as some heavier elements thanks to nuclear chain reactions. All the elements thus produced separate out into layers inside the star, like the layers of an onion. The heaviest are in the centre, the lightest migrate to the surface. Carbon makes its way to the surface of the star thanks to internal convection currents. During its last phase of life, the star expels part of its outer envelope, and carbon therefore reaches the star's atmosphere. In this way, some stars possess a mechanism whereby carbonaceous dust can condense around them at the end of their lifetimes. If the Red Giant should happen to become a supernova, the extraordinary explosion will propel all the carbon a vast distance away, to be dispersed throughout the cosmos. These wandering atoms and molecules may circulate and mix in interstellar clouds. A cloud such as this, rich in molecules and dust types, suddenly started to fragment and collapse in our Galaxy, some 4.6 billion years ago. One fragment, which we now refer to as the solar nebula continued to 'fall inwards' (accrete) forming the protosun, planets, and the other bodies that we collectively refer to as the Solar System.

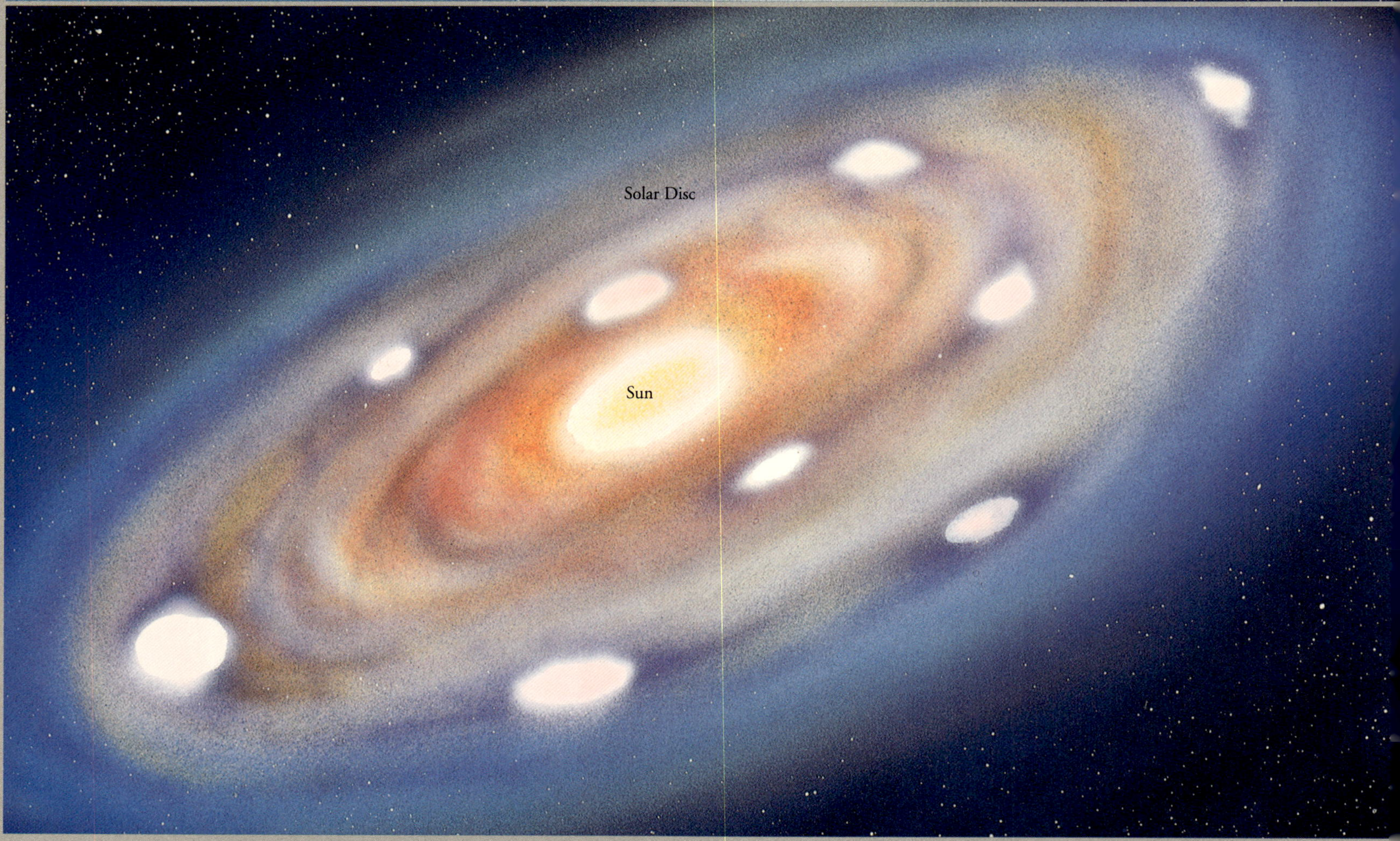

Diagram: from the initial seeding of nanodiamonds into the solar system by a supernova, 4.5 billion years ago, to the impact of a nanodiamond-containing meteorite in 1864.

A pre-solar cloud, next to a supernova. The supernova explosion emits a shockwave, which triggers the start of the protosolar nebula's contraction, permitting various different types of particle to penetrate it, including nanodiamonds.

The protosolar cloud condenses into the shape of a flattened disc, centred upon the Sun. At this stage in the solar system's evolution, the nanodiamonds were uniformly scattered throughout.

Most of the nanodiamonds would have been consumed when the Sun and its planets differentiated. Only the asteroid belt between Mars and Jupiter would retain evidence of the nanodiamond injection, because most of its small planetary bodies never melted.

A fragment of one of these asteroids becomes a primitive meteorite, and falls on Orgueil in 1864.

Pre-solar nanodiamonds: their strange destiny

When researchers discovered presolar nanodiamonds in meteorites, they realised the enormity of their discovery: they could actually touch the dust of ancient stars with their own fingers. Over the next few years, additional presolar grains were discovered. These robust mineral grains were a thousand times larger (around one micron in size), and included silicon carbide, graphite spherules, corundum (aluminium oxide), and titanium oxide. Given their sizes, it was possible to chemically analyse individual grains and assess their isotopic compositions. These showed that they overwhelmingly came from Red Giants, another type of main sequence star known as an Asymptotic Giant Branch star, and supernovae.

However, referring specifically to presolar nanodiamonds: where do they come from? Although it is difficult to analyse the grains individually given their size, an average analysis of several thousand revealed the presence of the Xe-HL anomaly. This is associated with a specific type of supernova explosion. However, it is equally likely that some of these nanodiamonds were formed at low pressure, in the cool atmosphere of carbon-rich stars. Initially, the scientific community was unwilling to accept this hypothesis, since it seemed that very high pressure was required to create diamond's tightly-packed crystalline structure (cf. Chapter II). A different type of synthesis was required, in order to explain how stars could create diamond from low-pressure gas plasmas. Inside a nebula, temperatures rarely exceed 700°C, and pressure is around one microbar. Inside the Earth, under similar temperature conditions, one billion times more pressure (15 kilobars) is required in order to cause diamond to crystallise.

However, the notion of low-pressure diamonds was not as absurd as it sounded: in the 1950s, scientists had already successfully synthesised diamond from plasma (extremely hot gas at low pressure). These conditions are actually similar to those in certain stellar atmospheres, particularly those of Red Giants and related stars, in the twilight of their existence. Diamonds made this way from gas plasma are called Chemical Vapour Deposition (CVD) diamonds (cf. Chapter VI). In this process, thin films of diamond are deposited from a carbon-rich gas mixture, at approximately 900°C and less than one atmosphere of pressure. This is a long way from the 1,200°C and 50,000 atmospheres necessary to crystallise diamonds in the terrestrial mantle. Therefore, astrophysicists concluded that the Orgueil nanodiamonds could well have been formed in these kinds of stellar atmospheres, by a natural process resembling CVD.

Nanodiamonds: from their formation to their fall to Earth

Around stars the carbon was transformed into diamond, and the other elements were trapped inside the diamonds' crystal structure as they formed, or were later implanted by a supernova explosion. The diamonds acted like miniature, high-security prisons for the rare gas atoms such as xenon, ultimately delivering them to us on a 'silver platter'. However, there are some pieces missing from this cosmic puzzle. We need to explain how diamonds from outside our Solar System ended up inside meteorites. One theory is that a supernova exploded not far from the protosolar nebula (figure 6), littering it with billions of microscopic diamonds. These nanodiamonds were thereafter incorporated into the matter that later became the Sun and its satellites. However, these dead star "fossils" only survived in the most unheated planetary bodies of the Solar System. Most of the terrestrial planets and minor planets (asteroids) have been heated, consequently losing their exotic presolar grains such as diamond. One particular asteroid was partially or completely shattered as a result of a collision, and some pieces developed Earth-crossing orbits. Eventually, in 1864, one such fragment fell to the Earth, near the village of Orgueil. As a result, years later, scientists would realise that our embryonic Solar System may well have been the neighbour of an exploding star...

The tears of the gods, and the secrets they contain

If the extrasolar nanodiamonds are present in meteorites, they may therefore be observable in space. As we saw at the beginning of this chapter, some telescopes are equipped to detect infrared radiation. Thanks to the analysis of this radiation, a multitude of chemical species and minerals have been detected in interstellar and interplanetary space and in stellar atmospheres. Although other presolar grains have been observed in this way (e.g. silicon carbide), nanodiamonds have not yet been conclusively detected. Everything may hinge around an infrared emission feature with a wavelength of 21 micrometres. This spectral feature has been detected around 12 Red Giants, and in odd carbon-rich stars called protoplanetary nebulae. The problem is to identify the material that is producing the spectrum. Astrophysicists, spectroscopists and theoreticians have pooled their efforts to find substances that are able to produce the same spectrum. There are, unfortunately, numerous candidates. These include silicon sulphide, hydrogenated fullerenes and, finally, nanodiamonds. The debate is still wide open at present. Theoretically, pure diamond absorbs infra-red energy poorly, compared to other materials. This is why it is so difficult to detect in space, compared to more absorbent materials. However, nanodiamonds are very different from other diamonds. They are riddled with structural defects, particularly surface defects and defects produced by nitrogen impurities. These defects make them more absorbent, and thus more easily detectable from an astronomical point of view. This is precisely the characteristic that is being used in an attempt to locate nanodiamonds in space. By a strange coincidence, terrestrial diamonds with high levels of nitrogen defects also have a spectral band in the 21 micron range. This band is strangely reminiscent of the signal detected by astronomers around carbon-rich stars (figure 7). The Orgueil meteorite's diamonds may therefore have been formed in this kind of distant star's atmosphere. If this is the case, the little village of Orgueil ("Pride", in French) richly deserves its name, as it was privileged to have been the first recipient of these interstellar jewels: specks of stardust from the dawn of time.

Whether they come from Red Giants (or related carbon-rich stars) or from supernovae, these diamonds are unique intruders in our Solar System. They are the oldest minerals known. Appropriately enough, the first Greek scholars believed diamonds to be the tears of the gods. These microscopic grains permit us to see far back in time, back to before the birth of our Solar System. A multitude of scientists from various disciplines have focused upon them: astronomers, spectroscopists, particle physicists, chemists and mineralogists. They are exceptional little grains and much is riding on them for the international scientific community. They open up new avenues for research and, one day, scientists will discover how to analyse nanodiamonds' isotopic contents, crystal by tiny crystal. This may help to unravel the mysteries of diamond formation in the atmospheres of far-off, long-dead stars. However, the enigmatic little gems are a long way from giving up all their secrets.

TOMAS·FEDRIANI·F·

CHAPTER IV

Tales of the diamond mines

Hubert Bari

Deep in our subconscious, alongside our other childhood memories, there is an image of a mythical diamond mine. It is the mine that belongs to Walt Disney's seven dwarves. The cheerful little gnomes, wearing their little caps, mine the rock with picks and shovels, collecting the gems that sparkle in the darkness. The multi-coloured diamonds in the rock are already cut! This beautiful scene was actually originally inspired by some unknown medieval manuscript illuminator. In certain ancient manuscripts, one can find equally brilliantly-coloured characters, picking at rocks in search of red, blue, white and green gems - only this time, they are on the surface. These fantastical representations are a far cry from the reality of diamond mining. There are mines on the surface (alluvial diamond deposits), and underground (primary kimberlite mines, 'bottomless pits' in Africa, Russia, Canada and China). In order to unveil the true secrets of diamond mines, we must delve deep into history: a history that is still being written by humanity's genius and greed.

A diamond mine. This picture bears no relationship to reality: it is a figment of painter Maso da San Friano's imagination (around 1532-1571). He decorated Francis I de Medici's studiolo in the Palazzo Vecchio, Florence.

India:

The oldest diamond producer

As many people know, for centuries India was virtually the sole source of the world's diamonds, apart from a small amount that came from Borneo. Humanity's passion for diamonds was born and nurtured in this vast subcontinent. Legends grew up around the stone, and travelled with the gem when it eventually spread abroad to conquer the West. Little is known about the ancient deposits. The Rajahs ordered their troops to protect them under armed guard, and they were rarely visited by foreigners. For many years, they were considered to be exhausted although, in fact, lovely stones are still occasionally found. The Indian diamond deposits tease historians by giving very little away in terms of documentary evidence and indisputable testimony. The oldest evidence comes from Marco Polo. He discusses diamonds at least twice in his book about the wonders of the world. The first tale is a version of the famous legend of the 'Valley of Diamonds', protected by serpents. The second is more true-to-life, in that it describes aspects of alluvial diamond mining: "In this kingdom, there are several very great mountains where diamonds are found[...] When it rains, the water flows in wild torrents through these mountains[...] When the rain has ceased and the water has gone, men go and search amongst the sands in the ravines from whence the water came, and thus they find enough diamonds". Although the book is totally inaccurate in terms of the geographical situation, it provides evidence of alluvial mining methods.

In the chapter about diamond deposits, we mentioned how the Ratnapariksha texts discuss six to eight places, of which only some correspond to identifiable diamond deposits. The others were probably centres of commerce or export posts for the gem. Three of the diamond deposits are in the Hyderabad region (in the state of Andhra Pradesh), near the Golconda Fort: Wajrakurur, south of Golconda, Wairagath to the northeast and Gana Coulour to the east. The output from the mines was initially concentrated in Golconda, which was reigned over by the Qutb Shâh dynasty from 1512 until 1687, when Mughal Emperor Aurangzeb conquered the fort. The town of Hyderabad itself was founded in 1590, and it very quickly supplanted Golconda and its fort, eleven kilometres away. Hyderabad became the centre of a very powerful kingdom which became independent after the Aurangzeb's death. The kings took the title of Nizam. Mir Osman Ali Khan Bahadur was the last Nizam, famous for being the richest man in the world in 1948, when his kingdom was forcibly integrated into the Indian Union. The last Nizam's fabulous jewel treasury reflects his country's bygone wealth, having been at the heart of Indian diamond production. Diamonds from this ancient kingdom's deposits are described as "Golconda" stones, even if they did not specifically come from that precise area. Even today, "Golconda" diamonds command a price premium, because this description implies a particularly rare quality.In addition to these three historic sites near Hyderabad, the Ratnapariksha texts often mention two others: Panna, in northern India (in the state of Madhya Pradesh), and Sambalpur to the east (in the state of Orissa). It is likely that there were other alluvial deposits, for which geographical names and traces have disappeared. Three of these five sites were visited by Jean-Baptiste Tavernier, the intrepid 17th-century adventurer and gem merchant who made six voyages to the Indies. His account of these voyages is exceptionally informative and, although Tavernier discusses the mines all to briefly, on the other hand he vividly describes the cultures of the countries he traversed. He evocatively describes diamond merchants, the methods of counting and payment, and the fiscal policies in force. Sadly, too many authors are content to mention Tavernier's voyages, without consulting the original, enthralling text - however florid the writing may be. This is a marvellous opportunity to make use of this exceptional text, written by an explorer who travelled to Japan, at a time when leaving one's home village was an adventure!

"Thus, I can say that I stole a march on the others, and that I was the first European to pave the way for the French to these mines: the only places on Earth where diamond is found. The first mine that I visited is in the lands of the King of Visapour in the province of Carnatica, and the place is called Raolconda, five days from Golconda, eight or nine from Visapour [...] This Raolconda mine was only discovered two hundred years ago or thereabouts [in the 15th century], as far as I can ascertain from the natives. The ground is sandy all around the place where the diamonds are found, and filled with rocks and coppices, a little like the outskirts of Fontainebleau. These rocks have crevices, sometimes the breadth of half a finger, sometimes of a whole finger. The miners have small, hooked metal implements, which they use to draw the sand and earth from these crevices, which they put in containers. The diamonds are found in this mixture. But these veins do not always go straight; sometimes they go up, sometimes they descend. The miners are thus constrained to break the rocks, whilst constantly following the trace of the crevices. After they have opened them all, and gathered all the earth or sand, then they start to wash it two or three times, and seek the diamonds therein. The purest stones with the whitest water are found in this mine but, unfortunately, to extract the sand from these rocks more easily, they give it great blows with a large iron crowbar. These blows produce flaws in the diamonds. [...] At seven days from Golconda, heading straight towards the sunrise, there is another diamond mine called Gani in the national language, and Koulour in Persian [...] This mine was only discovered approximately a hundred years ago and it was by the means of a peasant who found a simple point, weighing in the region of 25 carats, in the ground where he wanted to sow millet. As this kind of stone was unknown to him, and seeing some brilliance therein, he took it to Golconda. Happily for him, he addressed a person who traded in diamonds. The peasant told the trader where he had found the stone. The trader was most surprised to see a diamond of such size, given that the largest ones he had seen previously had been no more than ten to twelve carats. The noise of this new discovery soon spread all throughout the country, and some city-dwellers with deep purses started to excavate in the ground. There they found, and indeed still find, large stones in greater quantity than in any other mine. A number of stones from 10 to 40 carats are found in this mine, and even some many times larger, including the great diamond that weighed 900 carats before being cut, which Mirgimola gave to Aurang Zeb, as I mentioned previously [This sentence refers to the Great Mogul, which has since become known as the Orloff]. The first time that I went to this mine, one could see up to sixty thousand working there: men, women and children. They are employed for various tasks: the men to dig, and the women and children to carry the earth."

There is another valuable eyewitness account: Louis Rousselet undertook a great expedition to India in the 1860s. He produced a sumptuous work, The India of the Rajahs, decorated with hundreds of engravings taken from photographs. Rousselet himself pioneered this photographic technique during his trip, and his splendid photographic plates can still be seen today, at the Aquitaine Museum in Bordeaux. One of the engravings portrays diamond miners at work inside the Panna mine. The naked miners work at the bottom of a very wide mineshaft. They wade in knee-deep water, extracting gravel with picks and putting it into buckets. The mine was an alluvial deposit, so its fertile layer was covered with a thick layer of non-gem-bearing sediment. For this reason, vast shafts had to be dug to reach the diamond-bearing ore. These could be up to twenty metres deep. Rousselet described this process, along with its dangers, and goes on to talk about the mine's meagre yield: hundreds of cubic metres of earth need to be processed before the productive layer is reached. This productive layer is all too quickly exhausted. Then, there is no other solution other than to open a new shaft next to the first. Sometimes, the layer could be reached through sloping galleries and exploited using underground mining techniques. These galleries' entrances were protected by the local Rajah's soldiers. Another deposit was found nearby in 1827. This new source was believed to be alluvial for many years, but it is actually a primary deposit: the first primary deposit ever to be exploited, forty years before kimberlite pipes were discovered in South Africa. The rock was in such an advanced state of decomposition that it was not discovered to be a primary deposit until 1930. Today, it is the only diamond mine officially operating in India, and to date it has not proved possible to locate any other worthwhile primary kimberlite deposits in the sub-continent. However, alluvial diamonds are still found from time to time, whether through luck or persistence.

The Panna mine. Engraving, published by Rousselet in his book, The India of the Rajahs, 1875. Private Collection.

Borneo: a little-known deposit

The great island of Borneo is divided between Indonesia (Kalimantan state in the south), Malaysia (the states of Sarawak and Sabah in the north) and a few square kilometres which comprise the sultanate of Brunei. Diamonds have been mined there since at least the 10th century - possibly even the 7th century, according to archaeologists. The first authenticated documents to describe the Borneo diamond mines were written by a Portuguese, Feran Mindez Pinto, and date back to 1540. In his travel journals, Tavernier mentions that there was a thriving trade in diamonds in Batavia, a famous trading-post that eventually became the modern city of Jakarta, on the Indonesian island of Java.

"Finally, on the island of Borneo, the largest island in the world, there is a river known as the Succadan. Beautiful stones are found in its sands. They possess the same hardness as those of the Gouel river, or the other mines that I have mentioned [...] When I was in Batavia, one of the Company's principals showed me a simple point weighing 25 and one-eighth carats, a perfect gem that came from this river Succadan. I decided not to go to Borneo, mainly because the island's Queen does not permit strangers to take any gems, and there are great difficulties in exporting them. The few that are smuggled out are sold in Batavia."

Some time after Tavernier wrote these words, the Dutch East India Company acquired a monopoly over the trade in diamonds in Borneo. It is said that a 367-carat diamond - the Matan - was discovered in 1789. However, it is now thought to have been a piece of quartz. Borneo has never produced diamonds in large quantities.

Only small amounts of diamonds are mined nowadays, although this may change now that a mining company has been established in order to mechanise alluvial sediment processing. These fertile sediments are located in two main regions: west of Kalimantan, not far from the town of Pontianak, along the Landak river, and south of Kalimantan, close to the town of Banjarmasin, in the foothills of the Meratus mountains. The diamond-bearing rock is sedimentary sandstone, and it gradually releases its precious cargo as it is eroded by rivers. For this reason, mining has always been performed on a small scale. Families or groups of 'garimpeiros' (this Portuguese word, meaning 'gem-hunters' was initially used for Brazilian miners, and then spread throughout the world) dig up and wash the gravel. Conditions are difficult: the climate is equatorial, and the temperature is around 35°C for much of the year. Naturally, these operations only produce small quantities of diamonds, as have the initial attempts to mechanise the alluvial extraction process. One unfortunate company tried this in the 1980s, and the figures tell the tale: 5,300m^3 (more than 10,000 tons) of gravel was processed, yielding only 1,000 carats of diamonds (200 grams), accompanied by 470 grams of gold and 180 grams of platinum.

It is likely that the diamond deposits of Borneo will never be intensively exploited, although this is one less thing to worry about in an over-exploited island whose forests are being depleted at a dangerous rate. Nevertheless, as far as the history of diamonds is concerned, Indonesia is of undeniable importance. It maintained an active trade in spices with the Dutch, who colonised all of the Indonesian archipelago. This brought in enough money for most of the islands' kings to build up superb collections of jewellery. The National Museum of Jakarta has an extraordinary collection of diamonds in its vaults, from the majority of the ancient Indonesian kingdoms. Kriss knives were the most significant items of royal regalia, and all the collections had them. The kriss is a sacred knife, which is regarded as a kind of bridge between the earthly and spiritual worlds. The blades of these knives are reputed to have been forged from a mixture of two different sorts of metal: ordinary, terrestrial iron, and a nickel/iron alloy that was extracted from meteorites. These blades are of immense symbolic importance: the kriss' power is concentrated in its blade. As a result, the knives are protected by precious scabbards, usually carved from rare wood, with diamond-studded gold fittings, a little like a European reliquary casket. In addition to the kriss knives, the National Museum collection in Jakarta contains some superb brooches, necklaces and crowns; some of them contain diamonds weighing over 20 carats.

The principal jewellery-manufacturing centre in Indonesia was on the island of Lombok, off the island of Bali. The best jewellers worked there, and they made the majority of the splendid pieces that are on display today in the museum in Jakarta. Oddly, it was the Dutch that started the fashion for diamonds. They wore jewels set with Indian diamonds: hat ornaments, brooches and diamond-studded swords, for example. The Indonesian kings imitated them, using local jewels. However, it is impossible to tell whether the Dutch traded cut diamonds for spices and rough diamonds, or whether the kings gave the local diamonds to the Dutch, for them to be cut and later returned. In any event, the majority of the rose-cut diamonds in the Indonesian collection were cut in Antwerp.

The Dutch were tempted by the wealth of the jewellery workshops in Lombok, and they invaded the island in the late 19th century. Once it had been annexed, they began looting it, taking their plunder back to the Netherlands. It included innumerable diamonds from Borneo. When the Republic of Indonesia achieved independence in 1949, the "Treasure of Lombok" became the subject of intense diplomatic wrangling. Indonesia and the former colonial empire signed an agreement in 1970, whereby part of the treasure was returned. Today, this comprises the nucleus of the National Museum's jewel collection. However, some exceptional pieces remained in the Dutch Royal Cabinet of Curiosities, which was ultimately entrusted to the Royal Ethnography Museum in Leyden. The Lombok diamond, which weighs over 50 carats, is still there, languishing in a safe. The Rijksmuseum of Amsterdam has the 38-carat Banjarmasin, which remains the largest diamond known to have come from Borneo.

The Banjarmasin was taken by the Dutch from the Sultan of Banjarmasin's treasury. The diamond deposits on the island of Borneo were located in this Sultanate. The rough stone weighed 77 carats. It was cut into a cushion-shaped brilliant, weighing 38.22ct. It is now in the Rijksmuseum, Amsterdam.

Detail of a kriss (see photo number 3, following page).

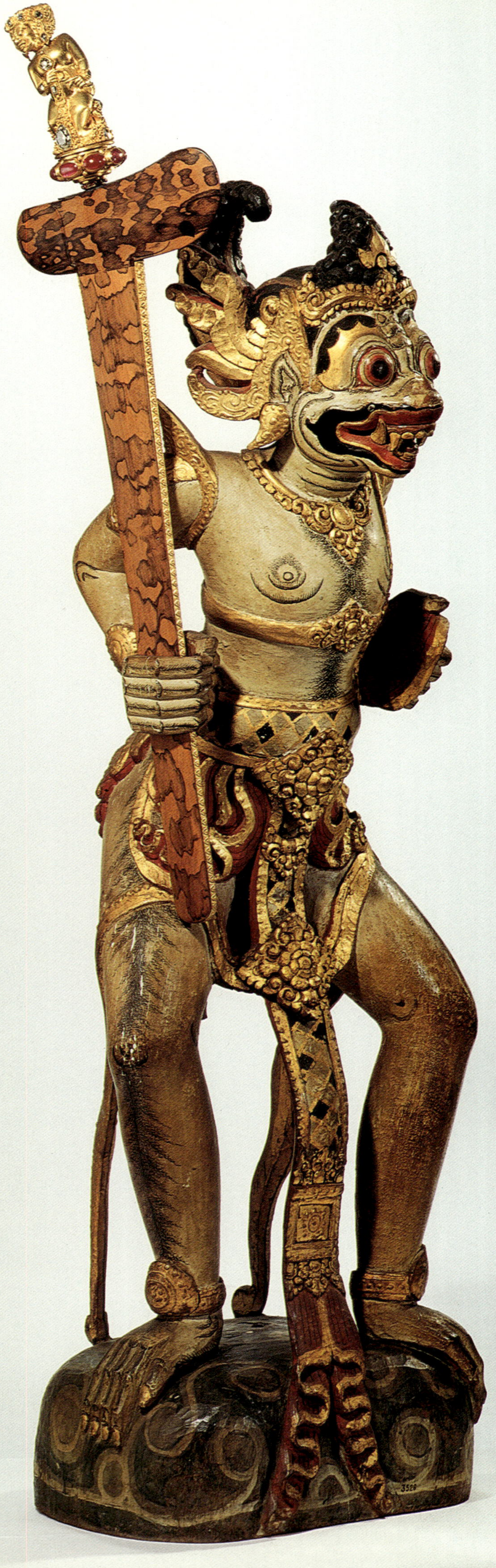

1

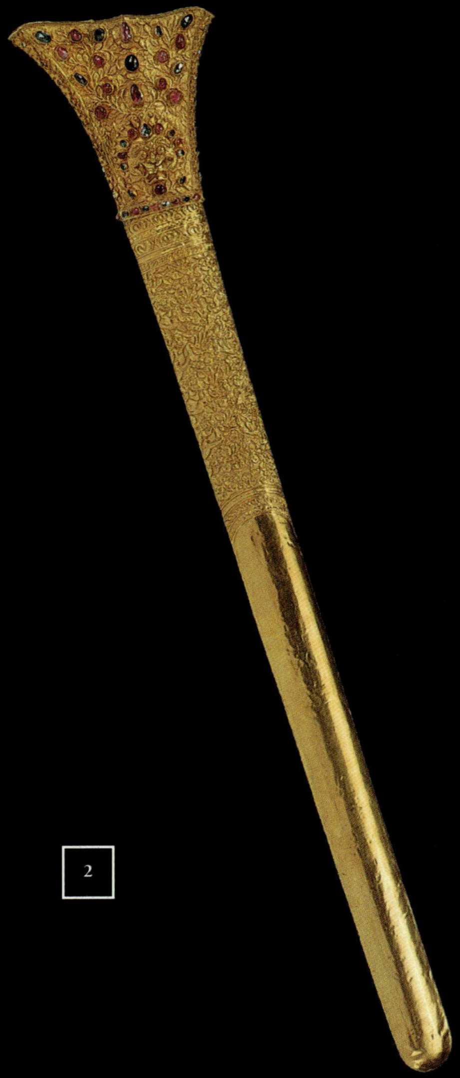

2

4

The National Museum in Jakarta hosts a marvellous collection of pieces studded with ancient-cut diamonds, mainly rose-cuts.

1. The monkey-god Hanuman. He was a hero of the Ramayana, an Indian epic dating back to around the 5th century, which spread to the Indonesian archipelago. He functions here as a kriss-holder. The statue was placed next to the throne of one of the kings of Bali. The kriss is embellished with a gold hilt, studded with rose-cut diamonds (a close-up is shown on the previous page). 19th century.

2. The scabbard for kriss number 3, in solid gold, rubies and diamonds.

3. Balinese king's kriss.
The remarkable blade displays a mixture of two metals, which are believed to be terrestrial iron and an extraterrestrial iron/nickel alloy from a meteorite. This sacred weapon united celestial and terrestrial forces. The hilt is in gold, set with rose-cut diamonds and rubies. 19th century.

4. Javanese kriss.
The hilt is adorned with a beautiful diamond plaque. The principal diamond is 16 mm long and appears to be blue. However, the bottom facets of the stone have been painted, to give it this colour. 18th century.

5. Balinese kriss (19th century), shown out of its scabbard. It normally held by the Hanuman statue.

6. Kriss from Borneo.
The hilt is in solid gold, and represents the mythical Indonesian eagle deity, Garuda. The scabbard is beautifully worked in gold, studded with diamonds. 19th century.

3

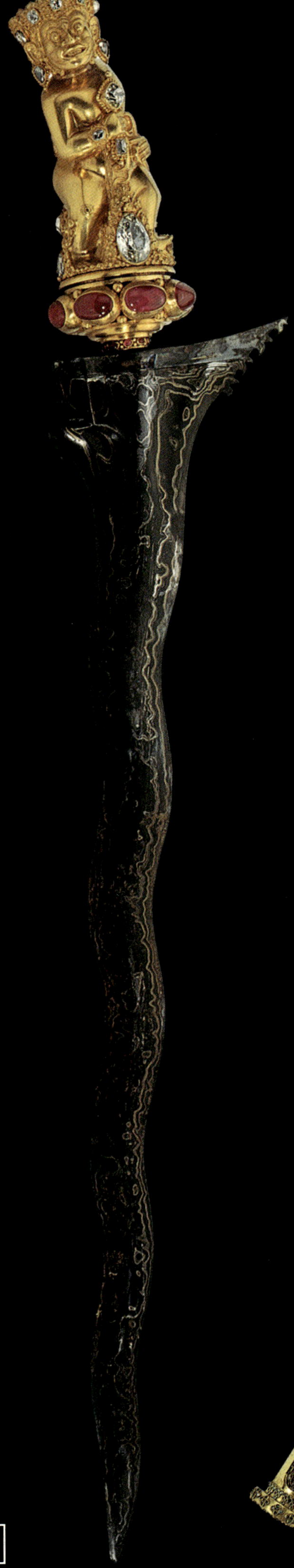

5

6

1. This brooch represents an eclipse. It is studded with some superb rose-cut diamonds. It was made in Lombok, from diamonds that were cut in the 17th century in Antwerp.

2. The crown of the Kingdom of Siak: gold, rubies and diamonds. It was used for the last time in 1894.

3. Two betel boxes. The delicate goldwork is studded with diamonds. They were made for royalty, and contained ingredients that were used in the preparation of betel leaves before chewing.

4 and 5. Two brooches from the island of Lombok. Each is set with a large cushion-cut diamond. 18th century.

6. Pectoral necklace, representing two intertwined dragons. The eyes are made of large, rose-cut diamonds, and the bodies are studded with small, Indian-cut diamonds.

1

2

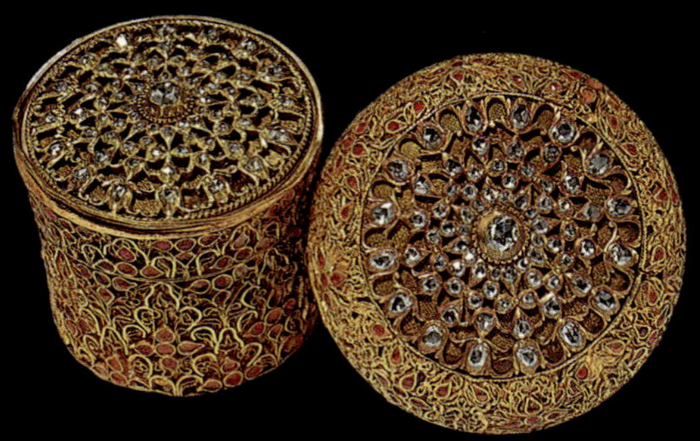

3

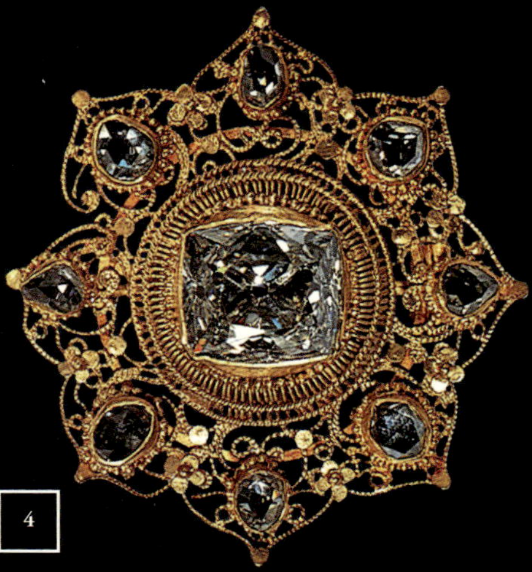

4

5

6

The timely discovery of diamonds in *Brazil*

Brazilian diamonds hit the market at a time when Indian production was rapidly declining and insufficient to meet Western demand. It is difficult to summarise the complex history of diamond mining in Brazil, even though it has been comparatively well-documented. We shall, however, make an attempt to do so here, because the story is a bitter tale that illustrates European greed with regard to its colonies. This is where the history of diamonds first takes a truly sinister turn.

The discovery of diamonds was never precisely dated, but it happened between 1726 and 1729, near Tijuco. This city subsequently became Diamantina. It is a splendid city, which today seems to doze along the Jequitinhonha river, flowing through the state of Minas Gerais, a hundred and fifty kilometres east of Belo Horizonte. This immense territory was particularly famous for its gold-bearing placer deposits, and thousands of poor miners (garimpeiros) tried their luck in Brazil, panning for the precious nuggets. Some of them noticed the presence of brilliant stones, which were obviously dense since they remained at the bottom of their pans, but they were unable to identify them. None of these garimpeiros had ever seen rough diamonds. According to tradition, a missionary was the first person to identify a diamond for what it was. He had supposedly started his missionary work converting Indians to Christianity in Golconda. A 1729 ordinance cancelled all the gold-panning concessions in this area "since small white stones, which are claimed to be diamonds, have appeared and continue to appear in various streams and rivers of the Serro Frio province". Therefore, in 1729 Brazil became the third nation in the world to produce diamonds, after India and Borneo. The news caused an immense stir in Lisbon, and a historian of the Portuguese Empire reported that "the discovery gave rise to splendid festivals, Te Deum masses and processions, celebrated both in Lisbon and throughout the kingdom: a great celebration, in accordance with the religious sensibility of the Portuguese people. The Government offered the first samples that it received to Rome. Ceremonies of thanksgiving to the Almighty were solemnly performed in the capital of the Catholic world. The Holy Father and all the Cardinals congratulated the King of Portugal. All the European monarchs congratulated him. It became a topic of conversation for the whole population. It was as if they had just discovered how to regenerate the universe and fill it with happiness."

The authorities were extremely harsh towards the garimpeiros who tried their luck prospecting. The mine concession process was a merry-go-round. Concessions were frequently annulled, and granted to the highest corrupt bidder. Taxes were extortionate. The tale of Brazilian diamonds does not portray the Portuguese Empire in a positive light. Initially, the profits were used to finance the extravagant lifestyles of King João V and his court, and for some time Brazil was a cash-cow that the cruel authorities milked excessively. The victims were not only the colonists, but also the slaves that worked in the diamond fields, who were savagely exploited. Very few of the local governors showed any sign of humanity. The detection of diamond-smugglers resembled witch-hunting: the law governing diamond-mining stated that an uncorroborated denunciation was enough evidence to prove illicit mining, which was punished by deportation to Angola on slave-galleys. There were considerable amounts of money at stake: miners were charged exorbitant fees, which increased in the 1750s. The tax authorities in Lisbon were corrupt, and in any case they knew nothing of the situation in the colony, seven thousand kilometres away. Brazilian complaints were ignored. Unsurprisingly, the earthquake that destroyed Lisbon on All Saints' Day 1755 was regarded as a punishment from God by the people of Tijuco.

Lisbon became increasingly greedy for tax revenues. In 1771, it implemented a new phase in diamond-field exploitation by launching the "Royal Extraction". A law was passed on August 2nd, 1771, under the name of the "Regulatory System for Diamonds". A single copy of the relevant legislation was sent to Brazil, bound in green leather: it became known as the 'Green Book'. It was reproduced and disseminated in Tijuco on January 6th, 1772. The Superintendent of diamond concessions and mine administration had discretionary power. He was assisted by a triumvirate of administrative treasurers. Every year, they would determine the places in which mining was authorised. They had a register of slaves, and used spies for the surveillance of the entire population, whose movements were monitored. Every soldier had the unlimited right to search the homes of people suspected of trafficking diamonds. All the hard-won concessions that had been granted earlier were invalidated and reassigned. In order to control the diamond trade more effectively, panning for gold was prohibited, since alluvial gold and diamonds are found together. Gold was the principal source of income for the prospectors, so the population's living conditions worsened even more. The procedure for diamond-trafficking and diamond-hoarding denunciations was broadened: from that point on, denunciations could be made anonymously, and did not even need to be signed for reprisals to begin. A denunciation could be personally presented to the Superintendent, who would supply an official receipt. This receipt gave the informant the right to gain the victim's concession, and for a slave to gain freedom. These signed receipts were thus invaluable, and therefore became the object of appalling black-market trading. Concessions were unjustly seized and transferred, sometimes even by sons who denounced their own fathers. The Green Book continued in a similar vein: it was a bitter pill for the miners to swallow, but for the Superintendents and administrators, whose privileges were clearly outlined in the legislation, it was an elixir ensuring vast wealth. This abhorrent text would regulate Brazilian diamond production for half a century.

The Royal Extraction was put to work, with 3,610 slaves distributed amongst twelve extraction centres. In the eighty years to 1843, 1,354,700 carats were officially collected, including at least eighty large and beautiful stones, that were reserved for the Crown. In the first few decades, the abundant diamond production had a perverse effect: because Indian production had dried up, Europe had become accustomed to exorbitant diamond prices and reduced supplies. The surge in production from Brazil

caused prices to fall. As a result, Lisbon set quotas for Brazilian diamond production. Naturally, this resulted in unemployment, and the impoverishment of the population in diamond-bearing regions. France and Spain declared war on Portugal in 1801, and this also had an important role to play in diamond history. In order to raise an army, the King of Portugal pawned Brazilian diamond receipts to banks in Holland and London. Napoleon rode roughshod over these pledges: after the Treaty of Madrid, he confiscated a large quantity of diamonds, and gave them to his brother Lucien. Marshal Junot also had a diamond windfall from royal stocks. This great influx of diamonds probably caused the future Emperor to develop his taste for wild extravagance, fuelling the production of dazzling Parisian jewels in the years to come.

When Portugal fell to Napoleon and the Royal court departed for Brazil, the situation changed. Judge Manoel Ferreira da Camara was appointed Superintendent in 1807, which improved the situation. Not only was Camara blessed with a degree of humanity, he had also travelled throughout Europe and learnt about mining during his education. For the first time, injustice and corruption were replaced with tolerance and competence. Meanwhile, the Independence movement grew in strength. The spirit of the French Revolution had spread to the Bahia coast, but it would not blossom until 1840.

John Mawe was an English explorer, who visited the Tijuco mines in 1810: his travel journal is a precious record of the situation in the diamond fields in the early 19th century. The book is beautifully illustrated with two famous engravings of gravel-washing. The 1816 edition provides some fascinating insights:

"The cascalho [diamond-bearing gravel] layer is composed of the same substances as that in the gold district. In many places, there are great masses of tumbled pebbles on river-banks. The pebbles are bound together by iron oxide, which sometimes conceals gold and diamonds. During the dry season, they work to gather as much cascalho as possible in order to occupy all the workers for the duration of the rainy season. When the cascalho has been taken to the side of the river from whence it

Diamantina, with its marvellous Baroque architecture. It is the former city of Tijuco, where the great Brazilian diamond adventure began. As the sun sets, modernity seems to seep away, and the city's true historic character is revealed.

Two rough diamonds, which were never taken from the King of Portugal's uncut diamond casket to be cut. They weigh 35 and 135 carats. Ajuda Palace National Museum, Lisbon.

Diamond mines in Brazil, at the end of the 18th century: the extraction of diamond-bearing sediment. The river, at left, has been diverted. The extraction site is supplied with rinsing water by a water-wheel. The slaves are depicted in blue. They are under the surveillance of superintendents, in red. They carry the gravel to a heap, in order for it to be washed. Ultramarino Archive, Lisbon.

came, it is piled into heaps of fifteen to sixteen tons each. Water is brought from nearby, and distributed throughout the area by means of ingenious, skilfully-built aqueducts. This is how the diamonds are washed: an oblong hangar is built, [...] covered by a thatched roof. A stream of water is run through the middle of the hangar, in a strong wooden channel, into which the cascalho is placed, two or three feet thick. Below and to the side of the channel, there is a wooden floor. It is twelve to fifteen feet long, extending the entire length of the hangar, and affixed by clay [...] This floor is divided into twenty compartments [...] There are some raised seats above the cascalho heap, for the supervisors. Once these have been seated, equal distances apart, the negroes enter the compartments. Each one is provided with a peculiarly shaped, short-handled rake. They use these rakes to drag fifty to eighty pounds of cascalho into their compartments, then they direct a flow of water over it. The cascalho is agitated and stirred unceasingly, and constantly moved to the upper part of the compartment. Once all the particles of soil have been washed away, the largest rocks are discarded, then the pebbles, and the rest is examined very carefully, in order to find the diamonds. When a negro finds a diamond, he straightens up, claps his hands and holds the stone between his thumb and index finger. The inspector collects it, and deposits it in a bucket, which hangs in the middle of the hangar, half-full of water. When a negro is fortunate enough to find a diamond weighing an octavo or 17.2 carats, he is garlanded with flowers and taken ceremonially to the administration, which gives him his freedom and compensates his master. The negro is given a new set of clothes, and is permitted to work for himself [...] The negroes are divided into troupes or work squadrons, each comprising two hundred individuals, and placed under the command of an administrator and other, lower-ranking officers. Each squadron has its own chaplain and surgeon. Although the current Governor has improved the negroes' food somewhat, providing them with fresh meat daily, which was not the case under his predecessors, I am nevertheless sorry to say that they are very poorly and stingily fed, and in general far more severely treated than those of other establishments that I have had the occasion to visit." In the mid-19th century, diamond production was in the order of 200,000 carats per year.

This first phase in the history of Brazilian diamonds is summed up by the relics of two different museums. The Diamantina museum in Brazil has slave "necklaces", made of iron chains. In contrast, the Ajuda Palace National Museum in Lisbon has the royal family's necklaces, made of gold and encrusted with Brazilian gems - alongside João VI's Order of the Golden Fleece, and Queen María Pia's suite of diamond star jewellery, of course. The Princesse de Joinville also had some magnificent Brazilian diamonds, which are currently in a private collection in Paris. She was the daughter of the last Emperor of Brazil. The royal family's descendants still cherish the memory of the venerated last Empress, who granted the slaves their freedom in 1870. This fundamental change in policy propelled the Brazilian mines into a new era, that of the independent garimpeiros, adventurous entrepreneurs whose energy is entirely based on their dreams of discovering a stone that will make them rich. This reckless energy is the fuel for diamond exploration in this vast country. The business is dominated by independent diamond-hunters, like the 19th-century American Wild West. Small family concerns dredge rivers and streams with little floating treatment plants. Sometimes, they work alongside bigger mining corporations, with their heavy machinery.

Nowadays, thanks to new deposits in the north, Brazilian diamond production has increased to one million carats per year. Companies explore continuously, in an attempt to find sufficiently rich primary kimberlite deposits. There are some potentially good future prospects amongst the ones that have been located so far, not far from the alluvial deposits. The 50 Million carats of diamonds mined in Brazil to date have virtually all come from secondary deposits. Riverbed gravels and silicaceous sedimentary rocks still regularly yield fine alluvial diamonds, and these discoveries fuel the dreams of rapid wealth that spur the garimpeiros on. Some of these are rare pink and red diamonds, which are often even more beautiful than pink Australian gems.

The monstrance from the Royal Bemposta Palace, in Portugal. It is an extraordinary masterpiece of Baroque goldwork, 1 m tall, studded with many Brazilian gemstones. The rays of the monstrance are set solely with diamonds (in their thousands), in accordance with Christian symbolism. National Museum of Ancient Art, Lisbon.

The President Vargas, a superb 48.26 carat emerald-cut that was cut from the largest diamond ever found in Brazil (in 1938). Robert Mouawad collection.

Brazilian diamond mines, late 18th century: the diamond-bearing gravel is washed by the slaves, under the surveillance of their supervisor. Ultramarino Archive, Lisbon.

Map of diamond concessions in the Diamantina region. The concessions are distributed along the Jequitinhonha river and its tributaries, which look like the veins on a leaf. Ultramarino Archive, Lisbon.

1 Cabeceiras do Rio Cabaçaco
2 Corgo da Lage
3 Corgo das 3 Barras
4 Riaxo Fundo
5 Corgo dos Macacos
6 Corgo do G.
7 S. Bartholomeu pequeno
8 Gopiaras do Frade
9 Corgo de S. Bartho.meu gr.de
10 Corgo dos Borbas
11 Corgo da Bocaina
12 Corgo do Capivari
13 Corgo do Mel
14 Corgo de S. Antonio
15 Corgo das Mortes
16 Giquitinhonha do Matto
17 Corgo do Diamante

Vertentes que formaõ o Ribeiraõ do Inferno

18 Corgo da Lage
19 Corgo de Gaspar Carvalho
20 Corgo da Roça grande
21 Corgo da Ponte da natureza
22 Corgo dos Canudos
23 Pombeiro
24 Corgo Motuca
25 Corgo Mãy d'agoa
26 Corgo de S.to Antonio
27 Corgo do Pelourinho e Bica
28 Rio de S. Francisco
29 Corgo Paciencia
30 Corgo Palmital
31 Corgo do Corralinho
32 Corgo do Pernambucano

Vertentes q̃ formaõ a Giquitinhonha do Campo

33 Corgo Pitrelsberbo
34 Corgo maravilha
35 Corgo Gavião
36 Corgo Comgonhas
37 Corgo [illegible]
38 Corgo do Crioulo
39 Corgo dos Porcos

Seguese o Rio Giquitinhonha athe a Barra q̃ o R. Pinhl. faz nela e detem ondem de S. Pedro

40 Corgo Caçapaõs
41 Biribahibas
42 Corgo de S.ta Maria
43 Corgo do Ferreiro
44 Corgo do Bomsuccesso
45 Corgo do Almeida
46 Corgo das Areias
47 Corgo da Chamambaia
48 Quebrado
49 Porcens
50 Monsoute
51 Lavra do Matto
52 A ponte do Giquitinhonha
53 Corgo do Ithumado
54 Carranato
55 Mendanha
56 Palmital
57 S.ta Catharina
58 Mangabaz

Vertentes que formaõ o R. Pinhal

59 Cabeceiras da Contenda
60 Corgo da Toca
61 Corgo do Loto
62 Corgo Agoa Limpa
63 Corgo dos Christães
64 Rio das pedras
65 Corgo do Pilam
66 Corgo Caldeirinha
67 Corgo dos Morrinhos
68 Corgo das Pombas
69 Corgo Pinho pequeno
70 Corgo da Formiga
71 Corgo de Joaõ de Macedo
72 Sammambaya Nova
73 Berberi
74 Corgo do Mulato
75 Corgo do Campo da Dona

Vertentes que formaõ o R. Manso

76 R. Manso
77 Corgo
78 Corgo Batatal

Seguese a Giquitinhonha the a Barra q̃ nelle faz o R. Caythé merim e fixa a demarcaçaõ

79 Corgo da Cangica
80 Cabeceiras do Caithemiri.
81 Corgo do Tixeira
82 Corgo do Caxambola
83 Corgo do Andayal
84 Corgo dos Macacos Gr.de
85 Corgo dos Macacos Peq.
86 Corgo das Almas o Grande
87 Corgo das Almas o Pequeno
88 Corgo do Buraco
89 Corgo dos Coquaes
90 Corgo do Inhahy
91 Corgo do Chaporra
92 Corgo do Gaviaõ S. Dom.os

Seguem-se os Rios Pardo e Parauna.

93 Cabeceiras do R. pardo gr.de
94 Corgo de S. Joaõ
95 Ribeiro da Areia, e da chapada
96 Ouro fino pequeno
97 Corgo ouro fino o grande
98 Corgo do Batatal e Gopiarý
99 Corgo de S. Ana
100 Corgo da Raiz
101 Corgo da Barras
102 Corgo da Contagem do Rib.

Seguem o R. pardo pequeno the fazer Barra no Grande

103 Cabeceiras do R. pardo peq.no
104 Corgo da Bandeirinha
105 Corgo de Joaõ Vaz
106 Corgo Braunas
107 Corgo do Bacalhao
108 Corgo do Capam
109 Corgo Danta
110 Corgo do Nuno
111 Corgo da Barra do Nuno
112 Corgo da Roça de Thome M.to
113 Corgo da chapada de Joaõ [illegible]
114 Corgo da Serra da Picada
115 Corgo da Melancia no Bueno
116 Forquilha honde fixa a Demarcaçam

R. Parauna

117 Corgo dos Gerais
118 Corgo do Pouzo Alto.
119 R. Genituba
120 R. Andrequicé
121 Corgo do Palmital de Lege
122 Corgo do Bom Succeso
123 Corgo do Morro de Luiz [illegible]
124 Cachoeira e Datas de ElRey
125 Corgo de Joaõ Pinto
126 Corgo do Peixe crú
127 Corgo da Roça do dito
128 Corgo do Bixo
129 Cabeceiras do chiq.
130 Corgo da Pitelha
131 Corgo do Cuyabá
132 Corgo dos Granetes
133 Corgo de Joaõ da Silva

Ribeiraõ da Area

134 Cabeceira do dito
135 Corgo da Bocaina
136 Corgo do Tamanduá
137 Corgo do Palmital
138 Corgo da Macaara
139 Corgo do Veado
140 Corgo de S. Patricio
141 Corgo do Tigre
142 Barra do Ribeiraõ da Area

South Africa

The words 'South Africa' and 'diamonds' have become virtually synonymous. The history of diamonds in South Africa is fascinating for many reasons. The volcanic rock which originally brought diamonds up to the surface was first identified here. These rocks are the remnants of the inner cores of ancient, extinct volcanoes; they occur in cylindrical masses, or 'pipes', that plunge deep into the Earth. This entirely new class of deposit enabled the geological nature of diamonds to be determined, which in turn led to the discovery of similar deposits in other African countries, Siberia and Canada. The exploitation of these pipes gave rise to utterly spectacular mines, thanks to the implementation of unique mining techniques. The immense holes thus created in the South African earth defy the imagination. In addition, these mines gave rise to a globally successful company: De Beers . Finally, of course, these mines have yielded some fabulous diamonds. A list of their names reads like the chapters of a fairy-tale: the Star of South Africa, the Excelsior, the Jonker, the Cullinan, the Centenary, the Tiffany... Reason enough to pause and reflect over this country's history. We shall start in the heart of diamond country: the town of Kimberley.

Erasmus Jacobs, shown alongside his wife.
He discovered the first diamond in Africa, in 1866.

Child's-play

The children of the first South African colonists did not have access to the shiny glass marbles that many of us remember. Their hard-working parents, mostly poor farmers, tried as best they could to work the land. The land was flat, harsh and unforgiving. Colonists tried to establish their farms as close as possible to sources of water, which were called Pan (lake) or Fontein (spring). The colonists were Europeans who had fled religious strife. They were primarily Dutch, with some Germans and a few French Huguenots. They tried to live a quiet life along the Vaal and Orange rivers in deepest Africa - virtually the end of the world. One summer day, in 1866, a little girl decided to play marbles in the courtyard of her father's farm, on the south bank of the Orange river. Her father was Daniel Jacobs, a Boer farmer. In the absence of marbles, she played with stones. Her elder brother, Erasmus, brought her some pretty stones from the river. One of them was white, and sparkled brilliantly in the sun... The family's neighbour, Mr. Van Niekerk, happened to be visiting. He noticed the stone, and offered to buy it: an insane, utterly absurd idea had just occurred to him. The little girl's mother, Mrs. Jacobs, refused to accept her neighbour's payment for the pebble, and gave it to him. Van Niekerk entrusted the pebble to an acquaintance, John O'Reilly, who took it to the nearest city. Everyone there scoffed at the idea that it could possibly be a diamond, and yet O'Reilly, unbowed, sent the stone to a keen geologist, Dr. Atherstone. In April 1867, he replied by letter, stating that the stone was indeed a diamond, weighing 21.25 carats. The stone was sent to London, and the Crown Jeweller confirmed the finding on July 1867. The pebble was cut into a modest, 10.73-carat gem. It was heavily flawed, but of enormous symbolic importance. Later, it became known as the Eureka. Years later, it was repurchased by De Beers, and presented to the government of South Africa. As for the little Jacobs girl, she was forgotten. Journalists did not bother to find out her real name, Frederika, and invented one for her: Nelly. Her brother is still commemorated as the first person to find a diamond in Africa. His photo was taken decades later, and it appears in all the diamond textbooks: it shows a stocky, bearded man in his fifties. The other half of the photograph, depicting his wife, is usually cropped off. They have the air of God-fearing folk, apprehensive about the wooden box camera that scrutinises them, astonished at the fact that a little pebble, collected years earlier, should be so significant that it was worth their photograph.

Confirmation

In the two years that followed, at least a score of other diamonds were found along the Vaal and Orange rivers. The great shock came when an 83.5-carat stone was discovered by a Griqua shepherd (the Boer colonists referred to Hottentot, Bochiman and Bantu tribespeople as Griquas). The young shepherd, called Swartboy, hid it for fear that his Master would confiscate it. He entrusted it to a friend, who took it up the Orange river to the De Kalk farm. He negotiated there with the same Mr. Van Niekerk whom we mentioned above, who gave him all that he possessed, namely 500 sheep, 10 bulls and a horse, valued at £500. It was March 17th, 1869: Van Niekerk found himself in possession of the first, genuine, large, perfectly gem-quality African diamond. He sold it for £11,200 pounds, making a considerable profit. The stone was cut in London into a superb 47.69-carat pear-shape, and was named the Star of South Africa. This discovery swept away any remaining doubts, and the inhabitants of the Vaal valley feverishly began to hunt for precious stones in alluvial gravels. They made sieves by piercing metal sheets with large nails, which resulted in large holes, thereby failing to trap diamonds weighing less than one carat! By then, it was 1870, and the diamond deposits were virtually identical to those of Brazil: prospectors searched the riverbed gravels for diamonds in the same way as gold-panners pan for gold, by washing the gravel on plates. It was a classic example of alluvial mining, and thousands of amateur prospectors quickly flocked to the area from other parts of Africa, Europe, Canada and even India. Commercial trading in tools and provisions was concentrated in a local city. Poignantly, it was named Hopetown.

'Dry' deposits in 'fountain' country

A great revolution in diamond mining was about to begin. It all started some time before 1870, possibly in 1869, on the Bultfontein farm. The farmer's children found some diamonds in the mud of a nearby pond, named Du Toit's Pan (after a French family that had previously established a farm there). They showed them to a prospector, who was probably called Anderson (sources disagree as to his name). Diamond-laced mud had been used to make the walls of a hut, and the prospector was stunned to see little sparkles of light, scattered around the hut's interior! The future Bultfontein mine had thus been discovered. The same Mr. Anderson went to visit the neighbouring Dorstfontein farm, on the other side of Du Toit's Pan. When he took geological samples, he found some diamonds and some garnets. The future Dutoitspan mine had been discovered. Unfortunately, one of Anderson's associates was too talkative and gave the game away, thereby starting a rush on the farms in 1870. A farmer in Jagersfontein discovered a 50-carat diamond in August that year, shortly after a gem had been discovered on a farm in Koffiefontein. Two more new mines had been found; they, too, would become famous.

In May 1871, a rumour started that diamonds had been found in a hollow in the ground, on land belonging to two farmers: the brothers Johannes and Diederik de Beer. The rumour proved to be correct: the stones were large and beautiful. Fortune-hunters rushed to the area, in the "De Beers' Rush". Two months later, in July 1871, a diamond was discovered at the foot of a small hill (Kopje), by the name of Colesberg Kopje, located at 3.5 km away from the De Beers' Rush. The finder was a cook called Damon; he had been drunk at the time. Mrs. Sarah Ortlepp, however, has a prior claim: she stated that she had discovered a diamond fifteen days earlier, during a picnic on the hill. Her family went on to cherish the diamond for many years, and it was recently presented to a Johannesburg museum. The Kimberley mine, which would ultimately become the famous Big Hole, had thus been located and named the "De Beers New Rush", or "New Rush" for short. Tents began to spring up everywhere, and nobody could have imagined that this fabric-and-wood town would have a proud future. The farmers were literally bowled over by the waves of prospectors in successive diamond rushes, and they sold all their properties for a few thousand pounds. The ones that tried their luck by taking mine concessions on their own ground ultimately failed. Only the De Beers name would live on and become famous, although the brothers themselves actually died before this happened.

The pioneers quickly noticed that these deposits had strange characteristics: they were dry, far away from rivers, concentrated in round or oval areas a few hundred metres in diameter, and the diamonds were located in a type of earth that did not resemble alluvial sediments in the slightest. Naturally, no-one realised that they were digging in a virtually bottomless deposit. They assumed that the diamonds had been concentrated there as the result of some unknown phenomenon. They felt that they had at best a year before reaching the bottom. The dry diggings had started.

Bottomless pits

Very quickly indeed, Colesberg Kopje had been flattened. The miners reached ground level, and found a layer of red earth: they assumed that this was the end of the party. They were in for a surprise. The red layer was barely thirty centimetres thick, and below that, they found a strange kind of crumbly yellow earth, which was even richer in diamonds. They had entered what they called the yellow ground. Things started to get organised. Concessions were distributed according to standard practices in alluvial deposits: each prospector had a terrain 31 feet (9.45 m) square, called a claim. The surface of the Kimberley deposit was therefore divided into a checkerboard pattern by a grid of wires. Four hundred and twenty claims were initially delineated, later growing to 620. Each was less than 100 square meters in size. Until 1876, a prospector was only allowed a maximum of two concessions. It was also forbidden to abandon the concession, even through illness. According to the jump rule, the first person to testify that a claim had not been worked for seven days could jump in and take it over.

From that point on, they began to sink their diggings into the ground. Imagine the situation: the surface area of the diamond-bearing zone was about the size of a football stadium, divided into 620 square plots, worked by 620 claim-holders and their assistants, all operating completely independently. Although it superficially resembled a neatly-delineated archaeological excavation, it was difficult to avoid anarchy. Some miners dug down more quickly, and neighbouring claims towered over them like walls, exposing them to the risk of cave-ins. The removal of mine tailings was an intractable problem. The miners on the edge of the pit had no problems, the others were surrounded by other claims, and inevitably had to pass over their neighbours' territory. Arguments and espionage took place; the situation was explosive.

From 1872, constraints had to be imposed, in the form of elevated roadways that passed by all the claims, two by two, from north to south. These raised roadways were used to transport mine tailings in wheelbarrows. In order to create the roadways, the organisers took half the length of every concession on either side of the route. The claim-holders would eventually get the land back, because once the mine reached down to the bedrock the roadway would eventually be demolished. Their haste was due to the fact that they believed the deposit to be alluvial, and that it would hence be quickly exhausted. As soon as they reached bedrock, it would be finished. And given that they had dug forty metres deep already, this could not be far away. Nobody yet understood that they were standing in the core of an extinct volcano, which reached right down into the heart of the Earth. This was hardly surprising: such a conclusion was new and unthinkable at the time.

By 1873, the miners had dug themselves in thoroughly. The diamonds had still not been exhausted. Neighbouring claims continued to collapse. The Kimberley mine began to look like an apocalyptic vision, with the men resembling termites and ants, scrabbling in the depths of a nightmarish pit. It was no longer possible to extract tailings using wheelbarrows. Winches were installed, powered by black natives or horses, to hoist the buckets of decomposed yellow rock up to the surface. At ground level, it was broken up with hammers and sorted by hand. There was no water for ore-washing. Soon, it became essential to widen the pit, to make the sloping sides more stable. Considerable quantities of earth had to be moved with shovels and pickaxes - as well as the heaps of mine tailings, which had not been dumped far enough away. It was always the same problem: nobody could have believed that it would go on for so long. They understood nothing, and were content to dig, guard their claims, spy on their neighbours, and complain about the price of tools, food and lodging in the town. The town itself had metamorphosed completely. Initially, as the hill was being flattened, it was assumed that it would need to last a year. Tents were adequate, and the mine was surrounded by a village made out of canvas. When they reached the yellow ground, the doubts began. How long would that last? The tent city was replaced with a sheet-metal city. The first small, pre-fabricated wooden house was shipped over from England. It is still there, in the grounds of the museum. Other buildings soon followed. The deeper they dug into compacted rock, the more the town became solid and permanent. The architecture was bizarrely linked to the rock strata in the mine: once they reached solid stone, buildings started to be made out of brick. The city was no longer called the De Beers New Rush: its new name of Kimberley had been imposed by an English proclamation on July 5th, 1873, in homage to the Secretary of State for the Colonies, Viscount Kimberley.

At the bottom of the hole, the miners continued to fight for themselves, like mindless burrowing termites. The Kimberley mine began to resemble Indian Pueblos in the Southern United States, with its rigid, checkerboard framework. However, there was one significant difference: the Indian Pueblos, with their superimposed square architecture, were built by a community. In contrast, the peculiar cubes at the bottom of the Kimberley mine were the result of selfishness and an absence of communal planning. Certain more enlightened individuals contemplated imposing their will on the situation, to sweep away the other termites and make their fortunes. They were Cecil Rhodes and Barney Barnato: two unusual Englishmen, who had begun to realise that these were no ordinary mines. They were worth taking risks for...

At the end of 1873, the Kimberley hole had begun to resemble a volcanic crater. The wheelbarrow roadways were collapsing on all sides. The rim of the crater was too high for buckets of ore to be winched to the surface by hand using ropes. The ropes were replaced by cables, and the remaining, unstable, raised roadways had to be demolished. The hole took on a new look once more, beginning to resemble the lair of some monstrous spider. It was spanned by hundreds of steel cables, which threaded down into every claim from the crater's rim. Every single one was operated independently. On the rim of the crater, the cables were strung over pulleys on posts, and wound around drums driven by horses. These were local versions of the horse-drawn winches that had been invented in the 16th century, in Saxon and Bohemian silver mines.

The De Beers archives preserve these early images, in stacks of wooden boxes that contain hundreds of photographic glass plates. They are invaluable records of this human adventure, the like of which we will never see again. The fragile glass plates reveal the Kimberley hole year by year as it grows, the claims and their strange cubist architecture, the roadways that rise and fall. Finally, the spider weaves her web, in an increasingly complex network that hoists up buckets and people. The web eventually comprised 1,600 cables: the situation could not continue any longer.

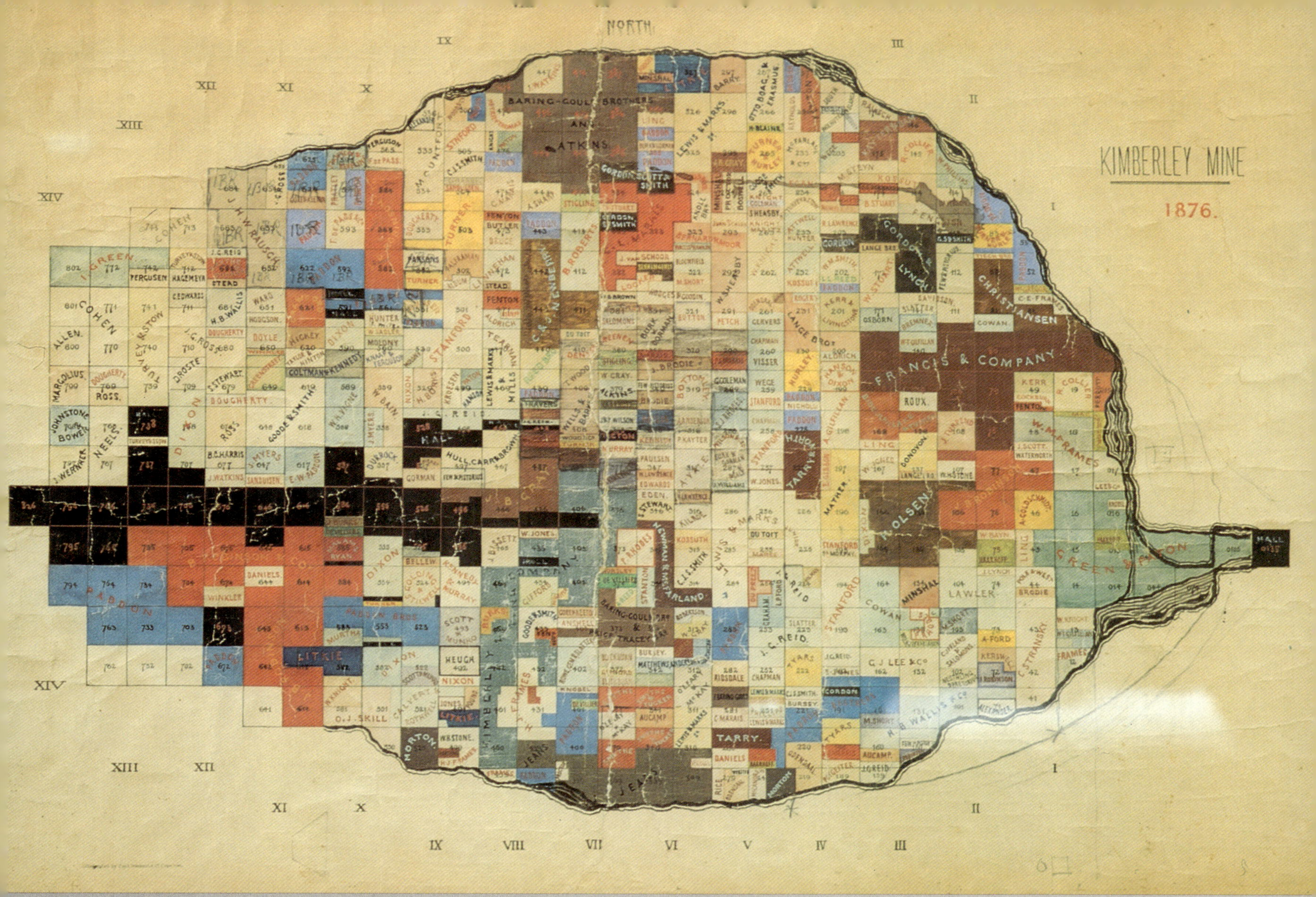

Map of the concessions in the Kimberley mine, in 1876. The patchwork effect is reinforced by the watercolours used to illustrate each claim. Africana Library, Kimberley.

The Eureka, the first diamond found in Africa, in 1866. This modest stone came from the banks of the Orange river. It is badly cut (10.73 carats) and of poor colour. It is also full of flaws - but its symbolic value is inestimable! Property of the South African Government.

The 47.9-carat Star of South Africa. The first large, gem-quality diamond found on the African continent, in 1869. Private collection.

The saga of diamond-mining in South Africa. The Dutoitspan mine, in 1873: a few tents, a few holes...

The life and death of the Kimberley mine. April 1872: the holes penetrate deep into the ground. It was still thought to be an alluvial deposit. Roadways have been built in order to allow men and wheelbarrows to pass.

1873. The concessions are being worked at different speeds. The result is an astonishing checkerboard architecture, with squares 9 m across.

1874. The holes are now too deep: each of them is equipped with its own, individual cable extraction system. A gigantic spider's-web begins to weave around the mine.

The cables are linked to horse-drawn wheels. Six hundred claims, the same number of wheels, double that number of cables: the edge of the pit is bordered by a wall of pulleys.

The hole begins to look like something out of Dante. Self-interest reigns. Several ambitious entrepreneurs begin to gather around the pit to contemplate their prey: the individual claim-holders' days are numbered.

1875. After millions of years, the hole looks like a volcano once more. The edges of the concessions are collapsing, and the claim-holders are dying out. It is impossible to manage six hundred claims. This sets the scene for the claims to be amalgamated: first, into several larger companies, and ultimately, into a single firm.

1875

1884. The amalgamation of the claims into one company has permitted more efficient, mechanised extraction methods to be implemented. This is a plot belonging to the *Compagnie française des mines de diamant du cap de Bonne-Espérance*, which occupies a crucial position in the bottom of the pit.

1903. The descent into Hell. The pit is now over 300 m deep. Underground mining installations are already in place.

The town around the pit began to get organised in the 1870s. The Bank of Africa, with its corrugated iron roof, has already set up shop.

The De Beers mine in 1884.

The Kimberley mine, the largest man-made hole in the world, was abandoned in 1914. It is now known as the Big Hole. It is 1,073 m deep. The water table is 270 m deep.

The Dutoitspan mine, in 1875. The land is sculpted by the division of the area into individual mine claims.

1879. The world supply of diamonds is too high. In an attempt to sustain prices, the Dutoitspan mine is barely being worked. It would re-open later, and is still in operation today.

Kimberley mine, 1892.
Ore treatment is now performed by the new Goodes machines. Diamonds are separated by slow centrifugation. This type of machine is still in use today.

The outskirts of Kimberley, 1885.
The ore is spread over a wide area, and left to oxidise slowly. It begins to crumble, and can be broken up by agricultural machinery, like clumps of soil. The diamonds are therefore released - and thieves start to congregate!

Bultfontein mine, Kimberley. The kimberlite is spread over the ground, and crushed by a steamroller.

It was quickly realised that the Orange river had carried diamonds from its source to the sands of the coastal desert, to the west. The rush started in 1908. The sand is carefully scanned for diamonds, which are often of fine quality.

The Big Hole, Kimberley, as it appears to tourists today. It can be viewed from a sort of springboard that juts out over the extraordinary crater.

The oldest corrugated-iron house in Kimberley. It was shipped over from England, and took over from the canvas and wood constructions that had previously been used. Eco-Museum, Kimberley

During their breaks, the black miners had to wear rigid, padlocked mitts, to prevent them from stealing diamonds. Engraving, taken from a photograph, published in Les Entrailles de la Terre, by E. Caustier, Paris, 1902.

The end of the termites

Once the pit reached a depth of sixty metres, half-measures were no longer enough. A complete solution had to be found. In 1876, the amalgamation of multiple claims was authorised for the first time. This resulted in the foundation of companies that gradually amalgamated with their neighbours. The miners were willing to sell: the ore had changed in appearance and become hard. They were having to resort to dynamite. They had reached bedrock, a strange kind of bluish-black stone. It had not yet been given the name of kimberlite, but was referred to as blue ground. The miners believed that the bottom of the pit had been reached. If people were crazy enough to want to buy their claims, then they should sell... In addition, diamond prices were dropping, so controlled production was important. Unfortunately, it was difficult to create a single mining company. It would take ten years of trying before the first shafts were dug around the crater and galleries were bored towards the centre to extract the ore from below. In 1881, the mine was divided amongst fifteen companies. Insane levels of speculation dramatically increased the value of the final claims, which changed hands for around £100,000, whilst the earlier claims had been purchased ten years earlier for a tenth of the price. The same madness affected the Dutoitspan, De Beers, Bultfontein and Jagersfontein mines, whose surface operations had been abandoned in 1872. The value of these claims had fallen to £50, yet a few months later it had risen to £15,000!

By 1883, there were several principal mining companies in the Kimberley Big Hole. The *Compagnie française des mines de diamant du cap de Bonne-Espérance* (French Company of the Cape of Good Hope Diamond Mines) had a strategic series of claims that split the hole in two. The Standard Company, Central Company, British Company and Barnato Diamond Mining Company surrounded it, eyeing it warily. Cecil Rhodes' De Beers Mining Company Limited was based 3.5 kilometres away, with a majority stake in the eponymous De Beers mine. The French Company also had a significant share in the Dutoitspan mine. However, it was quickly swept aside. It was one of the first companies to strive towards claim amalgamation, but the conniving Cecil Rhodes was already plotting to usurp it, through a series of complicated manoeuvres. He aimed to ensure that his De Beers company, named after the mine located on the old farm, was at the centre of the amalgamation. This occurred in several steps. Firstly, his company absorbed the French. Then, he began to negotiate with Barnato. In 1888, Barnato finally gave way, handing over his slice of the cake in exchange for a gigantic cheque, a majority shareholding, and the post of Governor for Life in the new company thus formed. De Beers Consolidated Mines was born. Dutoitspan and Bultfontein followed... and were immediately closed, in order to reduce the supply of diamonds, which was abundant. In addition to the idea of amalgamation, Rhodes had already seen the need to control the entire diamond market and to regulate supply, in order to be able to adapt to demand.

The rest of the story is less interesting: the mines were mechanised, the volcanic origins of kimberlite were recognised and the structure of these 'bottomless' deposits was therefore understood. Mining techniques were refined to their present methods: first, the volcanic cores are mined from the surface as far as possible, and later the mine is emptied from below, like an hourglass, by sinking an adjoining shaft and digging galleries to extract the ore from inside the pipe. Once the Kimberley mine had been consolidated, the company began to mine the blue ground (un-faded kimberlite rock). It was quickly realised that the blue ground rapidly deteriorates when exposed to air and water, far faster than most geological timescales: after only one or two years, the rock changes from being very hard to very friable. The areas surrounding the mines suddenly began looking very different: the kimberlite was extracted from the mine and spread out over a vast area, in a layer 20 cm thick. It was allowed to 'rot' there for a year, and 'ploughed' regularly. Naturally, the fields where the ore was spread were under constant supervision: diamonds were literally scattered on the surface. These new mining processes started in the 1890s. They were comparatively high-tech and industrialised and, as a result, required labour. The era of white pioneers was at an end, and De Beers began recruiting large numbers of black miners. This had also been one of the aims of successive amalgamations: not only to control the diamond market, but also to control the workforce.

The industry had therefore shifted away from self-employed workers, who were each responsible for their own claims, towards companies that employed large workforces. This created a new problem: the diversion of diamonds. The initial prospectors owned their own plots and therefore did not need to embezzle diamonds. In contrast, labourers could be persuaded, harassed or 'bought' by clandestine white traders, some of which were early prospectors who had left their claims. Diversion of diamonds to smugglers became so problematic that it threatened the company. Losses were estimated at 25% - sometimes even rising as high as 40%! Laws were implemented, but they started strikes. White employees refused to strip naked in special rooms and then wear company clothing while they were on the mine premises. A Scotland Yard envoy - one Bernard Shaw - came to South Africa to investigate. He proposed the only viable solution: the creation of mine compounds. The workers would enter the compounds to work and live, and would not be permitted to leave until a specified period had elapsed. This cut them off from all contact with the outside world. The French Company was the first to implement this system. It became widespread in the 1890s: De Beers had a controlling interest in all the mines, and so it could easily set up one compound per mine. There were many job applicants, even though the contract meant that workers had to remain virtual prisoners inside the compound for at least three months. Black workers were under close supervision, but they generally renewed their contracts. The pay was worthwhile, they were fed and housed, and job security was already a priority for the firm, as it helped to prevent theft. The compounds disappeared after the Second World War, and were replaced by European-style working towns. Some photographs

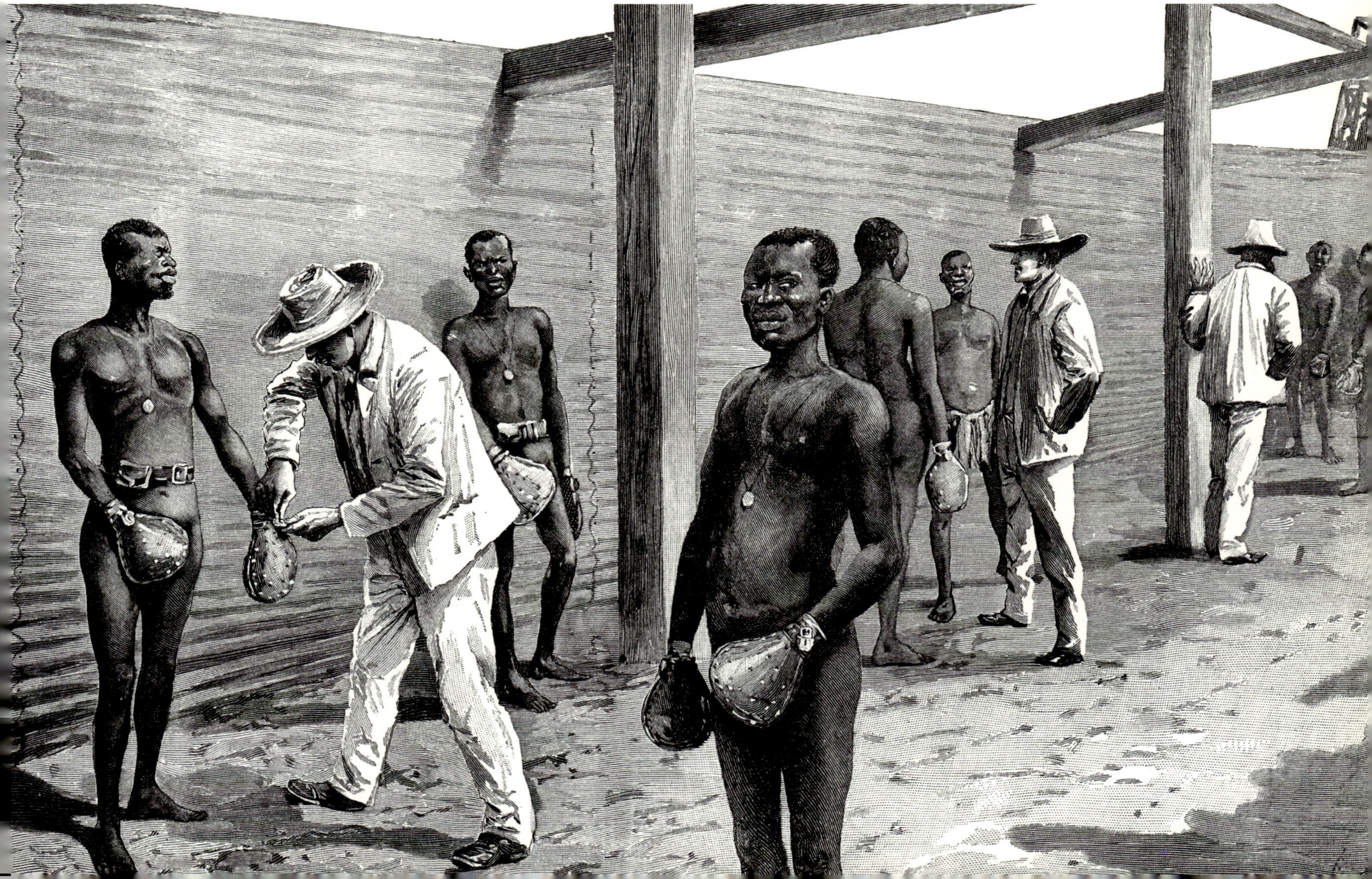

show black workers wearing rigid mitts over their hands in order to prevent them from stealing diamonds. This gives a somewhat distorted view of the compounds. In the 1940s, the workers' way of life was hardly to be envied - although the compounds included swimming pools, sports grounds and cooks - but they were in a better situation than early-20th-century coal miners, and living conditions were better than those experienced by many immigrants in European countries today.

The majority of the pipes in the Kimberley area were found in the 1870s. Wesselton was the exception: it was discovered in 1891. At the present time, Bultfontein, Dutoitspan, Wesselton and Koffiefontein are still being mined. Kimberley closed in 1914, and Jagersfontein in 1971. De Beers has opened a superb Eco-Museum around the Kimberley Big Hole: old houses and stalls from bygone Kimberley were transferred there, providing a picturesque impression of the mine's glory days. The Star of the West pub is not far away, and is still busy. It is a historic listed building, regarded as one of the most beautiful pubs in the world. The single most memorable moment of the trip, however, comes when a visitor steps out on to the viewing platform that juts out over the edge of the Big Hole. The view down from the top is utterly breathtaking. Humanity's lust for diamond is vividly illustrated by this immense, gaping space, heading down to the smooth, green water table. Thousands of human termites have been replaced by birds, which glide around the vertiginous circular cliffs. The hole extends a further 800 m deep below the surface of the water. A ten-million-cubic-metre-deep hole, for two thousand kilograms of diamonds, worn around the necks of people who have probably never held shovels in their lives.

Remote-controlled hole-boring machine.
Finsch mine, South Africa.

The Premier mine

Diamond history would not be the same without one particular mine. It is located far from Kimberley, 60 km north of Pretoria. It is the Premier mine, set up by a local construction tool merchant, Thomas Cullinan. After following the traces of alluvial diamond deposits upstream, he reached the original pipe. It was located on the Elandsfontein farm, which he acquired in November 1902. In January 1903, the kimberlitic nature of the deposit was recognised. T. Bell, a De Beers employee, foresaw great potential for the mine. However, a second De Beers agent thought that it was simply a fissure, and advised it to be dropped. In his defence, it has to be said that he was not permitted to enter the site and take samples, forcing him to jump to uninformed conclusions. He concluded that the deposit was a wild goose chase. Two years later, the goose laid a golden egg: the largest diamond ever found, the 3,106-carat Cullinan! De Beers ended up buying the mine in 1922.

The remarkable thing about the Premier mine is the size of the diamonds that are found there. They no longer keep track of the number of over-100-carat diamonds: over two hundred have been found. Various magnificent stones have been found in addition to the Cullinan. For example, the superb Centenary diamond was a 599ct rough stone, cut into a 273.85ct gem. The Golden Jubilee is the largest known cut diamond in the world to date (545.67ct), and the lovely, flawless, 137.02ct Premier Rose is one of the world's most beautiful diamonds. The Premier mine is also peculiar in that it regularly produces blue diamonds. These are not only priceless gems, but freaks of nature that are of interest to electronics researchers: they are semiconductors (cf. Chapter 2). As for the alluvial gravels that resulted from the pipe's erosion, they supplied the 721ct Jonker and the 287ct Pohl, both in 1934. The alluvial deposits are still in operation today.

Today in South Africa

De Beers has kept up diamond-prospecting activities ever since the days of the Kimberley and Premier adventures. However, two great modern discoveries (the Finsch and Venetia mines) were both discovered by others. The Finsch was located by two independent prospectors, Allistair FINcham and Wilhelm SCHwabel, who sold their lucky find to De Beers in 1963. The pipe was 17.9 hectares in size and open-cast mining began there in November 1965. Straight away, it began producing 3 million carats of diamonds per year. The hole got deeper, and a spiral pathway began snaking down into the pit, permitting huge trucks to reach the bottom and bring ore back up to the top. In 1990, Finsch reached a depth of 470 m, and underground mining commenced. In order to do this, the company dug a shaft that serves a tunnel in the shape of a ring around the pipe. From there, 46 galleries are dug out into the kimberlite, which is blown up and which breaks down naturally into these galleries. The ore is gathered up and transported through the ring-tunnel towards crushers and conveyor belts, which bring it to the base of the shaft. The pit continues to get deeper as the ore is extracted from below. Once every level has been blasted, the shaft is deepened, a new circular tunnel is dug, and the whole process starts again. To date, the crater has reached a depth of almost 600 m, and the Finsch mine has still at least thirty years of life ahead of it. Its production is kept at a low level (1.73 million carats in 1999), but this could be increased to 5 million carats per year with no problems.

The scene as one approaches the Finsch mine is remarkable. Firstly, the gigantic embankment catches the eye. However, attention rapidly shifts to the small mining town, beautifully located in the middle of the veldt. One can immediately detect a concern for the quality of life of the personnel, and respect for the environment. In the mine, safety concerns are religiously adhered to. Even in the apartheid era, De Beers had a reputation for being sincere in wanting to integrate black personnel into the life of the mines, and to ensure that they profited as much as possible from promotions. This was almost unthinkable amongst South African companies at the time. Nowadays, in the Finsch Mine, it is evident that these efforts have resulted in black labour being involved at all levels of the organisation. The workers' salaries are also remarkably high, in comparison to the national average.

Venetia is the richest mine of all. It was found in 1980, by prospectors out hunting for copper. It is the largest (12.7 hectares) of a group of pipes to the north of the Transvaal. Production began in 1992. In 1993, the mine's output reached a target of 5 million carats per year, decreasing to 3.4 million in 1999. The mine has a life expectancy of twenty years. Naturally, such a site requires a gigantic operation, which could only be assembled thanks to the power of De Beers. A large mine of this kind requires an investment in the region of $500 million. Not only are exploration costs very high, but the land must be stripped, the mine equipped and finally an extremely complex ore treatment plant built. Gigantic amounts of capital are invested before achieving a return on the initial investment. A mine like Finsch or Venetia requires more than 1,200 people in order to function, of which a third are management and engineering staff.

South Africa also produces diamonds from coastal and marine deposits. These spectacular deposits are also important in nearby Namibia. Geologists quickly realised that a layer at least two thousand metres thick had been eroded away from this part of Africa over millions of years. Inevitably, this process destroyed many pipes, whose diamonds were washed away by rivers. These rivers primarily flow towards the Atlantic, and the ocean beaches are particularly rich in diamonds. Moreover, the stones have already undergone a natural sorting process. Only the finest diamonds, free from inclusions and fractures, can survive this trip along the riverbed without being destroyed by the constant tumbling amidst pebbles. Therefore, the beaches are rich in gem-quality diamonds, which are worth more. Prospecting began in the early 20th century, but it intensified dramatically in the 1960s. Gigantic excavators were developed, which scoop up the sand from the beaches, and eject it once it has been stripped of its diamonds.
Off-shore diamond mining is even more spectacular. De Beers uses special

The Orange river flows to the sea. Over millions of years, it eroded the volcanic kimberlite cones. Diamonds were released by this erosion, and they ended up in the sand, along much of the west coast of South Africa and also Namibia.

The Debmarine company uses gigantic boats to treat undersea gravel deposits. The gravel is sucked up by remote-control robots that roll along the seabed.

On the other end of the scale, a scuba-diver from a small, independent company sucks up diamond-bearing undersea gravel by hand.

boats that go out into the ocean, suck up gravel from the seabed and process it in the boat. The boats themselves are ultra-sophisticated floating factories; an automated, remote-controlled vehicle patrols the sea-bed, holding the enormous suction pipe that leads up to the boat. These boats are used in Namibian waters. In Namibia, independent companies also undertake small-scale offshore diamond dredging. They cannot afford underwater vehicles, so they use small boats, with a crew of around ten people, of which at least two will be divers. The divers take the nozzle of the suction pipe down to the seabed. Sand and gravel is sucked up and roughly sorted on the boat. Large stones are discarded and the smaller gravel is put into sacks and delivered to a small treatment plant on dry land. It is a hard life: the divers can only go down twice a day, for health reasons. But the job can pay well, and there is no shortage of applicants...

It is true to say that South Africa still has opportunities available for small to medium diamond-prospecting operations, for investors who lack De Beers' financial muscle. The latter does not make a point of getting involved in small operations, leaving the ground free for others. There are numerous alluvial mines along the Vaal river, showing that the diamond extraction industry is still going strong. Between these small-scale mines, off-shore deposits and huge mines like the Finsch, the Venetia and the indomitable Premier (which will soon celebrate its centenary), South Africa still has many good years ahead of it.

Elsewhere on the African continent

Diamond deposits in Africa are by no means restricted to South Africa and Namibia: far from it. Pipes are also found in Lesotho and Swaziland, although their production is low. However, Botswana created waves by being the continent's first high-volume producer. The diamonds are from the two largest pipes ever found, Orapa and Jwaneng. It is difficult to undertake diamond-prospecting operations in this country because it is partly covered by the Kalahari desert, with layers of sand over fifty metres thick. As a result, the 106-hectare Orapa pipe was only discovered in 1967, and the 54-hectare Jwaneng pipe in 1973. The two sites produced 9.07 and 11.4 million carats respectively in 1999. A smaller pipe, Letlhakane, also produced 0.88 million carats that year. Unfortunately, the discovery of a kimberlite pipe does not necessarily mean success: it also has to be productive, which is often not the case. In all, 140 kimberlite deposits have been discovered in Botswana, but only three are worthwhile mining! The Finsch mine's logo is an eagle; in contrast, the Jwaneng mine's logo is a termite. This is because prospectors discovered diamond-associated minerals nearby by examining termite nests. These tiny insects dig very deep tunnels in search of humidity. They discard the extracted material as 'tailings' on the surface: by examining this material, prospectors can see what sorts of minerals are hidden deep below the Kalahari sand layer.

Diamond-hunters in Angola, in the 1980s. The blood-red colour in the water is due to iron oxides from the disturbed clay beds. It evokes the tragic fate of diamond-mining in this country: the civil war and diamond trafficking have bathed the country in the blood of innocent victims.

Zaïre and Angola, and to a lesser extent the Republic of Central Africa, are the other major African producers. They produce large quantities of alluvial diamonds. However, the instability of these countries has put them at the centre of a global discussion over the way diamond revenues are used. For some time, the international community and the diamond market have set up measures to exclude smuggled diamonds. This was prompted by the fact that the income from diamonds was being diverted to buy weaponry. Hopefully, the rebel militias in these "republics" will henceforth be deprived of precious gem revenues. Customers have been horrified by dreadful pictures of the conflict in Sierra Leone, and they have begun to demand that gems be certificated as "clean", rather than "conflict diamonds". Tragically, diamonds could have provided the funds for social development in these countries, but the money has been misappropriated. In contrast, with every day that passes, Botswana shows how the enlightened exploitation of diamond resources can ensure economic growth and development, to the benefit of the whole population.

Russian diamonds

The USSR was the first country to benefit from the South African experiment. Shortly after World War II, the extraordinary Professor Vladimir Sobolev made some brilliant geological deductions, which resulted in many prospecting expeditions along the Tungunska river in Siberia. The first pipe was found in 1953. It was not long before 400 had been discovered and mapped. The majority are not productive. However, the Mir ("Peace") pipe is an exception. It is 400 m x 600 m across. Enormous technical problems had to be solved in order to mine it, because the temperature in the region is -40°C for much of the year. The main problem was housing the miners and processing-factory workers. A city was built, supplied by a nuclear power plant. The Udachnaya pipe was discovered in 1955, inside the Arctic circle. Mining started there in 1967. Russian diamonds are of superb quality, and are partly marketed through De Beers. The State founded a powerful company to supply the gems, cutting workshops were opened, and the USSR simultaneously developed an entire industry to manufacture synthetic industrial diamonds. The USSR's collapse did not endanger this diamond industry, which had been built over several decades. Even today, production remains at around 16 million carats. The economic stakes are considerable, which explains the signs of a nascent drive towards independence in the mining republic of Sakha...

Three exceptional Russian diamonds: the 56.66-carat Terechkova, the 124.72-carat Allende, and the 32.65-carat Samantha Smith. Russian Diamond Fund, Moscow

Australia's surprising diamonds

It is a little-known fact that the Argyle mine in Australia is the world's largest diamond mine. In terms of quantity, it single-handedly produces one-third of the world's diamonds every year! Argyle's annual average production is around 35 million carats: 40 millions in 1998, and 29.8 millions in 1999. In other words, 8 tons of diamonds, or the equivalent of two hundred and fifty years' production from Brazil!

Argyle is clearly something special. It is located virtually at the end of the world. Getting to Sydney is already quite a trip. Even so, to get to Argyle, one has to travel a further three thousand kilometres west to Perth, and then another two thousand kilometres north to Darwin. After that, there is a trip in a jeep, across the baking desert to Argyle. The open-cast mine is in such a hot region, it feels like a furnace. Temperatures seldom drop below 40°C: in the 1970s, diamond prospectors had to be truly dedicated to locate the mine. Initially, researchers found some alluvial crystals in the mud at the bottom of creeks. Their attention was particularly drawn to two crystals, discovered downstream of the Smoke Creek alluvial zone. By methodically prospecting upstream, following the dry riverbed, they eventually discovered the diamonds' source. This happened on October 2nd, 1979. It was named AK1: Argyle Kimberlite number 1. Shortly afterwards, geologists were stunned to discover that it was not, in fact, a kimberlite, but another type of volcanic rock known as lamproite, which thus became only the second diamond-bearing rock ever identified. The next day, the world map of potential diamond deposit locations suddenly gained a whole smattering of additional red dots. The deposit had escaped De Beers' attention, as it was camouflaged under a layer of iron oxides...

After an investment of over £30 million the Argyle Diamond Mine was finally ready to mine its first stones in 1982. The productive area was terraced. The lamproite was in the shape of an enormous 'seam', approximately two kilometres long and five hundred metres wide. This resulted in a productive surface area of about 50 hectares. Today, the mine has become a wide, terraced valley. The seam is at the bottom; it is mined by gigantic machines. The rock is constantly being drilled, in order to follow the meanderings of the lamproite seam as it descends into the bedrock. To date, the seam has been mined to a depth of approximately three hundred metres. There are another one hundred and fifty metres to go. Once that point is reached, the Argyle Diamond Mine will have to make a difficult decision: to abandon the seam, or begin underground extraction operations. In fact, the mine does not have many good years left: production will be threatened by 2005-2006: in order to widen mining operations, they will have to remove more than one hundred million tons of unproductive rock. However, Argyle continues to break records in the interim. Given that it produces two to five carats per ton on average, every gigantic truckload of ore (190 tons) potentially contains a thousand carats of diamonds! Overall, the mine produces around twenty kilos of diamonds per day.

Ore processing is performed in the traditional manner: the rock is crushed into pieces around 1 cm across. These fragments are placed in vats, where the water is mixed with a fine ferrosilicate suspension. This raises the liquid's specific gravity to 3, which permits the rock to float whereas diamonds and other denser minerals sink to the bottom of the vat. The residue at the bottom is extracted: it accounts for 5% of the original crushed rock. The diamonds are then extracted (accounting for barely 0.0001%). This extraction is done using X-ray sorting, a process that is also used in most of the other mines. The ore is illuminated with X-rays, which cause the diamonds to fluoresce. When an electronic sensor detects fluorescence, it uses a puff of compressed air to eject the diamond into a collecting tray. The primary deposit does not operate in isolation: the alluvial deposits in the ancient riverbed are also being worked. These gravels produced 6% of Argyle's total production in 1998.

According to their inclusions, which have been studied and dated, Argyle diamonds are 1.1 billion years old and came from a depth of 270 kilometres: so far, so normal. However, their appearance and marketing set them apart. For a start, they are always small, often less than a carat. The two largest crystals ever found have been preserved in the mine's head office: they each weigh about 40 carats.

Half of Argyle's production by volume is of industrial quality, and the proportion that is used for jewellery varies widely in colour. Many are white, of course, but there are also some greyish-blues and many brown gems. These have become known as "cognac" or "champagne" colours. They are

A pink diamond brooch, made out of gems from the Argyle mine, Australia. Made by Ralph Esmerian, New York

The gigantic Argyle deposit. It is currently the largest diamond mine in the world.

quite unusual, to be sure, and have been heavily promoted using a clever marketing campaign. As a result, they have sold well. However, Argyle's reputation is based on its pink diamonds. It produces about fifty spectacular pink gems per year on average. Their colour ranges from purple-pink to almost red. They are rarely more than one carat in size, and are cut by the Argyle company itself. The finest stones are auctioned once a year to the highest bidder, in the Beau Rivage hotel in Geneva. These tenders are the Argyle mine's equivalent of De Beers' sights. The sales are conducted with the utmost discretion. The potential buyers are a very exclusive club: in order to take part in the process, buyers need to be able to spend at least £300,000 per carat. Before the sale, the stones are displayed in Sydney, Tokyo, Hong Kong, London and Geneva for publicity. A luxurious folder is produced, providing details of every stone, along with their gemmological certificates. This is accompanied by a simple form on a piece of paper, with a plain, anonymous envelope. Potential buyers fill in the form, with the prices they are willing to pay for whichever stones they wish to buy. The envelopes are gathered together at the Beau Rivage Hotel. The highest bidder wins, and must immediately honour the transaction with a bank transfer for the stated amount. Once the bank has confirmed the transfer, the stones are handed over. This is a unique market, quite separate from the normal diamond business: the rarefied sphere of fancy-colour diamonds.

As we mentioned earlier, the Argyle Diamond Mine manages its own operations. It has excluded De Beers and its Central Selling Organisation, the famous CSO (which became the Diamond Trading Company, or DTC, in 2000). Argyle worked with De Beers initially, but decided not to renew its contract in 1996, because it felt that the CSO was taking high profit margins from the goods. There was another important reason: prices for these small stones are generally low, and they fell further when Russia and Angola began producing similar goods. The mine therefore created its own marketing company, Argyle Diamond Sales, based in Perth. The rough diamonds are mainly distributed via Antwerp, except for around 20,000 carats per year, which the company cuts itself and sells to dealers. For the first time, De Beers' virtual monopoly over the global diamond industry had been dented, by a mine that was stranded at the end of the world.

Geologists used to consider Argyle as the exception that proved the rule. In 1999, they discovered a new exception in French Guyana: komatiite, only the third diamond-bearing rock ever discovered. It can contain up to a thousand diamonds per kilo, although unfortunately the crystals are tiny. It is not currently known whether this type of rock will ever prove to be economically viable.

New eldorados

Alluvial diamond deposits had been known to exist in Arkansas, USA, for many years. Naturally, it was assumed that there might be favourable primary deposits elsewhere in North America. A pipe was eventually found in Colorado, but Canada's vast Northern Territories proved to the great 'diamond Eldorado' for the new millennium. The story belongs to a single, obstinate man, Charles Fipke. He has become the most famous prospector in Canada. He had been searching since 1978, without outside funding, and ended up joining the Broken Hill mining company of Australia for the first test drillings. One of them produced a 142 m-long core, which contained 81 small diamonds: the Lac de Gras kimberlites had been found, 200 km south of the Arctic Circle. This started another diamond rush, and 125 companies descended on the spot. So far, they have found nearly 200 kimberlites, of which at least 14 are potentially viable.

The Ekati mine entered into production in 1998, and very quickly began producing almost 200,000 carats per month. So far, the largest diamond found weighed 47 carats, and most of the stones are sold independently of De Beers. A few dozen kilometres away, the Diavik mine is scheduled to start production in 2002. Canada should therefore quickly become the fourth-largest diamond-producing country in the world. However, it is not a simple operation: the climatic conditions are difficult, the native population's requirements have to be taken into account, and stringent measures have had to be put in place in order to safeguard the environment. These deposits are therefore very expensive to mine: over five years, the country's diamond research expenditure amounted to nearly 800 million dollars. Mr. Fipke, the famous prospector, did not have an easy life either. He became very rich, and went through the most expensive divorce in Canadian history. His ex-wife is still a shareholder in the companies.

The future of diamond production

Economists continue to study data on global diamond production, past and present. It is difficult to find data for the years preceding the African discoveries, particularly figures that date back to before De Beers' incorporation. The biggest gap in the data concerns production from India and Borneo. Brazilian diamond production was relatively well documented by the colonial authorities in Lisbon. At any rate, production figures prior to 1860 were comparatively insignificant compared to today's total; they account for less than the Argyle mine's yearly production! After a considerable amount of statistical number-crunching, an estimate has been produced for the world's total diamond production, from Antiquity to the end of the 20th century: five hundred tons. Until diamonds were discovered in Africa, annual world production was about 100,000 carats. Today, it is 100 million. In other words, one year's current production is equivalent to one millennium of Indian production!

These dizzying figures are set to rise even more, with the addition of Canadian production, continued production from Argyle, and excellent prospects in Russia. One might think that these increases will compensate for the inevitable decline of African producers. In fact, this may not be the case. The Premier mine is a good example: it has been in production for almost a century, and has become almost a symbol of the industry. Clearly, there is no reliable model for diamond production: Africa might remain the 'Diamond Continent' for a long time to come. The Botswanan mines may still be productive once the Canadian mines have been forgotten. The Orapa mine alone doubled production in 2000 to reach 12 million carats. The discovery of primary deposits has also affected statistics considerably. Alluvial placer deposits accounted for 100% of global production in 1870, and yet only account for 12% today! This was a triumph for the science of geology. One of the most remarkable intellectual feats was that of Professor Vladimir Sobolev of Russia. He correctly deduced the existence of diamond-bearing pipes in Siberia simply by making geological comparisons between Russia and Africa. A similar feat was performed more recently, when Russian geologists discovered the new Arkhangelsk mine. It is also known that there are diamonds in Lapland, which is hardly a geological surprise, but the environmental implications may be severe. Time will tell whether the Canadian pipes live up to expectations. In the meantime, prospectors continue to hunt after diamonds, dreaming of vast wealth.

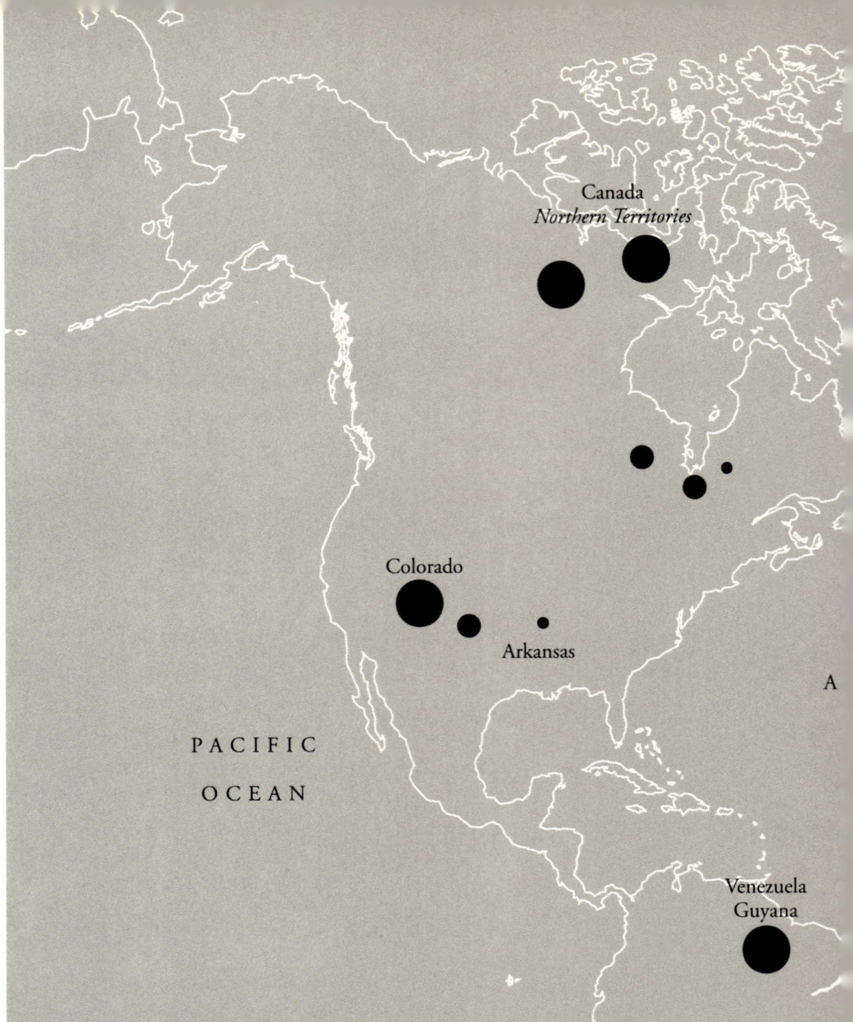

Global diamond production, 1988

(after Terraconsult, Antwerp, 1999, published in Lapis, Special Edition No. 18, 2000)

COUNTRY	TYPE (PRIMARY KIMBERLITES OR ALLUVIAL DEPOSITS	AMOUNT EXTRACTED (CARATS)	AVERAGE VALUE PER CARAT	TOTAL PRODUCTION, IN US DOLLARS
Africa				
Botswana	Primary	19, 798,000	80	1,583,840,000
South Africa	Primary	10, 228,000	94	964,500,000
South Africa	Alluvial	421,000	222	93,462,000
Angola	All. + primary	5,095,000	136	692,920,000
Zaïre	All. + primary	21,362,000	31	662,222,000
Namibia	Alluvial	1,460,000	267	389,820,000
Sierra Leone	Alluvial	900,000	140	126,000,000
Central African Rep.	Alluvial	550,000	211	116,050,000
Guinea	Alluvial	596,000	195	116,220,000
Liberia	Alluvial	256,000	105	22,576,000
Ivory Coast	Alluvial	166,000	136	22,576,000
Lesotho	All. + primary	53,000	167	8,851,000
Tanzania	Primary	93,000	150	13,950,000
Ghana	Alluvial	525,000	23	12,075,000
Total		**61,503,000**	**79**	**4,829,366,000**
Asia				
Russia	Primary	15,100,000	85	1,283,500,000
China	Primary	150,000	90	13,500,000
Indonesia	Alluvial	35,000	190	6,650,000
Total		**15,285,000**	**85**	**130,365,000**
Australia (Mainly Argyle)	Primary	**40,920,000**	**9.8**	**401,016,000**
The Americanas				
Brazil	Alluvial	1,400,000	46	64,400,000
Venezuela	Alluvial	3,50,000	128	44,800,000
Guyana	Alluvial	15,000	80	1,200,000
Canada (3 month's production)	Primary	250,000	130	32,500,000
Total		**2,015,000**	**71**	**142, 900, 000**
World Total 1998		**119,723,000**	**71**	**6,676,932,000**

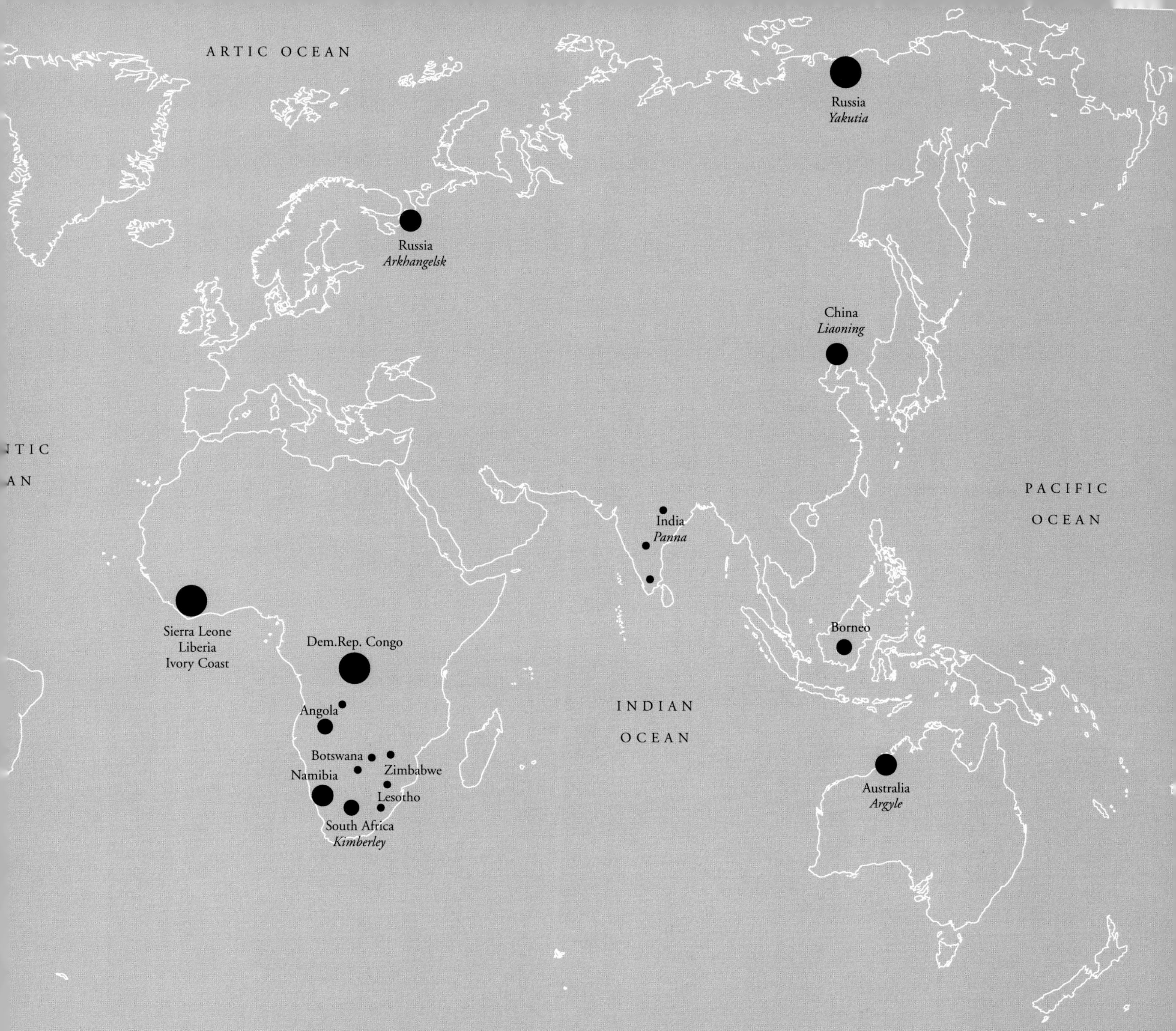

World map of diamond deposits, both active and extinct.

After Ian Balfour, Famous Diamonds, Christie's, 2000.

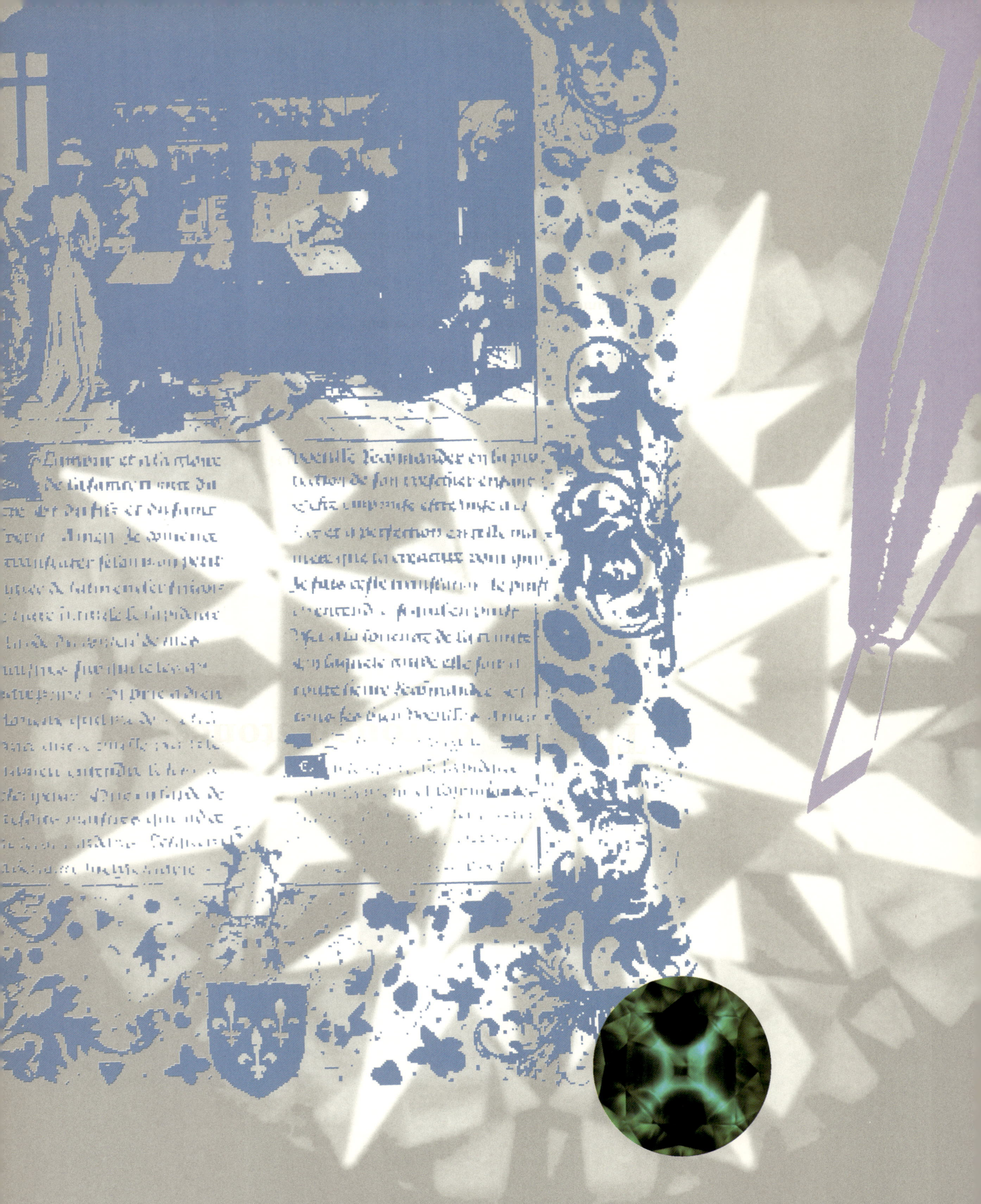

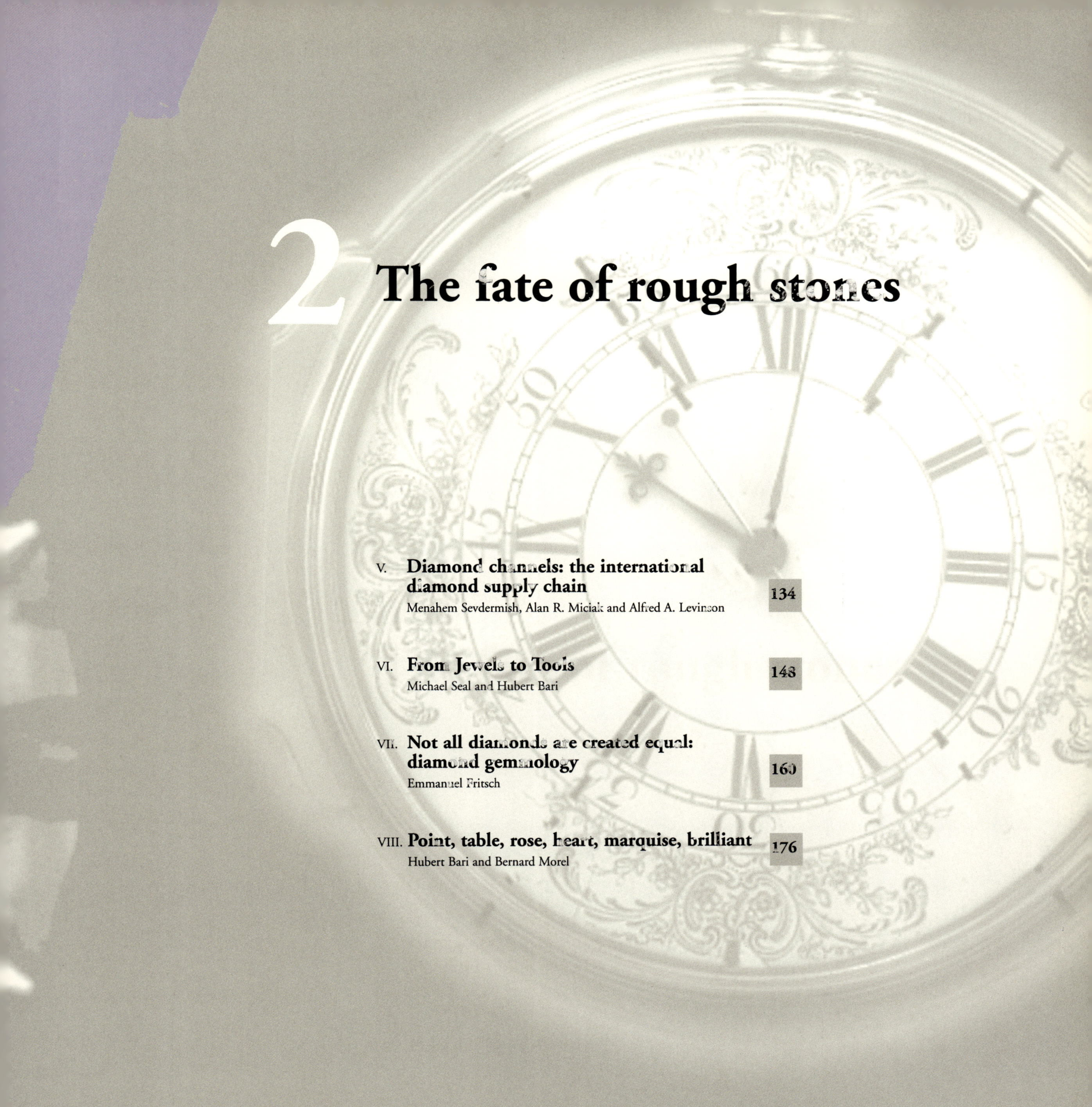

2 The fate of rough stones

A Lamour et a la gloire de la saincte trinite du pere Et du filz et du saint esperit Amen Je commence a translater selon mon petit engien de latin en cler francoiz Le livre intitule le lapidaire A laide du conseil de mes maistres sur qui ie les ay entrepris. Si prie a dieu glorieux quil me donne tele grace que ie puisse par tele maniere entendre le sens de lescripture Que en laide de mesdits maistres que ad ce me seront aidans Lesquelz La benoitte vierge marie

veuille recommander en la protection de son treschier enfant Ceste emprinse estre mise a effect et a perfection en telle maniere que la creature pour qui Je fais ceste translation le puist cy entendre si quil en puist user a la louenge de la trinite En laquele garde elle soit a toute heure recommandee et tous ses bien veullans Amen

Cy fine le prologue.

Cy sensient le lapidaire selon la verite et loppinion des Indois Ainsi comme les pierres precieuses cy apres escriptes sont esprouvees tant de fois

Menahem Sevdermish,
Alan R. Miciak &
Alfred A. Levinson

CHAPTER V

Diamond channels:
the international diamond supply chain

As with oil, that other famous carbon-based product, the international diamond supply chain is called the 'pipeline'. For a long time, the pipeline consisted of a single supply channel, virtually entirely controlled by De Beers. A channel is defined as the supply of the commodity from its source (in this case, the mine) to the retailer. Various events have conspired with global economic policy changes in order to promote the development of additional supply channels. Today, the global pipeline is a complex, multi-channel distribution system. Two of these new channels have appeared in recent years, following the discoveries of diamonds in the USSR and Canada. These economic factors are important: they display exceptional techniques and strategies, and show how the goods flow across the world. We must remember that diamonds are unusual: no other type of legal merchandise concentrates so much value in such a small volume. In addition, unlike the majority of raw materials, the supply and price of diamonds bear little relationship to one another. Diamond is therefore an exception to normal macroeconomic rules. How can this be? In order to understand the situation, we need to immerse ourselves in diamond history, once again.

Lapidary, a work supposedly by Jean de Mandeville, copied shortly after the death of its author in 1372. The book opens with a scene at a precious gem merchant's shop. The author gives advice on how not to be duped by these merchants. In the case of diamonds, Mandeville says it is better to receive rather than to buy. Indeed, the gem's protective force is strengthened if it is offered as a gift. In the 15th century, when the manuscript was transcribed, diamonds were sold in Venice and Portugal at these types of shops.

The birth of a giant. The De Beers name appears here in 1902 on a sorting building at the Kimberley mines. At this time the company had been in existence for fourteen years. No one could then have predicted the future glory of this name in the world diamond trade.

The beginnings of a single channel

Diamonds were discovered in South Africa in the late 1860s, and an enormous "rush" soon followed. As a result, thousands of prospectors and miners rapidly flooded the market with enormous quantities of diamonds. The market was unable to absorb them, and the price of the gem collapsed. Many of the independent producers were individuals or families, installed on their own small, 9m x 9m claims. Cecil Rhodes was the first to realise that this plethora of independent producers resulted in complete disorganisation. We have already seen how he plotted to amalgamate all these concessions into the hands of only one company. He began to execute his plan between 1870 and 1880, ultimately arriving at the foundation of De Beers Consolidated Mines Ltd. in 1888. He was already planning to not only control the mines, but also to regulate the marketplace. At the time, Indian production was minimal, and Brazilian production was in rapid decline. A syndicate, made up of London-based companies, regulated the sale of the diamonds from the De Beers mines. Little by little, this syndicate (known as "The London Diamond Syndicate") also purchased the production of other African mines. These were starting to become numerous: there were mines in South-West Africa (Namibia), the Belgian Congo (now the former Zaïre), the Gold Coast (Ghana), and Angola in 1923.

In 1930, the syndicate was hit by a major crisis: demand for diamonds dropped considerably. De Beers closed all its Kimberley mines in 1932, and the Anglo American Corp. took a stake in order to uphold De Beers' purchasing contracts. Various organisations began to undertake clearly defined roles: some are still operating today. For example, from 1930 onwards the Diamond Corporation (Dicorp) purchased the rough diamonds, whereas the Diamond Trading Company (DTC), which was founded in 1934, performed the sorting operations and managed the sale of the diamonds, via the 'sight' process. Dicorp and DTC later became the CSO (Central Selling Organisation), which managed the sale of De Beers' diamonds until the year 2000.

The diamond distribution process that developed was very original and remarkably clever. Basically, price fluctuations were regarded as normal in most other raw materials markets. However, the De Beers management realised that when diamond prices fluctuated, public confidence was battered: after all, diamonds are a luxury product, and they are also used for investment and hoarding purposes. De Beers' policy was therefore to promote price stability by controlling the supply of diamonds. The quantity and type of rough diamonds supplied to global diamond-cutting centres was continuously adjusted, whilst De Beers continued to purchase diamonds from the diamond-mining nations. Therefore, the CSO promoted stability and prosperity in the world diamond industry, by managing the supply of gem-quality rough. This unique economic role was implemented using a very simple system, the 'sight' process.

The sight process was a very original idea, and it regulated the sale of almost 85% of the world's rough diamonds until 1990. It is worth studying. The De Beers group established a "buyers' club" to purchase its diamonds, via the CSO (now DTC). The members of this club were the famous 'sight-holders'. It was a very exclusive grouping: the members were selected according to stringent criteria. There are currently around 120 of these diamantaires. They are diamond dealers, and they must have spotless reputations and unimpeachable financial credentials (amongst other credentials). The sight-holders each tell the DTC about their diamond requirements, specifying shape, colour, quantities and qualities. The DTC prepares batches of diamonds for them: it tries to meet their requirements, depending on the stones it has available in stock. However, it also considers a range of other factors, and prepares each parcel accordingly. Ten times per year, the sight-holders go to London to examine their specially-prepared diamond package. The final composition of the parcel is not solely a determined by the type of goods that the DTC has in stock: it also takes into account the global market situation, and the amount of stock in the market as a whole. Most of the world's gem diamonds therefore flow through a single, tightly controlled channel. From there, they go to the international diamond bourses (trading centres), then to diamond-cutting workshops and, ultimately, to the retail jeweller.

Diamond sorter in South Africa, early 20th century.

Children sorting diamonds at Kimberley, around 1900.

The headquarters of De Beers and the Kimberley mines, South Africa. The splendid historical building has been superbly preserved.

Between the end of the war and the start of the 1960s, this system functioned perfectly. Increased demand in the 1950s even made it possible to liquidate the stock of diamonds that the company had been forced to accumulate during the Great Depression in the 1930s. New mines entered into production. Between 1960 and the end of the 20th century, global diamond production increased fourfold! This was the result of the discovery of mines in Australia, Botswana and the USSR. These discoveries did not topple De Beers from its leading role in diamond production; indeed, even today the group single-handedly produces 43% of the world's supply, much more than any other single producer. The CSO's single channel also continued to work well. In fact, De Beers signed contracts with the new producers, who channelled their merchandise through its sights. All of the supply-side companies agreed that the system worked, and that there was no reason to replace it. It guaranteed price stability, even over the long term. This suited the customers, too. Likewise, the producer countries were happy because they had a guaranteed source of revenue: De Beers signed contracts to buy their rough diamonds. De Beers took on the responsibility of managing buffer stocks, to ensure price stability.

As a result, De Beers became an essential part of both the diamond mining and diamond trading industries. Its expertise allowed the company to locate and commercialise new deposits, like the Finsch and Venetia mines in South Africa and the Orapa and Jwaneng mines in Botswana. This enabled the company to maintain its strong position in diamond production. In order to sell more diamonds, the CSO began spending considerable amounts of money on diamond promotion. Almost immediately, one of the most famous advertising slogans of all time was born: "A Diamond is Forever". Even painters as famous as Picasso and Matisse produced illustrations for promotional campaigns, and diamond consumption rocketed across the world. This was particularly true in the largest market in the world: the USA. The diamond engagement ring became popular, single-handedly ensuring healthy gem sales. This promotional expenditure benefited the entire industry, not just the part that De Beers controlled. In fact, when consumers buy diamonds, they have no way of knowing which distribution channel the gems came from. It doesn't even occur to them to ask!

Ultimately, this single-channel pipeline is a remarkable feat of organization. All the companies adhere to a system whereby only one company ultimately controls the supply of diamonds. These companies include mines and diamond-cutters, individuals, companies or even sovereign states. Even the USSR used to be a member (its successor, Russia, still is). The CSO system functioned for a long time because, in exchange for exclusivity, it undertook various essential tasks that are very difficult to implement individually. The present-day DTC provides guarantees to producers that it will buy diamonds at a stable price; it sorts and evaluates rough diamonds with matchless skill; it performs scientific research that brings great benefits (automated sorting, quality evaluation, the detection of imitations and synthetic diamonds, etc...); it guarantees that buffer stocks will accumulate during periods of weak demand; it runs the stocks down when the market improves again; and it spends large amounts on diamond promotion.

These activities helped to ensure the extraordinary longevity of the single-channel distribution system. It has a unique place in the history of economics. The whole system worked relatively smoothly from De Beers' foundation in 1888 until 1992.

Sorting table at De Beers London.
Around 60% of the world's
diamonds end up on these tables.

Bill Goldberg, a famous New York diamond dealer,
examines a stone behind the windows of his
office in 47th Street.

Preparations for a sight in London.
The diamonds are placed in packets which
are then put into sealed boxes.

The diamond pipeline at the end of the 20th century

In 1985, cracks appeared in the system for the first time. They were caused by a dramatic industry development: the Argyle mine was commercialised, rapidly becoming the leading diamond producer by volume. In value terms, however, its production was far less significant. Argyle diamonds were primarily used for industrial applications. For this reason, the CSO could only distribute a relatively small proportion of Argyle diamonds through its 'sights'. However, a diamond-cutting industry was eventually established in India to cut very small (and mediocre-quality) gems, using low-cost labour. The other producers also profited from this, as they could send their lower-quality diamonds to India to be worked. In addition, the industry saw the birth of a new market segment, for small, bottom-of-the-range diamonds. This was promoted by intensive marketing activity, and specialised distribution networks were set up in the USA.

At the same time, diamond trading centres in Belgium (Antwerp) and Israel (Ramat Gan and Tel Aviv) grew considerably. They benefited from Russian diamonds that were outside the single-channel system. The crisis began in July 1996: the Argyle mine decided not to renew the contract that bound it to De Beers and the CSO. It had decided to market its own production (both high- and low-quality goods) through its own distribution channels.

Many people believed that the industry pipeline was destined to split into two major channels: one for high-quality goods, the other for low-quality. The unspoken consensus was that the boundary line would be drawn at around $160 per carat of rough. However, life turned out not to be so simple… The USSR had fragmented into independent states, leaving Russia with a source of very high quality diamonds, and a diamond industry that was capable of integrating all the operations in the pipeline, from sorting to cutting. This industry soon lost patience, fuelled by a new spirit of capitalist ambition. It decided to flex its muscles, by contravening the spirit of the purchasing contract that tied the former USSR to De Beers. It began 'digging' a new pipeline. To cap it all, developments were occurring simultaneously in Angola. Diamond-smuggling networks were being set up, making the situation worse. These events caused the old, single-channel pipeline to fragment into a multiple-channel arrangement. This was contrary to De Beers' wishes, and it surprised economists, who had assumed that the market would simply split into a two-channel system. However, the network of pipelines is still relatively simple, and it can be summarised as follows, into four parts.

The first part is the traditional pipeline, which continues to operate, channelling its rough diamonds through the DTC. It represents 60% or more of world production, and includes diamonds bought under contract from Russia and Canada.

Secondly, there is the Indian part. It cannot be accurately described as an Indian pipeline, because it is incomplete: India does not produce significant quantities of diamonds any more. It is quite remarkable that India, which had a monopoly on diamond production for 2,000 years, should have risen to play a significant economic role in the business again. Today, however, India has very little to do with the large, high-quality stones that it was famous for in ancient times. The Indian industry currently receives enormous quantities of rough, "near-gem" (i.e. low-quality) stones. These are mainly cut and polished into small, low-value brilliant-cuts. These rough gems come from all the mines in the world, but particularly from Russia and Argyle. Even the DTC is keen to distribute its own "near-gem" diamonds in this way!

Thirdly, there is the Russian channel. Russian capabilities are not limited to extracting, cutting and polishing diamonds. To some extent, Russia can even set them into jewellery and distribute them! It is unique in this respect. The Russian system was set up in the image of the traditional, complete channel. However, the Russians have relatively weak purchasing power. This tends to mean that

Coloured diamonds are sold by specialised dealers. One of them, Eddy Elzas in Antwerp, has built up the famous Rainbow collection.

most Russian diamonds are sold on the international market in the form of rough gems or loose, cut gems - including 50 % through De Beers!

Finally, the "Belgian-Israeli axis" forms the fourth part of the industry. It is perfectly integrated into the global, multiple-channel system. Large quantities of gems are marketed in the diamond trading centres of Antwerp, Ramat Gan and New York. These centres have multi-functional capabilities. They buy, cut and distribute diamonds from many sources: not only the DTC, Russia and Australia, but also diamonds from other producers outside the organised system.

Motorways and winding roads

One might think that the world's diamonds flow quietly along their chosen distribution channels. In fact, they can follow extremely complex pathways. A fine, gem-quality diamond can pass through half a dozen countries on its way from the mine to the ultimate consumer. For example, a diamond could be extracted from a mine in Botswana, sorted and evaluated in the country of origin and also at the DTC in England, sold to a Belgian sight-holder, set into jewellery in Thailand, and sold to a Japanese tourist on a holiday cruise in Martinique! Even so, this complex saga can quite easily take place in one single, 'traditional' distribution channel.

In some cases, a stone's gemmological characteristics determine the pathway that it will follow, regardless of where it was originally mined. For example, a very large, very valuable stone will probably be cut in New York, ultimately to be sold in one of the world's wealthiest countries, possibly in the oil-rich Middle East. Conversely, a small, low-quality gem will be cut in India, and will end up set in inexpensive jewellery in the USA or in a low-income country.

The Indian side of the business is by far the most interesting. As we have seen, it is not, strictly speaking, a complete channel. The diamond trade employs at least 800,000 people in India. It is organised into family firms that have an astonishing, pyramidal organisational structure, in which the Indian diaspora plays a key role. Family ties and agreements enable companies to spread networks of offices all around the world, wherever a family member has become established. Family ties have always been important in the industry, but nobody has ever pushed the logic as far as the Indian firms have. These vast extended families have set up company networks that operate like small, fully-fledged pipelines. Although they revolve around India, they do not require a single great trading centre like Antwerp or Ramat Gan. In fact, when diamonds enter into the Indian system, they usually follow a complex, vertical pathway. It starts with the parent company, which is usually based in Bombay. The parent company supplies a cascade of subcontractors. Each principal subcontractor in turn supplies a network of even smaller associate companies. The cutting can therefore be spread out over several villages: on the ground, an agent disperses the individual stones amongst several families for cutting. This cascade system allows the parent company at the top to cut enormous quantities of stones, without having to have a supervisor in charge of the process, or a commitment to the cutters and craftspeople at the bottom of the ladder. The latter are self-employed: if they have no diamonds to cut, they make no money. Once the diamonds are cut, they ascend back up the cascade, eventually returning to the parent companies. The parent company only has office space: all the work is done in rural areas, in places where the costs of living and wages are insignificant.

Naturally, the business does not stop there. Some of the more powerful parent companies have been able to develop powerful diamond-cutting companies, often helped by associate firms that are owned by other members of their extended family. Some Indian firms are DTC sight-holders, whereas others have access to the Ashton sales office in Antwerp, which sells rough diamonds from Argyle. Likewise, the cut gems can be marketed through family-connected sales networks. Together, these Indian company networks are thought to have over 1,000 sales offices, all over the world. Often, a son will purchase a stone in Africa or in Antwerp, and send it to his father in Bombay. The stone is dispatched to another son, who deals with the cutting side of the operation. The cut gem is sent out again, to another member of the family in charge of marketing. It could then go to companies owned by cousins, in the USA, Europe or Asia (mainly Hong Kong). From there, it may be sold to a jeweller who then sets it and sells it to the final consumer. Of course, there is a good chance that the jeweller would also happen to be another cousin! Although the Indian supply chain only began growing relatively recently, it is now extremely important. For example, 50% of the diamonds (by weight) in the world's jewellery passed through this Indian segment. Some Indian firms have been so successful that they have decided to open or acquire polishing factories in Belgium, in order to ensure higher quality standards. This industry's vitality will certainly continue to shape the economic landscape of the diamond market in the immediate future.

The current situation

Remarkably, the traditional distribution channel continues to function. It still helps to assure stability, although in the year 2000 it dealt with 'only' 60% of the world's diamonds (compared to 80% a decade earlier). The figures speak for themselves: the world produced a total of $7.5 billion of rough diamonds in 2000. The DTC bought $4.38 billion and sold $5.67 billion. To put this into context, the global sales figure for diamond jewellery amounted to $56.3 billion in 1999, including $13 billion that solely relates to the value of the diamonds contained in that jewellery.

In late summer in the year 2000, De Beers announced that it was implementing some far-reaching structural changes. The idea is to be more in tune with the marketplace by getting closer to the customer, whilst exploiting growth opportunities presented by the big luxury goods firms. It therefore created a new company: the DTC (Diamond Trading Company). The DTC took over from the CSO, whose initials disappeared after several decades of service. The new DTC also aims to ensure consumer protection, by establishing official distribution channels through firms that adhere to a 'best-practice' charter. By buying diamonds direct from recognised DTC sources, customers will be able to assure themselves that their gems did not fuel conflicts in unstable countries, that its cutting did not involve child labour, and that the gem is legitimate. In this way, the company aims to get closer to its consumers, which are more critical and responsible than ever before.

The crater at the Mir ('Peace') mine in Siberia

The Russian channel

In 1959, only a few years after diamonds had been discovered in Yakutia (Republic of Sakha), De Beers signed a contract with the government of the USSR. From 1992 onwards, however, the Russians started exporting small, poor-quality diamonds on the open market, outside the De Beers channel. Prices began to fall for this category of goods. Soon, significant quantities of diamonds were finding their way directly to cutting centres. The pipeline was leaking. Today, Russia accounts for 20% of the world's rough diamonds: the equivalent of 1.6 billion dollars. Supposedly, one-third is sold inside the country to Russian cutting factories, but there is no doubt that some of these rough diamonds are being diverted to other destinations. De Beers still has a share, in accordance with its Russian contract, but part of the production finds its way to private purchasers throughout the world. Roughly speaking, one can say Russian production is divided into three parts: one part supplies the DTC (former CSO), another part supplies Antwerp and Ramat Gan, plus some to India, and remainder supplies the local market. Although diamonds may initially escape from the traditional supply chain, they often end up re-entering it later on: after they have been cut in Antwerp or Ramat Gan, for example. Over the past few years, the Russian jewellery industry has undergone remarkable growth. Therefore, diamonds can be mined, cut and set in the same country. As with the traditional channel, poor-quality diamonds are either destined for industrial use, or sent to India. Clearly, the home-grown Russian pipeline was simply copied from the pipeline that De Beers had patiently constructed over the years. However, there is one important issue to remember: Russia's production is important enough (both in quantity and quality) for this channel to be a key part of the world diamond trade. However, De Beers has never looked like being completely cut out of the system: it provides tempting promises of price stability, and regular supply of a whole range of goods.

Canada: a new diamond pipeline?

Canada is beginning to emerge into the world diamond scene. It has some potentially rich mines that are only just beginning production. It could account for 10% of the world's production by value in 2003. This is probably just the beginning: diamond-prospecting operations are still coming up with highly promising findings. Inevitably, the country is faced with a dilemma: what should be done with these diamonds? If they are sold in the rough state, the country will lose out on the 'value-added' revenues that are apportioned by diamond-cutting. Moreover, diamond-cutting is a relatively new industry for Canada: it could present attractive employment opportunities for the population. Some cutting workshops have already opened, and jewellers have started to market 'home-grown diamonds'. If this system were to be extended, it might be possible to create a truly 'clean', conflict-free pipeline in Canada. This development depends upon several factors, primarily the quantity, size and quality of the diamonds that will ultimately be extracted from the mines, and of course the level of demand for them. De Beers is still important in this process because it is the only entity that has sufficient power to maintain buffer stocks: the nascent pipeline will be too weak for a long time to come. In value terms, 35% of Canadian diamonds go through the traditional CSO/DTC pipeline.

What does the future hold?

2000 was a year of surprises for the diamond industry, quite apart from the transformation of De Beers. It is difficult to predict the future for the diamond industry. The millennium celebrations resulted in unprecedented demand for diamonds. This was accentuated by an extraordinarily strong publicity campaign, orchestrated by De Beers. Diamond stocks melted away, and simultaneously all of the major operators in the global diamond market found themselves in a healthy financial position. Some of these companies have formulated lofty ambitions on the strength of this nest-egg: for example, the De Beers group is attempting to make acquisitions that will enable it to control 50% of world diamond production by value, compared to the 43 % that it holds at present.

These are not the only changes in the industry. Politicians are trying to change the way the diamond industry works. The international community has been shocked by the violence of certain African civil wars. Diamond money fans the flames of these conflicts, and politicians are trying to impose a code of ethics on the industry. The companies in the industry have adopted drastic measures to eliminate conflict diamonds from the market. A well-managed diamond business can, in fact, be a source of prosperity and stability for a country: Botswana is an excellent example of this. A code of conduct is necessary, in order to ensure rectitude in the industry. From now on, rough diamonds will be imported and exported with certification, attesting to their country of origin. Unfortunately, some independent traders have established extremely sinister business links, and it is currently impossible to guarantee that all the diamonds in the market are free from any taint of conflict. The industry is still trying to get its house in order. It appears that the problem concerned 4% of global diamond production. It is estimated that this figure has now been reduced to 2%. To date, it has proved impossible to develop laboratory tests that are capable of definitively identifying where a diamond came from: it is sometimes possible for parcels of stones, but loose single stones are far harder to identify.

There are many factors affecting the future of the diamond industry: the expansion of the Indian system, the potential of Canada, structural changes within De Beers… It is therefore difficult to predict what the future holds. However, it is possible to stay informed from day to day, by consulting the excellent website www.keyguide.net. It provides a list of all the De Beers sight-holders, and is a good source for industry news and gossip. www.diamondnews.com also has a great deal of information. www.Mondera.com is a fine example of a site that is creating an electronic distribution network for diamonds on the Internet. In order to find out about De Beers and its activities, the www.debeersgroup.com and www.debeers.ca websites are very useful. For information on the Argyle mine, www.ashton.net.au is a good place to start. www.gemkey.com is also worth a visit. Websites such as these enable us to find information on the diamond industry, and they may help us to predict its future.

A cutting workshop in the Mumbai region

A man founding discs for diamond cutting and grinding wheels at Surat, India.

CHAPTER VI

Michael Seal
and Hubert Bari

From Jewels to Tools

Many people still nostalgically remember the good old record player turntables and their black vinyl discs. But how many people realise that many tunes, such as the Beatles' "Lucy in the Sky with Diamonds" were only rendered audible thanks to a minor engineering miracle: a tiny diamond, tracing the undulations in a long, spiral, microscopic furrow. This technique and its characteristic scraping noise may have fallen into disuse, but it was not the only use that inventors found for this peerless gem over the years. Diamond is hard - very hard. In fact, it is one of the hardest industrial materials presently known. Everyone knows that, not least the industrialists who keep finding so many uses for it. Shaping, cutting, slicing, grinding, wire-drawing: the stone is second to none. Its properties are also turned upon itself: without diamond, it would be impossible to cut diamonds! Its hardness has been the main factor behind the development of a whole panoply of diamond tools. In the second half of the 20th century, however, it was discovered that this assemblage of carbon atoms had many additional extraordinary properties. This has provoked a resurgence of interest in the topic: in 1990, diamond was even nominated "Molecule of the Year" by the famous American journal Science, and today, this molecule is the subject of research topic for at least three thousand scientists around the world. These researchers' names may be added to the long roster of pioneers who repeatedly tried to make artificial diamonds, and who ultimately succeeded. These are exceptional people, whose story is worth telling. Diamonds are not mere fripperies. They are important in economics and technology, and continue to promote development in electronics and materials science.

Diamond, an irreplaceable tool

The Indians or the Chinese were probably the first to make use of diamonds, as cutting and engraving tools. There are documents dating from the 2nd or 4th century that attest to the use of diamond for engraving jade. The Chinese were astonished to find that the men of '*Fu-lin*' (Rome) would wear such a useful stone as an ornament. The celebrated *Intaille de Julie* gem carving (in the French National Library) is of stupefying magnificence, and only a diamond tool could have produced such artistry in a stone as hard as aquamarine. In Africa, some ethnologists believe that the rupestral patterns covering some rocks in the Kalahari Desert were made with diamond tools. These rocks have proved to be very durable, and the designs are of great precision. By using a splinter of diamond found at the site, mounted in a piece of wood, experimental archaeologists were easily able to produce engravings comparable to those on the desert blocks.

Naturally, when cutting diamonds, it is necessary to use diamond abrasives. Since the end of the 14th century, when diamond polishing was invented in Italy, people have needed diamond powder. Indeed, nothing can abrade the precious gem, except its own powder. People very quickly learned to produce diamond powder by hammering impure diamonds or diamond fragments between sheets of lead (to save all the dust). This powder is then kept in suspension in oil. This suspension was then ready for use in gem-cutting and, through the centuries, nothing fundamentally changed. Diamond powder thus became an essential item of commerce. In addition to cutting and polishing powder,

John Harrison's famous marine chronometer, made in 1759. Its ornate dial conceals a mechanism that uses diamonds, as bearings and at the tip of the escapement. Greenwich Observatory, Greenwich.

A batch of diamond crystals, mostly of industrial quality. The majority of them are either fibrous in structure, or aggregates of smaller crystals. Most will be crushed into abrasive grit. A small number of the best crystals will be used in jewellery.

there were also diamond engraving tools and, of course, the famous glazier's diamond. The existence of this tool is recorded in manuscript no. 165 of the St. Salvatore Convent in Bologna, dating from the first half of the 15th century: "If you want to cut glass or make little mirrors from a large one, take a diamond and scratch the mirror with the point of the stone and immediately dip the plate in water. As soon as you tap it with dexterity, it will break at the places where the diamond passed".

Much more recently, diamond came to be used as a cutting tool for lathes and milling machines. A diamond cutting tool was employed by J. Ramsden in 1779, for the manufacture of his high-precision astronomical instruments. He cut the dividing circles of his instruments and the steps of his micrometer screws in this way. Even more astonishingly, diamond was used in one of the most extraordinary human technological adventures: the invention of the marine chronometer. To avoid all friction and wear, John Harrison hit upon the idea of using diamond pivots and endstones in his prototype chronometer, the legendary H4. He had the diamonds cut by an unknown master, under conditions that remain mysterious. Furthermore, the tip of escapement which marks time at high speed is furnished with a curved surface diamond. No one knows how Harrison was able to obtain such an astonishing shape. He provided no explanation for his marvellous chronometer in his memoirs. But, thanks to this spectacular employment of diamonds outside the jewellery field, seafarers finally acquired an instrument that allowed longitude to be precisely determined, in 1759. This permitted secure navigation, and the making of exact maps of our planet.

However, the heyday of the industrial use of diamond occurred in the 19th century. This was the time of the Industrial Revolution, which generated enormous demand for manufactured products. These could not be manufactured or shaped with precision without diamond. The first patent for a diamond grinding-wheel was granted to A. L. Caverdon of Paris, in 1878. The use of coolant was described in a patent that was awarded to Carl Zeiss (Jena, Germany) in 1907, for "an improved tool for rough grinding or abrading glass", actually a diamond-loaded copper roller. Undoubtedly, however, grinding wheels made of cast iron embedded with diamond powder must have been used previously. The concave, diamond-charged, cast-iron wheels used by Pritchard in 1824 to grind diamond microscope lenses are a good example. Diamond saws, trepans, drills, and truing tools followed in the late nineteenth century, but diamond grinding wheels truly began to come into their own in the 1920s and 1930s. This expansion was the result of the invention of sintered carbide cutting tools, which were so hard that they could only be shaped by diamond. Such tools were in great demand for industrial and military production during World War II. Diamond became a strategic material. It was necessary for shielding tanks and various vehicles and for machining aircraft components. In the post-war period, demand carried over from tanks to cars, and from military to civil aircraft. An industry arose, based upon the hardness of these battle-winning materials, and tungsten carbide and diamond were the star products.

Drills (for piercing), trepans (for boring) and, of course, saws developed alongside grinding wheels. The history of this use of diamond dates back to Diderot, who mentions it in his Encyclopaedia (1751). In France, patents were filed in 1854 (supplemented in 1855) by the engineer Hermann. The engineer Leschot filed a similar patent in 1862. In this period, mines were more important than the oil industry. The 19th century brought many very important developments, not only in drilling machinery driving power but also in deep-shaft drilling techniques. Nevertheless, it was not until after the Second World War, and the explosion of oil-industry prospecting, that remarkable progress was made in trepans with diamond-set drill crowns. These trepans are used at the ends of trains of tubes that penetrate deep into the Earth, often from an ocean-based drilling platform. Such trepans were the beneficiaries of very precise design work: each diamond set in the crown occupies a precisely-calculated position based upon the characteristics of the cooling system and the flow of water that flushes drilling debris away. Today, tunnelling machines - monstrous machines that eat into solid rock - sometimes have diamond 'jaws'.

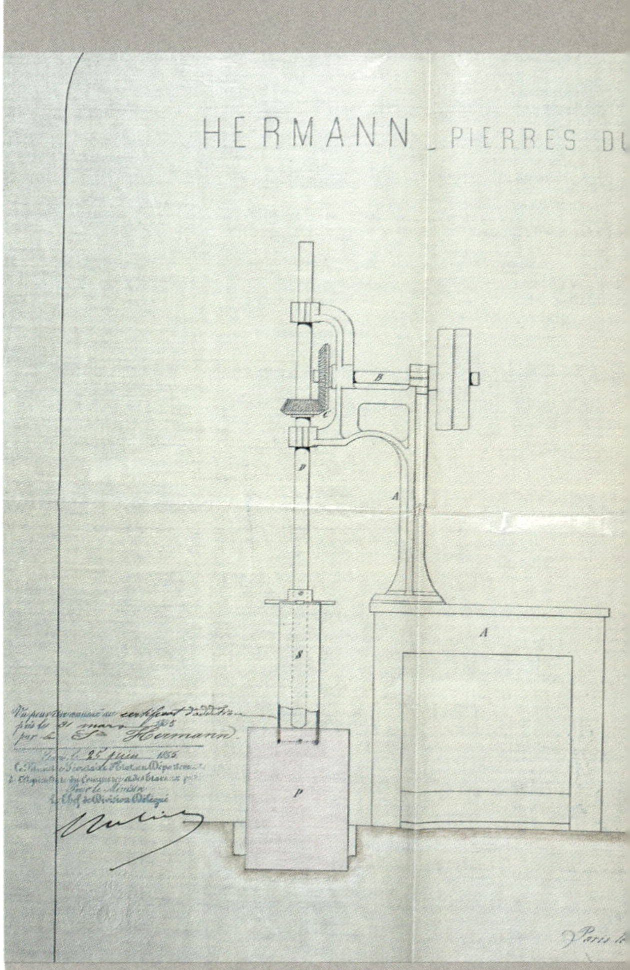

Saws may also be used to cut into rock. These were developed in France, first of all by Félix Frombolt in 1885. They were first used in a quarry at Euville (Meuse) in 1898. Quarries still use enormous quantities of diamond saws to this day. From tombstones to skyscraper façades, no slab of stone escapes the grip of the diamond. In the famous Carrara marble quarries, the giant blocks are cut with wires coated with oil containing diamond powder. On a much smaller scale, the high-precision cutting of silicon-chip wafers is performed using diamond tools, as is the cutting of pasta in the food industry. Finally, geological research would not be what it is today without the preparation of thin slices of rock, using diamond saws and abrasive powders.

Two drawings from the patent-application file submitted by Hermann, a French engineer, in 1854-1855. They display a hole-drilling machine, and a mechanism to dress grinding wheels. The diamonds can be seen in the pictures: they are drawn in grey, set in a blue framework. French National Intellectual Property Institute Archives, Paris.

One cannot end this description of the usefulness of diamond without mentioning a very special application, which has revolutionised the technique of wire drawing. To make wire from non-ferrous metals, one has to force the metal through a die which grows progressively narrow. The die has to be especially hard. We thus went from steel dies at the end of the Middle Ages, to tungsten carbide, then ruby (hardness 9), finally reaching diamond dies (hardness 10). A die is usually made from monocrystalline diamond, or a synthetic polycrystalline aggregate. It is pierced to the final diameter of the wire needed. The hole is, in fact, conical. The metal is forced into the die. The final straight part, the 'throat', determines the diameter of the wire that emerges, and also its quality: the surface condition of the die determines the surface quality of the wire. The only limit to the successful use of diamond in wire-drawing is the difficulty in drilling diamond dies to the correct diameter. The first patent was filed by Brockendon in Great Britain in 1819. However, it was again the French, Milan and Balloflet, who succeeded in perfecting a process for the manufacture of diamond dies, in about 1860. Today, millions of diamond dies are produced every year. The hole is precisely laser-drilled. This technology was developed in the USA in 1966, to replace the old method of electrolytic drilling.

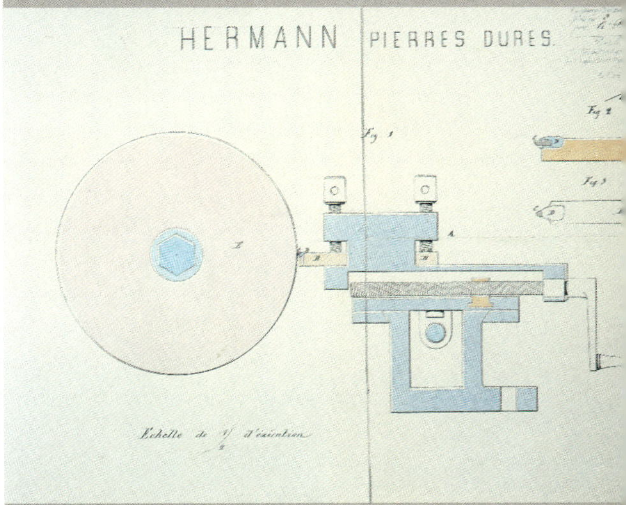

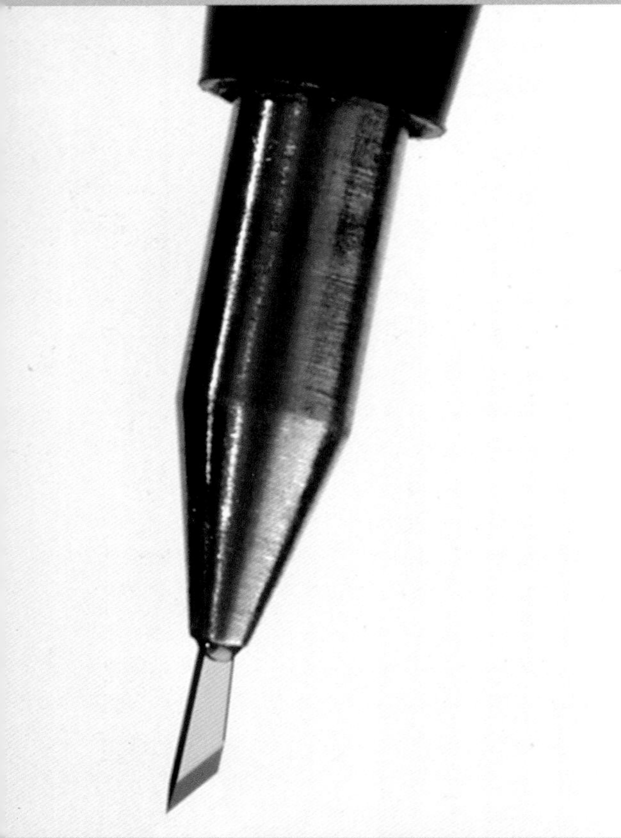

Astonishingly, diamonds are also used in medicine. This is perhaps the most extraordinary use for diamonds, and it has radically changed the practice of microsurgery. It was developed by one of the authors (Michael Seal), who has devoted 40 years of his life to the development of diamond technology. For him, bringing diamond scalpels to fruition was the most exciting development of his career. The main advantage of using diamond as a cutting tool is that it is a material that is both extremely hard and also fracture-resistant (as long as one takes the cleavage plane into account). Diamonds can be honed to a sharper edge than any other known material. This edge will resist the pressure exerted upon it, because of the extremely strong bonding of the carbon atoms. This is not the case with even the hardest steels: the weaker bonds are not able to prevent the edges from blunting or rounding off. Diamond scalpels have an almost unimaginable sharpness. Testing the edge by running one's finger over it is out of the question. A cut is inevitable, however little force is exerted. Surgeons are well aware of this: surgery with a diamond scalpel requires great dexterity, otherwise the cut will be deeper than intended. This ultra-sharp tool is particularly suited to ophthalmology: diamond scalpels are required for corneal incisions in nearly all the cataract operations performed in western countries. The diamond edge is so fine that it produces very clean cuts with less damage to the tissue, and thus more rapid healing. Finally, diamond has the property of naturally spreading the two edges of cut tissue, thus helping the surgeon to see the effects of the cut more clearly. Very encouraging results have been reported in hand, nerve, and heart surgery. Unfortunately, the uptake of diamond scalpels is restricted by the size of the blades and also by their very high cost. This is the case for blades produced from both natural diamonds and large synthetic diamonds, which are equally costly.

A surgical scalpel with a diamond blade, made by the Drukker company in Amsterdam.

A diamond knife, used to cut optical fibres. Made by the Drukker company, Amsterdam.

Ultimately, the solution to this problem of cost may come from diamonds that are produced synthetically from low-pressure gases (so-called CVD diamonds). However, these polycrystalline diamond aggregates cannot yet be polished in order to obtain a perfect edge. The ability to shape and polish this material, or even that of producing significantly large monocrystalline surfaces, would not only revolutionise surgery, but also all cutting tools, starting with knives. Razor blades coated with a CVD diamond film are already being sold commercially. The edge quality cannot be better than that of the underlying steel, but at least the diamond film will prevent it from becoming worn, and its life will be substantially increased. In the near future, the production of diamond-coated blades will become widespread such as the production of pure diamond blades.

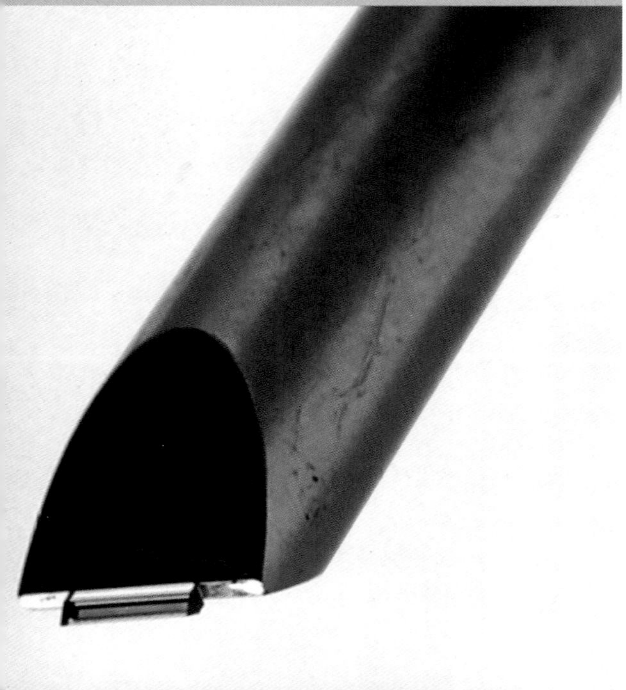

Diamond has so many uses that an entire industry has developed, in order to sort and make diamond powders. Sorting systems have been developed to categorise diamonds based on their crystal faces: some uses require octahedra, while others require more fibrous diamonds. All types of diamond, catalogued by shape and by form, are integrated in specialised grinding wheels. Similarly, people have developed methods to crush diamond, in order to obtain specific powders with grains that have a specific shape and character. Finally, some perfect stones have to be diverted from the jewellery industry, to make scalpels and some other very special and costly items. The most famous of these was the window for an optical instrument on the Pioneer Venus space probe. Diamond was the only substance that could be used in order to make a window capable of resisting the corrosive atmosphere of the planet Venus, which the probe penetrated in 1978. Furthermore, the window was particularly well-suited to its task, as diamond has the property of being transparent to infrared radiation. The diamond in the Pioneer window, 18.2 mm in diameter by 2.8 mm thick, allowed the probe to take images of the atmosphere for 40 seconds, before the probe fell to the surface of the fiery planet, along with its precious diamond. One can only imagine how much this little window might have cost.

As demand for the precious gem grew, it very quickly prompted scientists to search for ways of manufacturing man-made synthetic diamond. Their first steps differed little from the path that the alchemists of the Middle Ages and Renaissance followed, when they tried to make gold. This quest

A heap of diamonds, ready to be sorted at De Beers' headquarters in London. Most of the diamonds in this pile are destined for industrial use.

involved pioneering research into the world of high pressure. A specialist, Robert M. Hazen, wrote a book on the topic. It is a veritable novel of scientific adventure: The *Diamond Makers*. This book provides portraits of many of the scientists whose hearts leapt at the thought of artificial diamonds. These pioneers were Scottish, French, Swedish, and American, and it is worthwhile providing a synopsis of their story.

Diamond alchemists

The quest for the synthesis of diamond proved to be amongst the most fascinating adventures in the history of science. Everybody dreamed about it: diamond had always been worth much more than gold, and its composition (carbon) had been known since 1796, thanks to the work of the English researcher, Tennant. Nobody doubted that there must be a trick to reaching it. Charlatans applied themselves to the task at a very early stage, but the first serious candidate was a Scot, James Ballantyne Hannay. His position as director of a chemical enterprise left him the time and the material assets to pursue various experiments at high temperatures and pressures. It was during the 1870s that strange results on the dissolution of sodium in paraffin led him to imagine an unexpected way of synthesising diamond. In fact, he obtained a very hard, black, carbon-like residue from his experiments. From there, he tried to dissolve carboniferous materials in a furnace and observe their crystallisation as they cooled. He only obtained graphite. Meanwhile, news reached him of the discovery of the Kimberley mines, and the idea of remote formation of diamonds at great depths within the Earth. He therefore introduced pressure as a new factor in his experiments. Oils were introdu-

186 LE FOUR ÉLECTRIQUE

Nous avons disposé un four électrique en pierre de Courson, analogue à ceux que nous employons journellement, mais dont le fond portait une ouverture cylindrique de 6cm de diamètre. Les électrodes qui amenaient le courant avaient 5cm de diamètre; celle du pôle positif était creuse; elle portait, suivant son axe, un canal cylindrique de 18mm de diamètre dans lequel pouvait se mouvoir avec facilité une tige de fer, que l'on avançait ou que l'on reculait à volonté.

Ce four (fig. 39) était disposé sur deux tréteaux et en dessous

FIG. 39. — Four à grenaille.

se trouvait une marmite de fer, contenant du mercure sur une épaisseur de 10 cm, surmonté d'une couche d'eau deux fois plus épaisse. On commençait par faire jaillir l'arc, et l'on employait un courant de 1000 ampères et 60 volts. Lorsque le régime normal

Two pages from Moissan's famous book *The Electric Furnace*, published in Paris in 1897. The upper engraving shows the furnace in operation.
The lower engraving shows the residual crystals that appeared during Moissan's experiments, which he believed to be diamonds. In fact, they were silicon carbide, which is now known as moissanite.
Muséum national d'histoire naturelle, Paris, Chemistry Laboratory Library.

178 LE FOUR ÉLECTRIQUE

Les attaques se font par les procédés qui ont été décrits plus haut.

Nous avons obtenu ainsi les diamants noirs de la figure 31 et des diamants transparents.

Un de ces diamants transparents (fig. 32) mesurait 0mm,38, soit environ quatre dixièmes de millimètre dans sa plus grande longueur. Son aspect était tout à fait caractéristique; il tombait dans l'iodure de méthylène et, brûlé dans la petite nacelle de platine, il a disparu dans l'oxygène vers 900° en fournissant de l'acide carbonique. En retirant avec précaution la nacelle, du tube dans lequel avait été faite la combustion, on retrouva à la

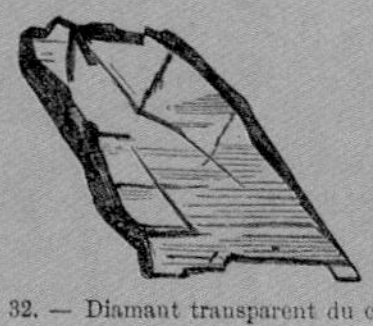

FIG. 32. — Diamant transparent du cylindre.

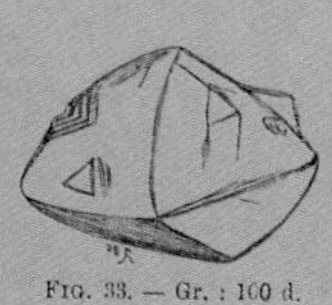

FIG. 33. — Gr. : 100 d.

place de ce petit fragment, une trace de cendres, à peine visible au microscope, ayant conservé la même forme et qui avait une couleur d'un gris ocreux.

Un diamant (fig. 33) d'une belle limpidité et bien cristallisé, provenant d'une autre préparation, a brûlé de même dans l'oxygène en ne laissant pas de cendres.

D'une façon générale, lorsque le fer employé dans ces expériences est bien exempt de silicium et lorsque le creuset ne renferme pas d'alumine, les fragments noirs ou transparents ne fournissent point de cendres par leur combustion dans l'oxygène.

Expériences faites dans la limaille de fer. — Il nous a sem-

ced into iron tubes, along with lithium. The tubes were then welded shut and heated to almost 1,000°C, whereupon the pressure rose considerably. Most of the time the tubes exploded, and more than once Hannay's laboratory narrowly escaped destruction. One of his assistants was wounded. At the beginning of 1880, nevertheless, there was a reward for all the risks incurred and for the destruction of all these furnaces. Minute colourless crystals were found at the bottom of a tube. Analysis removed all doubts: they were diamonds! Hannay published his results the same year in *Nature* ("Artificial Diamond") and in the *Proceedings of the Royal Society of London* ("On the Artificial Formation of the Diamonds"). Hannay's first diamonds were deposited in the Natural History Museum in London. The controversy continues to this day: are these diamonds natural or not? The most widely advanced hypothesis is that Hannay's technicians, tired of risking their lives, introduced natural diamonds into an experiment to speed up the end of the research! Michael Seal has studied Hannay's diamonds carefully, and is not so sure.

From there, we turn to the work of a Frenchman, Henri Moissan. After his apprenticeship at the *Muséum national d'histoire naturelle*, he obtained a post at the *École de Pharmacie*, where he worked for a long time on the characterisation of the element fluorine, which he was the first to isolate. In 1906, that earned him the first French Nobel Prize for chemistry. Moissan's second research project concerned synthetic diamond. He set out with an undeniable advantage: his mastery of high temperature work, thanks to the electric arc furnace that he was developing, which would ultimately revolutionise the research. Moissan was aware that diamond is the result of imposing high temperature and high pressure upon carbon. He reached these conclusions by studying natural diamond, as a good naturalist trained at the *Muséum* should. He was thus the first to notice that, in kimberlites, diamond is very frequently in a microscopic state, as a not uncommon constituent of the rock. Diamonds are thus not accidents in the rock, but are an integral part of it, through a process that people were beginning to think was volcanic. Now, whoever speaks of volcanoes speaks of heat! He also investigated the dissolution of metallic fragments from the Canyon Diablo meteorite (a famous meteor strike that created a crater in Arizona), and found microscopic diamonds there. His deductions are clear: shock means pressure... But, more than that, he noticed the association with a metal, an iron/nickel alloy that characterises this meteorite.

His observations led him to produce pools of molten iron in his furnace, which reached 3,000°C. He used these as solvents, to absorb the carbon placed in the furnace in the form of caramel (rather overcooked caramel, naturally)! After cooling, the mass of iron was dissolved in acid. The first experiments only yielded a black residue: a return to simple carbon. To obtain the pressure, Moissan had the ingenious idea of dropping the molten metal crucible into water. When brutally quenched in this manner, the metal developed a solid envelope around a still-molten centre. As the outer metal cooled, it contracted, creating high pressure in the centre of the sample. Moissan improved the process still further by quenching the crucible in molten lead, a better conductor of heat than water. The iron cooled more quickly, and the pressure rose further! After dissolution, the residues revealed microscopic particles, little crystals that Moissan believed to be diamond. His conclusions were published in his 1904 monograph *Le Four électrique* ('The Electric Furnace') and, to his death, Moissan remained convinced that he had succeeded in synthesising the gem. Alas, later analyses have proved that the micro-crystals were, in fact, silicon carbide. This mineral was discovered in nature later on, in the impact zones of meteorites, and it was baptised moissanite in the scientist's honour. Today, moissanite is produced artificially in large quantities, and is one of the most perfect diamond imitations.

During the course of Moissan's experiments, that same year (1904), a swindler pretended to have successfully synthesised large diamonds. This was the beginning of the "Lemoine Affair", which caused a furore in Paris at the beginning of the century. Using skills worthy of a conjurer, Lemoine made beautiful diamonds 'appear' in his experimental preparations. Sir Julius Werner, the representative of De Beers, was astonished and purchased the secret and exclusive rights to the process for a fortune: more than a million francs. Alas, very quickly De Beers discovered that the 'diamonds' produced by this 'scientist' actually came from its own mines: they had all the properties and appearance of natural diamond. Complaint, depositions, law-suit: the Lemoine Affair was born. On July 6th, 1909, the swindler was sentenced to six years in prison. People would have forgotten the affair completely had it not piqued Marcel Proust's imagination. He devoted part of his *Pastiches et Mélanges* to the Lemoine affair. These pages are bravura masterpieces of literature, recalling the better works of Saint-Simon, Michelet, Balzac, Flaubert, etc. Although Lemoine never produced diamonds, at least he can claim to have created several pearls... of French literature!

These alchemists' achievements should not be discounted: as a result of their work, pressure was incorporated into the process of diamond synthesis. In 1938, the theoretical research of Frederick Rossini and Ralph Jessup led to the publication of the first phase diagram, a diagram which delineated the stability zones of graphite and diamond under different temperature and pressure conditions. This work revealed that the required pressures were far higher than had been thought. The way was open for new practical research, founded upon a sound theoretical foundation that showed the way ahead. Berman and Simon produced a new diagram in 1953-1954, allowing the target, and the remaining difficulties, to be defined even more accurately.

The double victory

The true heroes in the adventure of diamond synthesis are the Americans and the Swedes. In fact, the Swedes arrived there first, although they never publicised their discovery and were thus officially dethroned by the Americans. In Sweden, diamond synthesis was achieved under the auspices of ASEA (Allmana Svenska Elektriska Aktienbolaget), which was inspired by a strange scientist's unusual project. This scientist's name - Balthazar von Platten - his personality, his monocle, and the incredible equipment that he developed would have been enough to inspire a scriptwriter. Von Platten developed equipment that could attain very high pressures, in an extremely baroque and ultra-secret context. This unprecedented and bizarre machine resembled an attempt to reconstruct the Earth in miniature. At its heart, there was a preparation that contained carbon. Six steel cones made up a spherical shape that surrounded this heart, and a mechanical press put the sample under pressure, thus recreating the forces at the heart of the Earth. The pressure bore down from all directions, whereas a standard press exerts a unidirectional force. The process was extremely complex. The spherical shape was composed of numerous elements, which had to be replaced after each experiment. The press that supplied the pressure was extremely heavy. The heat came from an envelope of thermite, a potentially explosive, combustible material that surrounded the carbon and metal heart. The first experiments, in the 1940s, were unsuccessful. ASEA dismantled the laboratory. Von Platten transferred everything to a beautiful palace in Stockholm, where he resumed his work. Nevertheless, after the war ASEA re-launched the project, but von Platten was only a consultant. On February 16th, 1953, the new project head, Erik Lundblad, performed an experiment at a pressure of 83,000 atmospheres that yielded the first diamond. Curiously, the project team - the Quintius Project - kept silent. In any case, the process was too complicated to permit the delivery masses of *Koh-i-Noors*, as von Platten had dreamed of when he put his ideas to ASEA for consideration.

In parallel, Percy Bridgman was exploring the world of high pressure in his Harvard University laboratory, with enormous success. Thanks to the development of new very hard alloys, like tungsten carbide, Bridgman was able to design extremely resistant cells. He exposed them to pressures attaining 70,000 and ultimately even 400,000 atmospheres. These new very hard alloys were made by the General Electric Company. Diamonds were needed to shape them, and the company suggested that Bridgman should perform research on the graphite/diamond conversion. Bridgman was a brilliant scientist, who obtained the Nobel Prize in 1946 for his work on high pressure. He frantically tried to perform the conversion, but without success. The tungsten carbide cells suffered a reduction in hardness as the temperature rose, and Bridgman was not able to reach the required combination of pressure and temperature. It was during this research that the ASEA team triumphed, but without publicity.

The final victory - that is to say, a diamond synthesis that was reproducible and adaptable as an industrial process - was achieved by a research team back at the General Electric Company. The team had been formed especially for this challenge, under the scope of an ultra-secret project called "Project Superpressure". The team leader was Anthony Nerad, who recruited Francis Bundy and Herbert Strong internally, from within GE. He added the two Robert Wentorfs (father and son), and then the person who was to become a key figure in the team, GE chemical engineer Tracy Hall, and finally also James Cheney. The laboratory was set up in Schenectady in New York State, where a giant press was soon constructed. The press anvils and the pressure cell where the force was applied were developed from Bridgman's work, but it was Hall who played a major role in determining the new shape of the anvils that would exert pressure on the cell. As Moissan had suggested, a metal was used as the carbon solvent on the day when they finally achieved their victory. This victory occurred four years after the project's launch, just as GE was on the point of putting an end to the project, whose costs had already been considerable. The 'Holy Grail' was reached in the night of

December 8th-9th, 1954. Two small diamonds were found in the metallic preparation. The rest of the story follows the classic procedure for every scientific discovery: repetition of the experiment by the same team, then by an independent team, process improvements... GE announced the news in a press conference on February 15th, 1955. The announcement released a storm of panic amongst jewellers and diamond dealers, who feared that their diamond stocks would be devalued to the price of coal! As De Beers shares dropped, those of GE rocketed up, a sign that synthetic diamond was seen as both an industrial and a commercial challenge. The process was improved very rapidly, and became routine. Bridgman visited the Project Superpressure laboratory during the summer of 1955 and was invited to make a batch of diamonds for himself, which he took away, fascinated. It was the detente after the victory, and Wentorf enjoyed it. He made diamonds from the most unexpected carbon sources. His most famous joke was to go to his usual grocery and buy his favourite peanut butter there. He placed a spoonful of the peanut butter in the press. Shortly afterwards, it yielded some small green diamonds! It took GE scarcely two years of development before the company launched the first man-made diamonds on to the market.

Today, diamond synthesis is disappointingly routine. Besides GE, the major producers are De Beers (in various factories in Ireland and South Africa, for example), and also the former USSR. There are batteries of presses around the world. Special ingredients are introduced into these presses and exposed to furnace conditions, and several minutes later they yield discs of metal that merely have to be dissolved away to reveal the diamonds. More than 100 tons of diamond are made this way every year. The ex-USSR remains very active in this field, and the laboratories that pioneered industrial diamond production have continued their research, with a view to overcoming the challenge of producing high-quality stones weighing at least a carat. This involves a growth process, based upon a seed crystal that is nourished by a reservoir of carbon-saturated metal. The process takes time, sometimes weeks, and the high pressure needs to be constantly maintained in order to reach several carats. It is not profitable. In its research, De Beers has achieved up to 30 carats! However, synthetic diamonds of several millimetres in size can be profitably grown in a few days, and these stones are used to manufacture wire-drawing dies. All these large crystals have a poor, brown-to-yellow colour, due to various impurities, essentially nitrogen. We should note that the production of synthetic diamonds for jewellery remains pointless: such stones' production costs are much greater than the cost of extracting natural diamonds, and the description "artificial" makes them impossible to sell. There is a perfect precedent for this: over the past century, the production of hundreds of tons of synthetic ruby has never harmed the market for the natural stone.

Synthetic diamond thus basically remains confined to the production of abrasive grit and crystals for saws, where it meets 90% of demand. The remaining 10% is natural, industrial-quality diamond, that is usually extracted as a by-product from diamond mines whose profitability is exclusively based on gem-quality diamonds. It is worth noting that one of the mixtures that the victorious GE team used in their tests led Robert Wentorf to the discovery of Borazon. This is the trade name for cubic boron nitride, which is almost as hard as diamond and which, unlike diamond, is stable at very high temperatures. Thus, in a few months, GE developed the two most exceptional abrasives in existence. Half century later, these products still dominate the market.

It is worthwhile mentioning an alternative method of diamond synthesis under high pressure: the explosive method. Whereas the methods previously described were inspired by those that prevail in the Earth's mantle, the explosive method copies the process by which diamonds are generated during meteorite impacts. The American company Du Pont, a leader in explosives production, distinguished itself by producing diamonds in some old abandoned mines, by submitting a metal and graphite mixture to the shockwave from the detonation of several tons of explosives. Once the resulting preparation is recovered, it is dissolved in acid, to yield diamond in the form of an extremely fine powder, much sought after for... the final polishing of diamonds!

Synthetic diamonds made by General Electric. Both rough crystals and brilliant-cut gems are shown. Remarkably, synthetic diamonds usually develop perfect cubic crystal faces, which is rare in nature. In this case, bluish and yellowish colours have been achieved, due to the inclusion of impurities.

Two scanning-electron-microscope photographs, displaying the diamond layers produced by CVD. By manipulating the deposition conditions, different crystal types can be favoured: the top photo shows a layer that is mainly made up of macles, whereas the lower photo shows an aggregate of cubic crystals. Paris-XIII University, Paris, High Pressure and Materials Engineering Laboratory.

CVD diamonds, or the triumph of low pressure

This was a surprise that appeared out of the blue: it is possible to make diamonds at low pressures. In fact, this technique may even have the greatest potential for the future. Bridgman had predicted that there was a very narrow window of possibility for diamond to grow under low pressure. Some American researchers had tackled the problem in the 1950s, with a few results that had remained unnoticed. The yield was extremely low. The principle is denoted by the acronym CVD (*Chemical Vapour Deposition*). The phenomenon also exists in nature: diamonds form in the coronas of stars under low-pressure conditions in a near-vacuum, as explained in Chapter III. The process consists in forming a gas plasma of carbon atoms at high temperature, and in causing their deposition on an appropriate substrate where they assemble themselves into the structure of diamond. In a way, it is the layer-by-layer construction of a diamond film. The first difficulties involved the tendency of the deposit to adopt random structures: sometimes graphite, sometimes diamond. Now, after decades of experiments, the process seems to have been mastered.

The CVD process most commonly yields a polycrystalline film, that is to say one in which there are myriad microscopic crystals, intertwined with each other. Current research is aimed at producing monocrystalline films, with a single crystal that would develop on the substrate. Researchers are also trying to solve the problem of finding a way to deposit diamond on any material whatsoever, at lower temperatures. Currently, the surface on which the carbon atoms are deposited has to be maintained at a temperature in the order of 800°C at best. This is not particularly high, but few everyday materials can withstand such heat. In future, this technique could have the potential to "diamondise" surfaces that are exposed to everyday wear. In this way, it is hoped that glass could be made completely scratch-proof - starting with spectacle lenses. All surfaces that are exposed to abrasion would ultimately become unusable.

However, in the future there may be alternative potential applications for the CVD process. By controlling the growth conditions of the diamond film perfectly, atom by atom, scientists will be able to make practical use of this mineral's conductive properties. It is the best heat conductor known, and incorporating layers of such films in an electronic circuit will permit waste heat to be removed much more efficiently. These films would not affect the circuit's function, because diamond is an electric insulator... but only when it is pure! Diamond can be made slightly conductive to electricity by merely adding impurities, such as boron, in tiny quantities (one in several million atoms). This ability of diamond to become a semiconductor will become the battleground of the future. Diamond would be able to dethrone silicon, providing integrated circuits that would be much more resistant to wear, and capable of functioning at high temperatures, since they would themselves dissipate the heat that they produce. The CVD process ought to be perfectly mastered, by 'knitting' together a regular, monocrystalline lattice according to a specified pattern, whilst also introducing impurities that would turn it into a semiconductor.

Numerous laboratories are involved in this research, and the race is on, between the USA, Russia, Japan, and Europe. In France, there is a national research programme that involves the Ministries of Defence, Higher Education, and Research. Several Parisian universities and research institutes are working in this field, in co-operation with equivalent institutions in Great Britain and Germany, in order to optimally exploit the results. Some private groups are also working on the technique. De Beers is already selling CVD diamond discs, which are used to make optical filters. These discs make use of diamond's extraordinary transparency to a wide spectrum of rays. It is actually the most transparent material known. It not only allows visible light to pass through it, but also radio waves, including microwaves, X-rays, ultraviolet and infrared. This property is of fundamental importance in the analytical processes, that De Beers is currently exploiting, even though it is currently a small niche. But there is no doubt that the market for diamonds made by the CVD process will develop strongly, as soon as the growth technique becomes more rapid. This is the major obstacle that must be overcome. At least several millimetres per day are required, more than a hundred times today's rate. The people who will overcome these problems, to achieve a rapid growth rate and accurate control of the deposit's structure, are assured a lucrative future.

CHAPTER VII

Emmanuel Fritsch

Not all diamonds are created equal
diamond gemmology

The *Deepdene* (104.53 carats) is a spectacular example of a diamond whose colour was enhanced by laboratory treatment (irradiation followed by heating) experimentally performed by the mineralogist F. Pough. The experiment was disclosed shortly before the diamond's scheduled sale at auction, in 1971. The sale was cancelled as a result!

We see diamonds being worn by Hollywood movie stars at film festivals, in jewellers' windows or in museums. It's easy to believe that they are all the same except for their size. Far from it! Diamonds weren't born equal in the heart of the Earth and, once a diamond-cutter is finished with them, they end up even more varied. It is the job of the gemmologist to identify them and classify them once they are cut. Gemmology is the science of gem appreciation, including diamonds. Gemmological testing is, therefore, the essential precursor to a commercial transaction: specialists evaluate the stones so that both parties can make an informed decision. This is not initially about price: the stones are classified into categories. There are regularly updated price lists that show what each category is worth. The most famous is the Rapaport Diamond Report, or 'Rap', founded by ebullient New Yorker, Martin Rapaport.

Quality criteria

Before they are made up into jewellery, diamonds are bought and sold in 'parcel papers'. These are sheets of paper that are folded in a specific way, in order to act as envelopes for cut diamonds. Let us imagine that we have been permitted to enter a diamond bourse, such as the one in Antwerp, one of the Meccas of cut diamonds. We see a number of these folded papers spread out over the tables. They are carefully examined by prospective purchasers. When we approach the table, to examine a group of papers that all contain diamonds of around 1 carat, we might be surprised to see that they all contain diamonds that look extremely similar to a layperson's eyes. However, the enthusiastic haggling that subsequently takes place is vivid proof that there are significant price differences between them. Why are certain diamonds more expensive than others? Four factors, known as the "four Cs" explain the price differences. They are Carat weight, Colour, Clarity and Cut. Obviously, the largest diamonds tend to be the most expensive. Therefore, carat weight is the most important value criterion. As we shall later see, even small differences in mass can result in significant price differentials. Colour (or, typically, the absence of colour) is the other fundamental factor influencing the price. It is true that most of the diamonds in jewellery appear to be colourless at first glance, but there are very subtle nuances, not always evident to the trained eye. Then there is clarity. The stones with the fewest visible flaws are more expensive. The presence or absence of inclusions, fractures, or visible defects of any kind is evaluated using a magnifying glass under 10 times magnification (10x loupe). Lastly, diamonds are supposed to sparkle! The factors that make one gem shine more than another are having a growing influence on price. These include the stone's cut, brightness, symmetry and proportions. To evaluate all these criteria, and consequently determine the classification of a stone, is known as "grading".

An expert carefully examines the clarity of a diamond using a loupe that magnifies ten times. A very beautiful rough crystal is being examined in this case.

International diamond clarity scales, determined through the observation of diamonds using 10x magnification using a loupe (based on GIA-CIBJO* equivalents, agreed March 9, 1977)

CIBJO scale		GIA scale
Loupe-clean	F	Flawless *no inclusions*
	IF	Internally Flawless *Minor surface imperfections*
vvs1 vvs2	vvs1 vvs2	Very Very Small Inclusions 1 Very Very Small Inclusions 2 *Tiny inclusions, very difficult to see with a 10x lens*
vs1 vs2	vs1 vs2	Very Small Inclusions 1 Very Small Inclusions 2 *Very small inclusions, difficult to see with a 10x lens*
si1 si2	si1 si2	Small Inclusions 1 Small Inclusions 2 *Small inclusions, visible with a 10x lens but invisible to the naked eye*
P1 (Piqué 1)	I1	Included 1 *Inclusions that are visible to the naked eye, without affecting brilliance*
P2 (Piqué 2)	I2	Included 2 *Large and/or numerous inclusions, easily visible to the naked eye*
P3 (Piqué 3)	I3	Included 3 *Large and/or numerous inclusions, very visible to the naked eye*

*GIA: Gemological Institute of America
CIBJO: Confédération Internationale de la Bijouterie Joaillerie Orfèvrerie (International Jewellery and Goldsmithery Confederation)

So small, and yet so valuable!

As we have seen, all other things being equal, a large diamond will be worth more than a small one. A diamond's mass is expressed in carats (abbreviated to 'ct'). A metric carat is worth 0.2 g. That may seem small, but it can result in a beautiful stone: a 1-carat round brilliant diamond is approximately 6.5 mm in diameter. There are very few other commodities that are weighed in such small units, except perhaps for some rare, life-saving pharmaceutical molecules. Many people would, of course, say that a diamond can change somebody's life!

It may seem strange that we are discussing mass, and not weight. Mass is a less familiar concept to most people, who think in terms of weight in their daily lives. In fact, weight is the result of terrestrial gravity acting upon mass. However, gravity varies a tiny but significant amount across the globe. As a result, measurements of weight are slightly variable from place to place. Mass, however, has the advantage of remaining constant. In order to measure mass, the balances need to be calibrated before use, in order to correct for variations in gravity, amongst other things. For these reasons, mass is the unit of choice in diamond transactions.

There are two types of carat, and it is important not to get them confused. The first is a unit of mass, whilst the other is an indication of the purity of gold and its alloys (pure gold is 24 carat, whereas an alloy containing 75% of gold is 18 carat, etc.). In America, the abbreviation for gold carats is, sensibly, a K, instead of 'ct'. The word carat, when referring to the unit of mass, originates from the use of carob seeds as counterweights in ancient times. These seeds come from the carob tree. They grow in pods, like peas, and have a remarkably consistent weight (around 0.2 g). The carat eventually became part of the international metric system and was standardised at exactly 0.2 g.The carat is sub-divided into hundredths, known as 'points'. The rules regarding the rounding-up of carat weights are very strict, and are actually more stringent than required by international scientific conventions. It is only permitted to round up the 'hundredths' digit of a diamond's mass to a higher number if the 'thousandths' digit is nine (instead of five or more, as is usually the case). Therefore, a 1.358-carat diamond weighs 1.35ct, and only 1.359-carat diamonds can be rounded up to 1.36ct. One can imagine a diamond-cutter's distress should he or she weigh a stone that has just been finished, and find that it weighs only 0.998ct!

Mass is the only grading criterion that is determined objectively, rather than by human eye. It is usually measured with very sensitive electronic balances. However, some jewellers still use the traditional precision balance, with its little metal weights. This is prettier, but less precise.

When a cut diamond weighs less than 0.2ct, it belongs to a special category: 'melee'. This is from the French word for 'mixed items' (mêlées), undoubtedly because these small stones are seldom stored individually, but generally wrapped together in a single parcel paper. In many pieces of jewellery, the valuable stones are surrounded by clusters of smaller gems, and the majority of these small stones are melee.

The price of a stone is generally proportional to its mass (all other quality factors being equal). Prices are usually quoted as a given amount per carat. However, there are 'psychological' values where the price jumps up suddenly, in particular at the round numbers, such as 1, 2 or 3 carats. For example, a 0.98ct diamond will be less expensive per carat than a 1.01ct stone. Conversely, 3ct stones are unlucky in Japan for cultural reasons. Lastly, it is well-known that the per-carat value increases the more the mass increases. For example, if a 1ct diamond is worth $10,000, a 2ct diamond will be worth much more than $20,000. As usual, it was Tavernier who first stated this law of exponential increase in the price of the stone, as its mass increases.

A row of strongly coloured diamonds, known as '*fancies*'. The stones are a selection from the Rainbow collection, from Eddy Elzas in Antwerp.

An exceptional diamond by anyone's standards: its colour (or rather, absence of colour) is perfect, classified as D. It is absolutely devoid of inclusions even when scrutinised under the magnifying glass: it is graded as '*flawless*'. It is beautifully cut as a heart-shape. Lastly, its weight, 101 carats, qualifies it for membership of the extremely restricted club of over 100-carat stones. This magnificent gem, owned by the Ben Moller company in New York, is worth around $11-$14 million!

Important nuances

The second significant factor in a diamond's price is its colour. One might ask: 'what colour, since diamonds are colourless?' In fact, they are not completely colourless (cf. Chapter 1)! There are two extremes, both perceived as valuable by diamond merchants: truly colourless stones, and strongly coloured stones.

Let us start with the first. Using a background that is as perfectly white as possible, a specialist's trained eye will be able to see barely perceptible tints of colour. The light is very important: light from a large, north-facing window is traditionally preferred wherever possible. In an office, a lamp that produces light that is equivalent in colour to sunlight will be adequate. To help in this delicate exercise, reference stones are placed on either side of the stone being graded. In this carefully-regulated environment, it is surprising to what degree it is possible to distinguish between different shades of colour, when concentrating hard. The international colour scale goes from D (colourless) to Z (distinctly coloured). Beyond this, there are the 'fancy-coloured' diamonds. Notice that the scale starts at the letter D! Some people think that it stands for 'diamond'. In fact, when this classification was proposed a long time ago by the Gemological Institute of America, there was another colour scale that used the letters A, B and C. This other scale is now obsolete, but it was decided to begin the new scale at D in order to avoid any confusion.

The grading of a near-colourless diamond requires a great deal of skill and training. For the stones that are most colourless, the colour is evaluated by looking at the stone from the side only, because the scintillation caused by diamond-cutting makes it impossible to see very weak shades of colour if the stone is looked at from the front. Colour tints only start to become noticeable under careful 'face-up' scrutiny when colour grades K, L and M are reached (these are known as the 'airline colours', after the Dutch carrier KLM). It has not yet been possible to develop an 'electronic eye' machine to replace humans in the colour grading process, despite the fact that people have been trying to develop one for half a century.

Inclusion in a brilliant-cut, enlarged 20 times. It is an olivine crystal.

At the other extreme, there are diamonds that have a distinct and obvious colour. These are known as 'fancy colours'. They are described by colour, with some qualifying remarks. There are fewer subdivisions, and the classifications are more recent. For example, an 'intense yellow' will be worth more than a plain 'yellow'. Certain colours are more highly valued than others: red is unquestionably the most expensive, and brown is the least expensive. Likewise, a red or orange tint often adds to the price, whilst a brown or grey component will reduce it. There is a commercial no-man's-land between the colourless and fancy-coloured extremes: stones classified between M and Z are very difficult to sell.

Unlike mass measurements, colour classifications are often difficult to establish. So are clarity and cut, which will be discussed below. These criteria can give rise to heated discussions between two graders at the same laboratory, let alone from one lab to another. They are, therefore, best regarded as subjective opinions rather than measurements. For the best stones, the opinion of several experienced specialists is required and the result is sometimes a compromise.

Reflections from the pavilion's facets, creating a pattern of hearts and arrows.
The pattern is revealed thanks to an optical device that uses special lighting.

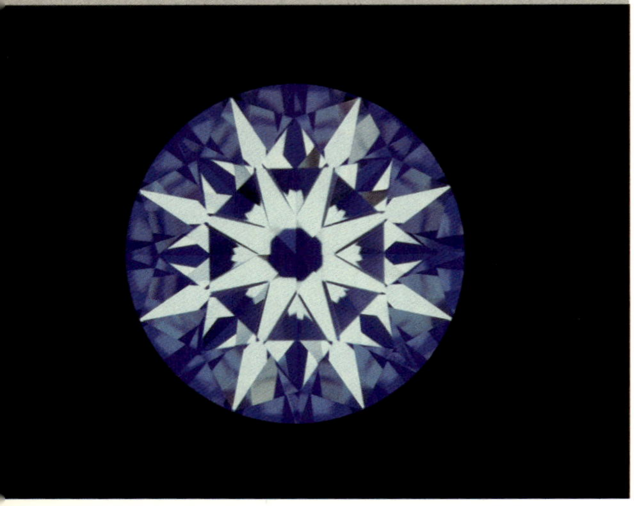

Inclusions and fractures

Diamonds are seldom flawless. The clearer they are, the more expensive they become. Sometimes, they contain 'inclusions' that disturb the play of light and mar the stone's beauty. These can include black spots (which are inclusions of graphite or metal sulphides), small crystals of other minerals, or defects, such as fractures or cleavages. But it is not simply a question of the presence or absence of defects. Their nature, number, size, colour (or contrast) and position in the stone all affect the gem's appearance, and thus the grading. For example, an incipient fracture that is located in an exposed place of the upper part of the diamond is at risk of being accidentally hit against hard objects in everyday use. It will be judged more harshly than a similar defect located in the lower part, which is hidden by the crown facets and generally protected by the gem's mount. It is thus a subtle process of evaluation, to which whole books have been devoted.

By convention, stones are graded using a magnifying glass (loupe). It provides 10 times magnification, and is optically corrected for distortions. The grader holds the diamond using special stone tweezers. With the other hand, the loupe is held very close to the eye (or the user's glasses!). The two hands are held against each other, and one of them rests against the face, in order to stabilise the hands and facilitate observation. Beginners are always surprised to find that experts tend to look out of one eye, but keep the other open. In fact, with a little practice, the brain learns to ignore the other eye and focus upon the important information from the loupe. It is much more comfortable to have both eyes open.

The impact of each detected imperfection is taken into account in the final grading. As with colour, there is an international clarity scale. It extends from F (flawless), to I3 (Included 3: see table p.162). Many parameters must be considered before the clarity can be graded. Out of all the diamond classification processes, it is probably the most difficult to automate. The diamond grader'sexpertise is critical.

Beauty worthy of Cupid

Not all brilliants have the same brilliance. The mark of a master cutter is a brilliant-cut stone that is rigorously symmetrical, with good proportions and a fine polish. In addition, the stone will not have been cut in order to retain maximum weight, but for maximum beauty instead.

The majority of diamonds sold today are cut in the round brilliant style (cf. Chapter 8). A series of ideal attributes for this cut have been established. They are based on proportions and symmetry. Since diamond's refractive index is constant (cf. Chapter 1), there is only a narrow range of proportions that will permit a good percentage of light to be reflected back towards the observer's eye. The pinnacle of this style of cutting is reached in so-called 'hearts and arrows' diamonds. When a brilliant is cut to the very highest standards, the pavilion facets will display a perfectly symmetrical pattern that resembles a cluster of hearts and arrows. Coincidentally enough, these are Cupid's attributes, which is highly appropriate given that diamond is the world's most popular engagement ring stone! This kind of stone is particularly highly prized in Japan, and a small optical instrument has been invented in order to display and evaluate the patterned reflections properly.

For a very long time it has been acknowledged that the quality of a diamond's cut is very important. However, only recently has the profession begun to attempt the standardisation of methods to evaluate a stone's beauty, in an attempt to make it a less subjective process. This research is still going on; it is not easy to put concepts such as a stone's brightness or scintillation into equations. In addition, non-round shapes are increasingly popular. These shapes also require evaluation criteria, but each shape has to be evaluated differently, which complicates matters. Colour and clarity grading criteria are also relatively recent in historical terms (they were introduced after World War II). It is therefore likely that antique family jewels will achieve quite disappointing results when they are graded. However, a jewel's or diamond's attractiveness isn't necessarily limited to its quality grades. They are simply a means of objectively comparing diamonds. Other aspects are excluded from the system, such as aesthetic, historical or symbolic value. These qualities are all subjectively determined, but they may be important for appraising value in some cases.

This small collection of Namibian brown diamonds is illuminated by "black light" (long-wave ultraviolet radiation), showing almost all the possible colours of diamond luminescence.

Colourful black light

In addition to the 'four Cs', there is another factor that is currently under discussion. In certain markets, customers do not like fluorescent stones, which constitute approximately a third of all cut diamonds. Fluorescence is the emission of light by a diamond when observed under ultraviolet radiation, or 'black light' (cf. Chapter 1). Some people dislike it, others adore it.

The most common argument is that the stone's fluorescence influences its appearance even under normal lighting conditions. This is generally false, except for a few special cases. On the contrary, taking the trouble to uncover a diamond's secret fluorescence can be worthwhile. It is a useful tool for the gemmologist. For example, blue fluorescence often offers a quick way of checking whether a diamond is natural. For the stone's owner, fluorescence can endow the gem with mysterious beauty under ultraviolet rays.

Well-treated diamonds

One of the gemmologist's most important tasks, even more so than diamond grading, is to make sure that the gems are neither synthetic, nor treated. As a result of developments in technology linked to World War II, many diamonds have been artificially treated in order to improve their commercial value. Most commonly, their colour is modified through irradiation and heating. This is usually restricted to the very specialised field of fancy-colour diamonds. Specialists have established tests to recognise the majority of these treatments. However, the tests are sometimes complex. Since the late 1980s, treatments have been developed that will not only affect a stone's colour, but also its clarity. High-refractive-index glass can be introduced into fissures in some diamonds, making them less visible, to obtain a more attractive gem. Simple methods have been developed to identify these procedures. In the late 1990s, new treatments were introduced that used very high pressure and temperature to turn certain brownish diamonds nearly colourless. Only a few thousand stones have been treated in this manner, often ending up as beautiful, high-quality gems. They are, however, clearly marked using tiny laser inscriptions. Scientists are currently refining complicated testing procedures in order to identify these treatments.

The impact of these treatments varies by country. The United States is the world's largest market, and news of new gem treatments can cause sudden agitation in the industry, but this reaction is often not long-lasting. In other countries, the appearance of certain treatments has never been documented, even though diamonds are examined there every day by qualified gemmologists.

A particularly good and fascinating example: intense red luminescence displayed by the famous blue Hope diamond (formerly known as the *Blue Diamond of the French Crown*) when subjected to ultraviolet radiation. Smithsonian Institution, Washington.

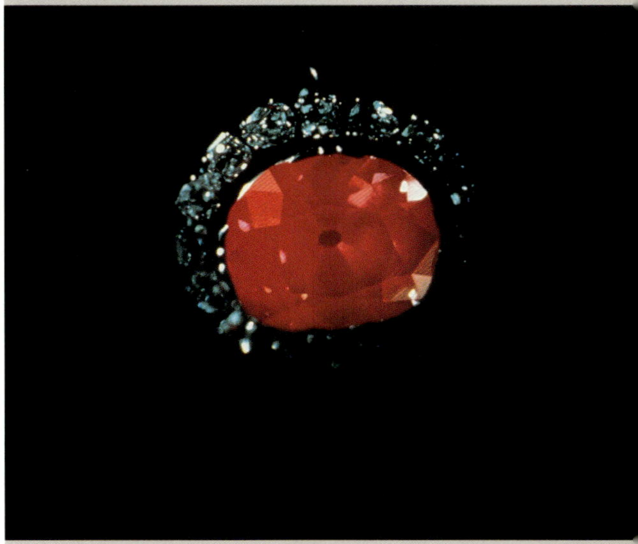

Genuine fakes

The general public perceives synthetic stones to be fakes. However, synthetic diamonds are, in fact, genuine diamonds: 'genuine fakes', so to speak. This is because synthetic gems are, by definition, of the same chemical composition and atomic structure as the equivalent natural gem. The principal difference is that a synthetic stone does not come from a mine, but has been entirely created in a laboratory: built up, atom by atom, molecule by molecule, thanks to crystal growth processes (cf. Chapter 6). Therefore, a synthetic diamond is a true diamond in the sense that it has the same overall chemical and physical properties as a natural diamond. It is a 'fake' because it was not made by nature, but by industry.

But then, if they resemble each other so much, how can they be recognised? A long time ago, specialists discovered the existence of subtle differences between these industrial products and their natural equivalents. Synthetic diamonds grow differently from natural diamonds. In particular, they develop true cube faces, which are unknown in natural gem diamonds (cf. Chapter 1), and they sometimes contain metal inclusions. Their crystalline defects can also be of a slightly different nature. This implies a whole series of zonations, inclusions and behaviours in luminescence that are invisible to the naked eye, but which can be rendered visible by well-equipped specialists. Therefore, gemmologists can usually recognize synthetics easily, and customers shouldn't be unduly worried about purchasing one unintentionally.

The filling of the fractures within diamonds with glass gave rise to a scandal in the early 1990s. However, it is easily identifiable thanks to the 'flash effect'. In light-field illumination, the filled fracture appears yellow-green, whereas under dark-field illumination, it typically appears purple to blue.

This thistle-shaped inclusion shows where laser drilling has been used to destroy an ugly black flaw inside a cut diamond. The 'stem' is the thin laser drill-hole. The 'flower' is the cavity caused by the inclusion's destruction. The 'leaves' are pre-existing fractures.

How is a synthetic diamond made? With pure carbon, and great difficulty. The process is a technological marvel. Extremely high pressures are required, (about 50,000 times atmospheric pressure) generated by presses which can be worth several million dollars. In addition, high temperatures (approximately 1,400 °C) are needed. It is necessary to control these parameters very precisely, which is not easy, and it requires great skill to manage the growth conditions inside the pressure cell efficiently. Synthetic diamonds are therefore expensive, more expensive than natural gem diamonds of equivalent quality. However, there are some on the market. They are, in fact, a direct consequence of the economic meltdown of the ex-Soviet Union. There were some teams of researchers there who had the heavy equipment and expertise necessary for this delicate task, and they decided to try to earn hard currency by making diamonds. They only produce small quantities, and their stones remain gemmological curiosities. Only a few thousand carats are on the market, compared to the annual production of a million carats of natural gem diamonds. Moreover, the stones are often small, and of average to poor quality. They are therefore not really a problem.

This photograph compares synthetic diamonds with natural ones. There are six colourless synthetic diamonds and two yellow ones, manufactured in the De Beers laboratories (1 to 1.56 carats), compared to four small brilliant-cut diamonds of natural origin. The De Beers synthetics were, of course, not intended for the trade. On the contrary, the company used this research to develop convenient instruments (the DiamondSure and DiamondView) that make it possible to detect synthetic cut diamonds.

Synthetic diamonds are created in a laboratory, and do not come from a mine. Coloured diamonds are the easiest to produce, particularly yellows. Contrary to natural diamond crystals, synthetic crystals show true cube faces, with flat sides and sharp edges. These rough and cut stones, of less than 1 carat, were made in the Sumitomo laboratories, Japan.

Many contenders, but only one true diamond

Diamonds are highly-prized, and very expensive. These are good reasons, therefore, to fake them. At first, similar natural gems were used as diamond substitutes: colourless topaz (aluminium fluo-hydroxy silicate), sapphires (aluminium oxide) or zircons (zirconium silicate). Even simple 'rock crystal' (quartz) was used for a long time. In addition, sometimes gems were misidentified in good faith. It is likely that many Portuguese colonists brought back topazes from Brazil that they believed to be diamonds. These natural gems remained in favour until the beginning of the 20th century.

However, industry had already produced some additional contenders. The first was lead crystal. This is a type of glass, more brilliant than the ordinary variety. It was also known as 'strass', after a French jeweller, George Frederic Stras (1700-1773), but its more common name is 'paste', after the French term *pâte de verre* (molten glass). This glass could have a piece of metal foil backing added to it, to increase its brightness further. Subsequently an additional technique was developed, whereby the glass was fused to a thin covering of natural garnet. This makes a sparkling stone with a hard, scratch-proof garnet top (a 'garnet-topped doublet'), which appears to be colourless because of the thinness of the sliver of garnet.

The development of crystal growth methods enabled Verneuil, a French chemist, to develop a process known as 'Verneuil' or 'flame-fusion'. This is particularly suitable for the synthetic manufacture of certain hard gemstones. It led to the manufacture of synthetic corundum in a variety of colours. Ruby is red corundum, whereas sapphire is blue corundum (the two gemstones are in fact exactly the same mineral). Colourless corundum could also be produced, as could colourless synthetic spinel, a similar mineral. These two substances could both be cut into imitation diamonds. They are both hard, but they can easily be identified as fakes.

After the Second World War, synthetic rutile was successfully produced. This had far more sparkle than synthetic spinel, but it was often yellowish and had too much dispersion (rainbow 'fire'). However, as with many other contemporary diamond substitutes, rutile would be marketed under many different trade names to increase its commercial appeal. There are at least 25 names for synthetic rutile (Titania, Rainbow Diamond and Kima Gem, for example).

The next step was to move on to products without natural mineral equivalents (see table on next page). The challenge was to find a colourless material, with about the same balance of brilliance, fire, and scintillation as diamond, but at a much lower price. In addition, some doublet stones made from various combinations of imitation materials were launched sporadically on the market. Nowadays, cubic zirconia (synthetic zirconium oxide) dominates the imitation diamond market. It is mass-produced in many factories worldwide in large quantities, so the wholesale price for the rough material has dropped to fractions of a cent per carat! So the gemmologist's work is made harder as he is confronted with a series of possibilities, from natural gems to zirconia.

Right at the end of the 20th century, moissanite was produced. It owes its name to Henri Moissan, the first French Nobel Prize winner for chemistry, who tried to synthesise diamond in the late 19th century (cf. Chapter 6). He initially studied at the *Muséum National d'Histoire Naturelle* in Paris, then occupied a laboratory at the Pharmacy School near the Jardin du Luxembourg, home of the French Senate. His high-pressure experiments caused the furnaces to explode, waking the Senators during the night. The story goes that they complained and tried to get him to perform his experiments elsewhere. Moissan never managed to produce diamond, but he did synthesise a type of silicon carbide, which was named 'moissanite' in his honour. Moissanite is found in nature under extreme conditions (such as meteorite impacts).

There are numerous diamond imitations. Some of them are displayed here, next to a natural diamond (first on the left). From left to right and smallest to largest: natural colourless sapphire, natural quartz (rock crystal), paste (lead glass), synthetic strontium titanate, cubic zirconia (synthetic zirconium oxide), and zircon (natural zirconium silicate).

Synthetic diamonds in various colours, produced by the Lucent company's laboratories. These remarkable diamonds are sold on the international market. However, they are 'marked' in order to certify their synthetic origin. They weigh about a carat.

Some man-made diamond imitations

Imitation type	Approximate date of introduction
Lead crystal 'paste', with or without foiled backing	18th century
Garnet-topped glass doublet	late 19th century
Synthetic colourless sapphire and spinel (Verneuil flame-fusion method)	1930
Synthetic Rutile	1950
Strontium Titanate ("Fabulite")	1955
YAG: Yttrium-aluminium garnet	1968
GGG: Gadolinium-gallium garnet ("Galliant ")	1971
Lithium Niobate ("Linobate")	1975

Green diamonds are a challenge for laboratories: is the colour of natural origin or not? It is seldom possible to tell for sure. This is the *Esperanza Verde*, probably of Brazilian origin. It is being studied in GemTechLab, Geneva. This 6.85-carat stone could reach a very high price if the natural origin of its colour could be demonstrated. Private Collection.

Laboratory techniques usually provide definitive results in uncertain cases. A Russian synthetic yellow diamond shows a cross-shaped growth pattern using the U-Visio technique, performed at Gem Tech Lab in Geneva. The results are clear, and diagnostic of synthetic diamond. On the other hand, using the same technique, a natural black diamond displays a natural growth pattern of concentric squares.

Laboratory-created moissanite is rather expensive to produce, and not always colourless. However, it was imposed a few years ago on the world market, to great fanfare, by an American company.

Contrary to popular belief, these imitations are easily identified by a qualified gemmologist. Their optical properties (optical character, refractive index, appearance under liquid immersion, luminescence, etc.) are all significantly different from those of diamond. Several thermal testers have been developed, permitting imitations to be identified using a sensor the size of a pen. Diamond conducts heat better than its imitations. It is, however, often better to simply apply some basic observational tests, rather than relying upon insensitive, badly calibrated or used instruments. The recent introduction of synthetic moissanite is a prime example. Elementary tests such as the feel of the stone, the shape of a water droplet on its surface, the speed at which it clears after being fogged up (by exhaling upon it), and the appearance of facet edges or unpolished surfaces can identify certain imitations. As in so many other matters, there is no substitute for an evaluation by a well-trained specialist.

It should be noted that diamond imitations are not always intended to mislead. Perfect copies of large diamonds are made out of spinel or colourless synthetic cubic zirconia for customer presentations or for display, while the priceless original is safely ensconced in a bank vault. The high cost of making a replica is largely cancelled out by the saving on the hefty insurance premium that would be charged for taking a large, genuine diamond out of protective custody. These copies constitute a reference as once a fine stone is sold to a private individual, it tends to disappear from public view. Sometimes, the only tangible reminder of its appearance is the replica. This is an ancient practice: the majority of 18th-century European monarchs had collections of crystal copies of famous diamonds, in order to be able to compare their gems with other famous stones around the world. Napoleon III's impressive collection of diamond replicas was unfortunately dispersed after his downfall. Only the replica of the Regent remains, in the *Muséum National d'Histoire Naturelle*, and you don't have to be a specialist to see that the Louvre's Regent is the original!

Don't panic!

Clearly, a diamond gemmologist's work has become increasingly more important and difficult since the 1980s. Although diamond is still simple to identify and grade most of the time, there is a rare but growing number of stones that require the use of laboratory techniques for correct identification. Conscientious jeweller-gemologists can no longer do it all in their workshops and are gradually beginning to go more and more often to physics laboratories. The relevant skills used to be taught from father to son, but today they are taught in professional courses at universities. Some people find this worrying, but it is the normal evolution of any specialist field, and it should reassure diamond-lovers. It proves that the profession is adapting to progressive change, and is seeking to keep up with events. This should help to ensure that purchasers can feel completely confident when they buy this glorious gemstone.

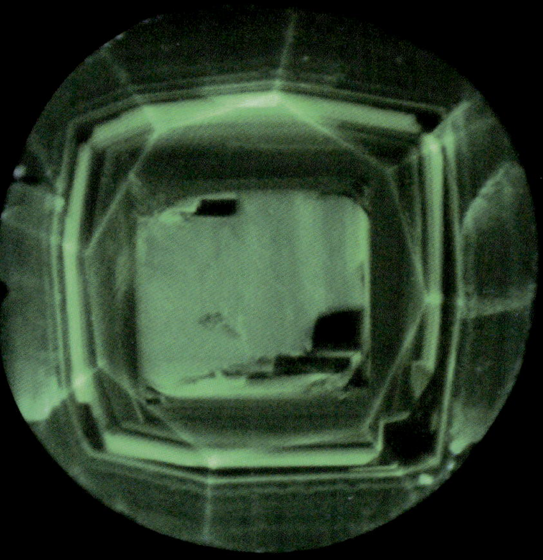

Gemmology laboratories love surprises: they are rare, and make daily research more interesting. Two exceptional diamonds recently passed through Gem Tech Lab of Geneva. One of them is a 31.31-carat oval 'chameleon' diamond. It is greenish-yellow in daylight, but turns yellow ochre when heated for 5 seconds in hot air at 110°C. The other is a splendid pear-shape, called the *Tavernier*. It is of Indian origin (Golconda), and weighs 56.07 carats. It changes colour according to the quality of the light. Under normal incandescent light, it is pinkish-brown. In daylight, it turns a subtle bluish colour, which appears to be somewhat fluorescent. Cartier set it in a necklace to commemorate the millennium.

CHAPTER VIII

Hubert Bari &
Bernard Morel

Point, table, rose, heart, marquise, brilliant...

It is important to remember that diamond's optical properties are only fully brought to light by the quality of its cut. Admittedly, however, even in the rough state it already displays a natural ability to reflect light. It also has a particularly bright lustre, known as 'adamantine lustre'. This term is used to denote a type of surface sheen, which can have various qualities, such as 'glassy' or 'greasy'. It is characteristic to every mineral. Topaz, which was sometimes confused with diamond by Brazilian miners, also has an adamantine lustre. Diamond also has high dispersion, the ability to split light up into the colours of the rainbow. This is what enables cut diamonds to display their famous, colourful 'fire'. These properties are enhanced by gem-cutting, as long as the specific optical properties of each gemstone are taken into account during the cutting process. With a diamond, the process is complicated by its extreme hardness. Diamonds can only be ground and polished with diamond powder. Moreover, diamonds are extremely rare, and a considerable proportion of each stone has to be slowly and painstakingly ground away during cutting. Therefore, the evolution of diamond-cutting, from natural crystal shapes to hand-worked objects of beauty, took a very long time indeed.

India or Europe?

One might think that India, the country of origin for diamonds, was the place where diamond-cutting was invented. Moreover, the story goes that Indian gem-cutters have known for over two millennia that diamond powder can be used to cut diamond. In fact, nothing could be further from the truth! None of the rare diamonds that reached Europe from India during antiquity were cut when they arrived, not even cursorily. Research shows that the same is true for the stones that arrived between the end of the 13th century until the mid-16th century. The 'secret' to cutting diamonds using diamond powder was only discovered in Europe in the late 14th century. The first cutting merely involved 're-surfacing' the small or medium-sized octahedral crystals that arrived, in the rough state, from the Indies via Italy. It was in Italy that the secret of diamond-cutting was discovered, either in Venice, Florence or Genoa: the cities whose merchants then held a monopoly on the import of Indian gems. The secret spread back to the land of the Maharajahs from Italy, probably spread by the ships that traded back and forth. Besides, the first sightings of cut diamonds in India do not seem to have occurred until the appearance of 17th- and 18th-century Mughal jewels!

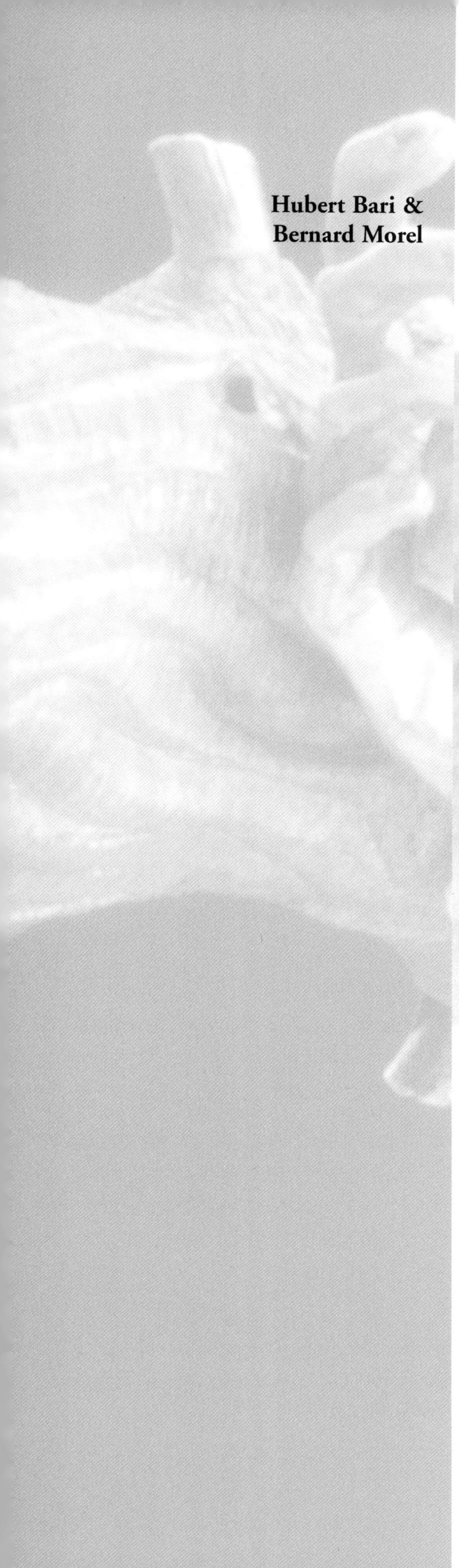

Reliquary, presented to Basle cathedral's treasury by the burgher Hallwyl. Strasbourg, around 1470. The golden masterpiece has Christ at its summit, crucified upon the cross with three diamond nails. It contains superb 15th-century point-cuts.

Illustrated plate from Max Bauer's treatise on gemstones, Leipzig, 1896. These two drawings show the original, 'Mogul-cut' shape of the *Koh-i-Noor.*

Having discovered the art of mastering the invincible stone, the Indians followed a very different path in their diamond-cutting techniques than the one followed in Europe. They generally limited themselves to polishing only a few facets, often resulting in a sort of oval shape, thereby preserving a little of the original, typically octahedral, crystal shape. Mughal jewels are studded with millions of them. Often, diamond rosettes surround a central motif of coloured stones. Indeed, spinels, rubies and sapphires, and later emeralds, were always popular in Indian jewellery. Given the rarity of large diamonds, small diamonds usually made up a closely-set, sparkling surface that was finished off with a splash of colour. Rubies or spinels were popular because of their red colour: the colour of blood, and therefore of life. The guiding principle behind Indian diamond-cutting was the conservation of maximum weight, at the expense of geometric perfection. It is known that the *Great Mogul* diamond (known today as the *Orloff*) was cut by Hortensio Borgis, an Italian expatriated in the Indies. He was expressly ordered by the Emperor to cut it with as little weight loss as possible, hence his choice of an 'Indian-style' high rose-cut. Nevertheless, too much weight was lost during cutting for the Emperor's liking. He refused to pay the hapless cutter, and had all his possessions confiscated instead! This anecdote proves that, in India, the choice of weight conservation over symmetry was related to power: the amount of power asserted by the sovereign was directly proportional to the stone's size. Stones were supposed to be big. They were intended to be seen from afar, at a distance dictated by protocol which, moreover, obscured any imperfections. It is precisely these imperfections that are valued today in ancient, historic gems, which not only possess a history, but also 'character'. In this respect, they are a world away from the gems that are being cut today, which are so pure that they have almost become geometrical abstractions. What contemporary observer would today seek to justify the butchery of the *Koh-i-Noor*, a gem whose real history, shorn of the legends that have accumulated around it, dates back to the 16th century? In 1852, Queen Victoria had the diamond re-cut, from a Mughal-cut that was highly characteristic of the 17th century and which weighed 186 carats, into a somewhat irregular and rather flat brilliant oval-cut that weighs 105.60 carats. A surface showing the wear of more than two centuries of history and tragedy was thus ground away forever.

Let us now close the chapter on India, and return to Europe where, having discovered the secret, gem-cutters busily devoted a few dozen years to testing new diamond cuts. This led to a blossoming of new cuts and shapes, according to the shape of the imported rough gems. Italy not only discovered the principles of diamond-cutting, but it also began to adapt ancient geometrical skills for it. These geometrical secrets were being rediscovered, in ancient writings that were flowing from monasteries and universities at the time. There can be little doubt that Renaissance Italian gem-cutters drew heavily upon the teachings of Euclid and Pythagoras. Thanks to them, they solved complex problems such as the determination of the correct angles, the symmetry, and the optical effect of a given facet upon the remainder of the stone. Italy lacked neither scientists nor geometrical publications, as one can see in the famous portrait of Brother Luca Pacioli, surrounded by crystallographic models and treatises on shapes by Leonardo da Vinci. It was also in Italy, particularly Venice, that the earliest editions of Euclid's *Geometry* first started to become popular. The technique of diamond-cutting spread very quickly to Northern Europe (Bruges, Antwerp) and, of course, Paris via the trading centres that Italian merchants maintained throughout Europe.

The problems faced by early diamond-cutters

When the first, rare, diamonds reached Europe, starting from the end of the 13th century, gem-cutters were still lacking in technical expertise, and were quite unable to work them. The trade had yet to be invented, and jewellers had to be content with setting rough diamonds in jewellery. Such stones were almost always small octahedral crystals. Although numerous pieces of medieval jewellery survive to this day, particularly religious jewellery, showing numerous other cut gems, it should be remembered that they have not been fully cut but merely given a surface polish. Their external form still generally resembles the original pebble outline, with only slight surface trimming. The normal shape applied to rubies, sapphires or emeralds was therefore the cabochon (a smooth, rounded shape), often irregular in outline. Although they may look primitive to our eyes, it is wrong to regard them as being of low quality - quite the contrary. These masterpieces were already highly prized in their time. Simply put, coloured stones, without any obvious play of colour due to their optical properties, were well suited to this technique. Achieving an attractive, rich colour was the only goal, and this quality is best displayed when the colour is spread out, and the stone is kept thick. With diamond, the situation is quite different: as it is normally colourless, its appeal comes from the reflective lustre of perfectly polished surfaces. Diamond-cutters realised this, and faced an additional complication due to the stone's hardness. Ruby and sapphire can be cut with a substance known as "emery", which is a powdered mineral known as corundum, the colourless or greyish version of ruby and sapphire. This mineral is found in profusion on the Greek island of Naxos, for example. At number 9 on the Mohs scale of hardness, however, it is quite incapable of making any impression on a diamond's surface.

Italian gem-cutters did not succeed in mastering this unconquerable mineral until the end of the 14th century. They finally forced it to take shape by means of grinding it on a polishing wheel, using diamond powder. To our knowledge, no 14th-century royal jewel inventory mentions any cut diamonds. That of King Charles V of France, dating back to 1379-1380, certainly includes many diamonds. The majority are small to medium-sized 'naïve' stones. The largest, described only as square and pointed, without any specified cut, were quite simply beautiful natural octahedral crystals. On the other hand, the 1413 inventory of the Duke of Berry, the King's brother, already contains numerous diamonds, with their cuts described in surprising clarity. The invention of diamond-cutting therefore occurred at some time between these two dates.

To date, European diamond-cutting has six centuries of history behind it. Needless to say, the variety of diamond cuts that have been tried is immense, and one cannot simply consider the standard round brilliant cut. To summarise all the different cuts in this book would be well-nigh impossible, however. Herbert Tillander devoted himself to the task, publishing his masterly "Diamond Cuts in Historic Jewellery 1381-1910" in 1995. It is the classic reference work in the field. An interesting conclusion emerged from his work: it is very difficult to date a piece of jewellery according to the diamond cuts it contains. The varieties of cut could have been in use for decades, or even centuries. At most, one can define various different phases in diamond-cutting history, which gradually lead from the point-cut to the modern round brilliant, via the table-cut and the rose-cut. Lastly, we will discuss a much-neglected aspect of diamond-cutting: the cutting of very large stones, which require highly specialised procedures in order to be faceted.

First steps

A stone arrived in medieval Europe, via Venice, that was harder than any other, extremely rare and therefore extremely valuable, which could only be cut with diamond powder, which was itself expensive. We can add another piece to the puzzle: the shape of the diamonds that reached Europe. Records state that the most highly valued stones in India were octahedral crystals, which were first reserved for royalty. Their export was consequently extremely restricted, hence smuggling began. In addition, the only stones that were supposed to reach Europe were the small octahedra and the flat fragments (cleavages and macles) that Indian princes permitted to leave the country. The first diamond cuts arose from these two categories of shape. The octahedra dictated the development of what is called the "point-cut". This cut is the same shape as the original octahedral crystal, but resurfaced into a double pyramid, with the angle of inclination of the faces modified to a greater or lesser degree. However, soon thereafter the point-cut was given additional facets by the abrasion of the edges and the creation of a table by grinding down a point. This shape probably resulted from the need to rectify some crystals, such as those whose pyramidal tip was damaged or broken. This grinding process resulted in the table-cut. This particular cut was the most prized shape from the beginning of the 15th century until the mid-17th century, if it was a perfect square or rectangle. The pavilion was generally pointed, whether truncated or not. When the table was large and the stone not very thick, the cut was known as a "mirror". The other rough shapes - cleavages, macles, etc. - were either cut into the shape of octahedra, or into small baguettes or, later on, rose-cuts.

The 1413 jewel inventory of Jean, Duke of Berry, is preserved at the St. Geneviève library in Paris. It is, without question, the most invaluable document displaying the evolution of the octahedron into the more complex shapes. This primitive inventory and its accompanying documents contain information on the jewels pawned, redeemed, bought or given away up until the Duke's death in 1416. No fewer than 1,200 jewels are listed, of which 81 correspond to jewels decorated with one or more diamonds. The text clearly distinguishes the octahedra from the cut diamonds: rough crystals are listed as "pointed dyament, not made", whereas cut diamonds are listed as "made". Here are some of the most interesting diamonds listed in the inventory. These examples provide incontrovertible proof of the existence of a fully developed diamond-cutting trade:

• Diamond of St. Louis: "[...] pointed dyament, known as the 'Dyament de saint Loys', sitting in a ring of gold [...]". This is one of the many examples of uncut diamonds on the list. Judging by the fact that the Duke paid 300 écus for it in 1408, it probably weighed around 5 carats.

• Mirror of Florence: "Item: one large round and flat dyament, made in the style of a miroeur, weighing approximately XXIIII caraz, which Monseigneur bought, in a gold cloak clasp, from Constantin de Nicolas, a Florentine merchant residing in Paris, the 29th day of August of the year 1409, for the sum of 6,000 golden *écus*". At the time, the aforementioned weight of 24 carats would have been highly impressive. It was a "mirror" with a broad, round table, resulting from a rough stone of the same shape. A simple bevel would have surrounded the round table. Given that the stone did not have a pavilion, the rough would have been a large, rather flat fragment, from 5 to 6 millimetres thick. In other words, it was perhaps the first ever "portrait diamond": a gem so flat, it could have been used as a glass to protect a portrait miniature.

• The Berri Point: "one pointed dyament, weighing XX carats or thereabouts, that he bought in a golden rose with another mirror dyament that he had put in a bear..."

• The Chartres diamond: "Item: a large pointed dyament cut with several lozange-shaped faces, that the chapter of the church of Chartres gave to my Seigneur."

• The diamond of King Charles VI: "Item, one flat diament cut with lozanges set in a gold ring given to the Duke by the King as a New Year's gift in 1412". This diamond and the preceding one are two of the first rose-cut diamonds ever recorded.

• The Genoa square diamond: "A large square and flat diament, weighing nineteen Genoese carats..." This is a square, mirror-table-cut diamond.

Page from Jean, Duke of Berry's jewel inventory (1413). It lists point-, table- and early rose-cut diamonds. Rough diamonds are described as "*non faits*" (not made) whereas cut diamonds are listed as "*faits*" (made). St. Geneviève Library, Paris.

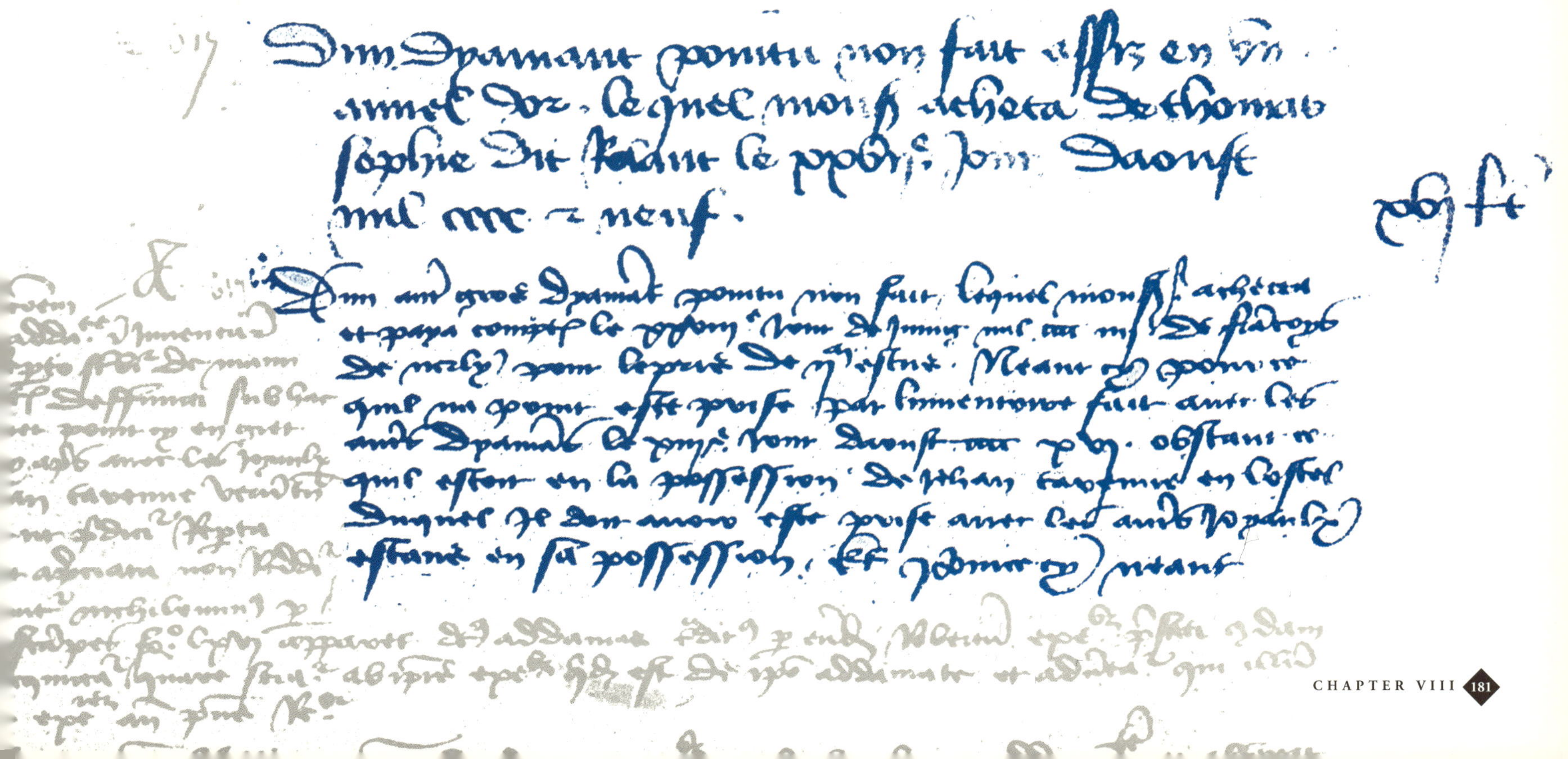

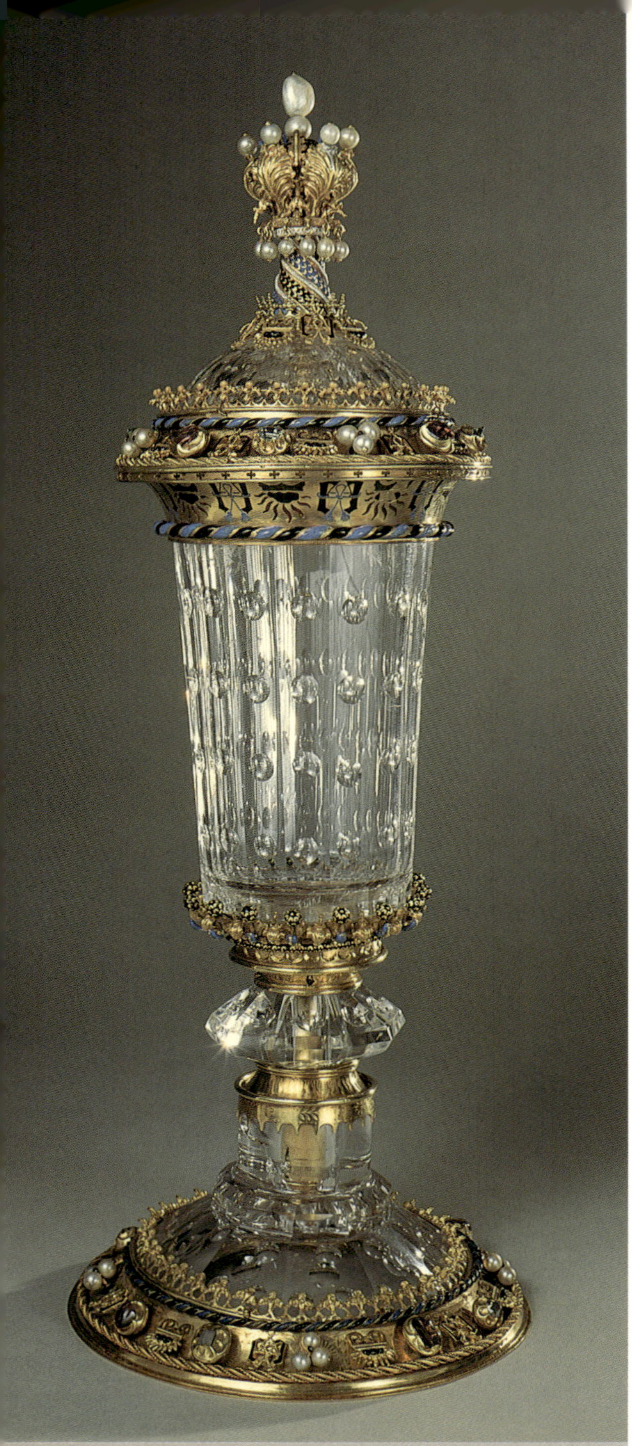

The great rock crystal cup of Duke Philippe the Good of Burgundy. It displays some very advanced diamond cuts, in particular onits base. Some of these are illustrated in Herbert Tillander's drawings below. Paris, first half of the 15th century. Kunsthistorisches Museum, Vienna.

It can be seen that, right at the beginning of the 15th century, diamonds were already being cut in a variety of ways. Admittedly, some rough crystals continued to be set in jewellery as they were, often in rings. On the other hand, lozenge-shaped facets had been developed, and the words "flat diament with lozanges" are virtually the definition of a rose-cut diamond. The frequently mentioned flat diamonds were probably cut from macles or small cleavages that were not highly valued in India. The inventory also includes assemblages of diamonds in jewellery, such as diamonds set into the shapes of the letters E and V, probably made from specially-cut baguette-shaped stones, with carefully determined angles. As for the "dyament by way of a mirouer", even at this early stage in the development of diamond-cutting, it is clearly a fully-developed table-cut. The mention of gem merchants is also interesting, because it testifies to the arrival in Paris of cutters originating from Italy, specifically from Genoa. Therefore, diamond-cutting techniques came from Italy to Flanders via Paris. Lastly, the mention of King Saint Louis' diamond should be noted. King Saint Louis died in 1270: this is the earliest-known mention of a diamond being owned by a monarch.

Therefore, at the dawn of the 14th century, diamonds could be cut, even if the number of diamond cuts and shapes available was somewhat limited. The quality and variety of diamond-cutting would henceforth evolve slowly, as can be seen in extremely rare surviving ancient jewels. Many old stones were subsequently re-cut, as techniques improved. That's the difficulty when studying ancient cuts. For this reason, museums like those of Dresden and Munich, which possess jewels that have not been disfigured, are exceptional. The Kunsthistorisches Museum of Vienna also possesses one of the rare pieces that display the development of diamond-cutting: the great rock crystal cup of Duke Philippe the Good of Burgundy, completed in the first half of the 15th century. Its base is decorated with 20 diamonds that display an astonishing variety of shapes. Although they are buried deep in a metal setting, one can still clearly see the gem-cutters' mastery. For example, they were able to create complex fleur-de-lys motifs with five diamonds. One can also see how diamond-cutters made the most of natural shapes: gems that were cut from octahedra can be clearly distinguished from those that were cut from dodecahedra. One particular multi-faceted pear-shape has exceptional brilliance and has remarkable fire for such an old cut.

On the subject of jewels that have a connection to the Burgundy court, we know of another remarkable example of a diamond with an unusual cut. It is the gem that embellished the *Three Brothers jewel*. The *Three Brothers* was a cloak clasp that was famous at the time. Its name comes from three extraordinary rectangular table-cut spinels that studded the jewel, of around 70 carats each, surrounding a 30-carat diamond. This was the largest-known diamond in Europe in the 15th century. It was bought by the Duke of Burgundy, Duke Jean the Fearless, shortly before his assassination in 1419. The stone was set in the centre of the *Three Brothers* under his successor, Philippe the Good. After the battle of Grandson, which Duke Charles the Bold lost in 1476, the Swiss victors ransacked the Duke's abandoned possessions and discovered a number of jewels, including the *Three Brothers*. A banker named Fugger acquired them, and had them depicted in several parchment watercolours, of which at least two survive. The *Three Brothers* was later offered to King Henry VIII of England in 1546, and ultimately purchased by Edward VI in 1551. The jewel was one of Elizabeth I's favourites, and it is shown in several of her portraits, and also as a bodice clasp on her funerary monument in Westminster Abbey. It disappeared from view after Charles I was overthrown and beheaded in 1649.

The *Three Brothers*, an extraordinary jewel that belonged to Charles the Bold. It was taken from him on the battlefield of Grandson in 1476. This watercolour was painted shortly afterwards. It shows what was then the largest diamond in Europe, of approximately 30 carats, in a faceted, four-sided point-cut. Basel Historical Museum, Switzerland.

The jewel's central diamond was of an unusually complex faceted shape, with each of its four sides coming to a point. This gave the gem remarkable brilliance. A watercolour that Fugger commissioned is preserved today in Munich, and it illustrates the cut beautifully. Its reflections gave the visual effect of a dark square in the centre. This is an optical illusion that is specific to any diamond cut in a double-pyramid shape that conforms roughly to the shape of the original octahedron. The lower pyramid fails to reflect light, thereby leaving a 'dark hole' in the centre, the size of which depends upon the pyramid's height. This 'black square' optical effect is clearly visible in the majority of 16th-century paintings portraying ancient diamond-cutting.

Marguerite Gonzaga, by Pourbus the Younger, around 1605. The princess is covered with diamonds, showing the full range of cuts that were in use before the invention of the brilliant-cut: points, rectangular and square tables, hearts, triangles...
Museo degli Argenti, Florence.

The spread of the point- and table-cuts

A significant political event occurred in the 16th century that changed the nature of the diamond trade: the Portuguese established bases on the Indian coast, at Goa, south of Bombay. These were commercial trading posts that were used to export spices and diamonds to Europe in large quantities. Diamonds became more numerous from that point on. They also became available in larger sizes. Renaissance portraits display a profusion of diamond jewellery, a trend which can be seen in the 17th-century portrait of princess Marguerite of Gonzaga, painted by Frans Pourbus the Younger around 1605. The young woman is literally covered with diamonds, all over her head, shoulders and chest.

These portraits all display two basic types of cut: the point-cut and the table-cut. The first was a modified simple pyramid shape, and the latter a pyramid with an abraded point. Point- and table-cuts became more widespread at the time because they arose from the use of octahedral crystal shapes: India was finally beginning to permit this type of crystal to be exported in larger quantities. The Residenz Museum in Munich and the Grünes Gewölbe in Dresden contain jewels with beautiful examples of such diamond cuts, often embellished with additional facets. The majority of the Renaissance's remarkable jewelled pendants are also decorated with table-cuts. By measuring the pyramids' angles, it is clear that these shapes resulted from cutting and are not natural crystal faces. Indeed, as we have seen earlier, diamond does not have same hardness in all directions and the natural octahedral crystal face is virtually invulnerable to wear. To make a highly reflective pyramid, 16th-century diamond-cutters would grind the stone in order to change the octahedron's four face gradients. In a natural octahedron, the angle between a crystal face and the 'equator' is 54°44'. Herbert Tillander's measurements of point-cut gems show readings that range from 45° to 60°. The natural octahedral face may be almost invulnerable, but merely cutting the gem at a 1° angle to the natural crystal face is enough to enter into a zone of reduced hardness that will enable normal gem-cutting to take place!

Point-cuts characteristically have a square outline, but they are also found in rectangles, triangles and even rhombuses. The finished outline depends on the original shape of the rough rock. Point-cut diamonds also spread to rings: the aggressively sharp, angular shape of this cut was perfect for embellishing such symbols of power and authority. Idle aristocrats sometimes used the points of their rings to engrave their names on window-panes, in châteaux and palaces. Point- and table-cuts proved to be so popular, their shapes were even used as decorative motifs in architecture and the applied arts. A famous house was built in Lisbon in the 16th century using "diamond point" masonry motifs. Unsurprisingly, the building belonged to Alfonso de Albuquerque, the viceroy of the Indies. There are also surviving pieces of Portuguese gold and silverware with these motifs, such as beautiful vermeil cups studded with "diamond points" on the bottom. However, the Diamond Palace of Ferrara remains the most striking example of diamond-cutting's influence on architecture.

1

3

1. A polished natural octahedron covers the summit of this elephant jewel. It is also studded with other table- and rose-cut diamonds. Dutch, late 17th century. Museo degli Argenti, Florence.

2. A startling example of the pointed diamond motif crossing over from jewellery into metalwork: a vermeil cup, studded with a constellation of pyramidal points. Portuguese, late 15th century, Foundation Ricardo Do Espirito Santo Silva, Lisbon.

Typical Renaissance jewels:

3. Pendant in the shape of a boat, decorated with many point- and table-cut diamonds. Germany, late 16th century. French National Renaissance Museum, Écouen.

4. Marriage pendant set with 21 diamonds. The central stone is a beautiful, classic table-cut. South Germany, around 1600. Rijksmuseum, Amsterdam.

5. Bear-shaped pendant, studded with point- and table-cut diamonds. Germany, late 16th century French National Renaissance Museum, Écouen.

6 Cockerel, decorated with rectangular and square point-cut diamonds, Flanders, 16th century. Rijksmuseum, Amsterdam.

7. Gold and diamond watch. The jewellery work is by Martin Duboule (1583-1639), early 17th century. Displayed with the case half-open, it is decorated with superb square and rectangular table-cut and triangular-cut diamonds. French National Renaissance Museum, Écouen.

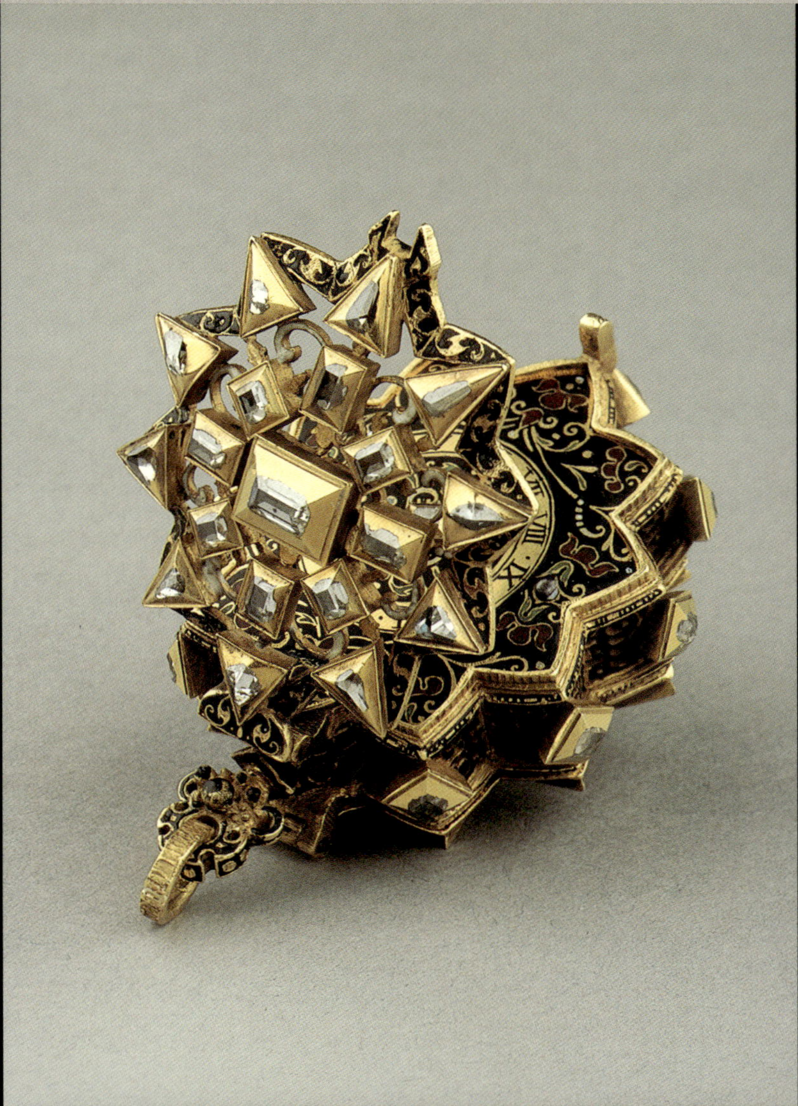

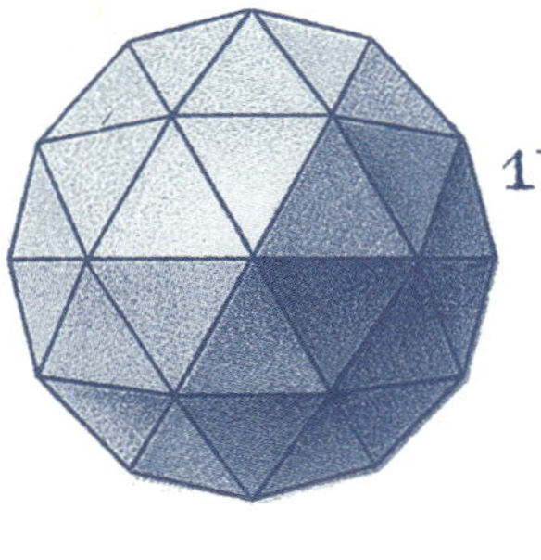

1 b

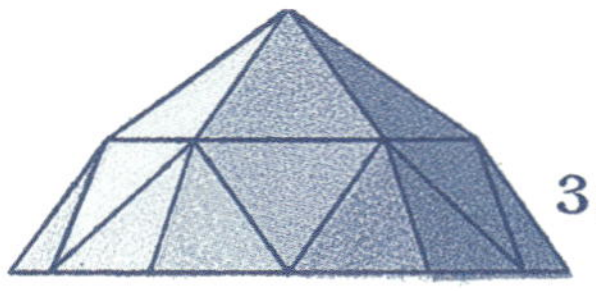

3 a

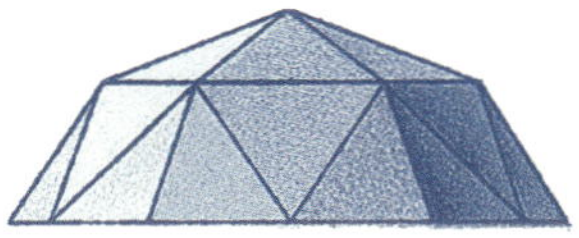

4 a

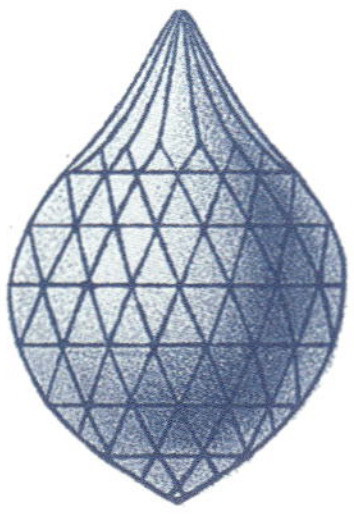

10

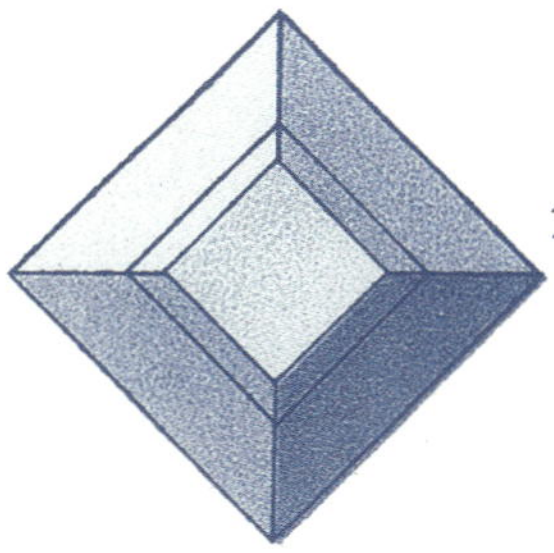

11 b

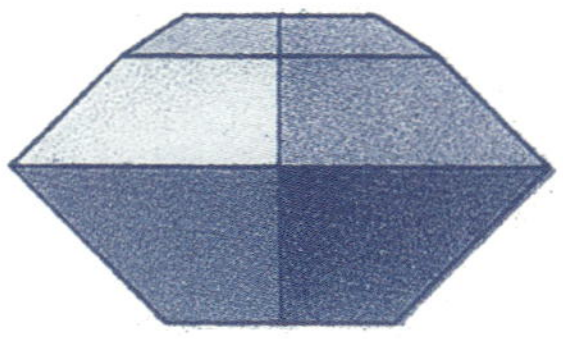

11 a

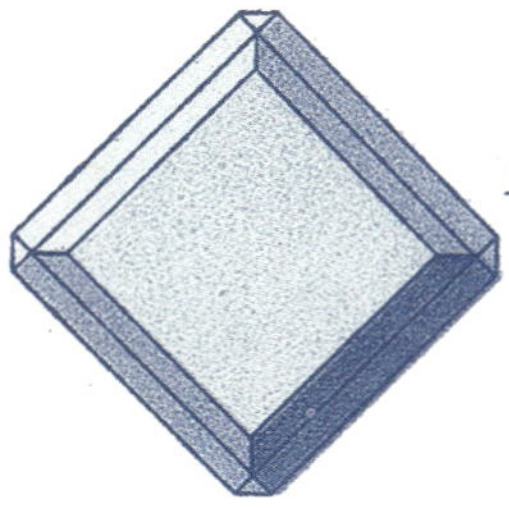

13 b

12 a

The rose-cut

The rose-cut was invented through necessity: cutters were forced to find some way of using the flattish rough diamonds (macles or cleavages) that India exported. These stones were thin, which made it impossible to cut them into a shape with a pointed upper side and a pronounced lower half. A flat-bottomed cut was therefore developed, which appears to have been inspired by the cabochon cut. Indeed, the rose-cut is effectively a cabochon with facets. The cabochon was characteristic of medieval gem-cutting. It was not until Gothic times that flat diamonds were cut, initially with three facets. Once the principle was established, skills improved until complex forms were obtained, with 6, 12, then 18 facets, and ultimately many more.

Rose-cut diamonds have an attractive sparkle, but they lack fire. Basically, the absence of a pavilion prevents the play of light inside the stone, and only surface reflection effects are possible. The light that enters the stone "leaks" from the back instead of being reflected forwards. In order to compensate for this, pairs of rose-cut diamonds came to be mounted back-to-back, to give double-rose doublets. Such doublets form the side petals of the double fleur-de-lys atop Louis XV's crown. The *Sancy* diamond formed the large central petal. The *Sancy* was itself a "double-rose" cut, albeit obviously in one piece. After the Coronation, the stones were removed from their setting in order to be returned to the Crown Jewel collection in the *Garde-Meuble*. Fortunately, copies were made during the process, and these copies were placed in the original setting, which is currently preserved at the Louvre. This piece is particularly interesting because it shows many of the other large, old-cut diamonds in the French Crown Jewels. These include eight large, bevelled square table-cuts at the top of the lilies in the bandeau (including five of the *Mazarins*, all of which were later re-cut as brilliants), the *Grand Mazarin* of 21.60 carats, and eight large double-rose pear-shapes. These were drilled at the tips and suspended between the crown's arches, and included *Mazarins V* and *VI*, of 23 and 20.26 carats respectively.

If they were sufficiently thick, the majority of old rose-cuts were later re-cut into brilliants. However, this resulted in considerable weight loss. For example, the *Mazarin IV*, a thick, high rose-cut of 24.92 carats, was re-cut into a brilliant under Louis XVI, and reduced to only 14 carats in the process. On the other hand, rose-cuts that were too thin to permit re-cutting into brilliant-shapes without massive loss of weight were preserved. Louis XVI retained almost 350 carats of them, and they were eventually used to decorate a marvellous rose-cut diamond sword-hilt, made in 1784. More recently, there has been renewed interest in this cut, and designers happily re-set old rose-cuts in contemporary jewels, such as the jeweller JAR, or Paul Flato in the 1930s.

A missing or poorly proportioned pavilion will cause light to 'leak' from the back of the gem. This was a major problem confronting Renaissance jewellers. To compensate for this effect, and to give the stone some sparkle, they came up with the solution of placing a reflective layer on the bottom faces of the pavilion or on the flat base of a rose-cut. This acted like a mirror. Since metal foil, mainly silver, was used, the term "foiled" was coined to describe this practice. The stone could also be enhanced by painting the pavilion with a coloured varnish, giving it a 'fancy colour'! Benvenuto Cellini's Treatise on jewellery and goldwork gives a lengthy description, explaining how to improve a stone's visual appearance by using these techniques to enhance its reflectivity and change its colour. French royal inventories often mention diamonds "painted" in blue, red, pink, etc. Once diamonds began to be cut in well-proportioned brilliant-cuts, they started reflecting light back to the eye using their natural optical properties, without any help from below.

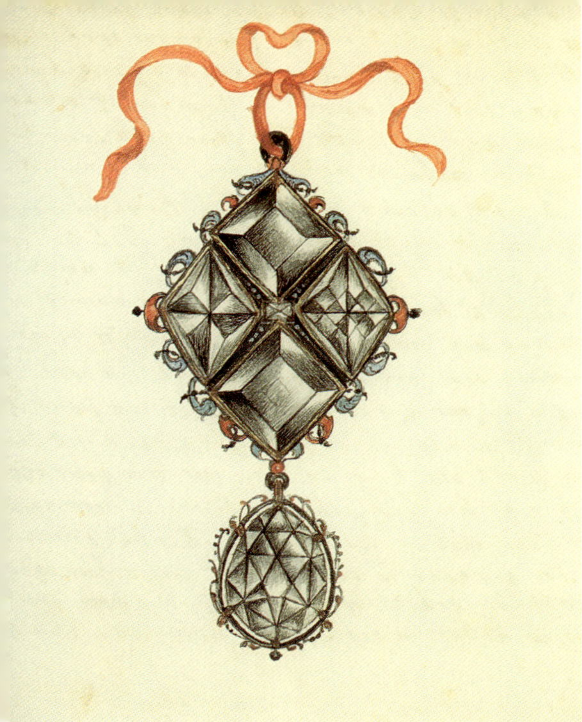

The Sancy is one of the most famous diamonds from the French Crown Jewels. It is a double-rose-cut. It was once set in the pendant to a jewel known as the *Mirror of Great Britain*, as depicted here. The Thomas Cletscher collection of illustrations, Boymans van Beuningen Museum, Rotterdam.

Diamond rings from the Indonesian island of Lombok.The stones have low pavilions, so the setting has a polished gold interior, which helps the stone reflect light.National Museum, Jakarta.

Paul Flato was a 1930s American jewellery designer. He re-set antique rose-cut diamonds in this superb bracelet. Private collection.

Illustrated plate from Max Bauer's treatise on precious gems, Leipzig, 1896. It is an anthology of the diamond cuts that were in use in the Renaissance. 1b, 3a and 4a are rose-cuts, 10 is a briolette, and 11b, 11a, 13b and 12a are variations on the table-cut.

15th-century Spanish gold cross, decorated with a baguette diamond-set inscription. The words "in *croce*" can be read at the top. The Louvre Museum, Paris, *Objets d'art* Department. Donated by Mr. and Mrs. Philippe Lenoir, Baron Adolphe de Rothschild.

Another superb jewel looted by the Swiss after the battle of Grandson in 1476: Charles the Bold's Order of the Garter. The motto "*Honi soit qui mal y pense*" (with archaic spelling) is written in baguette-shaped diamonds along the length of the garter, interspersed with eight large spinels. This exceptional piece also has a rose-cut, a very flat table-cut and two point-cut diamonds at its centre. Historical Museum, Basel.

Baguette-, briolette- and emerald-cuts

Baguette cuts appeared in the 15th century. The original versions were referred to in French texts as '*dos d'âne*' (saddle-shaped) cuts. They are basically elongated diamond shapes, with a lozenge-shaped cross-section, whose two long faces come together to form a ridge that supposedly resembles a saddle. The two "flanks" are sometimes faceted. Variations of this cut occur in many different lengths, enabling the use of diamonds in many different decorative designs, such as for writing letters. In the 16th century, pendants depicting the acronym for Jesus, IHS, were extremely popular. The letters were made from diamond baguette saddle-shaped cuts. These were also used to decorate pendants in the shape of miniature Saint George or Saint Michael figurines. Nowadays, a modern version of the baguette-cut is used to frame brilliants or make bracelets or chokers.

The briolette, a sort of faceted bead, was another very popular cut. It was often drilled, and could be used for pendants. The briolette was overshadowed by the development of the pear, a drop-shaped version of the brilliant-cut that was well suited for pendants. The briolette is, however, beginning to show signs of coming back into fashion today, in a minor backlash to the brilliant-cut's modern domination of diamond cutting.

The 'emerald-cut' is a shape that was originally designed for use with emeralds, which crystallise in elongated rods. The cut was adapted for use with diamonds: it consists of a cut-cornered square or rectangle, with tiers of facets on all four main sides. This cut possesses good brilliance, but unfortunately lacks fire. The emerald-cut is still used today, particularly for fancy-colour (or colourless) diamonds of good clarity. This cut displays the interior of a stone beautifully, but is not often used for poor-quality gems because it lacks complex, scintillating reflections that can sometimes be used to help disguise flaws.

The invention of the brilliant-cut

Historians are still divided over the question of who made the decisive steps in the evolution of diamond-cutting. The process has historically been attributed to 'Lodewyck van Berckem of Bruges', who worked in Antwerp. Was he, however, a historical or legendary character? It is impossible to say for sure. His statue still decorates the façade of a building in Antwerp, depicting him with a cut diamond in his hand. Some sources do not accredit him with having contributed a great deal to the development of the craft, and it is likely that they are correct. Other sources portray him as the originator of almost every significant innovation: the invention of the dop (a handle that holds the diamond for cutting), the innovation of securing the diamond to the dop using tin, the addition of castor oil to diamond powder to make an abrasive paste, and the introduction of the cast-iron grinding wheel! Surely, in a city such as Antwerp, where many diamond-cutters worked alongside each other as early as the beginning of the 16th century, developments must have been made constantly, resulting in remarkable technological advancement. This progress was eventually falsely attributed to one significant person due to blurred memories. It is probable that Lodewyck, who probably came from the Berckem suburb of Antwerp, was quite simply an ingenious diamond-cutter. None of the historical documents researched to date provides a definitive answer. There is a book, called "Wonders of the Western and Eastern Indies", written by Robert de Berckem, who claims to be Lodewyck's grandson. It was published in Paris in 1661. It makes great claims for Lodewyck's work, and is elegantly written, with a beautiful dedication to 'Mademoiselle', but it is, unfortunately, crammed with errors. It even makes the preposterous claim that his grandfather was the first to have succeeded in cutting diamonds, whereas in fact the 'secret' was already more than two hundred years old at the time the book was written! The author also had the nerve to omit any mention of a book that describes early diamond-cutting, and shows that these techniques were not restricted to North Europe. The text in question was written by Benvenuto Cellini himself, in his 1568 Treatise on jewellery and goldsmithery, published a century earlier. It provides an in-depth description of diamond-cutting: "a diamond is rubbed against another until one obtains the desired faces. The resulting powder is kept for later use. For this purpose, one sets the stone in lead or tin cups fixed on to wooden arms, and placed on a metal disc coated with oil and the aforementioned diamond powder". These words encapsulate the entire process of diamond-cutting: securing the stone in a dop, the use of diamond powder suspended in oil, and the metal grinding disc. The only remaining element for the development of the brilliant cut was to break with the practice of retaining maximum weight from the rough stone, in favour of maximising the play of light inside the gem.

Advanced versions of the table-cut, with additional facets on the corners, tend to suggest that the brilliant cut evolved gradually. All the brilliant-cut's characteristics are there: the reflective upper surface of the diamond, which would later be called the crown, and the lower half of the gem (the pavilion), formed from the bottom part of the octahedron. The final cut likely arose out of progressive experiments. Cutters must have noticed that certain shapes gave rise to astonishing optical effects, dispersing white light into rainbow-coloured 'fire'. Through trial and error, they determined the shape that had the best possible 'output' in terms of fire and brilliance.

The Wittelsbach Blue is the earliest-known diamond that merits the name 'brilliant-cut' (or 'old-cut' brilliant diamond, as cutters would now say). It is an extraordinary stone that belonged to the Crown of Bavaria before being sold in the 1950s. It only just escaped being re-cut into a perfectly proportioned modern brilliant-cut! It is a deep blue diamond, reminiscent of the *Hope* diamond, and it weighs 36.56 carats. Its oval form incorporates a wide table, a brilliant-cut crown and a pavilion with multiple facets in the shape of a star. Admittedly, its proportions are not ideal, but the beginnings are there. Incredibly, the stone's cut dates back to before 1664, when the gem was first mentioned.

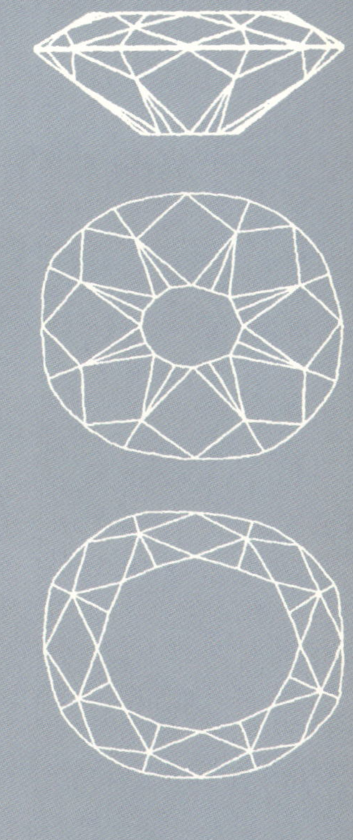

Schematic drawings of the *Wittelsbach Blue,* a splendid 36.56-carat stone that was the centrepiece of the Bavarian royal family's jewel collection. It is thought to be the world's oldest brilliant: cut at some time before 1664. Side view, pavilion view and crown view. After Herbert Tillander.

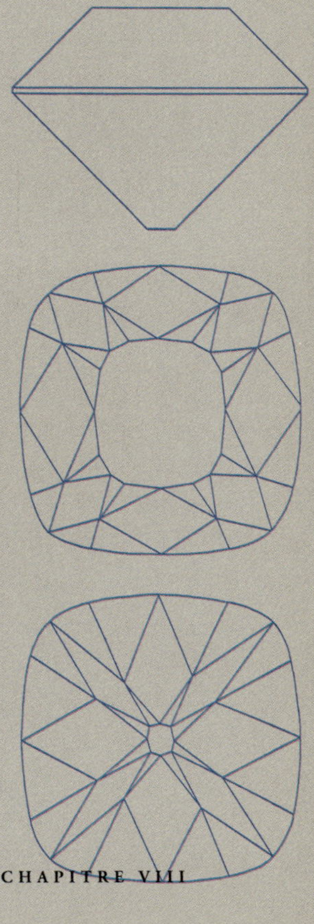

Lead moulds of the *Regent* diamond. These moulds were made during the cutting process, and as such are rare historical records. They show the progress of the work that culminated in one of the world's most beautiful diamonds. It is a marvellous 140.64-carat baroque brilliant, which is today in the Louvre. Sketches of its cut are also shown. The Natural History Museum, London.

The Regent diamond was the crowning glory of the French Crown Jewels. It was cut half a century after the *Wittelsbach*. It is the most marvellous known example of a cut that Herbert Tillander justly termed the "baroque brilliant". Out of all the different types of brilliant cut, this near-perfect variant survived up until the definition of the criteria of our modern brilliants. The Regent is the most beautiful and extraordinary example of its kind. Its proportions and the angles of its facets are perfect. The *Regent's* main angles are at 45°, on both the crown and pavilion. In addition to this balanced shape, the facets are perfectly symmetrical and the polish is absolutely flawless. The end result is that the 'baroque brilliant' cut gives off more multi-coloured fire than a modern brilliant, which generally looks 'colder'. Even though few were as fine as the Regent, these old-cut brilliants seem to possess just as much 'soul', with a distinct 'character'. Their cut was specifically designed to be viewed under the multiple pinpoints of light from candelabra, at a time when electricity, with its uniform, cold light (to which the modern brilliant cut is better adapted) had not yet been invented.

Lead moulds of the *Regent's* original rough stone are preserved to this day in London. The original stone weighed 426 old carats. It was discovered in 1698 in the Golconda region, and was purchased in late 1701 by Thomas Pitt, governor of the St. George fort in Madras. He sent it to London in 1702. It was entrusted to Joseph Cope, a diamond-cutter from the Jewish community in London. He was considered to be the only person in England able to undertake such delicate work. The cutting took him two whole years, from 1704 to 1706. Joseph Cope strove for perfection, which came at a price: the resulting yield was only 32%: 136 and 14/16ths carats remained from the original weight of 426 carats, a loss of 289 carats. But what a result! At the time, it was the largest colourless brilliant-cut diamond in the world, and it remains the largest old-cut Indian diamond in the world to this day. It is in the shape of a slightly rectangular cushion, measuring 31.58 mm in length, 29.89 mm in width and 21.05 mm thick, with a metric weight of 140.64 carats. With its incredible quality of cut, its exceptional clarity, its colour (or rather, its lack of colour), the *Regent* is still considered by many to be the most beautiful diamond in the world, even if its weight has been surpassed by several brilliant-cut gems of African origin.

In order to see baroque brilliant-cuts in all their beauty, one should go to the splendid Grünes Gewölbe museum in Dresden: it possesses thousands of diamonds that retain their 18th-century cuts. By studying ancient collections such as this one, it can be seen that the first brilliant-cuts were cushion-shaped, followed by ovals and pear-shapes. The diamonds cut from the famous Cullinan stone, in various shapes cut in 1908, could also be classified as baroque brilliants.

Two ancient brilliant-cut diamonds, seen 'face-up' and from the side, displaying two completely different sets of pavilion angles. With shallow pavilion angles, the stone seems bright overall, especially around the edges, but is slightly darker in the centre (the 'fish-eye' effect). With deep pavilion angles, the stone appears dark when viewed face-up. Approximately 15 carats each. National Museum, Jakarta.

The principles behind the different shapes

Cutting a brilliant-cut is a little like following an assembly line. There are a certain number of optical principles and rules regarding the placing of each facet on the stone. There are some possible variations from these principles. These permit the creation of fancy shapes and stones that are adapted to specific purposes. The basic modern brilliant-cut is currently the most widespread type. It is a round shape with 58 facets, including the table and the culet. Nowadays, thanks to mechanised cutting, it is even possible to cut diamonds of less than 1/1000th of a carat: 58 facets on a stone less than a tenth of a millimetre across! The round brilliant-cut is usually not appropriate for stones of over 10 carats.

Brilliant-cuts, showing how the principles of the brilliant cut can be adapted to various shapes, and two examples of the emerald cut.

The pear is a variant of the brilliant-cut which is particularly suited for elongated stones that will eventually be set in pendants. The marquise is a navette cut. It is said that its shape and name were inspired by the Marquise de Pompadour's mouth. Finally, there are triangle-cuts, and cushion-cuts, which are cut-cornered square or rectangular brilliants. The *Tiffany* diamond is a famous example of a cushion-cut. It has an extraordinary golden-yellow colour, and was cut in Paris with very thick proportions to deepen the colour. It has 90 facets.

It is generally believed that the modern brilliant-cut is the end result of centuries of diamond-cutting history. It integrates all the crystallographic properties of the stone, in order to maximise the visual and economic result. It also gets the most out of a stone, since a single octahedral crystal can be cut into two brilliant-cut diamonds. It has also benefited from highly advanced computerised optical research. The brilliance and fire have been maximised to virtually their full potential, and this cut is said to be unsurpassed. And yet... new cutting styles keep on appearing. Has the brilliant-cut become so standardised and impersonal that it has created demand amongst innovation-seeking customers for something different? Fancy cuts have appeared in the past few decades, and they are making their mark on the industry. The Princess cut is one of them: multiple small, wedge-shaped facets give rise to stunning brilliance. The family of "Flower" cuts is another group of new shapes. They were invented by the master diamond cleaver Gabi Tolkowsky to make the most of odd-shaped rough stones, and to camouflage faint colours under a dazzling play of reflections. The clever part of these cuts is in the multiplication of the facets around the culet. The profusion of sparkling reflections attracts the eye and obscures any deficiencies in colour. The flower cuts include the "Fire Rose", "Sunflower", "Zinnia", "Marigold" and "Dahlia".

This photograph perfectly illustrates the brilliant-cut's ability to split light up into the colours of the rainbow.

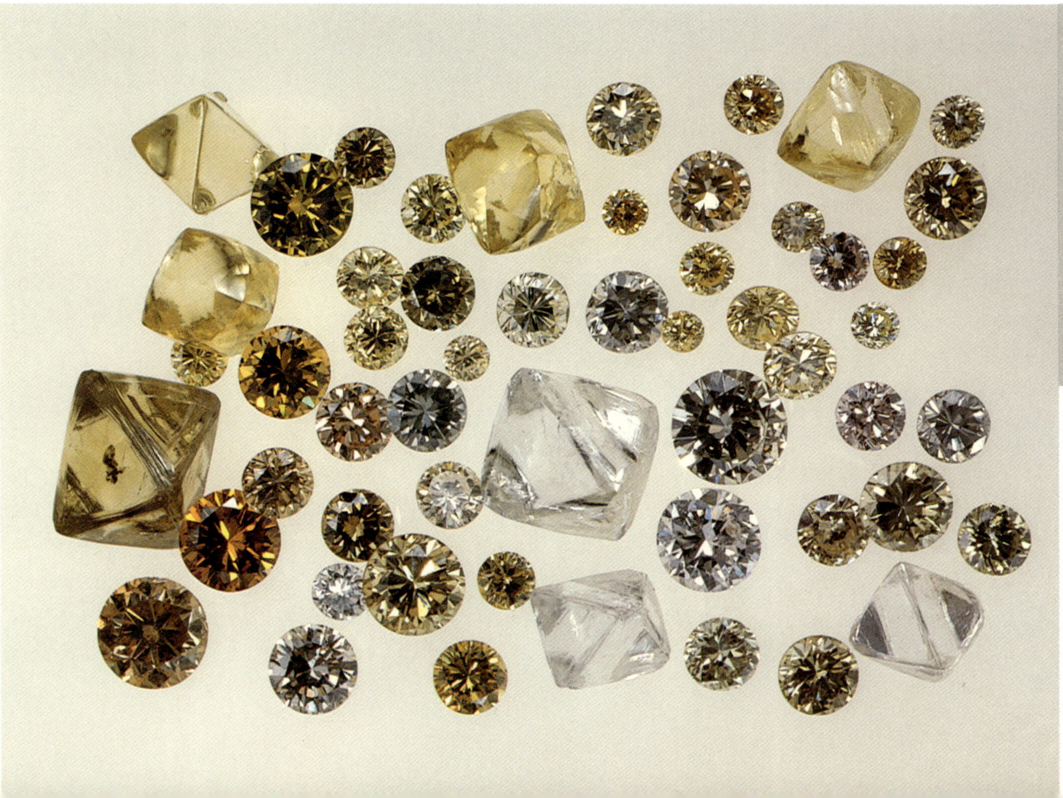

Octahedral rough diamonds. Two round brilliants can be cut from each octahedron.

Three stages in the cutting of the *Premier Rose*, a superb 137.02-carat pear-shape, cut from a rough stone that originally weighed 353.9 carats. William Goldberg supervised the process in 1978-79.

Cutting large diamonds

Round brilliant cuts are not suited to very large stones. They end up looking like car headlights, with a slightly unattractive, characterless appearance. It is usually necessary to tailor the cut to bring out the best in each large gem. In addition, cutting a monster stone, of several hundred carats for example, is a highly specialised activity. Such exceptional undertakings sometimes require up to four years of preparation and work.

Very large gems are usually irregular in shape, like big, partly dissolved ice-cubes. These huge rough stones must first be studied minutely, in order to reveal the impurities, inclusions and internal stresses that could cause them to shatter. It is also essential to locate the crystallographic axes, the cleavage planes and, finally, to determine the shape that will get the most out of the stone. The gigantic *Cullinan* diamond, for example, weighed 3,106 carats in the rough. It was decided to cleave it into three pieces. Joseph Asscher of Amsterdam was the master cutter in this case. He concentrated a lifetime's worth of skill into two hammer blows to split the gem apart. In contrast, the *Premier Rose* was sawn in two: it was a superb rough stone of 353.9 carats, cut in 1978. The *Centenary*, on the other hand, was neither sawn nor cleaved. The 599-carat rough was instead gradually ground to its preliminary shape by hand.

Special tools usually need to be devised every time such an enormous stone is cut. These need to be installed in a kind of bunker. This ensures both a high level of security, and the complete absence of extraneous vibrations. The dop, the handle that presses the diamond against the grinding wheel, is unusually large. The diamonds are affixed to the dop using a special paste. Formerly, molten lead was used, but this has been superseded by a composite cement mixture. A large polishing wheel, or 'lap', is also needed, along with special equipment to monitor progress. The *Centenary* was a fragile gem, so the dop contained probes that permanently monitored temperature changes and the stresses imposed on the stone. Before cutting can take place, a great deal of research must be undertaken in order to determine the stone's strengths and weaknesses, and the final shape that it will be given. Great master diamond-cutters excel in these difficult tasks: the Asscher brothers in Amsterdam (cutters of the *Cullinan*), William Goldberg in New York (cutter of the *Premier Rose*), Gabi Tolkowsky (cutter of the *Centenary* and the world's largest diamond, the *Golden Jubilee*). Currently, the most popular stone-cutting workshop is Benny Steinmetz's in Tel-Aviv and in Johannesburg, which is where the De Beers *Millennium Star* was born.

The story of the *Centenary* diamond's cutting shows the difficulties involved in shaping such a gem. Gabi Tolkowsky was selected as the cleaver because, at the time, he was reputed to be one of the best professionals in the field. This reputation was anchored in a long family tradition. His uncle Marcel had published a book in 1909 on diamond cutting. It is still an authoritative text, and it provided the first scientific assessment of the ideal angles for the facets of a modern brilliant-cut diamond. His nephew studied stone geometry and optics in depth, enabling him to go beyond his uncle's theories of brilliants and to invent the 'flower cuts', using unconventional angles for diamonds with slightly tinted colours. His fondness for innovation enabled him to conceive completely unconventional solutions for the cutting of the *Incomparable* and the *Golden Jubilee*, respectively 407.48 carats and 545.65 carats, two "cognac"-coloured giants.

When he saw the *Centenary* in the rough state, Gabi Tolkowsky immediately understood that its shape would complicate the cutting process. Its irregularity, protrusions, and a 'horn' sticking out from the surface would all conspire to create difficulties. By late 1988, he locked himself in a specially equipped vault in the heart of De Beers' Johannesburg diamond research facility, along with two polishing experts and a small team of technicians, engineers and guards. It took more than a year to simply prepare the necessary tools, which had to be sufficiently stable and robust. He examined the rough stone constantly. As a result of its crystallographic re-entrant angles, it was to risky to try sawing (which would cause vibrations), or laser cutting (which would generate heat). He finally chose to 'kerf' (trim) the stone by hand. This was done using a diamond blade set in a handle, like a kind of neolithic scalpel. In this way, Gabi Tolkowsky patiently eliminated all the irregularities himself. In all, 50 carats were removed, taking 154 working days. By then, the rough weighed 520 carats and was ready to be cut and polished. The final shape had yet to be determined. Innumerable drafts were prepared, in order to obtain the best yield for the final gem. An exotic, modified heart-shape was finally selected. The polishing wheels started turning in March 1990, and finally stopped in January 1991. In all, it had taken more than two years of work to fashion the final extraordinary 273.85-carat gem, with 247 facets: 164 on the upper crown, and 83 on the pavilion. It is the largest-known colourless modern-cut diamond. It is exceeded only by *Cullinans I and II*, neither of which had the benefit of modern computerised cutting technology. The result was a priceless, scintillating gem with glorious fire which was insured for 100 million dollars at the time of its public unveiling in May 1991. According to rumours, it may later have been sold to the Sultan of Brunei...

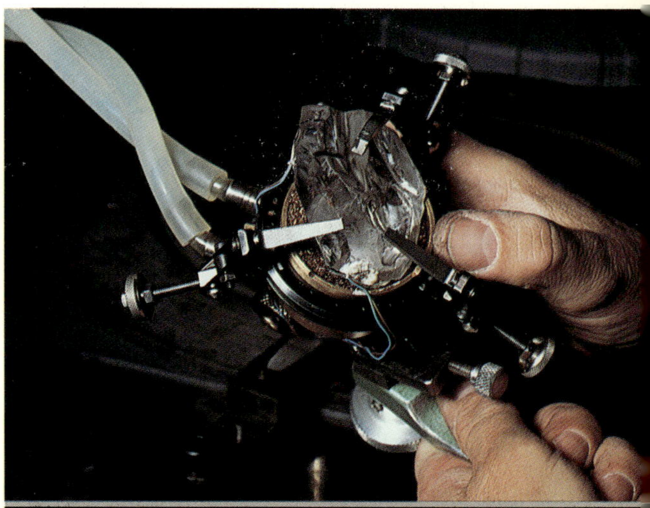

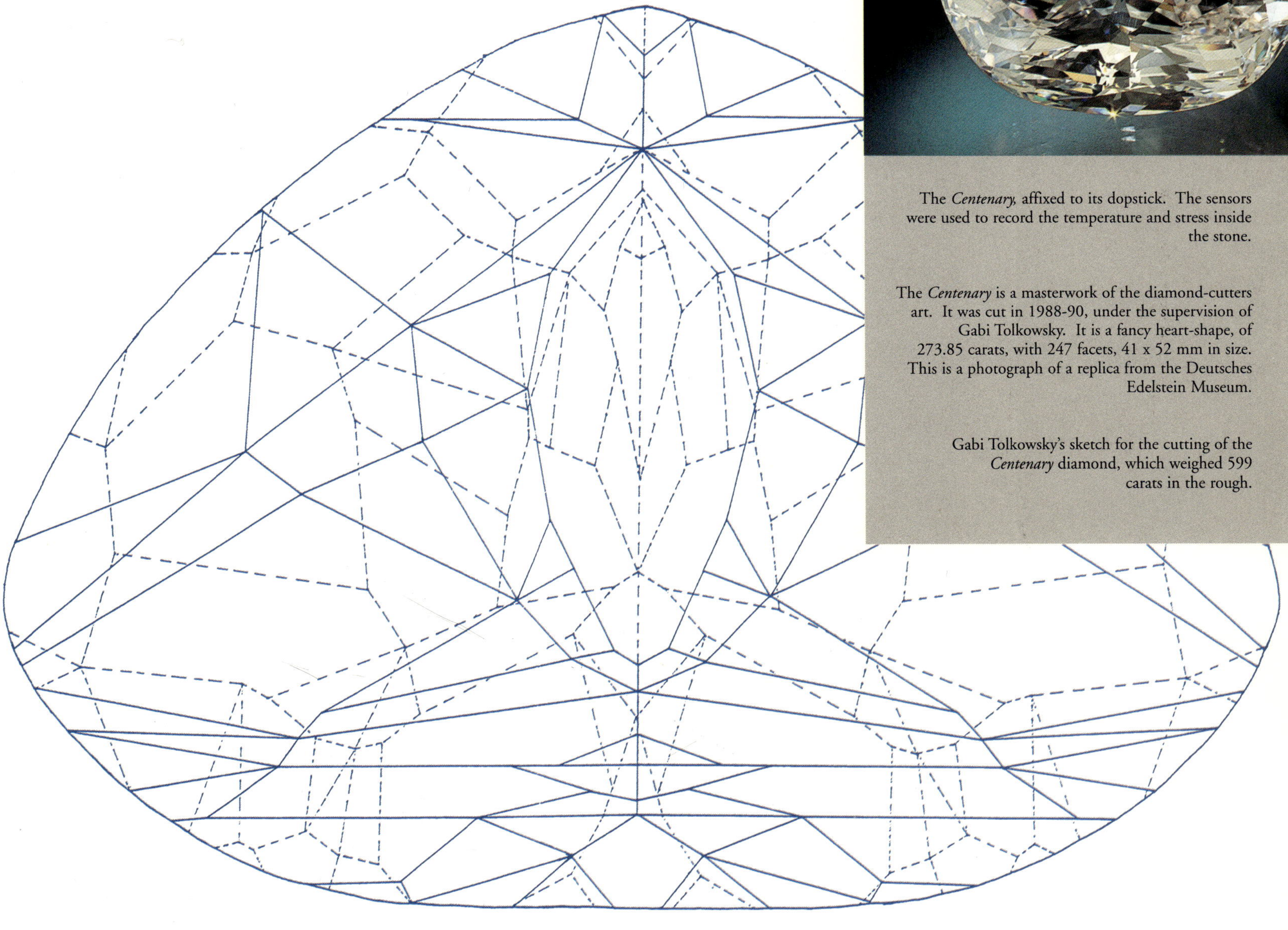

The *Centenary*, affixed to its dopstick. The sensors were used to record the temperature and stress inside the stone.

The *Centenary* is a masterwork of the diamond-cutters art. It was cut in 1988-90, under the supervision of Gabi Tolkowsky. It is a fancy heart-shape, of 273.85 carats, with 247 facets, 41 x 52 mm in size. This is a photograph of a replica from the Deutsches Edelstein Museum.

Gabi Tolkowsky's sketch for the cutting of the *Centenary* diamond, which weighed 599 carats in the rough.

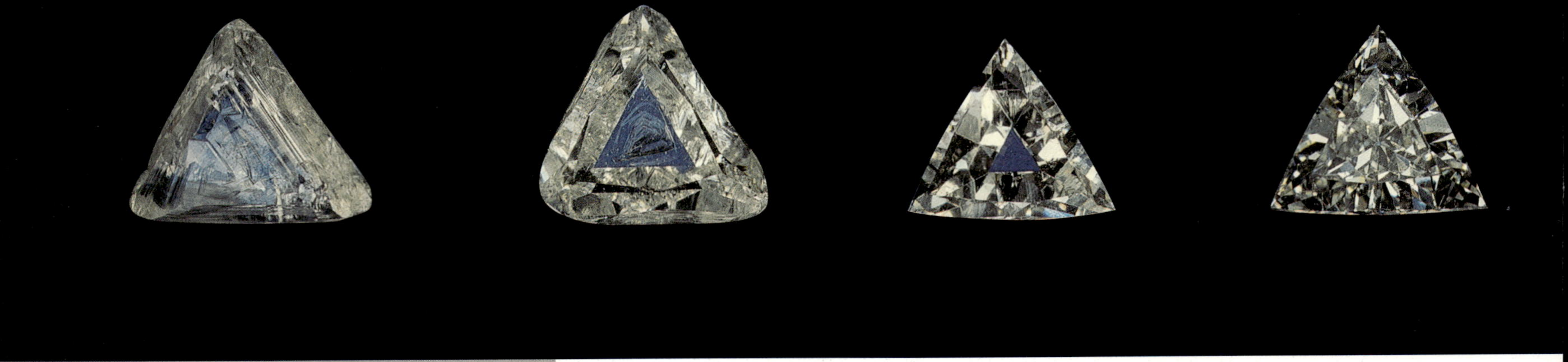

The artistry of modern diamond-cutting is shown here, working wonders on a triangular macle: various stages in cutting are shown, from the original rough to the final stone.

Brilliance at the turn of the century: Bordynckx, a Belgian gem engraver, revived the ancient Mogul technique of diamond-engraving for this superb butterfly with inscribed diamond wings. Bordynckx worked for Boucheron, a top jewellery firm in the Place Vendôme, Paris. He developed an extraordinary series of cut and engraved diamonds that helped to make the firm's reputation at the turn of the 19th century. New York, private collection.

How will diamond-cutting evolve?

Since the beginning, diamond-cutting has relied upon certain key processes which are not covered in detail in this book: the stone is marked with ink, it is cleaved or sawn, then the stone is 'bruted' (trimmed) to give its rough outline, and finally the facets are polished. This sequence of processes never varied, and it led diamond-cutting to its current limits, based around the principle of the round brilliant-cut. An angle would be modified here or there, a new shape might be introduced, but the basic principles remained. There was never anything truly new. However, in the past few years, new and completely revolutionary techniques have been introduced, which also contain elements of sculpture. These remarkable changes have come from technical innovations that have broken down the barriers constraining the diamond-cutter. Until recently, cutters could only place facets on the sides of a stone. Now that new technology has had an impact upon diamond sawing, and laser-technology has enabled the cutting of angles that penetrate into the stone, the possibilities are infinite.

Nowadays, many of the steps in the diamond-cutting process have been automated. Diamonds are sliced on serried rows of circular saws, or cut with laser beams. This professional cleaver's box is now just a souvenir. Cleavers used to split tiny diamonds in two using only these simple tools and a skilled hammer blow. This particular box belonged to Solomon Isaac Finsy (1875-1963), a cleaver working for diamond-cutters from Amsterdam and Antwerp. The boxes are used to house the diamonds, to guide the tools and to collect the fragments. The main tool is a wooden handle, to which a diamond was affixed with wax. A notch would then be ground in the gem, using the point of another diamond. An iron blade would be wedged in this notch, and the diamond cleaved in two by hitting the blade with a hammer. From the Wejer-de-Groodt and Kunz-de-Groodt collection.

This fancy star-cut was made possible thanks to the modern use of lasers in diamond-cutting.

In the past few years, remarkable star-shaped diamonds have appeared on the market. These are true technical marvels: classic geometrical shapes that sparkle with diamond fire. Stars have always been popular, as can be seen in the beautiful star tiara of Queen María Pia of Portugal. However, these stars were all made from a grouping of several diamonds and never from a single stone. Such a feat was inconceivable. Since then, however, a company has developed cutting processes that enable the cutting of re-entrant angles that form the notches between the points of each star, enabling the large-scale marketing of beautiful diamond stars. These corners were initially obtained by sawing, but are now shaped using a laser beam. The diamond vaporises at the point of contact with the beam, which can cut through the diamond from any angle, according to the wishes of the designer and the instructions of the computer programmer controlling the beam. The only limit is the underlying objective of diamond-cutting: to create a faceted stone that will maximise the beautiful play of light in a diamond.

The traditional brilliant-cut is an abstract shape that has no cultural significance. Diamond-cutters have used the new techniques to create shapes adapted to specific markets. For example, cutters have introduced diamond Buddhas to the Asian market. They have been very successful. The Buddha-shaped, faceted stone is perfectly in tune with the symbolic importance of diamonds in Buddhism: one fundamental Buddhist Sutra teaches that "The Buddha's truth is sharp, like a diamond". This is probably the future of diamond-cutting. Laser-cutting enables the creation of new shapes that are adapted to all the different global cultures. Diamonds could acquire new significance, more like an amulet or souvenir than a gemstone. Maybe we will soon find Madonna-shaped Virgin Mary diamonds on sale. Let's hope... not! In any case, the four-leaf clover, cut from a single stone, is already on the market.

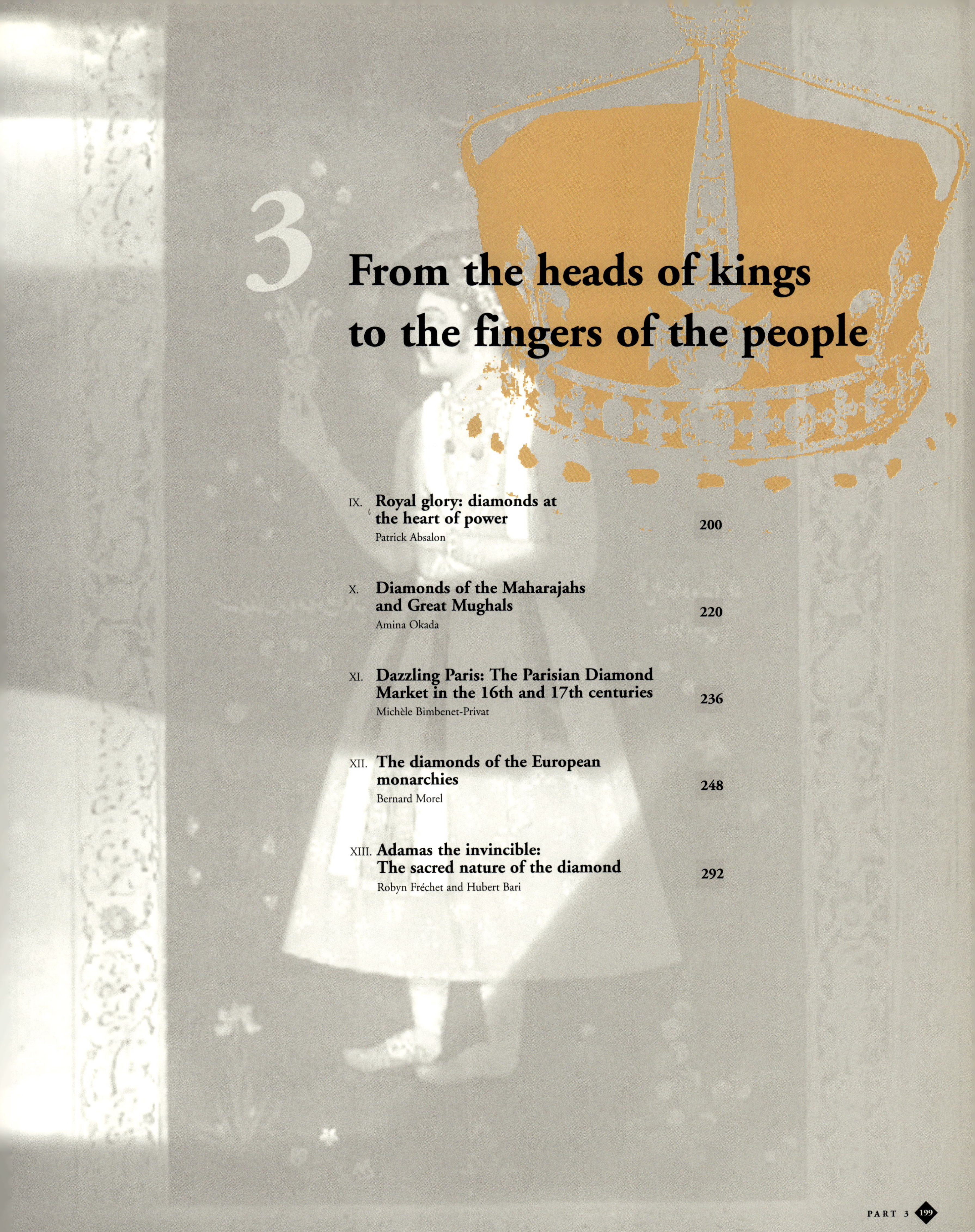

3 From the heads of kings to the fingers of the people

CHAPTER IX

Patrick Absalon

Royal glory: diamonds at the heart of power

It is said that Adamas, the indestructible stone, diffuses and concentrates infinite power. It is the 'third eye', that reveals the heart of the one who wears it, whether cut as a point or a brilliant, set in a ring, mounted on a crown, or worn on bodice in official court portraits. Its history is still being written, between dream and reality, poetry and science.

We are compulsively drawn to diamond's beauty and sparkle. However, its scarcity and price are not the only reasons for our fascination. Ever since Pliny' the Elder's time (23-79 AD), diamonds have nourished man's fantasies and been synonymous with power. Specifically, in the Western world, diamonds evoke two types of power: the power exercised by the grace of God, which is essentially male, and the power of seduction, which is essentially female. For some, particularly those who have experienced absolute political power, diamonds have become tangible symbols of their might. For others, ranging from Greek goddesses to Marilyn Monroe, diamonds and all precious gemstones are seductive, captivating symbols of beauty. However, at this point we should look at the practical implications of diamond's extraordinary structure, in order to explain why the stone became not only the king of gems, but the gem of kings.

'Pallas and the Centaur', by Sandro Botticelli (1444-1510). Pallas' robe is decorated with diamond ring motifs. Uffizi, Florence.

Diamonds and divine right

It all appears to have started with Pliny the Elder. In fact, he himself had been inspired by Theophrastus' *Treatise on Gems* (*ca.* 372-*ca.* 287). When Pliny wrote his famous *Natural History*, he already associated diamonds with non-human, divine forces. Here is an extract from his 27th volume, one of the best-known text on diamond: "[...]this invincible force scorns the two most powerful natural elements, iron and fire. It can only be broken by the goat's blood. Even then, the diamond must be soaked in the fresh, hot blood, and the blows must be numerous[...] Such an invention is certainly the work of the gods and nothing less than a divine favour. It is pointless to search nature for explanations: it is divine will".

The most interesting part of this text is not the allusion to the destructive power of goat's blood, which our readers are unlikely to experiment with at home. It is the author's desire to prove that diamonds (which could not be cut at that time) were amongst the many gifts that the gods had left to mankind: it was an expression of divine will. Pliny also believed that the gem grew inside gold, the quintessential precious metal that was worn by the powerful. Diamonds were not stones like the others and, as a result, they were expensive. He therefore wrote: "diamond commands the greatest price, not only among gems, but among all the goods of mankind. For many years it has been known unto kings alone, and not all kings, but only some".

In Pliny's time, diamond jewels were indeed virtually priceless rarities, almost exclusively reserved for the powerful. Some diamond-set Roman rings are known to have survived to this day, but they could all be worn on the fingers of one hand. Also according to Pliny, diamond's purpose was not only to reinforce the monarchs' display of power. It also had additional, unsuspected properties. These supposed properties would inspire medieval lapidaries for generations, to the beginning of the 17th century.

The Prime Mover made the diamond

All of diamond's virtues are summarised in Anselmus Boetius de Boot's Gemmarum lapidum Historia, published in Hanover in 1609. The book summarises centuries of exegetic interpretations, popular traditions, and the obvious influence of Theophrastus and Pliny the Elder. It also tries to disentangle the supernatural from the natural. Boetius de Boot was a healer in Emperor Rudolf II's court. Rudolf II was the King of Bohemia and Hungary, reigning from 1576 to 1612. He was the son of Maximilian II, and an aesthete and a connoisseur. He surrounded himself with artists, and accumulated an incomparable treasury. It is said that Rudolf believed that, by concentrating such beautiful items around his person, he would benefit from their power. He suffered from an unpleasant, chronic melancholy, and the hoard of riches was intended to alleviate his suffering. He had a passion for gems, such as emeralds and rubies, and especially diamonds. It is said that he cut them himself, by some mysterious process.

Diamond had some particularly astonishing uses, quite apart from its hardness, which was due to the fact that it was made from "most united matter". According to Boetius de Boot, these properties had nothing to do with mineralogical science. "all the supernatural effects that are produced by mixing common and precious gems can be attributed to God. Simultaneously, they can be used to express His wisdom, His power, and all the attributes that God possesses: thus, we awaken inside, and adoration and respect for His divinity are born".

Although he gives his text a scientific gloss, Boetius de Boot persisted in interpreting the natural sciences within an interpretative and theological tradition. Clearly, he was a man of his time, since the Catholic princes were leaving to fight against the Reformation. For Boetius de Boot, diamond remained an inalterable body. Its powder could be swallowed, and it would be returned as it had been introduced, in the manner of a cherry stone. It was therefore not a poison. Did it cure the plague, chase away poisons, protect against sorcery and "vain fears"? Did it bring "victory, constancy and force of spirit"? He wrote: «If one attributes something of the metaphysical or supernatural to this precious stone, it must be believed that this does not proceed according to its own temperament, essence, or nature, but according to the Law and the order of the Prime Mover".

Therefore, diamond is only precious becomes it comes from the Prime Mover, i.e. God. Boetius de Boot tried to locate the "historical" background to the stone's relationship with the Almighty while defining diamond as the receptacle of God's divine presence. This background lies in the stone worn by Aaron, Moses' brother and the first Hebrew priest. Whenever he entered the shrine, he would not only hold his blossom-covered staff in his hand, but also affix a "diamond" (according to Boetius) to his chest. The Bible does indeed mention that Aaron's breastplate contained twelve gemstones that were "beloved unto God". However, none of these were diamonds. There is not a shadow of a doubt about this: the holy texts provide precise descriptions. Diamonds were so symbolically important in Boetius de Boot's time that he hunted for potential biblical references to them. They could not have been known in Aaron's time.

Diamonds are, in fact, entirely absent from the Bible. It does, however, mention several other gems, such as ruby, carbuncle (garnet), and particularly sapphire. Indeed, the holy text mentions sapphire more than any other gem. It is as blue as the vault of heaven; when the God of Israel appears to Moses and Aaron, he does so upon a sapphire carpet (Exodus, 24,10); Heavenly Jerusalem will be built on emeralds and sapphires (Isaiah, 54, 11) and Yahweh's throne will be made from sapphire (Ezekiel, 1, 26). Saint John's Apocalypse finishes with a description of the heavenly city. The description mentions gold, pearls and several precious stones (Apocalypse, 21, 9-21), but not diamonds!

Two portraits of Henri III. In the first, he wears a diamond-set hat ornament. In the second, he wears a necklace set with point-cut diamonds. Drawings from the French School, 16th century. French National Library, Department of Prints and Photography, Paris.

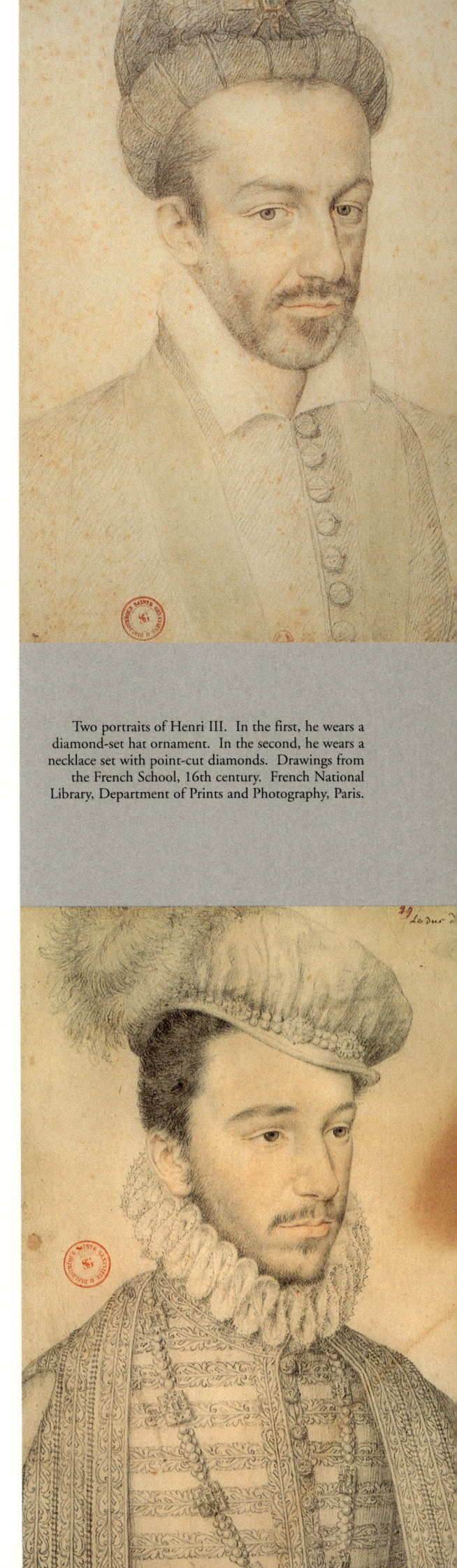

Portrait of Marie de Medici, by Scipione Pulzone (1550 - around 1622). She is depicted wearing a suite of pearl jewellery, set with a diamond plaque. There are matching diamond plaque motifs on her sleeves and her hair ornament. Palatine Gallery, Florence.

Boetius de Boot followed in an intellectual tradition that made diamond the stone of God, even though it is, in fact, absent from the holy texts. As a result, it was also the stone of monarchs or pontiffs. They made it their sacred gemstone: it was proof of their fidelity to God, and it was the sum of the human virtues ("innocence, constancy and power", according to Boetius de Boot) that they professed to possess. In this case, diamond was not only a precious stone that guaranteed superiority and bestowed certain virtues upon its wearer, it also educated the common people about certain attributes that the diamond-studded king evidently already possessed. When people adorned themselves with diamonds, the gems had a dual function: they were proof of the indestructibility and permanence of power, and they were a message to the world that the wearer remained faithful unto God.

Since diamonds were the stones of the Prime Mover, they were thus the legitimate stone of monarchs - particularly the French monarchs. The French monarchy, as all the monarchies based on a coronation ceremony, derived its powers from God. The French monarch's divine status dates back to Pépin le Bref's coup in 751. Pépin was supported by the Church, and anointed with holy oil during his coronation ceremony at Soissons. Pépin's wife, Queen Bertrade, was in turn blessed by Pope Etienne II in Saint-Denis. The pontiff then ordered that nobody from outside the royal family should ever be chosen as king, under penalty of excommunication. The divine right of kings was therefore born.

The king is the "son" of God and therefore wears diamond, the divine stone. As diamond-cutting, discovered in the 15th century, gave diamonds a new aesthetic, providing them with reflective light effects, and since this light was that which "illuminates mankind" (John, 1, 4), the divine light came to reinforce the idea that diamond was the gem of kings. This combination of hardness, invincibility and divine light resulted in the diamond becoming a symbolic element. The ruling classes used it to adorn themselves enthusiastically : terrestrial powers, who wished to associate themselves with a higher power.

Some dynasties made the gem their emblem: for example, rich bankers and princes in Renaissance Italy, such as the Medicis of Florence, the Estes of Ferrara and the Gonzagas of Mantua were. Cosimo de Medici (1389-1464) chose three interlaced diamond rings as his emblem. Lorenzo the Magnificent (1449-1492) added three feathers some years later "white Faith, green Hope, and ardent red Charity", according to Giorgio Vasari, the historian. These rings are prominently displayed in a famous Sandro Botticelli painting of Pallas (better known as Athena or Minerva). The diamond motifs are shown on the goddess' gown: she appears to have become a Florentine at a stroke and she is depicted subduing evil, in the incarnation of a hideous centaur. This masterpiece is preserved at the Uffizi gallery in Florence, and it contains both history and symbolism. It was painted around 1480, at a time when Lorenzo was experiencing some difficulties with the Papacy (Pope Sixtus IV allied himself with the Pazzi family, sworn enemies of the Medicis). Lorenzo then tried to ally himself with Ferdinand, King of Naples (the bay of Naples is seen in the painting's background), in order to win the battle. The diamond-studded Florentine was victorious, subduing their enemies in style. The painting also appears to be implying that Minerva is the protector of the arts, since the Tuscan city was the cradle of the Renaissance. Pallas stylishly subdues the centaur's barbarism, in order to allow beauty to triumph.

'*Symbola divina et humana...*', Jacopo Typhotius' collection of heraldic motifs (1601-1603). Many of the heraldic devices include a diamond ring motif. Cosimo I de Medici was the Grand Duke of Tuscany from 1569-1574. His emblem depicts three interlaced diamond rings, symbolising courage, endurance and valour. The motto is "SUPERABO" ("I will overcome"). Botticelli's painting also depicts this motif, on Pallas' gown. French National Library, Literature and Art department.

Agnès Sorel (around 1422-1450), Charles VII's favourite. She wears two diamonds, set in a forehead jewel. She is often still erroneously cited as the first woman to have worn a diamond ring. French School drawing. French National Library, Department of Prints and Photography, Paris.

Zeus made the ring

The diamond set in a ring is a symbol of fidelity to god. It displays the unbreakable bond between the wearer and a 'higher authority'. Whether in late 15th-century Florence or early 21st-century Paris, a diamond ring - particularly an engagement ring - symbolises one individual gaining power over another. The origins of this practice appear to date back to Greek mythology. The first stone-set ring was invented by Zeus, the ruler of the Gods, who commanded the world from the summit of Mount Olympus. The legend deserves to be told.

The Titan Prometheus, a friend of mankind, had offended Zeus during a banquet. He had given human beings the best pieces, and left Zeus the bones and scraps. Zeus was infuriated, and deprived men of fire as a punishment. The inventive Prometheus, however, stole some sparks from Apollo's chariot-wheel, and gave fire back to humanity. He was soon punished. He was chained to a rock in the Caucasus Mountains, and an eagle descended every day to devour his liver, every day for eternity. Heracles (also known as Hercules), who desperately searched for the Apples of the Hesperides, as one of his Twelve Labours, sought the advice of Prometheus, the Seer who told him where to find the Apples. As a gesture of thanks, the lionskin-wearing superhuman killed the eagle before leaving. Zeus was on the point of marrying the beautiful Thetis, and Prometheus warned him "if you marry her, the child born of your union will be stronger than you, and you will be overthrown". Zeus broke his engagement to Thetis, and pardoned Prometheus. However, in order to save face, Zeus ordered him to take a link from his chains, encrust a fragment of the Caucasus rock in it, and wear it on his finger forever, as a symbol of his debt to Zeus.

Therefore, this rudimentary rock-set ring was invented to symbolise an unbreakable bond between subject and master. In a diamond ring, the diamond is the quintessential symbol of power, whether divine power, fidelity or belonging.

When the Portuguese opened a trading post in Goa at the beginning of the 16th century, diamond imports from India increased rapidly. In 1725, the discovery of diamonds in Brazil increased the supply of the gem, which had become very rare. Diamond-set jewels became more commonplace, and their decorative value diluted the stone's symbolic link to God. However, even though diamond prices fell after mines were discovered in Africa in 1866, the stone's importance as a symbol of power did not diminish. The invention of the brilliant-cut gave the stone more sparkle and fire. More than ever before, diamonds were set in royal jewels: in kings' swords and crowns, and on women's collars and bodices. Diamonds developed a new role, as a tool of the art of seduction. Given their role in society, this was predominantly the prerogative of women.

The power of seduction and corruption

Here, again, we can delve into mythology to find an ancient evocation of jewellery's power of seduction. Although the allure of women in a state of virginal nudity is undeniable (as in the myth of Actaeon's lust for Artemis [Diana]), they are also alluring when they bedeck themselves with things of beauty, such as rich clothing or resplendent jewels. Let us consider the case of Hera (Juno), the wife of Zeus. She was often in conflict with her husband, but she was nevertheless drawn irresistibly to him when danger or loneliness loomed. The *Iliad* (song XIV) mentions that she supported the Athenians against Troy, whereas Zeus backed the Trojans and Priam, their king. Hera tried to tempt her husband by anointing herself with ambrosia, and beautifying herself with jewels and all her finery. She wanted to be able to summon her brother, Poseidon, to assist Agammemnon in his battle against Troy. She appeared before Zeus, he took one look at her, and "love at once conquered his befuddled senses". Zeus fell asleep from exertion after the consummation of their love, and Hera went to her brother Poseidon, who took up battle alongside the Athenians against Troy.

This history shows that the power of female seduction is trickery: it is a force that overwhelms the seductee's better instincts, when allied with the artifice of jewels and fine clothing. Monsieur de Valmont (*Dangerous Liaisons*) and Don Juan are examples of male seducers that use their intelligence. According to literary tradition, women merely use their outer charms. Not for nothing did Marie Leczsynska, Queen of France and Louis XV's consort, say: "with men, one looks at what thehave in their heads, and with women, what they have around the head".

Mary I of Tudor, the Catholic Queen of England, daughter of Henry VIII. She wears diamonds in her jewellery, but they are not there for vanity's sake. They are perfectly in keeping with her pious austerity. French School drawing. French National Library, Department of Prints and Photography, Paris.

Marie-Thérèse of Austria, Infanta of Spain and Queen of France, depicted in formal Royal garb by Charles Beaubrun (1604-1692). She wears some sumptuous diamonds on her corsage. National Museum of the Château of Versailles.

Versus luxus

Men, in all their ambiguity, simultaneously try to limit women to their role of seductresses, and yet condemn them whenever they believe they have been thus duped. The Bible tells how God punished women when they used and misused jewels and perfumed ointments. For example, the following extract shows how women of the depraved Jerusalem are vigorously condemned for their frivolous behaviour: "Moreover the Lord saith, Because the daughters of Zion are haughty, and walk with stretched-forth necks and wanton eyes, walking and mincing as they go, and making a tinkling with their feet: therefore the Lord will smite with a scab the crown of the head of the daughters of Zion, and the Lord will uncover their secret parts. In that day the Lord will take away the bravery of their tinkling ornaments about their feet, and their cauls, and their round tires like the moon, the chains, and the bracelets, and the mufflers, the bonnets, and the ornaments of the legs, and the headbands, and the tablets, and the earrings, the rings, and nose jewels, the changeable suits of apparel, and the mantles, and the wimples, and the crimping pins, the glasses, and the fine linen, and the hoods, and the veils." (Isaiah, 3, 16-23).

Women would not only have to renounce luxury, sparkle and adornment in order to reach God. Tertullius, the first of the great Christian writers (*ca.* 155 – *ca.* 222), wrote: "it is time to show yourself, dressed with the unguents and ornaments of the prophets and apostles. Take white for simplicity, and red for decency. Paint your eyes with reserve, and your mouth with silence. Place the word of God in your ears, and affix the yoke of Christ around your neck. Submit to your husbands and you will be adorned enough; occupy your hands with woollen-work, keep your feet in the home and you will have more pleasure than gold. Wear as clothing the silk of honesty, the flax of purity, the purple of decency. Thus adorned, it is God whom you will have as a lover" (The Dress of the Women, II, 13, 7).

The fear of adultery, which becomes a danger when the wife uses adornments to make herself beautiful, turns into obsession. Stripped of her jewels and perfume, the woman supposedly thus remains submissive to her husband. True virtue will be her luxury, and the words of Christ will be her gems. A clergyman, Abbot Gauthier of Savigny, published his *"Treatise against the love of jewels and the luxury of dress"* in Paris in 1779. He adapted the prophet Isaiah's words, from the Biblical quote above, and used them to inveigh against the love of ornamentation and sumptuous garments. Gauthier stated that "the Lord[...] shall make their diamond points fall away", naming Isaiah as his source, although the prophet never mentioned diamonds at all. This attitude is revealing: by mentioning diamonds, Abbot Gauthier modifies the Biblical text in order to denounce luxury most emphatically: this was because diamonds were the height of luxury at the time of Louis XVI. However, Abbot Gauthier goes even further in his diatribe against luxury. For him, a taste for ornamentation is a corruptor of the heart: it "dries up the source of alms[...] and nourishes vanity", thereby leading to sin. Ornaments should not be worn, whatever they are: on the contrary, "the body should be punished". Rather than adorning the outer body with jewels, "the man inside" should be bedecked with spiritual jewels. Here, Abbot Gauthier is quoting from the *"De Habitu Virginum"* of St. Cyprien (Bishop of Carthage, 3rd century AD). "If glorification of the body is required, it is only under pain of torture for a confession. When a woman is stronger than the men that torment her, when she suffers torture in the name of Jesus Christ, subjected to fire, or the cross, or the ravages of beasts, she will ultimately be crowned. These scars shall be the gems and diamonds that will truly embellish the body".

It goes without saying that Abbot Gauthier's anathemas cannot be understood without knowledge of the context in which the *Treatise* was written. Jewels and precious stones, including diamonds, were abundant in Royal treasuries, and these elements of 'vice' were beginning to penetrate into other layers of society. According to the Abbot, this is where the true danger lay. However, even he had to admit that it was nevertheless important for "ladies and girls of quality" to wear jewellery in order to establish their social status, because it was God himself who had "established the difference". Soon, the 'Affair of the Queen's Necklace' would come to a head, and the bells of Revolution would start to toll.

'Ferdinand II de Medici, Dressed as a Turk', by Justus Sustermans (1597-1681). Ferdinand II wears diamonds as a statement of his power, even whilst wearing this fancy dress festival costume. The fine gems are set in his turban ornament, and as buttons. Palatine Gallery, Florence.

From the private to the public sphere

As time went on, new sources of diamonds were discovered, and their brilliance and sparkle improved. Jewels became part of a decorative spectacle that formed part of a "universal coquettishness" that "contributes nothing to the wellbeing of mankind" (according to Louis Bourdea, see Bibliography by chapter). Up until the start of the Renaissance, this luxury (which was synonymous with power) had remained an intimate affair: diamonds were primarily private luxuries. However, the Renaissance was all about rediscovering a taste for ancient times, when style and spectacle had reigned. Displaying wealth to the world became a social necessity, all over again. The élite displayed their power conspicuously, and in magnificent settings: simple fabric headdresses gave way to gem-encrusted gold crowns, and the Vincennes Château was superseded by the Palace of Fontainebleau.

Diamonds therefore moved from the private sphere to the public sphere: kings, dwelt by myths, in quest of the origins, (i.e. the ancient times) used art in order to reinforce their prestige and power. Artists - including painters, architects and jewellers - played an essential role, and the artworks thus created were admired by an ever-growing number of people. Artists created masterpieces for all the European kings, just as François I had created the Crown Jewels of France for prosperity. The monarchs copied each other, and none of them could be certain that their possessions would remain unique and exclusive for long.

Diamonds and Politics

Monarchies created a world of images around themselves, in the broad sense of the term: breathtaking parades, luxurious entertainments and banquets, old master portraits and imposing equestrian statues in the hearts of cities. This richness undoubtedly reached a peak in Louis XIV's time. Voltaire described the extraordinary royal pomp of the Sun King's trip to Dunkirk and Lille in 1670, in his *Louis XIV's Century* (published in 1751). "The ancient Asian kings' pomp and grandeur was surpassed by the magnificence of this journey". Henri Baudrillart in his *History of Luxury*, added: "[Louis XIV] bestowed gold and precious stones in profusion to courtiers and ladies, who seized upon the slimmest pretext in order to speak to him". This brings to mind Pliny the Elder's description of Emperor Pompeius' triumphs: he ordered large quantities of pearls to be scattered amongst the Roman throng during his triumphal processions.

Diamond merchants worked in India, directly in service to the king. Their skills helped to bring diamonds into the public sphere. Tavernier was one of these merchants. He returned from his last voyage bearing some extraordinary gems, including the *Blue Diamond of the French Crown*, which was rapidly added to the crown jewels. Large stones, worn by Louis XIV, and the small ones, which the King distributed, turned Versailles into the most dazzling place in Europe. This trend grew in strength and further transactions continued to bring diamonds into the public arena. The purchase of the fabulous *Regent* diamond is a classic example of this phenomenon. This prestigious acquisition was, in fact, made in the interests of the State, and not in order to satisfy some royal whim (Louis XV was only seven years old at the time). For a definitive account of this episode, one can consult the 1717 *Memoirs of Saint-Simon*. He recounts how "he bought this diamond" (trying to take the credit for the transaction, rather more than he deserved). Mr. Law, an English banker, offered Philippe, Duke of Orléans, the Regent of France (Louis XIV's brother's son), to buy the diamond. The Regent was reluctant to purchase, considering the country's lamentable financial state. However, Saint-Simon claims to have been persuasive: "he [the Regent] was afraid of being blamed for making such a considerable purchase, when it was so difficult to provide for the most pressing items of expenditure, and so many people had to be left to suffer. I praised his sentiment, but told

Marie de Medici, Queen of France, by Frans Pourbus II the Younger (1569-1622). The Queen is covered in jewels. The Beau Sancy is set at the top of her crown. The Louvre, Paris.

him the following. Whereas an ordinary person would be considered reprehensible for spending one hundred thousand francs in order to adorn themselves with a fine diamond, the greatest king in Europe should not be judged by the same standards. The honour of the Crown had to be considered, and he should not let this opportunity slip: a unique chance to acquire a priceless diamond that overshadowed all others in Europe".

That same year, the diarist described Tsar Peter I's visit to the French court. The Crown Jewels were displayed to him: "on Monday 24th [May 1717], he went to the Tuileries early, before the King was awake. He visited Marshal Villeroy, who showed him the Crown's gemstones. He found them to be more beautiful and more numerous than he had thought, but he said that he was barely familiar with them. He claimed to think little of these beauties of splendour and imagination: especially those that he could not hope to match!". As we can see, the end of this intimate relationship with precious gems led to situations where the European courts began to compete with each other.

Dazzling official portraits

Diamonds were a major element of publicly expressed royal opulence. This is illustrated by many beautiful official portraits, representing men and women in their most beautiful court attire. It is clear, however, that this kind of image was not aimed at the peasantry, but at courtiers, ambassadors and the other distinguished visitors that came to the palace. Portrait galleries not only illustrated the history of the monarchy, they also showed the place that the portrait's subject occupied within it.

For example, let us consider the Louvre's royal portrait gallery. Judging by Toussaint Dubreuil's drawings, the portrait collection dates back to 1600. The final pictures were painted by Pourbus and Jacob Bunel. Let us look at what remained after the 1661 fire: one of Frans II Pourbus II's (known as 'the Younger') greatest masterpieces. He was a Flemish painter born in Antwerp in 1569, and he died in Paris in 1622. The painting depicts Marie de Medici, standing in her 1610 Coronation costume, covered with fleur-de-lys motifs, under a red damask canopy. She is, wearing a crown, and covered in pearls and diamonds. Bernard Morel describes the Queen's diamond and pearl jewellery in detail, in *"The French Crown Jewels"* (see Bibliography by chapter). The *Petit Sancy* or *Beau Sancy* is set at the top of her crown. The *Great Cross* at her bodice is from the French Crown Jewels; all the other gems were the Queen's personal property.

Claude Lefebvre (1632-1675): Philippe de France, Louis XIV's brother. He is depicted wearing the mantle of a Prince of the Blood Royal. He wears a large diamond, clasped at the centre of his extravagant bow tie. It was known as the 'Queen Mother': he had inherited it from Anne of Austria. Bordeaux, Beaux-Arts Museum.

Jean-Marc Nattier (1685-1766): Élisabeth-Alexandrine de Bourbon-Condè, Mademoiselle de Sens. She is depicted wearing a diamond necklace in a bow-knot design. National Museum of the Château of Versailles.

Jean-Martial Fredou (1711-1795): Louis Stanislas Xavier of France, the Count of Provence, painted in 1773. He would later become King Louis XVIII. He wears a magnificent diamond epaulette jewel. National Museum of the Château of Versailles.

Scipione Pulzone (1550 - around 1622): Christine de Lorraine, wearing diamond jewellery, with the diamond-set crown of the Medicis at hand. Uffizi, Florence.

Marie de Medici appears in an imposing presence. She is depicted standing in front of a half-domed, Renaissance-style niche, like some Virgin Mary from an Italian Old Master painting. Contemporary chroniclers noted the portrait's verisimilitude. Henri Sauval's *"History of the Antiquities of the City of Paris"*, written between 1650 and 1670 (see Bibliography by chapter), states that: "Marie de Medici's portrait was painted by Pourbus. It is the best in this gallery [i.e. the Louvre's Small Gallery]. Indeed, the clothing is so true-to-life, the diamonds embroidered upon it are so brilliant, the pearls so natural, the Queen's head so noble, her hands so beautiful and slender, that it is the most charming thing one could possibly see". Two centuries later, the poet and writer Theophilus Gautier agreed with him: he stated that the Pourbus was "a document of historical value". Pourbus' masterpiece also shows us that, by then, diamonds had also found a place upon the royal costume: they were not only set in crowns or necklaces, but also sewn on fabric. Admittedly, this had been done before on a smaller scale, but the painting depicts diamonds as the quintessence of luxury in dress, alongside the pearl. The bodice front, which resembles an inverted fleur-de-lys, is sumptuously decorated with table-cut diamonds. They were set in a new style, in order to display the gem and its reflectivity to best effect. Bernard Morel describes this style as "straight-edged, without large borders, enamels, chasing or scrollwork". Pourbus' superb painterly technique rendered these jewels beautifully. In order to depict the diamonds' brilliance, he contrasted painted shadows with thin white highlights, and punctuated the brushwork with small flecks of paint to suggest three-dimensionality. The majority of 17th-century artists also kept to this style of representational realism.

It is impossible to provide a comprehensive account of these court portraits, which display the wealth and splendour of kings, queens, princes and princesses. For the sake of categorisation, however, we shall merely point out that there are three main types of jewel in these portraits. In all cases, diamonds are the most precious gem. There are jewels that belonged to the treasury (which were assembled and broken up according to prevailing fashions), jewels from the sitter's personal collection (represented more or less accurately, according to the painter's powers of observation), and jewels that are merely figments of the imagination. The latter had two potential functions: beautify the sitter and/or act as attributes, such as the painted crown standing on a table next to Marie-Antoinette in the Jacques-Gautier d'Agoty portrait, which can be seen in the Palace of Versailles. When items from the Regalia are depicted alongside kings and queens, they are referred to as "honours". They often have symbolic value, and are not always accurate representations of actual jewels.

The portrait of Marie-Thérèse, Duchess of Angoulême, daughter of Louis XVI and Marie-Antoinette, is of similar quality to Pourbus' masterpiece. The Chamber of Deputies commissioned the Baron Gros (1777-1835) to paint this portrait in 1816. He was a "Pre-Romantic" artist, and a follower of the neoclassical painter David. The duchess is depicted some time after her return from exile. According to Tripier le Franc, she was still haunted by "the misfortune of her family and loved ones, which imprinted a profound sadness upon her". Her sparkling jewels, mostly set with diamonds, belonged to her personal collection. Some of the gems belonged to her mother, and some were gifts from her uncle, Louis XVIII. The gems had been set in modern style by the jeweller Ménière at the beginning of the Restoration: they comprise a tiara, drop earrings, a necklace and bracelets. The painting also depicts a crown on a green velvet stand. This was the most sumptuous portrait that Gros ever painted, and it testifies to the Bourbon family's return to grace: Louis XVIII, Marie-Thérèse's uncle, had been crowned the new King in 1814. The duchess literally sparkles in her profusion of diamonds. The scene is accentuated by the quality of the ambient light, which Gros depicted particularly skilfully. Finally, this official court portrait displays "the luxury of a royal residence, from the architecture to the accessories", according to Jean-Baptiste Delestre (see Bibliography by chapter), Gros' first biographer. Diamonds may signify wealth, but they do so as part of an ensemble: the image is intended to display the effect of an unsinkable historical dynasty.

Antoine-Jean Gros (1771-1835): Marie-ThÈrËse-Charlotte of France, the Duchess of AngoulÍme, painted in 1817. She is depicted in formal Court garb, wearing a magnificent suite of diamond jewellery. National Museum of the Château of Versailles.

Baudrillart's *"History of Luxury"* tries to explain the Western world's passion for diamonds. Many diamonds and gems were put on public display in the 1878 World Fair, to great public acclaim. Baudrillart wrote: "in addition to its beauty, diamond attracts attention like any other ancient artefact, like any other object from the Far East[...] and like the other objects that have inspired superstitious beliefs throughout human history". Clearly, this is the nucleus of diamond's mystique: it is an extraordinary gem that awakens and evokes deep-seated emotions, because it comes from near-mythical lands that inspire boundless fascination amongst explorers, artists and writers. Such ancient lands have always attracted explorers from afar, because they are supposedly ripe with riches that are ready to be plundered. Diamond's supposed powers and symbolism (political power and seductive temptation) is a direct result of these myths.

It is no coincidence that diamonds have been used by poets, and even Saints, in the evocation of some singularly lyrical images. For example, after having been Christ's tears, diamonds became the tears of the beloved in Gautier's *Enamels and Cameos.* In Marguerite de Navarre's *The Heptameron,* diamonds are the symbol of love. In Dante's *Divine Comedy,* diamond is the stone of Purgatory, because it deters demons. Lastly, in St. Theresa of Avila's *The Castle Within,* diamond is conflated with the mystical experience of meeting God:

"Diamond? It is the art of the ideal,
And its rays of silver, gold, purple and azure,
Incessantly radiate the two twinned lights
Of the most beautiful thoughts, of the purest love.
It carries the Spirit, and transmits history:
Yes, remnants of long-forgotten nations
It is the most brilliant treasure, and the hardest."

Alfred de Vigny, *The Oracles,* "Post-Scriptum", VI (March 28th 1862)

Diamond and platinum tiara, made by Chaumet for Hedwige de la Rochefoucauld's marriage to Prince Sixtus of Bourbon-Parma in 1919. Private collection.

Diamonds were still used as an expression of social status, even after the revolutions. Platinum-set diamond stomacher brooch, made by Harnichard for Cartier Paris. It is designed with drapery motifs, with five pendants. The central rosette contains a 'millgrain'-set cushion-cut diamond, surrounded by round diamonds. Commissioned by the Baroness de Gunzburg, 1909. "Art de Cartier" collection, Geneva.

Tiara, made by Cartier in 1910 for Élisabeth, Queen of the Belgians. It is set with diamonds, in platinum scroll motifs, and has a 5.84ct diamond in the centre. "Art de Cartier" collection, Geneva.

Diamond and platinum tiara in the 'Egyptian' style, made in 1934 for HH the Begum Andrée, third wife of HH Sur Sultan Mohamed Shah Aga Khan III. "Art de Cartier" collection, Geneva.

Diamond necklace, comprising a diamond chain and flexible palmette motifs, set at the centre with an articulated pendant, containing a 143.23ct emerald. Made in 1932 by Cartier London, commissioned by Lady Granard, the wife of the 8th Viscount Granard. "Art de Cartier" collection, Geneva.

CHAPTER X

Amina Okada

Diamonds of the Maharajahs and Great Mughals

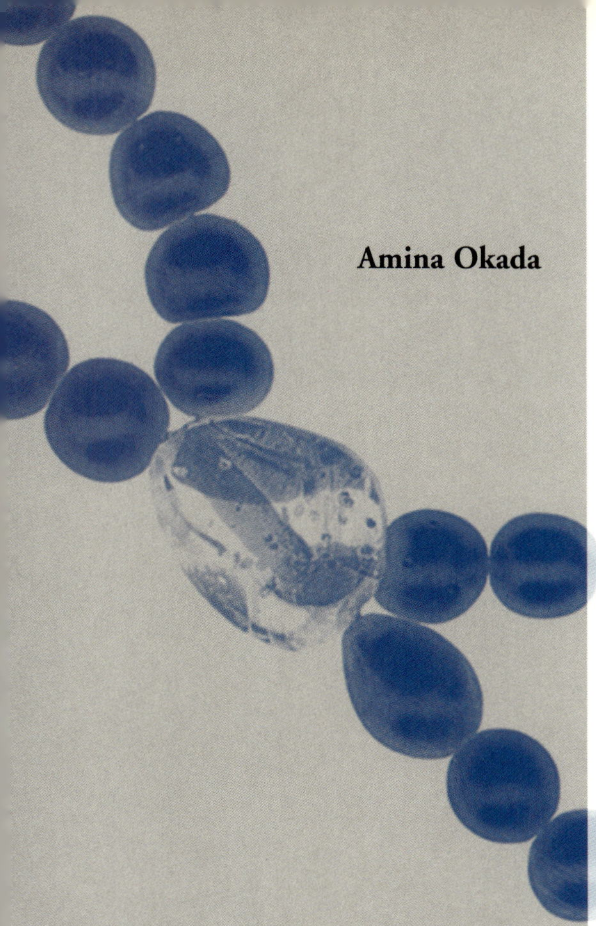

India is the motherland of gemstones. According to ancient beliefs, they are of divine origin: they came from the body of a demon (*Asura*) – known as *Bala or Vajra*, depending on the texts – who was struck down by the gods and whose mortal remains turned into "mountains of precious stones". The demon's internal organs each gave rise to a different stone. Diamonds came from his bones, pearls from his teeth, rubies from his blood, emeralds from his bile, sapphires from his eyes, cat's eyes from his voice, topazes from his skin, chrysoberyls from his nails, garnet from his lymph, carnelian from his chyme (stomach contents), and rock crystal and coral from his fat. Once the Asura's body had yielded its harvest of gems, gods and celestial beings seized the precious stones in order to introduce them to the three worlds. "Gods, *Yaksas*, *Siddhas* and Serpents plundered this cornucopia of gems. During their rapid flight through thin air, they dropped some. Because of their weight, the stones bedded down everywhere that they were scattered, whether in the sea, rivers, mountains or forests" (L. Finot, *General Bibliography*). This is how ancient gemmological treatises explained the geographical distribution of precious stone deposits in mountains, mines or riverbeds. In addition to gods and celestial beings, the star and planet deities, or *Grahas* ("the ones who snatch away"), also snatched items from these heaps of precious stones. Their hoards were deposited on specific celestial bodies, which consequently became associated with them: the sun with ruby, the moon with pearl, Mars with coral, Mercury with emerald, Jupiter with topaz, Saturn with sapphire, the eclipse demon *Rahu* with jacinth, *Ketu* the comet with cat's eye and Venus with diamond. In this way, precious stones became imbued with beneficial or malefic properties, according to the stars and planets with which they had become symbolically associated.

Diamond castes

Diamonds were tirelessly scrutinised and graded by meticulous ancient Indian gem-cutters. They were classified according to their shape, cut, weight, clarity, sparkle, colour and beauty. In addition, the various diamond colours determined the divinities to which the gem was consecrated, as well as the social caste that had the right to own it. Therefore, white diamonds were assigned to the *Brahmin* caste, red to the *Kshatriya* (nobles and warriors), yellow to the *Vaisya* (farmers and merchants), and black to the *Sudra* (servants). The *Agastimata*, a 6th-century gemmology treatise, states that "Diamond has four colours, corresponding to its castes. The diamond with a velvety sheen, like that of a conch shell, a rock crystal or the moon, is a *Brahmin*. That which is reddish, or coloured brown like a monkey, beautiful and pure, is called Kshatriya. Vaisya has a brilliant, pale yellow colour. Sudra shines like a well-polished sword: because of its sparkle, experts have assigned it to the fourth caste. Such are the signs which characterize the castes of a diamond" (L. Finot, op. cit.). Although they traditionally came from the *Kshatriya* caste, kings alone could wear diamonds of all colours, provided they were of spotless clarity and absolute beauty.

According to the Ratnapariksha, "A king who desires happiness must accumulate and wear jewels that have been thoroughly authenticated. A good jewel is a source of wealth for kings; a bad one is the source of evil". Furthermore, according to the Brihatsamhita of Varahamihira, "this is why

Exceptionnel Mughal jewel of imperial origin, with an engraved diamond. The necklace is of pearls and spinels, one of which is engraved with the name of Emperor Jahangir and the date 1609. The diamond in the pendant is surrounded by rubies, and encased in a jade frame. The engraved inscription on the diamond reads "Emperor Shah Jahan, warrior of the faith". Around 1630-50. Private collection.

Two extraordinary Golconda diamond pear-shapes. These stones are at the pinnacle of the diamond world, and virtually matchless: they are even larger than the famous Indore Pears, formerly owned by the Maharajah of Indore. It is almost unimaginably difficult to create a matched pair of diamonds of this quality, clarity, colour and size (56.64 and 57.53 carats). They are old gems that were slightly repolished recently. Their provenance remains a secret: which Rajah might have owned such a gloriously-matched pair of gems? Private collection.

jewels must be evaluated by experts, in order to read the destiny that is written within them" (L. Finot, *op. cit.*). The purest, flawless gems, blessed with perfect shapes and bearing certain surface markings (lakshana) were considered to be beneficial. Indians considered the octahedron to be the premier diamond shape. Diamonds were blessed with various properties and therapeutic attributes. These were listed in great detail, although sometimes with slight variations, in various texts. A beautiful diamond, in addition to providing health, happiness, richness and glory to its wearer, was also said to protect from epilepsy, to be an antidote to snake venoms and poisons – the gem was supposed to darken in contact with poison – or even render the wearer invincible. The qualities and powers of precious stones are central and recurring themes in ancient Indian gem texts, which were intended both for everyday use by jewellers and for the use of kings, since members of royalty were avid gem-lovers and wished to know about the stones' qualities and virtues.

Gemmological texts and literary sources

The oldest literary reference to Indian diamonds is in the *Arthashastra*, a famous treatise on the "Science of interests" written in the 4th century B.C. and attributed to Kautilya – a kind of Indian Macchiavelli who was one of King Maurya Chandragupta's most sagacious ministers. This treatise is primarily concerned with policy, administration, economic management and other affairs of state. However, Volume Two discusses a plethora of different topics, including roads, irrigation projects, fortress construction, tax collection, currencies, weights and measures, mines, manufacturing and, finally, gold, pearls and gemstones. Kautilya provides detailed descriptions of diamond deposits and localities in mines and rivers, in addition to interesting comments concerning the diamonds' value, quality and colours. The text implies that the state had already established control on the gem trade by the time of Maurya's accession (4th-2nd centuries B.C.).

Almost ten centuries prior to the oldest Indian gemmological texts (written around the 6th century A.D), Kautilya's chapter on diamonds and the gems testifies to the importance attributed to gemmological knowledge and the gem trade in India. In fact, India, particularly the Deccan area, effectively constituted the only source of diamonds in the world from ancient times until the discovery of diamonds in Brazil around 1725. There was some production in Borneo, but it is regarded as being negligible (see Chapter 4). Although the names and precise locations of the ancient diamond mines mentioned in gem texts remain difficult to identify and a matter of conjecture in many cases, the fact that they include the Golconda mines is enough to account for India's extraordinarily rich diamond production. This legendary richness would continue to supply the international trade until the beginning of the 18th century, when the deposits were exhausted, and would, to this day, captivate the imagination of the West.

Almost at the same time as Kautilya was drafting the Arthashastra, Alexander the Great's Indian campaign (327-325 B.C.) was underway. His exploits were the stuff of legends, and these legends incorporated many famous diamond myths – such as the story of the 'valley of diamonds', guarded by evil serpents. According to the story, Alexander managed to recover some gems through a cunning plan that consisted in throwing cuts of fresh meat into the valley. The diamonds stuck to the meat, and eagles and vultures carried them off in their claws. Alexander's archers would then bring down the birds of prey and recover the gems (see Chapter 13). This legend, which is also mentioned by Marco Polo in the 13th century and Niccolo de Conti in the 15th, is also told in the *Thousand and One Nights*. During his second voyage, Sinbad the Sailor escaped from the clutches of the giant Roc bird, only to chance upon a valley strewn with diamonds, but teeming with snakes. Moreover, Marco Polo specified that, in India, the most beautiful diamonds discovered in mines or riverbeds were reserved for the local sovereign: "Above all, do not believe that the diamonds that arrive in Christendom are the good ones. They go to the Great Khan, and to the kings and barons of

these various regions and kingdoms. This is because these have the world's greatest treasuries and buy all the costly stones. Those that arrive in our countries are merely the ones that they have rejected" (*La Description du monde,* Bibliography by Chapter).

View of the Golconda fort, not far from Hyderabad. The most famous diamond mines were located in this region.

This practice was documented well before the 13th century, and it was maintained during the centuries to come. It is often mentioned by foreign travellers or gem merchants, who went to India. In the 16th century, three Europeans travelled to the kingdom of Vijayanagar, in the heart of the Deccan. They were Fernao Nuniz and Domingos Paes of Portugal, and Jan Huyghen van Linschoten, an agent of the Dutch East India Company. They stated that, in Vijayanagar, diamonds weighing more than 10-13 carats were invariably destined for the royal Treasury. A century later, the French merchant Jean-Baptiste Tavernier visited the Golconda mines. He reported the same, and also specified: "I return to the management of the mines. Trade is freely and faithfully undertaken there. Two percent of every purchase is paid to the King, who also levies fees from the merchants for their mining permits" (Jean-B Tavernier, General Bibliography). This royal prerogative remained in force until the end of the 18th century.

Indian necklace, entirely set with diamonds. 19th century. Private collection.

Handwritten map showing Jean-Baptiste Tavernier's route in India. The diamond mines are towards the South-West of India, not far from the Coromandel coast. Bibliothèque nationale de France, Department of Maps and Plans, Paris.

The *Blue Diamond of the French* Crown brought by Tavernier to Louis XIV. It was stolen in 1793 during the French Revolution, disappeared for many years, and reappeared as the Hope Diamond. When recut to hide its true origins, its weight was reduced from 69.03 to 45.52 carats.
The Smithsonian Institution, Washington.

A Frenchman in the land of diamonds

During his Indian voyages, Jean-Baptiste Tavernier (1605-1689) visited four diamond mines in and around Golconda (see Chapter 4). Volume two of his famous book of *Voyages to Turkey, Persia and the Indies* is an invaluable historical record of gem extraction, mine leases, working conditions in the mines, the diamond trade and of the taxes that had to be paid to the king. Tavernier was conscious of the importance of his account and took legitimate pride in being "the first European to open the way for the French to these mines, the only places on Earth where diamond is found. His account, which is rich in picturesque and informative detail, constitutes an interesting counterpart to the technical writings and mystic revelations provided by ancientIndian gem texts. In particular, the French merchant set about making detailed comparisons regarding gem-cutting techniques and the way that gems were evaluated, since Indian methods sometimes differed from – or even contradicted – European ones. For example, when he visited the Kollur mines, "seven days from Golconda", where "up to sixty thousand people work [...] women and children as well as men", Tavernier notes: "With regard to the water of stones, it should be noted that whereas in Europe we use daylight to examine the rough stones, in order to judge their water and the qualities that they may have, the Indians use the night-time. They make a hole one square foot in size in a wall, into which they place a lamp with a large wick. By the light of this lamp, they evaluate the water and the clarity of the stone that they hold in their fingers. The water called celestial is the worst of all, and it is impossible to see it if the stone is brown. But in order that it should not be discovered on the grinding wheel, they have an infallible secret to examine the stone's water. It is to take it under a bushy tree and, in the shade of its greenery, one can easily discover if it be blue." (*Jean-Baptiste Tavernier, op.*

Jean-Baptiste Tavernier, by Nicolas de Largillière (1656-1746). The famous explorer travelled throughout the Indies to purchase diamonds for King Louis XIV. He is depicted in Eastern costume. Herzog Anton Ulrich-Museum, Braunschweig.

MIRZA MOLA

cit.). Jean-Baptiste Tavernier went to Turkey, Persia and the Indies to gather pearls and gems. These were destined for the Great Dukes of Tuscany or Louis XIV: the Sun King would buy 44 large and 1,122 small diamonds from him! In his travels, he inevitably crossed the path of the all-powerful Mir Jumlah. Mir Jumlah controlled almost all the diamond mines in the area, in his capacity as Governor of Karnataka and Minister for Finance of the Sultan of Golconda, Abdullah Qutb Shah. Tavernier reported that he had an interview in Mir Jumlah's tent, whereupon the devious minister tried to sell him "five small bags full of diamonds, of exceedingly blackish water and very small". He refused to acquire them, explaining to his host that Europeans esteemed nothing so much as "clear and white" diamonds (Jean-Baptiste Tavernier, *op. cit.*).

A crooked minister in the Golconda court

Mir Jumlah was the son of a humble oil merchant from Isfahan. However, in only a few years he succeeded in accumulating an immense fortune thanks to the diamond trade, and he had considerable power in the state of Golconda. Moreover, although the law stated that the largest diamonds discovered in the mines should be presented to the monarch, Mir Jumlah did not hesitate to appropriate the most beautiful gems, often only leaving the Sultan of Golconda the lower-value stones. This, however, did not prevent the Finance minister from being utterly intractable towards precious stone merchants. He would not tolerate any deviation from the law regarding the trade and taxation of diamonds. One Dutch report dating from 1643-1644 specifically states that Mir Jumlah required a Dutch trader to pay restitution in the matter of a diamond weighing 17.75 *manjali* (mangelins) –the reasoning behind the demand was that all gems exceeding a certain weight were the Sultan's property (O.Khalidi, Bibliography by Chapter)!

He was courted by foreign merchants, who feared his power and influence. Given that he enjoyed an immense fortune and had a personal army of some five thousand horsemen, twenty thousand infantryman and three hundred war elephants, Mir Jumlah could hardly avoid arousing the mistrust and jealousy of the Sultan of Golconda, Abdullah Qutb Shah. The Sultan felt, with good reason, that his sovereignty was threatened by the overweening power of his ambitious minister. Ultimately, Mir Jumlah betrayed his monarch by engaging in secret negotiations with the Mughal Prince Aurangzeb, who was viceroy of the Deccan at the time. Mir Jumlah finally pledged allegiance to Aurangzeb's father, Emperor Shah Jahan, in 1656. The Sultan of Golconda's treacherous minister did not, however, come to the Mughal court empty-handed. On the contrary, he presented his new masters with a fortune of gems and diamonds that he had illegally appropriated throughout his lucrative career. The French traveller François Bernier mentioned in *Voyage to the Lands of the Great Mughal* that the Mughal Emperor granted Mir Jumlah an audience, and describes the superb diamonds that were offered to the sovereign: "It was on this occasion that Mir Jumlah presented Shah Jahan a famous diamond, generally considered without peer from the point of view of its weight as well as its beauty." Two years later, in 1658, Aurangzeb succeeded Shah Jahan and was crowned Emperor. Mir Jumlah presented him with splendid diamonds, in accordance with his policy of self-serving generosity. Right up until his death in 1663, he continued to give diamonds to the Emperor, as documented by the Venetian Niccolo Manucci in his *Storia do Mogor*: "A eunuch accompanied a request with one gift that Mir Jumlah had deferred from presenting to the Emperor until his death. It was the largest and most perfect diamond in all the Indies [It was "*The Great Mogul*"]. Mir Jumlah had taken it for himself when he was in the service of the King of Golconda and controlled the province that was so rich in diamond mines, in his capacity as viceroy" (I. Amini, *L'Inde du Koh-i-Noor, Bibliography by Chapter*).

Mir Jumlah, called Mirgimola by Jean-Baptiste Tavernier. The crooked minister of the Sultan of Golconda controlled his master's mines. He drew all his power from this position and this miniature shows him proudly seated on his horse. French National Library, Department of Engravings and Photography, Paris.

On November 2, 1665, Emperor Aurangzeb granted Jean-Baptiste Tavernier the extraordinary privilege of examining these exceptional diamonds, and other equally magnificent gems. "As soon as I had arrived at Court, the two Courtiers of the King's Jewels, of whom I have spoken elsewhere, accompanied me to an audience with his Majesty. After making the usual salutations, they guided me to a small room at one end of the Hall where the King was sitting on his throne, and from where he could see us. I found the Head of the Jewel Treasury, Akel-Kan, in this chamber. Upon seeing us, he ordered four of the King's eunuchs to fetch the jewels, which were brought to us in two great gilded, lacquered wooden trays... The first piece that Akel-Kan put in my hands was the large diamond. It is a round rose-cut that is very high on one side. There is a small notch on the bottom edge, and a small crystal inside. It is of beautiful water, and it weighs three hundred and nineteen ratis and a half, which makes two hundred and eighty of our carats... When Mirgimola (Mir Jumlah) betrayed his Master, the King of Golconda, he made a present of this stone to Shah Gehan. It was in the rough state, and at the time weighed nine hundred ratis, which makes seven hundred and eighty seven and a half carats, and there were several flaws. If this stone had been in Europe, it would have been cut in another way, because one could have taken some good pieces from it. In this way, it would have remained heavier, instead of which it has been all ground away." (*Jean-Baptiste Tavernier, op. cit.*).

The Treasury of the Great Mughals

The Mughal Emperors, however, had not been idly waiting for Mir Jumlah to arrive with his gifts. They had accumulated a priceless collection of gems and diamonds in the royal Treasury. In 1636, they signed a treaty with the Sultans of Golconda, and imposed the payment of a substantial tribute. A large part of this tribute consisted of diamonds from the area's famous mines. Some fifty years later, in 1686 and 1687, the Mughals annexed the kingdoms of Bijapur and of Golconda, thereby becoming the masters of the diamond mines. The royal treasury of the Great Mughals contained legendary riches. There were many opportunities to augment the treasury: plunder from victorious campaigns, spoils of war, tributes presented to the Mughal crown, gifts from ambassadors and foreign monarchs, and presentations made by nobles and dignitaries under various circumstances (festivals, ceremonies, sovereigns' anniversaries). The Imperial chronicles and the sovereigns' own memoirs frequently testify to this constant and overwhelming passion for precious stones, particularly rubies, emeralds and diamonds. In addition to describing the exceptional gems acquired by or given to the Emperors, the memoirs sometimes mention the acquisition or gift of diamond mines, such as the Khokhara diamond mines in Bihar, acquired by Emperor Jahangir (1605-1627) or, strangely enough, a diamond mine presented to Jahangir by a zamindar from Khandesh. The monarch mentions in his memoir that "diamonds from this place are of a variety and beauty above all other kinds of diamonds, and are greatly appreciated by jewellers." (A. Aziz, *Bibliography by Chapter*).

The Mughal Emperors adored famous gems, and wanted them free from flaws. They refused to have mediocre stones in the royal Treasury. William Hawkins, an English merchant in India from 1608 to 1613, made an account of his voyage in which he recounts the difficulties experienced by the royal gem-cutters. The quality of gems supplied to the royal court was so fine, flawed stones were rare indeed. As a result, they had difficulty finding poor-quality diamonds that could be crushed into powder and used for cutting and polishing gem diamonds. Jean-Baptiste Tavernier's eyewitness account is the most precious record of the times, however: it is the only document that gives us an idea of the abundance and beauty of the Mughal royal treasury's diamonds. Moreover, the Frenchman accompanied his account with illustrated plates, showing sketches of the most remarkable gems and diamonds that he was able to see and acquire in the Indies – some of which were subsequently sold to Louis XIV. Emperor Shah Jahan had a true passion for gems. His treasury had

Mughal miniature from 1616-17, showing Prince Khurram, the future Emperor Shah Jahan, holding a turban plume in his hand. The plume is set with a diamond below an emerald. An identically-shaped Indian diamond appeared on the market in 1984. Victoria and Albert Museum, London.

This diamond was subsequently named the *Shah Jahan*. It weighs 56.71 carats and its shape makes it one of t he most extraordinary Indian diamonds: the gem-cutter made a sort of ridge that contains two drill-holes, enabling the gem to be sewn on to clothing, or attached to a jewelled ornament. Private collection.

شاه جهان

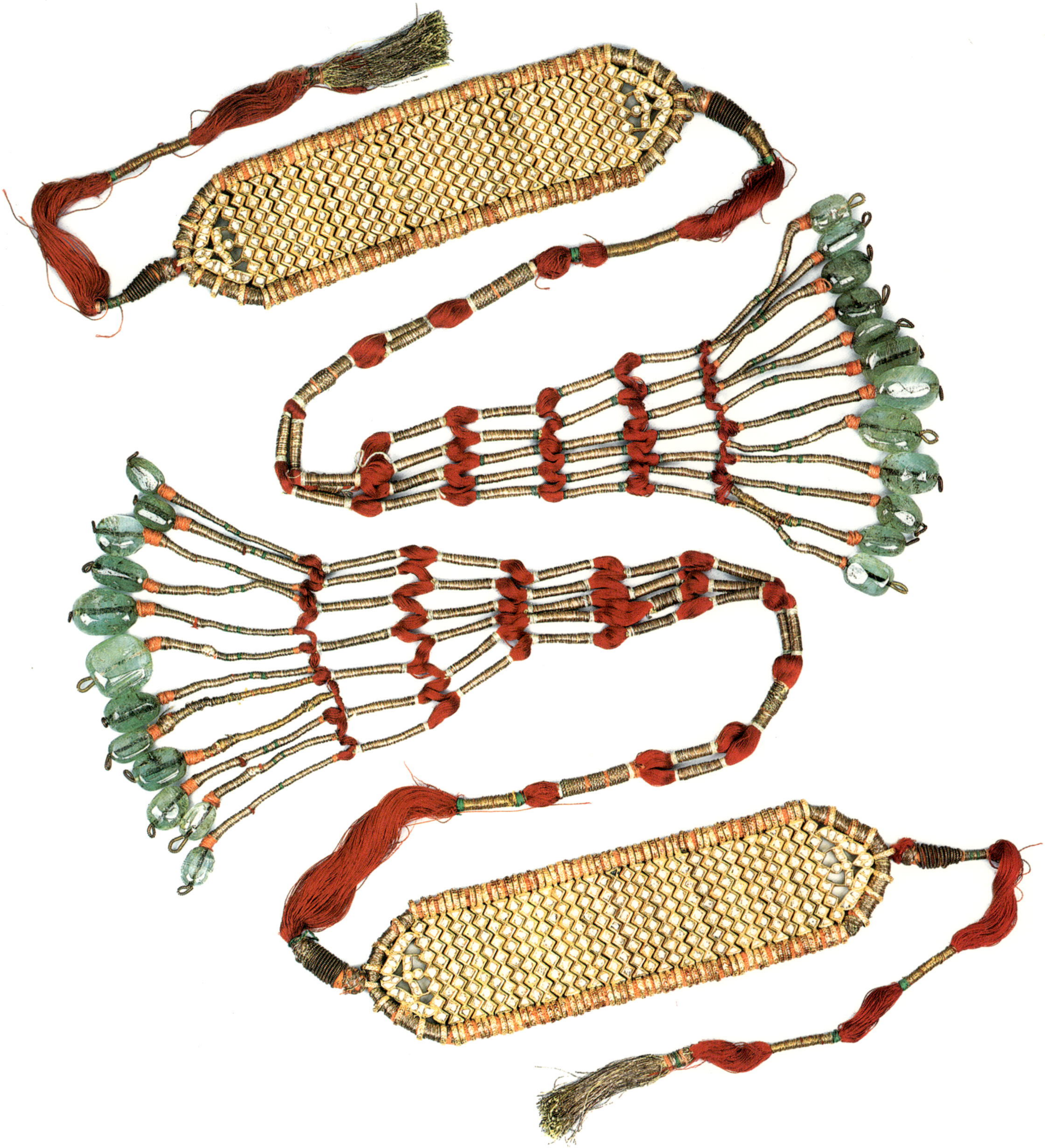

Pair of bazubands, bracelets that are tied around the upper arm. They are beautifully set with a mosaic of lozenge-shaped diamonds mounted in interlinked gold. 19th century. Private collection.

Turban ornament of the Maharajah of Patiala, early 19th century. It is made from table-cut and drop-shaped Golconda diamonds, with rows of emeralds. The setting is enamelled gold. Private collection.

Extravagant sword-handle, set with numerous diamonds in the preferred style of 19th-century Indian Rajahs. Private collection.

This diamond is currently known as the *Idol's Eye*, but it is in fact the Nassak diamond. It was set in the face of a statue of Shiva in one of the many temples around the town of Nasikk, 180km North-East of Bombay. In 1818, English troops conquered the city and looted the diamond. The stone was found and reidentified only recently: it had been re-cut in the interim. R. Mouawad Collection.

such a wealth of diamonds, rubies, emeralds and other precious and semi-precious stones that he studded them all over the silver and gold thrones in his palaces' royal audience chambers. The most famous Mughal throne is undoubtedly the *Peacock Throne* (*Takht-i Ta'us*), a sumptuous gold throne encrusted with a profusion of pearls, rubies, emeralds and diamonds. It was commissioned in 1628 – the year Shah Jahan was crowned Emperor – and completed in 1635. Tavernier described this peerless throne and, jeweller that he was, endeavoured to enumerate the gems encrusting it, and even to speculate upon the carat weights of some of them. Likewise, the bedazzled François Bernier left another description: "The king appeared, magnificently dressed, seated upon a throne at the end of the great *am-khas* hall. [...] His throne was supported by six large feet which are said to be of solid gold, set throughout with rubies, emeralds and diamonds. In truth, I could not tell you the quantity nor the weight of gems, because it is not possible to get close enough to count them and to evaluate their water and clarity. I can only tell you that large diamonds, amongst other things, are there in profusion, and that the throne is valued at four *crores* of rupees, if I remember rightly. As I mentioned above, a rupee is worth approximately thirty *sols*, a *lakh* is one hundred thousand rupees and a crore is a hundred *lakhs*. Thus the throne would be worth forty million rupees, which is approximately sixty million livres. Shah Jahan, father of Aurangzeb, is the one who had it made in order to display the gems that had accumulated in the Treasury over the years: the spoils of the ancient Pathans and Rajahs, and the gifts that the *Omrahs* are obliged to make every year during certain festivals. The effect of this throne does not match the materials. I believe that these two peacocks are covered in gems and pearls that are a Frenchman's works of trickery... He was a marvellous workman who, after having misled several European princes with his skilfully-made doublets, took refuge in this court where he made a fortune "(F. Bernier, Bibliography by Chapter).

The *Koh-i-Noor:* The brilliance and fire of history itself

The famous Golconda diamonds are associated with the sumptuous reigns of the Mughal Emperors. They ruled over Hindustan from 1526 to 1858, in varying degrees of power and splendour. These extraordinary diamonds are laden with history and mystery. They include the *Akbar Shah* (or *Jahangir*), the *Darya-i-Noor*, the *Shah of Ahmedabad* and the *Shah Jahan*. However, the *Koh-i-Noor* ("Mountain of Light") is undoubtedly the most fabulous Indian diamond. It has a uniquely complex and mysterious history that is interwoven with the history of India itself. Today, it is a Crown Jewel of Great Britain. It decorated the crowns of Queen Victoria and Queen Mary, and is currently set in the crown of Queen Elizabeth the Queen Mother, on display in the Jewel House in the Tower of London (see Chapter 12).

This Golconda gem is one of the most extraordinary diamonds in existence. Its origins are murky and remain a matter for interminable conjectures. It may have belonged to Ala ud-Din Khilji, Sultan of Delhi, in the late 13th century. His royal Treasury held so many jewels and precious stones, contemporary jewellers and poets stated that he reigned on an "ocean of gems". Certain historians maintain that the diamond subsequently passed into the ownership of Babur, the founder of the Mughal Empire. He would have obtained it upon his conquest of Hindustan in 1526, from the Rajah of Gwalior, Vikramaditya. Indeed, the first Mughal Emperor mentions an extraordinary diamond in his memoirs, which was considered to be worth "the expenditure of the whole world for two days and a half". But is this peerless gem truly the *Koh-i-Noor*? In all events, Babur then presented the diamond to his son, Humayun, who in turn presented it to Shah Tahmasp during his exile in Persia (1544-1555), in gratitude for his hospitality and military aid. At this point, all traces of the fabulous diamond are lost in the mists of time.

Around the middle of the 17th century, the diamond reappeared in the Mughal court; the Emperor Shah Jahan owned the gem, which was possibly offered to him by the extravagant Mir Jumlah. But the earliest firm historical sighting of the *Koh-i-Noor* occurs in 1739. This is the date of the looting of Delhi by Nadir Shah of Persia. In fact, the conqueror was so dazzled by its brilliance that he baptised the stone "Mountain of light" himself! Taking advantage of the weakness of the reigning sovereign Muhammad Shah (1719-1748) and of the slow disintegration of the Mughal Empire, Nadir Shah had easily overthrown the Imperial forces. The insatiable Shah subjected the city of Delhi to unprecedented looting, depriving the Mughals of the majority of their magnificent treasures and precipitating the demise of an already weakened dynasty. According to contemporary witnesses, some seven hundred elephants, ten thousand camels and ten thousand horses were required to transport the enormous hoard of spoils all the way back to Persia. Nadir Shah availed himself of nine gold and silver thrones encrusted with gems, including the Peacock Throne. He also took the gems and jewels of the royal Treasury, headed by the *Koh-i-Noor*, and an immense quantity of precious objects, valuable manuscripts, sumptuous fabrics, weaponry, gem-studded goldwork and silverware, and gold and silver bullion. Two thirds of the Iran Crown gems and jewels in Tehran originate from the Delhi looting and include the famous *Darya-i-Noor* ("Ocean of light") which weighs between 175 and 195 carats and the *Taj-i-Mah* ("Crown of the Moon") weighing 115.06 carats.

Upon Nadir Shah's assassination in 1747, the *Koh-i-Noor* was seized by one of his Generals, Ahmad Shah Abdali, who later became the sovereign of Afghanistan. The diamond passed down through the line of his successors until June 1813, when the unfortunate Shah Shuja was compelled to yield it to Ranjit Singh, the Maharajah of the Punjab and King of Lahore. Ranjit Singh took the *Koh-i-Noor* with him wherever he went. For a time, it was set in his turban, and then in an armlet, flanked by two smaller diamonds. In 1838, William Godolphin Osborne, who was the nephew of Lord Auckland, the Governor-General of the Indies, had twice the opportunity to admire the *Koh-i-Noor*, sparkling in all its glory on Ranjit Singh's arm. "The Lion of Lahore sat cross-legged on a gilded seat, wearing a simple white tunic, completely devoid of ornamentation except for one row of enormous pearls around his waist and the *Koh-i-Noor* or Mountain of Light upon his arm. The brilliance of the jewel was rivalled only by the intense, bright looks that he shot from his only eye as he warily inspected his courtiers [...] It is certainly a splendid diamond, almost an inch and a half in length and a little more than one inch wide, and rising up approximately one half-inch out of its setting. It is the shape of an egg, and set in a bracelet, between two splendid diamonds of half of its size. It is valued at 3 million pounds sterling. It is very brilliant and flawless. Ranjit Singh wanted to know how much it would be worth in England, and if we had ever seen anything so splendid." (I.Amini, op.cit.).

Ranjit Singh would never under any circumstances have agreed to part with the legendary diamond: it was his most prized possession. And in 1838, he could hardly have imagined that, some ten years later, the British would annex the Punjab and that his young son, Dhulip Singh, then twelve years old, would find himself obliged to present the gem to Queen Victoria. On July 3, 1850, the *Koh-i-Noor* was officially given to Queen Victoria by the president of the East India Company. It was displayed at the World Fair in 1851, alongside an array of other fine gems and jewels. However, although the prodigious size of the diamond fascinated the Crystal Palace's throng of visitors, its brilliance, on the other hand, left them somewhat disappointed. The Picture Post described the scene: "In spite of the most creditable efforts to make it sparkle, neither gas burners nor the sun can make this mountain as luminous as a display of well-cut diamonds. The Indian diamond is truly large, yet in general it does not reflect light. Over there, extraordinary proportions seem to be regarded more highly than transparency, brilliance and a reflective nature" (I Amini, *op. cit.*). Queen Victoria and her Prince Consort, Albert, hoped that the diamond's brilliance would be enhanced by recutting. Therefore, at their request, the *Koh-i-Noor* was recut on July 17, 1852, and reduced to its current weight of 105.60 carats.

The Koh-i-Noor diamond as it is today, having been re-cut from 180 carats to 105.6 carats.

Quite apart from the legendary *Koh-i-Noor*, whose history has yet to be fully unravelled, there are many other famous and historic diamonds that originally came from the legendary Golconda mines. These include the *Hope*, *Regent*, *Sancy*, *Grand Condé*, *Orloff*, *Hastings* and *Pigot*, amongst others. By the 18th century, the Nizams of Hyderabad, successors of Qutb Shah of Golconda, had accumulated an immense fortune from these mines. In accordance with the example set by their glorious ancestors, who had been Mughal Emperors, Sultans of the Deccan and sovereigns of the Rajput kingdoms, the Maharajahs and Nabobs of India had a true passion for jewels and gems, as well as a taste for pomp and royal ceremony. They tirelessly surrounded themselves with constellations of pearls, emeralds, rubies and diamonds, both on their person and in strong-boxes in their grandiose palaces. In the 1920s and 30s, caskets full of Colombian emeralds and Golconda diamonds were sent to the great Parisian jewellers, such as Cartier and Boucheron, who were commissioned to re-set them in platinum in the Art Deco style. The customers were Indian royalty, such as the Maharajas of Mysore, Patiala, Kapurthala or Nawanagar, and the gems included not only priceless personal jewel collections, but even the Crown Jewels!

Indian royal courts were fascinated by the West, and they welcomed European artists with open arms: full-length portraits of Indian sovereigns, dripping with diamonds and gems, were specially painted as a result, in addition to contemporary sepia photographs of self-important monarchs and princes who wanted to display their splendour, wealth and magnificence to the entire world.

Portrait of the Persian sovereign, Fath Ali Shah. He was a descendant of Nadir Shah, the conqueror of the Mughal Empire. The austere and bearded Fath Ali Shah is depicted covered with diamonds, particularly in his armlets. The gems are painted in cream-coloured pigment. The jewels' size has been exaggerated, in order to portray the sitter's power. In 1824, he had his name engraved on the famous *Shah* diamond, which is now in Moscow. Studio of Ali Mihr, around 1805. Louvre Museum, department of Eastern Antiquities, Islamic section, Paris.

Once the Indian diamond deposits were exhausted, the Maharajahs had to adjust to new discoveries of diamonds elsewhere in the world. The Maharajah of Nawanagar acquired this sumptuous and unusual golden-brown diamond. Its colour led it to be named the Tiger's Eye. It was found in 1913 in the Vaal river, close to Kimberley, and weighed 178.50 carats in the rough. The cut stone reappeared recently, still in its original Cartier turban-ornament setting. It weighs 61.50 carats. Private collection.

CHAPTER XI

Michèle Bimbenet-Privat

Dazzling Paris:

The Parisian Diamond Market in the 16th and 17th centuries

For many years, diamonds were so rare and mysterious that only the most famous Parisian jewellers had the opportunity to set them in jewels or ornaments for their wealthy and powerful patrons. Royal archives show that it was a common practice in the 15th-century courts of France and of Burgundy to offer a diamond as a gift for the New Year. Even though diamonds are far more rare than spinels, sapphires, emeralds or natural pearls, they are listed in the royal archives under jewellery, silver and gold plate expenditures. The *Burgundy Goblet* is the only surviving piece from Duke Philip the Good's rock crystal collection. It is still decorated with its original diamond-studded fleur-de-lis motifs (Vienna, *Schatzkammer*). However, although there are many documents describing "flat", "point-cut", "lozenge-shaped" or "square" diamonds, none explains exactly how they arrived at the Parisian goldsmiths' workshops, the trade routes they followed, or what the diamonds looked like to begin with.

Antwerp Merchants in Paris

The first known diamond supplier to the Valois kings was the Flemish merchant Josse Vezeler during the reign of François I (1515-1547). He was an internationally-renowned goldsmith from Antwerp, who exported precious stones, silver and gold plate and tapestries. He befriended the King of France and subsequently opened a trade in Paris, managed by his nephew, Pierre Vezeler. One of his most significant transactions occurred in 1532, when the goldsmith delivered a sumptuous dinner service with ceremonial cups in gold and silver, intended for the Franco-English meeting of Boulogne-sur-Mer. The *'St. Michael Cup'*, was the crowning glory of the service. It survives today, in the collection of the Kunsthistorisches Museum of Vienna. It is a high gold cup made in the Germanic 'Pokal' style. Not only does its structure seem to defy the laws of gravity, but it is also embellished with a staggering array of precious gems: 88 diamonds, 27 rubies, 2 emeralds and 123 pearls. Its lid is surmounted by an extraordinary statuette of St. Michael conquering the dragon, an allegory of the triumph of Christianity and a direct reference to the treaty agreed between the two sovereigns into 1532 to defend the Papacy against the Turks. A study of this golden figure, which is 'armed' with diamonds, displays the mastery of the diamond-cutters of Antwerp. The chest is set with a point-cut diamond, the stomach with a table-cut diamond, and the legs are set with two saddle-shaped diamonds. Contemporary Parisian cutters would not have been capable of such a technically complex operation.

However, the goldsmiths were in great number in Paris: towards 1550, there were 300 workshops in the city, mainly concentrated in the Pont au Change area, in the heart of the city. It reached the point that Henri II established a *numerus clausus*, which would last until the end of the *Ancien Régime*. Foreign observers remarked upon the concentration of goldsmiths, the result of booming trade in a prosperous market. Benvenuto Cellini, the great goldsmith himself, acknowledged in his *Treatise* that Paris was the "only city, aside from Rome and Venice, where one can learn the jeweller's trade in depth". However, although the reputation of Parisian goldsmiths is not in question, one has to recognise the limits of their skills. They were virtuoso engravers, excellent founders for casting and inventive jewellers, but they only knew how to set gemstones. There was not a single diamond-cutter amongst their number. They had to import gems that had already been cut, or sub-

The *'St. Michael'* cup, Antwerp, Josse Vezeler, 1532. The cup was made in Antwerp at the request of François I, who commissioned it for the Franco-English meeting of Boulogne-sur-Mer, as a prelude to an alliance against the Turks. The archangel illustrates the gem-cutting skills that were particular to Flemish jewellers. At that time, their French counterparts would have been quite incapable of cutting the three point-cut, table-cut and saddle-shaped diamonds in the armour. Kunsthistorisches Museum, Vienna.

contract the work to a dozen of Flemish gem-cutters based in Paris. Hans Yoncre is the best-known of these diamond-cutters coming from Flanders, as he was frequently mentioned in the Royal Silverware ledgers thanks to his deliveries of lavishly gem-set jewels, with large table- and triangle-cut diamonds. The archives also show the names of Volkart Van Barre, who cut a large, 4,000-ecu diamond in 1558 for the Princess of Lorraine's wedding, or of Hanriquez and Rodriguez, two families of Portuguese origin.

With regard to the import of rough gems, the role of the small Portuguese community in Paris should not be disregarded. The Portuguese had ruled the waves as a leading maritime trading nation for many years, and they were the ones who supplied European courts with mother-of-pearl, ivory, lacquer or oriental porcelain artefacts. Although their transactions are seldom documented, it is thought that the rough diamonds they imported from India also came through Flemish territory. In 1577 for example, a Portuguese merchant by the name of Diego Nunes d'Evora hired a Parisian lawyer in order to recover two "pacquetz or uzailles" of diamonds and uncut rubies that he had imported from Spain. He explained that the Spanish had confiscated them in Péronne on the way to Flanders. He nevertheless hoped to recover the goods, as the two packages carried markings and code number only known to himself. Drawings in the document's margin illustrate the two cryptic marks that proved his ownership.

Markings on the diamond packages lost by Portuguese merchant Diego Nunes d'Evora, July 26th, 1577. Documents describing the transportation methods that conveyed diamonds from their source to Europe are extremely rare. The merchant lodged this complaint in an attempt to recover the gem parcels, which were seized by the Spaniards between France and Flanders. It reveals one of the codes used by importers to distinguish their goods. National Archives, Paris.

The Jewels of the Italian Queen

Up until the end of the 16th century, the technical deficiency of Parisian jewellers regarding gem-cutting could be seen in the composition of the jewels they made. They sought to compensate for their lack of skills by producing more and more complex settings, embellished with opaque or translucent enamels, which imbued the gems with symbolic or moral meanings that were evident to contemporary observers but which are sometimes difficult to interpret today. For example, Queen Catherine de Medici commissioned a large emerald pendant from her goldsmith, François Dujardin, that had 'faith' as its theme (it had a motif of two clasped hands, normally symbolising friendship). The rationale for the design was that "the emerald is a fragile stone that is easily broken, like faith". The widow of the provost of Paris adorned herself with a diamond ring bearing the inscription *"Sic Adamentis Haeres Mihi Pectore Clavis"* (you hang round my neck like a diamond key). In the mid-16th century, Parisian jewels tended to be set with rubies or pearls rather than diamonds. Diamonds were usually reserved for the most expensive commissions. For example, Catherine de Medici gave a diamond ring to her daughter-in-law, Mary Stuart, and a "gem-set accoutrement" to her daughter, Marguerite de Valois, upon her engagement to Henri de Navarre in 1571. Even on this occasion, the Queen Mother tried to keep costs down, by entrusting the commission to François Dujardin. She wrote "it was the best price that I could achieve". There were two contrasting sides to the Queen's personality, which can be seen in the very close dealings that she had with her personal jewellers. On the one hand, she was austere and devout to the point of bigotry. On the other, she was sumptuously extravagant and authoritarian. The friendly letters that she wrote to François Dujardin survive to this day, enquiring after his health and personally describing the jewels that she wished him to make for her. For example, in autumn 1571, in preparation for the Christmas festivities, she ordered a suite of diamond and pearl buttons. She wanted them to be S-shaped, known as *fermesses*, symbols of fidelity and of a widow's loneliness. In the margin of the letter, she sketched a rough design for the required jewels and she described them thus: "make the S-shapes all in diamonds, with a pearl set in the centre, as shown in the picture, and if you need more gems to make eight buttons like this one, I will send you the pearl and the small diamonds". In his reply, Dujardin sent three designs he had created in accordance with her instructions.

On the other hand, Catherine de Medici didn't care so much for another of her jewellery suppliers, Mathurin Lussault, a Protestant goldsmith. The Book of the Crespin Martyrs is an early-17th-cen-

Design for a whistle, engraving by Etienne Delaune, around 1560. Initially a goldsmith, the Protestant engraver Etienne Delaune (1518-1583) is best-known for his designs of medals, tokens and goldwork, and which were created for the King and the court. This lasted until the Saint-Barthélemy massacre obliged him to take refuge in the German Protestant principalities. Perhaps these engravings of whistles represent actual commissions, or, more likely, design ideas. This design is based around four table-cuts and a rose-cut gem, with an extraordinary setting swarming with motifs and overflowing with ornamentation, as beloved by the French National Library, Department of Engravings and Photography, Paris.

Portrait of Elisabeth of Austria, Queen of France. Oil on panel, attributed to the workshop of François Clouet . As the object of a political alliance between France and the Empire, Elisabeth of Austria married King Charles IX in 1570. The jewels shown on this formal portrait differ only slightly from those of Catherine de Medici, and it appears that they reflect the prevailing fashion in the French court. Pearls dominate, and rubies and diamonds are still table-cut, set in thick, collet-set gold mountings. Musée Condé, Chantilly.

tury publication from Geneva. It describes how Lussault, along with all his family, perished in horrific circumstances during the Saint Barthélemy massacre on August 24 1572. Not only had the Queen Mother not offered him any protection, but two days after the killings she ordered his stock of jewels to be seized. The Queen's men searched for several hours before they finally found the hoard, which included Lussault's most beautiful jewels, hidden in the depths of his cesspool. After a Royal Commission declared that Lussault had been "slain alongside others of this so-called reformed religion, and the majority of his goods ransacked by the people", the Queen took possession of three coffers filled with plate and jewellery that had supposedly been intended for her.

Clouet and his circle painted portraits of the men and women of the Royal family in all their jewelled splendour. What is left of these pendant earrings, *tourets* (hat ornaments), earrings, fans with jewelled handles, *carcanets*, *cottoires* and other necklaces, and expensive suites of buttons in rubies and table-cut diamonds? Probably very little. This is because religious wars engulfed France from 1561, scattering the jewels to the four winds. At the time, the King himself was forced to pawn the Crown Jewels in order to pay his troops, despite the fact that the jewels were meant to be inalienable. In 1568, Charles IX secured a 180,000-*écu* loan from the Republic of Venice against three of the most important Crown Jewels. Bertrand Jestaz recently published a description of these pieces. There were two gold pendants that held the two largest diamonds in the Crown collection: the *Great Table of François I* and the *Large Table*. In addition, there was a large cross "embellished with five large and very beautiful table-cut diamonds, of which the central one is a high bevelled square, the one on the right similarly square with lower bevels, the one on the left slightly longer, the top one with large, slightly chipped bevels and the bottom table-cut slightly longer and very beautiful, with four other diamonds including a round and a flat at the top and three other faceted heart-shapes that comprise the foot of the aforementioned cross, making nine diamonds in total". Although the King of France failed to repay the debt in full, the three jewels were obligingly returned by the Venetians in 1574, subsequently pawned again, and never redeemed. Effectively, therefore, they had ceased to be used as jewels and were instead regarded as a source of ready money.

Full-length portrait of Catherine de Medici, oil on panel, attributed to François Clouet, undated. The Queen is covered with jewels, mainly comprising diamonds and pearls sewn to her clothing. She bears a large diamond cross at her bodice. Galleria Palatina, Palazzo Pitti, Florence.

Miniature portrait of Catherine de Medici, attributed to François Clouet, undated. At the time of her marriage to the future Henri II, Catherine de Medici had come to France equipped with a sizeable trousseau of precious stones and pearls. This portrait is a break from the usual austerity shown in her later portraits. Catherine wears a *touret* around her head, a *carcanet* round her neck, and a *berthe* on her dress. These three ornaments are made of alternating pearls and large table-cut diamonds. Victoria and Albert Museum, London

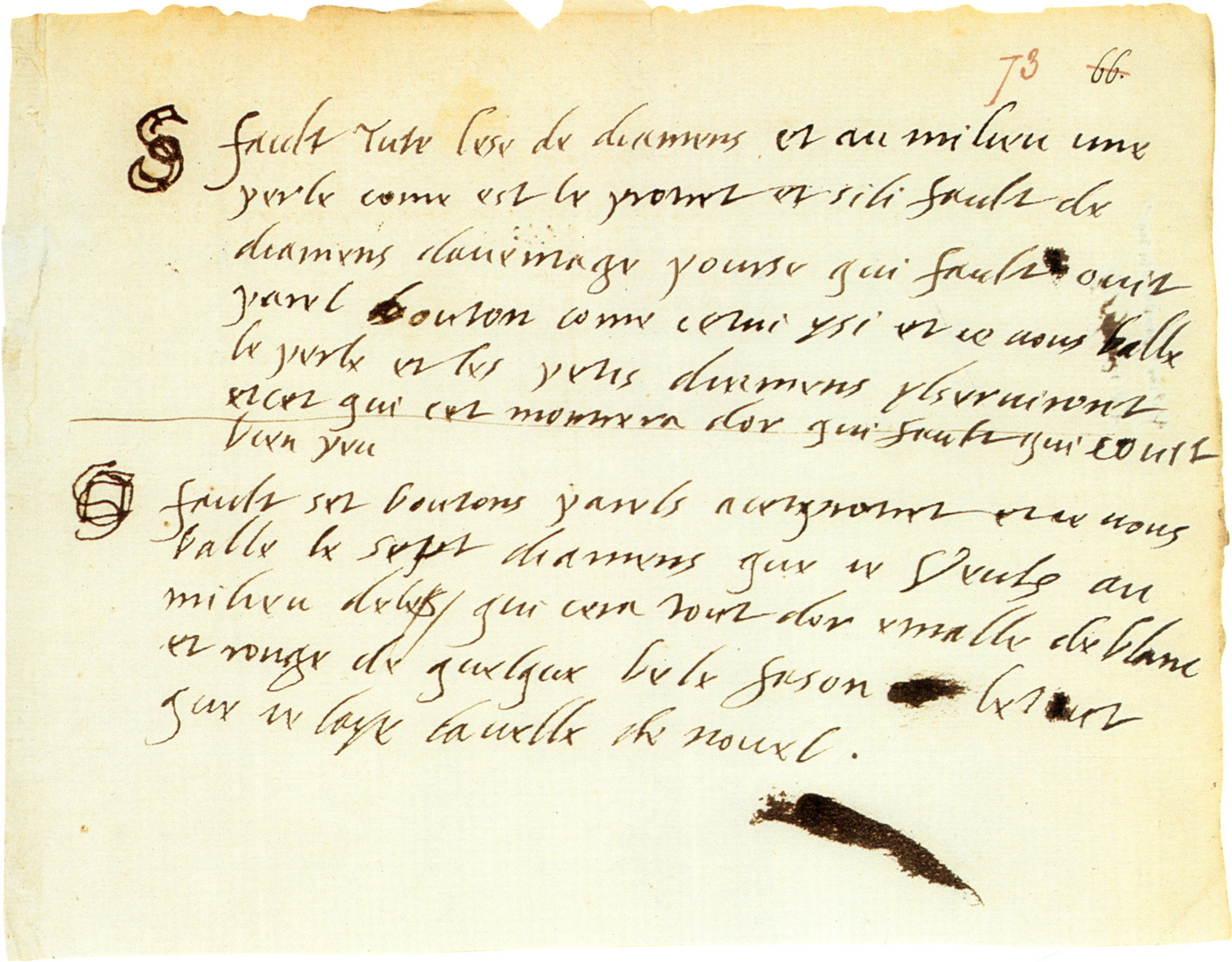

73 ~~66.~~

Il faut tute lose de diamens et au milieu une
perle come est le proint et sili faut de
diamens dauvantage pource qui fault ouir
parel bouton come celui ysi et ce vous balle
le perle et les petis diamens yl serviront
~~pieces qui est monstera dor qui faut qui court~~
bien pre

Il faut set boutons parels acetepoint et ce vous
balle le sept diamens que ie veule au
milieu de [illegible] qui sera tout dor emalle de blanc
et rouge de quelque bele fason les tout
que ie losse caualle de nouel.

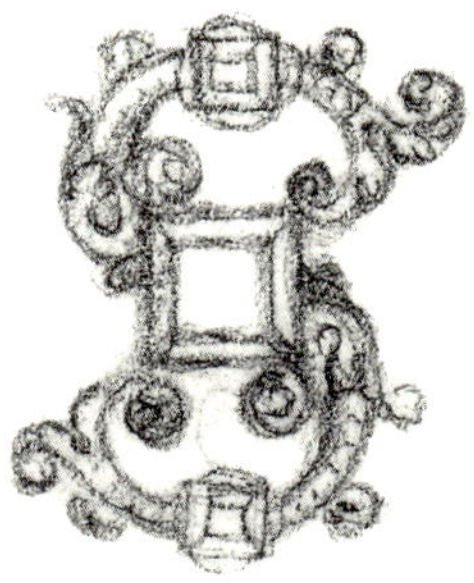

Letter from Catherine de Medici to her goldsmith, François Dujardin, and three sketches of jewels that he sent in his reply, 1571. The creative process that resulted in royal jewels is seldom so clearly outlined: Catherine de Medici's original message survives, in which she commissions diamond and pearl buttons from her jeweller, in her hesitant, Italianised French.In the margin, she has sketched the general shape that she requires. The goldsmith replies with three superb sketches that he drew himself in pencil. French National Library, Department of Western Manuscripts, Paris

Clandestine workers at the *Quai des Orfèvres*

In the last few decades of the 16th century, foreign political events came to have a profound impact upon the Parisian jewellery scene. The war in Southern Flanders, the devastation of the iconoclasts in 1566, the revolt against the Spanish, repression by the Duke of Alba on behalf of the King of Spain and, finally, the surrender of Antwerp in 1585: these events caused a mass of unemployed craftsmen to descend upon France, particularly goldsmiths and diamond-cutters from Antwerp. There was a massive influx of Flemish immigrants in Paris, but they were excluded from the goldsmiths' guild, which was protected by a *numerus clausus*. Some managed to find employment in goldsmiths' workshops, others worked illegally. Lapidary workshops for gem-cutting and clandestine forges for precious metal casting were set up in attics in the Pont-au-Change. Parisian goldsmiths shamelessly exploited the presence of the Flemish and grew rich at the expense of this foreign labourforce, unhesitatingly stamping their own hallmarks on objects that had been made illegally by others. This situation soon generated tension between the two communities, with the Flemish considering themselves unfairly restricted to subordinate positions. They attempted to obtain legal recognition on the grounds of their technical expertise. In 1584, Henri III tried to regulate the conflict by resuscitating an old and dying Parisian guild, the Glass-Cutters, and changing its name to "Lapidary-Workers". Gem-cutters could therefore achieve the rank of Master Lapidary, but at a price: they had to cease all their metal-working activities. From that point on, the lapidaries would cut and sell diamonds and other gemstones, and the goldsmiths would set them in jewellery. Although the jewellery trade itself was therefore left exclusively to the goldsmiths, they nevertheless contested the Royal decision so bitterly that the legislation would not be passed by the Parliament of Paris until 1600.

There were 29 members of the new guild. Unsurprisingly, fifteen were Flemish and four were Portuguese. The Flemish diamond cutters Jean Muittens, Gilles and Baudouin Baecler, Cornelis Deufle, Andri Pitten and Jan de Quillvalt were among the first Masters accepted into the guild. After that, the number of apprenticeship contracts grew rapidly. The documents are not detailed enough to allow the technical characteristics and practices specific to the Parisian workshops to be discerned. In 1632, for example, when the young René Moisin entered into the service of Master Lapidary Pierre Vimard, the contract specified that the Master would teach him the art of "grinding rough diamonds ready for the polishing wheel". The salary was meagre, at 9 livres per month, but the apprentice knew that, once qualified, he could make a great deal of money in this highly specialised field. In the first decades of the 17th century, Parisian jewellery incorporated a growing number of diamonds and precious stones. The creation of a professional class of wealthy Flemish lapidaries is the result of the expansion of the gemstone market.

The Kings of France themselves were partly responsible for the sea-change in the Parisian jewellery scene. Without hesitation, Henri III and Henri IV both recruited some of the most talented Flemish goldsmiths for their *Garde-Robe*. Josse de Langerac, Issac and David de Vimont, Cornelius and Nicolas Roger among others obtained the exclusive right to supply the Crown with gemstones. In 1595, the Venetian ambassadors to France were presented at court. This gave rise to many festivals and balls. The ladies of the court were "so heavily laden with jewels and precious stones, they could not even move" (J.-P. Babelon). Henri IV himself drew enthusiastically upon the Crown diamond collection. It is recorded that, in the most tender moments of his affair with Gabrielle d'Estrées, the King "placed on her finger the table-cut diamond ring that he received at his coronation ceremony: truly sacrilegious" (J.-P. Babelon). It is also said that, at the marriage ceremony of Madame Elisabeth, Henri IV's daughter, who became Queen of Spain in 1615, King Louis XIII "had in his hat a large diamond which was worth a hundred and twenty thousand *écus*, and an utterly priceless chain of rubies, emeralds, diamonds and other precious stones around his neck". The image of this King, bedecked with gold and precious stones, turns his usual image as an austere, sombre man of war on its head. In fact, Louis XIII's taste for diamonds was inculcated at an early age. He was only a young *dauphin* when his parents presented him with jewels and ornaments more appropriate for an adult than a little boy. The physician Héroard's *Journal* gives brief descriptions: a diamond insignia with an *aigrette* (in 1605), a diamond insignia and chain acquired by Marguerite de Valois at the Saint-Germain fair (1606), and even a diamond-studded watch, the Queen's gift in 1609, when the *dauphin* was only eight years old!

Another great royal innovation was Henri IV's installation of twenty-seven residences and five large workshops intended for the best craftsmen and artists of the time, in the ground floor of the Great Gallery of the Louvre in 1608. The concept of privileged artists with noble patrons was not new in France, but such a gathering of artists from different fields and backgrounds, who would be able to mutually influence each other, was unprecedented in Paris. It undoubtedly contributed towards the spread of the French capital's influence across the whole of Europe. The key innovation lay in the statutory privileges granted to the Gallery's tenants, to the enormous displeasure of the Parisian guilds: total independence, the right to become a Master craftsman without paying fees, or to train several apprentices at the same time, in order to become "a nursery for workmen" who would thereafter spread themselves throughout the kingdom. The idea, which also occurred to Colbert sixty years later, was to definitively install the best foreign professionals in Paris, in order to reduce the level of imports of luxury goods, which was extremely costly for royal coffers. With regard to jewellery, the Louvre's tenants included the goldsmith/enamellers Courtois and Bimbi from the Medici workshops in Florence, and Flemish jewellers such as Jean Vangrol. Thus Southern inventiveness and Northern technical expertise were combined in Paris, for the delectation of the royal family.

The diamond-lover

Marie de Medici deserved her reputation as a diamond-lover. She was quick to secure the services of François Dujardin, grandson of Catherine de Medici's goldsmith, who learnt his skills as an apprentice in Antwerp from 1600 to 1605. In January 1623, Dujardin went into business with his Flemish fellow goldsmith, Cornelius Roger, himself "goldsmith and guard of the cabinet of Anne of Austria", descended from the *Rogier* or *Rasier* family of Antwerp. For almost twenty years until their company was wound up in 1641, Roger and Dujardin kept up an impressive trade in diamonds, gems and pearls from Persia and India via Lisbon, Antwerp or London, through the channels of the East India Company or their own agents and local contacts. The precise trading practices for this business remain extremely obscure. It is known that, in 1641, they were faced with almost insurmountable difficulty in recovering two boxes full of diamonds that were stuck in the town of Laire, Persia, as a result of the death of their courier, a gem-cutter from Geneva called Abraham de La Combe. These diamonds were to be divided between Roger and Dujardin, a Venetian jeweller called Gallatin and a banker called Heuf from Amsterdam, representing the East India Company. There was a colossal amount of money involved: Dujardin and Roger's jewellery commanded prices that only royalty and the richest members of society could possibly afford.

A glance at some royal jewellery inventories, such as those of Queen Marie de Medici in 1609 or 1610, Marguerite de Valois in 1615 or Anne of Austria in 1666, is enough to appreciate the vast quantity of diamonds, precious stones and pearls that these French queens possessed. For example, Marie de Medici ordered a small baby's rattle in 1630 from Dujardin and Roger for one of her grandchildren, the child of Henrietta-Maria of France, Queen of England. The rattle was "in gold, enamelled in many colours, embellished with three hundred and fifty diamonds of varying sizes". Dujardin and Roger remained the foremost suppliers of the Queen Mother until her exile: after Louis XIII's death, the two goldsmiths asked for more than 109,000 livres for diamonds and gold chains that the Queen had never paid for. Anne of Austria, Queen of France, also appears to have

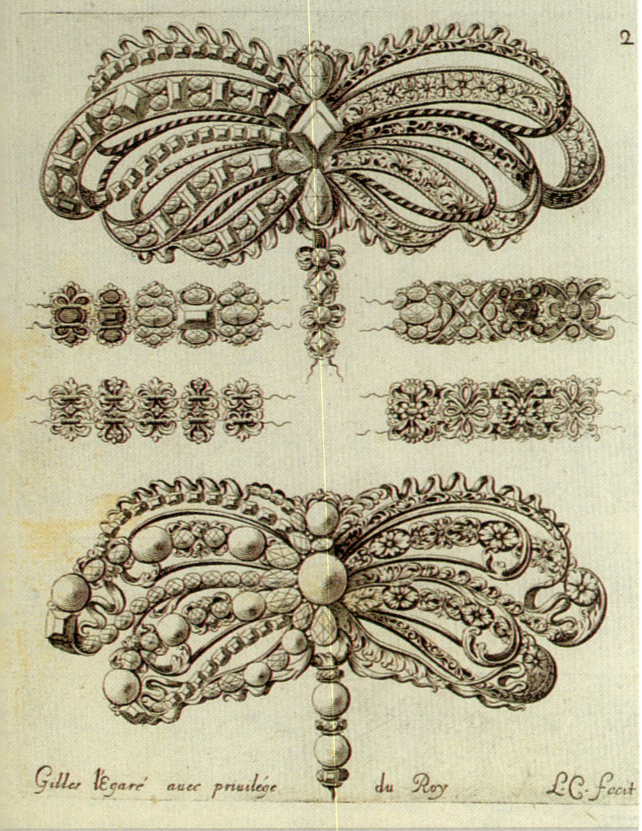

Plate of bow-knot jewellery designs, engraved by Gilles Légaré, 1663. The Protestant goldsmith Gilles Légaré was one of the suppliers to the royal family and the court, from 1657 until his death in 1663.
His jewellery designs were published by royal command in 1663. They clearly show how Parisian jewels were formed: precious gems on the front (shown on the left of the designs), enamelled floral decoration on the back (shown on the right). Museu Nacional de Arte Antigua, Lisbon.

been an important Roger and Dujardin customer, but her confidante Madam de Motteville revealed how her taste for diamonds was moderated by her pious generosity: "being extremely young and at the peak of her beauty, and as she did not have enough money to provide for all the alms that she wished to make, she surreptitiously used her own jewellery, breaking the chains as if they had been accidentally lost, in order to give them to the poor". In this way, precious stones, customarily associated with decadence and loose sexual morals, afforded this virtuous Queen the opportunity to put her soul to the test of vanity, as preached by Father Le Moyne in his *"La Dévotion aisée"*, the favourite book of devout women of the time.

In any event, the Royal court's suppliers found the fine jewellery trade far more lucrative than the foundry, chasing and metalwork trade, which was the bread-and-butter of the remaining goldsmiths in Paris. Upon his death in 1645, Cornelius Roger had 360,000 livres of credit at the company that he had formerly co-owned with Dujardin. In addition, he left an impressive stock of fashionable jewellery, comprising bow-knots, emerald and diamond pendants, pomanders, gem-set dress ornaments, agate carvings mounted in gold, presentation boxes with portrait miniatures and enamelled heraldic trophies, not to mention many other sources of income, plus the rank of Counsel Secretary to the King. It is clear that there was a growing gap between the King's principal goldsmiths, sustained by a network of customers of staggering wealth including foreign dignitaries, and the less fortunate goldsmiths in Paris.

Fashion trends in the 17th century

At that time, the fashion was for "bouquets of flowers, worn on the head". Marie de Medici had a complete set of such jewels, comprising marigolds, carnations, pansies and daisies. The goldsmiths from the Gallery of the Louvre also started a fashion for 'jewelled leaves', of which Balthazar Le Mersier, Jacques Caillart and Pierre Delabarre produced the finest examples. All of them also made a new style of jewel known as the 'pea-pod'. This became the name of a characteristic style of Parisian jewellery in the years 1620-1630. Its roots lie in botanical illustrations and the renewed contemporary enthusiasm for the marvels of Nature. The open pea-pods releasing their contents are incorporated within decorative bouquets, embellished with leaves, strewn with seeds and intertwined with tendrils. The goldsmiths set them with countless precious gems outlining the sinuous designs, with graduated rows of diamonds evoking the pods, clusters imitating flower petals and tiny gems for seed husks.

The number of Parisian designs grew, disseminating the pea-pod fashion beyond the circle of the craftsmen based in the Louvre. In 1628, for example, Pierre Marchand, a small goldsmith near the Arsenal, published an autograph collection of designs for aigrettes and pea-pod jewels. His work is less imaginative and inventive than that shown in the design collections of the King's goldsmiths but, as a conscientious workman, Marchand was careful to clearly depict the size and setting details of the precious stones: they are placed in what is now known as a closed, 'collet' setting. The majority of the stones are point-, table- and rose-cuts, the three most common cuts performed in Paris. Throughout Louis XIII's reign, pea-pods designs, which are published under the name of 'jewelled-leaf', became the original signature of the Parisian jewellery. They inspired goldsmiths across all the European Royal courts, who frantically tried to imitate the exquisite inventions of the Louvre's goldsmiths. These golden years mark the birth of the 'French style' of jewellery. The French court would lead the way in European style and fashion trends up until the end of the century. The Duchess of Orleans' letters still evoke the Berlin court's discreet fashion enquiries from 1691: "I cannot imagine who has led Your Excellency the Elector of Brandenburg to believe that one wears diamond aigrettes on hats over here. They are worn by neither the young nor the old. The only people I have seen wearing them have been dancers at the Opera. Therefore, I could not possibly send such designs to you. But there is one thing that is very popular, it is a brilliant diamond buckle holding the plume at the front, with large diamonds at the back that form a sort of clip.".

Little by little, the knots, pendants and presentation boxes made by Parisian goldsmiths acquired a coherent and fixed style. The front was reserved for the jeweller's skills: incredible numbers of gems would be clustered there, dominated by diamond rosettes, to the point that such clusters were habitually referred to as 'rocks'. The back was flat and smooth, but rich in polychrome floral decoration thanks to a vast palette of different painted enamels. The Parisian goldsmith Gilles Légaré put together a series of jewellery designs at the start of Louis XIV's reign, showing the front and back of each jewel side by side on the same engraving.

The diamond Cardinal

The patronage of high-ranking people of the State continued to promote growth in the diamond market and the development of diamond cutting. After the death of Anne of Austria in 1666, the goldsmiths who valued the Queen Mother's jewels were very pleased to discover rare examples of new diamond cuts amongst the collection, in particular "a large cross with a large modern-cut diamond in the centre, flat on the top and with facets below, with four heart-shaped diamonds and four other small gems", valued at 70,000 livres. Likewise, an inventory was also drawn up upon the death of Mazarin, a Cardinal and Minister to the King. Patrick Michel who produced a beautiful study of the collection, counted up to fifty rings set with precious stones. Cardinal Mazarin's correspondence is full of letters to his devoted goldsmith François Lescot, who was often sent to England, Flanders and Portugal with bags full of *écus*, to purchase diamonds and other products from the Indies. Mazarin had a genuine love of diamonds, immortalised in his legacy of the eighteen 'Mazarin' diamonds to the King (see Chapter 12). For example, here is his response, via Colbert, to Lescot's offer of diamonds for sale in August 1659: "Tell Lescot that I approve of all that he has said regarding the proposition that has been made, regarding a large diamond from the Indies that has arrived in the most recent Amsterdam shipments, which, following my answer to him, one might come to an agreement upon; because, if we hold firm to the price that he has asked for, I believe that there is no need to think twice about it. For the faceted heart-shaped diamond, it would be good if he could remember to send me the information about its weight, otherwise it would involve spending eight thousand livres without being informed; because often the price of these things is based on their weight, particularly when the diamonds are perfect. But should he tell you that it is at a good price and that it would be advantageous to buy it, please pay whatever Lescot requests. But I would rather that he not put it in the centre of the cross, as he proposed, unless one can make a setting for it whereby the gem would be detachable, without which the cross would be a waste" (P. Clément). This text vividly demonstrates the peculiar mixture of trust and caution displayed by Mazarin towards his favourite goldsmith.

Gold and diamond apprestat, France, around 1620. This large corsage jewel, in the classic 'pea-pod' jewellery style, comprises 208 diamonds, the majority of which are table-cuts, with a small number of faceted gems, mounted on a sheet of gold. Victoria and AlberMuseum, London.

The King's gems

Louis XIV's accession to power started a golden age for the Parisian goldsmiths who were in the service of the Sun King. These men included Jean Pittan, Louis Alvarez, Laurent and Pierre Le Tessier de Montarsy, Sylvestre Bosc, Philippe Pijart and Pierre Bain, whose workshop contained in 1702 "a saw for cutting diamonds, with copper bowl and bronze handles and bow", proof that some were true diamond-cutters in addition to the jewellers. Great voyagers travelled the roads of Persia and India for the King, in search of most beautiful diamonds. Jean-Baptiste Tavernier and Jean Chardin are the best-known of these. It was no longer merely a question of enriching the Crown jewel collection, or of providing precious stones intended for royal costumes, or jewels for the royal mistresses. There are many sources that describe the dazzling splendour of the King's attire. Some writers even dared to let slip an intimation of polite disgust in the face of such extravagance and, paradoxically, inclinations towards thrift: "the purchase of diamonds cost him 2,000,000 last year, an expense that he wishes to decrease further this year", wrote the worthy Marquis de Dangeau in January 1686. A single example is enough to take the measure of how disproportionate royal expenditure really was: for the Dauphin's marriage in 1680, Le Tessier de Montarsy sold the King more than 462,000 livres of precious stones. This included a suite of diamonds that was to be presented to the Dauphin, of 327,000 livres. That same year, the silver balustrade made by the Gobelins goldsmiths for the King's chamber, the heaviest and most prestigious element of Louis XIV's famous suite of silver furniture, cost the Crown only 100,000 livres.

Prompted by the ever-methodical Colbert, the King ordered the first of what would become known as the 'King's Gem Ledgers' in 1669. These catalogues are preserved today at the Ministry for Foreign Affairs, and they contain the complete inventory of the King's precious stones. One finds, for example, that in 1669 the King's diamond reserve comprised 1,302 rough diamonds and 609 cut diamonds, with their colours ("violet, verging on peach-blossom") and shapes ("helmet, marquise, heart-shape, table-cut") carefully noted. Colbert personally supervised the daily update of the inventory by hand-writing "correct" besides the entries (purchases from gem merchants) and exits (the King's gifts) of precious stones. This was because the ever-changing gem collection had political ends, just like the Crown Jewels, which were inventoried separately and themselves constantly enriched. Their purpose was firstly to impress. Therefore, when the Ambassadors of Siam were presented to Louis XIV in September 1686, the King took great care to ensure that he was "bedecked with diamonds of extraordinary size" which "are worth more than the whole of the Kingdom of Siam" (Sourches). Over the course of the following days, the King graciously displayed the Crown's gems to the Siamese, enjoying the admiration of his hosts, who acknowledged that the gems' beauty was beyond compare, "except for those of the Mogul Empire, which they had not seen". To say that Louis XIV had a passion for precious stones is more than an understatement. He travelled to see them, and discussed them with his ministers and his goldsmiths. He would be filled with enthusiasm for a fine jewel or, on the contrary, would be indignant at seeing an unpleasant diamond. So much so that Seignelay, one of his Ministers, preferred to submit mock-ups of potential jewels to him for approval before the pieces were cast. In 1685, he wrote to Le Tessier de Montarsy regarding a commission of diamond buttons. The King was so keen to know "every last detail" that Seignelay had to tell the goldsmith: "in order to ensure that it is to the King's taste, you should bring the gems to me tomorrow, arranged in wax" (P. Verlet).

The King's gems were more than an immense reserve of wealth. They also amounted to a means of government, because the King drew his 'presentations' from the collection. Any occasion might be enough to mark the Sovereign's benevolence and friendship. Gifts were made to France's foreign allies, foreign diplomats, loyal servants and even to the men of war with whom he clashed on the battlefield: during his career, the famous Duke of Marlborough would receive more than one presentation box with a portrait miniature. Quintessential Louis XIV gifts, these portrait boxes are true miniature political marvels. They were boxes only in name: they comprised an enamelled portrait miniature of Louis XIV, mounted on a gold plaque set with twenty, thirty, or sometimes even sixty diamonds, with another enamelled gold plaque bearing Louis XIV's cypher on the reverse. One can imagine the greed with which the recipients of these royal miniatures welcomed their gift. In 1703, for example, Louis XIV indicated to the Swedish diplomat Cronström that he wished to thank the Swedish architect Tessin, for having given him a painting. The two men pored over the details. Minister Torcy requested Cronström's opinion: would Tessin prefer a ring or a presentation box with portrait miniature? Cronström advised the presentation box. He wrote to Tessin, "it is likely to become like a mark of honour from His Majesty for your family". Prudently, he added: "I will go to see the keeper of the King's gems, Mr. de Montarsy, to try to ensure that you are given only perfect diamonds. I believe that I did well to recommend the portrait box over the ring, which would be only one stone; however beautiful it might be, it would barely be worth over four to five thousand livres. Thirty or forty gems would have to be very poor for them to be worth less than that...". It is, indeed, the intrinsic value of the diamonds that unfortunately resulted in the destruction of nearly all the royal portrait boxes. The recipients or their descendants usually had them broken up. To our knowledge, only three intact boxes remain today, worldwide. However, exactly 338 of them were supplied by Montarsis and his colleagues from 1669 to 1684, the date when the bookkeepers of the gem ledgers got tired of counting them... *Sic transit gloria!*

Presentation box with portrait miniature of Louis XIV, around 1670-1680. Richly set with 78 rose-cut diamonds, this portrait box was one of the many gifts that Louis XIV distributed during his reign, mainly to foreigners, to signify his benevolence, gratitude or thanks. In the centre of the medallion there is an enamelled portrait miniature of the king, surrounded and crowned with diamonds, with Louis XIV's cypher (two interlinked Ls) on the back, in enamel. Private collection.

CHAPTER XII

Bernard Morel

The diamonds of the European monarchies

When the first diamonds arrived in the West, European monarchs rapidly came to regard them as the most precious and coveted gem - and the most expensive. This was due to their scarcity, and particularly the discovery of diamond-cutting at the end of the 14th century. The monarchs never ceased to compete with each other in terms of jewelled splendour, although naturally some had deeper pockets than others. In this chapter, we will focus upon the principal European monarchies. Some of them were able to acquire magnificent treasures thanks to their finances, depending on the wealth of their countries. Some kingdoms will be omitted; whether because their jewel collections were dispersed without leaving an inventory, such as Spain, or because their collections are minor compared to those of other countries, such as France and England. For these reasons, we omit Italy, Belgium and Norway, which, in any case, did not have Crown Jewel collections. The old kingdoms of Central Europe, such as Hungary, Bohemia and Poland, are also omitted, partly because they were rapidly swallowed up by neighbouring empires, and additionally because their treasuries date back to the Middle Ages, and therefore do not contain any diamonds.

Diamonds reach the French court: 1300-1500

Until the first Crusades, European sovereigns only had a limited range of gems to adorn their crowns and jewels. These gems were inherited from Roman antiquity, and were far from the highest quality. Diamonds were not included in this list, of course. They had sapphires (which were often rather pale in colour), old Egyptian emeralds, garnets, old pearls and various semiprecious stones... Although the Crusaders captured Constantinople in 1204 and carried a hoard of gems back to the west, most of these were also of ancient origin and average quality, as can be seen on the famous *Pala d'Oro* of St. Mark in Venice. It was only then that the trade in gemstones from the East began to increase, thanks to Italian merchants and Middle-Eastern Arab middlemen. Sapphires were the first to arrive. They were of beautiful quality, from Ceylon and Burma. An incredible number of fine spinels soon followed, from Afghanistan. These sapphires and spinels were sometimes of great size, and the latter were reserved almost exclusively for monarchs, particularly French kings, who had a passion for spinels.

It seems that the first diamonds did not arrive in Europe until the time of St. Louis, in the second half of the 13th century. The majority of them were small rough octahedral crystals, and in truly minute quantities. This theory is based upon the Duke of Berri's 1413 inventory, which mentions a rough octahedron of around 5 carats, which was known as the *Dyament de saint Loys*. It had been purchased in 1408, for 300 gold écus. But was this attribution correct? The Saint-King had enormous prestige, and relics were passionately venerated at the time. It could be that the Duke of Berri was misled by the vendor, and this *Diamond of St. Louis* might, in fact, be the first known case of a diamond with a false historical attribution. This practice is still going on, endowing certain diamonds with a spurious history in the hope of increasing their worth.

In any event, rough diamonds only started arriving from the Indies in greater quantity in the mid-14th century. King Charles V of France assembled the Middle Ages' most fabulous treasury. Its 1379 inventory is very revealing, not only because of the number of stones, but also because of the fact that none of them had evidently yet been cut (cf. Chapter 8). It starts with a description of no fewer than 55 crowns and circlets. As far as we can tell from the inventory, these jewels contained the astounding total of 1,083 spinels, 236 sapphires, 705 emeralds, 4,250 pearls and 507 diamonds! All of these gems were rough dia-

Louis XV's Coronation crown (1722).
After the ceremony, the original gems were removed and replaced with copies. The *Regent* is set at the front, with the *Great Mazarin* immediately above it. The *Sancy* is set at the very top of the crown.

mond points (known as "naives"), except for the "very large and very thick diamond" set at the summit of one of the King's principal crowns, the "Crown with Square Gems". This was a beautiful rough octahedron, whose weight would barely have exceeded 20 carats. For the most part, the diamonds were set in the middle of three- or five-pearl clusters, to provide flashes of light in the midst of an abundance of coloured gemstones.

Apart from this large diamond, which was certainly the most beautiful in the royal collection and which we shall refer to as *Charles V's Diamond*, there were only two other diamonds that were exceptional for the period. They were also rough octahedra, and were set in rings: "521. A ring where there is a very large and fine 'dyamant', quite square", and *Jean the Good's Diamond* († 1364): "522. Another ring, where there is a large diamond, not of good water, not too fine, square, which belonged to King Jehan, the King's father". As far as diamond collections go, this was all that the richest sovereign in the second half of the 14th-century could muster...

The inventory also lists the crown of Jeanne, Queen of Burgundy (no. 10), Charles V's grandmother and the first wife of Philippe VI de Valois. She died in 1348. This crown was adorned with 63 spinels, 45 emeralds, 90 pearls and 48 rough diamond points. In all our research into ancient jewel inventories, this was the oldest diamond-set jewel that we could find. It could date back as early as the start of the reign, in 1328. Diamond-cutting was invented at the time of Charles V's death in 1380. This development rapidly led to Paris becoming the first of the world's great gem-cutting centres, not only for diamonds but for all other gems. Paris had Europe's greatest concentration of wealthy customers, not only the royal family, but also the principal feudal lords, who all had residences in Paris. Charles V had three brothers: Duke Louis of Anjou († 1382), Duke Jean of Berri († 1416) and Duke Philippe the Bold of Burgundy († 1404). The four of them, and later Charles V's son, Charles VI, were the most lavish princes of their age. They were all avid gem collectors, with almost unbelievably splendid collections. It is highly likely that most of the rough diamonds that arrived in Venice, Genoa or Florence very quickly went to Paris, where the majority were cut and sold. Unsurprisingly, therefore, the Duke of Berri's 1413-1416 jewel inventory lists many exceptional stones. Even at this early date, the majority of them appear to have been cut skilfully. The inventory lists 27 particularly significant diamonds, including the *Diamond of Saint Louis*, the *Queen of Sicily's Diamond*, *the Pope's Diamond*, *the Duc de Guyenne*, and *Charles VI's diamond*. Weights were recorded for only three of them; these were probably the heaviest, and their weights would have been considered exceptional at the time: the 24-carat *Mirror of Florence*, the 20-carat *Berri Point*, and the *Square Diamond of Genoa*, which weighed 19 old carats. The inventory shows that diamonds and rubies were priced at about the same per carat, and considerably more than spinels and sapphires. Because they were available in large sizes, spinels were more suited to the ostentatious luxury of the time. This is why spinels remained the principal royal gems. The Duke of Berri was obsessed with beautiful spinels, the majority of which were polished ('tumbled') pebbles. The inventory lists many of them, along with their purchase price. These figures allow us to compare the per-carat prices charged for spinels and diamonds at the time. The 24-carat *Mirror of Florence* cost 6,000 écus, or 250 écus per carat. The duke's largest spinel, the 414.5-carat Balas of Venice, had been purchased from the Duchess of Orleans, the king's sister-in-law, in 1407. The price was 17,500 écus, or 42 écus per carat. This was a discounted price, since her husband had just been assassinated on the orders of Fearless John, Duke of Burgundy, and she needed the money. The Duke's finest spinel, the 212-carat Duke of Berri, cost 16,000 écus in 1408, or 75.5 écus per carat. It was set in the centre of his treasury's most magnificent clasp jewel, surrounded by three diamonds, including the Berri Point, a large, flat, eight-sided diamond that had cost 2,500 écus, and the *Mirror of Berri*, a large, square, flat diamond worth 7,100 écus. The splendid Great Berri Pearl was suspended from the clasp, as a pendant. For the sake of comparison, a golden écu weighed 6.095 grams. The *Mirror of Florence* therefore cost the equivalent of 36 kilos of gold. However, the purchasing power of gold in the 15th century was three times greater than it would be in the 16th century, following the massive influx of American gold. In the Duke of Berri's time, a good horse would have cost 30 écus and, in today's terms, *the Mirror of Florence* cost the equivalent of 108 kilos of gold!

Since the Duke died without issue on June 15th, 1416, some of his treasures were sold to redeem his debts, and his estate was distributed amongst various heirs. However, his most beautiful gems, notably his entire collection of large spinels, went to his nephew, King Charles VI. When he sensed that his death was near, he had them set in a gold cross weighing twelve kilos, known as the *Pulcherrima Crux*. He presented it to the King in person, on June 8th, and asked him to keep it forever, as a memento of him. It was a vain hope, as the next year, on July 30th, the cross was stripped of its stones and sent to the Mint to be melted down... This was hardly surprising, since France was in a state of economic depression after its defeat at Agincourt in 1415, partly invaded by the English, and devastated by the civil war between the Armagnac and the Burgundy families. In only a few years, the mad King's Armagnac advisers liquidated all the treasure inherited from Charles V. As for the gems that the Duke of Berri had bequeathed, they were sold alongside the famous 'great crown' in 1417-1418. Virtually all the purchasers were Italian financiers, and nobody knows what ultimately became of the diamonds or the spinels. This was the first of the many great catastrophes that would befall the French Treasury throughout history.

As far as the 15th century is concerned, we have found hardly any other significant diamonds worth mentioning. France was ruined, and only recovered from its misfortunes at the end of Charles VII's reign († 1461). His successor, Louis XI († 1483), was only Valois to scoff at luxury. He preferred to use his gold for diplomatic missions and for the fight against Burgundy. The Dukes of Burgundy themselves (the famous grand dukes of the West), played their game well at the time of the Hundred Years' War and reigned over territories that were then amongst the richest in Europe, the finest being Flanders. Four successive dukes, Philippe the Bold († 1404), Jean the Fearless († 1419), Philippe the Good († 1467) and Charles the Bold († 1477) maintained by far the most sumptuous court of the entire continent, following in the great Valois tradition. Gem-cutters, of course, go wherever the luxury and the money are. For this reason, Paris lost its place as a great diamond-cutting centre, superseded by Bruges and then by Antwerp, in Burgundian Flanders.

At some time before 1412, Jean the Fearless had purchased the largest diamond to arrive in Europe in the whole of the 15th century. This was the turbulent year in which he was forced to pawn it with his jewellery and his gold dinner service. They were soon redeemed. At the time, the diamond was described as a large, pointed, square diamond, the size of a filbert (large hazelnut). The Duke was then mainly based in Paris, so it was probably cut there, at a date when the city still had many diamond-cutters. The rough octahedron was cut into a double pyramid point-cut with triangular facets, 16 mm in width. His successor, Philippe the Good, had it set in the centre of the famous Three Brothers clasp, alongside three table-cut spinels of about 70 carats each, and four very large pearls (cf. Chapter 8). Thanks to surviving watercolours of the jewel, the diamond's weight can be estimated at 30 carats. This was the most famous stone of its time, which we shall call the Duke of Burgundy.

Let us finish with the 15th century by mentioning the extraordinary "diament cut in the shape of a fleur-de-liz, in one piece", set in a ring, that René I of Anjou (1409-1480) gave to his wife on their wedding day. Clearly, a high degree of technical expertise must already have been developed by that time, in order to cut a fleur-de-lys out of a single diamond!

The 53.25-carat *Great Table of François I.*
Life-size reconstruction, by Bernard Morel.

The Point of Brittany (around 25 carats).
Life-size reconstruction, by Bernard Morel.

The triumph of diamonds in the 16th-century French Court

Once the Portuguese set up bases in Goa in the 16th century, the overland route to the Indies via Arabia was quickly abandoned. Diamond deposits were also being exploited much more effectively. As a result, diamonds started being imported to Europe in much greater quantities, including quite a few larger gems. Diamonds finally became the principal stones in royal treasuries, although large spinels still had their place. At the time, the French and English courts had the greatest wealth of exceptional stones. These were also cut in the most highly-prized shapes, such as point-cuts, square or rectangular table-cuts, and various other beautiful faceted shapes.

After the disaster of Pavie in 1525, the extravagant King François I was imprisoned in Madrid by Charles V. To secure his release, his two sons had to be sent there as hostages, where they remained until 1529. In order to pay the enormous ransom, his mother Louise de Savoie disposed of much of the royal treasure. The King was greatly displeased by the loss of many of his jewels. In order to avoid such disappointment in future, he decided to found the collection known as the Crown Jewels, on June 15th, 1530. From then on, these jewels ceased to be the sovereign's personal property, and become inalienable jewels of the State. These were, therefore, only presented "for enjoyment" to his new wife, Eleanor of Austria. It was a marriage of diplomacy: she was Charles V's sister.

In order to create the first Crown collection, King François I primarily used the jewels that he had inherited from his first wife, Claude of France, who died in 1524. This collection had survived the ransom process. She was Anne of Brittany's daughter († 1514). Claude of France had been the wife of both King Charles VIII and then of Louis XII. Most of the fourteen selected diamonds actually came from the ancient 15th-century ducal treasure of Brittany. Eleven of these large diamonds were set in Queen Claude's necklace, interspersed with ten clusters of fourteen pearls. They were valued at between 4,000 and 18,000 écus each, totalling 106,000 écus. The most expensive was a large heart-shape, flat on top and with a faceted underside. This was followed by four table-cuts, five point-cuts with various shapes, and the first marquise-cut diamond in history. This was the only stone in the necklace with a name: the *Eye or Spindle of Brittany*, valued at 10,000 écus. We traced this diamond to the reign of Louis XIV, although it had by then lost its name, and was listed as a "diamond cut in the shape of a boat, with facets on both sides", weighing 9.76 carats. It was later re-cut under Louis XVI into a 5.65-carat drop-shape, only to disappear during the Revolution.

The other three diamonds in the collection were even more important. The first of these was the *Beautiful Point*, which was later renamed the *Point of Milan*. It was set in an A-shaped pendant (Anne of Brittany's initial), alongside a large ruby. The inventory does not record its weight, but its valuation of 30,000 écus corresponds with about 30 carats. Then there was the six-sided *Point of Brittany*, set in a pendant with a drop-shaped pearl, valued at 25,000 écus (approximately 25 carats). Anne of Brittany had brought it to Paris in 1491 for her marriage with Charles VIII. She had had it re-cut in 1497 in Lyon: "to Jehan Cayon, a dyamentier of Lyon: the sum of 52 l. 10 s. for taking my lady's beautiful diamond point and putting it to the mill". The third was the *Table of Genoa*, also set with a drop-shaped pearl and also valued at 25,000 écus (approximately 25 carats). The fourteen large diamonds of the Crown Jewels were therefore worth a total of 186,000 écus, equivalent to 620 kilos of pure gold.

Of course, these were not François I's only diamonds. In 1532 he had some nineteen important gems in his private collection, worth a total of 143,000 écus. Four of them had been purchased from George Welzer, a well-known Antwerp diamond dealer who had travelled to France specifically for the transaction. Between then and the end of his reign (1547), the King purchased other marvellous gems, particularly the diamond that would be named after him, the *Great Table of François I.* He paid 65,000 écus for it, equivalent to 221 kilos of pure gold, and it was the largest diamond known in Europe at the time. It was a slightly rectangular square table-cut, thick and of 'full depth', i.e. it had a deep, pyramidal underside which was not truncated. The King also acquired the *Large Table*, which may have weighed up to 40 carats. The *Great Cross* was another important jewel, amongst others. It had five matching square table-cuts of between 15 to 16 carats, a round rose-cut of 10 to 11 carats, and three faceted 4-carat drop-shapes. This jewel was later worn by Henri II on his Coronation day, and it would subsequently be pawned in Venice in 1560 for 90,000 écus.

Upon the king's death, these splendid jewels passed into the private treasury of his successor, Henri II. Rather than permitting his wife, Catherine de Medici, to use them, he lent them to his beloved mistress, Diane de Poitiers. However, upon the accession of her son, François II (1559-1560), the Queen Mother added them to the Crown Jewels. They would be worn by the new Queen, Mary Stuart, and then by Elizabeth of Austria, wife of Charles IX, who died in 1574, and by Louise de Lorraine-Vaudémont, the wife of Henri III, who was assassinated in 1589. Tragically, this period of French history was marred by religious wars, which ruined the French monarchy. The Crown Jewels were pawned many times in order to pay the army, and they were in creditors' hands upon Henri III's death. These creditors were mainly in Florence and Venice. Henri IV, the new Bourbon king, spent several years defending his claim to the throne, and was unable to redeem them. The creditors sold the jewels... This was the second catastrophe to befall the French Crown Jewels. Later, Henri IV could only recover the diamonds from Queen Claude's necklace. The others were all lost without trace, except perhaps for the *Great Table of François I.* Upon Henri III's death, this diamond was in the hands of some bankers in Florence, still in its golden setting enamelled in black and white with a large drop-shaped pearl pendant. However, 30 years later, in 1619, Henri IV and Marie de Medici's second daughter, Chrétienne (or Christine) of France, married Victor Amédée, the son of Duke Charles Emmanuel I of Savoy. He gave her a very large diamond to mark the event. Christine became the Duchess of Savoy in 1630. Upon her death in 1663, she bequeathed her large diamond to the Crown of Savoy, by her will of April 5th, 1662. This gem is listed at the start of the 1679 inventory of the Treasury: "a large table-cut diamond, in a golden setting enamelled in black and white, in the antique style, weighing 54 carats, with three pendent pear-shaped pearls, including the *Pèlerine*, weighing 45 carats, the other two weighing 38 and 36 carats respectively". Apart from the two pearls, which must have been added later, this is exactly the same setting as for the *Great Table of François I.* It must have been sold in 1619 by the Florence bankers to Duke Charles Emmanuel I. It should be noted that the given weight of 54 carats was in Florence carats, which weighed 0.1972 grams, while the ancient French carat weighed 0.2055 grams. *The Great Table of François I*, which had been re-named the *Savoy*, actually weighed 53.25 metric carats: it was the first over-50-carat diamond known in Europe in the 16th century. It is not listed in the Savoy treasury's 1772 inventory: it may have been re-cut into a brilliant in the interim, or it may have been taken from the Treasury for financial reasons. From that point onwards, all traces of it have been lost.

Since the destinies of France and Spain crossed to a considerable extent, we should also mention another famous, large 16th-century diamond that has also disappeared: the *Estanque*, which Streeter called the *Diamond of Antwerp*. Philip II, the King of Spain, purchased it in late 1559 for 80,000 crowns during a trip to his territories in the Low Countries from Carlo Affetati, who owned a company in Antwerp. The King was making the voyage in preparation for his third marriage, to Elizabeth of France, daughter of Henri II and Catherine de Medici. The *Estanque* had arrived in Antwerp as a rough stone, and it was cut there into an a perfectly square table-cut. It had a particularly fine water, and weighed 47.5 old carats, equivalent to 48.80 metric carats. Philippe II gave it to his new wife just before she became Queen of Spain in Toledo on February 13th, 1560.

The Large Table (around 40 carats).
Life-size reconstruction, by Bernard Morel.

The Great Cross of François I.
Life-size reconstruction, by Bernard Morel.

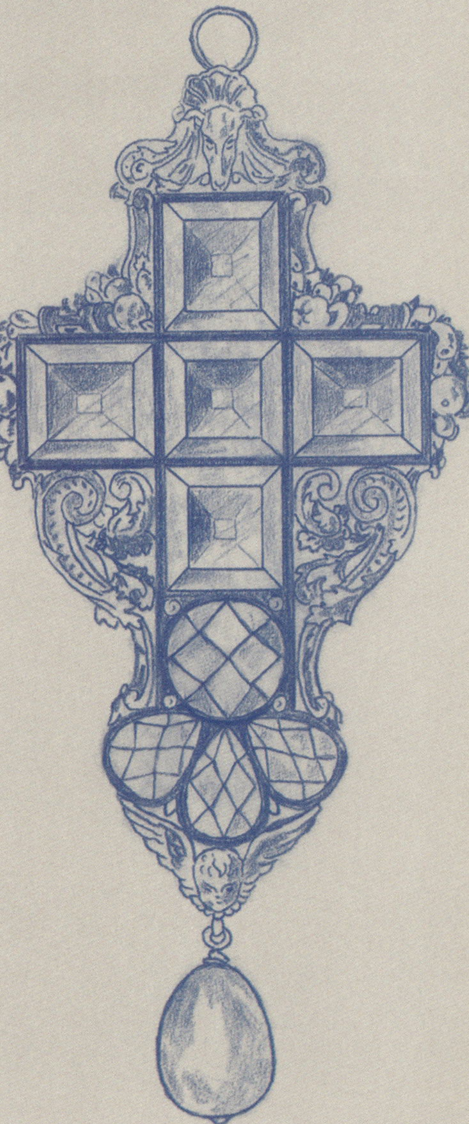

The Crown of Henrietta-Maria of France, Charles I of England's consort. The Sancy is set at the front, with the Mirror of Portugal below it. Ink and watercolour sketch by Thomas Cletscher. Rotterdam, Boymans van Beuningen Museum.

1509-1649: The treasures of Great Britain

Upon the death of Henry VII, the first king of the Tudor dynasty, in 1509, his son Henry VIII inherited a colossal fortune that enabled him to possess some fabulous jewels. His taste for luxury put a strain on its finances. However, after he broke with the Church of Rome and confiscated the immense wealth of the Catholic Church in England, he possessed the means to become the most extravagant monarch of his time, alongside François I of France. His great diamond and spinel chains were famous throughout Europe. After his death in 1547, his jewels were inherited by his son, Edward VI (1547-1553), and then by his daughters Mary I (1553-1558) and Elizabeth I (1558-1603). Elizabeth had an all-consuming passion for jewels, and in her official portraits, she is literally covered in them. Her death led to the accession of the Stuart dynasty, embodied by James VI of Scotland, the son of the tragic Mary Queen of Scots whom Elizabeth caused to be beheaded. He became James I of England (1603-1625). During his reign, the British crown jewels were the most glorious in Europe, particularly since the entire collection of the French Crown Jewels had just been dispersed and would only begin to re-form under Henri IV. James inherited Elizabeth's jewels, and increased them considerably. These were inherited by his son, Charles I, who was overthrown and beheaded in 1649. We shall now look at the principal diamonds of the British court, from Henry VIII to Charles I.

The oldest of these was the *Mirror of Naples*. It had been purchased by King Louis XII of France in Italy around 1500. Three months after the death of his wife, Anne of Brittany, in 1514, he gave it to his new and very young wife, Mary of England, Henry VIII's sister. Louis XII died on New Year's Day, 1515, and Mary returned to England, after having secretly married the Duke of Suffolk. The furious King Henry VIII confiscated his sister's treasury, including the *Mirror of Naples*, a table/mirror-cut of very beautiful water, valued at 60,000 crowns. Its weight remains unknown. *Anne Boleyn's diamond* was another French gem. François I had confiscated it from Baron de Semblançay, his Superintendent of Finance, who had been condemned to death for embezzlement in 1527. He had a summit meeting with Henry VIII in Calais in 1532, during which he gave the diamond to Anne Boleyn (Henry VIII's mistress and future consort). To Henry VIII, he gave a cross set with large diamonds. Anne Boleyn's diamond was described as "a very large and beautiful teardrop or spearhead shape", valued at 16,000 écus (approximately 20 carats). Henri VIII recovered it after Anne Boleyn's execution in 1536. This is the first historical example of a diamond that was said to have been cursed: after all, its first two famous owners had been hanged and beheaded, respectively...

Elizabeth I's most significant acquisition was *the Mirror of Portugal*, a long, rectangular, 26.07-carat table-cut diamond, obtained in 1589 against the promise of help to Antoine de Crato, the pretender to the throne of Portugal, who had been driven out of the country by Philip II of Spain in 1580. Upon James I's accession in 1603, the British treasury acquired several diamonds from the Crown Jewels of Scotland, including the *Great Harry*, also known as The *Stone of the Letter H of Scotland*. It is first mentioned in Mary Stuart's 1561 jewel inventory, drawn up just after her return to Scotland in 1560, after the death of her husband, François II of France: "a large H-shaped jewel, in which there is a large lozenge-shaped diamond with facets, and below it a large ruby cabochon with a little chain". Shortly afterwards, on 10th March 1604, the king bought the famous 55.232-carat *Sancy* diamond for 60,000 gold écus. He wished to wear it for his coronation entry into London, on the 21st March following. This fabulous stone's history is outlined in greater detail in the insert (p. 257). Throughout James I's entire reign, the *Sancy* was set as the pendant to a famous hat ornament known as the *Mirror of Great Britain*. The third version of this jewel is shown in Thomas Cletscher's famous *Sketchbook*, which is preserved in the Boymans van Beuningen Museum in Rotterdam. The *Sancy* was suspended from a large, sparkling lozenge made from four large diamonds that were set edge-to-edge, giving the appearance of a single large diamond: two large, square table-cuts that Cletscher estimated at 36 carats each, one flat-backed 12-carat rhombus and the 20-carat *Great Harry*. The *Mirror of Great Britain* was then the richest jewel in Europe, but it was not destined to remain so for long. Shortly after James I's death in 1625, his son, Charles I, needed money. He kept the Sancy, but sent the rest of the jewel to the Netherlands to be sold. This was in direct contravention of a 1605 decree of James I, which stated that his most beautiful jewels were to be part of a collection that was "indivisible and inseparate, forever hereafter annexed to the Kingdom of this realm".

The *Pinder* was the second most beautiful diamond acquired by the Stuart dynasty. The rough stone was purchased for 48,000 Dutch Florins in Constantinople by Nicolas Ghysbertij, representative of the United Provinces, on behalf of Pauwels Pinder, an ultra-rich businessman who was appointed British Ambassador to Turkey in 1611. The rough stone, of beautiful and very pure water, was brought back to the Netherlands and cut in Antwerp to a thick, slightly rectangular, perfectly-proportioned square table-cut. Pinder was ennobled in 1620, and he lent his large diamond to James I for official ceremonies on numerous occasions. He hoped to sell the gem to the King, for £35,000. The stone was then known as the *Great Diamond*, and it was ultimately purchased by Charles I in July 1625 for £18,000 - quite a discount, and with payment deferred until 1628! However, the King had, after all, granted Pinder many English monopolies... Another large diamond was given to James I by financiers in the City of London, hence its name: *The City*. It was a large, perfectly oval rose-cut. It had a particularly rare and unusual cut: the upper part of the stone was completely covered with small, lozenge-shaped faces, all of identical size.

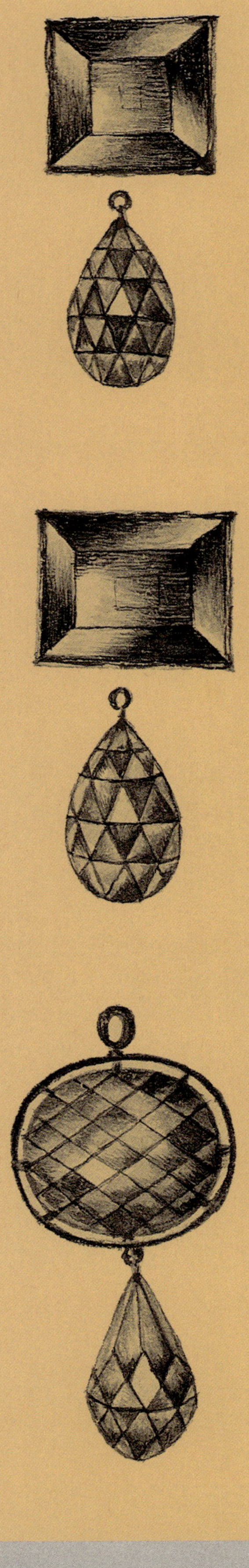

From top to bottom: the 34.3-carat Pinder, the 26.07-carat Mirror of Portugal, and the 27.75-carat City diamond. Drawing by Thomas Cletscher. Rotterdam, Boymans van Beuningen Museum.

The *Petit Sancy* or *Beau Sancy*

January 31st, 1589
The first mention of the diamond: it was pawned on this date by Nicolas Harlay de Sancy, in order to supply troops to King Henri III, who had promised to buy the gem from him.

1595
Nicolas Harlay de Sancy redeems the diamond, and tries to sell it.

March 1604
After a long and unsuccessful process of negotiations, the Beau Sancy is finally sold to Marie de Medici for 25,000 gold écus, despite its valuation of 49,000.

1642
The queen's jewels are sold after her death, including the Beau Sancy. They are purchased by Frédéric-Henri of Orange-Nassau, Stathouder of Holland. It will be passed down within his family for the next 60 years.

1702
The Beau Sancy is inherited by Frederick III of Hohenzollern, the first King of the new Kingdom of Prussia in 1701, under the name of Frederick I.

1702-1918
The Beau Sancy stays in the Prussian royal family up to William II's abdication on November 9th, 1918.

The present day
The gem currently belongs to the head of the House of Hohenzollern, HSH Prince Georg Friedrich von Preussen.

One of Cletscher's drawings depicts the *Pinder*, the *Mirror of Portugal* and *The City* together. The latter was estimated to weigh 27 old carats (27.75 metric carats). As for the *Pinder*, which Cletscher estimated at 36 carats, it later became the *Second Mazarin*, with a verified weight of 33 3/8 old carats, or 34.30 metric carats. The three stones had three splendid pendants, each of the most beautiful water. The *Pinder* had the smallest, which would become the 20.26-carat *Sixth Mazarin*. It came from a rough stone weighing 42 3/4 carats. The *Mirror of Portugal's* pendant would later become the 23-carat *Fifth Mazarin*, which came from a rough stone of 45 carats. These gems had been cut in 1632 and 1636 respectively, by Francisco Ghiot of Antwerp. He had later sold them to Charles I, for £5,000 and £6,000. As for the third pear-shape, suspended from *The City*, the original 42-carat rough stone had been purchased in Constantinople by Cletscher's father-in-law, Giacomo Ghysbertij, for 30,000 guilders. It was cut in Antwerp, as a briolette with a round cross-section weighing 22 old carats. This was the first-ever true briolette. It was then sold to James I, for £6,000. Clearly, in the first half of the 17th century, diamonds always arrived from the Indies in the rough state, since the secret of diamond-cutting had not yet spread there.

James I sent his son to Spain for a potential royal marriage, which never took place. However, thanks to this voyage, a list of jewels was made on July 7th, 1623. This is how we came to know the name of another large diamond from the British treasury, the Mirror of France: "A great table Dyamond sett in gould, called the *Mirror of Fraunce*". It has proved impossible to uncover this gem's origins, but its name brings to mind the *Large Table* of the French Crown Jewels, which had been cut as a mirror and pawned in Italy before 1589. This stone could have been later re-sold to Elizabeth I or James I.

The Protestant and parliamentary Revolution started against Charles I and was a catastrophe for the Stuart dynasty. Charles I was beheaded in 1649. In 1625, he had married Henrietta-Maria of France, the daughter of Henri IV and Marie de Medici. A superb open crown or "regal circlet" was made for the occasion, entirely set with diamonds. Thanks to Cletscher's 34th drawing, we can still see the details of its design. The *Mirror of Portugal* was set in the centre of the brow, and the Sancy was set in the fleur-de-lys at the front. In 1644, the Queen exiled herself to France. She took all the Royal collection of jewels with her, in order to raise money to help her husband. In 1645-1646, she pawned them to several creditors in Amsterdam and Rotterdam, including Cletscher. This collection included three anonymous table-cut diamonds, each of which with an estimated weight of 36 carats. The *Pinder* was one of them, and the two others were probably the *Mirror of Naples* and the *Mirror of France*. The latter subsequently disappeared without trace. Two other Cletscher drawings, numbers 5 and 6, show some of the most beautiful diamonds pawned in the Netherlands, which have likewise disappeared from view. The 5th drawing, for example, displays a pair of earrings with two large table-cut diamonds of 18 carats each, suspending two 10-carat pear-shapes with triangular facets. These two earrings are depicted either side of a splendid jewel known as the *Anchor*: a large, 20-carat table-cut, suspending an anchor comprising a peculiar stone with a pear- to lozenge-shaped cut and broad parallel facets, a long saddle-shaped baguette, and a briolette with a round cross-section.

Nobody in the Netherlands was willing to take on the *Sancy* and the *Mirror of Portugal*, but Henrietta-Maria had little difficulty in pawning them in France to the exceedingly wealthy Duke of Epernon, one of Henri III's former favourites. After Charles I's death, she was unable to honour her debts. This led to the breaking up of the most fabulous diamond collection of the early 17th century, mainly to the benefit of France, as we shall see later. As for the British monarchy, its diamonds would not shine again in Europe until much later, in the reign of Queen Victoria.

The *Sancy* or *First Mazarin*

Nicolas Harlay de *Sancy* was the first owner of both the Sancy and Beau *Sancy*, which are named after him. An important diamond collector, warlord, gifted diplomat and skilled financier, he was completely devoted to the monarchy.

June 20th, 1586
The first mention of the *Sancy* diamond, already owned by Nicolas Harlay de Sancy. He pawned it for Henri III's benefit.

Late 1594
Harlay de Sancy, who had become Superintendent of Finances, redeemed his diamond, and tried in vain to sell it to Henri IV.

March 10th, 1604
The *Sancy* is sold to King James I of Great Britain, for the sum of 60,000 écus.

1625
The *Sancy* is inherited by his son, Charles I.

1644
Civil war threatens the throne. Queen Henrietta-Maria exiles herself to France, taking the Crown's diamonds with her, including the *Sancy*.

1647
The *Sancy* is pawned to the Duc d'Epernon.

1649
Charles I is beheaded. The Queen is financially ruined, and cannot redeem the *Sancy*.

May 19th, 1657
Mazarin releases the Queen from her debts, thereby becoming the owner of the *Sancy*.

March 1661
Mazarin dies and bequeaths his most beautiful diamonds to the French Crown, with the proviso that they should be known as the Eighteen Mazarins. The *Sancy* is the *First Mazarin*. It is the largest diamond in Europe.

1661-1792
The stone belongs to the French Crown, and is frequently worn by successive Kings and Queens.

September 12th and 13th, 1792
On one of these two nights, the *Sancy* is stolen, along with most of the other eighteen Mazarins.

March 1794
After a long investigation, the *Sancy* is recovered and returned to the State's coffers.

1796
The Directoire needs money for its armies. The *Sancy* is pawned to the Marqués de Iranda in Madrid, in exchange for cavalry horses. Later, he sells it to Godoy, the Prime Minister of Charles IV of Spain.

1828
The gem is sold to a Russian Prince, Nicolas Demidoff, who dies a few months later.

1829
His son Paul inherits it, and tries to sell it without success. He marries Aurora Stjernvall, who keeps the stone after her husband's death in 1840.

1865
The *Sancy* is purchased by Sir Jamsetjee Jeejeebhoy, in whose family it will remain until the late 1880s.

1889
The diamond is acquired by a Parisian jeweller, Lucien Falize.

1892-1962
William Waldorf Astor buys it for his wife. The diamond remains in the Astor family until 1976.

1976
Following secret negotiations, the Louvre purchases the Sancy from the third Viscount Astor. It rejoins the *Regent* in the Apollo Gallery in 1978.

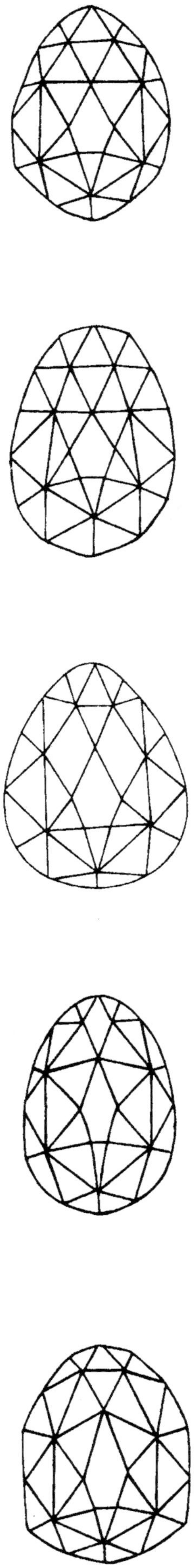

Five ancient drawings of the *Sancy's* cut: Cletscher (1626), Diderot (1751), Feuchtwanger (1589), Dieulafait (1874) and Bauer (1896). They all differ, but all of them correctly display the gem's characteristic five-sided table facet.

France in the 17th and 18th centuries: royal splendour to Revolution

In France, the Crown Jewels had been completely dispersed due to religious wars, which had definitively halted thanks to the Edict of Nantes, signed by Henri IV in 1598. He was barely interested in diamonds, and his most impressive purchase appears to have been a diamond plume worth 14,000 écus, in 1591. However, as part of the preparations for his marriage to Marie de Medici on December 17th, 1600, he was forced to re-establish the Crown Jewels for his new Queen. For this reason, he purchased 150,000 écus' worth of jewellery from various people. These included the Duke of Epernon, who sold him his great *Duke of Epernon* diamond for only 30,000 écus (it had been valued at 50,000). The *Duke of Epernon* became the Crown's principal diamond until Anne of Austria's regency. Her famous Rubens portrait, in the Louvre, shows her wearing the *Duke of Epernon* as a pendant at her bodice, with an enormous pearl drop. It was a large, square point-cut, whose rather flat lower part was covered with small, rhombic facets. It weighed between 40 and 45 carats. In addition, Henri IV had a large cross of 15 diamonds made, in commemoration of the ancient *Great Cross of François I.* It included 7 large table-cuts and three pear-shaped pearls. It can be seen on another famous Louvre portrait, this time by Franz II Pourbus the Younger. Marie de Medici is depicted in her Coronation robes, on May 13th, 1610, wearing the cross as a bodice pendant. This was the day before her husband's assassination, whereupon she became Regent of France until her son, Louis XIII, came of age.

Marie de Medici was obsessed with diamonds and pearls, and henceforth these gems would dominate the royal treasury, at the expense of spinels, rubies, sapphires and emeralds. In early 1610, she had an inventory of her personal jewels drawn up. They included 11,538 diamonds, a truly incredible figure for the time, not counting at least 4,000 very small stones. These included the *Grand Ecuyer*, a faceted rhombus "that the Grand Escuier [the Master of the King's Horses] gave to the Queen on the King's behalf when she married", as well as a great necklace of diamonds and pearls, worth 150,000 écus. Every New Year, Henri IV gave Marie de Medici a splendid jewel. These included the *Etrenne* of 1604, a large faceted heart worth 12,000 écus, the two *Etrennes* (1605 and 1606), two large table-cuts worth 15,000 and 12,500 écus, and the *Duke of Mantua* (1610), which the King had purchased from the Duke for 14,000 écus. Their weights were not specified. However, the Queen's most beautiful acquisition, the *Petit Sancy* or *Beau Sancy*, is known to weigh 35 metric carats, and its detailed history is set out in the insert (p.256).

Like his father, Louis XIII did not have a taste for luxury. He barely increased the Crown Jewel collection, merely re-setting the jewels in a modern style for his wife, Anne of Austria. However, on June 6th, 1636, Richelieu, the famous Minister of State, made a gift to the Crown. The gift was made six years before his death, and subject to his life interest. It comprised the large diamond that he wore on his finger, and the liturgical ornaments from his private chapel. The ornaments were of solid gold, set with 9,013 diamonds, 355 rubies and 29 pearls. The diamond, which was known as the Richelieu, was a large, thick 19.52-carat rose-cut shaped like a heart (a triangle with rounded corners), with a small table facet in the centre, flawless and with very beautiful crystalline water.

Upon the King's death in 1643, Anne of Austria became Regent of France until her 5-year-old son, Louis XIV, came of age. She made Cardinal Jules Mazarin her Prime Minister. This period was marred by the 'Fronde', a terrible civil war that lasted from 1648 to 1653. French finances, which were simultaneously collapsing as a result of the Thirty Years' War, were put to the test. Once more, the Crown Jewels were pawned, so that the monarchy could pay its Swiss mercenaries. The majority of the jewels were later recovered, with the exception of the most significant diamond, the *Duke of Epernon*. Once the Fronde came to an end, Mazarin became all-powerful and accumulated a colossal fortune that made him the richest man of his time. He was passionate about diamonds; so much so, that he has even been falsely attributed with the invention of the "*taille en seize*", a precursor of the brilliant-cut. In fact,

Peter-Paul Rubens (1577-1640): *Anne of Austria, Queen of France.* She wears the *Duc d'Epernon diamond* (40 to 45 carats) as a pendant jewel at her bodice. The Louvre, Paris.

he was only a connoisseur and well-informed amateur. He snatched up some of the most beautiful gems from the British treasury, that Henrietta-Maria had pawned. This was easy, since she lived off the French Court's charity. For example, on May 19th, 1657, he repaid the loan that Henrietta-Maria had borrowed from the Duke of Epernon using the Sancy and the *Mirror of Portugal* as security. The two gems therefore became his property. Likewise, *The City* diamond was brought back from Holland, only for Henrietta-Maria to give it to her sister-in-law, Anne of Austria, who kept it in her private treasury.

Upon his death in 1661, Mazarin bequeathed 18 large diamonds to the State. "His Eminence's intention was to gather together eighteen of the most beautiful large diamonds that exist in Europe. Having succeeded in this end, the aforementioned Seigneur gives and bequeaths them to the Crown, having His Majesty's approval; they are to be called the Eighteen Mazarins". In the same will, he bequeathed a bouquet of 50 diamonds to young Queen Marie-Thérèse, and another large diamond to Anne of Austria: the *Rose of England*, a 25-carat brilliant, also from Henrietta-Maria. Some of the eighteen *Mazarins* have individual names. For example, the first is none other than the *Sancy*. The adjacent table shows the shapes, names and weights of these famous stones, and also what became of them to the present day. On their own, the eighteen Mazarins were worth more than the rest of the Crown Jewels to which they were added. However, the lucky recipient, King Louis XIV, did not leave it there: Cardinal Mazarin was not only his godfather and political mentor, but he also gave him a taste for ostentation, and for diamonds. In 1665 he bought the famous *De Guise* diamond for Marie de Lorraine de Guise. It was a splendid, 34-carat rectangular table-cut of very beautiful water. In 1669, he undertook his famous transaction with Jean-Baptiste Tavernier, who had returned from his sixth and last voyage to the Indies: the King purchased 46 large and medium-sized diamonds, and 1,102 smaller ones. Tavernier provides us with engravings of the 20 principal diamonds. Three were rough, but the remaining 17 had all been rather crudely cut in the Indies, and one can see several characteristic mogul-cuts. This is the first historical record of the arrival in Europe of diamonds that had been cut in the Indies. Naturally, Louis XIV had all these stones re-cut in the European style by his diamond-cutter, Pitau. The most beautiful was a large, absolutely pure, deep blue diamond weighing 115.28 carats. It had been cut in the Indies, with large, irregular facets that conformed to the shape of the original rough. In 1673, it was re-cut by Pitau in a splendid heart-shaped, seven-sided brilliant with a star-shaped pattern on the pavilion. It was perfectly proportioned, and weighed 69 carats. Colbert provided it with a name: *The Blue Diamond of the French Crown*. Strangely, for as long as the *Sancy* remained the largest colourless diamond in Europe, at 55.232 carats, the *Blue Diamond* would be worth less. However, in 1791, it would be worth over three times more! As a result of re-cutting, only two of the other diamonds that Tavernier illustrated can still be recognised in the 1691 inventory of the Crown Jewels. The first was Tavernier's second-largest stone, the *Tavernier II*, was a square, very thick table-cut that had been cut in India. It was trimmed into a 43.80-carat stone. The second was a true brilliant marquise-cut weighing 13.61 carats, known as the *Eye of Tavernier*, which remained in the Crown Jewels until their sale in 1887. Also in 1669, Louis XIV made another purchase that was almost as significant as his transaction with Tavernier. He bought gems from a Dutch merchant named *Bazu*, who had also returned from the Indies. Pitau acted as the King's intermediary, purchasing a whole batch of pearls and precious stones including 14 large diamonds and 131 smaller ones. The largest was known as the Bazu, which yielded a thick, hexagonal 43.67-carat table-cut after re-cutting. It had a somewhat 'celestial' - i.e. slightly bluish - water. *The Bazu* become the fourth-largest diamond in the Crown Jewels.

Master Alvarez was a renowned Portuguese merchant of Jewish origin, who was said to have the most beautiful diamonds on the market. He provided a large quantity of them to Louis XIV. Alvarez was a member of a dynasty of merchants, and one of his ancestors had explored trade routes to India. The French National Library has preserved some strange travel journals, which may have been his father's. They describe a diamond merchant's journey to buy diamonds in the court of the Great Moguls, in Arabic, Italian and French. In 1678, Master Alvarez was commissioned to cut 12 large and 653 smaller diamonds. This is probably the date that the marvellous *Five-Sided Pink Diamond* was cut. From

The eighteen *Mazarins*

Name	Weight and cut in 1661	Weight and cut in 1791	Location
Sancy	55,232 double-rose drop	55,232 or re-cut	Musée du Louvre since 1976
Second Mazarin (Formerly the Pinder)	34,30 rectangular table-cut	25,37 rectangular brilliant	Stolen in 1792 then again in 1848
Mirror of Portugal	26,07 rectangular table-cut	21,71 rectangular brilliant	Stolen in 1792
Fourth Mazarin	24,92 heart-shaped rose-cut	14 rounded oval brilliant-cut	Stolen in 1792
Fifth Mazarin	23 double-rose drop	23 not re-cut	Brunswick Coll. 19th century
Sixth Mazarin	20,26 double-rose drop	20,26 not re-cut	Brunswick Coll. 19th century
Great Mazarin	21,60 square table-cut	19,07 square brilliant	Boucheron 1962
Eighth Mazarin	18,75 square table-cut	15,15 square brilliant	Sold to Boucheron in 1887
Ninth Mazarin	15,67 faceted marquise	15,28 marquise brilliant	Stolen in 1792
Tenth Mazarin	17,46 square table-cut	16,44 square brilliant	Stolen in 1792
Eleventh Mazarin	18,23 square table-cut	17,47 square brilliant	Stolen in 1792
Twelfth Mazarin	17,46 square table-cut	10,34 square brilliant	Stolen in 1792
Thirteenth Mazarin	13,36 square table-cut	10,53 rounded oval brilliant-cut	Stolen in 1792
Fourteenth Mazarin	11,65 rectangular table-cut	8,67 long oval brilliant-cut	Stolen in 1792
Fifteenth Mazarin	11,04 square table-cut	8,70 square brilliant	Stolen in 1792
Sixteenth Mazarin	9 square table-cut	6,16 square brilliant	Stolen in 1792
Sevnteenth Mazarin	21,96 flat, heart-shaped	21,96 not re-cut	Louvre Museum since 1887
EighteenthMazarin	22,09 flat, heart-shaped	22,09 not re-cut	Louvre Museum since 1887

Table, showing the eighteen *Mazarins* and how their cuts have changed over the years.

The eighteen life-size drawings, from a French textbook, show how they looked when they first became part of the French Crown Jewels, upon the Cardinal's death.

Napoleon I's reign onwards, this stone would be known as the Hortensia. It weighed 21.32 carats, and it was the oldest large pink diamond to reach Europe. Its cut was very similar to that of the *Blue Diamond*: a brilliant-cut crown, star-shaped facets on the pavilion and straight, sharply-angled edges. It is an immensely important gem in terms of diamond-cutting history, because it is the last surviving example of this particular type of Parisian cut. Alvarez probably also supplied the *Inch*, a strange half-brilliant (a brilliant-cut crown, with a flat bottom like a rose-cut). It was about an inch long (27 mm), and weighed 12.84 carats. He is also known to have supplied the *Alvarez*, a very long, medium-thick table-cut that weighed 13.36 carats. Alvarez was one of the writers of the 1691 inventory, along with a jeweller named Montarsis. Shortly before the inventory was written, Alvarez sold the King another beautiful gem, *the Peach Blossom*, a very wide, rather flat baroque brilliant that weighed 25.53 carats. It had a roughly pear-shaped, trapezoidal outline with rounded corners, and a faint pinkish water that resembled peach blossom, hence the name.

While the War of the League of Augsburg was underway, Louis XIV decided to have an inventory drawn up of the Crown Jewels in 1691, in order to establish the value of the collection. In order to pay his troops, he had already been forced to melt down the silver furniture of the Palace of Versailles, which weighed 27 tons. Fortunately, he was never compelled to touch the Crown Jewels, even though he had to pay the expenses of the War of the Spanish Succession, which he lost (1701-1713). On the other hand, he added nothing more to the collection between 1691 and the year of his death, 1715. However, there was more than enough already. In 1691 the French Crown Jewels comprised the most fabulous diamond collection in Europe; it contained 5,885 diamonds at a time when large stones were not surrounded by myriad small diamonds, as would later be the case, starting from the mid-18th century.

In 1715, Louis XV was only five years old. He was an orphan, and the great-grandson of Louis XIV. The regency was held by Duke Philippe II of Orléans, the Sun King's nephew. He wanted to inspire confidence in France's finances with a grand gesture. Therefore, after a council meeting held on June 6th, 1717, he decided to purchase the huge 140.64-carat diamond that Thomas Pitt had been trying to sell throughout Europe (cf. Chapter 8). The price was two million French livres, the equivalent of 745 kilos of pure gold at the time. The diamond was baptised the *Regent*, and was officially added to the State jewel collection two years later (by which time its valuation had tripled). "Today, on the fourteenth day of June, one thousand seven hundred and nineteen, a diamond has been added to this inventory; purchased in England, of the first water, weighing 546 grains, brilliant-cut, of slightly elongated square shape, with rounded corners and all its steps. There is a small crystal in its cleavage plane and a notch in its lower part. It is of inestimable value, but for the inventory, Messrs. Rondé, father and son, have estimated its worth at six millions. The aforementioned diamond has been given the name of the *Regent*". Thus, the world's most beautiful diamond became the centrepiece of the collection bequeathed by Louis XIV.

The *Regent* was mounted in the front fleur-de-lys in the ceremonial crowns for the coronations of Louis XV in 1722 and Louis XVI in 1775. The *Sancy* was set in the fleur-de-lys at the top. Apart from that, the *Regent* was kept as a single gem, which the King wore in his hat during official ceremonies. It would remain so until the Revolution. Louis XV purchased another large diamond, set in a ring, which he gave to his wife Marie Leczinska on their marriage, on September 5th, 1725. This was added to the State Treasury upon the Queen's death in 1768. *The Marie Leczinska* was a very beautiful, long rectangular cushion-cut. It was described as being very pure and of the first water. Its weight was not recorded but, given its 1774 valuation of 150,000 livres, it probably weighed approximately 25 carats. Although Louis XV left a number of Louis XIV's buttons, buttonhole florets and hat ornaments untouched, he had many of the collection's jewels remodelled, both for his wife and for his own use. In the 1750s, he commissioned the famous jeweller Jacquemin to create the famous "White Suite" and "Coloured-Gem Suite", each comprising an Order of the Golden Fleece, a plaque and a cross of the Order of the Holy Spirit, and an epaulette brooch. The Fleeces were the most sumptuous jewels. The

Life-size drawings of the crown and pavilion of the 69-carat *Blue Diamond of the French Crown*. Drawings by Bernard Morel.

The pale pink, 21.32-carat *Hortensia*. The Louvre, Paris.

Life-size drawings of the *Hortensia's* crown and pavilion, after Herbert Tillander.

The French Crown Jewel's most magnificent diamond: the 140.64-carat *Regent*. The Louvre, Paris.

Order of the Golden Fleece was founded in 1429 by Philippe the Good, the Duke of Burgundy. At the time, its badge was a gold necklace. In Louis XV's time, the Order was awarded by both the Austrian Habsburgs, who presented it to German princes, and by the Spanish Bourbons, who systematically granted it to their French cousins. In both cases, the decorations for the Order consisted of a large jewel that suspended a flaming flint motif, which, in turn, suspended the fleece itself. The fleece was depicted as a jewelled ram's skin. It was worn in the middle of the chest, hanging from a red ribbon.

The European Princes that belonged to the Order all competed to have the most sumptuous Golden Fleece. Louis XV was the outright winner. For the "White Suite", he had the 34.30-carat *Second Mazarin* re-cut into a 25.37-carat rectangular cushion-cut brilliant, and the 17.46-carat *Twelfth Mazarin* re-cut to a 10.34-carat square cushion-cut. He also added a 23.84-carat, slightly tinted rectangular cushion-cut, that had been re-cut from a 27.48-carat table-cut that belonged to Louis XIV, and a brownish 20.93-carat square cushion-cut that was purchased specially. This was the last acquisition of his reign. There were also 171 more diamonds and 80 rubies in the flame motifs, including eight brilliants that ranged from 2.44 to 4.43 carats. As for the "Coloured Gem Suite", its fleece was the most fabulous Order ever made. It had the *Côte de Bretagne* spinel in the centre. This gem had been specially re-cut for the Fleece by Jacques Guay, the best gem-engraver of the period: he carved it into a 107.88-carat dragon. Diamond flames spewed from its mouth. These flames were 'painted' in red, and were studded with four brilliant-cuts ranging from 4 to 5 carats, which surrounded the 69-carat *Blue Diamond*. Below this, there was a fleece, made of diamonds that had been 'painted' yellow. The dragon was set with jewelled wings and a brilliant-cut diamond tail that coiled around the *Bazu*, which had been re-cut into a splendid hexagonal brilliant, weighing 32.62 carats.

A touching reminder of Marie-Antoinette: the blue diamond that she wore in a ring. It weighs 5.46 carats. Private collection, New York.

Louis XV's superb "Coloured Gem" Order of the Golden Fleece, showing the Blue Diamond and the Bazu, as well as the Côte de Bretagne spinel. The life-size drawing by Bernard Morel shows how large the jewel originally was. The picture by Herbert Tillander shows its original colours.

Louis XVI did not add anything to the State treasury, although his wife, Marie-Antoinette, had some marvellous personal jewels. However, he did have numerous diamonds re-cut in 1786. These were old diamonds that had not yet been re-cut under Louis XV. The *Tavernier II*, for instance, a 43.8-carat table-cut diamond, became a 27.48-carat brilliant. To the fury of the Parisian gem-cutting community, this was done in Antwerp, which set the seal on that city's supremacy in the field. The diamonds returned in 1788. At the same time, 1,471 small, inferior diamonds were sold, and 3,536 small rose-cuts and brilliants were purchased. The new gems were used to make new, modern jewels for the King's use: a sword, suites of buttons, shoe and garter buckles, hat trimmings, a watch, and jewels that could be sewn on to the King's ceremonial garments. This was all that Louis XVI managed to have made before the Revolution started in 1789. An inventory made by order of the National Assembly in 1791 shows that two-thirds of the stones and pearls were no longer set by this date. There were 9,547 diamonds in the collection. The entire Crown Jewel collection was valued at twenty-four million livres or gold francs (which was equivalent to 7,012 kilos of 24-carat gold at the time). *The Regent* alone accounted for twelve million, the *Blue Diamond* (still set in its Golden Fleece) for three million, and the *Sancy* for one million. By late 1789, the jewels had been transferred from Versailles to the safekeeping of the *Garde-Meuble* (the Royal vault), which was in one of two buildings that had been built by Gabriel on the Place de la Concorde. Shortly afterwards, the third great catastrophe to befall the French Crown Jewels took place. In September 1792, over a period of four nights, a band of thieves seized a hoard of priceless objects, including almost all of the jewels. It was the largest break-in of all time. After two years of investigations, the State managed to recover two-thirds of the loot. However, France was at war, and ruled by the revolutionaries who had sent the King to the guillotine on January 21st, 1793. In 1794, the *Convention* sold five millions' worth of gems in Constantinople, using the Perrin and Cablat company as intermediaries. Shortly afterwards, between 1795 and 1799, the *Directoire* pawned the remainder all over Europe. As a result, thanks to theft, sale or the failure to redeem pawnings, France lost most of its treasure forever, including the *Blue Diamond*. This finally reappeared in London in 1812, owned by diamond merchant Daniel Eliason. In order to escape detection, it had been re-cut into a 45.518-carat oval brilliant, which would later be given the name of the *Hope Diamond*. It is now the centrepiece of the gem collection in the Smithsonian Institution, Washington DC.

The epaulette from Frederick Augustus III's rose-cut diamond suite. The king's Orders of Chivalry were suspended from silk sashes. When the king wore one of them, he would also wear this exceptional jewel along his shoulder to secure the sash. The sword handle is from the same suite; it is set with rose-cut diamonds. Made by Christian August and August Gotthelf Globig, 1782-1789. The Green Vault, Dresden.

German magnificence

Most of the ancient Crown Jewels of France no longer exist. However, the surviving Saxon Crown Jewels in Dresden give us some idea of what they must have originally looked like. The Duchy of Saxony became a kingdom in 1806, and this lasted until the monarchy was overthrown in 1918 at the end of World War I. Fortunately, the last King had preserved the marvellous jewel collection intact, in Dresden. It had been bequeathed by his ancestors, particularly Frederick-Augustus I, Duke and Elector of Saxony from 1694 to 1733, who was elected King of Poland in 1697, under the name of Augustus II. He is better known as Augustus the Strong. The jewel collection is dazzling, on display in a museum known as the Green Vault ("Grünes Gewölbe"). This was the name of the cellars in the royal Saxon castle, which had been specially built to hold the collection. Green vaults framed the windows, and the walls were covered in mirrors in baroque frames. Dresden was destroyed in 1945. However, several years later, the vaults were restored, and this unique treasury of jewels was placed on display once again. It is the most beautiful collection of royal jewels in Europe, and also the only one that is still in its original, specially-designed setting.

Augustus the Strong was on the throne during the last part of Louis XIV's reign. He followed Louis' example in most things, and was just as obsessed with diamonds. He was the one who purchased most of the diamonds in the Dresden collection. The most important of these was the 49.71-carat *Dresden White*, for which he paid an extraordinary amount. Allegedly, no one had ever paid such a high price per carat for a diamond up until that point. It came from the Indies, and it has a perfectly white and pure water. It is a slightly rectangular cushion-cut with slightly rounded corners, cut from a splendid octahedral crystal. It has a very unusual "scissor-cut" brilliant shape, which displays fine brilliance and very attractive fire. It is currently set as the principal stone in a magnificent diamond-studded epaulette, made for Elector Frederick Augustus III after his accession in 1763. Augustus the Strong also purchased the 39.46-carat *Dresden Yellow*, a slightly irregular oval brilliant-cut, and a thick, almost round, 21-carat brilliant-cut.

However, the *Dresden Green* is the most magnificent gem in the Saxon treasury. Strangely, in its day it was valued at less than the *Dresden White*, which would certainly not be the case today, now that 50-carat white diamonds are almost commonplace, and strongly-coloured diamond fetch exorbitant prices. It had been offered to Augustus the Strong by Marcus Moses, a London diamond trader, for £30,000 in 1726, but the transaction fell through. Ultimately, it was purchased it in 1741 by his son, Frederick Augustus II (1733-1763), who was also King of Poland under the name of Augustus III. He bought it during the famous Leipzig Fair, from a Dutch diamond-cutter named Delles, who presumably bought it from Marcus Moses. He appears to have paid 400,000 thalers, although some sources state that the price was only 200,000. Even so, this was a considerable amount. In fact, at roughly the same time, the immense Church of Our Lady of Dresden had been built for the cost of 288,000 thalers! The original rough stone might have weighed 100 carats; it came from Golconda, and was cut in London as an almost perfect, almond-shaped brilliant drop with a rounded point. It has 58 facets, and measures 29.75 mm long, 19.88 mm at its widest point, and 10.29 mm thick. Given that the gem weighs 40.70 carats, it is proportionately slightly shallow. The colour is a marvellous, uniform, strong green, with slight bluish undertones. The *Dresden Green* is flawless, and of the purest water. It is the largest and most beautiful green diamond in the world. Its colour is extremely rare, and its size makes it absolutely unique. Shortly after the purchase, Frederick Augustus II had it set in a Golden Fleece, by the famous jeweller J. F. Dinglinger. However, in 1768, Frederick Augustus III (the first King of Saxony, who died in 1827) had it re-set in a hat ornament, which still exists. It was made by the jeweller Diesshach, accompanied by hundreds of brilliant-cuts, including two round gems weighing a total of 35 carats.

As far as diamonds are concerned, the Dresden collection has two complete suites of jewels for men, and one for women. Each has its own display case. They are superb examples of the jewels that were then being worn by European sovereigns during official receptions. One of the men's suites is the finest collection of rose-cut diamonds in the world. The most important jewel is an epaulette, with 20 large rose-cuts and 216 smaller ones. The largest, the 41.77-carat *Rose of Saxony*, was also purchased by Augustus the Strong. The suite has ten jerkin buttons, and ten smaller, matching jacket buttons. Each button has a large central diamond, surrounded by smaller stones. The largest diamond in the buttons weighs 12.81 carats. There is also an Order of the White Eagle, adorned with a large rectangular 20.24-carat rose-cut, and a sword set with 779 rose-cuts, including a triangular gem of 8.33 carats.

In the women's jewels, there are several superb pieces made for Eberhardine of Hohenzollern, the wife of Augustus the Strong. The principal jewel is a splendid necklace of 38 brilliant-cuts in two rows, with a pear-shaped pendant at the centre. The total weight of the stones in the necklace is an extraordinary 489.44 carats. The pear-shape is known as the *Queen Eberhardine*: it is flawless and of very fine colour, and weighs 30.75 carats. There is an extraordinary bow-brooch, designed to be worn on the front of the bodice, covered with 51 large and 611 small brilliant-cuts. The central round brilliant-cut weighs 22.29 carats. Finally, there is a pin with a flawless drop-shaped briolette-cut, suspended from a fine branch set with small diamonds. The very long, 17.55-carat briolette is known as the *Saxon Drop*.

The Bavarian Crown Jewels were equally as splendid as those of Saxony. Like Saxony, the Duchy-Electorate became a kingdom in 1806, thanks to Napoleon. When the monarchy was overthrown in 1918, most of the jewels were taken away by the last King, Ludwig III. The largest and most beautiful diamond in the collection was the 35.56-carat *Wittelsbach Blue*, which was named after the ruling dynasty (cf. Chapter 8). It was the only other large blue diamond in the royal treasures of Europe. Its colour is superb, a uniform and intense sapphire blue, quite different from the *Hope* (formerly the *Blue Diamond of the French Crown*), as its colour is not as deep, and it does not have the same steely-blue undertones. It is of Indian origin, and flawless. Its history starts in 1664, when Philip IV of Spain betrothed his daughter Margarita-Teresa to his maternal uncle, Leopold I of Habsburg, Emperor of the Holy Roman Germanic Empire. The marriage took place in 1666. Philip provided her with a dowry that was primarily composed of Indian diamonds, including the blue diamond, which was probably cut in Antwerp. It was inherited several times by various owners, and eventually became part of the Bavarian treasury in 1722, as a result of the marriage between Archduchess Maria-Amelia of Austria (Emperor Joseph I's second daughter), and the Bavarian Crown Prince, Charles-Albert of Wittelsbach. Charles-Albert became Elector Charles-Albert I in 1726, and he had the diamond set in a Golden Fleece. In 1761, his son Maximilian Joseph III wanted a more up-to-date Fleece, and the *Wittelsbach Blue* was re-set in a magnificent jewel, studded with 700 other brilliants. Later on, in 1806, Elector Maximilian Joseph IV became the King of Bavaria. He commissioned Napoleon's Parisian goldsmith, Biennais, to create the insignia of his new kingdom - crown, sceptre, sword and orb. The diamond was taken out of the Fleece for this purpose, and set in the centre of the cruciferous orb at the top of the crown. However, this was a temporary setting, only used for Coronations. The rest of the time, the stone was re-set in its Golden Fleece.

This jewel remained in the Treasury in Munich until 1918, when King Ludwig III took much of the collection away with him. It then disappeared for a time without trace. Although Ludwig III died in exile in Hungary in 1921, his funeral nevertheless took place in Munich. The Royal Crown, re-set with the *Wittelsbach Blue*, was paraded in front of a Bavarian King's coffin for the last time. Unfortunately, following the enormous devaluation of the Mark, his heirs found themselves penniless. The Bavarian government, which had a certain degree of autonomy, agreed to sell part of the jewels that remained in Munich for their benefit. The sale took place at Christie's in London, in December 1931. It comprised 13 lots, including the *Wittelsbach Blue* (which had been unset from the Fleece and the Crown and replaced by glass copies). When the famous diamond failed to sell, the family found a buyer themselves, very discreetly. It reappeared in 1958 at the Brussels World Fair, although nobody recognised it. It was displayed by Antwerp diamond-cutter Remi Goldmuz. In 1962, Remi Goldmuz consulted a colleague, with regard to having it re-cut. The colleague, Joseph Komkommer, immediately recognised the gem's historical significance and dissuaded him. In 1964, it was sold to a German private collector, who wishes to remain anonymous. The 1931 sale also included the *Bavarian Cinnamon*, a cinnamon-coloured brilliant-cut weighing 30.25 carats.

The Residenz palace in Munich still contains some splendid jewels. The oldest is an extraordinary hat ornament in the shape of a trophy, made in 1603 by Hans Georg Beuerl of Augsburg for Elector Maximilian I the Great. It is the most extraordinary surviving example of a jewel set with large, square table-cut diamonds. It contains 245 diamonds and 6 large black pear-shaped pearls. The largest table-cut, the *Table of the Bavarian Trophy*, weighs 18 carats, which was very large at the time. However, the most eye-catching piece in the Schatzkammer (treasury room) is a large statuette of St. George slaying the dragon. It is a magnificent example of the goldsmith's art, from the late 16th century. The saint and his horse are covered with protective diamond armour, made out of table- or point-cut diamonds. It is undoubtedly the masterpiece of diamond-set Renaissance jewellery.

The other German states will not be covered here, as they did not accumulate enough sufficiently extraordinary jewels to warrant their inclusion. However, we should mention that the Royal House of Prussia inherited the *Petit Sancy*, as mentioned in the insert. The family still owns this marvellous diamond, although the last Wurtemberg King left his most beautiful jewels to the Historical Museum in Stuttgart. These are the *Harlequin*, a 22-carat pear-shape, set in a brilliant-cut diamond necklace, including the 20-carat *Wurtemberg Oval.*

Frederick-Augustus III of Saxony's hat jewel. It is set with the 40.7-carat *Dresden Green*, shown life-size. The Green Vault, Dresden.

Austro-Hungarian Splendour

The Habsburgs affirmed their power over Austria, and were Emperors of the Holy Roman Germanic Empire from 1438 to 1806, while also becoming Kings of Bohemia and of Hungary from 1526 to 1918. The most famous of them, Charles the Fifth, even became the King of Spain by descent. However, he ceded his German and Central European territories to his brother Ferdinand, and the Imperial title passed to this branch of the family. Later, the Napoleonic Wars obliged Francis II to renounce the title of Holy Roman Germanic Emperor in 1806, but in 1804 his territories were named the Austrian Empire, which he consequently ruled under the name of Francis I.

The principal diamond in the Austrian Crown Jewels was the *Florentine*. The early part of the stone's history is Italian, as one can tell by its name. The original rough stone had been confiscated at the end of the 16th century from the King of Vijayanagar (the present-day Narsingha, in southern India). His army had been conquered by the Portuguese Governor of Goa, Ludovico de Castro, the Count of Montesanto, who sent the diamond to the Jesuits in Rome for safekeeping. After long negotiations with Cardinal Del Monte, Grand Duke Ferdinand I of Tuscany bought it for 35,000 Portuguese gold écus. His son, Cosimo II de Medici, who had become Grand Duke in 1609, had it cut by Pompeo Studentoli, a Venetian working in Florence. The stone was completed on October 28th, 1615, and weighed at least 137.27 carats. It was a large, nine-sided, wide pear-shape with 144 radiating triangular facets. It was cut in the "double-sided rose-cut" style, like the *Sancy*. Although it was flawless, brilliant and with well-distributed fire, the *Florentine* was not of good water. It had a rather pale, slightly greyish, lemon-yellow colour. Cletscher depicted it in a drawing, alongside the *Sancy* and *Petit Sancy*. He had probably seen it in Florence. It remained in the Tuscan Grand-Ducal treasury until 1743, when it became part of the Austrian jewel collection.

But how did this come about? In 1735, François Etienne III, the Duke of Lorraine, exchanged his Duchy with the Grand Duchy of Tuscany, in accordance with high-level European political agreements. The Grand Duchy of Tuscany had a Medici Grand Duke, Jean-Gaston, who was against this decision and who died, most conveniently, in 1737. François III of Lorraine had married Marie-Thérèse of Austria in 1736. She was the daughter of Emperor Charles VI. Anne Marie Louise, Jean-Gaston's sister and the last of the Medicis, died in 1743. Following her death, François secretly moved many of the Tuscan Crown Jewels, including the *Florentine,* from Florence to Vienna. This was in direct contravention of the family pact that prohibited any of the Grand Duchy's chattels from being taken out of Florence. At the end of the War of the Austrian Succession in 1745, his wife, who was already Queen of Hungary and Bohemia, had him elected Emperor of the Holy Roman Germanic Empire under the name of Francis I. He was crowned in Frankfurt on October 4, and for the occasion he had the diamond set in the centre of his specially-made crown. The crown was subsequently broken up, and the *Florentine* re-set in a magnificent hat ornament, which survived until the end of the Austrian empire.

Charles I, the last Austrian Emperor, had to abdicate at the end of the First World War, on November 12th, 1918. He subsequently took many splendid jewels from the Viennese Treasury, which he regarded as the Imperial family's private possessions. These included the *Florentine*. The majority were later sold discreetly, but some of them were stolen by a criminal member of the Imperial entourage, who escaped to South America. It is not known exactly what happened to the *Florentine.* For a long time, it was believed that Charles I's widow, Empress Zita, was secretly keeping it, in case the Habsburgs ever returned to the throne. However, she died relatively recently and the stone did not reappear, so this theory has now been discounted. Unfortunately, it is highly likely that the *Florentine* was re-cut, whether it was sold or stolen. There is virtually no chance of it reappearing with its ancient cut intact, and nobody would be able to recognise it if it has been re-cut as an anonymous brilliant... Thus are the mighty fallen!

From left to right: the *Beau Sancy*, the 137.27-carat yellow *Florentine diamond*, and the *Sancy*.
Drawing by Thomas Cletscher.
Boymans-van Beuningen Museum, Rotterdam.

There was another important diamond in the Austrian jewel collection, the *Frankfurt Solitaire*. This was the largest white diamond in the collection, weighing 44 5/8 old Viennese carats, or 46 metric carats. This brilliant-cut had been purchased by Emperor Francis I in Frankfurt-am-Main in 1764, for 28,000 French gold *louis* (the equivalent of 196 kilos of 24-carat gold). The diamond was of the most beautiful water, but it disappeared after 1918, like the *Florentine*. The *Baden Solitaire* has also vanished: this was a very beautiful, 30.92-carat brilliant-cut. It was set as the clasp to a row of 114 large pearls. Although the old inventories do not say anything about its history, its name gives a clue to its origins: Francis I purchased it in the 1750s in the old duchy of Baden, probably in Mannheim. It is known to have been stolen in the Imperial jewel theft that was mentioned above. Many other marvellous jewels were also stolen, including *the Star of Este* and three diamond-set Orders of the Golden Fleece. The Star of Este was a perfect, white, 26.16-carat brilliant-cut. It later reappeared in the possession of King Farouk of Egypt. The finest Golden Fleece had belonged to Francis I: it entered the treasury upon his death in 1765. It was set with 150 brilliant-cuts of the most beautiful water, and it had the *Austrian Pink*, a marvellous 26.93-carat pink brilliant-cut, as its centrepiece.

Although Charles I removed all the Crown Jewel collection, he left the ancestral Habsburg treasures in the Hofburg Palace, in Vienna. These pieces are amongst the most beautiful in Europe. With regard to the diamond jewellery, Emperor Rudolf II's crown is one of the most interesting pieces. It was made in 1602 and cost 700,000 thalers, an enormous sum at the time. Other pieces include the sceptre and orb made for his successor, Matthias, in 1615. These jewels contain point- and table-cut diamonds. The crown's circlet has 8 particularly fine table-cuts, surrounded by a border of 20 smaller table-cuts, forming large, glittering square motifs. Another four are set around the orb, which is surmounted by a cross that contains some even larger table-cuts. These pieces are extremely rare and fine examples of early-17th-century diamond-set coronation regalia.

Brazilian stars in Lisbon

Let us now leave Central Europe, and shift our attention to Portugal, in the extreme southwest of the continent. At the end of the Aviz dynasty in 1580, the country was taken over by Spain. In 1640, the Portuguese rebelled. They took the Duke of Braganza as their king, under the name João IV († 1656). Moreover, he reconquered Brazil and Angola from the Dutch. He founded a dynasty that reigned until 1910, when the republic was introduced, overthrowing the last king, Manuel II. Thanks to the discovery of diamonds in Brazil around 1726 and the Royal diamond monopoly of 1772-1834, the Portuguese Crown Jewels rapidly became one of the most beautiful collections in Europe. In 1801, when France and Spain declared war on Portugal, the Prince Regent (future João VI) borrowed twelve million guilders from the Hope and Baring banks in Holland and London respectively. The loans used Brazilian diamonds as security. After the 1807 Napoleonic invasion, he left the country for Brazil, taking the majority of the Crown Jewels with him. However, he had left around 2,000 carats of diamonds, which were seized by General Junot. When João VI returned to Portugal in 1821, he brought back the surviving jewels from the collection. In 1822, Brazil declared itself to be an independent empire, but kept the Braganzas as the ruling family. Succession had passed from João VI to his elder son, dom Pedro, who became Emperor Pedro I of Brazil in 1825. When the monarchy was overthrown in 1910, Manuel II left the Crown Jewels in Lisbon. They were deposited in the State bank. There they remained until 1954, when an agreement was signed between the Salazar government and the members of the former royal family, regarding the division of the collection into State property and the family's personal property. This is how 115 of the most beautiful historic jewels found their way to the Ajuda Palace National Museum, in Lisbon.

Queen María Pia's magnificent diamond star tiara. The stars are mounted '*en tremblant*', on springs. Made in 1876 by Estevão de Souza. Lisbon, Ajuda Palace National Museum.

Joseph I's snuffbox is one of the finest jewels. He ruled from 1750 to 1777. The snuffbox was made in Paris, using the sovereign's own brilliant-cut diamonds. It is signed by L. Roucel and by Jacqmin, Louis XV's jeweller. Jacqmin also made the famous "White" and "Coloured Gem" Orders of the Golden Fleece for the French Crown Jewels. Jacqmin was so proud of his work that he couldn't resist the temptation of displaying the snuffbox to Madame de Pompadour, before delivering it to Lisbon via Madrid. It is made from chased gold, with small diamond scrolls, studded with emeralds and 28 large brilliants. The 29.07-carat *Joseph I*, superb colourless square, is the principal diamond, set in the centre of the lid. The King's walking-stick handle was commissioned in Paris at the same time. It is unsigned, but attributed to Jacqmin. It is also in chased gold with diamond-set scrolls, in the rococo style. It is surmounted by the *Cane Pommel* diamond, a colourless square cushion-cut brilliant weighing 24.23 carats.

In 1790, the Crown Jeweller, David Ambroise Pollet, made a very large *Golden Fleece* for prince João, the future Regent and ultimately King João VI. It is literally dazzling, and was of similar quality to Louis XV's destroyed "White" Fleece. It was worn by all the Kings of Portugal. It was 26.5 cm long (a record), and is set with several hundred white brilliant-cuts, 102 rubies in the flames, and a large, 48-carat sapphire. The largest diamond, the rectangular cushion-cut *João VI*, weighs 31.50 carats. There is also a fabulous military decoration in the collection, with 11 principal brilliant-cut diamonds, including the 30-carat *Marie I of Portugal.*

There is much more, apart from these four magnificent jewels. Like Dresden, the Lisbon collection also has a complete set of the jewels that were customarily worn by 18th-century monarchs. The fashion for these 'garment jewels' was started by France at the end of Louis XIV's reign and continued until the end of the 19th. There are large chains for the Order of the Tower and the Order of the Sword, many Orders and crosses from several different Orders of Chivalry, a gold sword with large diamonds, a cavalry sabre, large jerkin buttons and smaller jacket buttons, etc. All are studded with thousands of brilliant, glittering diamonds.

Amongst the womens' jewels, there is a particularly splendid corsage bow brooch. It dates from the first half of the 18th century, and is set with emeralds and diamonds, including the *Marie-Anne of Austria* (she was João VI's wife), a 23.89-carat intense yellow round baroque brilliant. There is also a necklace with 18 diamond-studded star motifs, and a matching tiara with an additional 36 stars. They were made in 1876 and 1878 by Estevão de Souza for Queen María Pia, Louis I's wife († 1889). Each star motif has a large brilliant-cut diamond in the centre. The principal diamond, known as the *María Pia,* is set in the central star in the tiara. It is a fine yellow cushion-cut brilliant, weighing 21.60 carats. Ambroise Pollet also made two rivières in 1787 for Marie I: one was set with 55 brilliants, weighing approximately 250 carats, the other with 32 brilliants weighing 150.35 carats. There is also a matching bracelet, of 18 brilliant-cuts. Finally, there is a superb pendant set with the *Lisbon Brown-Yellow*, a brilliant-cut pear-shape of brownish-yellow colour. It was cut in the 18th century and weighs 31.93 carats. It is currently surrounded by 16 brilliants in an 18th-century-style diamond bow brooch. This piece was actually made in 1950 by José Rosas Junior, as part of the restoration of the Portuguese Crown Jewels.

Strangely enough, the Portuguese Crown Jewels still preserve some items that are priceless pieces of natural history: two remarkable rough diamonds, weighing 135 and 32 carats respectively, as well as countless native gold nuggets, one of which weighs over 20 kilos! Finally, amongst the rare items contained in the collection there is a wooden casket mounted in silver, designed to hold diamonds. It dates back to 1844, and still bears the inscriptions "*Joias da Coroa*" ('Crown Jewels') and "*Diamantes Lapidos*" ('Cut Diamonds').

The Portuguese Crown Jewels' magnificent, 27 cm-long Order of the Golden Fleece. The smaller picture shows the reverse, displaying the magnificent quality of the jewellery work and the setting. Lisbon, Ajuda Palace National Museum.

Snuffbox, signed "Jacqmin, King's Jeweller - Paris" and "L. Roucel, Paris, July 29th 1756". 10 cm long. This spectacular masterpiece's lid is set with a diamond weighing nearly 30 carats. Lisbon, Ajuda Palace National Museum.

Bow brooch (6 cm long), suspending a 31.93-carat diamond. Lisbon, Ajuda Palace National Museum.

Queen Caroline-Matilda's watch and châtelaine, set with hundreds of diamonds. The movement is signed by Jodin, a Parisian watchmaker, and the jewellery work was done by J. F. Fistaine in Copenhagen, in 1767. Fistaine was descended from French Huguenots. Châtelaines were suspended from clothing like brooches, and were worn by both men and women. This piece shows the beauty of the kind of jewellery that was worn in France at Louis XV's court. Rosenborg Castle, Copenhagen.

The brilliance of the Northern nations

The Crown Jewels of Sweden are on display in the vaults of the Royal Palace in Stockholm. They are restricted to the regalia, including eleven crowns. The Royal family has private collections of jewels but, to our knowledge, these do not contain any historically-important diamonds. King Eric XIV's crown was made in 1561 by the Flemish goldsmith Cornelius van Weiden, who set up in Sweden in 1551. It is in heavily chased gold, richly encrusted with enamel, rubies, emeralds, pearls and diamonds. The crown was later altered and embellished many times. However, in 1970 it was restored to its original appearance, with the exception of eight large diamonds, which were kept in place. These large gems had been added in 1818 by order of Charles XIV, an ex-Marshal of France who founded the current reigning Bernadotte dynasty. The one in the frontal floret is the most interesting. It is a large, thick, rectangular rose-cut with rounded corners. It is cut in a very rare style, with horizontal tiers of identical triangular facets. It was probably cut in Antwerp at the end of the 16th century, or the beginning of the 17th. The *Diamond of the Swedish Crown* measures 14.5 x 17 mm, and weighs approximately 15 carats.

The most precious crown in the Swedish treasury is that of Queen Louisa Ulrika. It was made for her coronation alongside her husband, Adolphe Frédéric of Holstein-Gottorp, on November 26, 1751. It was designed by Jean-Eric Rehn, who had recently arrived from Paris. He had been inspired by a print representing the crown made by Claude-Dominique Rondé in 1725 for Marie Leczinska's wedding to Louis XV. Andreas Almgren was the Swedish goldsmith in charge of its manufacture. As with the French Queen's crown, he made it entirely from gems in '*à jour*' (openwork) silver settings. It is an exceptional piece, very much in the French style, used for Swedish Queens' coronations until 1873. The crown contains 695 diamonds in total. The largest rose-cut, the *Louisa-Ulrika Rose-Cut*, is in the centre of the frontal motif. It is of oval rectangular shape, and weighs 8 7/8 old carats.

Rosenborg Castle in Copenhagen houses the beautiful Crown Jewels of Denmark. Admittedly, it does not contain as many important diamonds as in some of the other European treasuries, but the pieces on display are exceptional in their profusion of diamonds with ancient cuts. Christian IV's crown, made in 1596, is an extraordinary masterpiece of delicately chased and enamelled gold. The goldsmith was Dirk Fyring, working to a design by Corvinianus Sauer. The crown is set with 54 pearls and over 900 diamonds. They are not particularly large, but they are in a range of fascinating late 16th-century cuts: square, lozenge or hexagonal table-cuts, and triangular and square point-cuts. In addition, it is one of the first jewels where diamonds are the principal decorative element, to the exclusion of all other gems except pearls. The collection also contains other pieces set with ancient-cut diamonds, such as horse trappings and swords. One particularly exceptional sword was used during ceremonies to ennoble knights.

The Order of the Elephant is the principal Order of Chivalry in Denmark. It started in the mid 15th century and was restricted to members of the Royal Family and foreign heads of Government. This elephant was worn on the end of a chain. Its palanquin and trappings are set with table-cut diamonds. Made by J. F. Fistaine, around 1722. Rosenborg Castle, Copenhagen.

The most beautiful diamonds in the Rosenborg collection are set in a magnificent suite of jewels. Queen Margrethe II is permitted to wear it for official ceremonies. It comprises a large bodice brooch in the shape of a bouquet of flowers, dating from the second half of the 18th century: flowers and foliage set with white and yellow brilliants are secured by a delicately swagged bow-knot. The suite also contains a matching necklace and earrings, from the 19th century. The necklace consists of a row of 38 large stones that suspends seven large brilliant pear-shaped diamonds, hanging from five-diamond clusters. The central round gem in the rivière weighs 20 carats, flanked by two diamonds of approximately 16 carats each, with the remaining stones graduating in size down to the clasp. The largest pear-shaped brilliant weighs 23 carats. The earrings contain two round brilliants of 14 carats each, with two pear-shapes of 15 and 12.50 carats. Together, these large diamonds are known as the *Danish Suite*.

Norway is a relatively recent kingdom, and does not have a diamond collection. Further to the south, the Netherlands does not have a formal coronation, but a simple enthronement ceremony before Parliament, in the presence of a crown, a sceptre and an orb, made for William I in silver-gilt and imitation gemstones. Although there are no Crown Jewels, this has not prevented the royal family building up a private collection of splendid jewellery. As far as diamonds are concerned, the collection includes a diadem and a large corsage brooch that are regarded as the finest suite of women's rose-cut diamond jewellery in Europe. The principal gem is a 40.60-carat pear-shape that was cut in Amsterdam from a rough stone that originally came from Borneo. It was purchased in 1677 by William III, consort of Queen Mary Stuart II, King of England and also Stathouder of Holland. At the time, it was called the *Great Heart*, although it is known today as the *Holland*. Upon the Queen's death in 1694, William kept the large rose-cut. Upon his own death without issue in 1702, it was inherited by his cousin John William the Frisian, entering definitively in the house of Orange-Nassau, the reigning dynasty of the Netherlands. The diamond was set at the top of the frontal part of the tiara in 1898, upon the accession of young Queen Wilhelmina. It is literally covered with other rose-cuts, including six larger gems. The matching corsage brooch is designed as large ribbon bows, and it contains eleven large principal rose-cut diamonds. This suite was worn for the last time by Queen Juliana, upon the marriage of King Baudouin of Belgium in 1960.

Christian IV's crown, made in 1596. It contains more than 900 diamonds in various antique cuts. Rosenborg Castle, Copenhagen.

Imperial France

We left the French Crown Jewels in 1799, when the *Directoire* had pawned the pieces that had survived the 1792 theft and the *Convention's* sales. These were not the only jewels that were pawned: the authorities confiscated gems from aristocrats who fled the country, leaving some stones behind them. Victor Amédée III, the King of Sardinia, had pawned his jewel collection in Amsterdam. When the city was occupied by French troops in early 1795, the jewels were seized.

In 1800, at the beginning of the Consulate, the first Consul, Napoleon Bonaparte, decided to put public finances in order. He decided to refund creditors as soon as possible. In so doing, he recovered the *Regent, De Guise, Fleur de Pêcher, Hortensia, Eye of Tavernier, Great Mazarin*, and the *Eighth, Seventeenth and Eighteenth Mazarins*. Unfortunately, the *Sancy* was beyond his reach. It had been pawned to the Marqués de Iranda in Madrid, and his heirs, having lost hope of being repaid, had already sold it to Godoy, the Prime Minister to Charles IV of Spain. On the other hand, the State had acquired the *King of Sardinia*, the finest diamond of Victor Amédée III, a 17.53-carat rectangular brilliant with a slight greenish-yellow tint. Three other important stones were seized from emigrants. The largest was the 28.51-carat *Chrysolithe Orientale* ('Eastern Peridot'). This gem had an unusual, 17th-century mixed cut: it was a cut-cornered square with a brilliant crown and step-cut pavilion. It was of yellowish-green colour, resembling the gemstone peridot, hence its name. The remaining two gems were the *Oblong Emigré*, a very pure and very white 17-carat oblong brilliant-cut, and the *Square Emigré*, a 16.95-carat white cushion-cut. In addition, another diamond was confiscated, and presented to the *Muséum national d'histoire naturelle* in 1796. It is a very fine and attractive canary-yellow diamond, known as the *Confiscated Yellow*. It has a rare cut from the 17th-century: a square table-cut based on the original octahedral shape, with small facets geometrically placed around small central table facets on both the top and bottom of the stone. It has remarkable sparkle and fire, unusually for a gem from this period. It was probably cut in Paris, and it is the only surviving example of its kind. It weighs 9.75 carats, and measures 11.5 mm long, 10.6 mm wide and 9.5 mm thick.

Standing portrait of Napoleon I, Emperor of the French, wearing the uniform of a Grenadier Colonel. The sword at his side contains the *Regent* diamond. Oil on canvas, by Robert Lefèvre (1755-1830). National Museum of the Palaces of Versailles.

Bonaparte was appointed Consul for life in 1802, and he commissioned a superb consular sword that was delivered in 1803. It was made out of chased gold, set with 14 large and 28 small brilliant-cuts. The chasing was performed by Odiot, and the setting by Etienne Nitot. The *Regent* was set in the front of the became: it had gone from being set in a royal crown, to a soldier's sword. This hilt the Imperial sword once the Empire was proclaimed, and Napoleon wore it when he was proclaimed Emperor of France on December 2nd, 1804, in Notre Dame Cathedral in Paris. In 1812, it was replaced by a new Imperial sword, made by François Regnault Nitot, with a heavily diamond-studded handle and hilt. The principal stones remained the same: they were replaced on the old sword with glass copies. The old sword is still on display in the Fontainebleau Palace.

In 1805, Napoleon decided to recreate the Crown Jewels, starting with the stones that had been recovered in 1800, some of which had already been reassembled on the sword. He started a re-purchasing policy that lasted until 1812. The final total expenditure was 6,600,000 gold francs. He demanded extremely tight control over expenditure, with detailed paperwork that covered even the tiny stones of 1/32 of a carat. By the end of his reign, the State jewel collection comprised no fewer than 57,771 diamonds, 5,630 pearls and 1,671 coloured gemstones! Napoleon's first important acquisition was a superb hat ornament, made by Marguerite in 1805. It contained a "long, square brilliant, with rounded corners, well proportioned, of fine, slightly milky water", weighing 26.33 carats, named the *Diamond of Napoleon's Hat Ornament*, or the *Napoleon* for short. It was the largest brilliant that Napoleon purchased; he paid 180,000 francs, the equivalent of 52.75 kilos of pure gold.

The Emperor's other most significant acquisitions took place in 1810. This was the year that he married Archduchess Marie Louise of Habsburg, Emperor François I's daughter. The French Crown Jewels had to be good enough for the Caesar's daughter! The most extravagant suite of jewels of the entire 19th century was therefore ordered from François-Regnault Nitot. It contained 13,067 diamonds, worth nearly four million francs. Some of them already belonged to the Crown, but the jeweller provided many additional gems. The *Aquamarine Diamond* was one of them: a very wide, 25.82-carat oval brilliant cut with a slight blue tint, hence its name. It was purchased for 137,000 francs (40 kg of pure gold), and set in the centre of the Empress' tiara, above the *Eighth Mazarin* and below the Fleur de Pêcher. The *Great Mazarin* and the *King of Sardinia* were set on either side, in diamond clusters. The diadem contained a total of 1,514 diamonds, weighing 830 carats and valued at 988,319 francs. The rivière consisted of a strand of 22 brilliant-cuts weighing 264 carats, with the 29.41-carat *De Guise* in the centre. The remaining 21 stones, including one of 19.25 carats and another of 18.56 carats, cost 874,500 francs. The two matching bracelets each had a portrait diamond in the centre of the clasp: they weighed 9.01 and 6.83 carats respectively and were of exceptional clarity. These two gems alone cost 100,000 francs. The larger stone, known as Empress *Marie-Louise's Portrait Diamond*, was presented to the *Muséum national d'histoire naturelle* in 1887.

The Emperor also added to his own garment jewels, which dated back to 1805, three major new diamond-studded jewels, and various other items, including a complete set of buttons. The epaulette was particularly splendid: it contained the *Hortensia* , then valued at 108,000 francs, accompanied by 12 large principal brilliant-cuts weighing 45 carats in total, along with 40 carats of smaller diamonds. Imagine the spectacle at an official reception: the Emperor would have worn the hat ornament, the superb diamond-studded necklace of the Légion d'Honneur from 1805, and the 1812 sword with the *Regent* set in the hilt, suspended from a sash of rose-cut diamonds. In addition, the Empress would have been at his side, wearing the dazzling suite of diamonds: the effect would have been quite breathtaking! Naturally, the Empress could also take her pick from the other Crown Jewels: after all, between 1810 and early 1813, François-Regnault Nitot had also delivered five complete suites of ruby, sapphire, pearl, turquoise and amethyst jewels. In order to make these pieces, no fewer than 32,808 diamonds had to be purchased! As if this were not enough, there was also a suite of pearl-studded jewels framing a set of cameos. The French jewellery business had virtually collapsed due to the Revolution, but thanks to this outpouring of luxury it had a record-breaking period for sales. As a result, it recovered its global pre-eminence, which it retains to this day.

In addition to all these official State jewels, Napoleon gave the Empress many other pieces, to add to her private collection. He wanted to ensure that she was the most bejewelled woman in Europe. He gave her the most important jewel for the birth of their son, the King of Rome. It was a magnificent necklace, purchased from François-Regnault Nitot for 376,275 francs (the equivalent of 110 kilos of pure gold). It comprised a row of 30 brilliant-cuts, ranging from 2.57 to 10.73 carats, with 9 large pear-shaped diamond pendants ranging from 3.86 to 10.40 carats. The pear-shapes were interspersed with 10 briolette-cuts, ranging from 4.24 to 6.94 carats. Marie-Louise took it with her when she left France after the fall of the Empire in 1814, along with the rest of her personal jewels. She often wore it in her capacity as the Sovereign of Parma and Piacenza: she had received this duchy in exchange for leaving her exiled husband. She died in 1847, and bequeathed it to her sister-in-law Sophie, Archduchess of Austria, who removed two of the diamonds from the necklace to make a pair of earrings. The collar was then inherited by her son, Archduke Charles-Louis, who kept it until his death in 1872. In 1948, a wealthy French citizen purchased it from the Archduke's grandson, Prince François-Joseph II of Liechtenstein. It was subsequently purchased in 1960 by the New York jeweller, Harry Winston. He sold it to Marjorie Merriweather Post two years later, and she bequeathed it to Smithsonian Institution in Washington, DC.

On the subject of the King of Rome: incredibly, he was dressed and adorned like a little Emperor as soon as he could walk. He was bedecked with 'miniature' versions of his father's jewels. However, it hardly seems appropriate to use the word 'miniature', when talking about a hat ornament that cost 98,297 francs! The principal diamond cost 60,000 francs alone. It was a superb, well-proportioned 14.51-carat square

The sumptuous necklace that Napoleon gave to Empress Marie-Louise upon the birth of their son, the King of Rome. Smithsonian Institution, Washington DC.

Brooch, made by Bapst in 1855 for Empress Eugénie. The two matching heart-shaped stones are the *Seventeenth and Eighteenth Mazarins*. Louis XIV wore them as buttons, along with the large, almond-shaped stone below them. The Louvre, Paris.

brilliant, of great purity and brilliance, known as the *King of Rome*. It was set in a cluster of 12 diamonds, suspended from two rows of four brilliant-cuts, each weighing over 4 carats.

This Imperial extravagance soon came to an end. After the Emperor's abdication at Fontainebleau on April 4th, 1814, the Bourbons returned to the French throne, headed by Louis XVIII, Louis XVI's younger brother. When told of Napoleon's landing at Golfe Juan on March 1st, 1815, and of his rapid advance upon Paris, the King fled to Ghent. He took the Crown Jewels with him, as a 'nest egg' in case things went badly for him. This was not the case: after the defeat at Waterloo, the "Hundred Days' Interruption" came to an end, allowing the King - and the jewels - to return. Unfortunately, France had been occupied by the Allies, and they imposed exceedingly onerous peace conditions. Louis XVIII was forced to offer massive bribes to certain Generals, including Wellington. Some of these bribes were paid for thanks to the State jewel collection: he gave Wellington a marvellous Order of the Holy Spirit, set with some diamonds from the Crown collection. Overall, the treasury lost 2,414 brilliant-cuts and 708 rose-cuts, including thirty of between 5 and 13.90 carats, worth approximately 700,000 francs in total.

However, Louis XVIII firmly believed in the grandeur of the State, and he worked to compensate for these losses. As a result, he went to Bapst and purchased several gems for the Crown Jewels, on November 29, 1818. These included two splendid matching opals weighing 77 carats, each worth 70,000 francs, and three important diamonds. The largest was the 22.86-carat *Louis XVIII Pear*, a long, trapezoidal pear-shaped brilliant-cut. It was of good water, very pure and brilliant, and was valued at 120,000 francs (35 kilos of pure gold). In addition, upon his death in 1824, the King bequeathed four gems from his private collection to the State. They had originally been part of the Crown collection, but had been stolen in the 1792 burglary. He had repurchased them through intermediaries during his exile in the Revolutionary period. They included the 107.88-carat *Côte de Bretagne* spinel, carved in the shape of a dragon, the only surviving stone from Louis XV's famous "Coloured Gem" Golden Fleece. There were also three diamonds, including the 25.37-carat *Second Mazarin*, valued at 240,000 on account of its great beauty. It was the only remaining diamond from Louis XV's "White" Golden Fleece. The three diamonds were immediately set in a hat ornament for his brother and successor, Charles X. Unfortunately, during the 1848 Revolution that overthrew Louis-Philippe, the jewel was stolen while it was being transferred from the Tuileries to the Ministry of Finance. Although a description was circulated amongst all of Europe's leading jewellers, it was never found...

Upon his accession to the throne, Louis XVIII appointed Paul-Nicolas Ménière as Crown Jeweller. Ménière had already held the title at the end of Louis XVI's reign. In 1817, he stepped down in favour of his son-in-law, Evrard Bapst († 1842). Bapst's uncle Georges-Michel († 1770), originating from Swabia, and cousin Georges-Frédéric († 1826) had learnt their trade at Jacqmin, Louis XV's famous jeweller. Needless to say, their work was of high quality. Evrard's son and grandson, Constant († 1852) and Alfred († 1879), remained Crown Jewellers until the end of the Second Empire. Constant's cousin, Frédéric Bapst (1789-1870) managed the workshops. Naturally, Louis XVIII had all the Imperial jewels broken up, as they held bad memories for him. He used the gems to create new pieces for himself. Since he and his brother (the future Charles X) had been widowers for some time, France needed some female representatives. In the event, there were two 'First Ladies': the wives of Charles X's two sons. Marie-Thérèse, Louis XVIII's niece, was married to the elder son, the Duke of Angoulême. Marie-Caroline de Bourbon-Sicile was married to the younger son: Charles, Duke of Berri, who was assassinated in 1820. Marie-Caroline bore a son, the future Comte of Chambord, who was the last member of the older branch of the Bourbon family. Some new jewels had to be made in order to ensure that Marie-Thérèse and Marie-Caroline were adequately bedecked with gems, befitting their status as Princesses of France.

The most sumptuous jewels, however, were made for the King and for his successors, set with the gems from Napoleon's garment jewels and Marie Louise's suite of jewellery, which had both been broken up. These masterpieces will not be discussed in detail here, instead, we will focus on the royal crown, which was the most extravagant and elegant in the world. It was designed by Evrard Bapst, and made by his nephew Frédéric for Louis XVIII in 1820-1821; later, it was slightly modified for Charles X's coronation on May 25th, 1825. The crown contained 5,206 brilliant-cuts, weighing 1,924 carats, 146 tiny rose-cuts, and 80 sapphires. The total valuation was 14,702,788.85 gold francs, including 12,000,000 for *Regent* alone, which was set in the centre of the great double-lily at the top of the crown. The lily's four petals were set with the 19.25-carat *Marie-Louise Rectangle*, the *King of Sardinia*, which had been re-polished to a weight of 17.40 carats, and two other brilliant-cuts weighing 14.64 and 14.39 carats. There were eight lilies around the crown, set with the *Louis XVIII Pear*, the *Aquamarine Diamond*, the *De Guise* (re-polished to 29.22 carats), the *Fleur de Pêcher*, the *Grand Mazarin*, the *Napoleon*, the *Oval Emigré* and the 18.56-carat *Marie Louise Oval*. The internal purple velvet cap was set at the top with the *Chrysolithe Orientale*. The crown's arches were set with eight principal stones, including *Louis XVIII's Pink Diamond* (15.96 carats) and the *Eighth Mazarin*; the six others ranged from 8.73 to 12.41 carats. After the July 1830 revolution, which overthrew Charles X, Thiers and the Orléanists forced Parliament to accept Louis-Philippe as the King of the French (but not of France) on August 9th. Louis-Philippe was the Duke of Orleans, head of the younger branch of the Bourbon dynasty, descended from Philippe d'Orléans, Louis XIV's brother. The new sovereign disliked ostentation. The Crown Jewels stayed in their jewel cases, and were never worn by the royal family throughout his entire reign.

Once the February 1848 Revolution overthrew Louis-Philippe, the Second Republic was born. According to a decree on May 9th, the Crown Jewels were supposed to be sold. The decree was never implemented. Louis-Napoleon Bonaparte was elected as President of the Republic on December 10th. He was Napoleon's nephew (the son of Napoleon's brother, Louis, and Queen Hortense, Empress Josephine's daughter from her first marriage). He was already secretly planning to restore the Empire, and naturally tried to prevent the sale of a collection that he wanted to use one day. In due course, he led a coup on December 2nd, 1851, which led to the proclamation of the Second Empire in 1852. He became Emperor under the name of Napoleon III (the King of Rome, who had died in 1832, had briefly acceded to the throne in 1815 as Emperor Napoleon II). On January 29th, 1853, the new Emperor married a Spanish aristocrat, Eugénia-María de Montijo de Guzmán, Countess of Teba: the Crown Jewels were about to be worn by one of the most beautiful women of the day.

The new Empress Eugénie asked for the Crown Jewels to be displayed to her. One by one, the fitted jewellery boxes were opened in front of her: she was star-struck. Most of the jewels were broken up: the pearl suite was completely re-modelled, and all the diamond jewels were dismantled, including the Royal crown, which was, of course, no longer appropriate. Charles X's marvellous Coronation sword was kept, as were some foreign Orders: they were still useful, because the Emperor had also been awarded these decorations. The coloured-gem suites that had been made for the Duchesses of Angoulême and Berri survived intact. At the start of his reign, the Emperor wanted to be crowned in Notre Dame Cathedral. He therefore commanded Gabriel Lemonnier to make an Imperial Crown in gold, emeralds and diamonds, designed as a circle of eight golden eagles. The eagles' wingtips met at the top of the crown, holding the *Regent*, which acted as an orb, surmounted by a brilliant-cut diamond cross. The circlet was set with eight large emeralds, interspersed with the same eight diamonds that had been set in the old Royal Crown's fleur-de-lys motifs. Since the ceremony ultimately never took place, these diamonds were replaced by paste copies and placed at the Empress' disposal. A smaller, matching coronet had been made for the Empress in the interim, and this remained intact.

A red leather box, bearing the inscription "Diamonds of the Crown". The Louvre possesses a whole collection of empty jewel boxes, as a result of the disastrous sale of the French Crown Jewels in 1887. The Louvre, Paris.

Eugénie therefore found herself with a fabulous collection of loose diamonds, which were entrusted to the Bapst company once again. They were turned into some truly marvellous jewels. There was a tiara in a 'Greek key' design, set with the *Regent*, an extraordinary suite of jewels in the shape of currant leaves (a girdle ornament, large bodice brooch and a garland for the corsage), and a large hair ornament with a fringe of pendants, with the Hortensia in the centre. As for the eight large historic diamonds from the Royal Crown, the *Aquamarine Diamond* was set in a large belt-buckle. The remaining gems were mounted in

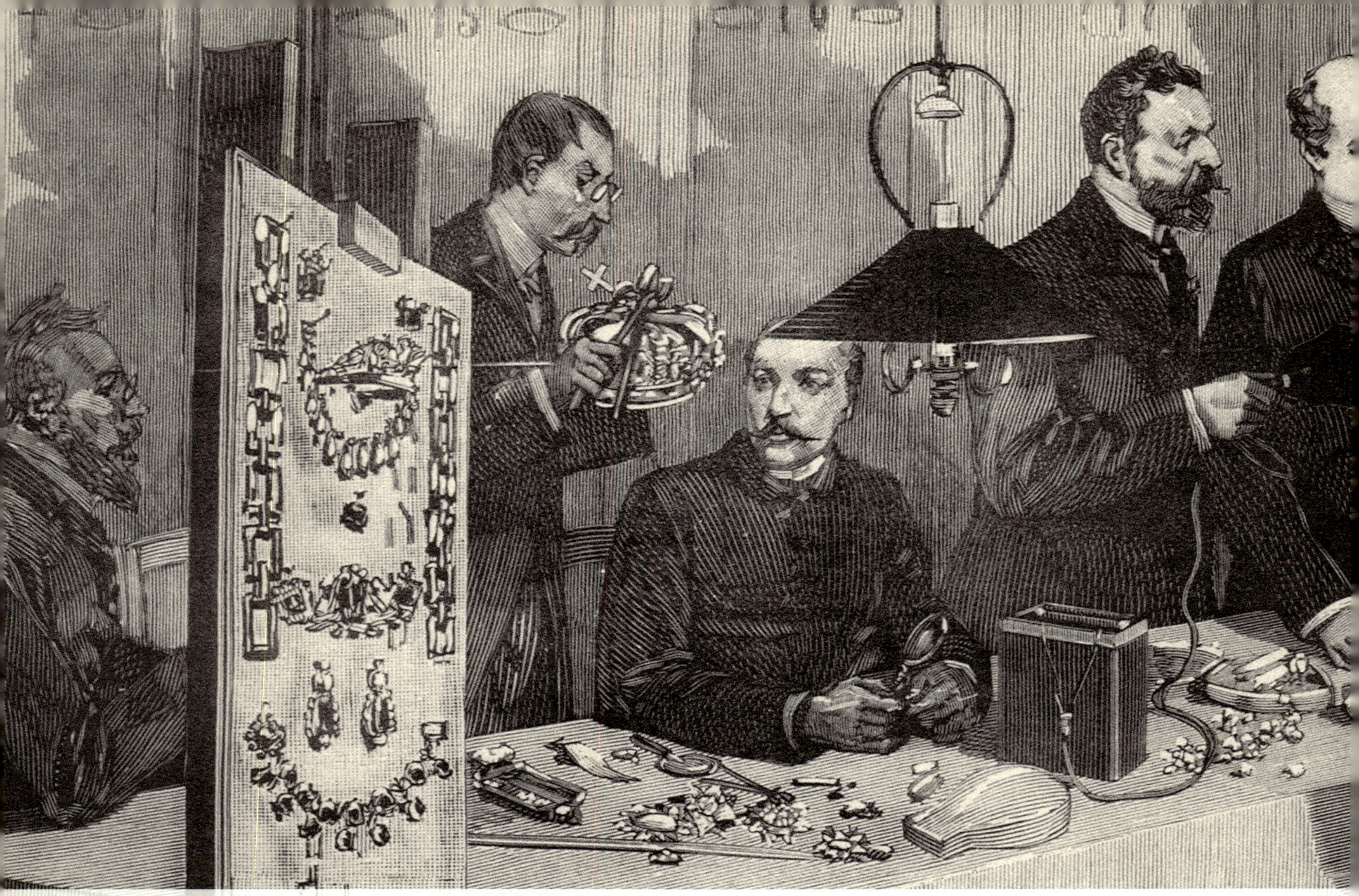

simple collets with little pendant hoops on the back, so that they could be sewn on to ceremonial costumes. Although the Crown Jewels had their chance to shine in all their glory at functions and imperial receptions, which were the envy of Europe, Napoleon III never added any significant diamonds to the State collection. Indeed, the example of the preceding revolutions would hardly have encouraged him to offer exceptional gems to the State, as he would not have been able to recover them in the event that he lost the throne. The only acquisitions that he made from his own pocket were the eight large emeralds for the Crown, and numerous small diamonds that were needed for the stylish modern jewels created for his wife. These amounted to only 103,409 gold francs in total. However, the Emperor gave Eugénie some marvellous personal jewels. She was obsessed with jewels, and gained the nickname "Empress Embellishment the First"! In spite of this, she turned down a 600,000-franc necklace presented by the City of Paris upon her marriage. It was made by Lemonnier, and had a superb, 23-carat heart-shaped brilliant in the centre. An equivalent amount was distributed to charity, at her request. When the Second Empire was overthrown, she went to England, taking her private collection of jewels with her. When in exile, she found herself short of money, and had to sell part of the collection at Christie's in London on June 24th, 1872. The auction fetched only 1,125,000 gold francs, much less than the jewels' true value. She also owned a large, pear-shaped brilliant known as the *Eugénie*. It weighed 51 old carats, and was given to her by Napoleon III as a wedding present. The gem had originally been given by Catherine II of Russia to one of her favourites, Potemkin. Napoleon III purchased it from the daughter of Countess Branitsky, Potemkin's niece. A diamond described as the *Eugénie* surfaced at auction recently. Although it was of almost identical weight, it was cut in the 17th-century Mogul style (genuine or imitation?). It seems unlikely that the two gems are the same. The Empress had sold the diamond privately to the Gaekwar of Baroda.

After the extraordinary extravagance of the Second Empire and the dispersion of Empress Eugénie's personal jewellery collection, we come to the fourth and final catastrophe to befall the French Crown Jewels throughout history. In 1875, the Third Republic commissioned an inventory of the collection. The diamonds alone comprised 51,403 brilliant-cuts, weighing 10,182.81 carats and 21,119 rose-cuts. The majority of the rose-cuts were very small and not weighed; the larger ones amounted to 484.14 carats. The jewels were displayed in two public exhibitions, at the Paris World Fair in 1878 and in the State Rooms of the Louvre in 1884, where they were admired by large crowds, providing ample proof of French supremacy in the jeweller's art. Despite this, the Government decided to sell them. It passed the Law of Alienation of the Crown Jewels in December 1886. It was a primarily political decision by the Third Republic, in an attempt to sabotage any attempt to restore the monarchy. The collection was therefore put up for public auction, in nine sessions from the 12th to the 23rd of May 1887. Because the Orders were official jewels, they were all dismantled, and the gems were sold as loose stones. Some of the suites of diamond jewels were considered to be too important, so they were broken up into smaller units in order to make the individual lots more

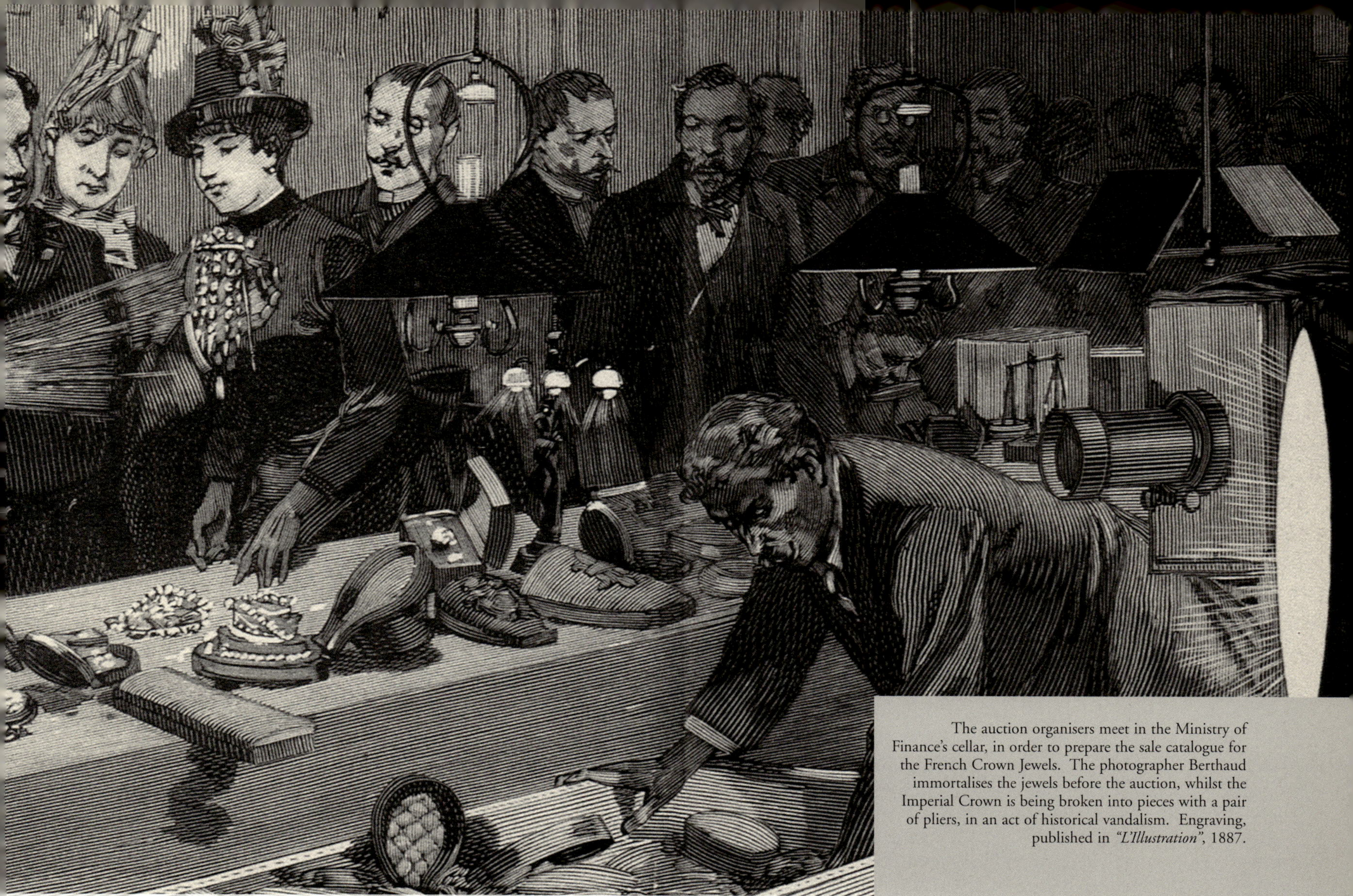

The auction organisers meet in the Ministry of Finance's cellar, in order to prepare the sale catalogue for the French Crown Jewels. The photographer Berthaud immortalises the jewels before the auction, whilst the Imperial Crown is being broken into pieces with a pair of pliers, in an act of historical vandalism. Engraving, published in *"L'Illustration"*, 1887.

accessible. Fortunately, the majority of the pieces were photographed, thereby creating a permanent record. The purchasers came from all over the world, and spent a total of 7,221,360 gold francs, including expenses. Tiffany & Co. of New York purchased some of the most beautiful diamonds, including the *De Guise*, the *Fleur de Pêcher*, the *Aquamarine Diamond*, *Louis XVIII's Pear-Shape*, the 20.03-carat *Marie-Louise Square*, the *Square Emigré*, the *Marie-Louise Oval* and the *Eye of Tavernier*. Boucheron bought the *Great Mazarin*, the *Oblong Emigré*, the *Marie-Louise Rectangle* and the *Eighth Mazarin*. Madame Asselin purchased the *Napoleon*, the Baron of Horn bought the *Chrysolithe Orientale* and the *King of Sardinia*, and a bidder known as Picard obtained *the Pink Diamond of Louis XVIII*. Since then, most of the jewels have vanished without trace. However, some of them occasionally reappear, such as the *Great Mazarin*, which was re-sold to Boucheron in 1962, before being sold on once again.

However, France did not lose everything. The Commission of Alienation requested that some jewels be preserved, in accordance with their historical importance or their artistic character - as if the remainder did not have any! They were distributed between the Louvre, the *Muséum national d'histoire naturelle* and the *Ecole des Mines*. In addition to the 107.88-carat Côte de Bretagne carved spinel dragon, the Louvre acquired several important diamonds. The principal pieces were the fabulous 140.64-carat *Regent* (thanks to its beauty and its prestige), the 21.32-carat Hortensia (because of its very rare colour), one of Empress Eugénie's brooches, the Dey of Algiers' Watch, and Charles X's coronation sword. The brooch was made for Empress Eugénie in 1855. It was set with 85 diamonds, including the *Seventeenth and Eighteenth Mazarins*, each weighing 22 carats, and a large, almond-shaped brown rose-cut weighing 15.67 carats, which had previously been one of Louis XIV's buttons. The jewel was only spared because it was mistakenly thought that it dated back to Louis XV's reign! The Dey of Algiers' Watch was embellished with 265 rose-cut diamonds. It was originally part of the spoils of war from the capture of Algiers under Charles X. Charles X's coronation sword, by Evrard Bapst, was kept because of the widespread admiration that it had received during the 1878 and 1885 exhibitions. It was decorated with 1,576 brilliant-cuts weighing 340 carats, the largest of 14.55 carats. The sword was valued at 241,875 gold francs in 1825. Tragically, it was stolen from the Louvre in 1976 and never recovered.

The Muséum national d'histoire naturelle received the lovely 9.01-carat *Portrait Diamond of Empress Marie-Louise*, 3 briolettes weighing 3.56 carats in total, and one of Louis XVIII's two great 77-carat opals, along with many coloured gemstones of lesser importance. As for the *Ecole des Mines*, its principal acquisitions were two loose brilliant-cuts, weighing 7.10 and 5.44 carats, that had originally been set in the Imperial crown. They were stolen in 1909.

Some items from the diamond suites in the Crown Jewels. The large bow brooch with pendants and tassels is shown in the centre. The large yellow diamond brooch at left contains the *Chrysolithe Orientale.* Photographed by Berthaud in 1887.

The bow brooch with pendants and tassels, as it exists today. It is in a private American collection.

At right, a photographic plate by Berthaud.
It was taken in 1887, and shows pieces of the great garland from the Currant-Leaf Suite, one of the Crown's most magnificent diamond suites.
Private collection.

At left, one of the pieces from the garland. It is part of the Metropolitan Opera's collection, in New York. It was converted into a brooch, and given to the opera diva Lucrezia Bori. Metropolitan Opera Guild archives.

Rivers of Russian diamonds

Glorious Russia! The Imperial court's splendour was legendary, and its sovereigns were the only ones in Europe able to compete with France on equal terms. By the eve of the 1917 Revolution, the Crown Jewels of Russia were the most imposing and marvellous in Europe - although it should be noted that, unlike France, they had not been ravaged by any catastrophes up until that point. Moreover, in Russia, the Tsarinas' private jewels, and even those of certain Grand Duchesses, were systematically added to the State jewel collection upon their deaths. Fabergé was the last Crown Jeweller: his firm created the famous and coveted Russian Easter Eggs for the Tsar. In 1913, he began a detailed inventory, only to be interrupted by the Great War. Later, Trotsky instructed him to continue the project, which took him from October 1921 until March 1923. Photographs were taken of every piece and wherever possible, the weight of each stone was recorded. The diamonds alone added up to 25,300 carats, including 70 very large gems weighing 1,500 carats, and 1,800 carats of gems ranging from 5 to 12 carats! Peter the Great († 1725) and his daughter Elizabeth Petrovna († 1762) accounted for 20% of the acquisitions. Catherine the Great, the Russian answer to Louis XIV, who reigned from 1762 to 1796, accounted for another 40%. 25% came from Alexander I († 1825) and Nicholas I († 1855), and the remainder from other reigns.

However, the Soviets could not resist the temptation to sell part of the collection at auction on March 16th, 1927 at Christie's in London. They did so anonymously, calling themselves "a trade union". Out of the 124 lots in the auction, half were jewels that had been confiscated from the private collections of the Imperial family, but the remainder included many State jewels of much greater importance. The sale raised 52,609 gold pounds sterling , but 30 jewels did not achieve their reserve prices and were re-sold secretly, including two tiaras and a brooch, which could have exceeded £75,000 on their own. In so far as diamonds were concerned, the auctioned jewels included the 41.38-carat *Russian Pink*, a splendid rectangular cushion brilliant-cut from India. It was of a fine pink colour, very brilliant and absolutely pure, and fetched £11,800. The Nuptial Crown, containing nearly 2,000 stones weighing approximately 300 carats, fetched £6,100. It had traditionally been used at Imperial family weddings; the diamonds were sewn on to the crown's fabric lining. However, the bulk of the collection remained in Moscow.

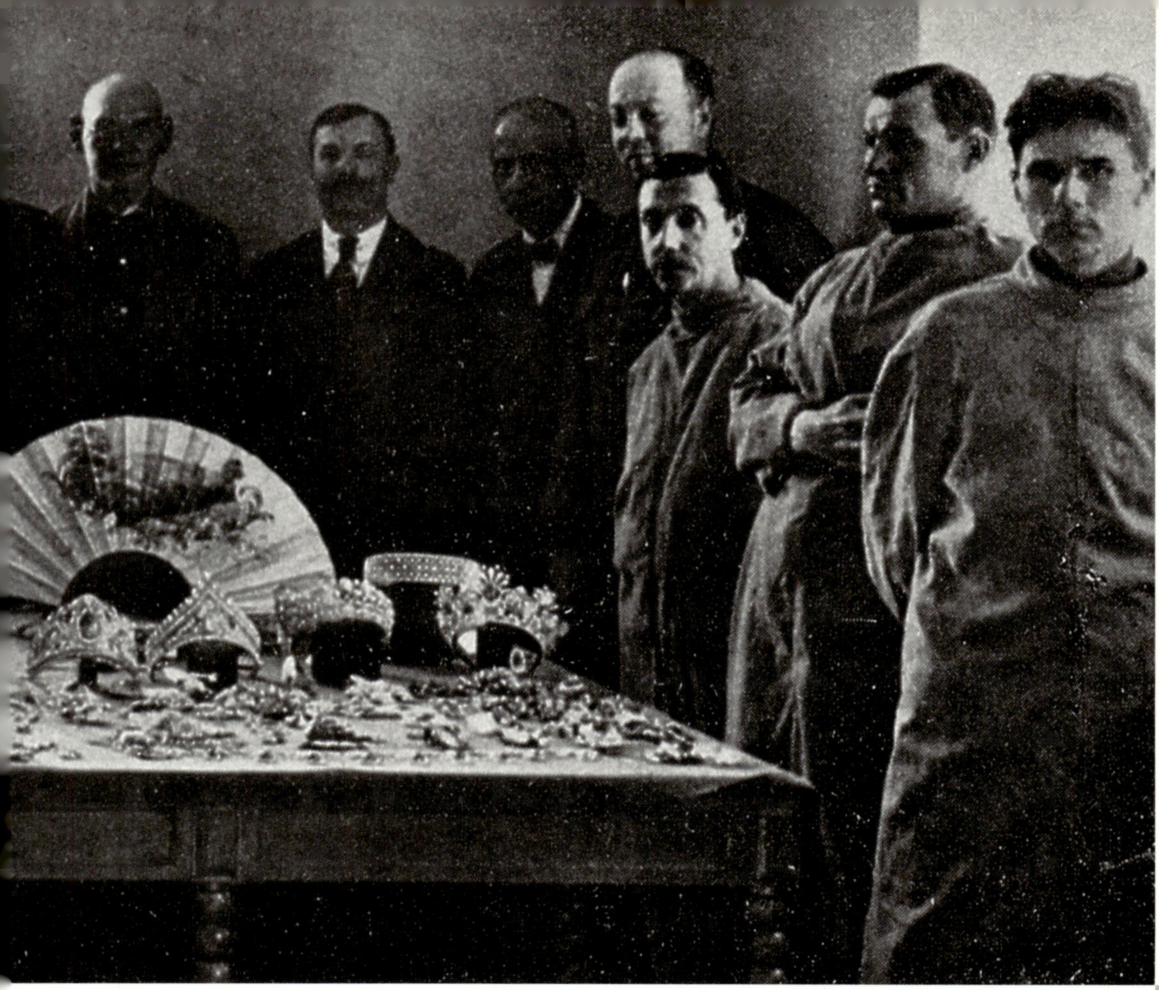

The Crown Jewels of Imperial Russia, displayed on a table, accompanied by the committee responsible for its safekeeping and inventory. Published in *"L'Illustration"*, 1922. Private Collection.

The Imperial Crown of Russia. Russian Diamond Fund, Moscow.

Unfortunately, many of these jewels were sold in 1932 on Stalin's orders. The transactions were performed in the utmost secrecy in Reval (which is now Tallin, the Estonian capital). The market conditions were particularly bad: the market was going through a period of crisis, and could barely absorb such a large quantity of stones. Connoisseurs could buy absolutely unique pieces at extremely favourable prices, such as the very discreet Swiss collector whose descendants still possess some of the most beautiful tiaras. The sale was so confidential that, even in the 1950s, when Soviet officials were asked for information about the State collection, they persisted in circulating a list of pieces that actually predated the 1927 auctions, backed up by the 1923 photographs! A considerable amount was lost in 1932. With regard to diamonds alone, the following items were sold: a tiara with 632 Brazilian brilliant-cuts weighing 273 carats, a rivière of 23 solitaires, including several Golconda gems, weighing 165.50 carats, and another of 45 brilliant-cuts, weighing 301.35 carats. These pieces almost certainly included 27 gems from Empress Joséphine's necklace that her daughter, Queen Hortense, had sold to Alexander I for 700,000 gold francs. However, the single most important piece was a 'slave necklace', which contained 36 large brilliant-cuts weighing a total of 487.50 carats. This worked out to an average of 13.50 carats for each stone, with the two largest gems weighing 33.28 and 27.25 carats! It was the most splendid necklace in Europe. The brooches contained some of the Collection's largest diamonds, including the 54.71-carat *Two Hundred Thousand Roubles,* which had been named in accordance with its 1878 valuation. It was a very white oval brilliant-cut from the Indies, with some small black flaws. The *Pink Golconda* was set in a flower-brooch, embellished with 120 carats of brilliant-cut diamonds. It was a thick, very brilliant gem of Indian origin and fine pink colour, weighing 38.75 carats. The 17.68-carat *Russian Pink*, a pink oval brilliant, was set in a jewel that could be converted from a brooch into a clasp. This jewel suspended a pendant that contained the 29-carat *Bitterman* diamond, a flat Indian pear-shape named after the Hungarian merchant from whom it had been purchased in 1834. As far as earrings were concerned, the three largest diamonds sold were the 40.50-carat *Russian Briolette*, a superb white briolette that had been cut in India, and a pair of cushion-cut brilliants from Golconda: one of pinkish water weighing 20.50 carats, and the other of white water, weighing 19.55 carats. And these were only the major pieces...

Three views of the engraved, 88.70-carat *Shah* diamond. Russian Diamond Fund, Moscow.

Fortunately, Stalin decided to preserve some of the most important pieces in the Kremlin, under the name of the "U.S.S.R. Diamond Fund". These included the regalia, particularly the Imperial crown made for Catherine II's coronation. It had been designed by Jérémie Pauzié, a jeweller from Geneva. He manufactured it in 1762, in conjunction with a French jeweller, Aurole. It was the most valuable crown of the 18th century after Louis XV's, which had been decorated with the *Regent* and the *Sancy*. In fact, it is possibly the finest in the world, although the British Imperial State Crown is admittedly embellished with the 317.40-carat *Cullinan II*. The British crown, however, was re-set in Queen Victoria's reign in a rather bulky design. The Russian crown is more elegant. It was inspired by the heraldic shape of ancient Western Imperial crowns, and is shaped rather like a mitre, in two hemispheres, studded with 4,936 diamonds weighing an incredible 2,929 carats! However, the true splendour of the piece is in the single arch that surmounts the crown. It goes from front to back, and is designed as a wreath of oak leaves and acorns. The front of the arch is set with the largest diamond, the 57.07-carat *Elizabeth Petrovna*, flanked by two pear-shapes of 13 carats each. The *Elizabeth Petrovna* is a rectangular, cut-cornered, white emerald-cut. It is very thick, and is set with its pavilion facing upwards. It had been presented to Empress Elizabeth Petrovna by the Merchants' Guild of Russia, in appreciation for having exempted the interior of the country from customs duties. The upper part of the arch is set with a superb white oblong brilliant-cut, weighing 42.34 carats, followed by a 17.80-carat slightly trapezoidal cushion-cut, a large pink marquise of 22.42 carats and an 18.83-carat rectangular cushion-cut. The back of the arch is set with the following, from bottom to top: a brownish-pink brilliant-cut trapezoid of 17.61 carats, a blue-white pear of 17.55 carats, a long, pale yellow rectangular cushion-cut of 13.06 carats, a flawless white brilliant-cut rhombus of 16.91 carats and a long cushion-cut of slightly bluish water, weighing 12.57 carats. The *Lal* spinel glistens at the top of the crown: it is an enormous polished pebble weighing 398.72 carats. Tsar Alexis Mikhailovitch bought it in Beijing in 1676.

The imperial sceptre was made for Catherine II in 1784, by the goldsmith Troitinski. It is made out of polished gold, with eight rings of brilliant-cut diamonds weighing 44 carats in total. The largest diamond in the Russian Crown Jewels, the *Orloff*, is set in the top, surmounted by the two-headed Russian eagle. In recent years, it was discovered that the *Orloff* is very probably the diamond known as the *Great Mogul*, initially described by Tavernier, who appears to have recorded its weight incorrectly. It had belonged to Aurangzeb, the last Indian Mogul Emperor from 1658 to 1707, then to Nadir Shah, King of Persia, who conquered India in 1739. Following his assassination in 1747, his empire broke down and the diamond disappeared during the disorder in Isfahan. It reappeared in the possession of an Armenian, Saphras, who sought to sell it in Astrakhan without success, before depositing it in a bank in Amsterdam. His nephew, Ivan Lasarev, a banker and jeweller from the Armenian colony in St. Petersburg, had a half-share in the diamond, and tried to sell the gem in Russia. Count Gregory Orloff, a favourite of Catherine II, purchased it from Lasarev for 400,000 roubles, payable in seven annual instalments. Seemingly, Catherine was displeased with him, and he hoped to give her the diamond in order to return to favour. He duly presented her with the gem on St. Catherine's Day in 1773. In fact, it is highly likely that Orloff was simply acting as an agent for Catherine: she gave him a marble palace in St. Petersburg in gratitude. The *Orloff* weighs 189.62 carats, and is the largest Indian Mughal-cut diamond in the world. Its cut is highly characteristic of the 17th century: extremely high, shaped like half an egg, with 180 tiered facets on the top and very few facets on the smooth, slightly curved base. It measures 47.60 x 31.75 x 34.92 mm. Fortunately, it never occurred to the Empress to have it re-cut into a brilliant: it would have yielded a stone of no more than about 100 carats, and it would have lost much of its historic value. As for the Imperial Orb, it is adorned with the *Paul I,* a superb pear-shaped rose-cut diamond from Golconda. It was cut in India, and weighs 46.92 carats.

We should also mention the other surviving items in the regalia, and the numerous garment jewels. They are literally covered in diamonds. There is a particularly remarkable neo-Gothic bracelet, in enamelled gold, containing a central full-length portrait miniature of Tsar Alexander I, painted on ivory. It is glazed by a large portrait diamond. The 25-carat *Portrait Diamond of Tsar Alexander I* originally came from India. It is triangular, and of extraordinary purity, measuring 40 x 25 mm across and 2.5 mm thick. It is one of largest of its kind in the world. Its large, perfectly polished table spans almost its entire surface, bordered by two rows of small facets. There are also two coloured diamonds of note: one is set in an early 19th-century tiara, accompanied by 400 carats of brilliant-cut and briolette diamonds. It was purchased by Paul I, and is extraordinarily rare and peculiar, with a faceted pavilion and a very large table. The gem is rectangular with rounded corners and very flat, even though it weighs only 13.35 carats, it has the surface area of a 100-carat gem! It is also unusual because of its unique soft pink colour, which has been accentuated by a red enamelled background- hence the gem's name, the *Blood Red.* The other coloured diamond is set in the famous *Great Bouquet* jewel, an 18th-century jewellery masterpiece. It is the *Tsars' Mauve Diamond*, a 15.50-carat brilliant-cut pear-shape of absolutely unique pinkish-purple colour.

Finally, the Crown Jewels of Russia have another extraordinary, unique piece: the famous 88.70-carat *Shah* diamond. This startling Indian gem was cut in the late 16th century by Indian gem-cutters, who kept very closely to the original oblong shape of the rough gem. It is 4 cm long. Three of the cleavage planes were polished, and the fourth has 15 facets. There is a groove, 0.5 mm deep, around the thinnest part of the stone, allowing it to be tied with cord and worn as a pendant. Its purity and transparency are extraordinary. The polished faces are beautifully engraved – a real technical feat – with the names of three of its former owners, and the three corresponding dates in the Hejirah calendar. The first inscription, "Burhan Nizam Shah II - Year 1000" (1591 in the western calendar) refers to the sovereign of Ahmadragar Province in the northwest of India. The second, "Dschechan Shah, son of Jahangir Shah, 1051" (1641) commemorates Shah Jahan, the Mogul Emperor of the Indies, while the third, "Nadschar Fath 'Ali Shah, Sultan and King, 1242" (1824) refers to the Shah of Persia, Fath Ali Shah. This is because the Indian Mogul Emperors' treasures were taken to Persia after the sack of Delhi by Nadir Shah in 1739. When the Russian Ambassador to Persia, the writer Griboyedov, was assassinated in 1829 by Persian fanatics, Fath Ali Shah was obliged to send Prince Chosrev Mirza to St. Petersburg with many gifts, in order to placate Tsar Nicolas I and avoid further bloodshed. The *Shah* diamond was one of them.

Interestingly, since the late 1960s, one division of the Diamond Fund has been devoted to making modern jewels, and even re-creating some of the pieces that were sold between the two World Wars. Siberian mines provide an abundance of diamonds and coloured gemstones that have been turned into rings, brooches, necklaces and tiaras, which have been added to the State collection, recalling some of the long-lost splendour of ancient Mother Russia. There are, for example, two reproduction tiaras that imitate jewels sold in London in 1927. One, the "Russian Beauty" is set with pearls and brilliant-cut diamonds (928 of them, weighing 137.95 carats). The other, the "Russian Field", is designed as a wreath of ears of corn and flax flowers and buds. It is set with 1,836 brilliant-cuts weighing 129.35 carats, and has a fine bright yellow cushion-cut in the centre, weighing 35.52 carats. The Fund also contains other modern gems: one particular Siberian diamond, a slightly bluish long octagonal shape of extraordinarily pure water (weighing 25.52 carats, and measuring 28 mm long by 18 mm wide) has become a symbol of the fund. It was illustrated in a recent publication, alongside a caption claiming that it was a 19th-century diamond from the Crown Jewels! There are many exceptional rough Siberian diamonds in the Fund. These are described in the chapter devoted to diamond mineralogy (cf. Chapter 1).

The Imperial Sceptre, set with the famous 189.70-carat *Orloff*, seen from the front and in profile. Russian Diamond Fund, Moscow.

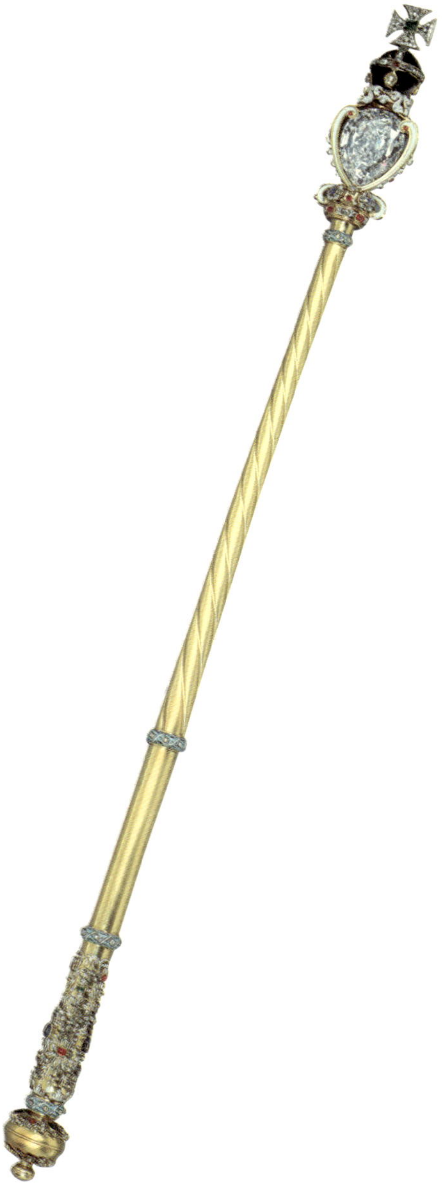

The crown made for Queen Elizabeth the Queen Mother (consort of George VI, mother of Queen Elizabeth II). The *Koh-i-Noor* is set in the centre.

The British sceptre, symbolising temporal power. It was made in 1661 and adapted in 1910, when the Cullinan I was added: the largest colourless cut diamond in the world. It is also known as the Great Star of Africa (530.20 carats). Jewel House, Tower of London.

The Kingdom of giants

We finish this chapter by returning to the United Kingdom: when we left off, the Crown Jewels had been completely destroyed after Charles I's execution. Queen Henrietta-Maria had left the Regalia - which dated back to the Middle Ages - in London, and Cromwell ordered everything to be broken up and melted down. New pieces had to be created for Charles II's coronation In 1661, when the Stuart dynasty had been restored to the throne. These included the 'St. Edward's Crown', which has been used for coronations ever since. It does not contain any notable diamonds. There were various other official crowns, which were used ceremonially until the end of the Stuart dynasty (Queen Anne was the last of the Stuarts, in 1702). However, all of them were set with rented diamonds. This was also the case in the early years of the House of Hanover, which became the ruling dynasty in 1714 (under George I). For example, the Crown Jewellers, Rundell and Bridge, made a very fine crown for George IV's Coronation on July 19th, 1821. The gemstones set in the crown were rented from Rundell and Bridge, for the sum of £6,525, equivalent to 10% of diamond's value. They also charged £735 in manufacturing costs. The principal diamond was a splendid, perfectly round 32.20-carat brilliant-cut, known alternatively as the *George IV* or the *Hastings*, set in the centre of the frontal cross patee. The two lily motifs on either side contained two other very fine and pure brilliant-cuts, the pear-shaped *Arcot Diamonds*, of 33.70 and 23.65 carats. They had previously been part of the private jewellery collection of Queen Charlotte of Mecklenburg, George III's consort. Mohammed Ali Khan, the Nawab of Arcot, had given them to her in 1777. Later on, the jewellers sold the *George IV* and *Arcots* to the Duke of Westminster. In 1930, he commissioned the Parisian jewellery firm Lacloche to set them in a magnificent tiara for his Duchess. This famous jewel was eventually sold at Sotheby's in London, in June 1959. It was ultimately dismantled, and the three diamonds were re-cut and sold separately.

The British Crown only began to acquire magnificent diamonds in Queen Victoria's reign (from 1837 to 1901). However, it should be noted that these were primarily gifts to the sovereign, requiring no expenditure beyond the cost of cutting and setting the gems in jewellery. For example, the East India Company gave the Queen the legendary *Koh-i-Noor* ('mountain of light') diamond in 1851. At the same time, she was also presented with the magnificent *Timur Ruby*, known as the 'Tribute of the World'. The Timur 'ruby' is, in fact, a polished spinel weighing 352 1/2 old carats. The *Koh-i-Noor's* history has already been discussed in the chapter on Mogul diamonds (cf. Chapter 10). We shall merely recall that the gem was, tragically, re-cut into a rather poorly-proportioned oval brilliant-cut, obliterating its historic appearance and, moreover, reducing its weight from 190.75 to 105.60 carats. In the early 20th century, South African diamonds began to flood into the global market. This was particularly timely, since Indian deposits had long been exhausted and those of Brazil were beginning to peter out. The British Crown Jewels were about to receive their most glorious acquisitions. On January 26th, 1905, the largest rough diamond of all time was discovered in the Premier mine, 20 miles to the northwest of Pretoria. It weight 3,106 carats, and was named the *Cullinan,* after the mine's chairman, Thomas Cullinan. The Transvaal government bought it in August 1907, for £150,000, and on October 17 they decided to present it to King Edward VII on his birthday. The gem was sent by ordinary parcel post to England, and entrusted to the Asscher firm of Amsterdam for cutting. It was successfully cleaved by hand by Joseph Asscher on February 10th, 1908, in what must have been an almost incomprehensibly nerve-wracking operation. Three gem-cutters worked full-time for eight months on the resulting fragments, which ultimately yielded 9 large and 96 smaller brilliant-cuts, all of the purest water. Initially, Edward VII was given the two largest gems; he immediately gave them to the State collection. The first was a 530.20-carat pear-shape with 74 facets, measuring 58.9 mm by 45.4 mm. It was named the *Great Star of Africa* by the King, and to this day it remains the largest white, cut diamond in existence. The second, known as the *Cullinan II*, was a rectangular cushion-cut with 64 facets, measuring 44.9 mm by 40.4 mm. It weighs 317.40 carats, and is the second-largest white, cut diamond in existence. Upon receiving the two enormous gems, Edward VII personally bought the *Cullinan VI*, an 11.50-carat marquise, which he gave to his consort, Queen Alexandra. The six other principal stones, the 94.40-carat pear-shaped *Cullinan III*, the 63.60-carat cushion-cut *Cullinan IV*, the

18.80-carat heart-shaped *Cullinan V*, the 8.80-carat marquise *Cullinan VII*, the 6.80-carat long rectangle cushion-cut *Cullinan VIII* and the 4.40-carat pear-shaped Cullinan IX, were ultimately purchased in 1910 by the Government of the Union of South Africa. On June 28th of the same year, they were given to Queen Mary, the consort of George V, who had just acceded to the throne following his father's death. At the present time, the Crown Jewels of the United Kingdom are divided into two groups. Only the first group, which primarily consists of the Regalia, is on display to the public in the Tower of London. The second group is not on display: it comprises jewels that were bequeathed to the State by Queen Victoria, King George V and Queen Mary, but which are held in trust by Queen Elizabeth II. In addition, the Queen also has a magnificent private collection of family jewels. The largest diamonds are in the Tower of London. The Royal Sceptre dates back to 1661. It was altered by Edward VII, who added the *Great Star of Africa*. We should add that, a few years ago, it ceased to be the largest diamond in the world and was relegated to being merely the largest gem-quality white diamond in the world. The King of Thailand's Sceptre was recently embellished with the *Golden Jubilee*, a brown diamond that is 15 carats bigger! The *Cullinan II* has been set in the centre of the Imperial State Crown's circlet since George V's coronation in 1911. The Crown itself was re-set for the Queen's coronation in 1953. None of the 2,872 other diamonds it contains is truly noteworthy, but the frontal cross patee is, however, set with the *Black Prince's Ruby* (a 163.22-carat polished red spinel), and the cross patee at the back is set with the 106.72-carat *Stuart Sapphire*. Queen Elizabeth the Queen Mother's Crown is the next finest crown in the collection. It was made in 1937, for George VI's coronation. Its frontal cross patee is set with the *Koh-i-Noor*, above the *Sultan of Turkey*, a 17.55-carat oval brilliant. The cross at the top of the crown was initially set with the 22.48-carat pear-shaped *Lahore diamond*, but Queen Elizabeth II uses it as a pendant to a diamond necklace, so it has been replaced by a copy. The Imperial Crown of India is also very fine and elegant. It was made during the Delhi Durbar, for George V's coronation as the Emperor of India, and cost £60,000, paid for by the colony. It contains 6,170 diamonds (a record for a crown), which have been used to embellish 4 sapphires, 4 rubies and 9 emeralds, all of exceptional quality.

The Queen frequently wears jewels from her well-known private collection, which includes the *Cullinans III* and *IX*. She has many tiaras and suites of jewels, in pearls and coloured gemstones as well as diamonds; the collection is the finest in Europe. The *Williamson* is the most recent important diamond to have entered the Royal collection. It was named after the Canadian geologist John Thorburn Williamson, who discovered a diamond mine in Mwadui, Tanganyika (today Tanzania) in 1940. He became the President of the mine, and in 1947 a 54.50-carat rough pink diamond was found there. Williamson decided to give it to Princess Elizabeth (later Elizabeth II) upon her wedding to Prince Philip of Greece and Denmark (later Duke of Edinburgh), later that year on November 20th. At the start of 1948, the gem was entrusted to the London firm of Briefel and Lemer. After three months' work, they produced a perfectly round, 23.60-carat brilliant cut. It was completely flawless, and of a fine and evenly-distributed pink colour. In her Coronation year, 1953, Elizabeth II commissioned Cartier to set it in a brooch of daffodil design. It has become one of her favourite jewels.

And so, we arrive at the end of this long voyage across six hundred years of history. These centuries have often been turbulent for the diamonds of the European monarchies. As we have seen, this story is almost entirely restricted to the distant past. Republics have swept away the majority of the monarchies, and the royal diamonds - at least, those that have not disappeared - now glitter inside museums' showcases or vaults. The same is true in the constitutional monarchies: ostentation is no longer considered appropriate. Our chances of seeing such magnificent gems sparklingagain depend largely upon the longevity of the current Queen of England. The *Koh-i-Noor* and the *Cullinans I* and *II* will glitter with every move of her successor's head. In order to see comparable gems, one would have to leave Europe and attend official functions in the monarchies of the Middle East or Brunei: oil sheikhs and their wives are adorned with the most recent large diamonds from African mines, as well as some historical stones. This is what happened to the Jubilee and Centenary diamonds and, in fact, the majority of the large gems that have disappeared from view in the last few decades.

Portrait of Queen Victoria, by François-Xavier Winterhalter. She wears a suite of diamond jewels, including a diadem that was part of her private jewellery collection (it was later dismantled), and a necklace that was later bequeathed to the Crown Jewels. The large jewel at her bust is the *Koh-i-Noor* itself, which had been re-cut to 105.6 carats. At the time, it was set in a brooch.

Official portrait of Queen Elizabeth II, by Sir James Gunn (1893-1964). She wears the Regal Circlet diadem. Her necklace has 25 brilliant-cuts, weighing 161 carats in total, with the 22.48-carat Lahore diamond as a pendant. The earrings weigh 13 carats each. They were re-cut from two Indian pear-shapes that were taken from the armlet in which the Koh-i-Noor was originally set. The Order of the Garter's gold collar is across her chest, suspending a diamond-set statuette of St. George. The 1937 Imperial State Crown and the Royal Sceptre are by her right hand: they contain the *Cullinan I* and *Cullinan II.*

iusque les propr
lateur & de ses pr
sont descriptes
ml. Il reste a di
chose a laide de n

CHAPTER XIII

Robyn Fréchet
& Hubert Bari

Adamas the invincible:

The sacred nature of the diamond

Because of their colour, brilliance, transparency and apparent inalterability, gems are fit for the gods, and only their most privileged earthly representatives. From a very early age, a highly specific literature evolved to discuss these exceptional substances. It was transmitted through lapidaries (gem texts) and encyclopaedias in all manner of languages: Greek, Arabic, Sanskrit, Latin, Persian and even Chinese. Diamond inevitably came to be accorded the most prestigious position in these texts. From the dawn of time, it has been revered for its hardness, for the mystery of its heavily-guarded Indian mines, and particularly for its rarity. Diamond was to engender a whole corpus of scientific and symbolic texts, particularly in the medieval period. These endowed the gem with a singular and sacred aura.

Pursuing diamonds through these texts is an exciting but complicated adventure. From the outset, the reader is presented with a formidable challenge: the designation of the stone itself is highly variable. By persevering through the inexhaustible lengths of library shelves devoted to the subject, the reader ultimately reaches a level of understanding that is sufficient to establish a picture of this mythical and sacred stone. This picture is somewhat distant from its mineral identity, which was not to be properly determined until the early 19th century.

The Book of the Properties of Things by Bartholomew the Englishman (ca. 1230-1240), in Jean de Corbichon's 15th-century French translation. The section on precious stones is headed by a miniature that reveals a fantastical mountain landscape, where gems were said to originate. The valley floor is studded with stones borne down by mountain streams. One can see beds of sapphires and rubies, as well as a bed of white stones, probably representing diamonds.

Offir est une region qui est situee es parties de Inde. Et dit Solin que en celle region les montaignes y sont. Et si y a moult grant habondance de pierres precieuses et de tous biens et de toutes et de toutes autres richesses que homme pourroit souhaiter. Mais en celle region il nest nul homme tant soit il fort et puissant soit sarrazin ou cristien qui y ouze habiter ne demourer pour la grant multitude et terrible oppression des bestes sauvaiges qui sont cruelles et horribles et venimeuses. et qui en icelle riche et noble region habitant que tout homme quilz rencontrent devourant transglotissant et mangeussent. Comme grans serpens et dragons vollans getans feu et venin par la gueulle et par les narines et lyons liepars tigres et lonnes cerues. Mais toutesfoiz les marchans qui vont et viennent en leurs vaisseaulx par la mer se enhardissent aucunesfoiz en aucune saison de lan de aller vagant et nageant au long des rivages de la mer a lendroit de celles riches et nobles montaignes dor qui sont en celle re

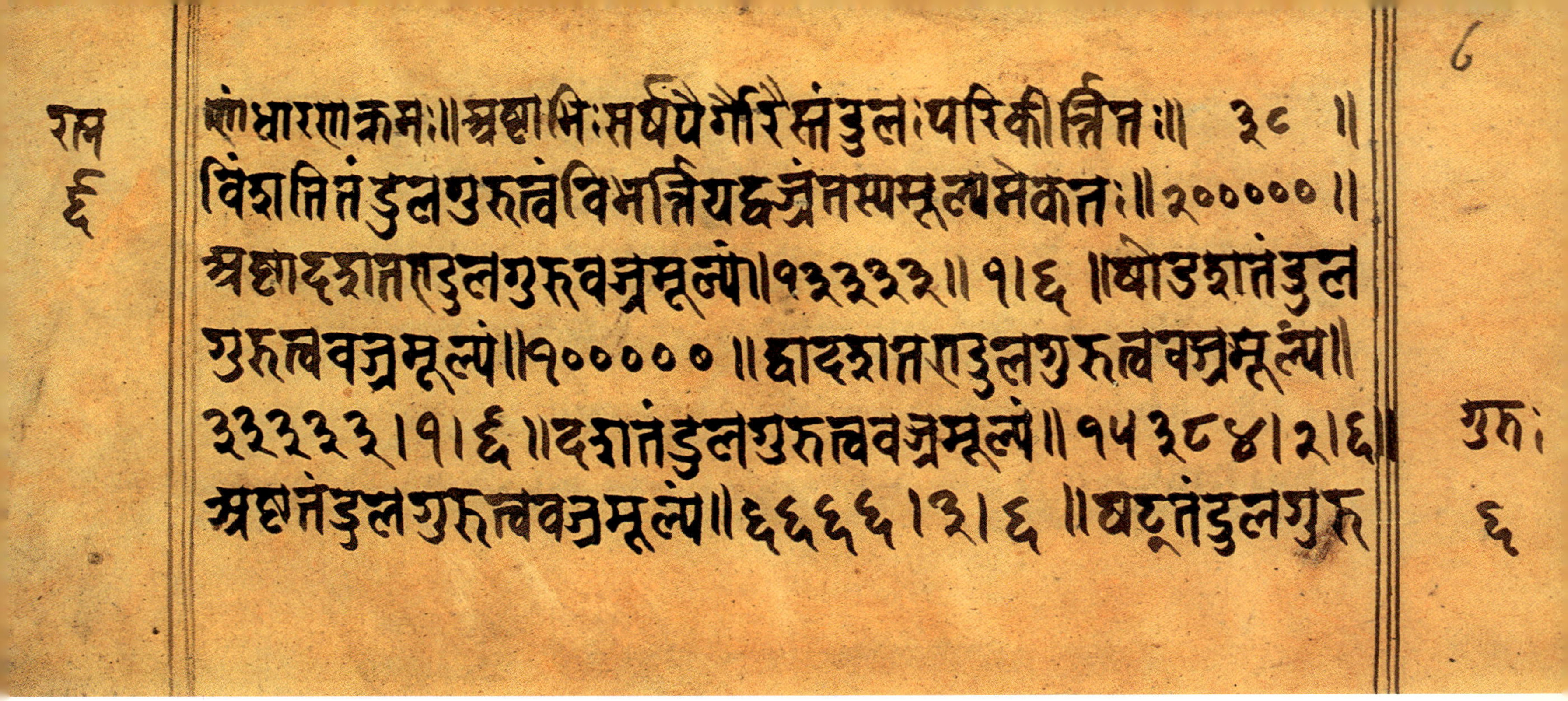

In the realm of Indra and Buddha

India, the ancient birthplace of diamond, naturally contains the earliest known corpus of sacred texts concerning the gem. India has always been a land dominated by a religion of multiple divinities and spirits, devoted to maintaining the world free of the chaos to which it was naturally destined. The cosmic energy necessary to maintain universal cohesion is supplied by the devotion and the offerings of the faithful. In a climate of continual fear of destruction, diamond's immovable nature and absolute hardness made it an indispensable attribute with which to honour the god Indra. Indra is somewhat analogous to the Greek god Zeus: he brandishes a thunderbolt. This is traditionally represented in sculpture by a mace, the ends of which could have been inspired by the natural form of diamond crystals. The Sanskrit term vajra denotes Indra's thunderbolt. Through semantic analogy, diamond also assumed this name. This is found not only in the surviving sacred texts (generally Buddhist), but also in the (generally Hindu) lapidaries.

The basic corpus of Hindu lapidaries is comprised of commercial manuals. The opening pages of these manuals are concerned with the forms of diamond crystals. Naturally, these works establish the quality criteria for rough diamonds, since diamond-cutting had not yet been discovered at the time. Market price, in turn, depended upon quality criteria. The texts use symbolism to embellish the gem's physical characteristics. Diamond's beneficial powers become sales pitches. They are attributed with the power to protect against various risks that assail humanity, such as poison, snakes, sickness and sinful behaviour. Buddhabhatta, the 6th-century author of one of these lapidaries, summarises the diamond's ability to pave the way to prosperity: "He who has a pure body, and who carries on his person a diamond that is sharp-pointed, without blemish and entirely flawless, shall daily increase his worth in happiness, prosperity, children, wealth, crops, cows and livestock, to the end of his life."

Some time later, Varahamihira completed his lapidary, the *Brhatsamhita*. It incorporates a warning against flawed diamonds. These supposedly attract the risks of loss of family, fortune and life. In contrast, a good diamond not only eliminates enemies, but also ensures vast wealth to royalty. For its part, the *Agastimata* reinforces the links between diamond and the divine realm. It recounts how, at the request of the thirteen gods, an *asura* named Bala was sacrificed for the benefit of the heavens: "Having ceded his entire body, the *asura* was struck by a thunderbolt on the head, from which sprang mountains of [different types of] gems". The first type of these gems was called *vajra* (diamond), and the text goes on to discuss eight excellent diamond mine-sites.

This illustration is from a manuscript (ca. 1480) of the *Secrets de l'Histoire Naturelle*. The artist has attempted to represent an alluvial site. Stone hunters dig with pickaxes, apparently oblivious to the snakes and dragons infesting the area. The text talkes of a site in India, where the mountains teem with incredible wealth. French National Library, Paris, Western Manuscript Department.

A page from a 19th-century Sanskrit manuscript of the *Ratnapariksha*, a famous Hindu treatise on precious stones in India. This page describes the relationship between a diamond's weight and its price. French National Library, Paris, Oriental Manuscript Department.

A Tibetan *Vajra*-diamond, probably 18th century. It is an exceptional and rare example of the vajra's symbolic nature, because it is sculpted in rock crystal. 20 cm long. Private collection.

Two views of a 26-cm-long bronze Vajra-diamond. This is an extremely ancient and remarkable depiction of a diamond-thunderbolt. When viewed end-on, one can see the slight resemblance to an octahedral diamond crystal. Klaten region, central Java, 9th-10th century. National Museum, Jakarta.

In contrast to Hindu literature, where a stone's commercial worth matters as much as its symbolic import, Buddhist texts concentrate upon the sacred and philosophical nature of diamond. Prince Siddhartha Gautama, the original Buddha, was born in the late 6th century BC. His philosophy was disseminated in two great ways: the *Hinayana* (the original Buddhism of the Small Vehicle) and the *Mahayana* (the Buddhism of the Great Vehicle). Buddha's teachings were recorded by his disciples in the form of sutras, the corpus of sacred Buddhist texts. *Sutra* is a Sanskrit term, denoting a cord upon which jewels are threaded.

The *Diamond Sutra* is the most profound *sutra* of the Buddhist pleiad. To be precise, its full name is the "*Sutra* of the perfection of wisdom, which cuts like the diamond thunderbolt". True wisdom is therefore characterised by its indestructible nature. The sutra is addressed to the venerable Subhuti. Subhuti was one of the ten principal disciples of Shakyamuni (the historical Buddha, silent sage of the Shakya clan). Subhuti was also the disciple who had achieved the most complete understanding of how to explain emptiness, or vacuity. Without ever referring to the stone itself, the *Diamond Sutra* is intended to show how to cut through illusion. By so doing, a disciple of the Buddha can understand the underlying reality that remains after illusion has been completely stripped away. This underscores the destructive power of the *Vajracchedika Prajna Paramita* (virtue of wisdom) dialectic: diamond cuts with an infinitesimal dissection that reduces appearances to nothing, as effectively as a volley of thunderbolts. Some 10th century manuscripts, found in the Dunhuang caves in the Chinese North-West, are embellished with the eight vajra guardian athletes, armed with their diamond thunderbolts. The British Library has a famous copy of the Diamond sutra that has been dated to 868: it is the earliest-known printed text. In the predication scene, which introduces the text, there is a depiction of two vajra thunderbolts on either side of the Buddha. The text itself was translated into Chinese by Kumarajiva in 402.

Ancient texts contain further allusions to the diamond. For example, *vajradhatu* is the term for the kingdom of awakened consciousness. This is quite distinct from the world of mere appearances, made of ephemeral phenomena. At the moment of Buddha's enlightenment, he sits upon a throne under the sacred tree. This throne is distinguished from any other throne by its adamantine quality, as encapsulated in the Sanskrit term *vajrasana*. Avalokitesvara, the *bodhisattva* of compassion, is also depicted sitting upon an adamantine rock. Avalokitesvara renounced Buddhahood in order to intercede for mankind. The bodhisattva's Chinese name (*Guan Yin* or *Guan Shi Yin*) specifically evokes the deity's benevolent eye on the cries of distress emanating from the mortal world. Avalokitesvara-Guanyin's intercession is beautifully described in a famous chapter of the *Lotus Sutra* entitled "The one who sees in all directions". A believer may escape from many catastrophes (including the collapse of diamond mountains) if he or she invokes the bodhisattva's name.

A third path of Buddhism - tantric Buddhism - developed in the first few centuries AD. Significantly, it became known as *Vajrayana* Buddhism, or Diamond Way Buddhism. By the 7th century, this third way had made its home in Tibet. It assimilated an entire, pre-existing, strongly animist religious philosophy, giving rise to Tibetan Lamaism. To attain awareness or enlightenment, Diamond Way Buddhism introduced psychic techniques based upon yoga. Adepts intensify concentration by reciting the sacred formula (*mantra*), and by practising meditation in front of a diagram (*mandala*) that represents the world. The *mandala* may be painted, sculpted or evoked in a pattern of sand or rice. Posture is important for concentration: hand gestures are codified, as are body positions. The best-known of these is the lotus position, which is more precisely termed the *vajraparyanka* or "diamond position".

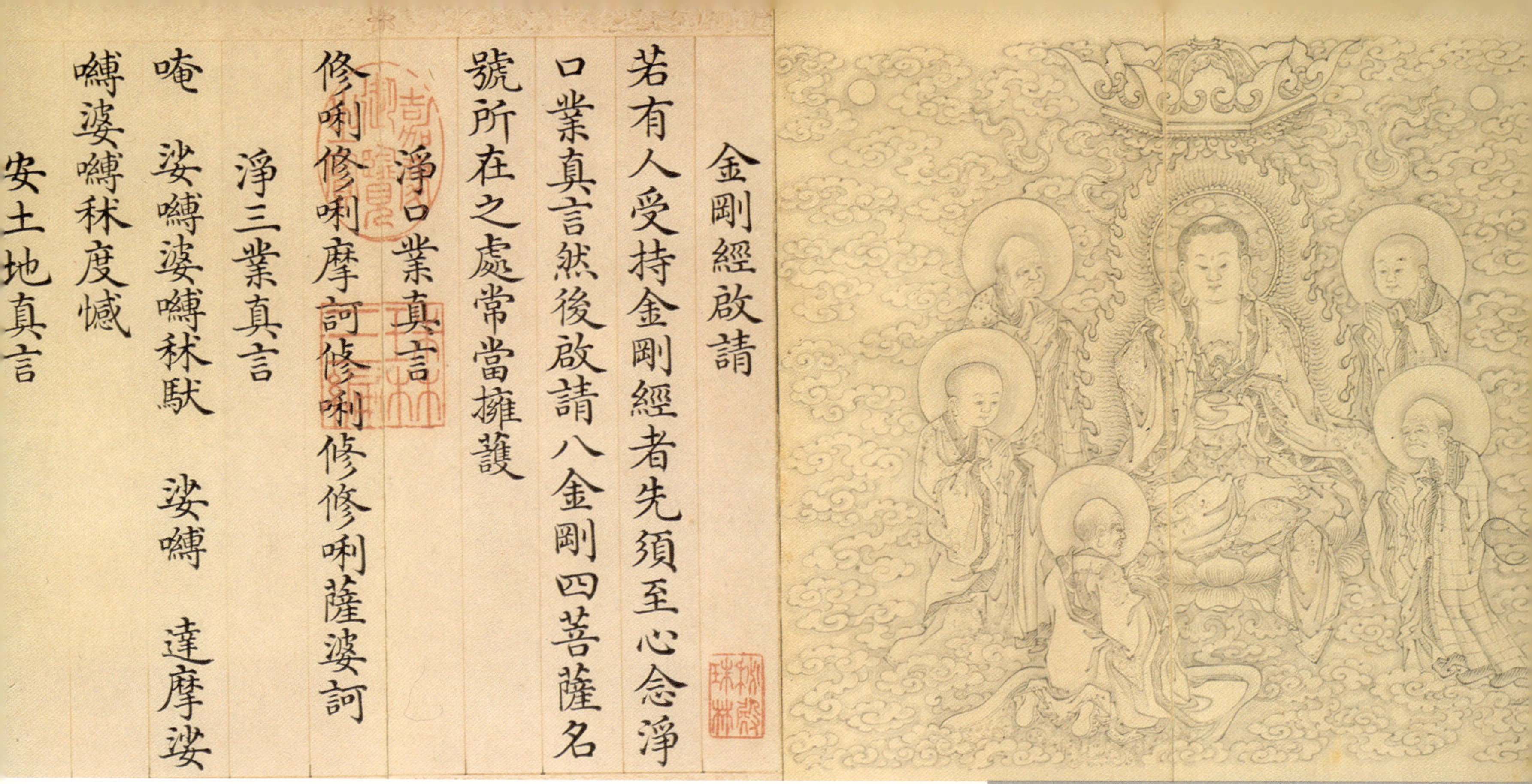

金剛經啟請

若有人受持金剛經者先須至心念淨
口業真言然後啟請八金剛四菩薩名
號所在之處常當擁護

淨口業真言

修唎修唎摩訶修唎修修唎薩婆訶

淨三業真言

唵 娑嚩婆嚩秫駄 娑嚩 達摩娑
嚩婆嚩秫度憾

安土地真言

A hand-written copy of the *Diamond Sutra*. This manuscript has 90 accordion-folded pages. The introductory drawing depicts Buddha, teaching a circle of disciples. The venerable Subhuti kneels before him. The text was translated by Kumarajiva, and the beautiful calligraphy was performed by Mien-ngen († 1822), Emperor Quianlong's grandson. Musée Guimet, Paris.

The *vajra*-diamond symbol is all-pervasive in Buddhist practice throughout Tibet and the regions under its influence (extending over more or less the whole of the Himalayan region). All cult members possess one, and carry it during religious ceremonies. In temples, *vajra*-diamonds may assume the form of fine bronze double-sceptres, sometimes up to several feet long. In rare cases, they are even made of more precious materials, such as quartz or jade, for example. A four-pointed variety exists, which is formed by crossing two vajra. Ceremonial practices require the celebrant to carry a *vajra* in the right hand, and a bell in the left. The bell has a *vajra* handle. This enhances the significance of the bell's role, as a metal cast that envelops emptiness -the object of the religious teaching. The bell symbolises awareness, engendered in the void, or rupture with the illusory world. The *vajra* surmounting the bell alludes to its original meaning: diamond is the means to attain awareness, since it cuts through the universe of illusion. The *Vajrasattva* is a common representation of the Buddha, in the lotus position and holding the bell and the vajra. The *vajra* motif is also displayed on ritual objects, such as the ewer and dagger. Skull-shaped ewers are used as containers for ritual offerings of the five ambrosia (whether made of real or symbolic foodstuffs). Many of the countless statues of the divinities in the vast Tibetan pantheon are depicted holding *vajra* attributes, and the symbol also appears on *mandalas*.

A manuscript of the *Diamond Sutra*. This document is from the Chengdu region of China, and dates back to 905-907. It is decorated with depictions of athlete-guardians who protect the text, brandishing their vajra-diamond weapons, shown here as tripartite maces. French National Library, Paris, Oriental Manuscript Department.

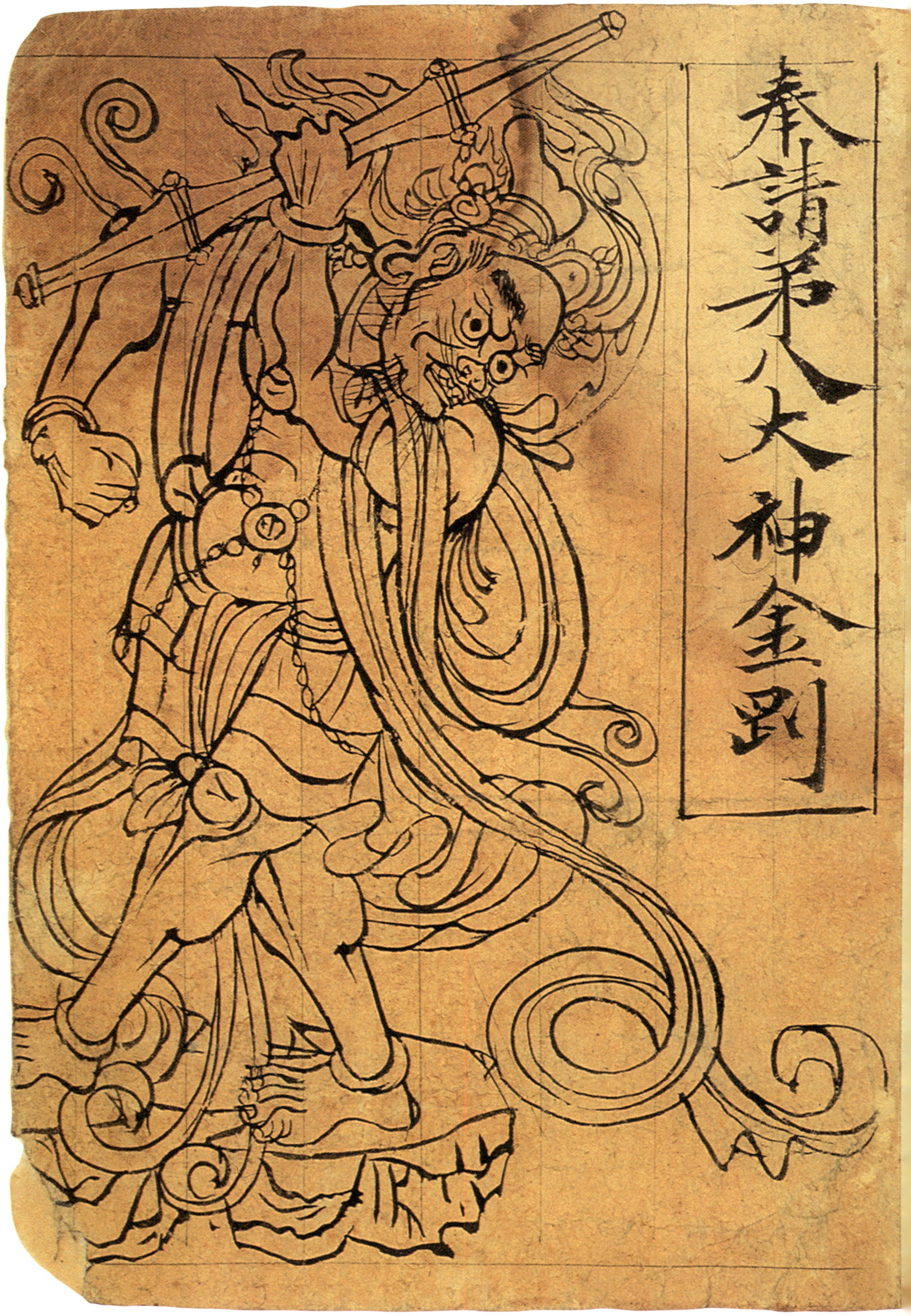
奉請弟八大神金剛

奉請弟七紫賢金剛

The sacred importance of the space at the heart of Tibetan tantric Buddhism, is also witnessed by the declarations of Padmasambhava. Padmasambhava was an 8th-century sage who is said to have founded the first Bsamyas temple. According to the *Sayings of Padma:*

> **...I accept the offer and gift of the Earth.**
> **King Khri Srong Ide'u btsan, make your idea a reality!**
> **Build a temple! The spirits will second your work.**
> **Padma the enchanter does not infringe the precepts.**
> **And off he flies, into the heavens pure.**
> **And wherever a Diamond Hero bore the shadow, the twenty-one non-human adepts [...] and the eight great planets and the 28 constellations of mountains and valleys gathered together earth and stones.**

This deified sage was of Indian origin. In Tibetan iconography, he is represented as a figure with a moustache, with an angry expression (to ward off the adversaries of Buddhism). His headgear is surmounted by a half-*vajra*, and he holds a full *vajra* in his right hand, leaving the left free to grasp the goblet of ambrosia, elixir of immortality. It is said that, when he executed his aerial dance, he cast a shadow on the ground that marked out, or consecrated, the area that was destined to receive the Bsamyas temple. This was his way of transmitting the power and permanence of the *vajra*-diamond into the very foundations of the future temple. A dance known as the "diamond-step" commemorates this event. Through this gesture, a potentially hostile space is transformed into a place worthy of religious practice.

This philosophy is perhaps the greatest symbolic evocation of the diamond in religious history and, remarkably, it took shape in a part of the world where diamond had probably never been seen. No actual diamond has been found in the ornaments of divinities, or in Tibetan monasteries' jewels and treasures. More than any other Buddhist practice, Lamaism discovered how to draw out diamond's singular characteristics of inalterability and indestructibility, rendering it a vital teaching tool. The technique showed how to abandon the commonplace view of reality; in this case, the physicality of stone itself, which is nothing more than an illusion. Although Western religious philosophy was also seduced by the symbolism of diamond's inalterability, it nevertheless never let go of the material reality of the stone and its commercial value: it was the possession of actual diamond which conferred power.

The great secret

The earliest references to the circulation of diamonds as merchandise are very ancient. As early as the first century AD, diamond is known to have been included in cargoes leaving the port of Bakare, situated at the mouth of the Nelkynda river on the Coromandel coast of South-East India. This is according to the *Periple of the Erythrean Sea*, a well-known navigation guide for the route from the Red Sea to the Indian ocean, written ca. 80 AD. In Justinian's *Digest*, a list dating from the 4th century AD, diamond is mentioned as one of the goods subject to taxation, alongside spices and drugs from India, silk fabrics, linen, Babylonian furs, cosmetics, leopards, panthers and eunuchs. According to the *Daily Acts of the Tsin Emperors* (265-419), diamonds circulated in the Far East at Dunhuang in 277. This observation is repeated in later Chinese encyclopaedias of pharmacopoeia.

These documents discuss the stone's commercial reality. In contrast, a body of written legends also developed around the stone. These legends tend to distance the diamond from any concretely identifiable source or mine. Reading these texts, one has the impression that the early Indian diamond barons consciously cultivated myths around the origin of these precious stones, in order to guard against the risk of deposits being pillaged. The tenacious legend of the Valley of Diamonds, which persisted for centuries, may be interpreted in this light. The earliest-known allusion to such a valley occurs in the *De Duodecim Lapidibus* (ca. 394) by Epiphanius, the Bishop of Salamis on Cyprus. This text, in fact, refers to another stone: the hyacinth or eaglestone (an ancient name for garnet). According to this legend, hyacinths were found at the bottom of an inaccessible ravine in Scythia. Joints of mutton were cast into the chasm, to which the stones adhered. Eagles flew down to seize the meat, and carried it off in their claws. In China, the legend had already become firmly associated with diamonds by the Tang period. At this time, the diplomat writer Zhang Yue (667-730) wrote his *Memoires of the Four Worthies* [502-519] *of the Liang Dynasty*. According to this text, the valley is located on an island in the Western sea of the Fu-Lin kingdom (i.e. the Roman empire). For the first time, Alexander became linked to the legend in a text that was attributed to Aristotle, but which was probably written by Luca ben Serapion (the son of Serapion, or the Pseudo-Aristotle), *ca.* 750. The text was transmitted through an Arab lapidary. It locates the valley in the Eastern Khorassan, and states that, when Alexander reached it with his men, the valley was protected by snakes capable of killing with their very gaze. According to the text, Alexander had the idea of holding mirrors before the snakes, so that they were killed by their own eyes. Having cleared access to the valley, the Pseudo-Aristotelian tale resumes the traditional sequence, with the pieces of flesh tossed into the valley, the stones adhering, and the birds bearing the meat away. Alexander and his men then retrieved the gems from the birds. In the 10th century, an Arab traveller located the Valley of Diamonds in the Kashmir region in his *Marvels of India*. In addition to the plague of serpents, the author specifies an additional challenge to explorers: a fire, burning day and night, summer and winter. Qazwini's version (1203-1283) moves the valley to Serendib (or Ceylon) and attributes the idea of using meat to recover the diamonds to Alexander himself. Qazwini warns that if the diamond is found contaminated by saliva containing venom from the vipers guarding the valley, it may break the teeth. His savant contemporary Ahmed Teifachi († 1253), takes the legend back to India, with no reference to either snakes or Alexander. The diamonds - dispersed in the valley as mustard seeds or barley - are carried off to the mountain heights by eagles, attracted to the meat. The story circulated in Persian and Turkish literature via the Pseudo-Aristotle lapidary, in the *Eskandar Nameh* (1196-1209), a section of the Five Poems, or *Khamseh*, written by the famous poet Nizami.

The renowned Catalan Atlas: this is a detail from a map of the world, drawn in Majorca in 1375. It shows the Valley of Diamonds as the source of a major river, with snakes protecting a lake, which is also the site of the Garden of Eden. French National Library, Paris, Western Manuscript Department.

In the early 15th century, a Parisian illuminated-manuscript workshop illustrated a famous copy of Marco Polo's travels, the *Livre des Merveilles du Monde (The Book of Marvels)*. It is preserved today in the French National Library. There is an illustration for the legend: it depicts the Valley of Diamonds, protected by serpents and surrounded by birds of prey. Travellers look for stones among

grant foy en buef et le tiennent pour sainte chose. Sy prennent du poil des
buefs sauvaiges et le lient au col de leur cheual. Et s'il est homme a pie il
met de ce poil a son escu. ou a ses cheveux mesmes. Si que par ceste raison est
ce poil chier et s'en fia asses. Car nul qui va en ost n'est asseur s'il n'a de ce poil
de buef. Car il avient que par cellui poil. chascun qui la soit sauue en bataille.
le. Or vous ay compte de ceste prouince de maabar une grant partie. Sy nous
nous partirons de cy atant. et vous compterons du royaume de mutfili
cy avant si comme vous pourrez oir et entendre.

Cy devise du royaume de mutfili.

Et quant l'en se part de maabar et l'en va entour mille
milles par tremontaines. si treuue l'en adonc le royaume
de mutfili. Et fu iadis a un roy. et depuis qu'il mourut bien
xl. ans avoit. adonc la royne sa femme l'ama tant que
onques depuis ne se voult marier a nullui pour l'amour
de son mary. Et en tout ce terme de quarante ans avoit tenu son royau
me aussy bien ou mieux que onques le tint son baron. Sy que pour ce
qu'elle amoit bien et iustice et paix estoit elle amee de chascun. ilz sont ydolatres et
ne font treuaige a nullui. il vivent de char et de ris et de lait. En ce royaume
treuue l'en les dyamans. et vous diray comment ilz ont moult grans mon
taingnes. et en yver fait moult grans pluies. et voient les yaues descendant
par ces montaignes a grant bruit faisant et par moult grans ruisseaux.
Et quant les pluies sont passees. et l'eaue des montaignes sont coulees sy
cherchent par ou l'eaue est coulee de ces ruisseaux et en treuuent asses. Et quant

the rocks, and speak with the region's ruler, Queen Mutfili. Oddly, the stones are red. This seems to suggest contact with the Epiphanius text, associating the legend with garnet.

Still in Europe, it is worth noting two Spanish references to the Valley of Diamonds myth, dating back to the 14th century. They appear to have been directly inspired through the Arabic manuscript tradition. The Spanish Lapidary was compiled ca. 1276-1278 for Alfonso X the Wise, the astronomer King of Castile. It describes how diamonds are found in the river when it is in spate, and borne to the surface by snakes (or rather creatures resembling worm-like snails, designated by the term *argollos*). The legend's universal circulation is proved by the famous Catalan Atlas, which depicts the valley between two juxtaposed mountains. The map's Jewish illuminator, attached to a Majorca workshop in 1375, includes a bird in the drawing. In its beak, it carries a morsel of meat, encrusted with stones. A river flows beneath, riddled with snakes. In the foreground, two men are shown cutting meat. A brief caption explains the diamond-gathering technique: "These men went to gather diamond, but as they cannot reach the mountains where the stones lie, they adroitly fling down pieces of meat. The birds eventually drop the stones adhering to the meat, and thus they can be collected. This is what Alexander saw."

The medieval priesthood realised that the myth had allegorical value. There are traces of the legend in a 13th-century preaching manual: it has been adapted as a moral example *(exemplum)*. There are no longer diamonds but pearls strewn at the bottom of the precipice, and the meat thrown into the chasm is that of a skinned goat. The valley is set close to the celebrated Crusader site, Damietta. The preacher transforms the whole story into an allegory of Christ descending into Limbo, to rescue souls that deserve to be saved.

From Antiquity to medieval exegesis

Diamond originally derived its name from the Greek term adamas, which was current in all the early Western texts concerning the stone. Lucretius knew the stone by this name in Cicero's time. Lucretius was the author of the first *De Natura Rerum* encyclopaedia. With astonishing intuition, he described diamond's structure, two thousand years before scientists established the truth. He speaks of *adamantina saxa* as a substance "amongst those solid and hard matters, formed of elements more closely hooked and held, knit deeply together by branched shapes (whose ramifications form between them a tightly condensed fabric)". This stone is notable, he writes, for its capacity to despise any blow, having the "density of rigid iron and bronze sockets that shriek out as they resist the door-bolts".

Pliny the Elder's (23-79) famous *Natural History* definitively established diamond's traditional properties, and imposed its most reliable identity in the term *"adamas"*. This term would be repeatedly used in texts until the Renaissance. Subsequent texts were, on the one hand, scientifically oriented, yet on the other hand they were also imbued with a sacred vocation, embellished and emphasised according to circumstances, but always faithful to the properties as they had been defined by the Latin scholar. The fact that diamond was demonstrably absent from all biblical texts did not discourage authors or textual commentators from exegetical comment. Paying no heed to any anomaly, they were driven to mention diamond because of its irresistible potential as a symbol in moral discussion. St. Jerome's (347-420) commentaries on Zachary and Amos are a good example. The twelve stones of Aaron's pectoral (Exodus 28: 15-21) and the gems that made up heavenly Jerusalem (*Apocalypse* 1: 18-20) are included in the earliest Christian lapidaries, such as that of Epiphanius. In such texts, adamantine references were not present. However, the temptation was too great. The *De Adamante Gemma*, a Greek text which was also originally attributed to Epiphanius but later reassigned to Anastasis the Sinaite, discusses a diamond that the priest supposedly wore on three major

Livre des Merveilles du Monde. This well-known illuminated text of Marco Polo's travels includes a representation of the Valley of Diamonds. Queen Mutfili watches the diamond-hunters in the famous valley, which is located in her kingdom. The birds seek the diamond-encrusted joints of meat and will carry them up to their nests in the mountain-tops. French National Library, Paris, Western Manuscript Department.

C. Plynii Secundi naturalis hiſtorie Liber. II.

Mundus & hoc qđ alio noïe celum appellari libuit: cuius circũflexu teguntur cuncta: numen eſſe credi par eſt. eternũ. immenſũ. neq; genitum. neq; interiturum unq̃. huius extera indagare. nec intereſt hominum: nec capit humane coniectura mentis: ſacer eſt. eternus. immenſus. Totus in toto: immo uero ipſe totum. infinitus ac finito ſimilis. omnium rerum certus: & ſimilis incerto. Extra intra cuncta complexus in ſe. idemq; rerum nature opus. & rerũ ipſa natura. ¶ Furor eſt menſuram eius animo quoſdam agitaſſe. atq; prodere auſos. ¶ Alios rurſus occaſione hinc ſumpta aut his data innumerabiles tradidiſſe mundos. ut totidem rerũ naturas credi oporteret. aut ſi una omnes incubarent: totidem tamen ſoles: totidemq; lunas & cetera etiã in uno & immenſa & innumerabilia ſidera: q̃ſi non eadẽ queſtiõe ſemper in termino cogitationis occurſura deſiderio finis alicuius. ¶ Aut ſi hec infinitas nature omnis artifici poſſit aſſignari: non illud idem in uno facilius ſit intelligi. tanto preſertim opere. ¶ Furor eſt profecto furor: egredi ex eo. & tãq̃ interna eius cũcta plane iam ſint nota: ita ſcrutari extera. quaſi uero menſuram ullius rei poſſit agere. q ſui neſciat. aut mens hominis uidere: quem mundus ipſe non capiat. ¶ Formam eius in ſpeciem orbis abſoluti globatam eſſe: nomen in primis & conſenſus in eo mortaliũ orbem appellantium: ſed & argumenta rerum docent. Non ſolum quia talis figura omnibus ſui partibus uergit in ſeſe: ac ſibi ipſa tolleranda eſt ſeq; includit & continet: nullarũ egens compaginum: nec finem aut initium ullis ſui partibus ſentiens: nec quia ad motum quo ſubinde uerti debeat: ut mox apparebit: talis aptiſſima eſt: ſed oculorum quoq; probatione ꝙ conuexus mediusq; quacunq; cernatur. cum id accidere in alia non poſſit figura. ¶ Hanc ergo formam eius eterno & irrequieto ambitu inenarrabili celeritate. xxiiii. horarum ſpatio circũagi ſolis exortus & occaſus haud dubium reliquere. ¶ An ſit immenſus: & ideo ſenſũ auriũ excedens tante molis rotate uertigĩe aſſidua ſonitus non equidem facile dixerim. non hercule magis q̃ circũactorum ſimul tinnitus ſiderũ: ſuoſq; uoluentiũ orbes: an dulcis quidẽ & incredibili ſuauitate cõcẽtus. nobis q intus agimur iuxta diebus noctibuſq; tacitus labit mũdus. ¶ Eſſe innumeras ei effigies animaliũ rerumq; cunctarum impreſſas: nec ut in uolucrum notamus ouis lenitate cõtinua lubricũ corpus qđ clariſſimi autores dixere teneꝝ: argumẽtis ĩdicat: quoniam inde deciduis rerum omniũ ſeminibus innumere in mari precipue ac plerũq; confuſis monſtrifice gignantur effigies. ¶ Preterea uiſus probatiõe. alibi plauſtra. alibi urſi. tauri alibi. alibi littere figura. candidiore medio ſuper uerticem circulo. ¶ Eqdẽ & conſenſu gentium moueor. nã quẽ Coſmon Greci nomine ornamẽti appellauerũt. eum & nos a perfecta abſolutaq; elegantia mundũ. ¶ Celũ quidem haud dubie celati argumento diximus: ut interpretatur. M. Varro. ¶ Adiuuat rerum ordo: deſcripto circulo qui Signifer uocatur: in. xii. animalium effigies & per illas ſolis curſu cõgruẽs tot ſeculis ratio. ¶ Nec de elementis uideo dubitari: quottuor eſſe ea. ¶ Igneũ ſummo. inde tot ſtellarum illos collucentium oculos. ¶ Proximum ſpiritus: quem greci noſtriq; eodem uocabulo aera appellant. uitalem hunc ac per cuncta rerum meabilem. totoq; conſertũ. cuius ui ſuſpenſam cũ quarto aquaꝝ elemento librari medio ſpatii tellurẽ. ¶ Ita mutuo complexu diuerſitatis effici nexum. & leuia põderibus inhiberi quo minus euolent. contraq; grauia: ne ruant: ſuſpendi leuibus in ſublime tendentibus. ſic pari in diuerſa niſu in ſua queq; ſubſiſtere irrequieto mũdi ipſius cõſtricta circuitu. quo ſemp

[Marginal notes, handwritten: An mũdus infinitus et an un[us] — De forma mundi — De mundi motu — Cur mundus dicatur — Cur celum — De elementis]

annual celebrations: Easter, Pentecost and the Feast of the Tabernacle. On these occasions, the gem would appear black if the congregation had sinned, or gleam like snow if the congregation had been virtuous.

Above all, the Church Fathers refer to diamond in texts concerning the judgement and contrition of sinners. They made use of its exceptional physical resistance to draw analogies with both the intensity of faith of the true believer, and the exceptional obstinacy of the hard-hearted sinner. According to St. Gregory's (560-604) commentaries on Ezekiel (Ezekiel III, 9), when confronted with the preacher's critical judgement, one should present a diamond face rather than a face of flint. In other words, one should repent with neither shame nor bitterness. In the *Regula Pastoralis,* Gregory asserts that two types of sinners (those who fear punishment, and also those who are unmoved by it), must be won over by gentle chastisement, like the diamond that is untouched by iron but which is tempered by unctuous goat's blood.

At least one of the Christian lapidary texts adds diamond to the standard list of twelve Biblical stones. This anonymous version, based on Marbodus' celebrated lapidary verse (thought to have been written prior to his appointment as Bishop of Rennes in 1067), distinguishes four varieties of diamond. They are listed according to their supposed sources (India, Arabia, Cyprus and Macedonia). This text, as well as those of Pliny and Damigeron, enumerates these sites, which give the stones varying properties. Indian diamond is weakened only by goat's blood, Arabian diamond can be shattered by a blow from an iron or steel hammer, whilst diamonds from Cyprus and the mines of the Philippi in Macedonia attract iron. This latter property was destined to provoke considerable confusion later, between *"diamant"* (diamond) and *"aimant"* (magnet).

Marbodus, and most of the authors he inspired, confined diamond symbolism to its moral interpretation. In contrast, other lapidaries stress a stronger association of diamond with the divine, as can be discerned in the following lines, cited from an anonymous lapidary:

[...]Tres tout cil qui ont dyamant	(Those who possess the diamond,
Plus volentiers vont Dieu amant,	Love God more willingly,
Plus aimment Dieu, plus i esgardent	The greater their love for God, the greater His for them,
Qui tel pierre vielt esprover	He who seeks to experience such a stone
Loialment se devoit prover.	Must loyally set to work to prove himself.)

This text is from a manuscript that is preserved today in the French National Library collection in Paris. The manuscript is bound together with an Anglo-Norman Bestiary (1210-1211) compiled by Guillaume le Clerc. The Bestiary itself also includes a section devoted to stones, in which the description of diamond is particularly interesting, because of the accompanying illustration. This illuminated miniature is a rare pictorial representation of the sacred significance apportioned to diamond. A rock encrusted with three diamonds is placed directly beside the Crucifixion. The text draws its inspiration directly from the anonymous text of the Pseudo-Hugh of St. Victor, itself inspired by some lines referring to diamond in the *Physiologus*, the most ancient of the Bestiaries, originating in Alexandria towards the end of the second century AD. Guillaume le Clerc's explanation of the assimilation of the diamond with Christ is as follows:

Li mons ou la pierre est trovee	(The mountain where the stone,
Qui tant est dure et esprovee	So hard and proven, is found
Senefie Dieu nostre pere.	Signifies God our Father.
La pierre qui moult par [nuit] est clere,	The stone shining everywhere
Doit senefier Ihesucrist	Must signify Jesus Christ
Qui por nous humanitei prist,	Who for humanity's sake came

Pliny the Elder's *Natural History.* The 37th and final volume contains a section on gems that describes diamond. This is the book that defined diamond's properties, particularly its hardness, from Antiquity until Lessing's time (in the 18th century). Illuminated manuscripts of Pliny's work are very rare, particularly printed ones such as this one, which was produced in Rome by Sweynheym and Pannartz in 1470. French National Library, Paris.

Religious texts starting addressing the link between Christ and diamond from the 12th century onwards. These writings justified the use of the gem in precious jewels, from the end of the Middle Ages up to the 17th century. The cross above is set with rectangular table-cut diamonds, with a rose-cut at the base. Probably Portuguese, late 16th century. National Ancient Art Museum, Lisbon.

Christ's trigram, IHS, inscribed in diamonds on a mid-17th-century Portuguese pendant. National Ancient Art Museum, Lisbon.

The Anglo-Norman Bestiary of Guillaume le Clerc. The lapidary section is decorated with an exceptional illuminated miniature. The Trinity - God, crucified Christ and the Holy Spirit (flanked by the Virgin and St. John) - is a visual counterpoint to the diamond-encrusted pillar alongside. French National Library, Paris, Western Manuscript Department.

En tenebres nous visita,	To visit us in the darkness
De clartei nous enlumina.	With brightness to enlighten us.
En la sainte letre lisons	In the holy scriptures we read
Celi q(u)' evangile apelons	He who we name Evangelist
Celi sauveres dist de soi	He the Redeemer, who says of himself
Je sui ou Pere et Il en moi	I am in the Father and He in me
Et qui me vient il vient mon pere	And he who comes to me comes to the Father
Qui nasqui de la Virge mere.	The one who is born of the Virgin Mother.)

Peter of Beauvais completed his bestiary before 1206, in which he expresses the same point of view, also relying on the text of Pseudo-Hugh of St. Victor: "The diamond [loving-stone (*pierre d'aimant*)] represents Jesus Christ, and the mountain of Orient where the stone is found represents God." This rock is assimilated to Christ, and announces his power, which reflects upon the worthy: "and, based on this word *adamante*, all the saints are named adamantini by the prophets, in the name of Christ". These saints' holiness is determined by their resistance in adversity, which allows Guillaume le Clerc to add:

Et cestes pierre entendeiz	(And this stone signifies that
Les apostres bons eureiz	The blessed apostles,
Les profetes et les bons sains	The prophets and the good saints
C'oncques ne furent faus ne fains,	Were never false nor feeble,
Oncques por torment ne flechirent	Nor ceding in the face of torment
Mais por Dieu martyr soufrirent	But for God's sake suffered martyrdom.)

These Earthly *adamantini* (representatives of Christ) seem to have their origin in St. Jerome's commentary on a passage from Amos' book (Amos VII, 7-8). This borrowing demonstrates how diamond was bathed in a biblical aura by the Church Fathers' exegesis. It also shows how its powerful symbolism became amplified over the course of the medieval period: the man (Christ) stands upon the adamantine wall (according to St. Jerome, the wall evokes the Saints and the Apostles, which are called *adamantes* because of their invincibility). He holds the rock (here specified as adamas) in his hand, which he casts into the midst of the people of Israel. This *adamas* was St. Peter, the strongest of the disciples, that even the gates of Hell could not resist. But if the rock had not been held in the hand of God, neither it (nor St. Peter) would have preserved its strength.

It may be extrapolated that, once the Church Fathers had taken control of diamond and linked it with biblical citations where it was originally never mentioned, there was nothing to prevent authors from using variants *ad infinitum*. The texts orient their symbolism around three of diamond's dominant qualities: brilliance, hardness and, strangely enough, its supposedly magnetic qualities.

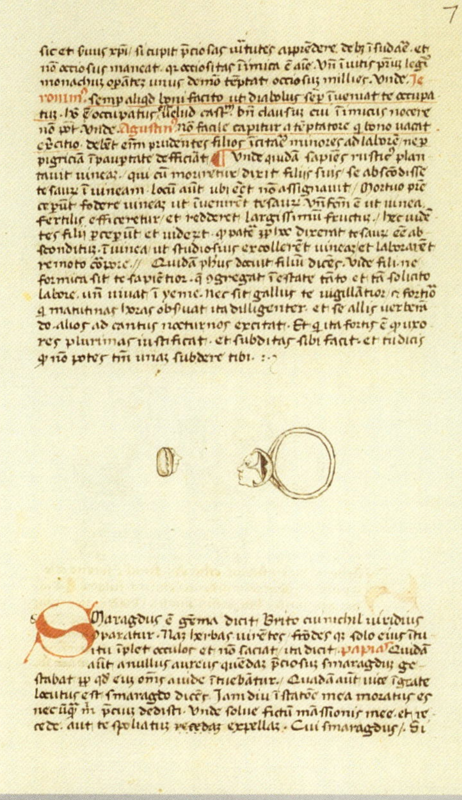

The Contemptus Sublimitatis or *Dialogue des Créatures*, 15th century. Fol. 7 shows the ring-mounted carbuncle and the [looking-]glass confronting each other. The carbuncle's properties, as described in the text, appear to be those of diamond. The verso depicts a jeweller setting a gem, possibly a diamond, in a ring. French National Library, Paris, Western Manuscript Department.

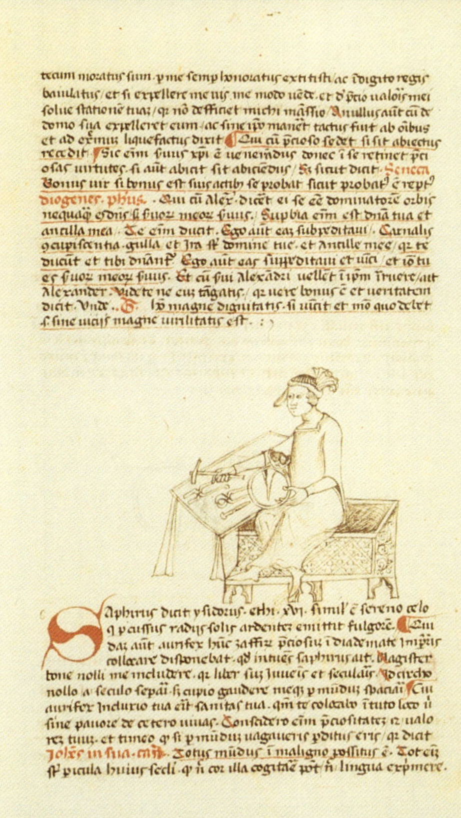

Diamond's brilliance and luminosity

According to the anonymous author of the *Physiologus*, diamond may be linked with divine power for one fundamental reason: its brilliance. Guillaume le Clerc extrapolates on this property:

On l'en trueve une pierre dure	(It is found to be a hard stone
Qant on la quiert par aventure	When seeking by chance
Mais ele ne luist pas par iour	But it does not light up by day
Car adonc pert sa resplendour	For it loses its splendour
Li solaus clers par veritei	The sun's brightness in truth
Li reboute sa grand clartei	Deprives it of its great clarity.

Since diamond's brilliance is eclipsed by that of the sun, authors concentrate on the diamond shining by night. In fact, diamonds do often possess a measure of luminosity, but this shows up only after exposure to ultraviolet light, which was naturally unknown to the ancients. It is therefore unclear where this insistence (that diamonds glowed in the dark) came from. However, these authors were probably unconsciously influenced by Indian stone merchants' accounts. These stated that, in order to determine a stone's quality, it was necessary to examine it in absolute darkness with only the light of a candle. This information was doubtless misquoted by too many merchants, leading to a false interpretation. The *Physiologus*' author made use of diamond's supposed luminescence in the dark to propose an analogy with the night-time birth of Christ in Bethlehem. The Pseudo-Hugh of St. Victor also noticed the symbolic potential of this property. He stated that the stone's luminescence cannot be discerned in daylight because the earth darkens its lustre, implying that Christ's descent among men was concealed by the divine glow of the angels, so preventing mankind from grasping the mystery of His earthly incarnation. Guillaume le Clerc simply postulates that, like the diamond, "The Lord visits us in the darkness, to illuminate us in His clarity". Peter of Beauvais expresses both points of view by concluding: "The fact that even if the stone does shine in daylight, we cannot see its clarity, represents the divine will to conceal Christ's incarnation, just as the fact that the stone shines at night signifies that Christ came down to man who was plunged in darkness".

On hardness and inalterability

Jeremiah's book already seems to imply a knowledge of the power of diamond's hardness, which is sufficient to engrave any other stone. According to a rare Syriac version of Ecclesiastes XVI, 4, God used a hard stone to divide light from darkness. These texts anticipate diamond's usefulness for cutting and grinding - a quality much appreciated by the Chinese, for jade-carving. Li Shizhen was a naturalist and doctor. He completed his great *Pharmacopoeia* in 1587, in which he describes how to sharpen a diamond point that has been blunted through use in stone-engraving. His prescription seems strange: it is simply a question of heating the diamond to red-heat, in order for it to recover its sharpness upon cooling. Arabic texts also applaud the stone's capacity to pierce, cut and polish all other stones. The "industrial" usefulness of diamond seems to have remained something of a poorly-understood paradox for early authors. In fact, the use of abrasive diamond grit for polishing, piercing and cutting implies reducing the stone to powder. But how can the hardest material be pulverised? After all, it was constantly lauded for its incomparable solidity. Mineralogy has since provided us with a scientific explanation: hardness is not synonymous with toughness. Diamond actually possesses directions of relative fragility ('cleavage planes') in its structure, which permit the stone to be reduced to fragments, each fragment conserving diamond's supreme hardness. This confusion between hardness and toughness originally stemmed from the ancient (and highly inaccurate) "anvil test": the stone to be tested was laid on an anvil and struck with a hammer. If it shattered, the diamond was declared a fake!

Traditional authors all concur that iron remains impotent in the face of adamantine hardness. Here, again, the Pseudo-Hugh of St. Victor provides a Christian interpretation of iron's weakness: "Iron is condemned to be as impotent as death, that the Lord vanquished with His spirit and His word, that which no other stone, nor human being, nor animal could do". Just as iron can do nothing to diamond, "so no man can contest God, who is everything", according to Peter of Beauvais.

But there was an exception to the rule. Diamond's indestructibility had a single, incontestable weakness to goat's blood. The medieval world never ceased to marvel upon it, yet no author seems to have been curious enough to check whether it was true. However, it is of course unlikely that any of the cited authors actually had an authentic diamond at their disposal, in order to try the experiment. However, at least one illuminated manuscript image seems to illustrate the test. The Fitzwilliam Museum in Cambridge owns an Anglo-Norman bestiary that contains an illustration, representing a man letting a diamond drop into a plate of blood. In this type of bestiary, the section on goats is found under the Latin name hircus, which describes a lustful and impetuous beast. According to Isidore of Seville, the animal's eyes look sidelong when the beast is animated by desire. However, since Pliny had already indicated diamond's sensitivity to goat's blood much earlier, the origin of the legend cannot be attributed to the Middle Ages, in the context of a God/Devil dichotomy. Not only is this supposed power mentioned by ancient authors, but also by the Chinese, who refer to the goat's ability to temper the stone. However, in this case the power is associated with the animal's horns rather than its blood: although the stone is capable of cutting jade, the Taoist Ko Hung (250-330) simply blew on a goat's horn to break the gem. One of Buddha's teeth, which was reputed to be a diamond, also faced this ultimate threat, but from the antelope's horn.

So the medieval West followed the lead of the original pagan Latin sources with regard to the goat's-blood issue, and turned it into a powerful Christian symbol. In an extraordinary feat of intellectual gymnastics, some authors transformed the goat's blood into the blood of Christ, in order to shatter the adamantine resistance of original sin. Helinand de Froidmont's sermons (ca. 1160-1229) use this image to exhort the sinner (who is adamantine in his stubborn resistance) to choose the path of virtue. "If the blood of the entrails of goats and oxen sanctifies, how much more so the blood of the lamb, the effusion of Christ's blood, designating his power to cleanse and to purify, has shaken the Earth, terrified hell and cleaved stones. And, in order that this blood reveal its moral significance, let it be known that, just as the diamond is cleaved by virtue of the blood of Christ, the obstinate sinner may likewise be tempered by penitence". The Norman bestiary of Philippe of Thaon (ca. 1123), on the other hand, retains blood and lead as symbols of corruption and sin, adversaries of the diamond-Christ. Moreover, for this author, diamond's power to attract iron is identified with the power of Christians to convert pagans.

The *Pen tsao Kang mu*, a vast botanical and lapidary encyclopaedia compiled by Li Shizhen, the Chinese naturalist and doctor (1518-1593). The description of diamond evokes the stone's quality of hardness and its usefulness for jade engraving, and its sole weakness: it is powerless before the power of the antelope horn, which will not spare even Buddha's adamantine tooth. Here, diamond is depicted (left-hand page) as three points or shards. The text contains the ideograms *sy gang chian* (stone, hard, metal). Private collection.

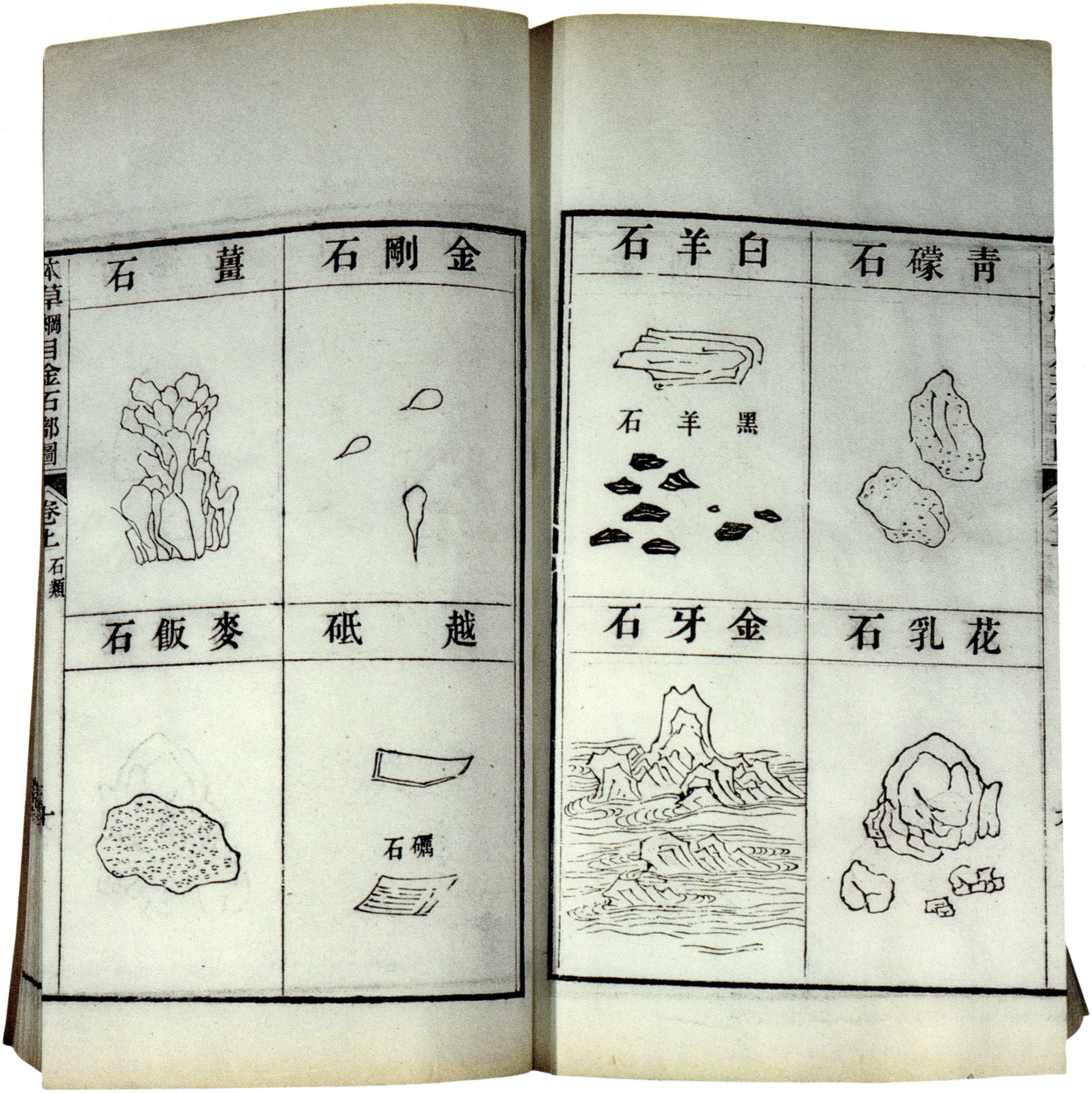

Hardness and invincibility

As we have seen, diamond was valued for its protective and salutary powers even in the earliest periods of its exploitation in India. This was also to be the case in the West. For example, the *Tournament of the Antichrist* (1230-1240) is a text by Huon de Méry, from the corpus of Medieval French Arthurian legends. The text identifies many of its protagonists by their headgear. The King of the Firmament is allocated the helmet of divinity, embellished with the circlet of judgement that contains carbuncles (garnets) and emeralds, whilst the Virgin bears a crown of the 12 most precious stones, engraved with the Holy scriptures. The diamond helmet is worn by the virtue of Patience. Her adversary, the Antichrist, wears a helmet furnished with a hollow diamond which Proserpine had offered to him as a pledge of love (to the jealous fury of Pluto). Pride also wears a diamond helmet. The tournament is blessed with a happy ending when the Archangel Gabriel successfully strikes the Antichrist's helmet, and dislodges the hollow diamond. In the German Arthurian tradition, diamond armour is renowned for its invincibility. However, in the case of Gahmuret, Parsifal's father, its vulnerability is exposed: the author Wolfram von Eschenbach tells how Gahmuret is beaten by his adversary, who renders his helmet as soft as a sponge by sprinkling it with goat's blood. In the De *Mineralibus*, Albert the Great (1206-1280), advises that diamond should be worn on the left-hand side of the body as protection against one's enemies. Diamond assures victory in justice and in war - but only if the cause is just. Jean de Mandeville's lapidary († 1374) and Jean d'Outremeuse's *Trésorier* (1382-1390) both cast doubt upon the reliability of diamond's protective abilities in battle. They both affirm, however, that a man is never struck down or killed if he wears a turquoise. Charles the Bold should certainly have borne this in mind: history shows that not even his famous 30-ct diamond, the largest then known in the West, could prevent his defeat at Grandson in 1476!

Diamond was also attributed with the power of protecting the home, as well as the person. Albert the Great advised that the gem should be placed on embers in the four corners of the house, in order to cast out demons. Diamond could confer its adamantine immunity on a fortress to maintain its invincibility; this is best illustrated by the diamond *(aimant)* rock upon which David's tower was built, according to the verses of *La Chevalerie de Judas Macabé* (1242-1269). The stone's protective function is obviously the justification for a host of talismanic jewellery pieces, in particular for pendants bearing the diamond-set initials of their owner. Brooches also provide a variety of diamond-embellished symbolic pretexts. For example, a jewel from Copenhagen's Rosenborg Castle shows cupid's arrow with a diamond-set tip. Likewise, the Museo degli Argenti (Silver Museum) in Florence has a jewel in the shape of a cockerel with diamond-set spurs, and the National Renaissance Museum in Écouen has a galleon-shaped pendant whose hull is literally smothered in diamonds. Jewels in the shape of St. George overcoming the dragon were also popular, and at least ten jewels of this type survive to this day. The knight is clad in diamond-set armour, ready to assault the fearsome dragon, the very symbol of evil, terrorising the town of Silene. The Residenz treasury in Munich has a marvellous example: the horse is also covered with diamond-set trappings. Its head is protected by typical Renaissance chivalric armour, with an iron spike at the front - although, in the jewel, the iron spike is depicted by a sumptuous point-cut diamond measuring a centimetre across. From invincibility it is only a short step to eternity. Bishop Meliton of Sardis († 190) provided us with the first text (the *Clavis* or *Symbolic Key*) associating diamond with the notion of eternity. This association occurs in the chapter on gems of a treatise that attempts to reconcile Alexandrine astrology with Christian philosophy. One thousand years later, Alain de Lille wrote the De *Planctu Naturae* in the 12th century. In it, the goddess *Nature* wears a crown surmounted by the diamond known as 'Eternity'. In this text, the diamond is given astrological attributes linking it more specifically to Saturn's orbit, sharing the planet's 'complexion' of coldness and dryness: "...The highest was the diamond. More economical of movement than the others, but more spendthrift of ease, delayed very long in the completion of its wide orbit. With such frostiness and great cold did it slowly move, that its form gave gentle proof that it had been born under the Saturnian star."

Portrait of Queen Sophie of Mecklenburg, mid-1570s. She wears a sumptuous array of diamond-encrusted gold jewellery. Certain pieces possess considerable symbolic significance. The diamond-set cross pendant necklace falling to her waist is rivalled by the superb diamond-set pendant on her chest. It portrays St. George on horseback, overcoming the dragon. Rosenborg Castle, Copenhagen.

Diamonds and immunity to ill-health

All Western medieval authors agree that diamond possessed power against poisons. However, the Islamic world is said to have used the stone primarily for piercing and cutting - and also poisoning. In the 16th century, there appear to have been several unsuccessful poisoning attempts using diamond powder. They were so ineffectual that Boetius de Boot wasted no time in dismissing the practice as absurd. The Pseudo-Aristotelian text seems to be the source of the myth that diamonds could treat bladder stones, a cure that was still promulgated in the 16th-century editions of the *Hortus Sanitatis*. Although Hildegard of Bingen (1098-1179) claims to cover medicine in her *Book of the Subtleties of Divine Creatures*, symbolic considerations seem to take precedence, particularly when it comes to stones and their salutary power against the devil. Hildegard explains the devil's hostility towards the mineralogical world, because precious stones reminded him of the lustre of those that he had left behind when he was stripped of God's glory. In addition, certain stones are born of the fire which became his instrument of torture. Finally, Hildegard singles out the diamond in particular: even the Devil had to admit that it resisted him. Her remedies recommend holding the diamond in one's mouth to avoid anger and lies - and also hunger, in moments of weakness during fasting-days. She also recommends that, in order to intensify its beneficial effect, one should hold the diamond firmly in one hand, while crossing oneself with the other! In contrast, Chinese and Arab authors strongly advise against sucking diamonds like pills, for fear of destroying the teeth. The *Lapidary of Alfonso X* further explains that this practice is dangerous, since the stones might be contaminated with traces of venom from the *argollos* worms that bore them up from the river-bed. This is the last remnant of the Valley of Diamonds legend.

The Book of Sidrac (1268-1291) assures us that the diamond has the power to restrain male semen from escaping the pregnant woman, and to preserve a child healthy in all its members. In John Trevisa's lapidary (late 14th century) in Oxford, this latter power also extends to adults, particularly with regard to protecting riders from breaking bones when falling from their horses: "Thou shalte not falle fro thine hors ne other beest, but that the bones shullen ge hoole who so be wellbelevyng."

Hardness as a source of strength and power

Certain 13th- and 14th-century Italian moralists are obsessed by the connections between gemstones and the personified virtues. Brunetto Latini wrote the *Trésor* (1266), devoted to advice on virtuous behaviour. In the second volume, he associates diamond with the cardinal virtue of Strength, thereby explaining her capacity to overcome daily adversity. This book's introduction discusses the four cardinal virtues, each of which is adorned with an appropriate precious stone that reflects the personification's qualities. A French illuminated cycle of the *Trésor* contains an exceptional illumination, depicting the relevant gemstones set in rings alongside each personification. The representation of Strength or *La Force* is shown with a diamond ring. The image compares the stone's power to that exerted by Samson when confronting the lion. The text emphasises the gem's ability to pierce all other stones and even metals, implying that Strength has comparable influence over all the other virtues. However, Jean de Meung's *Roman de la Rose* (1280) ponders whether even diamond might not be surpassed. In the battle for the castle, Pity's weapon is mercy, and the author implies that it could pierce diamond, since it is very sharp. One of the lapidaries (in verse) emphasises the Virgin's strength by including diamond in the centre of the third tier of her crown, which otherwise includes the twelve biblical gemstones. The crown's central tier is adorned with golden lilies (a reference to her virginity), whereas the uppermost tier contains white roses (an expression of her humility as Christ's mother).

La Fontaine de Toutes Sciences or *the Book of Sidrac* is an anonymous encyclopaedia composed after 1268. It takes the form of 613 questions and answers. This manuscript's lapidary section contains the long version of the mineralogical text. It includes a miniature illustration, depicting King Boctus, seated on a bench. He gestures towards a stone, possibly a diamond, that Sidrac raises to the light for closer examination. Late 13th century. French National Library, Paris, Western Manuscript Department.

Brunetto Latini's *Trésor*: introduction to Book II, on the virtues and vices from the *Nicomachean Ethics.* The miniature depicts the four cardinal virtues, each represented by the relevant precious stone mounted on a ring. One can easily recognise the pointed diamond at lower left. It is shown next to Samson overcoming the lion, to symbolise the Strength or *La Force* that diamond confers. This manuscript was copied around 1326 at Valenciennes, for Philippa of Hainault, who was betrothed to the future King of England, Edward III. French National Library, Paris, Western Manuscript Department.

Diamonds, magnets and attraction

The theme of 'attraction' is one of the most enigmatic topics in lapidary literature. As a symbol of eternity, diamond was already associated with the planets, but this was no justification for conferring magnetic properties on the stone. The *Abolays* is the first text in the *Lapidary* of Alfonso X, King of Castile (1276-1279). According to this text, diamond is the third stone belonging to the sign of Taurus, a sign which (along with Virgo and Capricorn) is associated with the unlucky, somewhat evil, planet of Saturn. In his *De Astronomia*, Raymond Lully (1232-1316), a Majorcan philosopher, also discusses the planetary virtues that spread on the Earth through plants and stones. The text mentions that "adamas attracts iron with celestial virtue and power, through the signs which are mobile and of adamantine and iron complexion. And the virtue of the polar star with *adamas* attracts iron and, because of this, *adamas* has the duty of reconciling the virtue of this star and the virtue of iron..."

Therefore, 'attraction' above all refers to diamond's supposed influence on the magnetic field of iron (and vice-versa). There is a considerable amount of literature on the subject. It confers diamonds a magnetic power over iron, or the capacity to remove the metal's magnetic properties. But is there any mineralogical reason to justify this long-lasting confusion between diamond (*diamant*) and magnet (*aimant*)? In fact, there is. The only known natural magnet (*aimant*) is the mineral iron oxide, or 'magnetite'. Like diamond, it is a very hard mineral. Like diamond, its crystals have brilliant, reflective faces and, again like diamond, it crystallises into octahedral shapes! The main visible difference is the colour: magnetite is black. However, this did not dissuade medieval naturalists, who certainly placed diamond and magnetite in the same family, form taking precedence over colour. In the same way, Indian gem workers mistook octahedral spinel crystals (magnesium-aluminium oxide), for red diamond. However, the assimilation of magnetite and diamond had far-reaching consequences.

In his Provençal encyclopaedia, Matfré Ermengaud (late 13th century) affirms that diamond has the power to demagnetise iron. He was not alone. In other texts, this neutralisation led to diamond possessing the power to attract iron. Not unexpectedly, one can also find references to diamond being used for navigation on the high seas, where the gem replaces magnetite to activate the iron in the compass! Such passages can be found in works by Thomas de Cantimpré (*De Natura Rerum*, 1228) and Vincent de Beauvais (*Speculum Naturale*, 1257-1258), for example. The same statement is even made by some authors who, it may be assumed, would have actually gone on such journeys. For example, Jacques de Vitry, Bishop of Saint Jean d'Acre, travelled at least as far as the Holy Land. He affirms diamond's magnetic powers with conviction, in his *Historia Orientalis* (ca. 1216). Jean de Mandeville went one step further, claiming that a compass could be used to detect a fake diamond, since the fake would not activate the needle as a true stone would. Naturally, preachers could hardly have been expected to resist the temptation to make use of this curious confusion between magnet and diamond! Pierre Bersuire compiled his vast manual, *Reductorium Morale*, at the pontifical court of Avignon in 1320-1350. According to him, the links between stone, iron and magnet provide an analogy of the power of Christ and the Virgin (diamond), whose presence neutralises the power of the devil (magnetic force) over the sinner (iron), through grace and charity.

Diamond rings originated in Roman times. This superb example was made in South-East Asia (possibly Vietnam). It dates from the 9th century, and is set with a natural, un-polished, rough octahedral diamond crystal. De Beers Collection.

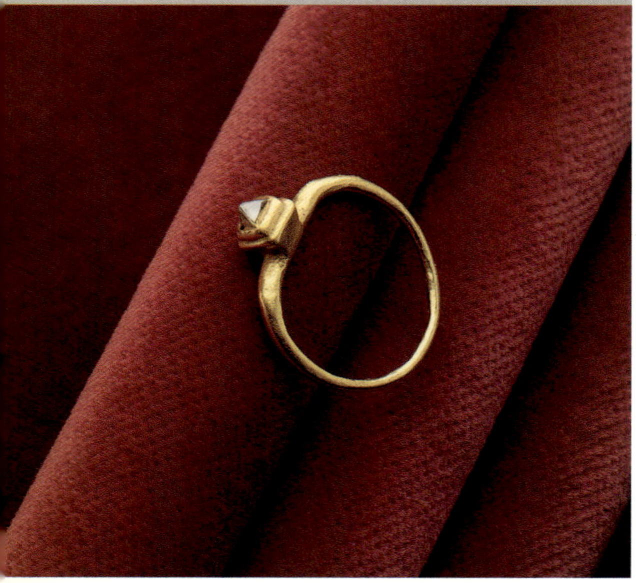

"Diamant - aimant - amant": can diamonds magnetise lovers?

Diamond eventually came to be implicated in the field of love - perhaps due to a confusion of Latin with Greek! The Greek *Adamas* is easily confused with *adamare*, the Latin verb "to love passionately". When one adds the confusing similarity of the French words "to love" (*aimer*), "lover" (*amant*) and "loving"/"magnetic" (*aimant*), we have all the ingredients for an explosive concoction of meaning!

Diamond's interference in amorous affairs seems to have commenced in the 13th century, with the relevant text in the encyclopaedia of Bartholomew the Englishman. In bk XVI of the *Liber de Proprietatibus Rerum* ("The Book of the Properties of Things", completed in Magdeburg ca. 1230-1240), he repeats (in ch. viii) the usual accounts of diamond based on Pliny and Isidore of Seville. However, he then goes on to introduce a few novelties, which he attributes to Dioscorides. If a women is incensed with her husband, their upset relations will nevertheless be pacified if she wears a diamond. A woman's fidelity towards her spouse may be tested by placing a diamond beneath her pillow in the conjugal bed. If she is virtuous, the diamond's presence will incite her to naturally turn to her husband in her sleep. However, should she be guilty, and therefore unworthy of remaining in the stone's presence, she will move away from him, to the extent of falling out of the bed. Strangely enough, there is no mention of submitting the husband to the same test! Bartholomew seems to have started quite a tradition. In England, James le Palmer, a treasury scribe of the Royal Exchequer, left us a compilation called the *Omne Bonum* (remaining unfinished at his death in 1372) in which, under the heading "*Adamanth*", he includes the Dioscorides description of magnetite that influenced Bartholomew the Englishman. In Italy, Cecco d'Ascoli's († 1327) long encyclopaedic poem, *L'Acerba*, discusses diamond after iron and asbestos (all under the auspices of Mars and Saturn). He also includes a reference to the "fidelity" test for errant wives.

In Guillaume Durand's priest's manual, the *Rational des Divins Offices* (Mendes, ca. 1286), we find references to diamond's symbolic importance when set in a ring commemorating the sacrament of marriage. He notes this custom's ancient origins: "A certain sage Proteus, seeking a sign of love, made a ring of iron and mounted a diamond (*adamantem*) on it, and in this way brides could be identified as married since, as iron tames, so love conquers all men, for there is nothing more insistent than love's passion. And, as diamond is unbreakable and love unquenchable and stronger than death, so it suits [diamond] to be worn on the ring finger, the vein of which comes directly from the heart." However, Guillaume goes on to admit that, subsequently, other stones have also been considered suitable for such rings. In the 14th century, Pierre Bersuire wrote an ecclesiastical text elaborating upon diamond's symbolism as proof of female fidelity, in identifying the husband with Christ and the wife with the soul.

Diamond rings were increasingly popular in the late middle ages as a result of this philosophical and symbolic heritage. Diamonds were listed in relative abundance in late-14th-century jewel inventories from wills and testaments. Therefore, contrary to popular belief, Charles VII's favourite, Agnès Sorel (1422-1450), was not the first woman to wear a diamond 'engagement ring'. The diamond nuptial ring already existed. According to a late-14th-century inventory, Charles V sealed his marriage to Jeanne de Bourbon with a diamond ring. So did René d'Anjou in 1420 when he married Isabelle of Lorraine under the sign of diamond. According to the 1498 inventory: "two little gold rings: one was used for our marriage to our redoubtable Lord and husband, God preserve him, and the other was given to us today[...] one of the rings has a diamond cut in the shape of a lily".

The Vatican manuscript commemorating the marriage of Constanzo Sforza and Camilla of Aragon, at Pesa in 1475, is incontestably the finest document to make reference to the diamond nuptial ring. A series of miniatures illustrates the whole symbolism of diamond as a guarantee of conjugal eternity. For example, one illumination portrays the divinity Hymen, represented by a fine young man who has lit two torches, linked by an outsize diamond-set nuptial ring. Hymen's tunic is embellished with diamond ring motifs, alternating with flame motifs. The picture is accompanied by a poem:

Due face in uno annello de ardente focho	(Two torches in a ring of smouldering fire
Doi volunta, doi cor, doi fochi insegna	Two wills, two hearts, two passions
Che siam congiunti in vincul de diamante.	Are joined in marriage by a diamond ring.)

Gold ring set with baguette-cut diamonds, outlining the letter M. This was possibly Duchess Marie of Burgundy's engagement ring. Kunsthistorisches Museum, Vienna.

Diamond ring. Portugal, early 17th century. National Ancient Art Museum, Lisbon.

'Lucida' engagement rings, by Tiffany. Tiffany has been remarkably successful at reinterpreting an ancient tradition, symbolically linking the 'indestructible' diamond to the eternity of the lovers' pledge. Tiffany & Co., New York.

Manuscript, commemorating Constanzo Sforza's marriage to Camilla of Aragon in 1475. The deity Hymen is depicted, consecrating a diamond-set ring. Vatican Library, Rome.

Love of man, love of nation

As the diamond ring became more popular, so it developed a rich emblematic destiny. The association of the ring and the diamond rapidly came to symbolise the 'engagement' between Royalty and State. A strange, anonymous, natural history text of Italian origin, dating from the first half of the 14th century, is a precursor to this emblematic association. It originally circulated in Latin, under the title *Contemptus Sublimitatis*. Later, a French edition was produced, under the title of the *Dialogue des Créatures*. The book covers various natural history topics. For each (whether relating to water, plants, stones or other elements), the text takes the form of a dialogue between two elements of opposing nature, each boasting of its superiority with respect to the other. In the mineralogical section, although diamond is not clearly identified, the 17th dialogue is very interesting. It is a dialogue between two gems: a carbuncle (garnet), and glass. The illustrations depict the gems set in rings, with faces on them, confronting each other. The carbuncle boasts about her nocturnal light, whereas the glass defends her own brightness and proposes a collaboration. But the carbuncle is not convinced of the benefits of such a union, and emphasises her outstanding hardness, comparing it unfavourably to the fragility of the glass. She underlines the nobility of her Christian ancestry, supported by Clement, Augustine and Jerome, which shelters her from the devil, but whom the glass must continue to fear. The glass is a citizen of the town where the devil no longer needs to labour since all its merchants are already in his service, while the carbuncle belongs to the monastic abbey and those who combat the devils, insistent but powerless to break in. It appears that the author may have mistakenly included the properties of diamond under the name of the carbuncle. In any event, this allegorical treatment of the stones paves the way for an emblematic future worthy of royalty.

This story is closely linked to an emblematic device conceived for King Ferdinand of Aragon (1452-1516). It makes use of this relationship between glass and diamond. The illustrations accompanying the motto "NATURA NON ARTIS OPUS" show diamond and glass in their natural state, with the following explanation: Ferdinand wanted to be judged by his nature, not by his profession, culture or education. Jacopo Typhotius listed an extensive collection of such mottoes and emblems in his "*Symbola Divina et Humana...*", which he published in three volumes in association with Anselmus Boetius de Boot (1601-1603). The text referred to the devices of both royal and church princes. Leafing through the three volumes, it is not difficult to observe the marked preference for diamond ring motifs, which symbolise the values that a prince pledges to his State upon his accession. Piero di Medici's emblem portrays a ring held between a falcon's claws, with the device SEMPER ("Always"). Cosimo I di Medici, Grand Duke of Tuscany from 1569 to 1574, had three intersecting rings as his emblem. They expressed courage, endurance and valour respectively, with the device SUPERABO ("I will conquer"). Matthias I Corvinus, King of Hungary between 1458 and 1490, had an emblem that portrayed a ring crowned with a star, accompanied by the device DURAT ET LUCET ("He endures and shines"). Finally, when Marguerite of Angoulême married Henri d'Albret, King of Navarre, in 1527, they commissioned an emblem depicting an engagement ring, formed from two cornucopias clasping a diamond. The device is SIMUL ET SEMPER ("Forever the same").

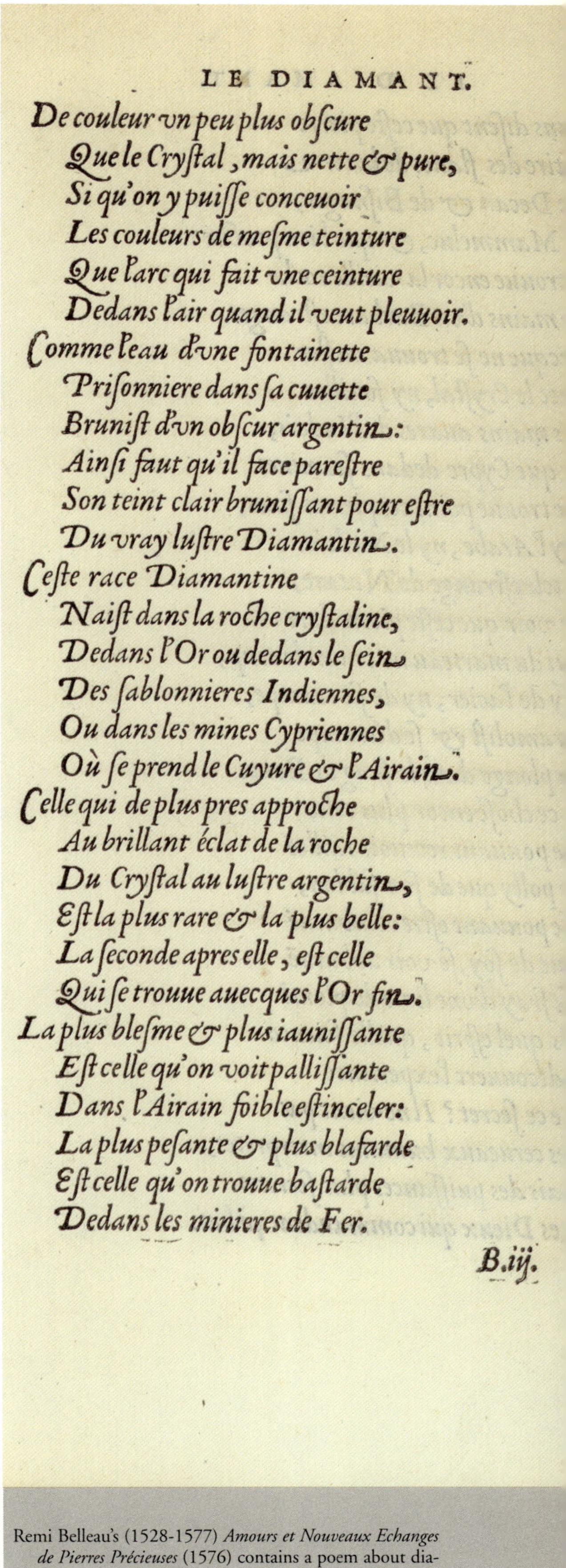
LE DIAMANT.

De couleur vn peu plus obſcure
Que le Cryſtal, mais nette & pure,
Si qu'on y puiſſe conceuoir
Les couleurs de meſme teinture
Que l'arc qui fait vne ceinture
Dedans l'air quand il veut pleuuoir.
Comme l'eau d'vne fontainette
Priſonniere dans ſa cuuette
Bruniſt d'vn obſcur argentin:
Ainſi faut qu'il face pareſtre
Son teint clair bruniſſant pour eſtre
Du vray luſtre Diamantin.
Ceſte race Diamantine
Naiſt dans la roche cryſtaline,
Dedans l'Or ou dedans le ſein
Des ſablonnieres Indiennes,
Ou dans les mines Cypriennes
Où ſe prend le Cuyure & l'Airain.
Celle qui de plus pres approche
Au brillant éclat de la roche
Du Cryſtal au luſtre argentin,
Eſt la plus rare & la plus belle:
La ſeconde apres elle, eſt celle
Qui ſe trouue auecques l'Or fin.
La plus bleſme & plus iauniſſante
Eſt celle qu'on voit palliſſante
Dans l'Airain foible eſtinceler:
La plus peſante & plus blafarde
Eſt celle qu'on trouue baſtarde
Dedans les minieres de Fer.

B.iij.

Remi Belleau's (1528-1577) *Amours et Nouveaux Echanges de Pierres Précieuses* (1576) contains a poem about diamonds. He dedicated it to Louise de Vaudemont, Henri III's young wife. Diamond represents certain values which will permit her to know constancy and fidelity. French National Library, Paris, Rare and Precious Book Reserve.

As an emblematic motif, diamond also appealed to an English poet and collector of engravings, George Wither. In his *Book of Emblems* (1635) dedicated to Charles I and Queen Henriette of France, the author recounts how he acquired a series of medallion-framed engravings from the Dutch. He attributed these engravings to a member of the Crispin de Passe family. Wither found the accompanying verse couplets somewhat inadequate - they related poorly to the images. Encouraged by his friends, he wrote a new series of emblematic poems. The result was a grand edition, which included an engraving dedicated to diamond, showing the stone placed on an anvil; an arm surges from a cloud, ready to strike the gem with a hammer. The poem that accompanies the engraving is a fitting conclusion to this examination of the symbolic literature that has accompanied diamond - the magical stone - over almost two millennia:

This is a well-knowne Figure, signifying,
A man, whose Vertues will abide the trying:
For, by the nature of the diamond stone,
(Which, Violence, can no way worke upon)
That Patience, and long-suffering is intended,
Which will not bee with Injuries offended;
Nor yeeld to any base dejectednesse,
Although some bruising Pow'r, the same oppresse;
Or, such hard streights, as theirs, that hamm'rings feele,
Betwixt an Anvile, and a Sledge of Steele.
None ever had a perfect Vertue, yet,
But, that most Pretious stone, which God hath set
On his right hand, in beaming-Majestie,
Upon the Ring of blest ETERNITIE.
And, this, is that impenitrable Stone,
The Serpent could not leave impression on,
(Nor signe of any Path-way) by temptations,
Or, by the pow'r of sly insinuations:
Which wondrous Mysterie was of those five,
Whose depth King Solomon could never dive.
Good God! Vouchsafe, ev'n for that Diamond-sake,
That I may of his pretiousnesse, partake,
In all my Trialls; make mee alwayes able
To bide them, with a minde impenitrable,
How hard, or oft so'ere those hamm'rings bee,
Wherewith, Afflictions must new fashion mee.
And, as the common Diamonds polish'd are,
By their owne dust; so, let my errours weare
Each other out; And, when that I am pure,
Give mee the Lustre, Lord, that will endure.

The Symbola Divina et Humana... (1601-1603), a vast catalogue of emblems pertaining to the princes and prelates of Europe. It was compiled and published by Jacopo Typhotius and Anselmus Boetius de Boot, and reveals a pronounced taste for the diamond ring motif in emblematic devices. Top: the emblem of Marguerite of Angoulême and Henri d'Albret, King of Navarre (1527). Below: the emblem of Matthias I Corvinus, King of Hungary (mid-15th century). French National Library, Paris, Literature and Art Department.

True Vertue, *firme*, *will alwayes bide*,
By whatſoever ſuffrings *tride*.

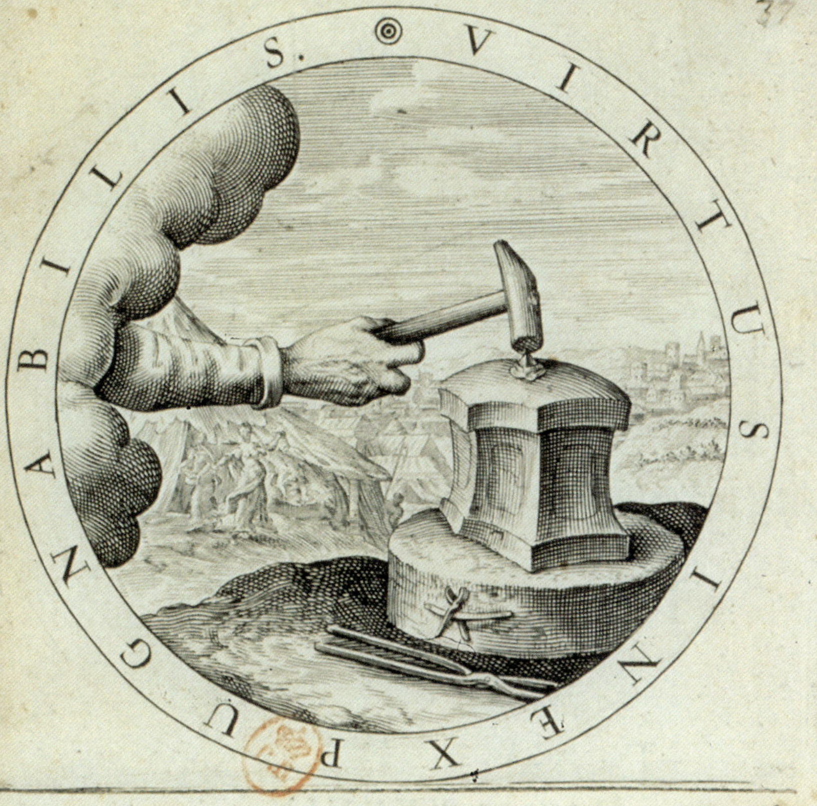

ILLVSTR. XXXVII. *Book*. 3

THis is a well-knowne *Figure*, ſignifying,
A man, whoſe *Vertues* will abide the trying:
For, by the nature of the *Diamond ſtone*,
(Which, *Violence*, can no way worke upon)
That *Patience*, and *long-ſuffering* is intended,
Which will not bee with *Injuries* offended;
Nor yeeld to any baſe dejectedneſſe,
Although ſome bruiſing *Pow'r*, the ſame oppreſſe;
Or, ſuch hard *ſtreights*, as theirs, that hamm'rings feele,
Betwixt an *Anvile*, and a *Sledge* of Steele.
None ever had a perfect *Vertue*, yet,
But, that moſt *Pretious ſtone*, which God hath ſet
On his right hand, in *beaming-Majeſtie*,
Vpon the *Ring* of bleſt *ETERNITIE*.
And, this, is that impenitrable *Stone*,
The *Serpent* could not leave impreſſion on,
(Nor ſigne of any *Path-way*) by temptations,
Or, by the pow'r of ſly inſinuations:
Which wondrous *Myſterie* was of thoſe *five*,
Whoſe depth King *Solomon* could never dive.
Good *God*! vouchſafe, ev'n for that *Diamond*-ſake,
That, I may of his *pretiouſneſſe*, partake,
In all my *Trialls*; make mee alwayes able
To bide them, with a minde impenitrable,
How hard, or oft ſo'ere, thoſe *hamm'rings* bee,
Wherewith, *Afflictions* muſt *new faſhion* mee.
And, as the common *Diamonds* poliſh'd are,
By their owne duſt; ſo, let my *errours* weare
Each other out; And, when that I am pure,
Give mee the *Luſtre*, *Lord*, that will endure.

Truth,

George Wither, *Book of Emblems*, London, 1635.
The emblem Virtus Expugnabilis is illustrated with an engraving by Crispin de Passe the Younger.
It represents a diamond on an anvil, threatened by a hammer. The commentary is a poem by Wither.
French National Library, Paris, Rare and Precious Book Reserve.

Jewellery

Mouawad Creations

Cartier Creations

Tiffany Creations

The name might not be familiar to the average person, but the Mouawad company is one of the great fine jewellers of the world. It is part of an extremely exclusive group: one of the leading jewellers to Middle Eastern royalty. The Mouawad name has been associated with jewellery for four generations. First, there was David Mouawad, a master watchmaker who established a shop in Beirut in 1890. He was succeeded by his son Fayez, who ensured the company's growth. Fayez was the first to incorporate gemstones into the watchcases and straps, thereby imbuing these everyday objects with a touch of magic and style. He also moved the business to Saudi Arabia in 1950. The quality of his work, combined with his personal charm and charisma, rapidly made him the exclusive jeweller to the Saudi royal family.

Fayez's son, Robert, is currently the group's President. He has continued to develop the company's jewellery business, and he also expanded its activities into Europe. Mouawad has established subsidiaries in Paris and Geneva. In 2000, the company opened its latest outlet: a luxurious jewellery shop in New Bond Street, in the heart of London.

Robert's own sons are carrying the tradition forward into the next generation. Fred, Alain and Pascal have opened up new worldwide horizons for the business, by launching an e-commerce site, Mondera.com. The site provides a simple and elegant way of distributing a range of products to the public, with diamonds at the forefront.

Mouawad jewellery has an exceptional, unique character, as if the perfume of Eastern spices had been transmuted into sparkling, crystalline brilliance. Diamonds are skilfully used to frame coloured gemstones, and nobody else can hope to match the quality of the sapphires, rubies and emeralds that the group uses in its jewels. But there is more to Mouawad than that. The Mouawad name resonates in the diamond industry, thanks to Robert Mouawad's association with the world's greatest historic gems. It is safe to say that nobody else has ever had as many priceless stones pass through their hands. The Mouawad name is inextricably linked with the finest diamonds that the Earth has ever seen. It is now difficult to compile an exhaustive list of the greatest diamonds currently set in Mouawad jewels. However, here a few of the most famous: the *Jubilee* (245.35ct), the *Premier Rose* (137.02ct), the *Queen of Holland* (135.92ct), the *Ahmedabad* (78.86ct), the *Idol's Eye* (70.21ct), the *Taylor-Burton* (69.42ct), the famous *Indore Pears* (46.39 and 44.14ct), the *President Vargas* (44.17ct), the *Tereschenko Blue* (49.92ct) and the *Excelsior* (69.98ct).

This passion for gems is absolutely unprecedented, and it is only fitting that the Mouawad name should be immortalised. Several gems now bear this title, including the *Mouawad Lilac* (24.44ct), the *Mouawad Pink* (21.06ct), the *Mouawad White* (48.28ct), the *Mouawad Splendour* (101.84ct), the *Mouawad Monolith* (104.02ct), the *Mouawad Polygonal* (106ct) and, lastly, the *Mouawad Magic*, an extraordinary emerald-cut of 108.81ct.

On November 16th, 2000, Robert Mouawad purchased a gem at auction in Christie's, Geneva. The atmosphere in the saleroom was electric, as he acquired the superb 60.19ct elongated pear-shape. Its colour and clarity are perfect, and it was named the *Mouawad Mondera*. In his own words: "this gem represents the link between a family tradition of four generations of jewellers, and the new economy, represented by Mondera.com".

These stones set the Mouawad Group apart from the rest. The company also sets the diamonds in magnificent jewels, in order to display the historic gems to best effect. The jewels themselves are dazzling and audacious works of art: this is amply illustrated by the extraordinary *Excelsior* and *President Vargas* bracelets.

The Mouawad Group has a keen eye for new business opportunities, and it is currently putting the finishing touches to its global structure. It has workshops in Jeddah and Bangkok, and its new workshop in Manila allows the company to produce a full range of fine jewellery products, including luxury objets d'art. The Group also incorporates the Robergé watch company: Swiss watchmaking precision, combined with richly jewelled settings. Recently, the Group has focused on mining activities and gem-cutting. However, this rapid expansion has not prevented the company from performing some truly remarkable philanthropic acts. For example, it financed the building of a new campus in California for the Gemological Institute of America, and the restoration of the Henri-Philippe Pharaon Palace in Beirut, which is where the Lebanese Act of Independence was signed.

Page 321 :
The magnificent *Excelsior I*, set in an extraordinary bracelet. The 69.68ct stone came from a 995.2ct rough that was found in the Jagersfontein mine in South Africa, in 1893. The Jagersfontein mine is famous for the colour and quality of its diamonds.

A sumptuous diamond cross-over necklace, containing two magnificent burmese rubies, weighing 37.01ct in total.

The *Mouawad Mondera*, a superb diamond acquired by the Mouawad company for the Millennium. It weighs 60.19ct.

1230 diamonds are set in the leaves of this necklace.
The pendant is a strange grey-green diamond of
284.38ct with milky glints.

These necklaces show the importance of diamonds in the jewellery industry, as highlights to coloured gemstones, such as sapphires or emeralds. The Mouawad company only uses the highest quality stones in its pieces.

Fancy intense yellow diamond ring, weighing 22.65ct.

The *President Vargas* bracelet.
The marvellous *President Vargas IV* diamond,
set in a bracelet against a background
of white emerald-cuts and black diamond brilliants.
The rough 'President Vargas' stone originally weighed
726.6ct: it was the largest diamond ever found in Brazil.
It was discovered in the Coromandel district,
in Minas Gerais, on August 13th, 1938.

Ring set with a pink, 15.07ct diamond ring.

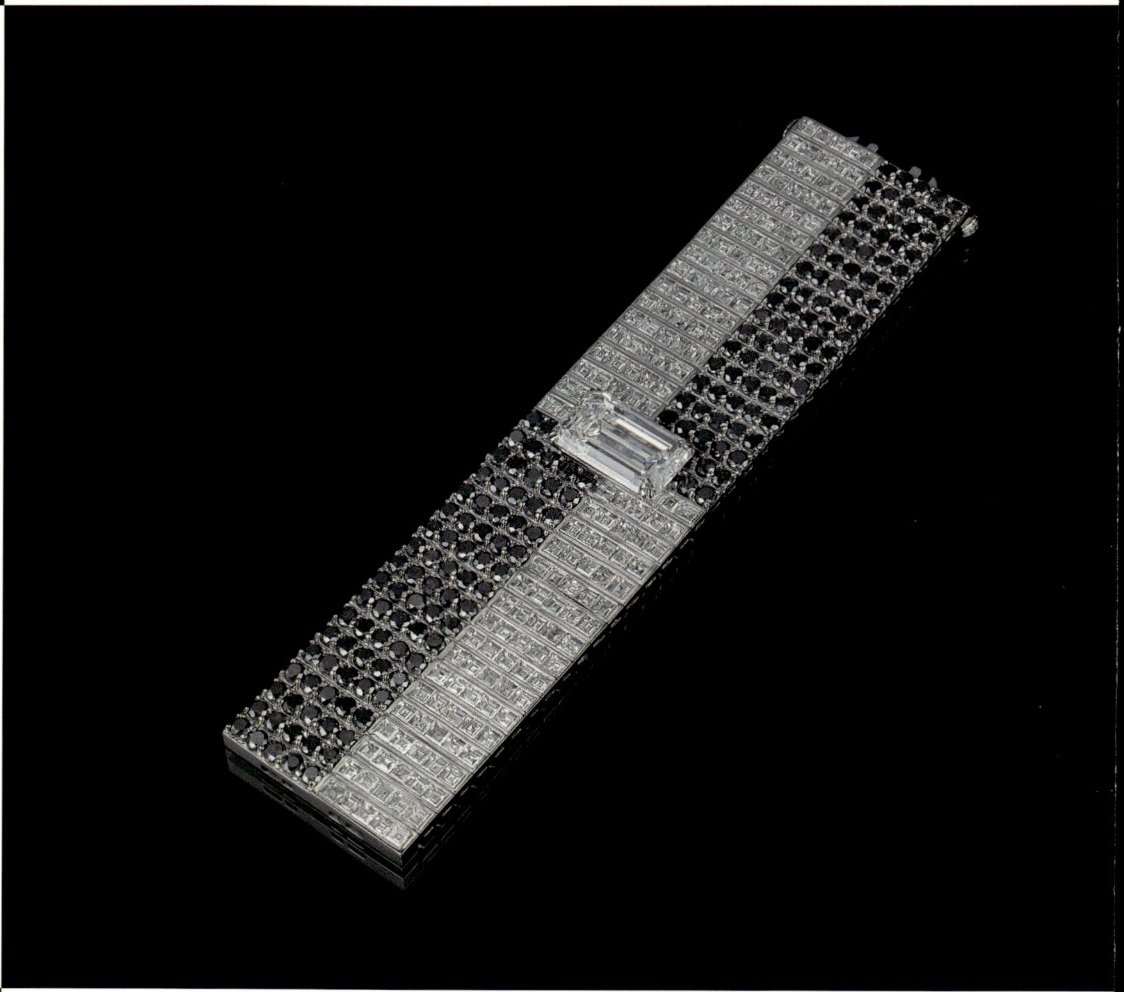

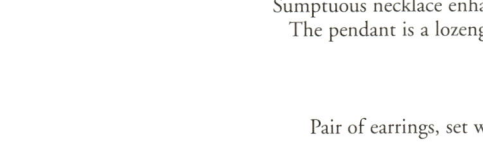

Sumptuous necklace enhanced with pink diamonds.
The pendant is a lozenge-shaped stone of 19.04ct.

Pair of earrings, set with perfectly-matched pear and oval-cut diamonds.

The Robergé watch company is part of the Mouawad Group. This extraordinary Robergé watch is set with a cluster of fancy-coloured diamonds. The watch 'glass' is itself a diamond! The fine quality of the movement is matched by the superb setting, making it both a precision watch and a piece of fine jewellery.

Superb brooch, containing a rare round diamond. The pendant is an extremely rare fancy pink stone.

Necklace, set with a rare yellow emerald-cut gem weighing 33.64ct, surrounded by pink diamonds

The *Tavernier*, a 56.07-carat pear-shaped diamond suspended from three strands of fine pearls, a yellow sapphire, grey pearl and a grey diamond. Designed by Micheline Kanou

One of Cartier's most famous flowers, containing the splendid Williamson Rose diamond which weighs 23.6 carats. This jewel was ordered by Her Majesty Queen Elizabeth II in her coronation year.

CARTIER CREATIONS

Cartier – a name that is synonymous with elegance and sophistication – expresses the very essence of French taste and the spirit of Parisian fine jewellery. The tradition of great names starting from humble origins is perfectly embodied by the Cartier story. Wandering around the busy stalls of the charming rue Montorgueil in the second arrondissement of Paris, who would imagine that the career of a great jeweller began here? But it was here, at number 29, that Louis-François Cartier opened his first workshop in 1847. As he gained more clients he decided to move to the more fashionable district of the capital. Louis-François was no designer, simply a skilled shopkeeper who laid down the base of the future empire. His son Alfred took over the business in 1874 and made the decision to go beyond merely repairing or improving jewels entrusted to him by his clients, including some of the aristocrats and leading personalities of the brilliant Parisian social scene at that time. Cartier moved to rue de la Paix in 1899 and set about developing an original style with the help of the best Paris workshops: the design of platinum settings around garland patterns and the renewal of the Louis XVI style to show diamonds in their full majesty. Louis Cartier, a partner with his father Alfred since 1898, launched the international development of the house with the help of his two brothers and orders flowed in at the time of the coronation of Edward VII in 1902. Jacques Cartier opened a shop in Burlington Street in London and then moved to New Bond Street in 1909. The New York outlet was opened by Pierre in the same year.

Great success followed as the creative genius of Cartier was combined with an unrivalled flair for business. Louis Cartier conquered the Russian nobility with exhibitions in St Petersburg. Jacques travelled to the Persian Gulf to hunt for rare stones and then on to India to captivate the rich Rajahs during preparations for the famous Delhi Durbar to celebrate the coronation of George V. The Indian princes were eager to show off their precious gems in new platinum settings. This was also the opportunity for Cartier to sell its exotic jewels to European clients. Pierre set out to conquer the meritocracy of the New World and sold the famous Hope diamond to Mrs Evelyn Walsh McLean.

Cartier began selling its models at the beginning of the 20th century although its own workshops were opened later. The Parisian workshop produced some prodigious creations for the international exhibition of decorative and modern industrial arts in the capital in 1925. Egypt, Persia, India and the Far East influence the designs of the period: always with a daring approach to captivate clients, Cartier flourished in the exceptionally rich inter-war years and created some marvellous jewels inspired by the discovery of the tomb of Tutankhamen.

Following the return to sobriety in the thirties, when white art deco reigned supreme, the post-war period of euphoria saw the return of a lively, colourful style inspired by wildlife and nature.

In most of the jewels created by Cartier the diamond obviously takes centre stage. The Diamant bleu de la Couronne de France and the famous Hope diamond are featured in Cartier settings at the Smithsonian Institution which also boasts the beautiful Etoile de l'Est (94.8 carats). The list of great diamonds set by Cartier in various jewels is long and can be summed up with a few famous names: the Etoile Polaire, the Etoile d'Afrique du Sud, two Mazarins, the famous Indian briolette of 90.38 carats, the Unzue blue diamond, the Pasha, the Nassak, the Porter Rhodes and, of course, the Jubilee, a fabulous diamond of 245.35 carats cut in 1897 for the jubilee of Queen Victoria. Cartier in London set the exceptional Williamson pink diamond at the heart of a flower-shaped brooch for the wedding of Princess Elizabeth, future Queen Elizabeth II. The series continued with the Cartier, a 69.42-carat pear diamond, bought from Parke-Bennett in New York and then bought by Richard Burton for Elizabeth Taylor, now known as the Taylor-Burton. This extraordinary trophy was crowned by a 107.07-carat pear diamond - the Louis Cartier – bought to mark the centenary of his birth in 1976.

A century after the jewel house first opened on rue de la Paix, the spirit remains unchanged: a constant search for renewal with the same commitment to quality. And diamonds are still as important as ever. In 2000 Cartier unveiled the marvellous pear diamond Tavernier, a historic pale sand-coloured stone with red glints that dates back to the era of the Moguls of Golconda. It was magnificently set in a pendant hanging from a subtly coloured pearl necklace.

The group is determined to defend the Cartier spirit and has taken great care to establish a history of the company. The archives that have been built up over the years provide historians with a valuable tool. Since 1900 every piece has been photographed in real size. The pictures are complemented by exact accounts and a collection of drawings from every stage of production. These documents are enriched by the Cartier Art Collection which is made up of exceptional pieces bought from clients or at auctions. The collection now features some 1,200 pieces which represent the changes in style and creative techniques over the years at Cartier. The sumptuous jewels and a rare collection of tiaras are all meticulously recorded and documented. The watchmaking section features some classical and precious timepieces in addition to exceptional 'mysterious' clocks where the hands turn inside a crystal seemingly unconnected with the mechanism. Other pieces include extravagant and practical items such as ladies' bags, decorated boxes, writing instruments, cigarette cases and so on. The Cartier Art Collection illustrates a range of different styles, including the most contemporary, and evokes the whole history of jewellery design. Since 1989 it has been invited to exhibit at many leading international museums.

Bouton de Rose brooch, Cartier Paris, 1965.
Petals set with jonquil diamonds with a brilliant in the centre. The leaves are set with emeralds and the stem set with diamonds.Cartier Art Collection, Geneva

Pyramide brooch with sapphire, Cartier New York, 1936.
Square brooch set with a faceted square sapphire.
The four sides are set with round diamonds with baguette diamond surrounds and alternate round and baguette diamond edges broken by a semi-cylinder of brilliants and baguette diamonds.Cartier Art Collection, Geneva

Palmier brooch, Cartier Paris, 1957.
Palm leaves set with round and baguette diamonds, 7 Burmese rubies of 23.12 carats, claw set diamonds, articulated trunk set with round and baguette diamonds. Cartier Art Collection, Geneva.

Serpent necklace, Cartier Paris, 1968.
Fully articulated jewel set with 2,473 brilliant and baguette diamonds with a total weight of 178.21 carats. The eyes are pear shaped emeralds, the stomach green, red and black enamel sheets.. It can be worn with either the diamond or enamel side on show.
Commission by Mexican actress Maria Felix.
Cartier Art Collection, Geneva.

Alligator brooch, Cartier Paris, 1975.
Articulated body set with 1,023 jonquil diamonds with a total weight of 60.02 carats with two emerald cabochons for the eyes. The second brooch is similarly constructed but with emeralds. The two brooches can be worn together as a necklace.
Commission by Mexican actress Maria Felix.
Cartier Art Collection, Geneva.

Noeud brooch, Cartier Paris, 1923.
Round centre and two Egyptian lotus designs in paving between two lines, set with round diamonds.
Cartier Art Collection, Geneva.

Brooch, Cartier Paris, 1930.
Set with round and baguette diamonds with a round diamond in the centre of a diamond-shaped motif.
Cartier Art Collection, Geneva.

Pair of bracelets, Cartier Paris, 1930.
Half-disks of rock crystal set with a single line of brilliants and three brilliants in a closed drop mounted on two circular platinum springs.
Commission by American actress Gloria Swanson.
Cartier Art Collection, Geneva.

Pendant from a large necklace made in 1909 by Cartier Paris for Mrs Cornelius Vanderbilt. Openwork round motif with millegrain setting old cut diamonds, claw-set central stone: two chains with an articulated central floral motif holding a hexagonal pendant set with old cut diamonds and edged with a line of brilliant diamonds. Five drops feature a round millegrain setting diamond and a claw set pear-shaped diamond. The original necklace can be seen in the Cartier archives in a splendid glass plate photograph.
Cartier Art Collection, Geneva.

Tiara, Cartier Paris, 1914.
Jewel in blackened steel set with pear diamonds, edged by graded rubies with two brilliant diamonds in each section. The rims features lines of graded rubies and brilliant diamonds.
Commission by Mrs Marghiloman.
Cartier Art Collection, Geneva.

The famous Tiffany diamond, the mascot of the famous American jewellery house. However, it is a very French gem! It was discovered by the French Diamond Mining Company in the Kimberley mines in South Africa.
This magnificent stone of 287.42 carats was unearthed in 1877 or 1878. It was sent to Paris where it was studied carefully for a year before being cut. The result is a cushion shaped diamond with 90 facets and a very deep pavilion that enhances the stone's natural yellow hue.
The diamond is shown here with the Bird on a Rock setting by Jean Schlumberger, a Frenchman, who worked as the principal designer at Tiffany.
Collection Tiffany & Co.

TIFFANY DESIGNS

Breakfast at Tiffany's – everyone knows this film based on the novel by Truman Capote which was strangely translated into French as *Diamants sur Canapé.* It was the opportunity for the delightful Audrey Hepburn to wear the magnificent yellow diamond that symbolises the most famous luxury name in America. Tiffany is an entire universe concentrated since 1940 in the shop on 57th Street and 5th Avenue in New York. A very American universe dating back to 1837 and which really got under way in 1841 when Charles Lewis Tiffany and his partner John Burner Young opened their small business to an investor, Jabez L. Ellis. The latter brought the necessary capital to allow the young firm to open an office in Europe. The idea was simple: satisfy the taste for luxury of the growing American middle class with the very latest fashions. American society was then going through a phase of profound change. The agricultural landscape carefully shaped by early settlers was giving way to big cities where the new wealthy classes were eager for all the comforts of modern living. Nothing was too fine for people who wished to impress their glorious social status on their guests during sumptuous dinners. Tiffany & Co. nurtured this desire with its magnificent tableware collections and was quick to branch out into jewellery. The firm took the official name of Tiffany & Co. in 1853 and has never looked back.

1887: *Annus horribilis* for diamonds in France but a splendid year for Tiffany. This year saw the disastrous sale of the French Crown Jewels. The stars of the world of fine jewellery crammed into the auction room. Interest was great since the jewels had been previously put on show during the Great Paris Exhibition of 1878. Charles Louis Tiffany admired them and recognised the superior quality of French jewellery. Nine years later he was not going to miss this unbelievable opportunity: he was on the front row for the nine sessions that were held from 12th to 23rd May 1887 to sell the 48 lots of France's greatest treasure. He left with some pieces that have marked French history: the De Guise, the *Fleur de pêcher*, four *Mazarins* and the *Mirroir de Portugal.* He bought more than a third of the collection and firmly established his reputation as one of the world's leading jewellers. The sale gave him the veneer of history that only Europe can give to the New World. Some pieces that were broken up by the French auctioneers were simply sold later in leather caskets with the words, 'Crown Jewels – Tiffany & Co. New York and Paris.'

The house of Tiffany continued to prosper and introduced the revolutionary concept of the claw-set diamond in 1886. The diamond is fully exposed and held in place simply by tiny claws. This was the beginning of the great saga of engagement rings, a truly American success story. Thanks to its rings, Tiffany & Co. is still one of the largest retailers of diamonds in the world.

The firm has retained a spirit of eternal youth and an ability for renewal without relying on the security that is brought by success. Tiffany is always ready to adopt new products such as Kunzite, named in honour of its gemmologist George Frederick Kunz, and Tanzanite, a new gem from Africa. Tiffany is constantly on the cutting edge when it comes to changes in fashion and design and the firm's designers are engaged in a never-ending quest for innovation. This policy is underpinned by the recruitment of brilliant designers such as the very influential Jean Schlumberger (1907 - 1987), born in Mulhouse in Alsace. He opened his own jewellery shop in New York in 1946 and joined Tiffany in 1955. Schlumberger was passionate about diamonds and worked on one of the most famous of all stones, the yellow *Tiffany* diamond, the mascot of the firm. He created the *Bird on a Rock* setting. The viewer is never sure whether the bird is simply standing on a rock or is about to try and fly away with the precious gem. This piece is the very essence of the designer's daring approach and the mischievous spirit of Tiffany. It is also a demonstration of the firm's passion for nature. This love affair began in 1889 with the series of orchids that were made for the Great Exhibition in Paris and it continues to this day. It is an eternal pact that unites the great jewellery house and the world around it.

Dragonfly necklace of three strands of pearls and a diamond dragonfly, 1997.
Tiffany & Co. Collection

Gold and pearl pin with a diamond fly, around 1875.
Tiffany & Co. Collection

Queen Bee brooch, pearl,
diamonds and rubies, around 1880.
Tiffany & Co. Collection

Golden Spider brooch, silver, pearls and
diamonds around 1875.
Tiffany & Co. Collection

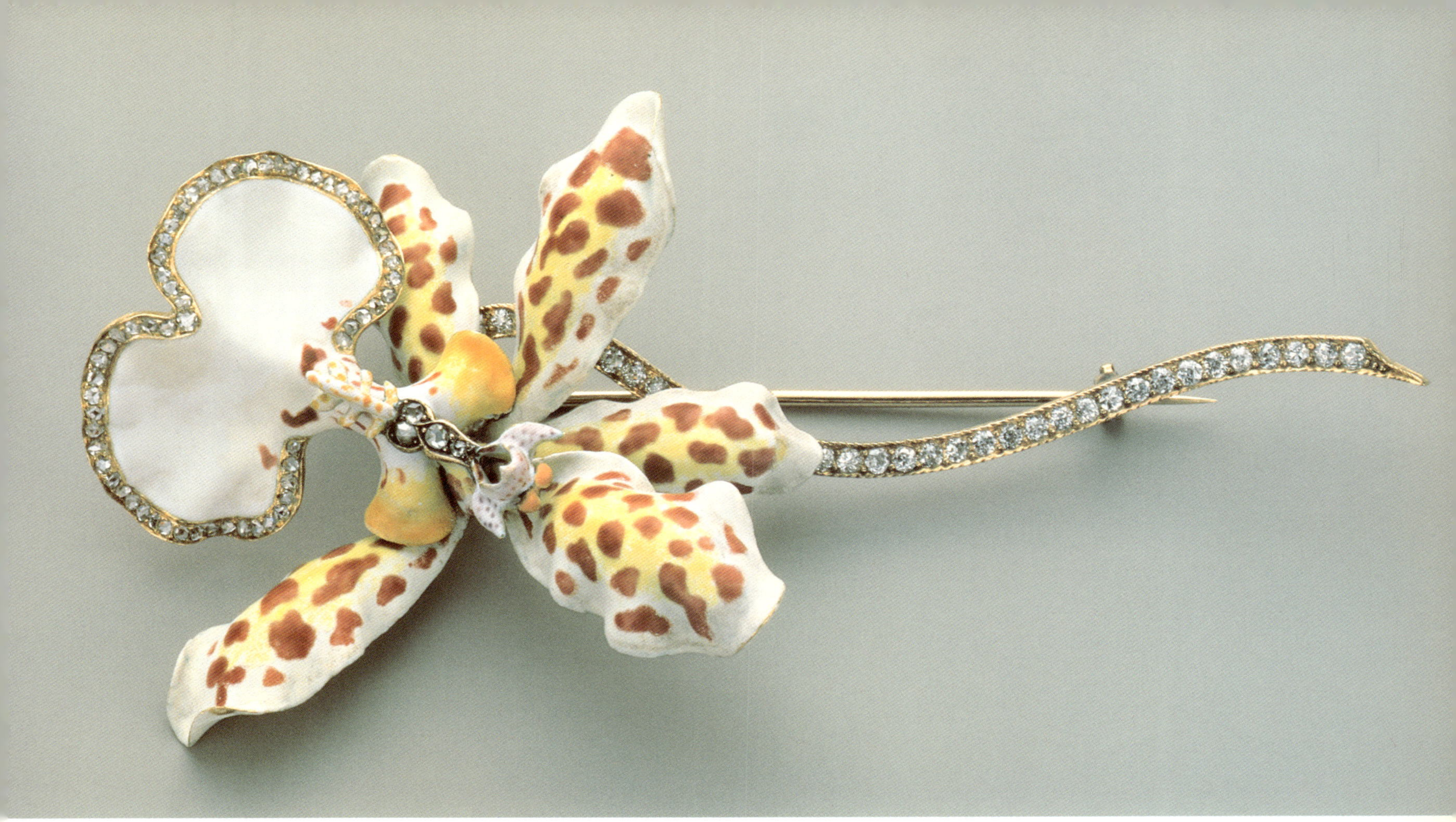

Two examples of the orchid series made by Tiffany for the Great Exhibition in Paris in 1889. The flower is in gold enamel, edged with diamonds and diamond-studded stem. The preparatory designs illustrate the observational skills of the firm's designers.
Tiffany & Co. Collection

GLOSSARY
ALL ABOUT DIAMOND IN 50 WORDS

1887 : the tragic year when one of the world's most fabulous diamond collections, the Crown Jewels of France, was sold at auction. The Third Republic decided to disperse the Louvre's incomparable hoard of jewels and historic gems, under the pretext of suppressing monarchist symbols. An incredible collection was lost forever.

beautiful water : an obsolete but exquisitely evocative way of describing a diamond of great clarity and limpidity: 'a diamond of beautiful water'.

blue ground : a term used by miners to describe kimberlite in its unoxidised, original state, underneath the yellow ground in the pipe.

boart : also written as bort, or boort. Non-gem-quality diamond, used in industry, primarily in the form of abrasive powders.

brilliance: a material's sparkle, caused by the reflection of light on its surface. The amount of light reflected depends upon the material's refractive index. Diamond has a very high refractive index, and is therefore very brilliant.

brilliant : a type of diamond cut. It includes the classic brilliant-cut, which is round and has 58 facets. The large, flat facet at the top of the brilliant-cut is called the table. The facets around the table are called the crown, and the facets on the lower part of the gem are called the pavilion. It is the most common cut for diamonds below 10 carats.

briolette : a drop-shaped gem cut with a circular cross-section and triangular facets. It is like a rose-cut, except that the facets go all around the surface of the stone

carat (ct) : from the Greek keration, which refers to the carob tree. In ancient times, merchants used carob seeds as counterweights to weigh gems. As late as 1907, the mass of the 'old' carat varied from one country to another: for example, the Parisian carat (0.2055 g) weighed more than the Florence carat (0.1972 g) or the Leipzig (0.205 g) carat. This confusion was bad for business, so it was decided to incorporate the carat into the metric system in 1907. Its mass was fixed at 0.2 g, and this is now the international standard measurement. The carat is divided into hundredths.

carbon : an atomic element. Its symbol is C, and it is the sixth element in the Periodic Table. There are many carbon compounds: it is the key element in organic chemistry. In the mineral kingdom, carbon exists in two pure forms: diamond and graphite. It is also present in many other mineral compounds, such as the carbonates.

carbonado : a dense, porous aggregate of small diamonds, of greyish or blackish colour. It is as hard as diamond.

cleavage : a property whereby some minerals have a tendency to split apart, along one or more well-defined planes in the crystal. These cleavage planes are related to the alignment of the molecular structure. Diamond has perfect cleavage parallel to its octahedral crystal faces.

CSO : acronym for the Central Selling Organisation, which distributed about 60% of the world's rough gem-quality diamonds. In 2000, it was replaced by the DTC, or Diamond Trading Company.

curse : an affliction that supposedly targets the owners of certain diamonds, in particular the Blue Diamond of the French Crown (now known as the Hope). However, after careful examination of the facts, no diamond has ever been proved to bear a genuine curse.

cushion : the most common shape for old or baroque brilliant-cuts. It has a rectangular or square cross-section, with rounded corners.

cut : the series of operations that turn a rough diamond into one that is ready to be set in a jewel. It incorporates various operations, such as sawing, cleaving, bruting (to form the general shape), faceting and final polishing.

CVD : acronym for Chemical Vapour Deposition, a process that is used to make ultra-thin layers of industrial diamond, synthesised from gas plasmas.

De Beers : the name of an industrial group, founded by Cecil Rhodes in 1888. He started by buying up thousands of mining concessions that shared the diamond 'pipes' in the Kimberley area, including those that were located on the De Beer brothers' farm. This consolidation enabled him to move on to underground mining, in the blue ground. He then decided to try to control production, in order to limit fluctuations in diamond prices. The De Beers Company underwent rapid expansion under Sir Ernest Oppenheimer, resulting in an extraordinary degree of control over this unique market.

diamond : from the mineralogical point of view, the shortest possible definition of diamond is "a mineral composed of pure carbon, which crystallises in the cubic structure".

dispersion : the 'prism effect', by which a colourless material breaks up white light into a rainbow-coloured spectrum. Diamond has high dispersive abilities and, when cut properly, it can display spectacular multicoloured 'fire'.

eclogite : from the Greek 'ekloge': 'choice'. Hard, massive rock, with green pyroxene and orange-pink garnet crystals that are visible to the naked eye. Its chemical composition is that of basalt. Diamonds are formed within eclogite, at great depths (at least 200 km below the surface). Eclogite is diamond's original mother rock.

fancy : a term that is used to refer to a diamond of intense colour.

fire : multi-coloured flashes of light, caused by rays of white light being split up into the colours of the rainbow when they travel through a diamond. See dispersion.

flawless : a term used to describe a diamond without any visible impurities or defects, even when examined under 10x magnification using a magnifying-glass.

Golconda : name of an Indian region or, more exactly, of a Mogul fort located not far from Hyderabad, in Andhra Pradesh. Golconda is the quasi-mythical, quintessential source of diamonds, even though the actual diamond mines were not located precisely in this area. If a diamond is thought to be from Golconda, it will command a price premium. Early Brazilian diamonds were initially imported to India before being re-exported to Europe as 'Golconda' stones. Professionals still refer to 'Golconda clarity', a kind of ultra-transparency that is difficult to describe.

goods : professionals use this word to refer to diamond merchandise when they are in public places, such as pubs in the London diamond district, or when speaking on the telephone. It is a way of concealing the conversation's subject-matter from eavesdroppers.

inclusion : a flaw inside a diamond, such as a mineral inclusion, crack or growth defect.

Kimberley : a small South African town, 400 km south-west of Johannesburg. This is where modern diamond history began. The first stones were found here in 1869, which soon resulted in a 'diamond rush'. The rock that brought diamonds up from the Earth's depths was discovered here for the first time, and named kimberlite. The De Beers company was founded here. It contains what is reputed to be one of the most beautiful pubs in the world: the Star of the West. Thousands of miners came here to quench their thirst with beer.

kimberlite : named after the town of Kimberley, South Africa. It is a type of volcanic rock that fills diamond-bearing 'pipes'. The pipes are the result of explosive lava eruptions, and measure a few hundred metres to 2 km or more in width. Their diameter tends to decrease with depth. In its original, pristine state, the rock is compact, blue or dark grey in colour, containing olivine, mica phlogopite, serpentine, and sundry rock fragments (eclogite and peridotite xenoliths) that were torn from the pipe walls, or which came from a great depth. Diamonds are found in this rock, but it yields only 1 carat of cut diamonds for every 200 tons of rock.

komatiite : a type of volcanic rock that is very rich in magnesium. It is amongst the oldest rocks on Earth. Diamonds were unexpectedly discovered in an outcrop of this rock in French Guyana, in 1999. The potential economic impact of this surprising find is not yet known.

lamproite : from the Greek lampros, shining. A magmatic rock that is rich in potassium. It contains a multitude of sparkling mica flakes. Explosive kimberlite eruptions contain carbonates, but these are, remarkably, absent in lamproite. As a result, the lamproite is very homogeneous, and it spreads in thick seams. In 1979, this rock stunned the sedate world of diamond geology, when diamond-bearing lamproite was discovered in Argyle, Australia. This outcrop became the largest diamond mine in the world, outstripping kimberlite deposits in quantity, if not in quality.

lapidary : a craftsman who cuts, polishes and engraves precious stones. It is also the name of a class of scientific literature in Roman times, which flowered again in the medieval period. These Latin, French, Arabic, Hindi and Persian texts discuss gemstones and their properties, in a symbolic context that now appears quaint and fantastical.

lustre : a property related to the reflectivity of light on a mineral's surface. When a gem has a high lustre, comparable to that of a diamond, this is referred to as 'adamantine' lustre.

macle : a grouping of two or more individuals of the same species whose orientation obeys strict geometrical laws. In diamonds, macles produce flat, triangular crystals. Special cuts have been developed in order to turn them into profitable gemstones.

marquise : a navette-cut variant of the brilliant-cut. It supposedly owes its name to the shape of the Marquise de Pompadour's lips.

mazel : a word spoken by Jewish diamond merchants when they conclude a business deal. It comes from a Hebrew expression ("mazel en broche"), and establishes an unbreakable pact between the buyer and the seller. No written contract is necessary. If anyone betrays such an agreement, they are expelled from the diamond business forever.

nanodiamond : ultra-microscopic diamond (10,000 times smaller than a grain of salt), found exclusively in some types of primitive meteorite. They can also be synthesised in the laboratory, in gas plasmas (cf. CVD).

pavilion : the lower part of a polished gem (the part which, in jewellery, is hidden by the setting). The upper part of the gem is known as the crown. It must have facets aligned in a specific way, in order for the stone to reflect the maximum amount of light. It ends in either a culet facet, or a point.

pear : a variant of the brilliant-cut, in the shape of a flattened drop.

pipe : a vertical, cylindrical volcanic 'chimney', filled with effusive magmatic rock.

piqué : a term used to describe a diamond that contains numerous impurities.

refraction : a change in the velocity and direction of a light ray. In diamonds, the carbon atoms are so compact that light decelerates dramatically when it enters the stone. This means that diamond's refractive index (the ratio between the speed of light in diamond and in a vacuum) is very high. This, in turn, allows a correctly-cut stone to reflect light and display the gem's characteristic brilliance.

rough : a word that is used to describe an uncut diamond that still retains its original crystallographic shape.

sightholders : a very select group of diamond merchants that go to De Beers headquarters ten times per year to purchase a box that contains a certain quantity of rough diamonds. 60% of the world's gem-quality diamonds are distributed in this way. In order to be a sightholder, one needs to be the head of a diamond-cutting company and have irreproachable bank references. There are currently approximately 120 sightholders, spread out amongst most of the world's major countries.

'naive' and 'made' point : terms used to indicate an octahedral diamond, until the 17th century. When the crystal was in its natural state, the term 'naive' point was used. From the 15th century, octahedral crystal faces started to be 'rectified' and polished: the term 'made' point was then used.

star : a famous person, generally female, who likes wearing diamonds! Also used to refer to a celestial body that produces diamond in one of the phases of its lifespan. These tiny crystals were probably formed in gas plasma during a supernova formation. Some of these diamonds were eventually incorporated into extremely rare meteorites, which then fell on our planet, billions of years later.

table : uppermost facet in a cut gemstone. It is surrounded by the crown facets. These crown facets lead down to the stone's 'girdle', the widest part of the gem that is gripped by the mounting's prongs. Early diamonds were table-cuts: octahedra with one point ground away. The table was, therefore, the first facet invented by gem-cutters. Later on, it became the main facet of a whole array of facets that were designed to allow the gem to refract light.

terrestrial mantle : layer of rock, comprising 63% of the Earth's volume, sandwiched between the Earth's crust and planetary core. Diamonds are formed in the mantle, from at least 150-200 km deep.

vajra : from a Sanskrit word, meaning "inflexibility, diamond". The term 'vajra' refers to something that is indestructible: it neither appears nor disappears. It is, therefore, the word used to describe diamond in ancient Sanskrit texts, particularly Hindu and Buddhist treatises. The diamond Vajra was transposed into a ritual object shaped like a sceptre, that is frequently shown in Buddhist iconography and used in Tibetan lamaist ritual.

yellow ground : a mining term, denoting the yellowish earth that results from kimberlite oxidation in the upper parts of kimberlite pipes, from the surface down to about 50-100 m deep.

BIBLIOGRAPHY

General bibliography

ALLEGRE (C. J.), *De la pierre à l'étoile*, Fayard, Paris, 1985.

BALFOUR (I.), *Famous Diamonds*, Christie's International plc, 2000.

BAPST (G.), *Histoire des joyaux de la couronne de France, d'après des documents inédits...*, Hachette, Paris, 1889.

BARIAND (P.) and POIROT (J.-P.), *Larousse des pierres précieuses*, Larousse-Bordas, Paris, 1998.

BERINSTAIN (V.), *L'Inde impériale des Grands Moghols*, Gallimard, , "Discoveries" collection, Paris, 1997.

"Diamant, der extreme Edelstein, das genial Werkzeug", *ExtraLapis,* n° 18, Munich, 2000.

FINOT (L.), *Les Lapidaires indiens*, Paris, 1896.

GAAL (R. A. P.), *The Diamond Dictionary*, 2nd Edition, Gemmological Institute of America, Carlsbad 1977.

HARLOW (G.), *The Nature of diamonds*, Cambridge University Press, Cambridge, 1998.

JANNETTAZ (E.), FONTENAY (E.), VANDERHEYM (E.) and COUTANCE (A.), *Diamant et pierres précieuses*, J. Rothschild Publishers, Paris, 1881.

MOREL (B.), *Les Joyaux de la Couronne de France*, Albin Michel, Paris, 1988.

Pliny the Elder, *Natural History*, translated and commentated upon by E. de Saint-Denis, Les Belles Lettres, Paris, 1972.

TAVERNIER (J.-B.), *Les six voyages de Jean Baptiste Tavernier en Turquie, en Perse et aux Indes*, Paris, 1679.

VLEESCHDRAGER (E.), *Diamant, réalité et passion*, éditions du Perron, Alleur, 1997.

WANNENBURGH (A. J.) and JOHNSON (P.), *Diamond People*, Norfolk House Publishers, London, 1990.

Bibliography by chapter

I.

The natural history of diamonds

FERSMANN (A., von) and GOLDSCHMIDT (V.), *Der Diamant*, Carl Winter's Universitätsbuchhandlung, Heidelberg, 1911.

KOIVULA (J. I.), *The microworld of diamonds: a visual reference guide*, Gemworld International Inc., Northbrook, 2000.

MOORE (M.), "X-ray studies of the growth of natural diamond", *Industrial Diamond Review*, vol. II, 1988, p. 59-64.

SUNAGAWA (I.) "Morphology of natural and synthetic diamond crystals", *Materials Science of the Earth's interior*, I. Sunagawa, Terra Scientific Publishing, Tokyo, 1984, p. 303-330.

WILKS (E. M.) and WILKS. (J.), *The properties and applications of diamond*, Butterworth-Heinemann, Oxford, 1991.

II.

Under the volcano: discovering the invisible

ANDERSON (D. L.), *Theory of the Earth*, Blackwell Scientific Publications Ltd., 1989.

NIXON (P. H.), *Mantle Xenoliths*, Wiley, New York 1987.

RICHARDSON (S. H), "Latter-day Origin of Diamonds of Eclogitic Paragenesis", *Nature,* n° 322, 1986.

RICHARDSON (S. H.), GURNEY (J. J.), ERLANK (A. J.) and HARRIS (J. W.), "Origin of Diamonds in Old Enriched Mantle", *Nature,* n° 310, 1984.

RICHARDSON (S. H.), ERLANK (A. J.), HARRIS (J. W.) and HART (S. R. E.), "Eclogitic Diamonds of Proterozoic Age from Cretaceous Kimberlite", *Nature,* n° 346, 1990.

RINGWOOD (A. E.), *Composition and Petrology of the Earth's Mantle*, Mc Graw-Hill, New York 1975.

SAUTTER (V.) and GILLET (P.), "Les diamants, messagers des profondeurs de la Terre", *La Recherche,* n° 271, December 1994.

III.

Diamond stardust

ANDERS (E.) and ZINNER (E.), "Interstellar Grains in Primitive Meteorites: Diamond, Silicon Carbide and Graphite", *Meteoritics,* n°28, 1993, p. 490-514.

HENBEST (N.), "Astronomers Catch the Diamonds in Stardust", *New Scientist* 1580, 1987, p. 30.

HILL (H.), *Les Nanodiamants dans les météorites primitives : un lien avec la matière interstellaire*, thesis for the Museum national d'histoire naturelle and the Institut d'astrophysique spatiale, 1998. *Les Météorites*, Cahiers d'histoire naturelle, Bordas, Paris 1996, 128 p.

NUTH (J.) and ALLEN (J. E.), "Supernovæ as sources of Interstellar Diamonds", *Astrophys. and Space Sci.,* n° 196, 1992, p. 117-123.

IV.

Tales of the diamond mines

JANSE (A. J. A. B.), "A History of Diamond Sources in Africa: part I", *Gems and Gemology*, vol. XXXI, n° 4, 1995, p.228-255.

JANSE (A. J. A. B.), "A History of Diamond Sources in Africa: part II", *Gems and Gemology*, vol. XXXII, n° 1, 1996, p.2-30.

LEVINSON (A. A.), GURNEY (J. J.) and KIRKLEY (M. B.), "Diamond Sources and Production: Past, Present, and Future", *Gems and Gemology*, vol. XXVIII, n° 4, 1992, p.234-254.

V.

Diamond channels: the international supply chain

SEVDERMISH (M.), MICIAK (A. R.) and LEVINSON (A. A.), "The Diamond Pipeline into the Third Millennium: A Multi-channel System from the Mine to the Consumer", *Geoscience Canada*, vol. XXV, n° 2, 1998.

VI.

From jewels to tools

HAZEN (R. M.), *The Diamond Makers*, Cambridge University Press, Cambridge, 1999.

MOISSAN (H.), *Le Four électrique*, G. Steinheil, Paris, 1897.

VII.

Not all diamonds are created equal: Diamond gemmology

Diamond grading course. Gemological Institute of America, Carlsbad, 1986.

ROSKIN (G.), *Photo Masters for Diamond Grading*, Gemworld International, Northbrook, 1994.

VIII.

Point, table, rose, heart, marquise, brilliant...

CASPI (A.), "Modern Diamond Cutting and Polishing", *Gems and Gemology*, vol. XXXIII, n° 2, 1997, p. 102-121.

KOCKELBERGH (I.), VLEESCHDRAGER (E.) and WALGRAVE (J.), *The Brillant Story of Antwerp Diamonds*, MIM Publishing Company, Antwerp, 1992.

TILLANDER (H.), *Diamonds Cuts in Historic Jewellery, 1381-1910*, Art Books International, London,1995.

IX.

Royal glory: diamonds at the heart of power

BAUDRILLART (H.), *Histoire du luxe privé et public, depuis l'Antiquité jusqu'à nos jours*, Hachette, Paris, 1878-1880, 4 vol.

The Jerusalem Bible, translated under the auspices of the École biblique de Jérusalem, 1998.

BOETIUS DE BOOT (A.), *Le Parfaict Joaillier, ou Histoire des pierreries: où sont amplement descrites leur naissance, juste prix, moyen de les cognoistre, et se garder des contrefaites, Facultez medecinales, et proprietez curieuses*, Adrian Toll, Lyon, 1644.

BOURDEAU (L.), *Histoire de l'habillement et de la parure*, F. Alcan, Paris, 1904.

CLAUDEL (P.), *L'œil écoute*, Gallimard, Paris, 1946.

COELHO (M. C), "St. Teresa of Avila's Transformation of the Symbol of the Interior Castle", *Teresianum*, 38, 1987, p. 109-125.

D'ALLEMAGNE (H. R.), *Les Accessoires du costume et du mobilier depuis le XIIIe siècle. jusqu'au milieu du XIXe siècle*, Paris, 1928, 3 vol.

DELESTRE (J.-B.), *Gros et ses ouvrages*, J. Labitte, Paris, 1845.

EVANS (J.), *Magical jewels of the Middle Ages and the Renaissance, particularly in England*, The Clarendon Press, Oxford, 1922.

GAUTHIER (F. L.), *Traité contre l'amour des parures et le luxe des habits*, A.-.M. Lottin l'Aîné, Paris, 1779.

GAUTIER (T.), *Guide de l'amateur au musée du Louvre*, G. Charpentier, Paris, 1882.

Homer, *The Iliad*, translated and edited by Mario Meunier, Albin Michel, Paris, 1956.

LECOQ (P.), "Perle, cristal et diamant chez A. de Vigny. Exploration d'un réseau d'images", *L'Information littéraire*, n° 27, 1975, p. 161-170.

LEVAVASSEUR (A.), "Les pierres précieuses dans *La Divine Comédie*", *Revue des Études italiennes*, N. S. 4, 1957, p. 31-100.

SAINT-SIMON (L. de Rouvroy, duc de), *Mémoires*, Gallimard, "Bibliothèque de la Pléiade" collection, Paris, 1947-1961, in 7 vol.

SAUVAL (H.), *Histoire et recherches des antiquités de la ville de Paris*, C. Moette, Paris, 1724, en 3 vol.

TERTULLIEN, *La Toilette des femmes*, Éditions du Cerf, Paris, 1971.

TERVARENT (G. de), *Attributs et symboles dans l'art profane 1450-1600, Dictionnaire d'un langage perdu*, E. Drose, Geneva, 1958.

TRIPIER LE FRANC (J.), *Histoire de la vie et de la mort du baron Gros*, Paris, J. Martin, 1880.

X.

Diamonds of the Maharajahs and Great Mughals

AMINI (I.), *L'Inde du Koh-i-Noor*, François Bourin, Paris, 1992.

AZIZ (A.), *The Imperial Treasury of the Indian Mughuls*, Lahore, 1942.

BERNIER (F.), *Voyage dans les États du Grand Mogol*, Fayard, Paris, 1981 (reprint).

KHALIDI (O.), *Romance of the Golconda Diamonds*, Mapin Publishing, Ahmedabad, 1999.

POLO Marco, *La Description du monde*, Klincksieck, Paris, 1955.

XI.

Dazzling Paris
The Parisian Diamond Market in the 16th and 17th centuries

ALCOUFFE (D.), “Le Maître aux dragons : les créations de l'orfèvre parisien Pierre Delabarre”, *Revue de l'Art* n° 81, 1988, p. 47-56.

BIMBENET-PRIVAT (M.), “Dessins inédits de François Dujardin, orfèvre de Catherine de Médicis”, *Gazette des Beaux-Arts*, t. CIX, June 1987, p. 191-196.

BIMBENET-PRIVAT (M.), “La vérité sur l'origine de la *Coupe de saint Michel*”, *Jahrbuch der Kunsthistorischen Sammlungen im Wien*, n° 97, 1993, p. 127-135.

CELLINI (B.), *The Life of Benvenuto Cellini*, translated by André Chastel, Scala, Paris, 1992.

EVANS (J.), *A History of Jewellery, 1100-1870*, London, 1953.

GUILMARD (D.), *Les maîtres ornemanistes, dessinateurs, peintres, architectes, sculpteurs et graveurs*, Plon, Paris, 1881, 2 vol.

HACKENBROCH (Yvonne), *Renaissance Jewellery*, Sotheby's Parke-Bernet, London, 1979.

HAYWARD (J. F.), *Virtuoso Goldsmiths and the triumph of Mannerism, 1540-1620*, Sotheby's Parke-Bernet, London, 1976.

JESTAZ (B.), “Les Joyaux de la Couronne mis en gage à Venise en 1569”, *Dubiis libertas, presented to Prof. Rémy Scheurer*, Gilles Attinger, Hauterive (Switzerland), 1999, p. 181-192.

LACROIX (P.), “L'Inventaire des joyaux de la couronne de France en 1560”, *Revue universelle des Arts*, 1856, p. 334-350, 445-456, 518-536.

LEITHE-JASPER (M.), “Der Bergkristallpokal Herzog Philipps des Guten von Burgrund”, *Jahrbuch der Kunsthistorischen Sammlungen im Wien*, n° 66, 1970, p. 227-242.

MICHEL (P.), *Mazarin, prince des collectionneurs: les collections et l'ameublement du cardinal Mazarin (1602-1661), histoire et analyse*, Réunion des Musées nationaux, Paris, 1999.

SOMERS-COCK (A.), “Louis XIV's Official Presents of Jewellery”, *International Silver and Jewellery Fair and Seminar*, London, 1985, p. 10-14.

WEIGERT (R.-A.) and HERNMARCK (C.), *Les Relations artistiques entre la France et la Suède, 1693-1718. Nicomède Tessin le Jeune et Daniel Cronström, Correspondance (extraits)*, Stockholm, 1964.

Exhibitions

A Sparkling Age, 17th century diamond jewellery, Antwerp, Diamond Museum, 1993.

L'Orfèvrerie parisienne de la Renaissance. Trésors dispersés, Paris, Panthéon Cultural Centre, 1995.

Princely Magnificence, Court jewels of the Renaissance, 1500-1630, London, Victoria and Albert Museum, 1981.

XII.

The diamonds of the European monarchies

BAPST (G.), *Histoire des joyaux de la Couronne de France*, Paris, 1889.

Inventaire des diamants de la Couronne, Imprimerie Nationale, Paris, 1791.

Le Trésor de la résidence de Munich, Official Guide , Munich, 1995.

Rosenborg Castle, A Guide to the Danish Royal Collections, Official Guide, Copenhagen, 1999.

Royal Treasures, Palacio nacional da Ajuda, Lisbon, 1992.

STREETER (E. W.), *The Great Diamonds of the World*, London, 1882.

SYNDRAM (D.), *Das Grüne Gewölbe zu Dresden*, Koehler & Amelang, Munich/Berlin, 1997.

TWINING (L.), *A History of the Crown Jewels of Europe*, London, 1960.

XIII.

Adamas the invincible

Alain de LILLE, *Book of Alain on the Complaint of Nature* (translation: Douglas M. Moffat), H. Holt, New York, 1908.

Albertus Magnus, *De virtutibus herbarum lapidum et animalium*, Amsterdam apud Iodocum Ianconium, 1655.

Alphonse X, *El Primer Lapidario de Alfonso X el Sabio*, pub. Maria Brey Marino, scientific committee José Luis Amoros Portoles, Arte en el lapidario, Ana Domingues Rodrigues, Madrid, 1982

Barthélemy l'Anglais, *De rerum proprietatibus Minerva*, Frankfurt, 1964.

BEGUIN (G.), *Les Peintures du bouddhisme tibétain*, in “Catalogue des tantra du musée Guimet”, Réunion des musées nationaux, Paris, 1995.

Epiphanius, *De Gemmis* (Georgian version, fragments of the Armenian version and the Sahidic Coptic version, by Henri Devis), Christophers, London, 1934.

BURIDANT (C.), *The Translation of the Historia Orientalis by Jacques de Vitry*, French Manuscript 17203, French National Library C. Buridant, Klincksieck, Paris, 1986.

CARDANUS (J.) (Hieronymum CARDANUM), *Somniorum synesiorum omnis generis insomnia explicantes libri IV*, bound with *De Gemmis et coloribus*, Basle apud Henricum Petri, 1561.

DAMIGERON (latin translation), in *Lapidaires grecs*, trad. Robert Halleux, Les Belles Lettres, Paris, 1985, p. 238-239.

Le Dialogue des Créatures, translated by Colart, Mansion du *Dialogus Creaturarem*, 14th century, Pierre Ruelle, Royal Academy of Belgium, Brussels, 1985, p. 115-116.

Dioscoride, *The Greek Herbal of Dioscorides*, Robert T. Gunther, Oxford, 1934.

DURAND (G.), vicar of Mendes, *Guillelmi Duranti Rationale Divinorum Officiorum I-IV*, A. Davril, pub. T. M. Thibodeau, *Corpus christianorum* 140, 1995.

ERMENGAUD (M.), *Le Breviari d'Amor*, pub. Peter T. Ricketts, Westfield College, London, 1989.

FERY-HUE (S.), “Sidrac et les pierres précieuses”, *Revue d'histoire des textes*, vol. XXVIII, 1998.

FREDERIC (L.), *Les Dieux du bouddhisme, guide iconographique*, Flammarion, Paris, 1992.

FRIESLEBEN (H. C.), *Der Katalanische Weltatlas vom Jahre 1375 nach dem Bibliothèque Nationale, Paris*, Stuttgart, 1977.

GARCIA da ORTA, *Colloquios dos simples [...]*, J. de Endem, Goa, 1563.

GAUTIER de BELLEPERCHE, PIEROS du RIES, *La Chevalerie de Judas Macabé*, Jean-Robert Smeets, Gröningen, 1955.

Grégoire le Grand, *Moralia in Job*, French translation by C. Morel, 1986-1990, *Sources chrétiennes* 327-360 ; *Regula Pastoralis* III,13, French translation by J. A. Boutet, 1928.

Hildegarde de Bingen (1098-1179), *Livre des créatures divines*, translation by Pierre Monat, J. Millon, Grenoble, 1988, p. 262-263.

HUON de MÉRY, *Le Tournoi de l'Antéchrist de Huon de Méry*, pub. Georg Wimmer, French translation by Stéphanie Orgeuer, revised by Jean-Pierre Bordier, Orleans, 1995.

LAUFER (B.), *The Diamond: a study in Chinese and Hellenistic folklore* (Anthr. XV, 1), Field Museum of Natural History, Chicago, 1915.

LEVI (K.), *La Puissance de l'amour, six siècles de bagues de fiançailles en diamant*, The Diamond Information Center, London, 1988.

Lucrèce, *De Natura Rerum*, livres I à III, translation Alfred Ernout, Les Belles Lettres, Paris, 1990.

MANDEVILLE, *Voyage autour de la terre*, pub. Christian Deluz, Les Belles Lettres, Paris, 1993.

NECKAM (A.), *De Naturis Rerum* (1154-1220), pub. T. Wright, Longman Green, London, 1863.

OHLY (F.), *Diamant und Bocksblut : zur Traditions und Auslegungsgeschichte eines Naturvorgangs von der Antike bis in die Moderne*, E. Schmidt, Berlin, 1976.

PANNIER (L.), *Les Lapidaires français du Moyen Âge des XIIe, XIIIe et XIVe siècles,* 1882, Fac-similés Slatkine, Geneva, 1973.

The Periplus Maris Erythraei (introduction, translation and commentary by Lionel Casson), Princeton University Press, Princeton,1989, p. 85.

Philippe de THAÜN, *Bestiaire*, E. Walberg, Lund, 1900.

PHYSIOLOGUS, F. Sbordone, Milan, 1936, p. 102-107.

Pierre de BEAUVAIS, *Bestiaire*, pub. Guy R. Mermier, A. G. Nizet, Paris, 1977, p. 54.

POLO Marco, *Le Livre des merveilles*, French Manuscript 2810 from the French National Library, Paris (Commentary: F. Avril, M.-T. Gousset, J. Monfrin, J. Richard, M.-H. Tesnière, with contributions by T. Reiner), Éditions Fac-similés, Lucerne, 1995.

Pseudo-Aristote (Luca ben Serapion), see the ROSE (V.) study, *Aristoteles de lapidibus und Arnoldus Saxo*, Zeitschrift für deutsches Alterthum NF VI, 1875.

RABAN MAUR, *De rerum naturis sive/De Universo,* Cod. Cassin. 132 Archivio degli Abbazia di Montecassino, commentari a cura di G. Cavallo, Turin, 1994.

RICHARD (F.), *Les Cinq Poèmes de Nizami, chef-d'œuvre persan du XVIIIe siècle*,Anthèse French National Library, Paris, 1995.

RICHARD (F.), *Splendeurs persanes, manuscrits du XIIe au XVIIe siècle*, French National Library, Paris, 1997.

Sérinde, terre de Bouddha, exp. au Grand Palais, Paris, 1995, Monique Cohen, pub. Jacques Giès, Paris, 1995.

SNELLGROVE (D. L.), *The Hevajra Tantra: a critical study*, Oxford University Press, London, 1959.

STUDER (P.) and EVANS (J.), *Anglo-Norman Lapidaries*, Édouard Champion, Paris, 1924.

TESNIERE (M.-H.), "Le Reductorium Moral de Pierre Bersuire", *L'Enciclopedismo medievale*, Michelangelo Picone, Ravenna, 1994.

Thomas de CANTIMPRE, *Liber de Natura rerum*, Helmut Boèse, W. de Gruyter, Berlin, 1973.

WITHER (G.), *Collection of Emblems ancient and modern, quickened with metricall illustrations, both morall and divine, and disposed into lotteries*, London, 1635.

ZINK (M.), *La Prédication en langue romane avant 1300*, Honoré Champion, Paris, 1976, p. 358.

Jewellery

CHRISTIE'S, auction sales catalogues.

D'OREY (L.), *Five Centuries of Jewellery, National Museum of Ancient Art, Lisbon*, Zwemmer, London, 1995.

KRISHNAN (U. R. B.) and KUMAR (M. S.), *Dance of the Peacock, Jewellery Traditions of India*, India Book House Ltd., Mumbai, 1999.

NADELHOFFER (H.), *Cartier*, Éditions du Regard, Paris, 1984.

PRODDOW (P.), FASEL (M.), *Diamonds, A Century of Spectacular Jewels*, Abrams, New York, 1996.

RUDOE (J.), *Cartier*, Somogy Éditions d'Art, Paris, 1997.

Tiffany Retrospective, Designs from Tiffany & Co., 1837-1999, APT International Inc., Tokyo, 1999.

PHOTOGRAPHIC CREDITS

Bischhofsheim Archives/MNHN 138-139

De Beers Archives 112 to 119, 122

National Archives 239

H. Bari 22, 37 (top), 71 (top), 95, 120, 121, 140, 151, 154, 197 (top left), 282-283, 295

D. Behl 9, 127, 189 (bottom right), 196 (bottom), 284 (right), 285 (left)

M. Bernaz 284 (left), 285 (right)

J. Bradley, MVA, Inc./H. Hill 84 (bottom)

MNHN Central Library, Paris 15

French National Library, Paris 14, 134, 205, 224 (top), 226, 239 (bottom), 241, 292, 294, 295 (top), 301, 302, 304, 306, 307, 312, 313, 317 to 319/Print Collection 203, 206, 207

St.-Geneviève Library, Paris 181

Vatican Library 44, 316

R. Capdevilla 79 (bottom left)

Cartier/N. Welsh 217-219, 332 to 337/M. Feinberg 330 (top)

Central Gem Laboratory, Tokyo 166-167

Le Cercle des Arts/N. Rachmanov 126, 287 (right), 288, 289

Rosenborg Castle, Copenhagen 277, 278, 311

Christie's 160, 191 (top), 223 (bottom), 229 (top), 230, 231, 247

A. Collins, King's College, London 168

A. Cossard 172 (top)

DR 42 (top and centre), 123 (top and bottom), 152, 165, 220, 256, 309

DTC 17, 20, 24, 27 (top), 32, 35, 40 (left and right), 41, 108, 111 (bottom left and right), 123 centre, 125, 136, 137, 141 (top right and bottom), 145, 153, 162, 193 (top), 194, 195 (top and bottom drawing), 314/P. Johnson 74, 77, 103 (top), 128, 141 top left, 147, 223 (top)

E. Elzas 143, 164-165

K. Färber 8 (full page), 42, 216, 222, 235, 321 to 329

Ricardo do Espirito Santo Silva Foundation 186 (n° 2)

E. Fritsch 170

Gemological Institute of America, Carlsbad 43

Gem Tech Lab 174-175

A. Gicquel 158

P. Gillet/ENS-Lyon 51

Mouawad Group 10, 11, 105 (bottom), 232

T. Hammid 12, 156-157, 164 (bottom), 171, 172 (right), 224 (bottom), 265

J. Hatleberg 169

Herzog Anton Ulrich-Museum, Braunschweig/B.P. Kelser 225

Instituto Português de Museus, Lisbon 105, 244, 305 (top), 315 (centre)/J. Pessoa 305 (bottom)

J.I. Koivula 58 (centre and bottom)

Kunsthistorisches Museum, Vienna 236, 315 (top)

Lapilazuli/C. Creutz 38, 80, 98 to 101, 103 (bottom), 104, 106, 107, 189 (bottom left), 192, 272, 274-275, 296

Malin/Pasachoff/Caltech 85

B. Morel 261

Boymans van Beuningen Museum, Rotterdam/T. Haartsen 189 (top), 254, 255, 271

Historical Museum, Basel 176, 183, 190 (bottom)

Muséum national d'histoire naturelle, Paris 57, 59, 71, 178, 188/H. Hill 84 (top and centre)/P. Lafaite

50 (top), 83/J. Lossel 21, 50 (bottom), 56 (top, centre and bottom), 79 (top and bottom right)

National Maritime Museum, Greenwich 148

Natural History Museum, London 191 (bottom)

Quattrone 186 (n° 1)

Réunion des Musées nationaux, Paris 186 (n° 3), 190 (top), 208, 211, 212 (bottom right and top left), 215, 238, 257, 262, 263, 296, 298-299/Arnaudet 280, 281/Beck-Coppola 248/J.G. Berizzi 258/G. Blot-J. Schor 278/H. Lewandowski 212 (top right), 234/R.G. Ojeda 187 (numbers 5 & 7)

S.E. Richardson 57 (top), 58 (top), 65

Rijksmuseum, Amsterdam 97, 186 (n° 4), 187 (n° 6)

The Royal Collection/HM The Queen 25, 233, 290, 291, 330

V. Sautter & S. Haggerty 61 (top and bottom)

Scala 92-93, 184, 201, 204, 210, 212 (bottom right), 240 (top)

J. Scovil 55, 195 (centre), 197 (top right)

Smithsonian Institution, Washington DC 23 (bottom), 37 (bottom)

Staatlische Kunstsammlungen, Dresden 266, 269

Tiffany & Co. 8 (inset), 315 (bottom), 338 to 343

Kunsthistorisches Museum Treasury, Vienna 182

E. Van Pelt 26, 28 (right), 29, 36, 30, 31, 39, 150, 193 (centre and bottom), 196 (top), 279

Victoria and Albert Museum, London 229 (bottom), 240 (bottom), 245

The drawings on pages 46, 48, 52, 54, 66, 68, 70, 72, 86, 88, 89 are by Valérie Stetten and Dominique Dehoux.

Printed by Industrie Grafiche Editoriali Musumeci S.p.A.,
Quart, Val d'Aosta, Italy,
September 2001